EVEREST
EXPEDITIONS

EVEREST EXPEDITIONS

Originally published in three volumes:

EVEREST: SOUTH WEST FACE

EVEREST THE HARD WAY

EVEREST: THE UNCLIMBED RIDGE

(*with Charles Clarke*)

Chris Bonington

Weidenfeld & Nicolson

LONDON

This omnibus edition has been edited by Margaret Body.
Some diagrams and maps in the original volumes have been omitted
due to space limitations and to avoid duplication.
For a photographic account, see *Chris Bonington's Everest*,
published by Weidenfeld & Nicolson in 2002.

Everest: South West Face first published in Great Britain in 1973 by Hodder & Stoughton
© 1973 Chris Bonington

Everest The Hard Way first published in Great Britain in 1976 by Hodder & Stoughton
© 1976 the British Everest Expedition 1975

Everest: The Unclimbed Ridge first published in Great Britain in 1983 by Hodder & Stoughton
© 1983 Jardine, Matheson & Co. Ltd

This edition first published in Great Britain in 2003 by Weidenfeld & Nicolson

A CIP catalogue record for this book
is available from the British Library.

ISBN 0 297 82936 X

Typeset by Selwood Systems, Midsomer Norton

Printed in Great Britain by
Butler & Tanner Ltd, Frome and London

Weidenfeld & Nicolson

The Orion Publishing Group Ltd
Orion House
5 Upper Saint Martin's Lane
London, WC2H 9EA

EVEREST
EXPEDITIONS

Contents

The challenge of Everest, showing the ridges and faces by which the mountain has been attempted from the 1920s to the present day. Mallory tackled the North Ridge from Tibet. Hillary and Tenzing's 1953 first ascent was made from Nepal by the South Col. The Americans mastered the West Ridge by the Hornbein Couloir on the North Face in 1963. By the 1970s the challenge had shifted to the South West Face.

KEY

1 Changtse	**6** Second Pinnacle	**11** South Col	**16** Hornbein Couloir
2 North Col	**7** Final Pinnacle	**12** Lhotse	**17** South Summit
3 North East Ridge	**8** North Face	**13** Pumo Ri	**18** South Pillar
4 North Ridge	**9** West Ridge	**14** Western Cwm	
5 First Pinnacle	**10** South West Face	**15** Nuptse	

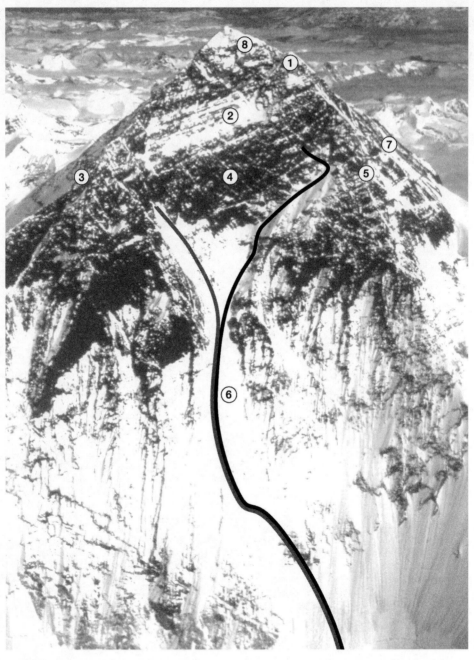

▬▬▬▬ Japanese routes:
Spring 1969, Spring 1970

▬▬▬▬ International Expedition
route in Spring 1971. International
Expedition in Spring 1972 and the
Japanese of Autumn 1973, which
followed the same line but tried to
traverse right on to the South East
Face

1 South Summit
2 Summit Snow Field
3 West Ridge
4 Rock Band
5 South Pillar
6 Great Central Gully
7 South East Ridge
8 Hillary Step

The South West Face of Everest showing the routes taken by earlier expeditions in their attempts.

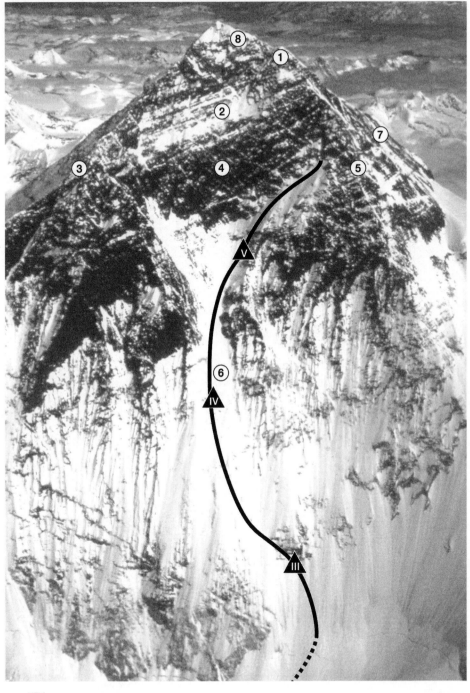

KEY

———	Climbing with fixed rope
▪▪▪▪▪	Climbing without fixed rope
▲v	Camp

1 South Summit   **5** South Pillar
2 Summit Snow Field   **6** Great Central Gully
3 West Ridge   **7** South East Ridge
4 Rock Band   **8** Hillary Step

The South West Face of Everest showing the route and camps on our 1972 attempt.

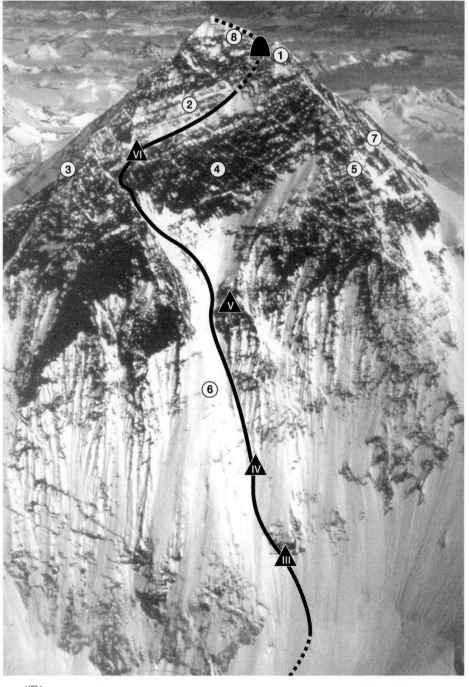

KEY

———	Climbing with fixed rope
▪▪▪▪▪	Climbing without fixed rope
◖	Doug and Dougal's bivvy on way down
▲ V	Camp

1 South Summit
2 Summit Snow Field
3 West Ridge
4 Rock Band
5 South Pillar

6 Great Central Gully
7 South East Ridge
8 Hillary Step

The South West Face of Everest showing the route and camps on the successful 1975 climb.

EVEREST: SOUTH WEST FACE

In memory of Tony Tighe

Contents

Foreword

by Lord Hunt of Llanvair Waterdine, CBE, DSO

It is a truism that success can be perceived in different ways. Some achievements in the field of adventure have, unfortunately, been marred by the controversies to which they have given rise, either during or after the event; conversely, there have been great enterprises where the goal has not been reached but which, nevertheless, have captured the public imagination and been acclaimed as triumphs.

Scott's journey in 1912–13, failing in its purpose to be the first to reach the South Pole, failing in the struggle to return, is one such example. The disappearance of Mallory and Irvine not far below the summit of Everest in 1924, is another. There is no doubt that tragedy or injury enhances the impact of such adventures in the public mind; the French first ascent of Annapurna, successful in the evident sense of reaching its objective, was the more sensational for the suffering through frostbite of Herzog and Lachenal on their way down the mountain. Other examples can be found in pioneering journeys on the oceans or in the air. Heroism and tragedy inherent in these stories have so fired the minds of people everywhere that they have lived on to inspire succeeding generations.

Bonington's story is of a different order. Here was a team of Britishers and Sherpas who were forced to a halt on the great South West Face of Everest by winter, cold and wind and who returned unscathed to tell the tale. True, tragedy did occur in the Khumbu Icefall, but this sad episode falls outside the context of the expedition itself.

Many mountaineers can match the sentiments of Chris Bonington and his team mates, which he expressed to me in a letter written, doubtless in circumstances of extreme duress, from Camp 4 at 24,600ft:

By the time you get this you will know whether we have succeeded or failed. Being realistic I think the latter in strictly material terms is the most likely, but in terms of effort, human relationship and self-sacrifice I feel our attempt on the South West Face has been well worth while …

I don't think anyone has succeeded in contending with the elements over such a period of time, at such altitude, on previous expeditions … We're still in good spirits, whatever the outcome.

I was much moved by this letter, both for the simple ring of sincerity it contains and because it evoked similar feelings which I have experienced on turning back after nearly reaching the top of a high mountain.

But what I find intriguing, and heartening, is that the accolade of achievement should have been accorded spontaneously to this group of splendid young men by a wider public without comparable experience. It is greatly to the credit of the news media that the story should have been portrayed in such a way as to enable people to discern and accept a truer meaning to success than that of reaching the top of the world by the most difficult way. The combination of individual skill, courage and endurance with the cohesion which enabled this party to strive in unity and harmony against all the odds, only to prove the impossible, has come loud and clear through television, sound radio and newspaper reporting of the 1972 Everest expedition.

But it is in no sense to underrate the quality of the various news media to suggest that only through the genuine account of someone who lived through those testing weeks high on the mountain face last winter, can the listener or reader gauge the true measure of these men. No one who has experienced the appalling conditions prevailing at high altitude in the Himalayan winter can doubt that Bonington's team was stopped in their tracks at the ultimate limit of human achievement imposed, for the time being, by natural forces.

In a world as conditioned as our western civilisation by material values, sporting records and tangible rewards, it is good to be made aware that, more important than all these things, is the spirit which moves individual people and the strength of moving together.

This is one of the great stories of our time.

JOHN HUNT
18 March 1973

The Grenadiers of Nepal

Some talk of Walt Bonatti, of Dougal and of Don,
of Smith and Joe or Patey, and even Bonington,
They are the game's great hard men, the short ones and the tall,
but I could write screeds on the heroic deeds of the Sherpas of Nepal.

Up in the Sola Khumbu, south west of Everest,
there lives a brand of hillman, the strongest and the best.
I've climbed with famous Tigers and many a budding star,
but they're not as tough, made from the same stuff, as the man from Namche
  Bazar.

You think you are a hard man, as strong as strong could be,
you'll carry more than he can, but listen hear to me,
he'll take your load twice over and when he sees you drop,
he'll pick up you and your rucksac too and go till you're both at the top.

You've risked your life there's no doubt, on an overhanging wall,
but have you tried your axe out on a great big bad ice-fall?
You'll take a chance a few times making sure the route goes through,
but certainly not fifty days on the trot like the Sherpas have to do.

You think maybe you're special, maybe you're just naive,
for at a certain threshold you'll find it difficult to breathe,
So now you're sucking oxygen, what's so special about that?
I know a man won't take air from a can, he's from the village of Ghat.

Some talk of Ed or Tilman, I couldn't name the lot,
there's many a great hillman whose name I have forgot,
But of all the unsung heroes who's the bravest of them all?
I've tried to explain, but I'll say it again – the Sherpas of Nepal.

DAVE BATHGATE

1

Beginnings

The gully stretched endlessly in front of me; six steps, a rest, breathless in the snow – then another six steps. Aware of Ang Pema just behind me, determined not to let him overtake, not to weaken, I looked up and the top seemed to get no closer; concentrated on the snow in front of my nose. Ten steps this time; I succeeded in making eight, and then lay panting against the snow. My heart was beating so hard that I thought it would burst; time and distance slipped by slowly. The top was just above – just ten slow steps – and suddenly, after two months' effort with the same magnificent view, a new world opened out before me. It was 1961 and I was on Nuptse, the third peak of Everest. We had been climbing its South Face, and this day was our fulfilment – we were going for the summit.

My first impression was one of boundless space, of a sea of brown rolling hills, flecked by the occasional snow cap, reaching to a distant horizon. There was no haze, each distant undulation was etched sharp in the cold, thin air. In a way this view is even more striking than that of Everest, just the other side of the deep gorge described by the Western Cwm. Its summit is a mere 900m (2950ft) above where we were standing that day – less than the height of Snowdon – a squat black pyramid, veined with snow and ice, towering above the void of the Western Cwm. And we turned right, Ang Pema and I, to follow the ridge of Nuptse to its highest point, 7879m (25,850ft). The summit, a corniced snow cap, left just enough room to sit down. I collapsed, thankful that our own struggle was over, uncomfortably aware that I had reached my own limit, that those extra three thousand feet to the summit of Everest would be beyond my capabilities without the use of oxygen.

From the summit of Nuptse we had a unique view of the South West Face of Everest, but that day I'm afraid I cannot claim to have formed an immediate ambition to tackle it. We had been too close to our limits on this 7879m mountain to entertain thoughts of technical climbing at even greater heights. In 1961 we weren't ready for the South West Face of Everest. And so we turned away from the summit of Nuptse and, strangely, the memory that clung in my mind was not that of the squat pyramid of Everest but of those boundless arid hills of the Tibetan plateau which seemed to stretch for ever to the very edge of the world.

Everest, however, exerted its own special magnetism on others, even after it had been climbed by John Hunt's party in 1953. The Swiss, who had made two valiant attempts in the spring of 1952 and the autumn of 1953, returned in 1955, both to repeat the South Col route up Everest and make the first ascent of Lhotse. The Indians and the Chinese attempted the mountain in 1960; the Indians admitted failure in the face of high winds, whilst the Chinese claimed success on the pre-war North Face route. The Indians made a further attempt in 1962 but were once again defeated. Then in 1963 came the massive American Everest expedition, with a budget of $405,263, and twenty team members. They repeated the South Col route, and then Tom Hornbein and Willi Unsoeld, in what was almost a mini expedition within the expedition, climbed the West Ridge to traverse the mountain and come back down by the South Col.

This was an outstanding achievement since they made their build-up with a comparatively small group of Sherpas and support climbers, and had a top camp at only 8300m (27,250ft), giving them a long and arduous summit push up completely unknown ground. It was unlikely that they could have retreated back down it, had they failed to make the summit. In 1965 the Indians returned once more and this time were luckier with the weather, putting no less than nine climbers on the summit by the South Col route. It was around this time that climbers began to think of the South West Face of Everest. It was an obvious challenge – the highest face on the highest mountain in the world.

Though at this stage big wall climbing in the Himalaya had barely started, the South Face of Nuptse was probably the biggest and most diffi-cult face that had been climbed up to this point in time. Most of the diffi-culties were concentrated in its lower parts, on an ice ridge that pierced the lower defences of the wall, reaching a height of approximately 6400m. Above this, the face opened out into a series of snow arêtes, slopes and gullies that led to the summit. We had used about 2400m of fixed rope, but nowhere had the angle been steep enough to necessitate jumars – which was just as well, for in those days we had never even heard of them. On the one short vertical rock section, we had made a rough rope ladder.

The first time I had heard the South West Face of Everest mentioned as a possible objective was in the summer of 1965. I was climbing with John Harlin, the American climber who swept through the European climbing scene in the early sixties. He was one of the most colourful and controver-sial figures of the post-war years. With the physique of a Tarzan, far-flying ambition and imagination, an overpowering personality and tremendous determination as a climber, in the course of a few years he put up several routes that represented a definite step forward in alpine techniques. In effect, he was bringing to Europe the climbing techniques developed on the sheer granite walls of Yosemite by a small group of Californian climbers and then adapting them to alpine conditions. We were planning to tackle the Eiger Direct that summer, and did a number of training climbs together. John was always full of far-fetched schemes, some of which remained castles in the air, but others surprisingly came off. At one stage we were planning a two-man assault on a series of peaks down the line of the Rockies and Andes, using a light plane to get from climbing area to climbing area. The project was to last eighteen months, and would have included a dozen first ascents. He also talked of the South West Face of Everest, dreaming of an international expedition. We never got further than dreams, however, and neither of us got down to any detailed planning, or even had any real concept of just what such a project could entail.

I backed out of the Eiger Direct project that autumn, worried about the prospects of a winter attempt on the face, of which I, personally, had no experience. I was also dubious about the practicality of John's plans. At this stage he wanted to make an alpine-style single push up the wall, without using any fixed ropes. This was something that I felt was probably impractical under winter conditions.

Anyway I came back into the climb on a more professional level when I was asked to go out as photographer for the *Daily Telegraph Magazine*. Becoming more involved in the actual climbing than I had originally intended, I ended going about three-quarters of the way up the face. The climb changed from a blitzkrieg push to a drawn-out siege, using fixed ropes, and snow holes for camps. In fact, the climbing was very similar to Himalayan climbing, without the problems of altitude, but with cold that was probably more extreme than in the Himalaya and technical difficulty that was considerably greater.

It was on the Eiger Direct that I came to know Dougal Haston; we'd met in passing in Chamonix and Leysin, but somehow both of us had been reserved, regarding each other, no doubt, as potential competitors. On the Eiger Direct, however, we spent a certain amount of time together, sharing snow holes and doing some climbing on the face. Dougal was single-minded and even then knew exactly what he wanted to do in life – to climb to the limit – and knowing this, he was very easy to work and climb with. There was no manoeuvring for position on a climb to get the best pitch, or to avoid some of the harder or more dangerous work. He just took everything as it came.

Tragically John Harlin was killed in the final stages of the climb; we had lost a good friend and mountaineering lost one of its most colourful and imaginative innovators. Had he lived, he would undoubtedly have gone on to many other exploits, one of which could have been the South West Face of Everest.

But he had kindled an interest in Dougal and myself. We both got frostbite on the final day of the climb, Dougal fighting his way out of the wall in a storm, and myself sitting on the summit waiting for him to arrive.

We spent a few weeks in the London Hospital under the care of Michael Ward, who was doctor on the 1953 Everest expedition and has become an expert in mountain illnesses and injuries. Part of our treatment was to be immured in a hyperbaric oxygen tank for hours on end. This entailed being shut into a cylinder shaped like a space capsule, into which was pumped pure oxygen. You couldn't take anything into the cylinder with you because of the danger of static electricity igniting skin or clothing and sending you up in a puff of smoke, and so you just lay there for hours on end. The thoughts of both of us turned to Everest – but at this time neither of us had any experience of large-scale organising. I had been on two Himalayan expeditions, to Annapurna II and Nuptse, but at this stage taking on the overall responsibility of leading an expedition was too much for me. I just could not see myself in this role. And so we needed a leader, and who better than Michael Ward. He had been to Everest, had the right contacts with the mountaineering establishment and yet seemed forward-looking and modern in his approach. We asked him whether he would like to lead such an expedition and he expressed interest – but there were other problems. The Nepalese government had just banned mountaineering in Nepal. This was mainly due to the increased tension on the Nepalese-Tibetan frontier created by the Indo-Chinese war. The fact that there was no immediate chance of going to Everest and, even more I suspect, the fact that none of us at this stage was fully committed to the idea of organising such an expedition, meant that it simply faded away, one of those projects that never really got off the ground.

But others were thinking of Everest's South West Face in a much more determined way. The Japanese were planning to go to Everest at the first available opportunity to attempt the face. They already had a great deal of experience in the Himalaya; in most years the number of Japanese expeditions to Nepal is equal to the sum of all the other expeditions from different nationalities. In addition, an increasing number of Japanese climbers had been coming to Europe to extend their knowledge and experience of high standard technical climbing.

2

The Japanese Everest expedition

1969–70

Nepal opened its frontiers to climbers once again in 1969, and that very same spring, a small Japanese team went to Everest to make a reconnaissance of the South West Face. The party included Naomi Uemura who was to be involved in the subsequent international expedition. They climbed the Icefall, taking ten days to do it, and had a close look at the face to reassure themselves that it was feasible. The following autumn they came out with a larger party to make a reconnaissance in force. This time the party numbered twelve, led by H. Mihashita, and once again Uemura was a member. Their aims were to get as high as possible on the face, and to gain experience of altitude for a full-scale attempt in the spring of 1970. The team gathered at Luglha, the air strip four days' march from Everest, on 4 September, having been flown in by chartered plane. They established Base Camp on the 16 September, and by 28 September, had climbed the Icefall and established Camp 2 at the foot of the face. It took them a further fortnight, until 15 October, to establish Camp 3, just below a rock buttress on the lower slopes of the South West Face, at a height of 7000m. The face had a good covering of snow, and they were not unduly troubled by wind. They succeeded in establishing Camp 4 in the middle of the gully at a height of 7500m (24,600ft), where there was just enough snow to carve out platforms for their tents. However, they determined to bring out alloy platforms for their spring attempt. Above Camp 4, the Great Central Gully runs up towards the Rock Band, dividing after about 245m, with the left-hand prong of the Y running up towards the left-hand end of the Rock Band, where a deep cut gully leads up towards the West Ridge. A narrower chimney seems to go up to the left-hand end of a snowfield that stretches across the upper part of the face to another gully at the right-hand end, which in turn leads up towards the South Summit of Everest. The right-hand fork runs up towards a long snow ramp which leads across the bottom of the Rock Band to its right-hand edge.

The Japanese chose the left-hand fork, and climbed over hard wind-packed snow to establish Camp 5 at a height of 7800m (25,600ft) on 29 October. Once again, there was just enough snow to carve out a tent platform. Masatsugu Konishi and Uemura moved into the camp and on 31

October reached a point just below the Rock Band. On the following day, two other members of the team, Nakajima and Satoh, reached the same point and forced another pitch. They had now fulfilled their objective, being confident that a route could be made through the Rock Band with sufficient build-up of supplies at their top camp. They had been extremely successful, and had probably been fortunate with the weather, in that they were barely troubled by the high winds that seem to dog most post-monsoon attempts on Everest, or other mountains of over 8000m. It must be noted, however, that to reach the foot of the Rock Band, at a height of approximately 8000m, without any intention of getting higher, is considerably easier than pushing on above, for the real problem is sustaining an extended line of communications to supply climbers out in front for the final push.

Uemura stayed on at Khumjung throughout the winter, making arrangements for the spring attempt, and getting the full benefit of staying for a long period of time at the same altitude as the Sherpas. Living at a height of around 3350m, you undoubtedly gain a great deal of benefit from fast acclimatisation, while living much higher than that is probably a mistake. Hillary led an expedition in 1961 which wintered at 5800m before attempting Makalu without oxygen. In this case, the climbers were very definitely badly run down after their long stay at altitude.

The Japanese spring expedition was a massive affair. It numbered thirty-nine Japanese of whom nine were representatives of the media and had a grand total of seventy-seven Sherpas, twenty-six being designated as high-altitude Sherpas for work above Camp 2 in the Western Cwm. The leader was Saburo Matsukata, a man of seventy years of age. He led the expedition from Base Camp and some of the problems that occurred later on in the expedition might well have arisen from this cause. They set out with a dual objective, to climb Everest by the South Col route as well as attempt the South West Face. To make the mountain still more crowded, the Japanese skiing expedition also planned to reach the South Col to make a ski descent from as high on Everest as possible.

The expedition moved into Base Camp in mid-March, after an acclimatisation period, and started work on the Icefall on 24 March. It took ten days to make a route through the Icefall and, on 4 April, Camp 1 was set up at the mouth of the Western Cwm. The expedition was dogged by ill-fortune however. On 5 April, six Sherpas of the Japanese skiing expedition were killed in the Icefall, and then, on 9 April, another Sherpa of the Everest expedition was killed. The entire expedition, and particularly the Sherpas, were badly shaken by these two accidents. I was on the South Face of Annapurna at the time, and several of our Sherpas had relatives amongst the casualties. Not surprisingly, they were deeply shocked by the accident;

the impact on the Sherpas with the Japanese expedition must have been even greater.

The leader of the Japanese expedition, Matsukata, only reached Base Camp on 11 April, after these crises had occurred. One cannot help wondering just how effective was his control over events during the course of the expedition.

In spite of the accidents in the Icefall, the Japanese succeeded in maintaining the momentum of the expedition, and established Camp 2 at the foot of the South West Face. This becomes in effect an advanced base camp for any expedition attempting Everest, whether it be by the South West Face, the West Ridge or the South Col. Ironically the common route up through the Icefall is by far the most serious and dangerous part of any climb on Everest from the south. It is like playing Russian roulette and, however careful an expedition is in making the route, it cannot avoid a certain element of objective danger. The risk of an accident occurring increases statistically with the number of people going through an icefall. In the case of the two Japanese expeditions, there must have been around 150 people going through the Icefall at one time or another and, of course, the Icefall Sherpas make the trip daily throughout an expedition to keep the Advanced Base and high camps stocked.

The Japanese had decided to tackle the South East Ridge (the original route climbed in 1953) as well as the South West Face. This would give them a more guaranteed chance of success and might serve as a good descent line for the face assault team, should they succeed.

The team now divided into two distinct parties, with the face team even having a separate Advanced Base Camp, slightly closer to the face itself than that of the South East Ridge team. They only nominated the members of each at this point, however, and the split was done by the leadership of the expedition. The selection was not well received by all members.

In his official report on the expedition, Hiromi Ohtsuka stated: 'It would have been better if the grouping of the members were decided beforehand according to their own wishes, although it was necessary to observe the condition, aptitude and intention of every member.'

The selection was announced on 17 April. Nine members of the team led by Konishi, leader of the autumn reconnaissance, were selected for the face, and sixteen members were chosen for the South East Ridge. What immediately becomes evident is that the South East Ridge had priority in Sherpa strength for the initial route-making and build-up on the Lhotse Face. In addition, Uemura, who had been to the high point on the South West Face in the autumn and was probably the best acclimatised member of the entire team, having spent all winter in Sola Khumbu, was apportioned to the South East Ridge.

The expedition had fallen into the trap of having split objectives and was concentrating on the almost certain success of repeating the South East Ridge to get the first Japanese on the summit of Everest. In doing so they were prejudicing their chance of success on the greatest challenge of all, the South West Face.

The South East Ridge team had their share of setbacks. On 21 April they had their own expedition's second fatality, and the seventh of the two expeditions on Everest at the time. Narita had a sudden heart attack while eating his evening meal at Camp 1, and died before even his companions sitting beside him could do anything about it. The entire team was badly shocked by the tragedy. Ohtsuka writes:

Every member hearing the news was in a state of great shock, Narita being one of the strongest and youngest [aged twenty-eight] member of the expedition, it was unbelievable as to how such a thing could have happened. We remember him that afternoon waving to us with a smile and therefore his death seemed to be a dream.

Although he was not in good condition at the time of establishing base camp he recovered completely by going down to Lobuche to take some rest for a week. He resumed his work with other members at this stage. Was it because he wasn't acclimatised? I was quite concerned over this question. But our doctors judge this accident may have no relation with the high-altitude sickness, though this is not certified.

Narita's death put back their schedule still further, for all the members of the team went back to Camp 1 for a farewell ceremony, and eleven went all the way down to Tukura, one day's march below Base Camp, where they cremated the body.

But the climb went on. By 28 April they had reached the South Col on the South East Ridge route, though on the South West Face progress was lagging. Ropes had only just been fixed up to the site of Camp 3, at a height of 7000m. During this period the situation was discussed at Advanced Base and, because of the way the expedition was slipping behind schedule and the growing amount of sickness in the team, it was decided to put off the South West Face assault, and concentrate all efforts on the South East Ridge.

Four days later, on 1 May, Hiromi Ohtsuka, no doubt pressured by the South West Face team, changed his mind once again, and formulated a new compromise plan to allow both teams a chance of reaching the summit. The outline of the plan read:

(1) Both the South West Face and the South East Ridge projects will be carried out.

(2) Face Camp 4 (8000m) will be established just below the Rock Band in the South West Face by 12 May.

(3) The summit assault from the South East Ridge will be carried out twice on 11 and 12 May.

(4) Matsuura and Uemura were assigned for the first summit assaulting members. The second assaulting team would consist of a member and one Sherpa.

(5) 350 kilos of equipment and food will be carried up by Doi, Kamiyama and 16 Sherpas to Camp 5 of South Col.

The South West Face team still had a low priority. Progress on the South East Ridge was now swift, however, and on the 11 May, Matsuura and Uemura reached the summit of Everest on a perfect, windless day. The following day, Hirabayashi and the Sherpa, Chotare, also reached the summit.

Things were not going so well, however, on the South West Face where Camp 4 was established on 6 May, using duraluminium frame platforms. On 8 May, Konishi and Yoshikawa reached a height of 7800m, once again taking the left-hand route explored by the autumn reconnaissance team. Two days later, on 10 May, Kano and Sagono with two Sherpas pushed the route out higher. There was much less snow than there had been in the autumn; instead, there were broken rocks of an unpleasant slatey nature. They were forced to take off their crampons and left their ice pegs behind, at a height of about 7900m. It was pure rock-climbing from here, and conditions were ideal – windless and comparatively warm. They reached an altitude of 8050m (26,400ft), just below the Rock Band, at the point where a comparatively easy-looking ramp stretched left towards the crest of the West Ridge. A narrow chimney forked right through the Rock Band, to arrive on a broad snow ledge that stretched back, right to a gully that would have led to the South Summit. It would have given difficult climbing, but they were confident that they could climb it and, having reached this point, the pair dropped back down towards Advanced Base Camp for a rest. On the way down, just below Camp 3, Kano was injured by a falling stone. That same afternoon Nakajima, at Camp 4, was also hit by a stone. Hiromi Ohtsuka, who seemed the effective leader of the expedition, being up at Advanced Base, decided to call off the attempt on the South West Face on the grounds that the stonefall was too dangerous and that in the time available before the arrival of the monsoon they would be unable to force the Rock Band and put in a summit assault. He therefore resolved to concentrate the teams' effort on making two more assaults on the South East Ridge. This also enabled their single woman member, Seluko Watanabe, to establish a world female height record, in reaching the South Col. They ran out of good weather however, and on 20 May the expedition was called off.

Might the expedition have been successful if they had concentrated from the start on the South West Face? One cannot help feeling that this might well have been the case. In the circumstances, the leadership of the expedition seems to have concentrated on getting to the top of Everest by any means and, consequently, gave the more exacting objective a lower priority. The stonefall, which was quoted as one reason for calling off the expedition, does not seem to have been much worse than that which either the Germans or ourselves experienced in 1972. Hiromi Ohtsuka was aware of these problems and in his summing up of the expedition states:

As deputy leader of the expedition, I would like to state some of the characteristic problems of the expedition and the possibility of the South West Face.

(1) Our expedition was a large force consisting of 39 members, including nine reporters and cameramen. At the Base Camp the members came close to 120, including the Sherpas and local Sherpas. There were more than 60 members living together even at Camp 1 and higher. A 39-member expedition is too large to work as a cohesive unit. One leader should not have more than 12 to work with otherwise there will be a lack of common bond among the members. Furthermore, the pleasures of mountaineering will be stifled.

(2) Our expedition consisted of two distinct groups which had the same objective to acquire the summit of Mt Everest but with a different route and different tactics. This scheme has made the expedition into such a large size. The necessity of such a big expedition should be considered with restraint in the future. I want to pay tribute to the American expedition which scaled the summit both from the South East Ridge and the West Ridge. I have come to know how hard it is to keep close co-ordination between the two teams with different tactics. If there is a need to set up an expedition with a similar set up as ours, it is necessary to set up two distinct ones beforehand, under the powerful organisation committee of the expedition. And there are reasons to believe that even such an organisational set up has its own setbacks.

But the Japanese came away with the belief that success on the South West Face was possible, with the right kind of expedition. Subsequent expeditions to the South West Face might well have been advised to study and act on Ohtsuka's advice.

3

The International Everest expedition

Spring 1971

The International Everest expedition was next in what had become a long queue for Everest. I first became involved in the venture in April 1969 when I received a letter from Jimmy Roberts, a retired Lieutenant Colonel in the Gurkhas who ran a trekking business in Nepal, telling me he was going to attempt the South West Face and asking my advice on equipment. He was joint leader with Norman Dyhrenfurth.

At the time I was organising an expedition to the South Face of Annapurna for the spring of 1970. I already knew Jimmy well, having been with him on Annapurna II in 1960 when he was leader of a combined services expedition. It had been my first Himalayan expedition and I had been very impressed by his style of leadership. Though dogged by ill-health, and unable to go above 5000m on the mountain, his sound judgment, planning, and incisive leadership had been instrumental in ensuring our success. I couldn't help being tempted by the possibility of going to Everest in 1971 and therefore asked in my reply whether there was any chance of joining the expedition. I had a letter back a couple of weeks later, not only welcoming me aboard but suggesting I should take over the climbing leadership. A few weeks later Norman Dyhrenfurth was on his way to Europe from the States, and he broke his journey at London Airport. He had a flashing smile, the looks of a film star specialising in rugged but slightly glamorous adventure, yet at the same time he was obviously a man of considerable warmth and sincerity. His record, both in Himalayan experience and as an organiser and fund-raiser, was impressive.

He had been to the Everest massif three times – twice to climb Everest (1952 and 1963) and once to make an attempt on Lhotse (1955). He had also climbed Dhaulagiri in 1960. Like John Hunt, he had carried loads high and distinguished himself as a tactful and diplomatic leader. There was also no doubt that he and Roberts were well matched. Dyhrenfurth, with his resourcefulness in getting financial support, his skill in public relations and his ability at handling the press, was the ideal front man, while Roberts, with his Army background and his great rapport with the Sherpas, was perfectly suited for the job of dealing with the vast logistical back-up to the expedition.

I felt honoured by the trust that Norman and Jimmy had placed in me, but I was able to spare little thought for the expedition itself. My own attempt on Annapurna now filled my horizon. Although I had twice been to the Himalaya, I had never before led an expedition or undertaken such a gigantic responsibility of organisation. Besides, in 1969 it seemed doubtful whether the International expedition would ever take place, since the Japanese who were making the first attempt might well have been successful. Already, that autumn there were disagreements over the composition of the team and the goals of the expedition. This was partially caused by the way the expedition had evolved and mutated over a period of years, changing both in form, composition and objective.

It had started off as a small group of people who happened to come from different countries but knew each other well; they had decided to go on an expedition together. The co-founders were John Amatt, who came from Wilmslow in Cheshire, and Leif Patterson, a Norwegian. They had met in Norway in 1965 when they were members of teams attempting first ascents on the gigantic Trolltind Wall, one of the most impressive rock walls in Europe. They met again in Peru in 1966 and discussed the possibility of forming an expedition. Patterson was already planning a trip to Antarctica and so they decided on this as a venue. The fact that it was to be international in character was almost coincidental. But then the Antarctica project fell through and they looked round for other objectives and decided on the Rupal Face of Nanga Parbat. At this stage the team numbered six, none of whom had climbed before in the Himalaya. Amatt therefore came up with the idea of inviting Jimmy Roberts to be their leader, to give them the benefit of his considerable Himalayan experience. This also fell through, however, since the Germans had succeeded in getting permission to attempt the Rupal Face in 1970. They therefore decided to go for the South West Face of Everest. It was a big step from Antarctica, particularly for a comparatively inexperienced team.

It was at this stage that Norman Dyhrenfurth became involved in the expedition. He had been thinking of an International expedition to Everest completely independently – in fact had had the idea from way back in 1952, before the mountain had even been climbed. He wrote to Jimmy, who had been his transport officer on the American Everest expedition, inviting him to join him. At this stage Dyhrenfurth's expedition was no more than an idea, while Jimmy had an expedition, albeit a comparatively inexperienced one with little expertise at fund-raising or large-scale organisation. And so Jimmy welcomed the suggestion and proposed that he and Norman should join forces as joint leaders.

The merger made the expedition feasible on practical grounds, since it seems doubtful whether the original group could possibly have gathered the necessary funds or have coped with the mammoth task of organising a major expedition, the members of which were scattered all over the world. Norman Dyhrenfurth plunged into the task with enthusiasm, however, broadening the scope of the expedition to include climbers from all the alpine nations and from Japan. It now became truly international, but this also brought many problems.

It was at this stage that I came into the enterprise. Norman proved himself a brilliant co-ordinator, keeping everyone informed with a series of long and detailed newsletters. Inevitably, however, he had to make many of the decisions himself, some of which were dictated by sheer economic necessity. The trouble with having embarked on an International expedition was that no one national body could be expected to take responsibility for the expedition in the way, for instance, that the Mount Everest Foundation had taken my own Annapurna South Face expedition under its wing. This meant that Norman Dyhrenfurth became financially responsible for the expedition, which began to escalate in cost almost with the speed of the Concorde project.

The team now began to expand very quickly. He invited Michel and Yvette Vaucher from Switzerland, Pierre Mazeaud from France, Wolfgang Axt and Leo Schlömmer from Austria, Toni Hiebeler from Germany. They were all well-known, accomplished mountaineers with impressive records behind them. And yet I was getting increasingly worried about the way the expedition was going. Appreciating Norman's need to increase the numbers participating in the expedition to bring in further finance, I was impressed by the fullness and frequency of his newsletters. What worried me was whether I was going to be able to control a group of climbers of this calibre, all of whom would presumably want their turn out in front, and all of whom would have come with dreams – or the determination – of being in the summit party. My own authority would be tenuous, and I could even end up in an uncomfortable position as go-between for the expedition leadership and the climbing members.

During the course of the Annapurna expedition, I experienced quite enough problems even in guiding a group of people most of whom I knew very well and all of whom spoke the same language. Moreover, they had a strong vested interest in getting on together, both in the sense of wanting to maintain long-standing friendships and needing to work together on future climbing ventures. In addition, I was desperately tired, both from the experience of organising and leading an expedition, and the actual climbing itself. It was while on Annapurna that I decided to withdraw from the International expedition.

I broke the news to Jimmy Roberts on my return to Kathmandu. Having already recommended Dougal Haston as a possible member, I now suggested Don Whillans as my replacement. On getting back to England, I began to have some doubts about the step I had taken. Could I afford to turn back from such a considerable mountaineering challenge? Jimmy Roberts came to see me in August to ask my advice about equipment for the expedition, and with this level of involvement I could not resist the temptation to ask whether I could come back on board. Both Jimmy and Norman very kindly welcomed me back, but once in the team again, things seemed, if anything, blacker.

At that point, the expedition was resting on very shaky financial foundations, and the team, although studded with well-known names, seemed to lack cohesion. In a way I envied Don and Dougal who had no worries about the financial side of the project, since all they had to do was to go along and climb. I, on the other hand, was inevitably to be involved in fund-raising and working for the media. But what would happen if the expedition ended up with a gigantic debt? I should certainly have felt obliged to shoulder my share of it, yet could have ill-afforded to do so. My serious doubts about the outcome of the expedition, and my own role within it, forced me out once again. I did have one more chance of going back in, when the BBC asked me to go out as their reporter, but I had crystallised my own doubts about the venture and therefore resolved to stay out.

By February 1971 the expedition was ready to set out for Nepal. Just getting it organised had been a magnificent achievement by Norman Dyhrenfurth. The team was well equipped, had the most sophisticated oxygen system, developed by Dr Duane Blume, ever to be used in the Himalaya, and the project was financially viable, largely as a result of the participation of the BBC. The team had also had some further additions on the climbing side, with Carlo Mauri from Italy, Uemura and Ito from Japan, both of whom had been members of the previous year's Japanese Everest expedition, and Harsh Bahuguna from India. The team on setting out from Europe numbered twenty-two, backed up by a large media team of eight, of whom several were experienced climbers.

Before I pulled out of the expedition I had expressed some doubt about the size of the party, stressing that I felt twelve to be the maximum number of climbers I could cope with on the South West Face. In addition, of course, I wanted a strong Sherpa force to perform the task of load-carrying. Norman therefore suggested having a secondary objective, but rather than merely repeat the South Col route, he was more ambitious, planning to go for the true West Ridge of Everest. This had been attempted in 1963 during his American Everest expedition, but Hornbein and Unsoeld who made the West Ridge route had strayed on to the North Face to avoid some of the difficulties of the ridge line. At the time Norman's decision to attempt two routes seemed the only practical course, though with hindsight one can see that this was one of the most serious fundamental mistakes of the expedition. The team was weaker in numbers than that of the Japanese in 1970, yet was tackling a more ambitious secondary objective. The International expedition had fifty-five Sherpas, compared to the seventy-five that the Japanese had had. This number was to prove barely sufficient to sustain a single assault on the mountain.

But in mid-February 1971 when the team assembled in Kathmandu chances of success seemed good. The entire team walked out to Base Camp from Kathmandu in preference to flying to Luglha, the air strip that is only four days' easy walk from the Everest Base Camp. In this way they were able to acclimatise at a steady rate and, perhaps equally important, get to know each other. They also paused at Pheriche, just short of Base Camp, for further acclimatisation. So far everything seemed to be going well; morale was high and there was a fine spirit of camaraderie within the team. Friendships were fast forming, many of which were to last through the well-publicised differences that were to occur later on.

Dougal Haston, though, was slightly perturbed by the light-hearted way in which the majority seemed to treat the venture; he had the feeling that many saw the trip as a holiday and were little aware of the grim discomfort and effort that inevitably form a major part of any Himalayan expedition. There were also some heated discussions on the route to be taken on the South West Face; the American contingent, particularly Colliver and Peterson who were full of the big wall climbing ethic cultivated in Yosemite, were talking blithely of forcing a route straight up the centre of the Rock Band.

Norman Dyhrenfurth believed in a democratic form of leadership and wanted to give everyone the maximum satisfaction in their role on the expedition. There had been some complaints on the previous year's Japanese expedition that the two teams to tackle the South West Face and the South Col route had been selected without consulting the members. Dyhrenfurth allowed the team to make their own choice. Below is the form it took.

South West Face	West Ridge
Evans (USA), Co-ordinator	Axt (Austrian), Co-ordinator
Colliver (USA)	Bahuguna (India)
Ito (Japan)	Teigland (Norway)
Uemura (Japan)	Eliassen (Norway)
Haston (UK)	Vaucher (Switz.)
Whillans (UK)	Mme Vaucher (Switz.)
Schlömmer (Austria)	Mauri (Italy)

Hiebeler (W. Germany)   Isles (USA)
Peterson (USA)   Mazeaud (France)
                                         Steele (UK)

The title of co-ordinator given to John Evans and Wolfgang Axt is indicative of the problems that Dyhrenfurth was going to meet in controlling the members of the team. With such a large number of talented climbers, all of whom had established a personal reputation in their own country, it seemed inadvisable to appoint any one of them as leader over the others.

Dyhrenfurth planned to work mainly between Base and Advanced Base, in a co-ordinating role, while Roberts stayed in Base, keeping the Sherpas and porters moving systematically up the mountain to supply those in front. It was decided that the Sherpas would be divided into two equal groups, working independently of one another, their deployment being decided by their respective co-ordinators working with Roberts.

The expedition's Base Camp was established on 23 March, and the team immediately started work on the Icefall, which was especially dangerous that season. It was a fortnight before they had managed to force their way through this maze of tottering séracs. At this stage everyone was working well together. Each day two parties would go up into the Icefall, while back at Base Camp the others either rested or worked on the gear and food. The latter was to prove a considerable problem. Wolfgang Axt had been given the unenviable job of organising the food. He is a health fanatic and the diet reflected his beliefs. There were huge quantities of pumpernickel and various other health foods which the other climbers found to be totally inedible at altitude. A more serious factor was that the food had not been pre-packed in ration packs. This had to be done at Base Camp, and since the packages were not sealed it was inevitable that as the food found its way up the mountain, the most attractive items were pirated. As a result, by the time it reached the front climbers, they were left the remnants that no one else fancied.

Once the Icefall had been forced, the route was quickly pushed out to Camp 2, and the lead climbers of the two parties started work on their respective routes. It was already becoming uncomfortably evident that there were barely enough Sherpas to support these two efforts. On the American Everest expedition the climbers had taken an active part in load-carrying, particularly in the early part of the venture; on this expedition, however, there was a strong school of thought amongst the climbers that they should do as little carrying as possible, saving their strength for the summit bid. There was also growing friction between the two teams, the West Ridge team feeling that the face team were getting priority of Sherpas for their build-up. In addition, the approach to the West Ridge from the Western Cwm was proving to be more difficult than it had been in 1963. Even in the face team, there was some trouble. Schlömmer felt that Don Whillans and Dougal Haston, who were pushing out the route towards Camp 3, were hogging the lead, and complained accordingly.

In spite of these problems that were beginning to show themselves, it is just possible that the expedition could have succeeded on at least one of the routes without a major rift, had they been spared an appalling accident followed by an unusually savage and prolonged storm. Wolfgang Axt and Harsh Bahuguna had been working out in front trying to establish Camp 4 on the West Ridge. They had been working at altitude for some time and both were getting tired; the weather was beginning to deteriorate and so they decided to return to Advanced Base Camp. Axt described what happened next to Norman Dyhrenfurth in an enquiry held after the accident:

We were not roped during the descent, there was no need, there were no difficulties at all. Since I knew Michel [Vaucher] and Odd [Eliassen] had placed fixed ropes on all the steeper sections, I left my climbing rope and my harness and karabiner at the new camp. At first Harsh went ahead. Around 2 p.m. the weather turned bad. Soon we were caught in a raging storm. When we reached the long rope traverse I took over the lead and got across it hand over hand. It was very long and tiring as hell. At the far end I waited for Harsh to follow. Voice communication was impossible, the storm was much too strong. I waited for a long time, perhaps as much as an hour. My hands and feet lost all feeling. Then I saw Harsh tied into a fixed rope with a harness and karabiner, groping his way round the last corner of the steep ice slope that separated us. He waved with one hand. Everything seemed OK, no indication of any serious difficulty. I was really worried about frostbite so I went down. Just before I got to the camp I heard his screams and alerted everybody. I couldn't have gone up as I was completely done in.

When he was asked why he did not stay with Bahuguna:

I had no idea how bad things were with him, and besides what could I have done without a rope or karabiner? Harsh had taken his gear but I would have had to go back hand over hand over that long traverse. I simply didn't have enough strength in me for that and my hands and feet felt like blocks of ice.

Immediately, a rescue party set out and reached Harsh some hours later when it was already beginning to get dark. The conditions were savage, with the wind and snow gusting across the slope. Harsh was semi-conscious, hanging by his harness on the fixed rope, his anorak and upper clothing pulled up exposing his body to the storm. Vaucher and Eliassen tried to lower him straight down to easier ground, since it was impossible to get him back across the traverse. Unfortunately they ran out of rope before he reached the bottom of the slope. He was lying helpless on the slope, suspended by the rope. Whillans, with considerable courage, cramponed, unroped, across to him. Harsh was now unconscious, very close to death. Even if they had managed to get him down, it is unlikely he would have survived the journey back to Camp 2. There was nothing Don could do to get him down and so he had to make the agonising decision to abandon a man who still had a spark of life left in him.

The storm did not abate and the party at Camp 2 were trapped there for a further ten days. They were unable to recover Harsh's body till the end of the storm and it was left hanging there, a grim reminder of the tragedy. In the enforced idleness of days spent in sleeping bags, the members of the team had ample opportunity to brood over Harsh's death. Food was short; everything became covered in spindrift, with gear and sleeping bags getting progressively damper.

During the storm Mazeaud and Mauri had come up with the suggestion that they should abandon the West Ridge, which was obviously going to extend the limited resources of the expedition too much, and instead go for the South Col. Dyhrenfurth was unhappy about the suggestion, but against his better judgment agreed that there should be a vote amongst the West Ridge team. Peter Steele and Eliassen voted for abandoning the alternative route altogether and going for the face, while the rest of the team voted for the South Col route, and Dyhrenfurth endorsed this decision.

The first task once the storm ended was the grim one of taking down Harsh Bahuguna's body. Several members of the team also were forced back to Base Camp, weakened by sickness. The remnants of the two parties started work on their respective routes. After a few days, however, it became increasingly obvious that there simply weren't enough Sherpas to support two separate attempts; indeed, there were barely sufficient for the face. Jimmy Roberts strongly recommended that the South Col route should be abandoned; Norman Dyhrenfurth, having agreed to let the 'Latins' have their way, was unhappy about going back on his word but soon realised that he had little choice in the matter. Fair to the last, he held another vote, even allowing the Sherpas to have their say. The Sherpas voted overwhelmingly in favour of the face route, preferring a straightforward line, protected all the way by fixed ropes, to the much longer way by the South Col.

Mazeaud, Mauri and the Vauchers were furious, suspecting intrigue. They retired to Base Camp and Yvette Vaucher even pelted the unfortunate Dyhrenfurth with snowballs. After a series of savage arguments the four decided to withdraw from the expedition. Hiebeler also was forced to withdraw for reasons of health rather than protest. Several more members of the team were knocked out by illness and never really recovered. Peter Steele, the doctor, was kept hard at work with a whole series of ailments, the most serious of which was a virus infection, a rare type of glandular fever, which attacked almost every member of the expedition. Dyhrenfurth was struck down and was so ill that he had to return to Europe, leaving Jimmy Roberts in charge. John Evans, the face co-ordinator, was also affected. Only Whillans, Haston, Ito, Uemura, Schlömmer, Axt and Peterson remained untouched.

Don Whillans was the obvious choice as successor to John Evans as climbing leader and he now took over. They returned to the face at the end of April. Don and Dougal went out in the lead, supported by Uemura, Ito and the Sherpas. They quickly established Camp 4, using the platform left by the Japanese, on which they pitched Whillans Boxes, then pushed on up towards the Rock Band. On the 1970 attempt the Japanese had gone to the foot of the gully on the left-hand side of the Rock Band. They failed to find a suitable camp site. Whillans therefore decided to follow a route that led across towards the right-hand flank of the Rock Band, since there seemed more hope of finding a suitable camp site. They discovered one on the right-hand side of the Great Central Gully leading up the Rock Band at a height of approximately 8000m. Above this a system of ledges and snowfields led across to the right-hand side of the Rock Band.

There was some criticism within the team and from the press that Don and Dougal were hogging the lead, refusing to let anyone else go out in front. It undoubtedly would have been better for morale if another climbing pair had been able to take a turn at making the route. Schlömmer and Axt did offer to help, but unfortunately there was an altercation between Schlömmer and Whillans after the former asked Don to send down a Sherpa to carry up his personal gear, which Don refused to do. The two Austrians claimed that Whillans and Haston refused to let them go out in front whilst the Britons put in a counter claim that they would have been only too glad to be relieved if only someone had come up from Camp 5 to do this. It is interesting that Uemura and Ito did not seem anxious to go out in front but were well content to give the two Britons their loyal support. The Sherpas, led by Pembatharke, also did a magnificent job in the final days of the expedition, working without any supervision from the climbers, most of whom had either given up or were convalescent at Base Camp. Peterson did a good job in the running of Camp 3 and John Evans, having recovered from glandular fever, returned to Camp 2 but was not able to do much to influence events.

Meanwhile Don and Dougal had succeeded in establishing Camp 6 (8290m/27,200ft) at the foot of a narrow gully, filled with snow, at the right-hand end of the Rock Band. Whillans went round the corner and saw that there was a comparatively easy way across to the South Ridge. They would certainly have had a much better chance of climbing this than of climbing the Rock Band itself, but they rejected the thought. After all the arguments they had had about going for the face rather than the South Ridge route, he felt it would have left Haston and himself open to charges of hypocrisy.

The supplies coming up to them, however, had now thinned down to a trickle. They needed three bottles of oxygen a day at Camp 6, one each during the day to climb with and a bottle shared at night. They succeeded in climbing about 90m up the gully but then ran out of rope. It was painfully obvious that they were not going to get sufficient supplies to make a sustained effort on the Rock Band, let alone making a summit bid once that was climbed. Don had reached the high point and came sliding back down the rope to Dougal. 'I think we've had it,' he said.

And so, admitting defeat, they turned back, returning to Base Camp and all the accusation and counter-accusation that was to follow the expedition.

The arguments and the desertion of the four Latins have undoubtedly clouded the real causes of failure. The decision to go for two objectives when there was barely sufficient Sherpa support for one was certainly the greatest factor. This might have defeated both attempts even if the weather had been perfect. The death of Harsh Bahuguna, linked with the ten-day storm, put the lid on it.

4

The European Everest expedition

Spring 1972

One expedition had failed and the next was ready to step into the breach. Dr Karl Herrligkoffer, a Munich doctor with a long record of expedition organisation behind him, had permission to attempt Everest in the spring of 1972. He contacted Don Whillans, Dougal Haston, Uemura and Ito, while they were still in Nepal, inviting them to join the team. He knew them only by reputation, and in inviting climbers whom he did not know, from another country, and who did not know the other German and Austrian members of his climbing team, he was already sowing the seeds of potential dissension which had bedevilled and, in part, damaged the chances of success of the International expedition.

Herrligkoffer, a controversial figure in the German climbing scene, first came into prominence in 1953, when he led the expedition that made the first ascent of Nanga Parbat; this was a 'German mountain' in much the same way in which Everest had become a 'British mountain', with a succession of pre-war attempts on its northern flanks. Before the Nanga Parbat expedition he was completely unknown on the German climbing scene and only had limited experience as a mountaineer. His interest in Nanga Parbat seemed to have been created by the fact that his stepbrother was Willi Merkl who led and died on the disastrous 1934 attempt when nine climbers and Sherpas were killed in a storm. Although his expedition had been successful, it was also bedevilled with arguments and controversy, particularly between the famous Austrian climber, Hermann Buhl who reached the summit in an incredible solo bid after Herrligkoffer had called the expedition off and the climbers back down to Base Camp. The argument was so savage that it led to the law courts.

But this did not deter Herrligkoffer. He led a succession of expeditions in the next few years, six of them back to Nanga Parbat to attempt the mountain on its other faces; three of these were successful with ascents of the Diamir Face, the Rupal Ridge and finally in 1970 the Rupal Face. Yet most of these expeditions were bedevilled with arguments and the Rupal Face expedition was extraordinarily similar in its pattern to that of the original ascent, with the brilliant young Austrian climber, Reinhold Messner fulfilling the same role as had been taken by Hermann Buhl. He also made a solo dash for the summit, followed by his brother Günther, who caught up with him near the top of the mountain. They had then found that they couldn't get back down because of the difficulty of the climbing and therefore took the desperate course of descending the Diamir Face on the opposite side. Sadly, Günther was killed by an avalanche on the way down when nearly in sight of safety. Once again arguments flowed between summit climber and leader over a series of misunderstood signals. Once again the expedition ended in the law courts.

Part of the reason for the misunderstanding was perhaps the fact that Herrligkoffer never went far beyond Base Camp, was essentially an administrator rather than a climber and seemed to have little in common with or understanding of many of the climbers he invited on his expedition. To help finance and organise expeditions he had founded the German Institute for Exploration.

And so, to Everest. When Don and Dougal received this invitation, both knew about Herrligkoffer's background, but in just the same way as Buhl and Messner, they decided to join an expedition about which they were not too happy, simply because this was the only opportunity they were going to have to go to Everest in the foreseeable future.

I became involved in the expedition later on that autumn, when I received a letter from Dougal. He had just been to see Herrligkoffer in Munich, and told me that Herrligkoffer would extend an invitation to myself to join his expedition. Apparently he was having difficulty in raising funds – difficulties which were aggravated by the distrust for his expeditions held by the majority of German climbers, and also a large part of the media in Germany. Dougal had mentioned that I had good contacts with the British media and could probably help him with fund-raising as well as the actual climbing. At this stage I was organising an expedition to the Trango Tower, of which Joe Brown, Hamish MacInnes, Martin Boysen, Will Barker and Paul Nunn were to be members. The Trango Tower is a magnificent rock obelisk of 6250m (20,500ft) which would have given superb rock-climbing of a slightly larger-than-alpine scale. The team was obviously going to be very compatible, and the expedition would have been sheer fun. However, we were having trouble in getting permission from the Pakistan government. At this stage, I was still hopeful that we might pull it off, and therefore stalled with Herrligkoffer to give me time to see whether we were going to be able to go for the Trango Tower or not.

I actually met Herrligkoffer for the first time at the end of November, when he came over with several members of his team to take part in Don Whillans' 'This Is Your Life' on television. Talking with him between rehearsals, both Dougal and I were badly shaken to learn how little he appeared to know about the problems presented by Everest or, for that matter, how limited was his knowledge of Himalayan history or Himalayan mountaineering in general. I couldn't help feeling that his sole interest lay in his own expeditions and the comparatively limited fields which he had covered. It was quite obvious that money, at this stage, was very short and that preparations for the expedition had barely got off the ground. He had had an abortive expedition to attempt to climb the North Flank of Rakaposhi that summer and had presumably only just finished closing it down.

Herrligkoffer himself could speak only very limited English and the other climbers could speak none at all. They were certainly very different in appearance from the average British climber; short hair – not surprising when later we learned that most of them were in the Austrian Army – fairly square clothes, and a look of earnest clean living. Since I could still not commit myself, I kept out of any of the plans or discussion. Don, on the other hand, after the programme, had a long session with the Germans and tried to get across the need for greater British participation if Herrligkoffer was to hope for more money from Britain whilst, at the same time, trying to get the planning on to a sound footing. A couple of weeks later, the fate of our Trango Tower trip was finally sealed. Due to hostilities on the India-Pakistan border, we were informed by the Pakistan government that we did not have permission.

And so, what next? Go to Everest – even with what was obviously a thoroughly unsatisfactory expedition, which promised even more chances of failure than that of the international one? I was tired of standing down from expeditions; had even regretted, during its course, my withdrawal from the International expedition. And so I decided to go along. After all, I was a writer and a photographer. There would certainly be plenty to write about on Herrligkoffer's expedition. He needed money, which meant selling book rights, television rights, newspaper rights in this country and, possibly, the US and I was probably in a position to sell these rights on the basis of my own reputation after writing up the Annapurna expedition.

I went over to see Dr Herrligkoffer with my agent, George Greenfield. George had helped us get the money for the South Face of Annapurna and was undoubtedly the most experienced, effective expedition agent in the business. He helped Sir Vivian Fuchs with his Trans-Antarctic expedition; Wally Herbert on his crossing of the North Pole, Sir Francis Chichester, Robin Knox-Johnston, and many others. As we flew out to meet Herrligkoffer, just before Christmas 1971, I couldn't help feeling uneasy. My motives for joining this expedition were a long way from the simple mountain challenge. This was professionalism – raising money for an expedition, writing about it and making sure that I got a fair cut of the proceeds for my writing and work for television companies.

We met Herrligkoffer at his flat in Munich. It was beautifully furnished in that slightly heavy German style, with good antiques, and its walls surrounded by statues and friezes, presumably collected on his Nanga Parbat trips. Herrligkoffer himself, with his bristling military moustache, heavily lined face and his swept-back white hair, was a severe rather cold figure. There was little feeling of shared anticipation of a great adventure. I realised we were negotiating like a group of businessmen over copyrights and how to raise money.

That afternoon we discussed and came to an agreement on the split of media rights. We left with no feeling of friendship, and I with very little enthusiasm for the expedition. Nevertheless, in the next six weeks, George Greenfield and I set about raising the necessary support for the German-British Everest expedition. Both the BBC and ITN were interested, as were several publishers and newspapers. There is no doubt that we could have raised a large part of the money that Herrligkoffer needed.

Now it became increasingly difficult to deal with him and it became quite obvious that he was trying to raise funds himself which cut across the copyrights we were arranging on his behalf, in order to be independent of the British contribution. In some ways I don't blame him, but he should have told us in the first place, instead of accepting our offer of help, allowing us to raise support for him, and then revoking our verbal agreement at the last moment.

In January I went off to the Alps with Dougal Haston to make an attempt on a new route on the North Face of the Grandes Jorasses. It was a wonderful escape from the financial manoeuvring we had landed in, to the clean simplicity of a big mountain challenge with a small group of friends. Dougal and I discussed Herrligkoffer's expedition whilst tucked in a small ice hole about a third of the way up the North Wall of the Grandes Jorasses. We both resolved to withdraw from the expedition. At this stage Herrligkoffer still had no oxygen, nor had he ordered any Sherpas from Nepal. The expedition seemed to have no hope of success, and there seemed little point in joining a doubtful cause which was likely to give us only a series of unhappy experiences.

Don Whillans stayed on in the expedition. He also had many doubts about Herrligkoffer, but nevertheless had a deep and burning desire to reach the summit of Everest. Perhaps in some respects his motives were material, as mine had been. Such an achievement would undoubtedly have crowned his career as a mountaineer and established him in a very strong position. I suspect he was very aware of both this and the actual financial rewards which would have accompanied his success. But his desire to go to the top of Everest was much more deep-rooted. Throughout his climbing career, he has always favoured bold, very obvious lines; has never really bothered with a contrived route which works its way subtly up a rock face or, for that matter, up a mountain. Climbing with him over a period of time, I had found that whereas I simply enjoyed the process of climbing, and provided I was climbing, worried little about the nature of the climb, Don would only set out on a climb which he felt was worthwhile. In recent years he seemed to have lost interest in British rock-climbing, although he put up some of the best and hardest routes in Britain in the fifties. His interests had gone further afield. He had also become genuinely interested in travel for its own sake. In 1968 he had taken part in an unsuccessful attempt to climb the South Face of Huandoy. He told me subsequently that the most enjoyable part of the trip for him was the return down the River Amazon. Everest, to him, was much more than the means of making a good living or establishing himself in the climbing firmament. It represented the ultimate superlative – the ultimate strong and simple objective. To attain it he was prepared to cope with an expedition which was anything but ideal in composition.

While I was still with the expedition, we had a fourth member to choose. Don was already established as the leader of the British contingent, but we consulted with each other, in spite of an element of stress which had entered our relationship after the Annapurna South Face expedition. We had both, separately, thought of Doug Scott as the best choice for the fourth member of the team.

Doug was an extremely powerful climber with a long record of pioneering behind him. Son of a Nottingham policeman, he started to climb at the age of twelve, having borrowed his mother's clothes-line. At the age of sixteen in 1957 he had his first trip to the Alps, arriving full of ambitions to do new routes, but being avalanched off the first climb he attempted. Undeterred he continued climbing and exploring, putting up new routes on the limestone outcrops near Derby, hitch-hiking as far afield as Morocco to look at the Atlas. In 1959 he left school to go to Loughborough to train to be a PE teacher, then returned to Nottingham, getting married at the age of twenty, to teach in a local secondary school. He stayed there for the next ten years, climbing to the full, mainly with a small group of Nottingham climbers, and also taking out many of his pupils to introduce them to the hills. He remained for a time outside the main stream of climbing, partially through the fact that he tended to remain with the same group and partially through his appetite for original climbing and expeditions; he preferred to go off to the further ranges rather than hammer the trade routes in the Alps. He organised on a shoestring budget expeditions to Turkey, the Tibesti in the Sahara, the Hindu Kush, where he made the first ascent of the 1500m high South Face of Badaka (6850m), and Baffin Island.

He also became increasingly interested in the American approach to climbing, making in 1971 the first British ascent of Salathé Wall in Yosemite – probably one of the most beautiful rock climbs in the world. He was powerfully built, weighed thirteen stone, played rugger regularly and kept fit throughout the year, running and climbing. With his proven performance at altitude and expedition experience he seemed a good choice for Everest.

Once Dougal and I had withdrawn from the team, Don looked around for a replacement, and chose Hamish MacInnes. Hamish was an old friend of mine. We had first met in 1953, when he took me, little more than a novice, on the first winter ascent of Raven's Gully. Since that time we had made an abortive attempt on the North Wall of the Eiger in 1957 (it would have been my first alpine route) and both of us had met Don Whillans for the first time when we set out to attempt the South West Pillar of the Drus. Don probably saved Hamish's life when he hauled him in a semi-conscious condition up most of the climb, after Hamish had been hit on the head by a falling stone. The following year Hamish and Don made the second British ascent of the Walker Spur of the Grandes Jorasses.

Hamish has had one of the most fascinating lives of any post-war British mountaineer. He is called, by his friends, the 'Old Fox of Glencoe' and is a complete individualist who has always carved his own path, regardless of what popular opinion might be at any one time. Shortly after our ascent of Raven's Gully in 1952, Hamish took off for New Zealand with that other very hard Scottish climber, John Cunningham. They took assisted passages out to New Zealand, but only stayed there for a few weeks before working their way on a boat to India, bound for no less than Mount Everest itself. They had heard that the Swiss expedition which had made attempts on Everest in the spring and autumn of 1952 had left dumps of food and oxygen all the way up the mountain. The two Scots were hoping to use these for a super-lightweight attempt. By the time they got in position, John Hunt and his Sassenachs had already beaten them to it, so they exchanged their objective to Pumo Ri, a very attractive, unclimbed, 7000m peak, immediately opposite the Everest Icefall. The entire expedition had been on a shoestring. They had jumped the Nepalese frontier, had employed a Sherpa to help carry their gear for a short time, but dismissed him when he complained of carrying a load of over 30 kilos. They were already carrying 40 kilos each. They parted with the Sherpa without ill-feeling, and the latter even presented them with a fork, since they were being forced to use pitons as eating utensils.

They lived off the land, on rice and tsampa until they reached the foot of the mountain, and then bought a goat to act as mountain rations. Hamish had a lightweight Boy Scout's sleeping bag and they had a threadbare tent for their high-altitude camps. Perhaps it was just as well that they were avalanched off the lower slopes of the mountain and were forced to abandon their attempt.

After a couple of years of climbing and lumberjacking back in New

Zealand, he returned to Britain. An abortive attempt on Rakaposhi with Mike Banks and some yeti-hunting in Kulu followed. He had taken photographs and was also beginning to make films. In the past few years he has established himself in his fox's lair in Glencoe, running a climbing school in the winter, manufacturing rescue equipment and organising the Glencoe Mountain Rescue Team. Today he is a world authority on mountain rescue.

Hamish was an ideal choice, since he had good contacts with both BBC and various newspapers and was therefore able to raise the funds required by Herrligkoffer as entry into the expedition. The position was still as confused and as unsatisfactory as when Dougal and I had pulled out. Herrligkoffer had originally planned to travel overland, but of course as a result of the Indo-Pakistan war, the frontier was still closed. At this stage he had no other means of transport; neither did he have sufficient oxygen equipment, or bottles, for the expedition, even though they were now only a few weeks from departure date. Lieutenant Colonel Jimmy Roberts, who probably had some of the best high-altitude Sherpas in Nepal in his employ, was not prepared to let him use any of these; the reason for this was concern for the safety of the Sherpas. At this point, however, Herrligkoffer did have one windfall. Senator Dr Franz Burda, who ran the German publishing firm Bunte, stepped in to cover him financially. This must have relieved Herrligkoffer from many of his financial worries and, of course, enabled him to do without the British media coverage which I had organised.

Don Whillans flew out to Munich to spend a week with Herrligkoffer, hoping that he would be able to give him the benefit of his experience on the face, and to discuss equipment for the expedition. Unfortunately this trip was to prove partially abortive. Herrligkoffer was heavily committed with his day-to-day medical practice and was also involved in a long-drawn-out lawsuit with Reinhold Messner – a by-product of the Nanga Parbat expedition. As a result Don had very little chance of advising Herrligkoffer, spending part of the time in court with him – to show Don what could happen to him, if he failed to toe the line, no doubt! At all stages Herrligkoffer was extremely secretive about his plans and did not even condescend to show Don full equipment lists for climbers and Sherpas. In failing to do this, he was going to land himself in a great deal of trouble on the expedition, since as an economy measure he had not budgeted for giving the Sherpas adequate down clothing and sleeping bags. During this week's meeting, Don had emphasised how important it was to equip the Sherpas with good gear on any Everest expedition.

Somehow, the expedition got off the ground. Don had found a good contact for oxygen cylinders which, ironically, were made in Germany, flown over to Britain to have valves fitted by Sabre Safety, a small oxygen equipment firm at Aldershot and then filled with British Oxygen. These bottles were still considerably cheaper than the French bottles, available to Herrligkoffer. The British contingent also secured for the expedition a number of tents from Blacks of Greenock, and the vital Whillans Boxes from Karrimor. They had also equipped themselves extremely adequately with Don's specially designed one-piece suits, Neoprene foam overboots, and all the other equipment they were going to need on the mountain. Their gear was to prove considerably superior to that used by the Germans.

It was on-off right to the last evening before departure. I have a feeling that Herrligkoffer was beginning to regret ever having invited his trouble-some British members. Doug Scott had taken all the oxygen bottles and tentage to Munich in a hired Transit van. Herrligkoffer seemed to have taken an immediate dislike to Doug – perhaps because of his long hair and slightly hippie appearance. He phoned Harold MacCarthy, who was his contact in Britain, to say that he wanted to drop Doug Scott from the team. Don relayed back immediately that if Doug went, Hamish and he would drop out as well. Demand and counter-demand now flickered back and forth between Munich, London and Rossendale, where Don lived. Many of the quibbles were financial; the root of the problem perhaps lying in the fact that there was none of the loyalty of friendship, or even of a united cause, to join the German-Austrian contingent with that from Britain. Don had been very frank with Herrligkoffer all the way along, putting his cards on the table, that he was a professional mountaineer and therefore needed to make some money out of the expedition. His view was identical to my own when I joined and then dropped out of the expedition. Don and the other members of the British contingent wanted to cover the cost of their individual contributions which Herrligkoffer had raised to £1000 per head and perhaps make some money themselves. This, of course, would involve extra work on their parts in writing, filming and sending film back. Herrligkoffer on the other hand, seems to have regarded this as 'profession-al money-grabbing'. He did not make any profit personally out of his expe-ditions. Presumably he didn't need to, since he had a good medical practice. He put all the profits from his expeditions into the Deutsches Institut für Auslandsforschung – a charitable institute, run by him from his own home address, and whose main function seemed to be to finance his many expeditions. All members of his expeditions had to sign a very full contract which, in actual fact, was similar to the one used by myself for the Annapurna South Face expedition, whose chief sponsor was the Mount Everest Foundation. In some ways you can't blame Herrligkoffer for expecting to have full copyright, plus that of all the photographs. On the other hand, he had invited climbers from a different country who had no allegiance to his institute, or to German mountaineering, and it was understandable that they would want to get hold of their own pictures and have the facility to write in their own country. This is really where the contradiction arose, in trying to form what had now become an almost bi-national expedition.

Don, Doug and Hamish were still arguing with Herrligkoffer over the financial ins-and-outs of the expedition right up to the last evening before flying out to Kathmandu to join the expedition. Hamish was in London trying to confirm with *The Observer* and the BBC the contracts that he had made with them on behalf of Herrligkoffer. Don was having a riotous farewell party in Rossendale, being dragged away every half hour or so from his cups to give his opinion on the latest gambit. It was at this stage that Don very aptly coined Herrligkoffer's nickname of 'Sterlingscoffer'. But Herrligkoffer, presumably, still needed the money that Hamish had managed to raise from the BBC and *The Observer*, and therefore finally an agreement was reached between the two parties.

It was hardly the happiest atmosphere in which to start an expedition. Don and Doug still hoped that perhaps everything would turn out all right once they reached the mountain and financial differences had been put behind them. The three British members of the team flew out, direct from London Airport, to Kathmandu on 12 March. Most of the remaining members of the team had already assembled in Kathmandu, and some of them were already at Luglha air strip ready to establish Base Camp. Herrligkoffer arrived a few days after. Don had a further shock on reaching Kathmandu when he learned that he had been demoted from the position of joint climbing leader, which he had been led to expect, leaving Felix Kuen as climbing leader of the expedition. The expedition had also acquired another name and was now known as the European Everest expedition. Presumably this was on the basis that the team comprised ten Germans, seven Austrians, three British, one Swiss, and one South Tyrol climber. The Continental element, however, were all essentially Austro-German, and the expedition split was definitely bi-national, with all the risks of 'them and us' creeping in when decisions became controversial.

By the time the three British members of the team flew into Luglha with Herrligkoffer, Base Camp was already established. The British team was amazed at the way Herrligkoffer ignored all the normal precautions one takes with acclimatisation. Herrligkoffer, keen to get to Base Camp as quickly as possible, rejected suggestions that they should stop for a day or so on the way up from Luglha to Base Camp, which is about 5330m (17,500ft). He insisted on pressing on and told the British that if they wanted to stop they would have to cater for themselves. Small things, but all abrasive to future relations. As a result of this course of action Herrligkoffer was showing some signs of altitude sickness on the way up. The Base Camp manager, Professor Huttl, had already collapsed from the altitude, perhaps partially as a result of rapid height gain, and had to be helped back to Luglha and then returned to Germany, taking no further part in the expedition. In addition, the British members of the team had been unlucky with their health in the early stages of the expedition. Don had trouble with his old recurring complaint of vertigo and was forced to retire to a sleeping bag on reaching Base Camp, while Doug had been knocked out with dysentery. Hamish was busy sorting out all his film equipment ready for the climb. As a result, the British members of the team were unable to take an active part either in the climbing or the load-carrying in the first few days of the expedition.

On 29 March, just three days after Herrligkoffer and the British had reached Base Camp, trouble erupted with Sherpas. Over the years Sherpas have come to expect a high standard of equipment. This, undoubtedly, has become one of the perks to be had from an expedition. A high-altitude Sherpa who is going out on two expeditions a year – one pre-monsoon and one post-monsoon – can expect a complete set of gear each time, and of course can sell this gear at the end of the expedition. Herrligkoffer was accustomed to the Hunzas, whom he had employed on Nanga Parbat in the Karakorum. These porters are not nearly so sophisticated as the Sherpas. On the whole, they don't give as good value for money as the Sherpas do in the shape of determination, enthusiasm and expertise, but along with this, they do not demand quite so much. Herrligkoffer, no doubt, had planned the equipping of the Sherpas on much the same lines as had proved satisfactory with his Hunza porters. In spite of the warnings which Don Whillans had given to him, he had only sufficient down gear for the fifteen high-altitude Sherpas who would be going up on the South West Face. There were insufficient foam mattresses, and he had omitted to bring out double sleeping bags even for the high-altitude Sherpas; there was no down clothing for the Icefall Sherpas at all. The argument that ensued was undoubtedly motivated by the poor relationship which had already developed between the Germans and the Sherpas. The Germans tended to shout at the Sherpas and to bully them and, of course, to make matters worse there was a language barrier, since although most of the Sherpas spoke a smattering of English, none of them could speak German and few of the Germans could speak English. The Sherpas were demanding more down clothing, refusing point blank to go any further on the mountain without it. Herrligkoffer, perhaps not unreasonably, explained that they had no more down clothing, and that therefore they could not give them any. (We were to have a very similar argument with the Sherpas during our autumn expedition.) This very nearly ended in complete deadlock and probably would have done but for Don Whillans, who got on extremely well with the Sherpas, and their excellent liaison officer, Mr Pandi, who negotiated between the two parties in the argument.

Eventually Herrligkoffer resigned himself to rushing back to Germany to collect more down equipment, and chartered a helicopter from Kathmandu to pick him up at Base Camp to speed his journey. He was very bitter when, on his return from Germany with the down clothing which had been demanded, many of the Sherpas simply took the equipment and hid it away in their tents for resale after the expedition, and continued to use the old equipment which they had said was inadequate.

No sooner had this problem been solved than another row reared its head. On the evening of 1 April, there was a meeting at which the lack of activity of the British members of the team was discussed. Don was summoned from his sleeping bag, still badly stricken with vertigo, to answer for the British. He put the case very strongly that everyone needed to acclimatise at his own rate, but the Germans remained uninterested, convinced that the British were saving themselves for later on. The real crux of the matter was the basic distrust between the two parties. Felix Kuen was a close friend of Schlömmer, who had been on the International expedition. There had been no love lost at all between Schlömmer and Don, and the former had given his version of the story to Kuen. There is no doubt that the Austro-Germans arrived on the expedition with a very strong prejudice against the members of the British team and Don in particular, being firmly convinced that their one intention was to reach the summit of Everest for their own personal satisfaction and glory.

At this stage an unofficial member of the expedition arrived – Mischa Saleki, a Persian who had originally been invited by Herrligkoffer to join the expedition, but at a later stage had been dropped from it. Mischa was extremely bitter, since he had put in a lot of work raising money for the expedition, in Persia, and had also obtained a certain amount of equipment. In Doug's words:

It was hardly surprising that he was in a particularly vindictive frame of mind when he arrived, determined to avenge himself for the humiliation he felt he had received in the face of his friends in the Persian government (which was sponsoring him in part), as a result of the leader's treatment. It was clear that if Saleki were allowed to give vent to his feelings, there would be some serious repercussions. Between us, we managed to talk him round to helping the expedition to be a success, and he became calmer when he realised that he had at least three sympathetic companions to confide in.

On 4 April, Felix Kuen, Adolf Huber, Werner Haim and Leo

Breitenberger moved up to Camp 1 to make the route up to Camp 2. This foursome became known as the Big Four, since during the first part of the expedition they stayed in the lead, using the rest of the team as load-carriers to support them. It was a similar step to the one taken by Don Whillans, Dougal Haston and the two Japanese, Ito and Uemura, on the International expedition the previous year. There was one big difference, however, since in the case of the International expedition, it was unlikely that any other climbing pair could effectively have taken up the role of lead climbers. But on this expedition, there were other candidates for the lead, though at the time the Big Four moved out in front, Don was still suffering with his ear trouble. He attempted to do a carry up to Camp 1 on 5 April but only made it halfway before being forced to retire. Fortunately, in the next few days he recovered fully, and the other two were also becoming increasingly well acclimatised and fit.

On 10 April, the British trio moved up to Camp 1, to be hit by a savage storm which very nearly caused several casualties on the mountain. Don had set out behind the other two and was caught in the white-out near the top of the Icefall. Only a freak break in the storm enabled him to see the tent at Camp 1 and reach the others; if he had not found it, he would have had an extremely unpleasant night out.

Up at Camp 2 the Austro-Germans were even more severely hit. The tents were not sufficiently strong and the plastic groundsheets quickly disintegrated as a result of the combination of wind and cold. The tents filled up with snow from underneath. The lead climbers had a desperate night and next morning retreated to Camp 1. They recovered quite quickly, however, and returned to Camp 2 once the storm was over. From Camp 1 the British trio made five carries before moving up. Doug Scott suspected that Kuen was trying to keep them one step removed from themselves out front, the whole time. On 17 April, he wrote in his diary:

Radio call from Felix taken by Peter Bedner. Felix wanted five Sherpas to come up in a few days to stay at Camp 2. Seems to be edging us out, wants us to stay here at 1 to keep Sherpas moving up loads. Suits us just now, as long as he doesn't turn round when he's in the shit – i.e. down with altitude sickness, no supplies coming up, etc., and ask why we are not at the front. Seems to alternate in his thinking between us hogging the lead and not doing anything.

Perner's parting shot while I'm on the way down, was to say that Felix and Don must get together, and Felix thinks that Don is lazy!

Meanwhile, the Big Four started work on the South West Face, running the fixed rope up to Camp 3 quite quickly and then moving up. Their progress now began to slow, and it took them six full days to make the route up to Camp 4. Back at Camp 2, their Austrian support group began to get impatient, demanding a turn out in front. The British trio were quite glad to be out of the line of fire for once and let the Austro-Germans fight it out amongst themselves.

The lead climbers were now undoubtedly beginning to tire. Huber developed a sore throat and had to descend to Base, while Breitenberger who was also on the verge of collapse was finally forced down. The British trio were appalled at the way the lead climbers bullied and shouted at Breitenberger to try to keep him going. They were more like a group of drill sergeants bullying new recruits than climbers on the highest mountain in the world. Don now suggested that Hamish, Doug and he should move up to Camp 3 and establish Camp 4. Felix Kuen agreed to this in return for a promise that the British, under no circumstances, would go beyond Camp 4. He seemed determined to deprive them of the glory or satisfaction of doing any lead climbing.

April was now slipping by and the team were undoubtedly behind schedule if they were to make an effective bid for the summit, in spite of having had one of the best seasons for years. Part of the problem was the fact that only a limited number of the Sherpas had been persuaded to come up into the Western Cwm, since they still had insufficient gear and equipment. As a result the build-up of supplies, even at Camp 2, was inadequate. The push up the face had also been on the slow side, especially when one considers that the fixed ropes left by the International expedition were still in place on the route from Camp 3 to 4, and then up to 5; they only had to use a comparatively small amount of their own rope to link stretches which were either covered in snow, or where the rope had been damaged.

There was so much work to be done in building platforms at Camp 4, the British trio, with Horst Schneider, moved up to the Camp on 30 April, and in the next two days put up two boxes and three platforms. Two of these had been brought out from Germany and were based on a design which Don had sketched for Herrligkoffer on his visit to Munich before the expedition. The other platform was already in place and was easily renovated. In view of their promise, they returned to Camp 2, having completed their task, to find that the expedition had been deprived of yet another climber. Werner Haim had been hit on the knee by a rock and had to be taken down to Camp 1. This was particularly unfortunate since Haim, as well as being a first-class climber, got on well with the British members of the team and acted as something of a mediator between them and the Huber-Kuen duo.

It was at this time that Herrligkoffer returned from Germany with the down gear demanded by the Sherpas. This precipitated another crisis. The lead climbers, who admittedly had been out in front for a lot of the time, while the British members of the team had been down at Base Camp, were now extremely tired. They felt the need for a rest, and Herrligkoffer's arrival in Base Camp seemed a good moment. Michel Anderl, the deputy leader, called the whole team back down to Base Camp to welcome Herrligkoffer, and put on a good show for him. Don was appalled at this decision, since time was now running out fast; the weather was excellent, and this seemed the time for an all-out push. He favoured staying up, with as many Sherpas as possible, to keep the route going. Kuen and the German leadership rejected this suggestion and told him to come down with the others. Don, however, decided to stay on and naturally Hamish and Doug stayed with him. They were not alone, however, since Adi Weissensteiner (who had taken over the unenviable job of controlling the Sherpas), Adi Sager and five Sherpas stayed at Camp 2. Hamish, Doug and Don now resolved to move up to Camp 4, to try to establish and stock Camp 5, supported by the Sherpas. Unfortunately, however, the latter objective proved impractical since the Icefall Sherpas, and those working from Camp 1 to 2, had mostly gone down to see the homecoming celebrations for Dr Herrligkoffer. Doug Scott takes up the story:

The casualty list was now growing, and in theory at least, we were fortunate to have the Doctor back. Leo Breitenberger was sent back to Kathmandu in the helicopter which came to collect Haim. According to Herrligkoffer, Breitenberger had pulmonary oedema, but in fact, he turned out to be suffering from pleurisy, while Haim came back to Base Camp two weeks later, having recovered from a suspected shattered knee joint! However, the doctor did not tend many more patients before he, too, had to be evacuated. He had flown up to 15,000ft and had a mild heart attack from the physiological strain this entailed.

Horst Vitt, the German diplomat, had already died from pulmonary oedema, having tried to reach Base Camp too quickly to take over from the unfortunate Professor Huttl. Mischa Saleki also joined the list of evacuees, though for a different reason. Unable to stand the derision which came his way any longer, he stowed away in a helicopter, according to German press statements. Considering the machines only seated two, he must have made himself very inconspicuous, if not invisible, and presumably almost weightless! (Incidentally, these were the highest helicopter comings and goings ever recorded as far as we know.) Finally, Hans Berger had gallstone trouble and severe pains in his bladder, but with suitable treatment he was able to come back towards the end.

On the credit side, Peter Bedner recovered from a wrongly administered cholera injection which had plagued him throughout the expedition. Luckily, a visiting band of German professors had diagnosed his problem and had treated him correctly. Peter was at last able to reach the face after being posted for weeks at a time at the lonely Camp 1. Meanwhile, we went up to Camp 4, and in the next few days fixed 500ft of rope up to Camp 5, using the remainder of the International expedition's rope which Dougal and Don had placed the year before. We dumped ropes, tents and oxygen at the site and chopped out a platform for two tents.

Their action in staying up at Camp 5 was severely criticised, and even described as 'sabotage' by Kuen and Herrligkoffer. Kuen states:

Finally the Englishmen left the Camp that they had already occupied for ten days. For sleeping they had used up fifteen large bottles of oxygen, in addition to a whole lot of provisions and yet in ten days they had merely laid 40m of rope between Camps 4 and 5 and set up a Whillans Box and a platform. They had forcibly taken away from the Sherpas, who were on the route between Camp 3 and 4, flasks of oxygen and used them up in Camp 4. The Britons had grievously upset the provisioning plans of Camp 5 and intentionally or unintentionally had sabotaged it.

Accusation and counter-accusation. Doug Scott assures me that they only used four bottles in the entire period and that the other bottles which Kuen found when he returned to Camp 4 had been uncovered when they had dug out the platform, having been left from the International expedition. The British trio were doing their best to uphold their part of the bargain, and keep the expedition going. In a period of ten days they were at Camp 4, they made the route up to Camp 5. Doug and Hamish went out the first day but, unfortunately, Hamish was forced to retreat with stomach trouble. Doug carried on, climbing solo, going higher than he had ever been before, using the fixed ropes of the International expedition as far as possible, joining one or two gaps with the fresh rope he was carrying. He went up to a height of almost 7925m (26,000ft), to the head of the Great Central Couloir which is short of the point where one traverses right to reach Camp 5.

The next day Don went out with him and they made the route all the way up to Camp 5, where they started digging out a platform. Then they made one or two further carries to Camp 5. Admittedly, they did spend a long time at Camp 4 without making appreciable progress. There was, however, some bad weather during this period and they experienced a certain amount of trouble with the Sabre oxygen equipment which Don had had specially developed for the expedition.

When Kuen and Huber arrived on 10 May, there were more arguments. In Doug's words:

Huber and Kuen arrived at Camp 4, armed with a plan they had worked out at Base Camp. In effect it placed us in Camp 3, and Sherpas in Camp 4 with Peter Perner or

Adi Weissensteiner if the latter's cough would allow it. Horst Schneider and Adi Sager were to go to Camp 5 and Kuen and Huber to 6. When all was ready two of us were to be allowed to join them at the front in an attack on the summit. But just how we could get enough oxygen and other equipment up there, to support four climbers, was not explained, and we grew suspicious. We had a feeling that we were being edged out again. So we worked out a compromise plan, which put us in support of the summit pair, with one other Austrian accompanying us in Camp 5. After Kuen and Huber had made their bid, we four of the support party would have a go.

After some debate, this proposal was accepted and Kuen and Huber moved up to 5. Unfortunately, Schneider and Sager were not satisfied with the new arrangements and they went to persuade Kuen to revert to his original plan. The crunch came when Schneider and Sager returned from their mission. Schneider said, 'You British are in trouble. Kuen says you must go down to Camp 3 or he will come down, call off the Sherpas and end the expedition.' Next day we went down to Camp 2 and later to Base Camp. We had come to the end, and reached the point where personality differences could no longer be ignored. Both Schneider and Sager refused to carry for Don; even the equable Peter Bedner said he was fed up with acting as a Sherpa for the British.

It must be noted that the British trio had not insisted on having the first attempt at the summit; they had merely asked to support the summit pair from Camp 5, and that they should have the second summit attempt. The relationship between the Britons and the Austrians had become so bad, however, that the split had now spread from not only between them and the Big Four, but to one between them and most of the other Austrian members of the team.

On a mountain such as Everest, when one has reached the point where one pair, or group, believe that others are saving themselves solely for a summit bid, teamwork becomes impossible. It is ironic that Don, with Doug and Hamish, felt forced to take the same controversial step that Mazeaud, the Vauchers and Carlo Mauri took on the International expedition. On the other hand, on this occasion, the British trio had taken a very full and active part in the expedition, and in the later stages had done their best to make a series of compromises to keep the expedition going.

The British trio reached Camp 2 on the morning of 15 May and then that afternoon were amazed by the arrival of Felix Kuen and Huber, back at Camp 2. This was particularly ironic in the light of his threat that unless the Britons dropped back to Camp 3 he would come down and call off the expedition. One wonders whether he had lost his nerve, finding that he was out in front by himself. In an article in *Bergsteiger* he described how his sleeping bag in Camp 5 was surrounded by a crust of ice within breathing range, and stated that 'life here is unbearable'.

The three Britons had had enough, however, and went down to Base Camp the next day. Two days later, 18 May, a last attempt to reach the summit was begun. Kuen, Huber and Berger climbed straight from Camp 2 up to Camp 4, and then, on 19 May, Sager, Bedner, Schneider, Huber and Kuen moved into Camp 5. They now had five Sherpas carrying loads straight through from Camp 2 to Camp 4, but supplies were undoubtedly thin on the face and there was certainly insufficient oxygen equipment for a protracted assault. On 21 May, the five Austrians, with two Sherpas, moved up to Camp 6, once again using the ropes left by the International expedition for most of the way. Kuen, Huber, Sager and Schneider all planned to stay that night in a single two-man tent, which they had erected at Camp 6. While Schneider and Sager erected the tent in a cleft in the cliff, Kuen, together with Huber worked his way round the corner of the rock tower to an almost horizontal stretch leading up to the snowfield. They were thus planning to bypass the true difficulties of the Rock Band on the South West Face, to take the escape route which Don had discovered the previous year. It was now getting dark, so the pair returned to the already crowded two-man tent.

That night the weather broke and it began to hail, the temperature sinking to −40°C. The weather was still very bad the next morning and the team had insufficient reserves of either stamina or food and equipment to sit it out and wait for the bad weather to subside, so on 22 May they decided to turn back and abandon their attempt.

It is an academic point whether Kuen and Huber got higher than Don and Dougal the previous year. They had traversed round the corner while of course Don and Dougal had climbed straight up into the gully which seemed to penetrate the Rock Band. The two Austrians claim to have got to a point higher than that of the two Britons, but this is unlikely in the light of the route which they followed. It certainly is not worth wasting any time in conjecture on whether they did or did not.

And so another expedition to the South West Face ended in acrimony and arguments. Looking at all three expeditions dispassionately, whoever was right or wrong on the different sides of the argument, the leadership of each expedition seemed to have made several basic mistakes. The Japanese, in 1970, were undoubtedly an extremely strong and well-organised expedition, but had split their objective between the sure South East Ridge route and the South West Face. Their team, large though it was, was still not big enough to sustain two independent attempts and, as a result, had had to decide upon which one to give priority. They had decided, with some argument within the team, to give priority to the South East Ridge route, to make sure that they put a Japanese on the summit of Everest. They did, at least, have partial success by reaching the summit, and, perhaps equally important, they did return to Japan as a united party.

The following year the International expedition compounded the Japanese mistakes by taking out an expedition which was, if anything, slightly weaker than that of the Japanese, and yet at the same time tackling two objectives. One of these was the West Ridge of Everest, which was considerably harder and therefore demanded greater logistic preparations than the South Col route. Even so, the International expedition might well have succeeded had it been more fortunate with weather and had it been spared the tragic death of Harsh Bahuguna. The storm which had occurred in the middle of the expedition shattered the fragile unity of the international team, and caused the defection of Pierre Mazeaud and his friends. It is extraordinary how each expedition repeated mistakes which could perhaps have been avoided, had the expedition leaders analysed the previous expeditions.

Herrligkoffer was at least going for a single objective, but the structure of the team was probably potentially more dangerous even than that of the International expedition. In effect, there were two groups – the British trio and the Austro-Germans plus the rest of the expedition. The Austro-Germans, even though several of them were not enamoured of Herrligkoffer's leadership, remained essentially loyal to the leader's directive. The British group, coming from a different environment, without any of the automatic ties of loyalty that bound the Austro-Germans, were inevitably more critical. It seemed to me, when I was considering whether to pull out of the expedition or not, that a lack of sound preparation before the expedition, and this bi-national split during the expedition, could make failure almost inevitable. Sadly, this proved to be the case. The failure of these two international expeditions has led to an automatic condemnation of all international climbing enterprises. I suspect that in the case of Everest, this could be justifiable. So many pressures are brought to bear on the Everest climber, particularly one going for the South West Face. For a start, the expedition must inevitably be large and therefore expensive. If the money is raised from the media and commerce, naturally they want a return in publicity, and it is this very publicity that imposes the greatest pressures on the climbing members of the team. There is even a touch of the international golf tournament with individual members being given star category in the reporting and, in the event of success, the pair reaching the summit are lionised, to the inevitable exclusion of the other team members who helped them to get there. There is nothing new in this. The publicity following the pre-war Everest attempts was every bit as intense as that which follows today's epics. In 1953, it was Hillary and Tenzing who received the accolades for reaching the summit of Everest. Who, today, remembers the efforts of George Lowe in forcing the route up to the South Col – or Evans and Bourdillon who made the first summit attempt?

Immediately the purist will say that no climber worth his salt will be concerned with such sordid matters as material rewards, fame, or a position in history. But this attitude is unrealistic; even the most modest of people like to have their efforts recognised in relation to the contribution they have made to the success of a venture.

It seems to me essential that the leader who selects a team must know the members of that team extremely well. Only then can he assess how far each member will co-operate with the others, and estimate to what degree they will be prepared to sacrifice their own ambitions for the good of the team as a whole. It is unlikely that you are going to be able to assemble a team of totally unselfish easy-going people, since the talented climber needed for forcing a route to the summit, by his very nature, will have strong ambitions and is probably quite an egotist. It is essential, therefore, to get a group together who can accept each other's role within the team, and each other's ambitions, and who will also be prepared to compromise in the face of conflict. It is undoubtedly a lot easier to assemble such a group from a single country, simply because most of the climbers one knows to that degree will come from the same country as oneself.

Were these three expeditions a total waste of time? Certainly not – each expedition learned something more about the mountain. In Doug Scott's words, summing up what he learned on his first trip to Everest:

To me, the trip gave rise to few delusions of grandeur; I am simply glad to have been able to go up the Icefall unscathed, and to have entered the Western Cwm, that incomparable valley of snow lying between the iridescent ice of Nuptse and the hanging glaciers of the South West side of Everest. Each day I expected to succumb to the altitude; I examined myself minutely each morning for sore throat or other symptoms. Thanks to Don's guidance, all three of us acclimatised slowly, and after more than two weeks and four carries up to Camp 5, we went well to the end. One of the driving forces was a personal curiosity to find out how high one can go before the stomach starts to heave, the legs fold under, the head aches and the mind hallucinates.

Once back home the bad memories fade; one's slides and photographs bring back the haunting beauty of rock and ice swept by winds and avalanche and scorched by strong sunlight. It is an area of stark beauty where nothing grows; no trees, no flowers, no lichens even; it is a place where man's confidence is quickly shattered by a slight disturbance in the atmosphere which may transform the once quiet face into a whirling mass of spindrift, sending its insolent invaders scuttling to their tents, battered by the fury raging outside.

And so, climbers continued to dream of the South West Face of Everest, and in most of them, this whole mixed range of motivations encompassed a full span between idealism and materialism.

5

Preparations for our own expedition

Autumn 1972

The lure of Everest and the attraction of leading my own expedition had proved too much for me, even during the course of the International expedition.

I had been trying to get permission to attempt the South West Face, ever since I heard of the failure of the International expedition of 1971. The problem was that a dozen other climbers, from different countries, had the same idea. The Nepalese authorities only released a list of firm bookings for Everest in the New Year of 1972. Most of these applications had been in for some years and, as a result, we weren't even on the end of the list. An Italian millionaire called Guido Monzino had Everest for both the autumn of 1972 and the spring of 1973. He was planning to make a reconnaissance in the autumn and then a full-scale attempt (apparently only on the South East Ridge, not the face) the following spring. The Japanese Rock Climbers' Club had Everest for the autumn of 1973, the Spaniards for the spring of 1974 and the Japanese Ladies for the spring of 1975. I already knew that the British Army had put in an application for Everest, and were hoping to get permission for the spring of 1976. It seemed an awful long time to wait, though there was some possibility that some of these expeditions might fail to materialise.

My contact in Kathmandu was Mike Cheney, who was assistant to Jimmy Roberts. He was a bird-like little man, with a slightly high-pitched voice which disguised an extraordinary level of courage. Having been in the Gurkhas, he had retired to take up tea-planting in India. He had then contracted cancer and was warned that he had only a couple of months to live. A resolve to get the utmost out of life in the time left to him, made him decide to go and settle in Nepal, and he drove there by Land-Rover in defiance of his doctors, who had told him he should be in bed. Like Francis Chichester, by refusing to bow down to a seemingly fatal disease, he somehow succeeded in defying death. On reaching Nepal he started working for Jimmy Roberts. Mike had access to all the latest information on expeditions' comings and goings in Kathmandu. Consequently, he was able to help me in putting in applications to the Nepalese government, and also indicating any possibly vacant slots.

In January 1972, just after I had pulled out of Herrligkoffer's expedition, it seemed possible that Monzino might abandon his expeditions altogether. I hoped for the spring slot of 1973, since tackling Everest in the autumn presented a large number of problems. There are two periods in which you can climb in Nepal and they have very different characteristics. The pre-monsoon season is squeezed between the clearing of the winter snows, round about the beginning of March, and the arrival of the monsoon at the end of May: the post-monsoon season starts at the end of the monsoon – any time between mid-September to early-October – and then trails off into the gathering winter cold. During the pre-monsoon season, the weather tends to be more unsettled than post-monsoon. However, there are two advantages in climbing in the spring. Firstly, the temperature is getting progressively warmer during the course of the expedition, so that when the team are in a position to make a summit bid, hopefully before the arrival of the monsoon, the weather is also at its warmest. In addition, the winds in the spring do not seem to be anything like as serious as they are in the autumn. In the autumn you have the converse effect; when the team starts off it is relatively warm, in the immediate lee of the monsoon and then, as they climb higher up the mountain, it gets progressively colder. Thus, when they are ready to make a bid for the summit, the weather is considerably colder than when they started. Much more serious, however, during the autumn, are the high-altitude jet-stream winds which seem to blow continuously at an altitude starting at round about 7500m (24,500ft). It is for this reason that the record of expeditions attempting mountains of over 8000m in the post-monsoon season has been very poor. The only mountain of this category to be climbed was Cho Oyu (8153m/26,750ft), on 19 October 1954 by a very small, compact Austrian expedition led by Herbert Tichy. There was, however, practically no technical climbing on this mountain – it being little more than a very high-altitude fell walk.

The story on Everest in the post-monsoon season has been depressing. In 1952, the Swiss made two attempts to make the first ascent of Everest. Their first attempt in the spring of 1952, an expedition led by Dr Edouard Wyss-Dunant, was very nearly successful when Raymond Lambert and Tenzing, who was to climb Everest in 1953, made their summit bid from Camp 7 at a height of 8300m. They reached a height of 8560m, roughly 288m below the summit, but were going so slowly, mainly because the oxygen system was defective, that it was obvious to them that they would not be able to reach the top and then get back before dark. They were therefore forced to retreat back to the South Col.

Having been so close to success, they resolved to return in the autumn. This expedition was led by Dr Gabriel Chevaley, and the climbing leader was now Raymond Lambert. Norman Dyhrenfurth joined the expedition as photographer and film cameraman. Base Camp was established on 2 October, but they only succeeded in repeating the route through the Icefall and establishing Camp 3 at the head of it (our Camp 1) on 14 October. On 20 October, their Camp 4 (our Camp 2) was established, in the middle of the Western Cwm. They were undoubtedly getting rather late in the season, and were further delayed by an unfortunate accident to one of their best Sherpas, Mingma Dorji, when a sérac on the Lhotse Face collapsed and swept him away. Several other members of the team were injured at the same time. Partly as a result of these delays they only reached the South Col on 19 November, when Lambert, Reiss and Tenzing, with seven Sherpas, did a carry up to it. On 20 November, the three climbers moved upwards, towards the South East Ridge, but were met at a height of about 8000m by a hurricane of polar temperature and intensity – a barrier which it would have been near-suicidal to cross. They had no choice but to retreat. The following year, in the spring, John Hunt's expedition succeeded in climbing Everest.

Norman Dyhrenfurth returned to the Everest massif in 1955, as leader of an International expedition, which attempted a direct route up Lhotse from the Western Cwm. They, too, were defeated by savage winds in the post-monsoon season. The only hopeful factor in considering the post-monsoon season for an attempt on the South West Face was the experience of the Japanese in the autumn of 1969. They did not have any particular problems with wind at all. Whether this was a freak season, or whether they were getting some shelter from the positioning of the South West Face, it was impossible to tell, but it did give some rise for hope. The experience of the Argentinian expedition in the autumn of 1971 certainly was not encouraging, since they also were defeated by savage winds once they reached the South Col of Everest. Earlier than the Swiss had been in 1952, they established Base Camp on 15 September and found the Icefall with a good covering of snow which made progress easy and faster. They took a mere three days to climb the Icefall against the fortnight taken the previous spring by the International expedition, and by 21 September, had established Camp 3 at the foot of the Lhotse Face at a height of 7000m. Then on 30 September, they had severe storms which put down very heavy snowfall – at Base Camp 50cm, Camp 1 – 1.70m, at Camp 2 – 1.50m and at Camp 3 an incredible 2m. These heavy post-monsoon snowfalls definitely seem to be a feature of this period; most of the time the sky is clear, and even though there is high wind there is blue sky. When it does snow, it snows very heavily indeed and, as a result, the damage caused by a couple of days' snowfall lasts for several more days before an expedition can recover itself and get moving again. The Argentinians were increasingly troubled by high winds and snow as they climbed the Lhotse Face, but in spite of this, they succeeded in reaching the South Col on 28 October, and actually established Camp 5 there on the 29th. The wind was very savage, however, at 160 kilometres an hour, the temperature –38°C and they could make no further progress. Their tents were being torn to bits by the winds, three Sherpas had frost-bite, and so they, also, had to surrender to near-impossible weather conditions, abandoning their top camp on the South Col on 31 October. Their leader, Lieutenant Colonel Captiva Tolosa, did give us some grounds for hope, however, since he told us that the South West Face seemed to get some shelter from these very high winds.

Another reason why I did not like the idea of trying the South West Face of Everest in the autumn of 1972 was that we would have no time at all to organise the expedition, since we could not really get under way until we had learned the fate of Dr Herrligkoffer's expedition. From initial reports in March and early April, they seemed to make good progress and there was the probability that they could well climb the mountain. I very much doubted if they would try the true South West Face, but even if they managed to get round the escape route which Don had spied in 1971 and reach the summit of Everest, we would probably have had considerable difficulties in raising funds for an attempt on the true South West Face route.

The other factor was that I felt that the quality of the Sherpa support was vital to our chances of success. The best and most reliable Sherpas available in Nepal were, without doubt, employed by Jimmy Roberts of Mountain Travel. I had already asked Jimmy, as well as Mike Cheney, whether they would be interested in being involved in the expedition. At this stage they had to warn me that the autumn was at the height of their trekking season, that therefore neither they, nor their Sherpas would be available at this period. Jimmy and Mike were hoping that Monzino might withdraw altogether, and we might be able to get the spring slot for ourselves. We were not the only climbers who were trying to jump the queue. A representative of the Spanish expedition, which already had permission for 1974, armed with a letter from Prince Carlos of Spain, was rumoured to have arrived in Kathmandu, pressing their cause for going out a year early. They, of course, were in front of us in the queue. Mike Cheney also warned me that the Canadian Alpine Club were trying for permission for Everest, though when I wrote to them their President assured me that he had never heard of any such plan. This manoeuvring for the mountain had very little to do with real climbing, and yet, strangely, it had its own special fascination, though at times it became downright frustrating. At this stage the only person involved in my plans was Dougal Haston who was always mildly amused by my obvious enjoyment of the wheeling and dealing of trying to get the mountain. Dougal was quite happy sitting back in Leysin, skiing and climbing, and waiting to see what the fates would bring.

Then in mid-April we learned that we would almost certainly be able to get the post-monsoon slot in 1972, for Monzino had definitely withdrawn. Monzino, however, still had his options open on the spring 1973 slot. Though I felt that we had to commit ourselves to this certain chance rather than hope that Monzino would withdraw in the spring also, I was still extremely worried about the prospect of trying to organise a South West Face expedition at such short notice, in such a doubtful period of the year, with the likelihood that we would not have the best Sherpas. It was obvious that a South West Face of Everest expedition would cost something in the region of £60,000 – a lot of money to collect in the course of a few weeks. But then I had another idea. Why not attempt Everest by the South Col route, with a lightweight expedition? This would mean that there would be nothing like the same financial involvement, and yet the challenge would be there, and probably with a small expedition it would be very much more fun. Immediately, I attacked the new concept with enthusiasm. Just how small can you pare down an Everest expedition? The ultimate, of course, would be one man, on his own. This had been tried back in 1934 when Maurice Wilson attempted to climb Everest from the North. No experienced alpinist, he was a dreamer and mystic, who slipped into Tibet in native dress, with three Sherpas and a single pony carrying all his equipment. He reached Camp 3 on the north side of Everest, at a height of 6400m without any difficulty, but his porters, not surprisingly, had never taken his attempt very seriously, and now refused to go any further. Determined not to give in, however, he made several attempts to reach the South Col and finally died of cold and exhaustion. His body was found in 1935 quite close to Camp 3. There was another solo attempt in 1947, by a Canadian adventurer called Earl Denman. He claimed to have reached 7000m (23,000ft) – a height higher than the North Col of Everest, but there was no evidence to back up his claim. He was only away from Darjeeling for five weeks.

The scale of Everest is so vast that it is difficult to conceive of a successful solo attempt. All the expeditions to Everest have been on the heavy side, with strong back-ups of Sherpas. The only exception was another unofficial expedition of four climbers, three Americans and one Swiss, led by Woodrow Wilson Sayre, a grandson of the former US President. Their declared objective was Gyachung Kang, a magnificent peak of 7952m (26,089ft) which in itself was probably beyond their capabilities. The party was comparatively inexperienced, poorly equipped and had no porters. Reaching the Gyachung Kang region, they slipped over the Tibetan frontier on to the Rongbuk Glacier, and succeeded in climbing well above the North Col of Everest to a height of 7600m (25,000ft). This was a remarkable achievement, but the attempt was fairly heavily castigated in conventional climbing circles. Ramsay Ullman in his official book telling the story of the

American Everest expedition, declares:·

In retrospect, as told by Sayre, the exploit was all fun and games. It made lively reading in *Life* magazine and a good story on the lecture circuit. But it is exactly this sort of hare-brained adventuring that makes the general public think all climbers are mentally deficient. And it hasn't the remotest resemblance to what true mountaineers mean by 'mountaineering'.

But I wonder. There are quite a few mountaineers today who are beginning to feel that this type of expedition is true mountaineering, while the massive, hopefully well-organised, expeditions are getting quite a long way from it. Another challenge on Everest, of course, is to try to climb the mountain without oxygen. This is the only way that a truly lightweight expedition could succeed, since the weight of the oxygen bottles needed on the upper slopes of the mountain mean that you need a fair number of load-carriers and consequently the size of the expedition must inevitably escalate. There is a certain appeal in the thought of man, unaided, reaching the summit of Everest. It would undoubtedly be a really huge challenge, since from all the evidence gained so far, particularly from the pre-war expeditions, the height of 8500m (28,000ft) seems to be a critical one without the use of oxygen. The climber who tries to reach the summit of Everest without oxygen is certainly taking huge risks, not only with his life but perhaps also with his future health – he would be making a super-human effort on a body and brain starved of oxygen. Nobody knows just how much damage would or would not be caused by this effort.

These, then, were the lines on which I was thinking for an attempt on the South Col route of Everest. I put a great deal of thought into the matter and finally came up with what I felt was the minimum practical number for an attempt using oxygen – a climbing team of four climbers supported by two others, since you would need someone at Base Camp and at Advanced Base Camp in the Western Cwm. But this could not be a true four-man team; I intended to use oxygen and so inevitably the logistic load on just four men would be much too great. Therefore, one had to bring in some Sherpas as well and I planned on using six Sherpas. The team, then, would total twelve men – by no means minuscule as expeditions go, but still very much smaller than the average.

I based my planning on what I had learned on the South Face of Annapurna. One factor which made it very much easier was that the route was known. Also the length of time it would take to set up each section of the route between camps was fairly predictable. My calculations started with a hypothetical two climbers at the top camp – which would be at a height of approximately 8360m (27,600ft) – with a tent, sleeping bags, gear needed for the night and the oxygen bottles they would need for the assault the next day. You then work out how many carries it is going to take to get the pair into that position, together with the number of bottles of oxygen required by the climbers carrying the loads. You add this weight to the weight of the tentage of the penultimate camp on the South Col, the amount of spare oxygen bottles and so on, that are going to be required there, and so you can work it out, all the way down the mountain.

A theory I worked out was that having established Camp 2, the Advanced Base Camp, in the Western Cwm, you can climb Everest in eight days, given perfect weather; two days to ferry requisite gear to Camp 3 at the Lhotse Face and establish four climbers and six Sherpas; two days to climb, fix ropes where necessary and ferry gear to Camp 4, halfway up the Lhotse Face. Climbers, using oxygen from the foot of the face, would move up to Camp 4 with two Sherpas; two days for the four climbers to move up to Camp 5 on the South Col, and one day to establish two climbers in their high camp on the South Ridge. The support pair at Camp 5 would move up to Camp 6 on the day of the assault, and have a chance of either making a second attempt or a second ascent.

As far as the Icefall was concerned, we should, of course, need as much in the way of ladders and fixed ropes as would a mammoth expedition. The big difference, however, was that we required only just a limited amount of equipment to go through the Icefall, since we were only maintaining approximately twelve people above the Icefall for a very limited period. I proposed to make the route through the Icefall, and then use all the climbers and the six Sherpas over a period of around four to five days, to ferry all the gear required for the assault on the mountain, up the Icefall, and then from Camp 1 up the Western Cwm. In theory, this build-up only takes about ten days.

There were many question marks, and yet many attractive features in this plan. For a start, there would not be the slightly invidious distinction between lead climbers, who have got to be saved at all costs from exhausting themselves, and support climbers and Sherpas who do all the load-carrying. Even though we would be employing Sherpas, the climbers in this situation would have to do as much carrying as the Sherpas. Because of this, I thought there would be a greater integral unity in the team with the bonus, of course, that all four climbers would have a very good chance of reaching the summit of Everest. There were also a lot of problems. A small party would be much more severely affected by some of the heavy snowfalls which could completely obliterate camps on the route. In the light of our actual experience on Everest in the autumn, it is questionable whether a small party could have maintained its drive over the period of time involved, and of course, it would have been impossible to have kept open the route behind Camp 2 while the thrust beyond it was going on. Therefore, if we had run out of supplies at Camp 2, because we were there longer than anticipated, the expedition would inevitably have failed.

Anyway, the concept of this four-man expedition was exciting. It had less of the overtones of high finance and heavy publicity that a South West Face venture would inevitably entail. It was also possible to start organising it before we knew the outcome of the Herrligkoffer expedition. We could even contemplate carrying out this expedition whether or not Herrligkoffer succeeded. And so I went ahead with my plans, formulating them towards the end of April 1972.

Dougal was already a party to the scheme; the question was, who else to invite? Besides myself, there would be two other so-called lead climbers. I decided upon Nick Estcourt and Mick Burke. Both of them had been with me on the South Face of Annapurna and we had climbed together over a period of years.

Nick was a computer programmer aged twenty-nine, with two children. He was essentially an amateur climber, with a very traditional background – public school, Cambridge University, president of the Cambridge University Mountaineering Club, and then a job in a large organisation. My invitation, however, posed him a very real problem, since he had got permission to come with me to the South Face of Annapurna in 1970 and he was naturally afraid that his employers might take exception to his going on another long trip only two years later. The lure of Everest is irresistible, however, and Nick asked for leave of absence, knowing full well that it probably wouldn't do his career any good and, at the same time, that he wouldn't get it with pay. In this respect he probably made the greatest sacrifice of any of our little group, since the others whom I was going to invite were either 'professional' mountaineers who could only benefit from the expedition, or were more independent. Nick had performed extremely well on the South Face of Annapurna – reaching a height of round about 7300m (24,000ft). He had plenty of drive, was tremendously competitive by nature, and yet had an extremely strong conscience. I asked him to act as treasurer of the expedition, since he was always extremely methodical and had, at times, an almost pernickety sense of money values – but then, this is what you want in a treasurer.

Mick Burke had also been with me on the South Face of Annapurna, and we had climbed together on other occasions. Mick originally came from Wigan, from an essentially working-class background, leaving school at sixteen to go into an insurance office. At the same time, he had started to climb and quickly abandoned the security of an office for the freedom of living up in the Lake District, taking odd jobs as labourer or barman. He had never been a brilliant rock-climber, but had considerable determination over anything he really wanted. As a result, he had made several out-standing routes, particularly on larger mountains. It was he who instigated the first British Cerro Torre expedition in 1967, when Dougal Haston, Peter Crewe, Martin Boysen and he made a very strong attempt on what might well be the world's most difficult mountain. He then made his way over-land up the Americas to California, and was the first Briton to complete a climb on the famous El Capitan, Yosemite's, and for that matter, the world's, finest rock wall. He made the first British ascent of the Nose of El Capitan, leading all the way, and taking up as a second man Bob Wood, a talented climber who had no experience at all of Yosemite's big walls.

It was round this time that Mick got married, and started thinking of the future. Although he had practically no experience in filming, he decided to make his career in films, and managed to get a place at the London Film School. Since then he had gone steadily forward, taking an active part in making the film on the South Face of Annapurna, then going out as assis-tant cameraman on the ski-traverse of the Alps, led by Alan Blackshaw in the spring of 1972. There were also straight professional jobs, working in ordinary television feature films. Mick had been with Dougal and myself on the North Face of the Grandes Jorasses, when we had tried to make a new route up the side of the Walker Spur that same winter. He and I had always had a slightly odd relationship. He was argumentative, and, perhaps having left school at sixteen and without a comfortable middle-class background behind him, he was fiercely aware of what he considered were his rights and his position in the world of the climbing rat-race. Frequently we had fero-cious arguments, usually over money, and yet both of us had the capacity to lose our tempers, blow up at the time and then very quickly simmer down and see the other's point of view. Our friendship had remained intact over a period of years. I had been particularly impressed by Mick on the North Face of the Grandes Jorasses; he had come with us on this primarily as climbing cameraman, and had been very happy to fill this role while Dougal and I did most of the lead climbing. We got to a point where Dougal and I were ensconced in a little two-man snow hole, a third of the way up the face. There was no room for three and we had therefore sent Mick down to the hut, well below the bottom of the wall, with the promise that we would wait for him when the weather was sufficiently good to make a summit bid. All three of us could go to the top of the North Face together, and Mick could get the climax to the film he was making. And then the weather had improved unexpectedly and both Dougal and I felt that we could not lose a day in waiting for Mick. We set out without him, while he spent a complete day struggling and wading through thigh-deep snow to the foot of the wall, and climbing up the fixed ropes to our high point, to receive a little note to say that we had abandoned him. In his place I think I would have been absolutely livid at this betrayal, yet Mick took it wonderfully philosophically, fully appreciating and understanding the position that we felt we had been in. This incident, plus some other very good times I had with Mick in the mountains, influenced me in inviting him to join our team. He also, of course, would be a first-class climbing cameraman, since we had no intention of taking with us a big separate media team such as had accompanied the 1971 expedition.

In addition to my four lead climbers, I envisaged making the push above Camp 2 with our Sherpas. I needed two more climbers in a support role, who would act as long-stops and run the basic administration of the expedition while we were making our summit bid. Mike Thompson, one of my oldest friends, was an obvious choice. He had been with us on the South Face of Annapurna, in a similar support role. In his mid-thirties, an anthropologist by career, he was a reasonable, without being an outstanding, mountaineer, and was wonderfully good at getting on with other people. Mike and I had been to Sandhurst together and both of us had tired of the Army at roughly the same time. The Army released me without argument, but had felt that Mike was of greater value to them, partly because he was just completing the course at the Royal Military College of Science at Shrivenham. Mike struck on an original way of getting out of the Army by standing for Parliament. Every citizen in the British Isles (at that time anyway) had a constitutional right to stand for Parliament, yet no soldier was allowed to go in for politics, so the Army had no choice but to release him. It cost Mike about £250 by the time he had lost his deposit and paid his solicitor's fees. He even had the satisfaction of getting fifty votes in the Middlesbrough West by-election! In the spring of 1972 he was bridged between his career as an anthropologist and that of a property tycoon, just having bought a splendid derelict mansion in Bristol which he was converting and renovating. The lure of Everest, and particularly a small lightweight expedition, was too much, however, and he agreed to come with us.

The final member of the team was our expedition doctor. I had already come to know Peter Steele, who had been the doctor on the International expedition, before I withdrew from the team. Peter, a doctor who had never been able to settle down to a steady routine of medical practice, had spent his time as an outback doctor in Labrador, then went to Nepal to work in a hospital in Kathmandu, and visited Bhutan, working in that wonderful closed land of mountains. His wife and young children accompanied him on all these adventures and he gave the impression of being a tightly integrated family man, at the same time as having an adventurous disposition. He had the double advantage of being able to speak fluent Nepali, had obviously been very good at handling the Sherpas in his experience of the International expedition, and had as wide a knowledge of high-mountain illnesses as one could possibly desire. My invitation placed him in a dilemma, since he had at last decided that it was time for him to settle down to more steady medical practice. However, for Peter, also, the lure of Everest proved too great and he agreed to come with us.

So there we were in May 1972 with permission to climb Everest reasonably assured, an exciting concept of a small expedition, and an enthusiastic team. And yet the presence of the South West Face still nagged at me. What we were trying to do was exciting and interesting and, I suspect, would have been a great deal of fun, in spite of the immense physical and mental demands which such a lightweight expedition would inevitably impose. But the South West Face was still there! As May dragged out, it became increasingly evident that the European expedition were getting into severe difficulties, and then, at the end of May, came the news. The Britons had pulled out and, a few days later, the entire team had withdrawn from Everest. The South West Face was still unclimbed.

My mind was in a turmoil for a period of about ten days. We could be sure of raising sufficient funds for our South Col expedition – a strong body of climbing opinion in Britain strongly approved of its concept, being tired of the massive, heavily publicised expedition. It would certainly bring infinitely fewer personality problems and afford greater personal satisfaction, as I should have a very good chance of reaching the summit of Everest myself, if we were to be successful. And yet, the fact remained that we would be following the route that others had climbed before us. Admittedly, no one had climbed Everest in the autumn; admittedly our expedition was going to be considerably smaller than any other expedition and so the odds we were piling up against ourselves would be that much greater. But these were artificial obstacles. They weren't the same as that unclimbed 600m above the high points of the two previous expeditions on the South West Face. The South West Face of Everest obviously represented a massive problem of technical climbing at high altitude, together with the logistics of getting all the gear, food and oxygen cylinders up to the foot of the Rock Band, and the problems of holding together a group of men under these circumstances. Nevertheless, the entire concept of the South West Face expedition, with all the complications, its challenges and its problems, was still extremely attractive – perhaps merely because the challenge was so very great. And so, in mid-June, I came to my decision. We changed from a relatively simple concept of a small expedition, to an all-out assault on the South West Face of Everest.

From the day I made that decision, we were to have approximately eight weeks to increase the size of the team, raise all the extra money required – approximately £60,000 – and get together the mass of equipment that such a large expedition would involve. The scale of the thing we were about to undertake was tremendously exciting, even though the odds seemed to be stacked against us. The first thing was to adapt my basic planning to the larger objective. We were obviously going to have to increase the size of the team, but I was anxious to keep it as compact as possible. On the South Face of Annapurna I had had, in effect, eight lead climbers, who were capable of and therefore expected and needed to share the lead. There were also three support climbers, two of whom were competent mountaineers and yet were obviously not of the same standard as the other climbers and therefore quite happy to adopt the role of support, without having any aspirations to go out in front. Because we had taken with us a comparatively small number of Sherpas – a mere six – the lead climbers also had to double up in a load-carrying capacity. This was primarily because the technical difficulty was so great on the South Face of Annapurna that we could not visualise being able to use the Sherpas to any great degree above 6400m and this, in fact, was the case. The Sherpas never carried above Camp 4, at 6583m and by far the most arduous carry was up the Ice Ridge in the centre of the face, from Camp 4 to Camp 5. The climbers, therefore, had to take turns in lead climbing and load-carrying. There's no doubt about it, the lead climbers also proved to be the best load-carriers. The dual role, however, proved too much for most of the team, and by the end of the expedition there were hardly any fit members left.

The situation on Everest was very different. We knew from the experience of the previous expeditions that there was no technically difficult hard climbing, up to a height of 8230m (27,000ft). We hoped that at least some fixed ropes were still usable, and even if they were covered in the post-monsoon snows, the very presence of these snows would make climbing on the lower part of the face still easier. Therefore, the pressure on the lead climbers would be less. At the same time, because of the easier angle and the sheer scale of the logistic problem, it was essential that we used a good number of Sherpas for ferrying gear up the mountain. It seemed to me that we did not want to have too many lead climbers, since the real challenge of the climb was above the site of Camp 6 at the foot of the Rock Band, and it was unlikely that I was going to be able to employ more than four climbers to tackle this and then make the summit bid. The rest of the climbing below that point was comparatively routine and therefore would give the climbers who first went up and fixed ropes on this section, comparatively little satisfaction. I therefore arrived at a figure of six lead climbers of which, initially, I envisaged being one, to go out in front to take it in turns to make the route on the mountain. This would give me a reserve of two good climbers.

The next question was how many more climbers to have along as support. I decided we would need a further four. The job of the support climber is not so much that of load-carrier, but of managing the different camps on the mountain. I planned to put the burden of load-carrying on the shoulders of our Sherpas – to employ enough of them to be able to make a fast build-up of supplies to the Western Cwm and then up the face itself. On the question of Sherpas, I arrived eventually at a figure of forty, having started with a figure considerably lower than this. My thinking about the expedition comprised a series of expansions from my original concept of a mini-expedition to climb the mountain by the South Col and I suspect this was partially because I did not want to escape too far from this concept; I preferred to keep our own South West Face venture as compact as possible, partially on an aesthetic level and partially on one of sheer finance – the more people we had, the more it was going to cost.

And so, for my choice of a team. In the first instance, I was looking for three more hard climbers to join Dougal, Nick Estcourt and Mick Burke. This immediately raised vast problems of selection. There were so many first-class climbers in Britain and it very quickly became evident that my choice would excite much interest and a certain amount of public criticism. For the simple fact that the mountain was Everest, that we were going on the South West Face rather than the South Col route, and that I intended to select all my team members from this country, gave us the status of a national expedition, whether we liked it or not. Indeed, we needed it, since it was largely on this basis that we were able to raise the necessary funds in such a short time.

I now wanted to add four more members to the six we already had. At this stage I envisaged two of them being lead climbers so that I should have, in effect, six potential leaders and four who would adopt support roles. Although there are a huge number of very talented climbers in this country today, there are comparatively few who have real high-altitude experience. From this point of view, both Doug Scott and Hamish MacInnes were obvious choices, since they had both performed well on Everest, reaching heights of nearly 8000m. There was also some hope that their acclimatisation would carry through to the autumn. I therefore invited them to join me for the autumn attempt and they both accepted promptly. I had to think harder about my support climbers. They were going to prove particularly important, not only for keeping things going on the mountain, but also for helping me fling the expedition together in approximately eight weeks. Back in January, when I had been discussing the question of team selection with Dougal, he had suggested Graham Tiso as a possible person for this role. Graham was running a very successful climbing shop in Edinburgh and was also one of the main importers of specialised climbing equipment in this country. In addition to this, he was an extremely sound steady mountaineer, with a long record of Scottish winter climbing behind him. Dougal vouched for his steadiness, and I did know him slightly – we had climbed together many years before in Glencoe, and I had met him on several occasions since. One of my biggest problems was going to be obtaining all the specialised equipment, some of which was in short supply, in time; Graham was an obvious choice and therefore I invited him. The only factor that gave me some food for thought was the worry that Graham's personality, the ebullient self-confidence of the successful businessman, might be a little too overpowering. In the event, he fulfilled an absolutely vital role in the expedition, not only in getting the right gear together, but also on the mountain itself. We found that we worked well together, and built up a strong friendship.

My final support climber was to be Kelvin Kent. When I was organising the Annapurna South Face expedition, I decided that I needed a person who would, in effect, be a Base Camp manager – whose role would not take him much above Base Camp, but who would take on all the day-to-day administration to leave me free to be anywhere on the mountain. The ideal person to adopt such a role seemed to be an Army officer, one who ideally spoke fluent Nepali. Not knowing such a person, I had therefore approached Charles Wylie, who had been on the 1953 Everest expedition and was a lieutenant colonel in the Gurkhas, to ask his advice. He had recommended Kelvin Kent, then a captain in the Royal Signals, stationed with the Gurkhas in Hong Kong. He was just coming to the end of a tour of duty and Charles assured me that he was both dynamic and an extremely good organiser. I took Kelvin entirely on his recommendation, and we only met personally when we arrived in Kathmandu. Kelvin fulfilled an outstanding role on the Annapurna expedition, even though he had never been on a mountain before. In the end, he reached a height of just over 6583m carrying loads to support the lead team, though his chief and most important function was his handling of our Sherpas and local porters, and his general day-to-day administration of the expedition. I knew that I could rely upon him to fulfil the same function on Everest when things would be considerably more complicated and when we should have many more porters than we had on Annapurna. When I phoned him he had only recently returned from another expedition which had just completed the crossing of the Darien Gap in the Americas. He was about to take on a new job in the Army as company commander at Sandhurst. Characteristically, though, he responded to the challenge and accepted my invitation.

Another essential person was Jimmy Roberts. I wrote to him as soon as I decided to change my objective from the South Col route to the South West Face, to ask whether he would be prepared to change his mind and join us, in spite of the pressures of work which I knew his trekking firm would be under. Very fortunately for us, Jimmy could not resist the opportunity of going to Everest once again, and agreed to become my deputy leader. This meant that we would have the benefit of his vast mountaineering experience and also would be guaranteed as many of his best Sherpas as he could possibly spare. Having Jimmy with any expedition would also make any relations with the Sherpas very much easier.

This then was the team as I now visualised it. From the moment I announced our intention of changing our objective to the South West Face, and the team I had selected, the phone didn't stop ringing. Everyone wanted to know why I hadn't included Don Whillans. His name had come to be associated with Everest as a result of his part in the two previous expeditions, and therefore people tended to take it for granted that any expedition to the South West Face of Everest must include him. He is undoubtedly an outstanding mountaineer but the real strength of a team is decided not by the ability of any one member, but by how well that team manages to integrate as a single unit. I did not feel that Don would have fitted into the team I had chosen, a feeling that I knew was shared by a majority of the team, particularly those who had been on the Annapurna South Face expedition.

I was now presented with a further problem. Mike Thompson phoned to tell me that he had been thinking very seriously about the expedition and his role in it. He felt that because he was trying to get established in the academic world, at the same time as developing his property in Bristol, he really could not come. The change of plan from the mini-expedition to the full-scale assault of Everest no doubt influenced his decision, since for Mike having fulfilled a support role on the South Face of Annapurna, the same role on this expedition would merely have been a repetition of all the misery which must inevitably accompany a high-altitude siege, with none of the recompense and elation that our original small-scale adventure promised. I could fully understand Mike's feelings, and immediately started looking round for a substitute.

Our first reserve for the mini-expedition had been Martin Boysen who had also been a member of the Annapurna South Face team, and was a very close friend of mine. I therefore felt obliged to ask him whether he wanted to come on the expedition to replace Mike, even though I knew it would be very difficult for him to accept the invitation, since his wife was due to have a baby while we were away, and he had only just started teaching in a new school. For these reasons, Martin had to regretfully decline the invitation.

And so, who else to ask? There was certainly any number of fully qualified talented mountaineers in Britain. I did not want a brilliant lead climber for this replacement since I felt, and this proved the case on the mountain, that what we were really short of was good steady supporters. At the same time, I wanted someone who could take the lead if necessary. This would also have the advantage of giving us three lead pairs besides myself, yet freeing me for a support role, which is probably best for the leader of the expedition. In our discussions in January, Dougal had suggested Dave Bathgate, an Edinburgh climber aged thirty-one who had made a considerable impact on Scottish winter climbing and rock-climbing in the early and mid-sixties. He also had two expeditions behind him, both of them to Peru, one to climb Alpemayo and the other to make an attempt, with Don Whillans, Brian Robertson and Ian Macecheran, on the South Face of Huandoy. I knew Dave moderately well and had always been impressed by his quiet, unselfish manner. By profession he was a master-joiner, working in partnership with his brother, and this meant that he would probably be able to get the time off. Therefore I invited him.

A few days after this, on 17 June, we had our first expedition meeting in North Wales. It was to coincide with the Alpine Climbing Group Dinner at Llanberis. All the team except Kelvin Kent, who was still in Germany serving with the British Army on the Rhine, and Graham Tiso, managed to attend the meeting, which we held in the very best tradition at the Pen-y-Gwryd Hotel, the home of many of the 1953 Everest expedition's training weekends and meetings. In spite of his decision to withdraw from the expedition, Mike Thompson had put in an immense amount of work on our behalf, planning the food, and he attended the meeting as well. We got through all the formalities, had a look at prototypes of some of the equipment, including a special new box tent which Ultimate Equipment made as a rival to Don Whillans' Box (which of course had been developed in the first instance for the Annapurna South Face expedition), and everything seemed settled.

Next morning, yet another blow. Peter Steele, in his own charming apologetic way, came to me and told me that he was desperately sorry but he also had had second thoughts about the expedition. The thing which really affected Peter's decision was the change from the concept of the mini-expedition to the siege of the big face. As far as he was concerned, it would have been just a repetition of 1971, albeit, hopefully, without any of the rows and dissension. He had been attracted by his role on the mini-expedition, where he would have been the only Nepali-speaker with responsibility beyond that of medicine. Now I had brought in two more Nepali-speakers and administrators in the shape of Jimmy Roberts and Kelvin Kent. I could fully appreciate how he felt, especially as I knew he was also negotiating for a new job in medicine. So I accepted his resignation without any feeling of bitterness at being let down. This was made even easier for me by the fact that Peter was able to recommend someone who sounded a really excellent substitute.

Barney Rosedale was a friend of Peter's who had also worked in Nepal. Peter assured me that Barney could speak good Nepali, was dynamic and a very pleasant person. I telephoned Barney who agreed to come and see me at my home in Cheshire, and the moment I set eyes on him and had my hand gripped in one of the most powerful handshakes I have ever experienced, I took an immediate liking to him. With a shock of untidy, dark hair, intense almost haggard features which were lightened by a warm, spontaneous smile, Barney radiated both energy and sheer human kindness. He had only done a limited amount of rock-climbing and a bit of trekking in Nepal. This didn't seem to matter, since the position of the doctor on a peak like Everest is not high up on the mountain, but at Camp 2 or Advanced Base Camp, ready to receive any casualties. His knowledge of Nepal, combined with the fact that he was now thirty-five and had a broad experience of medicine, most of which was spent doing interesting jobs in the outback of Africa or Nepal, made him the perfect choice. Moreover, he was used to making diagnoses on his own, without a hospital or other doctors to whom to refer for a second opinion. His enthusiasm and dedication were demonstrated by the fact that his wife was due to give birth to their first child only two or three days before the date of our projected departure, and yet he was still prepared to go with us.

And so, now we had a complete team. We also had about eight weeks to put together the entire expedition. Even more to the point, we still had nothing like the £60,000 it was going to cost, and my agent, George Greenfield, who was one of the greatest optimists I have ever met, was worried whether we should ever be able to get it. The most frightening thing was that we were going to have to commit ourselves to expenditure before we actually had the money, since we were going to have to order all our equipment and our transport at the same time as trying to raise it. On the South Face of Annapurna I had had these financial worries taken away from me, since the Mount Everest Foundation had given us their total sponsorship. This meant that they took on any financial risk in return for taking any profits which we might make. In actual fact, Annapurna will probably have made between five and six thousand pounds by the time all the royalties of the book have come in. There didn't seem time to get this kind of support for our present expedition, however, and anyway I had received some indication that it was unlikely that the Mount Everest Foundation would want to undertake such a big risk again. The fact was we were going to have to find almost twice as much money for Everest in a very much shorter time and also, we were going to have to take on the risk ourselves as a group of comparatively impecunious climbers. I had learned a great deal from the Annapurna South Face expedition, both means of fundraising and also basic expedition organisation. On Annapurna I had been a bit of a one-man band, handling the fund-raising, most of the equipment, and all the transport. Mike Thompson had taken care of the food and Don

Whillans had acted as equipment designer and did a certain amount of co-ordination work with firms. Nevertheless, the main burden had fallen on me. This had proved too much, especially as once one gets involved in the finicky details – sizes etc. in equipment – it is very easy to lose sight of the broader picture of the expedition. Determined that this should not happen on Everest, I therefore gave Graham Tiso the onerous job of getting all our equipment together. In the early stages he was helped by Doug Scott, but then Doug, a keen climber, wanted to go off on a trip to Baffin Island and as a result Graham handled most of it himself, helped by Dave Bathgate in Edinburgh. Then, Mike Thompson having resigned from the expedition, Kelvin Kent took on the food organisation as well as getting all our communications equipment. He attacked the task with efficiency and enthusiasm.

It would be impossible to relate the day-to-day crises which we met in organising the expedition. Our two biggest problems, at such short notice, were getting an effective oxygen system and also getting the gear out to Nepal in time. On the oxygen front I had decided to use the demand system developed by Dr Duane Blume for the International Everest expedition. Both Dougal and Don spoke very highly of this system, and it seemed to answer all our requirements. (The system is described in detail in Appendix D.) The firm who makes it, Robertshaw, did a special rush job for us, and succeeded in getting all the components over to Britain in early August. The question of oxygen bottles presented a greater problem. We could not possibly have afforded to use the American bottles, which were both expensive and would also have to be transported to Britain on their way out to Nepal. We therefore had to find a British firm, and were extremely lucky to come across Luxfer Limited, who offered to make the bottles for us at a very competitive price in the time available. Valves to fit the American system, however, had to be sent all the way over from the States, and this entailed a fair number of panic phone calls across the Atlantic. Eventually, we got all the valves fitted and the bottles filled by British Oxygen, the day they were due to be flown out to Kathmandu! We had not had time to actually marry one of the reducer valves to a bottle, and only tried out the completed system in Kathmandu.

But by far the greatest problem was one of time. The days slipped away with terrifying speed. I wanted to get out to Nepal as quickly as possible, to be at the Everest Base Camp immediately the monsoon ended. Reading through reports of the previous expeditions during this period, it seemed possible to get excellent weather in early September, before the official end of the monsoon. The more work we could do on the Icefall and on the lower slopes of the mountain in the early stages, the more hope we should have of getting high on the face before the winter cold and winds set in. The other factor was that the sooner we could get out there, the sooner the members of the team could start acclimatising and the more leisurely could this acclimatisation period be.

Normally expeditions fly from Kathmandu to Luglha. This is both easier and also quite a bit cheaper, since airfreight to Luglha costs less than employing porters to carry loads. However, since we were planning to make our approach march through the monsoon, we could not possibly guarantee getting ourselves sufficient good weather for the plane to be able to fly into Luglha. Jimmy Roberts therefore recommended that we should make the 170-mile approach march all the way from Kathmandu. This also would have the advantage that the team members could slowly get fit and acclimatised in the course of the march. I therefore planned on leaving London on 21 August. There was no question at all of sending our gear out by sea, and I had to resign myself to the expense of flying it out. In this respect, BOAC proved extremely co-operative and, without their efforts, we should never have got it into Kathmandu in time. They even flew one of their cargo planes out of schedule to Delhi to carry our oxygen, since they could not carry this on one of their scheduled passenger flights.

I had sent Kelvin Kent out to Kathmandu in advance, in order to clear all our equipment through Customs – in itself a marathon task. The gear actually left Britain by cargo plane on 16 August, and by 21 August it had been flown into Kathmandu and cleared through Customs – a really brilliant piece of work by Kelvin and Jimmy Roberts. We were ready to leave for Kathmandu on 22 August. I, personally, felt singularly unready for the most physically exacting climb of my career. I don't think I have ever worked so hard before in my life – not only had I been putting the expedition together, but I had also been completing – way over deadline – the second volume of my autobiography, and actually typed the last words in the hotel bedroom in London on the morning of my departure.

In those last few weeks I had worked to a routine, getting up at around 3.30 a.m., working on my book until about 11 a.m. and then transferring to the expedition, to work on that, very often until 9.30 or 10.00 at night. In the final stages I had a secretary, Betty Prentice, working full time in my office at home, to help cope with the huge volume of letters, phone calls and general administration which the expedition involved. Kelvin Kent and Graham Tiso had been under similar pressure.

I had been greatly helped in my money-raising efforts by Bob Stoodley, a friend who was chairman of a group of garages in Manchester. He wrote several thousand letters to firms up and down the country, asking for contributions and he also promoted a signed cover scheme, by which we promised to send covers back to anyone who contributed. He and his secretary Diana Lister put in an enormous amount of work on our behalf, without any thought of personal gain. Our financial backing was now beginning to look more stable. Thames/ITN had taken up television rights, *The Observer* had taken up newspaper rights and we had sold the book rights both in Britain and the United States; the Mount Everest Foundation had given us an extremely generous grant and we had also received the support of the Sports Council with a grant through the British Mountaineering Council, the first time that an expedition had ever received such support. We were still about £10,000 short of my budget estimate and it was at this point that we received an unexpected windfall from Rothmans who contributed very generously.

As I walked up the steps into the VC-10 which was going to take us to Kathmandu, I felt some of the worries that had beset me in those last hectic weeks fall from my shoulders. Despite the tight time schedule, Graham had succeeded in ensuring that we were as well equipped as, I felt, any expedition which has left these shores. We were also fairly solvent, and the team had a feeling of excited anticipation and friendship which boded well for the future.

6

The approach march

25 August – 7 September

The journey out preceding an expedition is a kind of limbo period. On my first two expeditions to the Himalaya, I had travelled out by ship – a little 10,000-ton passenger liner run by the Anchor Line, called the S. S. *Cilicia*. The charm of a boat journey, especially if one is unattached, is the way it lengthens this limbo period and all you have to worry about is eating, drinking and having the odd affair to speed the quiet passage of days and nights. The modern way, by plane, is almost too frenetic – the limbo is just a few hours in the air, before descending upon a new world, new problems and new challenges.

For us they were busy hours, for we had four thousand postcards to sign as part of our fund-raising campaign. We flew via Tel Aviv and Teheran, security men searching the plane and us for hidden weapons and bombs. It seemed ironic that with all the improvements in fast jet travel and cheaper fares, when opportunities for travel and adventure should be much easier, political conflicts were limiting the number of places to go and how to get there. In actual fact, the pre-war mountaineers and explorers had greater freedom. They were able to wander through the wilds of the Karakorum into Tibet and the back of China, areas which are closed to us today. We were met at Delhi by the BOAC station manager, who, just a few days before, had whisked our 7250 kilos of equipment, oxygen cylinders and food through the airport and on to Nepalese cargo planes. Soon we were in the air again, this time on a Boeing 727 bound for Kathmandu.

I couldn't help feeling a little sad at the pace at which Nepal seemed to be catching up with the rest of the Western world. Twelve years before, in 1960, we had flown in from Patna, on an old Dakota, to land on a dusty air strip with a battered tin shed at one end of the field to act as air terminal. Now, the Royal Nepalese Airlines had just purchased their first jet airliner, and were in the process of lengthening their runway to take the big Boeing 727. The airfield itself was like any other modern airfield – long concrete runway, with its modern air terminal building. And yet that day we had one of the most magnificent flights in the world, as the plane carved its way over the patchwork quilt of cloud, through which one could see the brilliant green of monsoon-fed fields and the occasional patch of water. And then on the northern horizon – at first almost a continuation of the puff balls of white cloud – we saw the Himalaya. Dhaulagiri, a squat pyramid; the sprawl of the Annapurna range – the South Face of Annapurna itself, the mountain on which we had spent so many weeks just two years previously; Machapuchare, shapely and slender, dwarfed by the great mass of mountains behind it. Annapurna II, the mountain I had climbed in 1960, looked in some ways the finest of them all, standing in splendid isolation to the right of the Annapurna massif. I was excited, and yet my excitement was a little bit deadened, partly from a heavy mental and physical fatigue which still hung on me; partly perhaps from the fact that I had now flown this journey three times.

We landed at Kathmandu at mid-day; the ladder was pulled to the door of the plane and a group of the local press corps crowded around it. There was no sign, however, of Jimmy Roberts or Kelvin Kent. Everyone was very friendly and we trailed over to the passengers' entrance, the press corps clicking away with their cameras, myself tired and slightly confused, trying to gather my thoughts for the inevitable press conference. Jimmy Roberts and Kelvin arrived a few minutes later. Kelvin, characteristically, immediately took charge and shepherded us like a group of sheep into the arrival hall, where he started to chat up the Customs men to get our gear through quickly and easily. At the same time, the reporters wanted their press conference there and then. What did I think our chances were? Why had the International expedition failed? Was there a chance for international climbing? Why hadn't I taken Don Whillans? And so it went on, with me trying to field the questions tactfully and clearly, without treading on any toes. By the end of the conference I felt limp and yet there were still more decisions to be made.

I had been determined to move out of Kathmandu as quickly as possible, and consequently we were only going to have two days there before starting out on the approach march. In this respect, Jimmy and Kelvin, helped by Dave Bathgate who had flown out two days in front of us, had done a fine job, not only in getting all our gear through Customs, but also in sorting out the loads, getting our coolies ordered, and everything ready to move on the scheduled date. I wondered if any expedition, especially one of our size, had ever moved through Kathmandu so quickly. And then to the Shankar Hotel. Set in well-kept gardens, this was an old Rana palace, down the front of which were the mock Greek colonnades that the ruling aristocracy in Nepal had loved so much. We plunged into the dark coolness of our rooms, but even now there was no question of relaxing; there were too many different things to deal with. Jimmy had produced a very workmanlike plan, based on my own original planning brief, but actually going into details on the deployment of porters. I had to check through this so that I could at least make some sensible comments. The decisions to be made – how many extra cook-boys to take – how to split the team – most of these, fortunately, had been sorted out by Jimmy and Kelvin, and I was very happy to go along with them. There was the subject of our budget. Having only just raised enough money, already we were discovering we had underestimated on many things. Inflation gallops as fast in Kathmandu as it does in Britain.

There were also discussions with Liz Hawley, who was to be our agent in Kathmandu. She was a very formidable lady who some years ago came to Kathmandu as a freelance writer for *Look* magazine, fell in love with the place and decided to settle there, since there was a real opening for an efficient local correspondent. She obtained the position of Reuter correspondent and also helps to run the bookings side of a safari-type hotel in the Terrai, the jungle area of Nepal. She had made herself almost indispensable to expeditions who want to get out their news to the magazines or television companies which have sponsored them. In doing this there was a split loyalty between her commitment to Reuter, who provided her daily bread and butter, and her temporary employers for whom she acted as agent. It was, however, a loyalty which she succeeded in bridging remarkably effectively. I still had to thrash out several intricacies involved in getting the news out as quickly as possible and at the same time, satisfying the Nepalese authorities that they received the gist of any important news before it reached the world's papers. These were problems I could have dispensed with happily. Somehow, having left Britain, one's actual reaction was to want to drop all thoughts of day-to-day administration and the media, and get down to the comparatively simple and much more exciting problems of climbing a mountain. If you decide to lead an expedition, however, this is one of the prices that you must inevitably pay. I also had the responsibility of writing articles for *The Observer*. The first one was due to be produced for the next Sunday, and I ended up writing it at five in the morning of the day of our departure.

At last, on 25 August, we were ready to set out on the approach march. We were to have with us altogether 400 porters, recruited from villages around Kathmandu. This would have been too large a body to travel in one group, particularly at the height of the monsoon when many camp sites are waterlogged, and the porters need to find shelter in the houses of villagers. Jimmy therefore proposed splitting the party into two groups with all the climbers accompanying the first party, with 200 porters and then the rest following under the command of Pertemba, one of his best Sherpas. I was not too happy about this, since the loss of one vital load could influence the outcome of the expedition. In addition, there was the problem of handling money and keeping a day-to-day check on expenses. This difference of opinion brought home to me, as leader of the expedition, one potential problem in my relationship with Jimmy. He, of course, had been leader of my first Himalayan expedition, the Combined Services expedition to Annapurna II; later he had been joint leader of the International expedition. Some of our best high-altitude Sherpas were his employees, and they understandably looked to him as their boss on the expedition. This could have led to a difficult situation had Jimmy and I failed to get on together, and following those first few days when Jimmy had had to make most of the decisions in my absence, I could not help feeling a little worried that perhaps I was losing control of the situation. In fact, there was no danger of this, largely because of Jimmy's loyal friendship. We had a meeting to discuss the approach march, and since most of us were apprehensive at the prospect of half the expedition gear travelling out to Base Camp unattended, I finally allotted Barney Rosedale to stay behind. With him would be Mick Burke, who was coming out to Kathmandu a couple of days later, and Mick's wife Beth, who I had agreed should accompany us to Base Camp.

She was coming out at her own expense as far as Kathmandu, and besides being a delightful easy-going girl who could get on with anyone, she was also a trained nurse. This meant that she could have a very real function in the expedition, helping Barney and holding the fort at Base Camp, looking after any convalescents that Barney should send down from higher up the mountain. She had flown out with us, and would await Mick with Barney in the second party. Doug Scott, as it turned out, also went with them, having contracted a stomach upset on the morning of departure. There were, therefore, six of us in the first party: Dave Bathgate, Kelvin Kent, Hamish MacInnes, Dougal Haston, Graham Tiso and myself. Jimmy Roberts was still tied up in the trekking business, but was going to fly out to join us at the beginning of October.

The first leg of our journey was along the newly built Chinese road, which wound its tarmac way into the valley of the Sun Kosi, and then on up towards the Tibetan frontier, and eventually to Lhasa, the capital of Tibet. We bumped and shook in Jimmy Roberts' Land-Rover for sixty miles, to the small village of Lamosangu, where all the expedition loads had been sent out the previous day. The Sherpas had spent the night there and were in the process of sending off the porters. A little group of local reporters was grouped around the start of the footpath which was to lead over ridges, down valleys on the 130-mile walk to the foot of Everest. It was a good feeling to shoulder a pack-frame and contemplate the simple day's objective of walking a few miles through the green terraced fields of Nepal to the night's camping spot. At last my own responsibilities were, for a time, almost over. Kelvin managed the day-to-day administration of the expedition with wonderful efficiency, and all I had to do, like the rest of the members of the team, was to walk through the Nepalese countryside, absorbing the host of sights, sounds and smells of this unspoilt, pollution-free land. I, for one, desperately needed the approach march, both to get physically fit, since I had had practically no exercise before the expedition, but – more important – to build up the mental stamina which I was going to require once we reached our Base Camp. Once there, I would have to make decisions constantly, and take on the full responsibility of running the expedition.

We had set out in a bright spell in the monsoon, and the sun blazed down, hot and heavy, through gaps in the piled clouds which still clung to the higher hills. Everything was green – a green much richer than anything one saw in the drier pre-monsoon season. The hillside, however steep, was carved into terraces, each one with a low mud wall imprisoning the waters of the monsoon rains. The rice shoots grew in a thick green carpet, in each one of these terraced pools. There was a constant trickle of running water from the many streams coursing down the hills, and the houses clustered in little groups, brown earthen walls with a veranda across the ground floor, small wooden-slatted windows and roofs made from weathered wooden slats or thatch. Although the Everest route had now become a tourist trail, particularly in the post-monsoon period, with the constant march of trekkers, there seemed hardly any change at all from when I had walked the same path back in 1961. The Nepalese were as gentle and courteous as ever – the Nepalese girls with their golden nose studs and ear-rings had a shy and gentle beauty. The first day there was a soft kind balm in the air after our weeks of wheeler-dealing, frantic worry and activity. We were already slip-ping into the easy, methodical routine of the approach march, resting beneath our umbrellas, stopping about three o'clock in the afternoon for the evening's halt.

Our first was at the side of a small lake of opaque brown waters, with a little ruined hut on a peninsula which jutted into it. The Sherpas pitched the tents, which we resited in the shade of a tree. Suddenly, there was a distant roll of thunder and the clouds billowed around us until the hills were engulfed, and there was just a small touch of blue immediately above us. Then that vanished as well, and the rains came down in a steady ham-mering torrent. Within seconds the ground was running in water. One crisis immediately presented itself. We had packed all our gear in reinforced cardboard boxes, which were especially designed for packing kippers, fish and similar products. Very quickly it became evident that they were not going to stand up to day after day of being continually soaked and then man-handled on our porters' backs; it was essential to find some way of keeping them off the wet ground, and here our aluminium ladders came in useful. We had altogether 45ft (1.5m) sections of ladder, and these were tied into bundles of three to make 27 kilo loads. By laying them out in a plat-form on the ground, we were at least able to keep all the packages clear of the water and cover them with a tarpaulin.

That first night was chaotic, yet strangely enjoyable, as we crouched under a leaking Stormhaven tent, trying to avoid the drips, waiting for a much-delayed supper to arrive. There had been a lot of talk of losing the spirit of adventure with massive expeditions to Everest – but we had very little feeling of being a large expedition. There were just seven of us crammed into the tent, and another four, two days behind. This was the sum total of the European climbers, in fact, less than we had on Annapurna, where there had been eleven climbers but also a four-man tele-vision team. On Everest we weren't bringing out any media people, but were going to do it all ourselves. This added responsibility undoubtedly increased the sense of unity felt by the entire team. It rained all night, but it was strangely reassuring to lie in one's tent and hear the monotonous soporific drumming of rain hammering on canvas. There was something very simple, very sensual about it. I dropped off into a deep sleep, more relaxed than I had been for the past eight weeks.

We were to have forty Sherpas on the expedition, plus several cook-boys and six mail-runners to carry film, mail and stories down to the air strip at Luglha. The Sherpas themselves were divided into two categories, that of high-altitude Sherpa, who would expect to carry loads on the South West Face itself, and Icefall porter, who would be responsible for carrying the gear up to Camp 2 in the Western Cwm. Of our fourteen high-altitude Sherpas, most of them were with us on the approach march. We were responsible for paying them from the day we met them in Kathmandu until the end of the expedition. They received 15 rupees a day, plus their keep, in addition to all their equipment for the climb. The Icefall porters also received 15 rupees a day and their keep, but could be equipped on a more modest scale, since they would only be going as high as Camp 2 and would only be employed from the day they joined the expedition near Base Camp. I was planning to promote ten of the best Icefall porters to the ranks of the high-altitude Sherpas, once we saw how they performed in the Icefall and had brought out additional clothing and gear to make this conversion. The reason for this policy was that often some of the young Icefall porters are keen to get themselves established and have more drive than the older established Sherpas; by promoting them in the field, it seemed that we should be more certain of getting the best men for the high carries.

We had two sirdars, Pembatharke being the chief sirdar who would pri-marily be in charge of directing the Sherpas on the mountain itself, while Sona Hishy, a younger man, was to be our administrative sirdar, looking after our supplies from Base Camp, and helping to make the approach march run smoothly. This pair highlighted the changing role and development of the Sherpas. Pembatharke was very much a Sherpa of the old style. He could neither read nor write; had a rugged simplicity in his attitude to life and yet, at the same time, was highly intelligent and shrewd. He certainly had a magnificent climbing record. With the Indians on Everest in 1965, he reached the South Col on two separate occasions; as a member of a German expedition attempting to climb Annapurna I from the South by its long South East Ridge, he had reached their top camp, at a height of approximately 7160m. Then in 1970, he had come with us on the South Face of Annapurna. For this expedition he had not been sirdar, though he was undoubtedly the strongest personality and the strongest climber amongst the Sherpas. This had led to some tension, and towards the end of the expedition he had even become something of a trouble-maker – I suspect because he had resented his subordinate position. Even so, he had worked outstandingly well. On the International expedition he had been made face sirdar by Jimmy Roberts, and had been extremely successful in this role, loyal to Don and Dougal in organising and keeping the Sherpas going on the tenuous line of communications behind them.

His opposite number and, in theory his assistant, Sona Hishy, was very different. Aged twenty-six, he had been educated at one of the Hillary schools, spoke and wrote good English, and had even visited the United States. He had done more trekking with tourists than he had climbing on expeditions. Whilst Pembatharke had a magnificent physique, and looked the very prototype of a leader of men, Sona Hishy was tall, slender built, and was a very much more complex character. He was extremely efficient, but was also to prove to be the Sherpa shop-steward, finding it difficult at times to reconcile his loyalty to us as – in effect – part of the management, with his loyalty to his fellow Sherpas.

Sadly, Pembatharke was the only Sherpa we had from our little Annapurna South Face team, since Jimmy was heavily committed in this autumn period to trekking, and most of the Sherpas we had had on Annapurna were also extremely good in this newer role which the Sherpas had taken. He had, however, allotted to the expedition some of his most outstanding high-altitude Sherpas, whom we were to get to know better as the expedition went on. Doug Scott had also recommended some of the better Sherpas from the spring expedition, and Jangbo was to give a particularly outstanding performance.

The routine of the approach march quickly fell into a well-defined pattern. The monsoon was certainly back with us, the rain by now having thinned out to a drizzle through the veil of mist. The porters, as they set off, looked like modern-style ghosts, each one shrouded in a plastic sheet which we had issued to keep both them, and perhaps more important, their load dry. At first there was a babel of sound and argument, particularly as the three naiks, who were the representatives of the Himalayan Society in charge of the porters, and our own Sherpas argued ferociously about who had, and who had not, been paid. Kelvin, in the middle of the argument, bore the full brunt of this, trying to sort it out and come to some agreement with them. I was happy to stand back, take photographs and just absorb the strange beauty of the mist-enshrouded scene.

That day we had our first taste of the Nepalese leech. Dave Bathgate describes them in his diary:

The average leech is about one inch long, has a sucker at both ends of its tubular body and travels along by somersaulting from sucker to sucker. The leech likes to sit around on dry rocks and pathways and on plants that overhang the track. Perched on one sucker, it extends itself to its full length and waves about, rather like a weed in a pool, and attempts to attach itself to a victim.

There seem to be two main types of leech common to the mountain region of Nepal, one black and the other brown, often with a yellow strip along its length. The brown one is the larger of the two, but both multiply their dimensions tenfold once gorged. The leech can slither through the smallest of apertures. It can easily enter a boot through the lacing, and penetrate most woollen garments. Once they have latched on properly they are most difficult to detect. The larger ones can cause a prickly feeling which sometimes gives them away, but if this is not felt, they will already have used a local anaesthetic to reduce the pain while extracting the blood. If undiscovered, a leech can suck away quite happily for days, then drop off, leaving the victim bleeding freely from the wound. A leech wound should be treated just like a cut, as in damp humid climates, any kind of wound usually takes much longer to heal. If a leech is discovered just as it has attached itself to the skin, it is quite difficult to pull off, and usually it will attach itself with the free sucker to the fingers. A drop of salt on the leech will cause it to detach itself without leaving a bleeding sore. Sketofax or any other, similar insect repellent, liberally applied, will generally deter the leech. Salt or insect repellent rubbed into the boots or on the skin is about the only safeguard, and these soon become ineffective because of walking through water or the skin sweating.

We all became thoroughly neurotic about the leeches, which in some areas seemed to cling to almost every blade of grass and would get on to the walls of the tents at night, then drop with unerring precision upon the heads of their unsuspecting victims. It took us fourteen days to walk to Namche Bazar – a journey which is well known and well recorded. Today, hundreds of trekkers follow this trail. Making it during the monsoon gave it special character, at times an acute level of discomfort, which still managed to have a charm of its own. We never got a glimpse of the mountains throughout the approach march and yet, deprived of these further vistas, one's eye was drawn to the luxuriant green of the vegetation on either side of the path, tangles of spiders' webs encrusted with jewel-like droplets of water, and the wealth of flowers which are not present at other drier seasons.

Our route lay parallel to the spine of the Himalaya, and consequently there was a series of climbs and descents over subsidiary ridges, each undulation taking us slightly higher. A constant, imperceptible change in the style of layout of the terraced fields, the wildness of the woods and vegetation became apparent as we gained height. Our stages on the walks were all fairly short – round about ten miles a day, and some even less. This was primarily to enable the porters, who were carrying anything up to 36 kilo loads, to keep up with us. Walking in the monsoon season had many disadvantages – paths like ice rinks presented constant hazards for the barefooted porters who were soaked to the skin for most of the time. Whereas we had our tents and sleeping bags to retire to at night, they would have to find shelter in the porches of villagers' houses, with only damp blankets to keep them warm. We were paying them the equivalent of 50p per day, but they had to find their own sustenance and accommodation at night. This does not seem much; but was quite a bit more than they would have earned had they been working for a Nepali merchant.

On 3 September – the tenth day of the approach march – we dropped down to the Dudh Kosi valley. The previous day we had crossed a pass of over 3000m in the cold and drizzling rain. We now wound our way down slippery paths to the deepest bed of the valley at a height of little more than 1500m above sea level – our lowest point for several days. Then having reached the iron suspension bridge over the boiling waters of the Dudh Kosi, where the big plaque declared 'Made in Aberdeen', we knew that we were now going to gain height steadily up the valley as we walked into the heart of Sherpa country. For the last few days there had been a transitional period, where Sherpa houses, or even Sherpa villages, were jumbled with those of the Nepalis in the lower foothills. The Nepalis are essentially of Indian ethnic background, Hindu by religion, with delicately moulded features, slightly reminiscent of those of the Malays or Burmese. Sherpas, on the other hand, are essentially Tibetan, having overflowed the watershed that divides Tibet from the Indian subcontinent. There are similar encroachments all the way along the Tibetan frontier with Nepal, the people having the same common Tibetan language and broad mongoloid features, yet with distinct differences in their customs and behaviour. The Sherpas form probably the largest, and certainly the best-known, ethnically Tibetan community in Nepal, based on Sola Khumbu, the upper valley of the Dudh Kosi. Before climbers started going to Everest in the 1920s, the

Sherpas' economy was based on a combination of subsistence farming in the sparse gravelly fields of the mountains, and trading between Tibet and India. They already had a substantial colony in Darjeeling at the start of the road to Everest from the Tibetan side, and it was mainly Sherpas who were employed for all mountaineering expeditions before the war – not only in the Everest region, but also across to the Karakorum. With the Communist invasion of Tibet, part of their economy was seriously disrupted. This loss in trade, however, was already being replaced by their role of high-altitude porters, as an increasing number of expeditions came to Nepal to climb in the Himalaya. Then, from the mid-sixties onwards, another development still further increased their relative wealth. Trekking became more and more popular. One of the early founders was Jimmy Roberts. In the last few years trekking has boomed, and an increasing number of Sherpas have found trekking more remunerative and less arduous than mountaineering expeditions. Nevertheless, there are still a few Sherpas, Pembatharke is undoubtedly one, Jangbo another, who prefer the rugged adventure of climbing on a Himalayan expedition to the more sophisticated and inevitably subservient work of looking after rich American tourists on treks through Nepal. Others of our Sherpas, however, very sensibly looked upon prestigious expeditions, such as one to Everest, as useful stepping-stones in their careers as trekking Sherpas. Ang Phu, who was twenty-three and one of our most outstanding Sherpas, had been to the Hillary school, spoke fluent English and was a first-class organiser; he was determined to do as well as possible on the expedition, in order to establish his reputation and name.

The attitude of the Sherpas to a mountaineering expedition varies from person to person, as no doubt it does amongst European climbers. The Sherpas, like most mountain people, have never been able to afford the luxury of being romantic about their mountains. Apart from anything else, having lived amongst them from time immemorial, they tend to take them for granted. The romantics are the affluent city-dwellers, be they Japanese, Indian, European or American, who come to the mountains to escape from their over-sophisticated complex lives.

Sherpas themselves are in a very similar position to that of the Swiss peasant in the 1850s, and indeed, their way of life and living standards today are probably identical. Their interest in the mountains, as with the Swiss, started only when outsiders came and offered to pay money for their help. The difference between the Sherpas and the Swiss, however, was that when the early-Victorian alpinists started venturing into the Alps, they knew even less about the problems of mountaineering than the Swiss peasants they took with them. The Swiss peasant, therefore, initially assumed the role of guide and expert in the mountains, a role he was to keep until the end of the nineteenth century, when an increasing number of mountaineers began to feel the need for dispensing with guides and to seek out adventure for themselves. The Sherpas were employed as carriers rather than guides. The mountaineers who came to the Himalaya already had a background of climbing in the Alps or their own countries; consequently, they were the experts, and had to look after the Sherpas in the mountains, rather than vice versa. There have been, of course, some notable exceptions to this. Tenzing, who accompanied Hillary to the summit of Everest, was able to climb with the European members of the team on a level footing, especially of course, as he had already been most of the way up Everest before the British team ever got there. With recent developments in mountaineering in the Himalaya, disparity between climbers and Sherpas has become greater. Now that mountaineers are tackling high standard technical problems at altitude, there are comparatively few, if any, Sherpas who have the technical knowledge even to think of taking part in the lead climbing and they might even have difficulty in coping with the fixed ropes on particularly steep sections. For instance, on the South Face of Annapurna, we were unable to use our Sherpas above a height 6580m since they were obviously unhappy at the prospect of tackling overhanging jumar pitches. It was interesting that here it was our younger, less established Sherpas who did finally offer to try the precarious route from Camp 4 to Camp 5; in the event, we found we were unable to use their services, since they were needed lower down the mountain.

The attitude of the Sherpa to mountaineering is inevitably practical and materialistic; and it is most unlikely that a group of Sherpas would ever go off and climb a mountain on their own, for fun, as we do in Europe. They cannot afford such a luxury. With a good expedition, however, they enter into the spirit of the climbing. In my experience, the only time that Sherpas actually made an ascent for the fun of it was on our expedition to Annapurna II in 1960. We had left two of our Sherpas, Urkein and Mingma, at our penultimate camp on a shoulder of snow about 300m below the peak of Annapurna IV, which we had to bypass on our way to the summit of Annapurna II. With nothing to do for a couple of days, they decided they might just as well go and climb Annapurna IV, and went off, made their ascent and even left a bamboo wand, with a dirty handkerchief tied to it, on the summit.

On our own expedition to Everest this autumn, we had a certain amount of conflict with the Sherpas. Very often this came about through our different motives for climbing Everest, and the difficulty on both sides in understanding what the other was trying to do. For a start, the Sherpas regard every European expedition as vastly rich, since who else could possibly afford the luxury of doing anything quite as pointless as climbing a mountain. The very resources we display, the mounds of gear we bring in, the standard of life we adopt on the mountain, all contribute to this impression. The richest Sherpa, after all, is probably living at a lower standard than some of the poorest-paid workers in the countries which send out mountaineering expeditions. They come from a society where money has only very recently been used as the main means of doing business. Straight barter still forms an important part in their economy. The actual wages of the Sherpa are, in effect, in two parts – the money you pay him which, in actual fact, is not very much – 15 rupees per day – and the equipment you give him. To us, as organisers of a mountaineering expedition, this equipment is purely functional, enabling us to climb the mountain. To the Sherpa, however, it is a lot more. It is part of his wages which he can exchange for either further goods or a straight cash transaction at the end of the expedition. Throughout Sola Khumbu, the old traditional forms of dress are fast vanishing and the average Sherpa or Sherpani will be wearing down trousers, or a down jacket and various other items of expedition gear. Since this equipment can only come in limited quantities with expeditions, its value has become very inflated. A down jacket, for instance, is valued at 300 rupees, or nearly three weeks' pay.

The Sherpas have become accustomed to a certain scale of issue laid down in outline in the rules of the Himalayan Society, but this has almost become a minimum issue – the Sherpas have come to expect more. Dr Herrligkoffer had had a great deal of difficulty with the Sherpas because he had not given them the gear which they were accustomed to using. The reason for the complete lack of understanding on either side was that Herrligkoffer had failed to realise the equipment he was giving the Sherpas was every bit as important as the salary he was paying them, to gain their full co-operation. We also had similar problems on our expedition. Team members, including myself, were very often exasperated by what often seemed to be rather petty claims by the Sherpas – whether it was for more cigarettes or for double sleeping bags, when, in fact, the single good quality sleeping bag we had given them was, in our view, perfectly adequate. It seems probable that the Sherpas took a few perks – taking perhaps a percentage of the sale of firewood or rice – or in the payment of our coolies. We often became very indignant about this, but once again, this was part of a system which they have always practised. Provided one maintained a level of control which allowed the turning of a blind eye to a certain degree, one could ultimately gain a perfectly satisfactory relationship. To me, the main factor was that whatever the Sherpas or the porters expected, they were doing a great deal for us, and the pay we were giving them was by no means exorbitant – whether it was for one of our coolies who carried a 36 kilo load, during the course of the approach march, or the Sherpa going through the dangers of the Icefall day after day, knowing full well that there was a good statistical chance of a fatal accident.

Sherpa society is undoubtedly becoming very much more sophisticated, with the growing invasion of visitors to Sola Khumbu. The area is becoming increasingly accessible, not just to trekkers, but to tourists, with the introduction of air strips. The air strip at Luglha has been in existence since 1967. Now they are building another air strip, just above Namche Bazar in the very heart of Sola Khumbu. The first hotel, built by a Japanese entrepreneur, is now completed and taking its first guests. No doubt there will be more in the future and Sola Khumbu will become more and more like a Swiss valley. The Sherpas themselves naturally want to share in this bonanza. They are by no means simple or primitive. They have a long history of trading behind them and have always known how to strike a good bargain, and yet at the same time, they have had, and hopefully will continue to have, a rich sense of humour and a real warmth of personality. Unless the flow of tourists, trekkers and climbers into Sola Khumbu stops altogether, the people and the region must change and develop to meet this flow. Two important factors emerge, one being that the Sherpas themselves should benefit from the change, rather than a group of foreign operators or people in Kathmandu; and the other is the fervent hope that, in exploiting the development of a tourist industry, they don't destroy the very landscape, way of life and architecture which attracts the tourists in the first place.

In this respect, Sir Edmund Hillary has done a vast amount to help, and has certainly put back into Khumbu a great deal of what he gained personally in reaching the summit of Everest in 1953. Over the past few years, he has set up a network of schools to give the young Sherpas a sound basis of education. He has also set up a small hospital at Khumde, has built a number of bridges and has helped to encourage local industries. As a result of this, together with their monopoly of the job of high-altitude porter on mountaineering expeditions, and a near monopoly in the trekking business, the Sherpas are probably one of the most prosperous groups in the whole of Nepal.

In the last days of our approach march towards Namche Bazar, the capital of Sherpa country, we stopped for lunch and in the evenings in Sherpa houses. The basic construction of these houses had not changed very much in twelve years but there were small, yet very important changes. In 1961 none of the houses had glass in their windows. Consequently, the actual window frames were very much smaller, allowing only a glimmer of light into the rooms. The crops were also limited to maize, barley and potatoes. In the autumn of 1972, however, it was very noticeable how many other vegetables had been introduced into Sola Khumbu – onions, cabbages, carrots, beans, just to quote a few. We even passed a beautifully laid-out market garden down the Dudh Kosi valley, which was being worked by a Japanese couple who had settled in Sola Khumbu, primarily with the intention of supplying fresh vegetables to the Japanese hotel above Namche Bazar. The actual structure and layout of the houses themselves, though, hadn't changed. The more prosperous ones were uniformly built on a two-storey basis; the lower storey, without windows, devoted to store-rooms and byres for their cattle and sheep, and a narrow, wooden staircase in almost pitch dark, leading up to the first-floor, living area. This was almost always open-plan – a spacious room, lit by small windows, though in the case of some of the more modern houses, the windows had been enlarged because of the inclusion of glass. At one end would be the cooking fire on a large stone slab, without any kind of chimney stack; the smoke was allowed to find its way through the stone-tiled roof – a primitive form of space heating. The walls of the room would be lined with rough-hewn cabinets, filled with cooking pots, bowls, chang pots and booty from previous expeditions. At one end of the room there would be a little shrine, and the size would be a good indication of the wealth of the owner. A ceremonial prayer drum might hang from the ceiling and an array of brass cups would be lined in front of an altar. The room itself would be full of smoke. It is not surprising that many of the Sherpas suffer from eye complaints – and yet the houses are comparatively clean and have an atmosphere of comfort and homeliness and, what is more important, hospitality.

We reached Namche Bazar on 6 September. The village is formed in a crescent built into a wide, open bowl in the hillside. Although the administrative capital of the country, with a police station and a Nepalese administrator, it is no more than a large village. There were changes here, however, since 1961. In those days we didn't see a single European for the entire period of the expedition, after leaving Kathmandu, but today Namche Bazar has become a tourist centre, with three or four little restaurants serving omelettes, tea and chang at inflated prices. There are also a couple of shops selling carpets and other tourist-orientated goods. It was at Namche Bazar we paid off our 400 porters who had been recruited from around Kathmandu, to take on local Sherpas. This, as much as anything was a question of trade-union job delineation – once in Sherpa country you employ Sherpas. Most of our newly employed porters were women, who carried exactly the same loads as the men. Some of them were ancient crones who looked in their sixties, and others were young girls who could have been no more than thirteen or fourteen years old. They all seemed to regard their projected journey, firstly to Tengpoche and then to Base Camp, as a glorious, well-paid holiday, a very similar attitude to that of the hop and fruit-pickers in Kent. We also took on a certain number of yaks.

These could carry a double load, 70 kilos or more, but you paid the yak-owner for the number of loads carried.

I had determined to have a couple of days' rest at Tengpoche, a day's march from Namche Bazar. This is the site of the main monastery in the Sola Khumbu region, and must be one of the most idyllic spots in the world. The monastery is perched on the crest of a tree-clad ridge round which swirls the Dudh Kosi. It is surrounded by snow-clad peaks; to the north-east is Everest itself, peering over the great South Wall of Nuptse, flanked on its right by Lhotse; but at Tengpoche, even more impressive is the view of the mountains which tower immediately above it, Tamserku, a shark's fin of fluted ice, and Kantega set slightly further back, with steep, seemingly impregnable walls guarding its summit. Today, with modern transport, the European climber can be at the foot of Tamserku even faster than you could have reached the heart of the Swiss Alps a hundred years ago. In many ways this represents the most exciting climbing of the future, when small groups can go off and climb mountains like these without any of the heavyweight organisation required for mountains the size of Everest. At the moment this is impossible because the Nepalese authorities are only able to allow a limited number of peaks to be climbed. They issue a list each year of the peaks that climbers can apply for, but no doubt in future years the number of peaks which they will open up to expeditions will be increased.

We had now reached a height of 3650m. I was very aware of the importance of acclimatisation. In the original 1953 Everest expedition, John Hunt established an acclimatisation camp at Tengpoche, where they spent a period of two weeks, exploring the glaciers in the immediate vicinity and climbing minor peaks up to a height of about 5640m. This undoubtedly benefited the team later on in the expedition. This approach is strongly contrasted to Herrligkoffer's planning, the previous spring, when he flew his party into Luglha and then tried to push them as fast as possible up to Base Camp. As a result, he had acclimatisation problems in the early stages of the expedition and caused a lot of unnecessary stress. We, unfortunately, were unable to take as leisurely an acclimatisation period as John Hunt since we were going to have to make the maximum possible use of the comparatively warm days in the immediate post-monsoon period. However, my timing, so far, seemed to have worked out well. The monsoon, obviously, was still not over when we reached Tengpoche; the mountains were shrouded in cloud, and it was drizzling gently. I decided, therefore, to spend three days at Tengpoche, to enable our second party to catch up with us, and for everyone to dry themselves out, get their gear sorted and get used to the increased altitude.

We stayed in a small, pre-fabricated hut which had been left by the

Indian expedition of 1965. The grass round us was lush and green from the monsoon rains, and we caught tantalising glimpses of the mountains as the clouds rolled back and forth. Our own little group had felt a comfortable homogeneous unit on the approach march, but it was good to see Barney, Mick, Beth and Doug on their arrival two days later.

Doug had walked all the way from Kathmandu barefoot. With his hair down to his shoulders, held back from his eyes with a head band, and a short unkempt beard, he looked a cross between one of the early Christian martyrs and a modern-day hippie. He had a wonderfully warm and simple idealism and interest in the people around him. Inspired by the scenery about us, and the character of the Sherpas, he cooked up a scheme to organise a climbing school in Khumjung for the Sherpas to give them the necessary technical know-how to be able to work as guides in the rapidly expanding tourist industry that was developing in Sola Khumbu.

There was a further addition to the team in the form of Tony Tighe. He was a close friend of Dougal's – an Australian, who had got part-way through his studies in architecture before feeling the wander-urge and leaving Australia to visit Europe. He had ended up at the Club Vagabond in Leysin, Dougal's base, and the temporary home of many world-travellers. Tony had settled there for a couple of years, earning enough money to live helping out in the bar and finally taking over as bar manager. I had met him a couple of times and had spent one superb day with him, skiing down the Vallée Blanche on the Mont Blanc massif the previous Easter to rescue some gear which we had left on the North Face of the Grandes Jorasses. He was a natural mixer, easy-going, very outward-looking and unselfish. He had written to me just before we set out on the expedition, telling me that he was planning to travel overland to India, and would be in Nepal at the same time that we would be there. He asked whether there was any chance at all of joining up with the expedition to help at Base Camp.

It is always useful having a few voluntary helpers who have joined the team on an informal basis and I had therefore accepted his offer. He was to contribute a great deal to the work of the expedition during its course.

We had nearly come to the end of our journey and the climbing was about to begin. The summit pyramid of Everest, like the keep of a medieval castle, peered tantalisingly over its curtain wall formed by the crenellated ridge of Nuptse, and greater corner bastion of Lhotse.

Would we be able to race the winter winds and cold to its top?

7

Acclimatisation and planning

8 September – 14 September

I had not been able to relax entirely on the approach march, for I had spent much of the time, as I wandered in the rain through the Nepali countryside, thinking of how we were going to climb the South West Face and talking to the others of my plans. I had already made a draft plan; this was necessary in assessing the number of Sherpas we would require, and the amount of gear and oxygen we should obtain. I based my planning largely on the experience of Dougal on the International expedition, since Doug and Hamish, on the European expedition, had only reached the level of Camp 5. The first fundamental problem was that of how many camps we should use. Dougal recommended having a seventh camp above the Rock Band, and this seemed to make good sense, though even before leaving Britain, as I tried to make a detailed analysis of how we should establish, stock and then maintain this seventh camp, it was beginning to become obvious that with the numbers we had available – ten climbers and forty Sherpas, which might seem a small army – we should still barely have the manpower to succeed in doing this.

Oxygen was at the core of the problem. Each cylinder weighed 7.5 kilos and contained just over a 1000 litres of oxygen, enough for about four hours. We planned on letting the climbers use oxygen from 7000m (23,000ft) upwards, to try to keep them going for the final summit push, while the Sherpas would start using it from Camp 5 at 8000m (26,000ft). The problem is that once a climber or Sherpa is using oxygen, his effective payload is reduced to about 7 kilos, since his oxygen cylinder for climbing takes up half the acceptable load of around 16 kilos. To achieve a fast build-up from Camp 5 upwards, one would need a large number of carriers at each camp to maintain the flow. A further complication was presented by the fact that the camp sites have a limited capacity. This was especially the case at Camp 4 (7500m/24,600ft) which had room for only three platforms.

During the approach march, in the course of several discussions with Hamish and Dougal in particular, we decided we should have to abandon the concept of a seventh camp and plan instead on fix-roping the Rock Band from Camp 6, then making a summit bid from this lower camp.

Another fundamental decision, which to me had never seemed in doubt, was our choice of route up the Rock Band. The Japanese had headed for the left-hand side of the Rock Band, where there are two clearly defined breaks, one a ramp leading out on to the West Ridge, and the other a deep chimney-like gully cutting up through the Rock Band. Doug Scott had named it Gardyloo gully during the European Everest expedition, and had suggested, even before we set out, that this might offer a possible line of ascent. Dougal, on the other hand, had been to the very foot of another gully which pierced the defences of the Rock Band on its right-hand side. He described this as being filled with snow and looking comparatively straightforward. It is interesting to speculate just why Whillans and Haston abandoned the Japanese line up to the left, to make their long traverse below the Rock Band over to the right. One of the key problems was that of camp sites and in the spring of 1970 the Japanese had failed to find a suitable camp site for their Camp 5 at the foot of the Rock Band. There was insufficient snow on the face to cut out a platform, and they had insufficient alloy platforms to construct artificial standings for their tents. Don had detected possible sites for Camp 5 on the right-hand side of the Great Central Gully, and Camp 5 was duly established there. From their site of Camp 5, however, it would have been extremely difficult to get back across to the left-hand fork of the gully. The route to the right, across the foot of the Rock Band, however, seemed fairly straightforward, and so they had adopted this.

Since there was a line of fixed ropes, which we might well have been able to use, and since the gully through the Rock Band did not seem too difficult, there appeared to be no doubt that this was the route we should take.

The plan in principle, therefore, seemed clear-cut. My logistic calculations, made back in England before the expedition, are in Appendix B. We had even tried to work them out on a computer. A friend of mine, Ian McNaught-Davis, was managing director of Comshare, a computer company which rented out terminals to firms who could then use the central computer. He was an outstanding climber, having made the first ascent of the Mustagh Tower in 1956 with a very small and compact expedition, but more than that, he was one of the most ebullient characters on the British climbing scene. He had taken part in most of the BBC's climbing spectaculars, usually taking the part of the happy clown, a foil to Joe Brown's silent proficiency. With his immense capacity for outrageous fun, in this instance the thought of working out our planning on his computer like a giant war or business game, appealed to him mainly for its own interest and at the same time as a possible piece of public relations for his firm. David Walkworth, one of his best programmers, was given the task of working out a program for climbing Mount Everest. Sadly the pressure of work in getting the expedition together in those last few weeks was too great for us to be able to take our computer game through to its logical conclusion. I have a feeling that if we had, we should have discovered back in England that we didn't have the logistic power to establish a seventh camp.

There was nothing magic or gimmicky in using the computer. You could not work out a program and then leave the machine to climb the mountain. We used it essentially as a very sophisticated calculating machine which could reduce the hours that I ended up spending in my tent during the approach march working out each step of the climb. In the event, we found that it was impractical to plan in detail too far ahead, because invariably circumstances intervened to dictate a change in plan. On the other hand, by having the outline plan based on carefully thought-out principles, and by playing through what, in effect, was a projected course for the expedition, we were in a position to alter our plans within a sound framework.

I had made my initial plans on the basis of climbers and Sherpas, without troubling about who would do what job, and how each person would fit into the role allotted to him. Now I was going to have to give people their roles on the expedition and realised all too well how critical this could be.

My team was selected on the basis that I had six lead climbers, any one of whom would be capable of reaching the summit of Everest, and who would also expect, and need, to have a share of the lead climbing if his morale and interest in the climb were going to be sustained. These were Dave Bathgate, Mick Burke, Nick Estcourt, Dougal Haston, Hamish MacInnes and Doug Scott. Then there were five of us who would have to be in support. Initially, I had given myself the role of lead climber, but then had increasingly felt that it would be better for me to stay in support, as far as possible, in the camp just below that of the lead climbers. On the South Face of Annapurna, I had found it difficult to conduct the expedition from the front, when I was forcing the route out, for then my mind was too involved in the immediate tactics of the climb, of working out the next few feet of ice or rock, rather than the operation as a whole. Back in the tent at night, the nervous exhaustion of lead climbing had been so great that it was still more difficult to pick up the strands of the entire climb. Another factor was the inevitable resentment felt by other members of the team if you spent too long out in front. Equally, though, I had found it difficult to control the expedition from Base Camp. On the South Face of Annapurna we had our greatest personal crisis towards the end of the expedition, when I had pushed Don Whillans and Dougal Haston out of turn to the front to make the final push. There had been a lot of hard words over the radio, and a certain degree of misunderstanding which would never have occurred had I been at the penultimate camp instead of being sick at Base Camp. And so for this climb, I resolved to stand down from the lead, but to stay as near the front as long as I could to maintain effective control.

My other support climbers, Graham Tiso, Kelvin Kent and Barney Rosedale, were going to be extremely important, for each camp needed one European climber in residence to supervise the Sherpas, allotting loads, maintaining their morale and taking the radio calls. As it turned out, I could have used more climbers performing this role. The lead climbers were not suited by temperament to such a job, and anyway I needed to keep them as fresh as possible for the final push. My support climbers, on the other hand, could gain sufficient sense of fulfilment in feeling that what they were doing was worthwhile. In addition, they all had extra administrative responsibilities and, in the case of Barney, medical ones also. On the logistic front, I merely gave Graham the list of gear I wanted at different camps and it was he who worked out the order of the loads that went up the mountain and then kept a check on their flow through the expedition. Kelvin had a constant responsibility in looking after our relations with the Sherpas and the day-to-day administration. Once Jimmy Roberts arrived at Base Camp, Kelvin was then able to move up the mountain to Camp 2, which by this time had become an Advanced Base Camp, leaving Base Camp and its many problems in Jimmy's capable hands. His presence, advice and authority with the Sherpas were to be invaluable throughout the middle and later stages of the expedition.

Having settled on the lead climbers, I had to decide how best to employ them, whether to make pairings fairly permanent or completely flexible. I decided that if pairs got on well together, it was best to let them stay together. Another factor to be taken into consideration was that we had a responsibility to film for ITV and Thames Television, and therefore, ideally, there should be someone interested in filming prepared to concentrate on this task in each team. Mick Burke was taking overall responsibility, but the important thing was to have a camera at the front at all times where things were likely to happen, and therefore everyone needed to be capable of having a go with it. Hamish MacInnes, also a very competent cameraman, had got some magnificent film for the BBC in the spring attempt. It would therefore have been unfortunate to pair Mick and Hamish together, thus over-concentrating our filming talent. I also had to take into account how compatible each pair was going to be and how they would supplement each other's experience.

At the same time as deciding on the composition of the pairing, I had an even more basic problem to resolve. This was how far to plan ahead the sharing out of the lead climbing to ensure that team members felt, as far as possible, that they had had a fair share and consequently might end the expedition with a feeling of satisfaction. One of the factors on Everest was that we could predict movement fairly accurately from the experience of the previous expeditions. I knew that there was comparatively little technical difficulty until we reached the foot of the Rock Band. It was the Rock Band and the summit bid, which I hoped would immediately follow, that provided the real challenge of the climb – but it seemed unlikely that more than four climbers would have a chance of trying it.

I evolved a revised plan during the approach march by which we should first climb the Icefall with all members of the team having a turn out in front; then I intended to move pair one up to Camp 1, to make the route to Camp 2 in the Western Cwm. Since this was little more than walking, I planned then to allow them to make the route on from Camp 2 to Camp 3 at a height of 7000m (23,000ft). They would then go down for a rest and pair two would move into Camp 3, erect the boxes there and make the route to Camp 4 at 7500m (24,600ft), fix the ropes and then return to Base for a rest. Pair three would then move up to Camp 4, dig out the platforms left by the Germans, erect their boxes and make the route up the Great Central Gully to Camp 5 at 8000m (26,000ft). I estimated that the route-making between camps would take between one and two days each, since either the fixed ropes from previous expeditions would still be in place or, if they were covered in snow, the very presence of the snow would make the climbing that much easier. The method of making the route is that the lead pair goes up and leaves a continuous line of rope all the way up the face, anchored at intervals by snow anchors, ice screws or rock pegs. Everyone subsequently climbs the fixed ropes using jumar clamps.

Having reached Camp 5, the logical thing would be for pair one to move back up, to make the route from Camp 5 to 6; pair two to have the first try on the Rock Band and, if it was as straightforward as Dougal led us to believe, I believed that, provided they felt capable, one must let them make a first attempt on the summit. This would leave pair three rested and fresh to make a second ascent or attempt, depending on the success of the first attempt.

My problem was to decide upon the pairing, and then whether to just explain phase one, up to the establishment of Camp 5, or explain my entire plan. There were pros and cons for either course. If I merely explained phase one, I should have greater flexibility in changing the plan round and adapting it to the performance of different pairs. At the same time, however, I should have created a state of greater tension in the early part of the expedition, since everyone would have been working out their position on the mountain, and their relative chances of tackling the Rock Band or making a summit bid. By explaining the full plan, I was committing myself to a definite pattern of action, but once each pair had accepted their role, I could hope that they would then work to the full within it. I decided, therefore, to follow this latter course.

I then spent many an hour considering the pairing. Dougal and Hamish, who had known each other in a casual kind of way over a good many years, had never actually climbed together. On the approach march, however, they obviously got on, and by the time we reached Tengpoche, they also seemed particularly fit and to be acclimatising well. I decided to pair them together. Of the remaining four, I knew that Nick Estcourt and Mick Burke did not get on particularly well; they were too different in temperament and background – Nick precise, almost niggling over small details but tremendously conscientious, Mick more slap-dash, easy-going on the surface, but very pushing underneath. Nick and Doug did not know each other over well, and since Doug had travelled out on the second party, they did not have the opportunity to get to know each other any better during the course of the walk in. There had already been points of mutual irritation, however, with Nick's logical mind rubbing against Doug's more emotional approach to questions of basic principle. Doug and Mick, on the other hand, got on well together; they bickered constantly in an almost light-hearted, playful way; they undoubtedly made a good team.

This left Nick and Dave Bathgate, who, although they had only known each other casually before the expedition, got on very well together. Dave, like Nick, was extremely methodical and precise, with a highly developed conscience and a perfectionist attitude to any job he undertook. And so I had three pairs who, in the course of the expedition, worked well and happily together.

The next question was more difficult – sorting out the batting order. This was not merely a question of settling on the relative strengths and abilities of each pair and arranging them accordingly, it was more a question of fitting each pair for their specific task, working out how well they were suited to it, and how easily they could accept it. Pair one would be having the least satisfying task, since they would merely be establishing the lower part of the face and then making the route from Camp 5 to 6. I was hoping however that, having made the route, they would also be able to stay up in support for the summit bids, working until they were completely finished. In a way, acceptance of this role required the greatest level of unselfishness and the highest degree of reliability, for the direct rewards were less obvious. I decided to cast Nick and Dave for this somewhat unenviable task, for I knew I could rely totally on their loyal support in what, at first glance, seemed a lesser role. In addition, Dave had less high-altitude experience than the other members of the team. There was little doubt in my mind that Dougal and Hamish were by far the most experienced pair, and Dougal particularly was recognised by the entire team as having the greatest drive on the mountain. If you like, he was acknowledged by all to be at the top of the pecking order. There was very little to choose as a pair between Doug and Mick, and Dave and Nick. Doug did have the advantage that he had been to 8000m and Mick, who at the beginning of the expedition was probably the least fit, and had certainly climbed the least in the last year or so, had an amazing single-minded determination which had enabled him to screw out of the bag some very impressive performances over the years – his first British ascent of the Nose of El Capitan and, even more applicable to Everest, his achievement in leading all the way across the Rock Band on the South Face of Annapurna. Another factor which I had to take into consideration was that since Mick was chief cameraman of the expedition, I wanted to give him the maximum chance to get the best film possible, since we owed this to ITN and Thames who had sponsored us.

Bearing all these considerations in mind, I decided to designate Mick and Doug as pair two, with the responsibility of making the route from Camps 3 to 4 and then from 6 up the Rock Band with the first summit attempt, holding Dougal and Hamish back for the final summit attempt. This made sense and because of the latter pair's complete self-confidence, they would be able to cope with a reserve role, knowing full well that on them would rest our main chance of reaching the summit of Everest. I had a feeling that the chances of Doug and Mick could be no more than outside, after the effort they would require to make in forcing the Rock Band.

I announced the plan once the second party had caught us up at Tengpoche. Naturally Nick and Dave were disappointed at their seemingly subordinate position in relation to the others, but it is a tribute to their loyalty to the concept of the expedition that they accepted their role without argument and fulfilled it with enthusiasm.

And so, at Tengpoche, when we were still fifteen miles from our objective, we had a plan which was to provide the basis of our efforts on Everest. The three days' rest was well spent, drying out our equipment and sorting out gear for the climb ahead. The climbers were going to use one-piece down suits, covered by a windproof outer suit. The suit had originally been designed by Don Whillans and was ingenious, having a zip round the interior of the leg so that the climber could remove or put on the suit over boots and crampons. A small slit down the back, closed by a zip, enabled him to relieve himself without taking the suit off and baring his backside to the icy blast. I had made one or two important modifications to cater for the extreme cold and wind that we were going to encounter during an autumn attempt. These included increasing the down content of the suit, having all flaps over zips padded in down and, most important, incorporating a Ventile (cotton) inner layer, underneath the outer layer of the windproof suit. This ensured that the suit was totally windproof. One thing we had failed to notice in the rush before leaving Britain, however, was that the outer suits did not have hoods. We were fortunate in having Beth Burke with us, and she hand-tailored hoods to fit all the members of the team. We had issued our Sherpas with the more conventional down jackets and trousers, with windproof outers. At the same time, Hamish was sorting out all our oxygen gear, adapting our pack-frames with a special set of straps to hold the bottles rigidly in position, and making one or two modifications on the equipment itself to strengthen what seemed some weak joints.

During our stop at Tengpoche, we visited the Chief Lama of the monastery to receive his blessing and to make a presentation of money to the monastery. I described this in my diary on the 10 September:

At 11.30 a.m. we had to go up and make our official visit to the Lama at Tengpoche monastery. The official visit of the expedition is a way of giving a presentation of money to the monastery, and it is also an opportunity for the Sherpas to be blessed by the Lama. The Lama lives not in the main monastery building, but in a little side building. We went through a low door to a little yard with marigolds and flowers in window boxes around it into the Lama's room, which was sparsely furnished with low divans round the whitewashed walls and a table in the middle. The divans were made from rough cut wood, with Tibetan carpets on them. The Lama was sitting there, waiting to receive us, in his dark brownish robes. He was perhaps in his mid-thirties or early forties and had a look of tranquillity about him. I was ushered in first and made my namaste (greeting) to him, bobbing my head; Kelvin and Hamish came in afterwards and did the same. Then all our Sherpas trooped in, in what seemed to be an order of seniority – Pembatharke first, followed by Sona Hishy and then Phurkipa, the eldest of our Sherpas, and finally all the others. As all the Sherpas came in, the older ones went to him and bowed right down in front of him to have their heads touched, but the younger ones completed what was almost a yoga exercise, going right down on their hands and knees, touching the floor with their heads, and then back into the standing position – doing this three times before coming forward for the blessing. Each had with him a white ceremonial gauze scarf, in which was wrapped his offering. Between them, the fourteen had raised 280 rupees as a gift for the Tengpoche monastery. We ourselves gave another 500 rupees for not only Tengpoche, but also the Khumbu monasteries. Having gone through this ceremonial we all sat down, and the Lama talked to us as a group. Kelvin, being able to speak Nepali, got into quite a deep discussion and the Lama was able to put across his own religious attitudes. He showed, I think, that even in these seemingly primitive surroundings, how much broader his religion is than that of many Christian priests and prelates. He said how there could be only one God, but that man had found many different ways of trying to reach him and to worship him. He then went on to talk about expeditions, saying how on the two previous expeditions, because the climbers had started arguing and quarrelling among themselves, this had led the Sherpas to become discontented, and therefore the expeditions had failed. It would be very cold for us, he said, going in the autumn, but in spite of this we should remain united.

We sat there, eating biscuits and drinking tea, for about an hour. During that time some of the tranquillity and the settled peace of the monastic's existence had rolled over us. We then visited the main gompa, and were shown the inner sanctuary, a room on the first floor. It was lined with magnificent garish mural paintings of devils, wheels of life, and other pictures associated with their mythology. Down one wall was the main altar, with three incarnations of Buddha, and glass cabinets full of idols, many of which seemed to have a strong Hindu influence in their design. On one side of the room was the monastery library, with parchment rolls tucked into little square compartments. The Sherpas, once again, went through their obeisance in front of the altar, and we admired the pictures, and made a further contribution to the upkeep of the monasteries.

We left Tengpoche on 11 September; the monsoon clouds had rolled in once again and we could see no more than the dripping trees on either side of the path and rough stone walls disappearing into the mists. That night we stopped at Pheriche, a little collection of one-storey huts in small fields, only occupied in the summer months. The following day we walked up to Lobuche, in a rain that slowly turned to snow as dusk fell. Dave Bathgate describes the day in his diary:

There are some advantages to the depressing weather. The day started off as usual. Swirling damp mists and visibility about 100 yards, the altitude making it that wee bit colder and turning the rain to sleet as we climbed. The consolation of walking through magnificent scenery that can only be beheld in the imagination, is that one is forced to study the immediate surroundings, particularly the piece of ground in front of your nose. You walk, head down, brolly up, threading through the moraines, climbing as you peer past the boulders into the murk. Now, couldn't this just be Scotland: like some part of Sutherland to be precise, where the moraines are still not quite covered in vegetation. But stepping into a pile of yak dung you are brought back to reality. This is Nepal. This is 15,000ft up in the mountains on the last few days of the walk into the Everest Base Camp. Yak dung is everywhere in neat piles.

Suddenly you are aware of the colours. You are walking on a carpet of yellow butterwort, little yellow stars, all interlocking, and between is green. Under a clean granite rock there are pink pom-pom flowers and one or two bright purple blooms like our bluebell. The moraine walls are covered in juniper and sheltered by the bush are edelweiss and large yellow-petalled flowers like buttercups. There are plants like fluted columns, large, leafy, green things, little clusters of red buds and many other wonders of the alpine scene unidentifiable to the layman; a paradise for the botanist; an entomologist would have a field day. Countless millions of butterwort (an insect-devouring flower) can't be wrong. The geologist would also weigh himself down with samples of a fascinating nature; here is granite and quartz; evidence of iron and copper or schist; the stream beds are full of 'pearls' for him.

All this that has been brought to my attention would otherwise have gone unnoticed if the big hills had shown themselves.

Lobuche was no more than a couple of yak herders' huts in a little valley at the side of a glacier. I had planned to send the porters straight through from Lobuche, by Gorak Shep, up to Base Camp with Hamish MacInnes and Dougal Haston, who seemed extremely well acclimatised and who were keen to press on and start reconnoitring the Icefall. On the other hand, I had wanted to give the rest of the team as much opportunity as possible to acclimatise, and therefore considered spending another two or three days at Lobuche, at a height of 4875m, so that each member of the team could acclimatise at his own rate. The following morning, however, 13 September, we had no choice in the matter. It had snowed hard all night and our porters had had a rough time. With insufficient shelter in the two yak huts for all of them, we had had to make improvised shelters from piled-up loads and tarpaulins and the Sherpas and Sherpanis spent the night huddled beneath these. In spite of the cold they seemed to enjoy the experience, regarding the whole affair as a light-hearted adventure, even though most of them had little more than a blanket each in which to wrap themselves.

The next stop would have been Gorak Shep, which was not much higher than Lobuche, but in an even bleaker situation. From there to Base Camp was a three-hour walk and in the event of another bad night at Gorak Shep it would have been difficult to persuade the Sherpas to walk this distance the next day, so I decided to let them stay at Lobuche. At least it gave us a chance of issuing all their equipment to the Icefall Sherpas who had now joined us. Very quickly the camp took on the appearance of a bazaar, as Graham broke open the boxes and lined them up like a series of market stalls. Our temporary porters, who were going to carry the gear up to Base Camp, acted as an audience, watching the hand-out in a spirit which was both light-hearted and critical. This was the moment which had caused the crisis on the Herrligkoffer expedition, when the Sherpas had discovered that they had insufficient gear with which to climb the mountain. I was just praying that they would be happy with what we presented to them. You could tell at a glance the difference between our high-altitude porters who had been employed all the way from Kathmandu and the Icefall Sherpas whom we had only just hired. The latter were less well dressed, their clothes the relics of previous expeditions; very few spoke English and they looked altogether rougher and surprisingly, perhaps, older than our high-altitude porters. Jimmy Roberts' Mountain Travel Sherpas looked like mountain guides – they barely condescended to use the clothing which we had issued, preferring for the approach march gear they considered more elegant. Some of them, Pertemba particularly, reminded me of French guides, with smart peaked cap and well-cut breeches.

The proceedings started with a little ceremonial speech from myself, in which I described a bonus scheme we had worked out to give the Sherpas an incentive to carry their loads up the South West Face. I also promised magnificent baksheesh in the event of success. The speech was relayed in Nepali by Kelvin, through Sona Hishy, who gave it in Sherpa. The speech appeared to be well received, and then we lined up all our newly recruited Sherpas and handed out all their equipment. That afternoon the camp resembled a factory, as Graham with one group of Sherpas assembled pack-frames; other groups fitted crampons to boots or tried on their new gear. Inevitably, the odd item disappeared, as Sherpas helped themselves, or swapped one item of gear for another. They all seemed satisfied at this stage with what they had been issued.

The following day dawned fine, and for the first time we saw the magnificent setting which surrounds Lobuche. Looking back down the valley, the twin peaks of Kantega dominated the deep-cut gorge of the Dudh Kosi. Further over to the right was Taweche, a beautiful fluted peak almost climbed by Hillary's schoolhouse expedition in 1963, and just to the right was that of Tsolatse, which was still virgin. Immediately above us were some lower, rocky peaks which would have been attainable if only we had had more time. We did, however, climb the nearest summit, which must have been at a height of about 5480m. We plodded up grassy slopes which were a mosaic of alpine flowers and mosses, and then scrambled up a rocky little ridge to the top. We had been well rewarded for our purgatorial march through the monsoons by the sheer variety and beauty of the vegetation, which would soon die in the dry autumnal air. From the summit of our little peak we gazed across the Khumbu Glacier to the incredible turreted ridge of Nuptse which concealed Everest and the Icefall. Many tourists who have come only this far have made the mistake of thinking that this was Everest itself – it certainly looked sufficiently high. And then, on up the Khumbu Glacier, the 7160m (23,400ft) summit of Pumo Ri was a shapely pyramid of snow and rock; this had been climbed by a German expedition in 1962 and was to be the target of a French expedition from Chamonix while we made our attempt on the South West Face of Everest. One couldn't help having a slight feeling of envy for them. We were under no illusions about the type of climbing we were going to have on Everest – a great deal of hard work, with comparatively little exciting climbing. On the other hand, a mountain like Pumo Ri would obviously yield superb technical climbing, at an altitude low enough to enjoy it. Nevertheless, the scale of Everest made up for it – the problem we were tackling was so huge that this very challenge made it all worthwhile.

That day the porters and yaks moved on, up to Gorak Shep, the standard staging post on the way up to Base Camp. They were accompanied by

Graham Tiso and Nick Estcourt, together with five of our high-altitude Sherpas, whilst Dougal and Hamish, with half a dozen Sherpas carrying their tentage and personal gear, moved straight up to Base Camp. And so, on 14 September, little more than three months after we had conceived our expedition, the real climbing of the mountain was about to begin.

8

The Icefall

16 September – 20 September

So far luck had been with us – our timing seemed perfect; 14 September to all intents and purposes marked the end of the monsoon. Jimmy Roberts had seen many monsoons in Nepal and had a theory that its end was often marked by a heavy snowfall down to 4000m. He appeared to be right, for the snow of the previous few days had reached all the way down to Pheriche, which is just on the 4000m mark. Now the sun blazed from a cloudless blue sky and had that special, autumnal quality. In spite of the heat of the sun there was a clean-cut bite to the air, which removed all traces of haze. It was as if you were looking at the distant peaks through a magnifying glass. And it was on the 14th that Dougal and Hamish, feeling almost no effect at all from the altitude, made the long walk from Lobuche to the site of Base Camp.

Base Camp on Everest is a bleak place; it is situated on the glacier itself, amongst rocky debris carved by the glacier in the previous millennia. It resembles a vast derelict granite quarry, whose unworked stones have been left in haphazard piles, the rocks comparatively young and unweathered, edges unrounded by erosion of wind and weather. There was rock dust everywhere, as if from a recent blasting. At close quarters it is a stark, almost ugly place contrasting with the austere beauty of the surrounding mountains; but even these mountains offer little relief, for their appeal is one of chill remoteness, a beauty unrelieved by softness. No grass in sight, none of the brilliant alpine flowers and mosses that we had seen at Gorak Shep for the last time for some months; this was a wilderness of rock and snow and ice, whose only reminder of man was the worst possible – man's pollution of almost anything he touches. The area round Base Camp was marked by the previous expeditions to Everest. Their rubbish was everywhere – rusty tins, plastic bags, decayed packing cases.

Yet that first night the very austerity of the setting must have seemed precious to Dougal and Hamish. Both had been there before, but on the two previous occasions there had always been a mass of people around them. That afternoon, though, the Sherpas carrying the tentage and climbing gear had dumped their loads and returned to the main party camped at Gorak Shep, leaving just the two of them in a small orange tent, at the head of the Khumbu Glacier. A few days later this was to become a little village of tents, with a population of over fifty. Then, inevitably, some of the magic must be lost, for this is the problem of all large expeditions; the atmosphere of the mountains, the emotion they inspire in us, the feeling of easy friend-ship that you get when just a few are sharing this, are very dependent on empty solitude.

Over the way was Pumo Ri, snow traced buttresses stretching up towards its corniced summit. Immediately above was Khumbutse, foreshortened because of its proximity, with none of the classic proportions of Pumo Ri; then to its right, within easy reach of Base Camp, the pass of the Lho La, the way into Tibet and the Rongbuk Glacier. An occasional rattle, slightly muted, betrayed falling ice tumbling from its piled séracs and the western spur of Everest.

But it was the Icefall which commanded their attention – as indeed it does the attention of any visitor to the Everest Base Camp. The Icefall is a natural continuation of the Khumbu Glacier, as is the Western Cwm. It is a gigantic frozen river, the source of which is on the slopes of Everest and Lhotse. The Western Cwm must rank as the most inspiring cirque to be found in any mountain range in the world, squeezed as it is between the flanks of Everest and the incredible wall of Nuptse. The Icefall is the gateway to Everest, a vast frozen cataract, tumbling 900m between a sub-sidiary spur of Nuptse and one from Everest. Had it been water it would have been a gigantic waterfall, but as ice it is even more impressive. The huge but slow pressure of the glacier in the Western Cwm inexorably thrusts the ice before it, over the drop of the Icefall, breaking up the smooth-flowing river of ice which forms the bed of the Cwm into a convo-luted chaos of ice walls, towers and pinnacles, all of which must eventually topple. Dougal and Hamish had to find a route through this maze. In addi-tion to their knowledge of the risks and the problems, now, in the autumn, we had some grounds to hope that it would be both easier and safer than it had been in the spring. They could see that many of the crevasses which seam its surface before the monsoon had been filled in. We knew that the Argentinians, the previous autumn, had found it comparatively easy and had forced the Icefall in a mere three days, compared with the fortnight it had taken the International expedition and the ten days spent by the European expedition. It was easy to imagine the wonder and, at the same time, the trepidation of Eric Shipton's reconnaissance party, who first climbed it in the autumn of 1951. Entering the Icefall undoubtedly has an element of Russian roulette. There is no possibility of making a safe route through the Khumbu Icefall. All you can do is to try and pick out a route which is as safe as possible, but there will always be sections which are threatened by ice towers which, sooner or later, must collapse. You just hope that no one happens to be beneath them when the inevitable collapse occurs. If climbers and Sherpas only had to go through the danger area once during an expedition the risks would be comparatively slight – not much greater than the risks presented to any alpinist working his way through a hanging glacier in the European Alps or any other mountain region in the world. The problem with the Everest Icefall is that some climbers must go through these danger areas almost every single day of the expedition. As a result, the chances of an accident occurring are increased considerably, as the death-roll on Everest has sadly proven. It is the Sherpas who are exposed to the greatest risk, particularly the Icefall porters whose job it is to keep Camp 2 fully stocked with food and gear throughout the expedition.

Dougal and Hamish spent a further day gazing at the Icefall through binoculars, resting to ensure that their acclimatisation was as complete as possible. Nick Estcourt and Graham Tiso, with all our porters and some high-altitude Sherpas, walked up to Base Camp from Gorak Shep, and that day the camp became a Base Camp indeed. The following day, the 16th, we first set foot on Everest in earnest. Dougal, Hamish and five Sherpas carrying 1.5m sections of alloy ladders, rope, snow stakes and deadmen (not corpses, but plates which are buried in the snow to provide a compact yet very reliable anchor), set out before dawn. There was no breath of wind, but in the dim light the temperature was in the region of –10°C; the snow was firm underfoot, points of crampons snicking into its hard surface. They had picked out a line the day before and now zig-zagged steadily up, through the gentle undulations of the approach to the Icefall. The harsh angularity of the ice was hidden by the covering of monsoon snows and they were able to make rapid progress, bridging the occasional open crevasse with one of their ladders. Hamish was in his element; being, perhaps, a frustrated structural engineer, he revelled in making complex pulley systems, bridges and anything mechanical. By mid-day they had reached a point almost halfway up the Icefall, having found a route that seemed completely free from objective danger. However, the sun was now hammering down, and not only was the hard snow being softened into a thigh-deep morass, more important, the sheer heat of the sun burning down into the giant reflector provided by the Icefall and the Western Cwm had an enervating effect which sapped the will and made any movement a trial. They retreated, therefore, well content with their day's work.

That same day I walked, with Dave Bathgate, up to Base Camp from Lobuche. I was able to forget for a few happy hours my overall responsibility for the expedition in the excitement of walking to the foot of Everest. That evening I commented in my diary:

This morning dawned magnificently; the monsoon certainly seems to be over. Dave and I set out early, along the moraine which flanks the Khumbu Glacier, past an array of miniature alpine flowers and plants picked out by the early-morning frost. From Gorak Shep, the route goes on to the glacier itself, past giant white fins of ice that look like the sails of yachts, and over a sea of rubble-strewn ice. The gleaming white of the ice fins was enhanced by the drab grey of the glacier around. It is a bleak, almost lunar landscape. The Icefall itself is completely hidden until you are almost at the end of the Khumbu Glacier. It turns a tight L-turn, and it is only near its end that you see it – and what a chaotic mass of ice it is. Dougal and Hamish must be somewhere amongst it. We missed the way to the camp and went much too high – very nearly reaching the foot of the Icefall. I was beginning to feel quite tired, and so was Dave. We were both slipping around a bit and feeling the altitude. We realised at last that the camp could not possibly be in front of us, looked back, and only after a very careful search were we able to see the camp site. It made you realise what a really huge scale this area is – there was just a collection of tiny matchboxlike tents lost in the barren waste of rubble on the dying glacier.

In spite of having a bad headache, Graham Tiso had been at work all day, sorting out the mass of expedition gear which was to go up the mountain. We had altogether five tons of gear which was destined for the Western Cwm. There were 170 bottles of oxygen, of which I estimated we should use approximately ninety, the rest were a reserve. There was – or rather should have been – 15,000ft (4500m) of fixed rope, several hundred pitons, dead-men, snow stakes, ladders and all the paraphernalia for laying siege to a big mountain. Graham had done an outstanding job in getting all the gear ready in time for the expedition, but had made one vital mistake in failing to check the quantity of rope delivered to him against what had been ordered. Consequently, instead of 15,000ft of fixed rope, we found our-selves with 5000ft (1500m) – not nearly enough to climb the South West Face of Everest, and barely enough for use in the Icefall. The impact of this shock was softened by the discovery that Graham was, in fact, fallible! He was quite a bombastic soul, accustomed to ruling his business with a hand which was both very firm and yet, at the same time, had a touch of fun in it. Having the total self-confidence of all successful businessmen, he was happy to assure all of his infallibility. All was not lost, however, since we knew that Jimmy Roberts had about 3000ft of rope back in Kathmandu, and we immediately sent a message asking if we could borrow this, and for a further 6000ft (1830m) to be airfreighted out to us from England. There were one or two other minor omissions, such as the fact that we had forgot-ten to supply our Sherpas with water bottles. This was easily rectified by sending down to Namche Bazar and Khumjung, and buying them from the Sherpas. There must be enough equipment stashed away in Sola Khumbu to equip almost an entire Everest expedition, though the prices tend to be inflated. We also tried to buy some rope locally, and Lindsay Strang, the New Zealand doctor who ran the Khumde hospital, succeeded in obtaining a 1000ft for us, but this was only in lengths of 80ft or so.

On 17 September, Dougal and Hamish, with a group of Sherpas, went back into the Icefall, setting out even earlier than on their first visit. By dawn, as the rest of us got out of our sleeping bags, we could see them – tiny, black dots, dwarfed by the immensity of the Icefall. They were making good progress, having reached their high point, a good halfway up, before dawn. Once again, they moved steadily, picking their way across some avalanche debris, where they had stopped the previous day, and then climbing up a series of comparatively straightforward snow slopes to the foot of the final steep section before the top of the Icefall. A sheer wall of ice barred their way. Hamish cut his way up the steep little snow gully, but by this time the heat of the sun was upon them – enervating, blazing heat, which softened the snow and exhausted the climbers. They managed to look over the top, however, and found themselves confronted by a series of moat-like crevasses. They came down that night, encouraged by their progress, but also warning us that the next section was going to be difficult.

It was now to be the turn of Dave Bathgate and myself to go into the Icefall to force the last section. In my diary I said:

I must say, I am a little apprehensive, in that I hope I don't make a mess of it, not having been in the Icefall before. Hamish and Dougal, of course, are real old hands, whilst Dave and I are novices. Still, we'll have to do our best.

There is a real feeling of friendship within the team – of people working together, and I only pray we can keep this up. It really is tremendous. Obviously, there are going to be pressures; bound to be conflicts (I have had one with Mick), and so on. But these we shy away from when we have them, realising how bad they are, immediately suppressing them. You seem to find that when people have had a little row, they make special gestures to show this. Such as the other day, when Mick and I had a flare-up – Mick made a special point afterwards, by shoving some of the stuff I had left outside my tent in the rain, inside, to prevent it getting wet. I think it is these small things which are terribly important.

Once again, from my diary:

18 September, 1972: I woke up this morning at about one o'clock, going over the various problems of the expedition. I dropped off to sleep and was woken again by a cook-boy at four o'clock with a cup of tea – certainly a civilised way to start a day's climbing, since we also have breakfast in bed. I got up at about 4.45 a.m., went over to the Sherpas and found they were all ready, and just going through their reli-

gious ceremony. In this, each one has a little thread put around his neck and an incantation is made over him with a burning ember, to protect him for the day on the mountain, and in the Icefall. Throughout the day, as long as the Sherpas are on the mountain, they keep small fires of smouldering herbs burning, and very often you will notice a Sherpa by one of them, muttering prayers.

Eventually we got going, just as it was getting light, at about 5.15 a.m. Seven load-carriers accompanied us, carrying ladders and other bits of climbing gear. We plodded through the dim light of the dawn – it seemed just pleasantly cool, but I suppose it was very cold, because there was no wind at all, and was absolutely clear and very dry. I felt slightly unco-ordinated and still had a slight cough, with discomfort at the back of my throat. I stumbled across the broken rocks of the moraine, to the point where the Sherpas were gathered, putting on their crampons. They just leave their crampons, ropes and ice axes out on a few rocks – which is all very fine of course, unless there is a big snowfall, when I think they would find it very difficult to locate them. It's something I am going to have to make an issue about with the Sherpas.

Being unco-ordinated, I stood on my hand with my cramponed boot, cut my hand, leaving blood spewing out over everything. Having put my crampons on, I started walking and felt a lot better. I must say, I seemed to be going the fastest of all the party. Of course, you've got to remember, though, that most of the Sherpas were heavily laden, whilst we, the climbers, were not. We have noticed that as they plod up the Icefall they mutter their prayers. I was with Dave Bathgate; Nick Estcourt was coming up behind with Phurkipa, our 'road-mender', to improve the route.

Phurkipa was the oldest of our Sherpas. Then fifty-five, he had been on innumerable expeditions, including the spring Everest trip with Doug. It had been Doug who had recommended him. In the spring, Phurkipa had earned the title of 'road-mender' for he had taken charge of the Icefall throughout the expedition, repairing and renovating the route as necessary. He was to have this function on our trip as well and was to do an excellent job.

We wound our way up through the Icefall, following the trail made by Dougal and Hamish. Technically, it was fairly easy and comparatively safe, for the route was not threatened by any precarious séracs, though at one point it crossed the debris of what must have been a huge avalanche from the walls of the Everest Spur. There was a large number of crevasses, which they had bridged, and Dougal and Hamish had done well to make such good time. The place where they had actually ended the day was below a big sérac wall. Dougal had already warned me that they had tried to go up a blind gully. We could see the tracks, but this did not seem to lead anywhere except to a huge crevasse which would require a large number of ladders to bridge. Dougal had mentioned going round to the left, up an alleyway which was below some very loose-looking séracs. It seemed a dangerous area and, as we looked, a sérac higher up collapsed – this convinced us.

Then I was tempted by the wall immediately above, which looked solid enough to use a ladder straight up it. I worked my way across, and brought Dave to me and he went to the foot of the wall itself. We started to get our ladders ready – we had five sections altogether – when one of the most impressive avalanches I have ever seen came off the very summit of Pumo Ri. There was a great cloud of windblown powder snow which billowed across the glacier and seemed about to engulf Base Camp itself. But we were concentrating on the route in front, and after a struggle with our five ladders, bolted them together. This was a style of climbing I had never undertaken before. Pushing up a 9m (30ft) ladder from a comparatively narrow snow ledge is no joke. It was just as well we had six Sherpas with us. With all of them pushing and heaving, we finally succeeded in balancing the ladder against the wall; it reached a point about a metre below the top.

With true courtesy, partly because I wanted to get some pictures, I gestured to Dave to have the honour of climbing the ladder first. It was a matter of balancing delicately up it – it was still very unstable. He succeeded in putting in an ice piton about two-thirds of the way up, where it came in close to the ice, fastening the ladder to it with a rope, and now that there was no risk of teetering backwards, climbed more rapidly to the top. After a bit of step-cutting, he pulled out on to the top of the sérac wall. This had taken us about three hours. I was uncomfortably aware of the speedy progress which Dougal and Hamish had made the previous day, and was worried that we were going so slowly. From the top of the sérac wall, things did not look at all hopeful. There was a wide depression immediately in front of us of unstable-looking snow that led to another mass of séracs; to the right, a sérac tower curled up and there was a feeling of unpleasant insecurity wherever we looked. Finally, I picked on a line going to one side of a depression. Even on seemingly easy ground, one stepped forward very, very carefully, always uncomfortably aware that one might go rocketing down into a deep hole. Always there was the suspicion that the entire mass of ice could collapse around one like a pack of cards.

It is strange how one's attitude to a route through a glacier or the Icefall changes. The first time through, one's progress is slow and nerve-racking, but once the route is made, though it gets no safer, one treats the glacier in an increasingly blasé manner until finally something happens – a sérac collapses and, perhaps, a man dies.

Another small wall barred our way. This was to be the only real climbing I was to have on the entire expedition – a mere 6m (20ft) vertical ice wall. I cut a step, kicked in my crampons, forgot the altitude for just a few minutes, in my concentration and apprehension, as I worked my way up the sérac wall; I pulled over the side, kicking in my front points, and reached the crest. Once I had fixed the rope, Dave followed up quickly, and we looked further ahead.

The view was not encouraging. We were on a little ridge which reminded me of the crest of a breaker, frozen into immobility, brittle, fragile, about to tumble on to the lesser waves around it. To our left, this was linked with the next line of breakers by a ridge of wafery ice towers, all on the point of collapse. To the right, a trough stretched round a corner, into a broken area that was like a choppy sea. Nothing seemed stable, nothing sure. I tried the ridge to the left, but the sun was now burning down from the empty sky, sapping the will, destroying strength and energy, softening to the consistency of candy floss, the snow which bound one pinnacle to another. That way seemed no good.

'Have a look at the ridge on the right,' I told Dave.

He set out, probing the snow in front of him with a long alloy pole whose function was to act as a handrail on crevasse bridges – the most effective way of feeling for hidden crevasses. I sat and stewed in the sun, trying to keep my eyes open, aware that I had been awake since three o'clock that morning. The rope trickled through my fingers. At last we came to the end of the rope, Dave secured it at his end and I clipped a jumar clamp on to it and followed the line of his tracks, most of them deep in the heat-softened snow.

'It doesn't look too good from here,' he warned me.

It didn't; the well defined trough had disintegrated into a chaos of holes and towers that looked ready to collapse at any instant. We returned to our starting point at the top of my 6m pitch. To me, the best hope seemed straight down into the trough, to climb the other side, flanking two square-cut sérac towers which, at least, looked a good deal more solid than anything around them. A snow slope led to one side of them, but the problem here was that if one of the towers did collapse, no one below would have a chance of survival. I made a half-hearted step down into the moat which guarded them, but the snow was frighteningly soft and our own strength and determination was waning fast. We looked at each other and decided to return. I have always been intensely competitive in my climbing and could not help feeling disappointed in myself that I had not made better progress. In actual fact, during the next few days, other groups had a struggle to make much further progress in any one day. The top of the Icefall was to prove the crux of this part of the route.

Leaving even earlier than we had the previous day, on 19 September, after their day's rest, Dougal and Hamish once again went out in front. We were discovering that it was almost impossible to climb after mid-day – it was so hot. They reached my high point, and then Hamish indulged in his passion for complex engineering. He shared the same worries that I had had in the choice of a route going down into the moat and then climbing the other side. (This was the place where Tony Tighe was to be killed at the end of the expedition.) Hamish tried, therefore, to avoid this by making an incredible suspension bridge from several sections of aluminium ladder, across the side of the tottering sérac which I had avoided the previous day. It was a magnificent piece of engineering. Having bridged the gap they climbed a steep gully, laddered over the steep wall and got to a point where they could look across the top, over one crevasse, to what they thought would probably be the end of the Icefall.

That day they came down well satisfied. Up to this point, rather as on the spring expedition, Doug Scott had acclimatised slowly and, weakened by his attack of dysentery on the approach march, he had spent a couple of extra days down at Gorak Shep to give himself a better chance of acclimatising. However, he was now feeling better and on 20 September, with Dave Bathgate, Nick Estcourt and myself, we planned to go up and make the final push to the top of the Icefall.

In the early stages of the expedition almost all of us, with the exception of Hamish and Dougal, had stomach upsets, or short periods of sickness. I was struck in this manner that night, and when the time came to get out of bed I found I had lost all my strength. I spent the entire day in my sleeping bag, dosed with a variety of pills from Barney Rosedale. Meanwhile, Doug, Nick and Dave pressed on, up to the high point which Hamish and Dougal had established. Unfortunately, all the ice screws which anchored Hamish's suspension bridge had melted the previous day and so there seemed no choice but to drop the ladder across the bottom of the moat and accept the threat of the two towers above. Having done this they climbed to the top of the gully to rejoin the route made by Hamish and Dougal the previous day, and which we all hoped was to bring us to the end of the difficulties. As is so often the case, this did not prove to be so, and it was necessary to make another long traverse along an undercut ridge of ice, back towards the centre of the Icefall. The trio had one of their first personality differences at this point. Doug was still feeling the altitude first thing that morning and had started out very slowly, with Nick and Dave out in front making the route. He caught up with them once they were slowed down erecting ladders. In my diary that night, after I had heard the story, I wrote the following:

Doug caught up, apparently with a new lease of life in him, pushed ahead, took one look over the top and said, 'Ah, lots of crevasses here, still, the site of Camp 1 is much further on.' Nick, however, was convinced that they were already at the site of Camp 1 – in fact they had an argument – but Doug wouldn't listen, and Nick stood down, uncertain perhaps of his own rightness, since Doug had been there before; also, Doug probably has the stronger personality. They plodded off for a mile and a quarter up the Western Cwm, about 500ft higher, trying to find a site.

They found another camp site which they discovered after crossing some dangerous areas, and got very close in to the side where there was the risk of avalanche, before turning back. Then, of course, they were absolutely exhausted, for it was now getting late. Meanwhile, they had another flaring argument – this time about the one-piece suits. Doug had been the original exponent of the one-piece suit, after using it on the spring attempt. Some of the team undoubtedly felt that the Erve down jackets and trousers, which we had issued to the Sherpas, were considerably superior. Anyway, Nick tried to relieve himself – the trouble is, because of the size of the slit in the back, you can't relieve yourself and have a pee at the same time, which is what you usually want to do. Nick, in a fury of rage, took his suit off, hurled it down and stamped on it, cursing it and telling Doug exactly what he thought of one-piece suits. This evening Nick admitted that the argument he had with Doug was not really about the one-piece suit at all, but was against Doug having made a false decision to push on against Nick's better judgment. Then, of course, there is a deeper connotation to all this, because I had given Dave and Nick a less attractive role than Doug and Mick, with very little chance of reaching the top.

These tensions and minor flare-ups might seem very petty when written down after the expedition – things better buried and forgotten, far from the spirit of the hills and the romance of true adventure; but if you do forget them you ignore the very reality of what an expedition is like – the tension that climbers come under, both from the point of view of personal ambition, the ways in which their differing personalities interlock, and the physical and mental stress they are under.

At first, Nick and Doug, without a doubt, got on each other's nerves, neither fully understanding or respecting the other. Nick was the more aggressive because he had been given a subordinate role in establishing Camp 6, and he felt that Doug took his, more attractive role of climbing the Rock Band too much for granted. The important thing, to my mind, was the way that in the course of the expedition, each came to respect and like the other, even though they recognised the differences in each other's personalities. An expedition is comprised of a pattern of tensions in human relationships. If these get out of hand – as they did both on the International expedition and the European expedition – the results are unhappy. If they can be contained, however, usually by the basic respect of members for each other, these little explosions during the expedition's course simply act as minor eruptions and, perhaps, even as a necessary safety-valve.

And so, on 20 September, we had actually forced the route through the Icefall, taking a mere five days. We now seemed well ahead of schedule. The weather was perfect, there were no signs of the post-monsoon winds, and we were all beginning to talk of reaching the summit before the end of October. The climbing now seemed very much more predictable and I could start trying to follow the logistic plan which I had originally worked out in Britain and modified during the course of the approach march.

9

Teething troubles

21 September – 29 September

We had climbed the Icefall, but that was barely a start. The route still had to be made safer for the porters in order to start ferrying the five tons of oxygen cylinders, climbing equipment, tentage and food through to Camp 1 and on to Camp 2, our base of operations at the foot of the face. Although Camp 1 had yet to be established, we were still ahead of schedule, for it was now 21 September, and it was on this day that we made our first big carry, with twenty-five Sherpas, to Camp 1. At the same time, Dougal and Hamish went out in front to improve the route where possible. At this stage I was worried about Graham Tiso's acclimatisation and I persuaded him to do a carry, as much as anything so that he might become accustomed to physical work at altitude. Until this point he had been working flat out, organising all the equipment into loads to go up the mountain in the correct sequence. He explains his work and the effect of that first carry in his diary:

The effect of altitude here [Base Camp] is for the head to start thumping like fury, it wasn't too bad in the evening, though whenever I sat up the next morning, my head really started to go. However, this symptom soon went away and I felt perfectly fit. I expected that the Sherpas would want to start building their shelter and making tent platforms and other things, but fortunately they had to wait until the glacier started to thaw and loosen the boulders, so I did have the help of all of them for about three hours, and we were able to get the loads unpacked and sorted out. This was a tremendous help. They left me about mid-day, but that was fine. Since then, I managed to sort all the camp kits, the mugs, the stoves, the dixies and everything that is to go up to the various camps, segregated them all, and packed them into loads. Then I had quite a lot of paper work to do, sorting out the actual order in which everything goes up. It's incredibly complex, this; if you take Dave, Nick and four Sherpas, who have gone up to stay today – one can't be absolutely certain that a Sherpa carrying a load up the Icefall is actually going to make it to the camp – it is possible that he might dump his load part-way there – so the tents they would be using had to go up the day before. This means we've always got to work one day ahead of ourselves, actually working this so that you don't send up a tent the day before, that someone was sleeping in the same night. It's a nightmare, and it took me a very long time to work it all out. I think we really should have given this some thought; this has been a bit of a blunder, although not a serious one, in our whole planning that we hadn't, in fact, allowed for enough tents for everyone to sleep at Base, and at the same time to start moving tentage up the mountain. If we hadn't had the four North Face tents and the Pete Carmen tent extra, we would have been in the difficult position of having to send tents up the hill the same day they were to be used that night – hoping that they got there. Anyway, by the skin of our teeth, I managed to work it all out so that a tent is vacated the night before it goes up the hill. I also had to work out all the schedules; then of course there were the changes of plan! Chris approaches very diffidently and says – 'I've been thinking about this point of the plan…' and I have to start thinking rapidly of reasons why he can't do that, because it would alter my plans. Then we have a little battle, and eventually settle for a compromise. It's all been very interesting.

I've really lost track of days – it's the 22nd according to my watch now; I just don't know how many days doing all this has taken. Anyway, I have now got it to a pretty good state of organisation. I've managed to grab Tony as assistant, partly because I'm going up the hill myself and I'll need somebody back here who knows something about the equipment that's left. With his help, I got all the loads sorted out, and him fully briefed. Then Chris was insisting I had to go up and do some acclimatising in the Icefall. That was yesterday. I had the option of going up at six o'clock with the porters, five o'clock with Mick and Barney – who were doing some filming – or with Hamish and Dougal, who were just going to do some tidying up on the route. Believe it or not, I opted for the four o'clock start – only because of the heat. Breakfast was served in the tent at twenty past three – a most incredibly heavy pancake, which sat like a great log on the stomach; then dressed and followed Hamish and Dougal's light up to the bottom of the Icefall – that's about twenty minutes' walk through the boulder field before one actually comes on to ice – and there, had to stop and put crampons on. We found, incidentally, that the Primus Gas lanterns are absolutely fabulous for this purpose – it's just like the olden days in the Alps; a gas lantern gives far more light than a torch, and as there are no real difficulties in the lower section of the Icefall, it's great. You get to the start at about half past four and flog on, up the now well-beaten trail, until it gets light at about half past five.

Up until this time I was feeling quite OK, that's an hour and a half's walk – perhaps something like a 1000ft of rise – and then I began to feel the altitude. I hadn't had any trouble at all with altitude since arriving here. Nick was flat out for one day, and other people have been pretty dodgy. You get out of breath if you start running around the boulder field, but that's to be expected – you just have to take things steady. I just kept plodding up the Icefall, but it really started to clobber me after this hour and a half – between half past five and six o'clock. It's a question of doing one step – then a second – then a third – and you're panting after only five minutes; I was timing myself, I could manage five minutes moving at that pace before I just had to stop, panting, to get my breath back. It was depressing because the legs weren't tired, it was the breathing which was the trouble.

Anyway, I carried on; I was just wondering how far I was going to go, was getting despondent, and then I got to the bottom of the big ladder – or Chris's Folly, as it's been called. It's the first real obstacle. Hamish and Dougal took a wrong turning and were confronted with this big crevasse – this was Chris's answer, he'd stuck up a 25ft [7.5m] ladder, straight up a vertical cliff. I met Hamish and Dougal at the bottom of the ladder – they'd been playing around, looking at things to see if they could make the route safer. They said it was about half an hour from this point to Camp 1 – 'One or two difficult bits in it, we don't recommend you to go.' So I thought at least I would climb the ladder and have a look and see what was over the other side. I was breathing perfectly normally, because I'd been standing at the bottom, waiting for them to come down it. And then I climbed this 25ft ladder, and just about collapsed on the face as I got to the top, puffing and panting; it was as though I'd run a mile in four minutes. Once I got to the top of the ladder, I got one or two photographs and then bombed off down – coming down is dead easy – you could almost run. I was pretty shot by this time, but as I'd come down in about an hour, this wasn't surprising.

Staggered into the mess tent, and started moaning and grumping about how hellish I felt, and they all said, 'Ah, you'll feel a hell of a lot better the next time you go up.' I don't think I'll manage to get up again. Chris has been up for the second time today and he said he felt just like I did the first time up – the second time you really begin to enjoy life. Nick said the same thing. Going up again tomorrow, I'll do a carry right through to Camp 1, then I'll move up to Camp 2 the next day, so I hope that what they say is borne out. It's funny, the body somehow seems to adapt to this lack of oxygen in the air.

It is very easy to forget the day-to-day details of an expedition and even easier to forget one's own interpretation of events as they occurred, particularly when in the decision-making position. Looking back, it is too easy to justify decisions in the light of the outcome of a certain action, forgetting the immediate pressures with which one was confronted, the change of mood from one day to another, the shifting pattern of personal relationships. All too easily this can be smoothed out into a bland, retrospective picture, and it is only by referring back to one's diary that it is possible to capture the true mood of each day of the expedition. I kept a diary, using a Sony TK 40 cassette recorder. It became my confessional – almost a psychoanalyst's couch – physically easier than writing a diary, certainly less self-conscious. In many places I have used this verbatim, to give the feeling of what it was like – not in retrospect, but actually being there, at the time. Inevitably, much of the diary is concerned with my own command problems and decisions, my opinions of other members of the team, and the role I felt they could best fulfil. This is my comment for 22

September:

Usually I get to sleep and then wake up at about midnight, or one o'clock in the morning, and start going over all the expedition problems. Certainly, yesterday was bad vibes day, and there really was tension, with arguments and conflicts all through the day. Dougal and Hamish had gone off early to make the route safe. The porters had set off after them. I felt appalling, with a bad headache – perhaps through reading too much. I had taken two codeines in the early hours of the morning and another two later – probably too much, as I definitely felt muzzy first thing. Mick had sent back a mass of film and I got up at about 7.30 and wrote a short ITN report.

I did a bit more work, trying to sort things out and then it was lunchtime, with row number one of the day. Mick said he wanted two porters for doing some more filming in the Icefall. I said we just couldn't spare two porters for this – we could spare him, but we needed the manpower. We had a tearing great row, both of us going to extremes, and at the end of it Mick's hands were trembling and he was as tensed up as I was. We then simmered down a little, finally arriving at a perfectly reasonable compromise. At this altitude, especially with the kind of work we have to do, we just can't afford this kind of throw-away of nervous tension. It's funny, Doug Scott was sitting in on the row and did his best, in his own way, to quieten it down by just asking quietly, 'Well, what do you want?' I don't think, in actual fact, that this kind of reasonable approach really works – it emerged that Mick didn't really need very much – I think Mick almost needs this slap-on confrontation.

We got through the remainder of the morning satisfactorily and I did a bit more work, but not very much. At teatime there wasn't so much a row as just tension through a misunderstanding of different points of view. I outlined the general plan; when people were going to be moving up the mountain and then, having done this, put across the point that I would like climbers to do some carrying as well, even though they couldn't carry anything like the loads of the Sherpas. I thought it would be a good thing – it showed willing. At certain stages I think it might be absolutely essential. Immediately this opened up opposition; Dougal obviously didn't like it – neither did Hamish. They had done four days in the Icefall now, probably thought they deserved a rest and were bored by carrying, and they said so. I made my point, that we still needed to do a certain amount of carrying and eventually we arrived at a compromise solution, where Dougal and Hamish agreed to renovate the Icefall while they are down here, freeing the Sherpas for actually carrying – as good a compromise as any, probably. Anyway, we settled that one.

The weather, at this stage, had begun to look quite threatening – it had clouded over much more than it had done on previous days. A minor irritation arose when I just double-checked that the Sherpas who were destined to move up to Camp 1 knew they were going up. I had actually gone over all this with Pembatharke and Sona Hishy the day before, yet the Sherpas in question didn't know anything about it – they were just carrying ordinary loads up. This was particularly annoying, since we had actually briefed Pembatharke and Sona Hishy. Anyway, we sorted this one out – we thought.

Then Graham came to me with a problem. This was another tension thing – slightly shambolic. We had these eleven conversion kits, and had said we would like a say in the actual selection of the Sherpas to be elevated to high-altitude Sherpas. We got them lined up in a rather casual kind of way, and whether the sirdars felt themselves affronted that we had not left it to them, I don't know. I suspect we should have just left it to Pembatharke to make the selection, to emphasise his importance. Lined up, it was difficult to remember one individual Sherpa from another, but finally we made a selection of eight men who might, or might not, be the best. The next thing was to give them their extra equipment; we'd given them lightweight padded Terylene jackets – useless, but rather attractive, and I think the Sherpas like them; we'd also given them waterproof jackets and this had obviously rankled with the original high-altitude Sherpas, since they had not had waterproof jackets on the approach march. Now Sona Hishy pointed this out to Graham Tiso. [This led to one of the most serious crises we had on the entire expedition.]

It all started so innocently. I had gone over to see Sona Hishy and Pembatharke, with Kelvin, to discuss two small quite easy points, one, the fact that apparently Sona Hishy had complained that in up-grading ten of our Icefall porters into high-altitude porters and giving them additional kit, they now had two items more than the original high-altitude Sherpas, who had not been given the padded ski-jackets and waterproof jackets. This, of course, was completely ignoring the fact that the high-altitude Sherpas had been given Morlands boots, Ronson lighters and wrist-watches, plus one or two other extras. Anyway, we agreed that we should take the jackets back from the Icefall porters.

It was twilight, and we were sitting immediately outside the cook-shelter, a big, yellow tarpaulin stretched over stone walls with a long wooden pole as an eave. People were going to and fro, and then Sona Hishy, out of the blue, said, 'The Sherpas going up tomorrow are not happy about only having one sleeping bag. They want two sleeping bags – they're very cold in one sleeping bag.'

I immediately replied that this had all been discussed. I told him, 'We've all got the same sleeping bag – the Fairy Down sleeping bag, and the climbers are just using one sleeping bag. This is perfectly all right, and you can always get into your down suits if it's very cold.'

Sona Hishy replied, 'The Sherpas say that the down suit is outside clothing – it doesn't count. Other expeditions have given them two sleeping bags and you yourselves have two sleeping bags. We also want two.' [This is true, in so far as we had a lightweight Terylene bag which we had used on the approach march.]

'Look, Sona Hishy,' I replied, 'we explained at Kathmandu.'

Sona Hishy immediately said, 'Roberts Sahib said we were going to have two sleeping bags.'

Now this is absolutely true – originally, we had planned on everyone having a lightweight sleeping bag from Blacks, for the march, but Blacks, because it was for Everest, had made the biggest flock sleeping bag that has ever been made. Fifty of these had been produced, and we had decided that they were useless – they were so bulky and heavy. We made the fatal mistake of getting lightweight flock sleeping bags just for the climbers' use on the approach march, deciding to give the heavy bags to the Icefall porters as their main sleeping bag. In the rush at Kathmandu we had neglected to explain the change to Jimmy.

There has always been a big sleeping bag 'thing' in the Himalaya. I remember on the American Everest expedition, when the Sherpas were superbly equipped (I suspect better than ours were), there was also trouble, and they almost had a strike over this. One reason is that the sleeping bags do reach a very high market value in Sherpa country. [In the event, we were to find that you did need a double sleeping bag on the mountain.]

But the Sherpas were absolutely vehement about this – perhaps defensively aggressive – because, as the argument developed, they emphasised again and again that it wasn't the value of the extra sleeping bag they were worried about, it was the fact that they were cold at night. It's just possible that the Fairy Down bag is too large a bag, and it might well be that they are a bit cold.

Anyway we scratched and racked our brains – the argument flowing this way and that, with various suggestions being made. Then we said we could not provide extra bags immediately – we hadn't physically got them. I told Sona Hishy to call all the Sherpas and they all materialised. They'd obviously been talking about it – they looked tense, rather angry, gathering in a little group, all jabbering away in Sherpa. The trouble is, Kelvin can't understand Sherpa, only Nepali. All of them wanted another sleeping bag, and various things were suggested. I thought this was definitely a money thing and said, 'Well look, we'll fly the sleeping bags out from England – it will take about a fortnight – I'll cable straight away. The weather doesn't look as though they'll be needed on the mountain in that time,' which – hopefully – was true. But they wanted the sleeping bags immediately and were not prepared to shift until they had them.

The ringleaders were Ngati, who looks obstinate, with a squat, pushed-in type face, standing arms akimbo in his very expensive Erve Duvet which we have given him; Pertemba, to my surprise was also backing this up quite vehemently; Tenzing as well – and Ang Phurba, a sprucely turned out individual, wearing very smart, Austrian ski-pants, given to him by an Austrian expedition. We argued and argued and argued. At one stage I said they were asking the impossible – we did not have this gear, and if they insisted on it we'd just have to go home. But Sona Hishy had the answer to that:

'You can't afford to do that, Sahib. All it means to us is that we've lost a couple of thousand rupees if you sack us all – but for you it means many, many thousands of rupees.' [This of course was absolutely true.]

The argument got even more serious. I can't understand Nepali, but they were getting to the stage when they were being downright rude and insulting to Kelvin before I eventually thrashed out the various possibilities with them. They said they wouldn't go up the mountain the next day without an extra bag and there seemed to be only one solution. I collected ten lightweight bags from the rest of the team and said, 'Right, you can have these right now.' They had got their bags, and had on their part won, but I went back to a very bitter, disgruntled expedition, who felt I had stood down much too easily. I don't think so – I think if I'd stood out we'd have had a situation where they just wouldn't move up the mountain. At least we've got them moving without any worry or fuss.

That night I felt exhausted from my efforts, isolated from the rest of the team who would have liked their say in the argument, without appreciating just how critical were the negotiations or how disastrous it would have been to have had a three-cornered argument. It had been bad enough arguing with the Sherpas as a group. That night, depressed, disillusioned, I spoke into my 'confessional':

Climbing Everest is a logistic problem – it's a man-management problem, a complex labour problem, and there's just a little bit of climbing in it too. If we can pull it off, we shall have climbed the mountain – it will be a challenge and I shall breathe a sigh of relief – but there's going to be little or no enjoyment in it.

And yet the mood changed from day to day, with the coming of the sun in the lee of the storm, whether it be one of words or the forces of nature. Next day, on 23 September, I taped:

Kelvin came to my tent at about 6.30 – I was just having breakfast, ready for the walk up the mountain. I felt very apprehensive, because I couldn't hear any of the Sherpas and wondered whether we had another Sherpa strike! Kelvin told me that he had been up until 2 a.m. with the Sherpas in the kitchen. They had gone through everything and had got it all off their chests – I think this big row was necessary. Kelvin felt that it was, as much as anything, the fact that they are frightened of the Icefall. This is undoubtedly true, from the way they pray incessantly as they plod up the Icefall, the way they burn their incense before setting out, and hold their religious ceremonies. I think they have been building up tension about this and then, additionally, the sleeping bag thing is age-old – they've had trouble on practically every expedition about it. Anyway, the big row had come up and Kelvin had gone through it. Once again that night, the main arguers, or trouble-makers, were Sona Hishy, Tenzing – with whom he shares the same wife – and Ngati, who is related to Sona Hishy. Pembatharke, once again, was very good, shrugged and even looked fed-up when Sona Hishy got going on one of his tangents. I think Pembatharke might have been even more positive in our favour but for the fact that he has been feeling lousy for the past three or four days, with an infected leech-bite in his leg, which Barney has been treating. He hasn't been able to get out of Base Camp and doesn't like this at all. Pembatharke is a man of action and very loyal to us.

Anyway, it all seems sorted out. I set out later, plodding steadily; coughing quite a lot, but I must say I felt fairly OK, and as I went up, felt better and better. I overtook a couple of Sherpa groups, pausing to ask the leader of one of them whether he spoke English. He did, and told me he had been on the Argentinian expedition. I asked whether the Icefall was better or worse now, and he said that the route we have made is superior. They seem to appreciate the fact that we've chosen a good route and a safe route for them.

Then I caught up with Kelvin – typical Kelvin – who was not only carrying a half-load similar to mine, a 16lb [7 kilo] food box, but was also carrying nine foam mats. He was going slowly and steadily and I stayed with him for a while, but when he stopped to rest I carried on up. At the top of the long ladder I waited for about twenty minutes to make sure he was all right, and then went a little beyond.

It is quite incredible, the most amazing sight anywhere in the world. There are great areas of tumbled ice – huge blocks, the size of office blocks almost, all jumbled together – great shattered areas as well, gleaming white in the snow, deep, dark, green-blue shadows – and I think we have picked the only possible route through it. Hamish reckons, and I can see this, that we can definitely avoid one of the dangers; just short of the ladder there is a bad sérac tower that could kill someone, and we can get round it. We're going up the day after tomorrow to do this. Then the route drops into a kind of moat below another very big sérac which, if it did collapse and you were below it, you'd have had your lot; the trouble is, you're about four minutes underneath it. We're going to try to work a kind of aerial ropeway to avoid this as well. We'll see about that the day after tomorrow.

Plodded on up and was now meeting some Sherpas coming back down. Just beyond this point I'd been picking up quite a lot of gear on the way up – odd bits of rope etc., so that we have everything at the top together. Met Dave and Nick, who were coming down to meet us to collect our loads from us and carry them up the last little bit. This is the kind of friendly gesture that is tremendously warming and, I think, an important thing within an expedition. Nick and Dave are obviously very, very happy and excited to be there, at the mouth of the Western Cwm – neither of them has ever been there before – and they're going to find the route up to Camp 2. Four Sherpas are on their way to join them. We now have a great dump of gear – fifty-six loads – actually at Camp 1. It's not as many as I had hoped, but it's good, considering we're only a week out.

Doug had just set off down and I asked him to wait for me so that we could go down together. We could try to rescue some more fixed rope on the way down, and then send it up to give us enough to do the run-out to Camp 5, come what may.

Even though Graham had got 10,000ft short, it didn't seem to matter so much today. It was good going down with Doug and I must say the more I do things with Doug, the more I respect him. For instance, we'd got back to the top of the ladder and there were three long marker poles left there. He said he might as well get these back so that they can be picked up, so he collected them and went back up the hill to leave them with a bunch of marker-flags which a Sherpa would have to come down and pick up from Camp 1. We worked quietly and efficiently together, as a good team, with neither trying to dominate the other.

Everywhere, the atmosphere in the camp was good and very happy. Mick had been doing some filming with Dougal and Hamish, doing some fill-ins. Unfortunately, Tony Tighe, who is a really great chap, and has worked very, very well within the group – a strong, robust kind of character – has slipped and has torn his hand.

I saw Sona Hishy and took him aside and gave him a long, long talking to. Basically, I think he is unsure of himself – perhaps apprehensive of the climbing. He certainly wants the approbation of his fellows, and I think that although he has worked hard (there's no doubt about it – he's worked well for us), when they were all grumbling about the sleeping bags, etc., he couldn't resist the temptation of being the ringleader. I tried to get across to him – and gilded the carrot very lavishly – that this expedition was as important as the original British Everest expedition, and that he could be a Tenzing if he worked for us and with us. I gave him a lot of bull about the book – how it will be sold in every country in the world – and this, that and the other, then, looking him straight in the eye, said, 'By Christ, if there's another happening like last night, you'll regret you ever heard anything about this expedition.' Whether I got through or not, I don't know – it's always difficult to tell with the Sherpas. He is one of these semi-sophisticated Sherpas, having been in America for six months and is particularly hard to deal with. Certainly all the other Sherpas seem happy now – mildly apologetic, almost, about last night. They've all got their sleeping bags and I think, with a bit of luck and several days' good weather, we'll be able to get the momentum going and get everything working well.

Everyone seems very relaxed and at the moment things are good – no doubt there's going to be a lot more crises – no sooner do you get one good thing going than something else happens. But today I liked walking up the hill – I felt acclimatised – it was enjoyable playing around with the ropes and it was a super, happy, carefree day.

I have described these two days in detail, not in retrospect, but as they happened. At times the pressures of holding the balance within the team between individual members and the Sherpas, seemed to fill the horizon, but then, in the escape from Base Camp, just by walking through the Icefall to Camp 1, all the adventure and beauty of the mountain re-asserted itself.

This pattern was particularly strong for myself and, perhaps, to an even greater extent, for Kelvin, who had the day-to-day contact with the Sherpas and the job of passing on my directives. I tried to keep out of this as much as possible, so that when a serious deadlock did occur I could enter into the argument as mediator, trying to find a compromise solution which would enable us to continue the climb.

Meanwhile, up at Camp 1, Nick and Dave were having their share of problems. They had moved up to the camp with four Sherpas on 22 September, but the following day the weather began to show signs of change, with clouds swirling through the Western Cwm. Snow merged into cloud, making it almost impossible to pick out a route through the array of moat-like crevasses which stretched across the valley. They resolved to wait for the weather to clear, but next day, the 24th, there was no improvement and it had snowed during the night. Dougal and Hamish, setting out early to repair the route, discovered, about halfway up, that a big area of the Icefall had collapsed; ladders were twisted, ropes torn asunder – the entire area was as if an earthquake had struck it. In the driving wet snow the pair decided that it would be too dangerous to try to get any of the Sherpas across and so they turned everyone back. Our first repulse on the climb. Was this the last kick of the monsoon? Where was that perfect post-monsoon weather?

The weather continued to deteriorate, but even so, we succeeded in ferrying twenty-five loads up the Icefall, with Dave and a couple of Sherpas pushing down to meet the porters just short of the area of the collapse. Dougal and Hamish, assisted by Phurkipa, had made a good job of repairing the route. I, hoping to have recovered sufficiently from the cold and general malaise which had hit me, set out that morning with a half-load – a mere 16lb – but I seemed to have lost all my strength. Every step was an effort; it was as if I were at 7000m. I struggled up to the point where Dave had come down to meet us, and then returned to Base to collapse into my sleeping bag. Doug went on, up to Camp 1, where they had now erected one of our two magnificent Palace tents – a big frame tent one would expect to see on a Riviera beach rather than at the head of the Everest Icefall. With transparent plastic windows, it was about 2m high, and had two sleeping compartments which provided a touch of luxury in these bleak surroundings. It was difficult to imagine yourself on the Riviera, however, for even this early in the season, the temperature at night dropped to –10°C. During the day, however, in the sun, the interior of the tent became oven-like, for the sun still gave plenty of heat and there was little appreciable wind. That night Dave commented in his diary:

Nothing for it but to have a swig of whisky. One bottle came up with the loads today. We were really touched when Doug Scott mentioned that this was the last bottle, but then he put his foot in it by saying that Base Camp had treated themselves to some of the goodies from the Fortnum and Mason's box. By the time Doug left our Palace, half the bottle was gone. His parting remark was, 'Christ, you don't half get pissed easy at this altitude!'

Nick and Dave were left on their own in the big Palace tent, the Sherpas sleeping in the smaller Vango tents. As dusk fell it began to snow hard and they resolved to get up at intervals during the night to dig out the tent, particularly to clear the snow from the very gently eaved roof. They woke at midnight and forced themselves out into the blizzard, no pleasant task in the middle of the night. Having cleared the tent they dropped off into a deep sleep, only to be awakened again at four in the morning as the roof of the tent, forced down by the snow, touched their faces – rather like one of those nightmare stories of Edgar Allan Poe. They were lucky to get out at all, but managed to put their boots on and, crawling to the window of the tent, got out there. In the confusion Nick had forgotten his gloves and, as a result, was nipped by the frost. It was lucky it wasn't worse.

They spent the rest of the night digging out the Palace tent, which was now almost totally derelict, and then erecting a Whillans Box. By the time the 6 a.m. radio call was due they were shaken and near exhaustion – a state not improved by the fact that we, at Base Camp, failed to come on the air. We, too, had been having our crises, for several tents at Base Camp had collapsed in the night. My own role had not been particularly heroic, as I described in my diary on 26 September:

During the night it snowed steadily, and I woke up to Mick's voice saying – 'You want to watch it, the tents are all collapsing under the snow – you need to get dug out.' Then Barney got up. Barney's tent had not actually collapsed, but was very nearly buried in the snow. Mick and Beth's pole had collapsed and they had been short of breath before Mick got out. Kelvin, also, was completely trapped; he had an elaborate extension on the end of his tent – his radio house – and this had collected snow and the poles had broken. I think he was quite shaken and worried – it took him half an hour to get out, and Barney finally had to help him.

Barney turned out to be an absolute tower of strength, rounding up the Sherpas, getting shovels and trying to dig everything out. The cook-shelter had also very nearly collapsed. I wondered whether I should do the heroic thing and get out of bed – the Great Leader and all that jazz – but finally decided that it was much more important for me to get better quickly, so I snuggled down into my sleeping bag and stayed in my tent, which seemed stable. I think this happened to nearly everybody, because even Dougal said he thought of going out and helping Mick to dig himself out, but finally abandoned the idea. Anyway, Barney, a few Sherpas and

Kelvin, eventually sorted everything out. Beth and Mick ended up sleeping with the Sherpas and Sherpanis, for we have staying with us ten additional porters who came up carrying loads yesterday; Beth commented on the high smell of them all.

This morning tea was delivered as usual; it's snowing hard – I reckon about 3ft of snow has fallen already, and there's a lot more about. At least this bad weather spell gives me a chance to try to recover and throw off this cold and relax completely. I feel a lot better today, but think I may need two or three days more to recover completely.

Evening – 26 September 1972
In my sleeping bag – it's about 8.15 p.m., after quite a pleasant day. It stopped snowing around about mid-morning. A steady Scrabble school got going, with Dougal, Tony Tighe, Mick and Doug. I retired to my tent and started working out the best thing to do. As I thought about it, I was definitely a bit worried about Dave and Nick. There's no doubt about it, they haven't got the same breadth of experience that Hamish and Dougal have; they definitely sounded a bit worried about pushing on up the Icefall, or up the Western Cwm – worried about the avalanches and everything. I wanted to get Hamish up there at least. Another problem was getting the tent repaired.

So I decided to push up Hamish, Mick and Graham, to enable Graham to get the tent repaired, Hamish to act as adviser to Dave and Nick, and Mick to get some film. I called Hamish into the tent and talked this over with him, but he definitely didn't like the idea of going with anyone but Dougal. He and Dougal have formed a superb pairing, in the same kind of way, almost, that Don and Dougal clung together on Annapurna. But this, I think, is a much better, more well-ordered and equal pairing, with each respecting the other. I agreed that Hamish and Dougal should go up together to support Nick and Dave. Although worried about Mick's reaction to this, whether he would start getting all aggressive, wanting to be out there filming, I finally decided that we would keep him back – I don't want more people than absolutely necessary out there in front.

Then we started working out ways of repairing the tent at Camp 1. Someone – I think it was Graham – suggested that they send the broken frame back down here and meanwhile, another frame is taken up to replace it. We could then repair the frame down here, and use it as a permanent Base tent. This had the advantage that we did not have to send Graham up.

I sat down and worked out the basic movements this afternoon. With a bit of luck, everyone will be moving up in two days' time and I sincerely hope I shall be fit and well enough to keep going for the rest of the expedition. I announced my plan just before supper, and Doug, very characteristically and very nicely, said, 'Well, can't Dave and Nick make it to Camp 2 by themselves?' I know he was thinking of their disappointment if they were to feel themselves outclassed the moment Dougal and Hamish got there. Nevertheless, I think we've got to make sure of getting the right site for Camp 2, and of getting there as quickly as possible. Anyway, they have got one day to do it – maybe this will act as a spur to them – they might just do it tomorrow, before Dougal and Hamish arrive, in which case it will all be finished. Then, of course, they will be going on by themselves to establish Camp 3.

27 September 1972

Yesterday evening there was a good forecast – the weather cleared with the evening, and it was a brilliantly clear, very cold night. We were called slightly late this morning, about 5.30 a.m., and Mick, Doug and two Sherpas set off. Mick got about a hundred yards away from the camp and said, 'Appalling this, we'll never get up.' I then sent two Sherpas to increase their party to six, and they kept going.

Nick came on the radio at 6 a.m., sounding very abrupt – I think he was probably in a bad temper, feeling rather self-righteous about how hard they were having it, how easy we were having it, and how much we were expecting from them. Anyway, they said that they were going to send three of them forward and two down to break trail. There was no sign of the trail-breakers until about 9.15 a.m., when they appeared at the top of the ladder.

This evening, at the five o'clock call, Nick said they had got about two-thirds of the way up the Western Cwm, in very bad conditions – very deep snow, very heavy going. When I said I was sending Hamish and Dougal up to give them a hand he said 'Oh', obviously resenting the inference. I'm not sure how I could have put it better, or more kindly – I just said 'to give you a hand, perhaps – you've already had two days at it'. Anyway, tonight both Mick and Doug talked about this. Mick is obviously very worried, and I think this must have got into Nick's mind, as well, that Hamish and Dougal will be pushed in front whenever others are a bit slow or, perhaps, if the issue seems to be in doubt. Perhaps I didn't get across well enough the fact that at this stage of the game it's just a matter of pushing the route out, and when you have the manpower to do so, it's ridiculous to leave a large party just sitting doing nothing at Base Camp. If the front pair are delayed, it's much better to use the climbers to help with the climbing when they're not carrying loads.

The night of 28/29 September

In my conversation with Doug and Mick yesterday we arrived at a plan, in principle, and this is one of the issues which could cause argument. As Doug and Mick, very sensibly, pointed out, if they spend two days on the Rock Band and then find it's going to take longer, what do we do? Do I pull them back? If I try to pull them back at this stage, there will inevitably be an argument, with Hamish and Dougal impatient to get up there in front to force the route. I think, therefore, providing our communications system is working effectively, and providing Doug and Mick are making some kind of progress, somehow I am going to have to keep them going on the Rock Band – even if it takes four or five days – pumping up more oxygen so that they can do it. What we want, in a way, is to put our 'B' team out in front first, giving them the first chance of getting to the top of Everest, though the odds would be very much against them because, of course, they will have exhausted themselves on the Rock Band. They've got this huge carrot of making the first British ascent of Everest, but on the other hand, Hamish and Dougal will be in position for the final push when, and if, they are exhausted. This could create great pressures, because Hamish and Dougal, champing at the bit to get out in front, will also be critical of the progress being made by Doug and Mick, perhaps fearful of losing the ultimate accolade of making the first ascent. It's going to take a lot of controlling of these two pairs, but I think this could give the ingredients for the greatest success.

29 September 1972

After a really good deep sleep, I was woken up at 6 a.m. The massive doses of Vitamin C seem to be succeeding in getting rid of my cold, though I am coughing quite a bit even now. By this time Dougal and Hamish had already set out; I went to the kitchen and, after a Sherpa breakfast, waited about for a while, planning to go up with the Sherpas. They showed no signs of getting ready fast enough, so I finally set off by myself. It was still very cold – there are extraordinary temperature contrasts here at Base Camp, ranging from about –11°C first thing in the morning, to the seventies once the sun hits us.

I plodded up – certainly going infinitely better than the previous occasion, when I had stalled and staggered back down. Kept going, slowly and steadily. I had only a light load, just a cine camera belonging to Hamish and a few bits of film, but I passed some bamboos which had been left on the side, so decided to take them up too – a really awkward load because they stuck straight up above my head, and every time I got on a steep bit they stuck into the snow.

I caught Graham up about three-quarters of the way up. He'd set out about an hour and a half earlier, and was going very, very slowly. He really is finding load-carrying a very hard, purging experience. He was muttering to himself, swearing that this was the last time he would ever carry up. I gave slightly too tart a reply, saying, 'Well, if you're not going to carry, then you're really not much use to anyone.' Immediately I realised how wrong this was, because in fact Graham is extremely useful and important, just in getting all the gear organised.

Having plodded behind him for a bit, I passed him, then passed the Sherpas and kept going to the top. I found it hard work because of the heavy snowfall – even though the trail had been broken yesterday, Dougal had had to break it again afresh – which just shows how strong and fit he is. I was very tired by the time I reached Camp 1.

Camp 1 is a fantastic situation. It's on a huge block between great crevasses – completely safe though, because it's right in the centre of the glacier, well away from the big avalanches which could come down either from the Nuptse or Everest faces. Dougal and Hamish were already there. Hamish had felt very rough on the way up, caused, he thought, by his breakfast, and so Nick and Dave had been left to make the route by themselves. They had set out earlier, with their four Sherpas, and with a bit of luck will have made the route to Camp 2 and sited the camp. I waited up there. There's a very impressive load now – already eighty-five loads, and another thirty-five coming up today, making it a hundred-and-twenty.

Graham staggered up and said he really could not face doing this again, so he's staying up here tonight, and I hope, tomorrow, will get all the loads organised. At the moment they're in a great big heap, an absolute shambles. I waited for the porters to arrive, all thirty-five of them; this is one of the biggest carries, I should say, ever to have been made through the Everest Icefall.

A week had gone by since we had first reached the top of the Icefall, and although still only two-thirds of the way up the Western Cwm, we were all optimistic. Surely that snowfall must be the last heavy snow of the season! We now looked forward to weeks of uninterrupted sunshine – hoped that we should be able to get into position to make our summit bid before the winter cold winds became too intense. The next day I was planning to move up to Camp 1 with a strong force of Sherpas and the rest of the lead climbers. We were on the move once again.

10

Up to Camp 3

30 September – 8 October

'I know it's inevitable, but I can't help resenting the arrival of the big team,' said Nick. 'When there's just two of you and a few Sherpas, you live a hell of a sight better, and you get on together so much better – especially with the Sherpas. I feel we've really established some kind of rapport with them, especially Jangbo and Pertemba.'

I could sympathise with Nick's feelings. We were standing just above Camp 1 which now resembled a small village, with the big Palace tent dominating the cluster of two-man tents standing around it. It had been re-erected that day, on the undamaged frame brought up from Base Camp; a Stormhaven tent had also been erected, and a babble of voices intruded on the peace of the late afternoon. The surrounding scenery was the same as it had been for the last three days or, for that matter, from time immemorial, but the mere presence of the tents and the sound of twenty-five people somehow diminished the sensuous quality of mystery which is such an important part of the beauty of mountains. As always on any big expedition, the satisfaction of isolation can only come in small doses though during the course of the expedition, as camps are established, the lines of communication become more extended and the numbers are stretched up the length and height of the mountain, the feeling of solitude returns. Certainly, we were not a big expedition by Everest standards, but in those early days, when the entire manpower of the expedition was first compressed into Base Camp and then spread between Base and Camp 1, we still felt we were on an overcrowded planet. But Nick and Dave could look forward to escaping from the crowds – if only for a short time. It was 30 September and on the following day they were going to move up the Western Cwm to establish Camp 2.

A week had gone by since we had succeeded in climbing the Icefall, but a single day's heavy snowfall, combined with a few more days of bad visibility, had set us back about four days – days which did not seem to matter too much at the start of the expedition, but which were to prove all-important later on. The previous day Dave and Nick, helped by Hamish and Dougal, had marked out a route through the maze of crevasses which guard the lower part of the Western Cwm, and now we were ready both to push them up to Camp 2, so that they could start work on the face itself, and to start ferrying loads up the Western Cwm to Camp 2. I had moved up to Camp 1 that afternoon, with Doug Scott and fifteen Sherpas, to join the five climbers and four Sherpas already in possession.

Next morning, on 1 October, the entire party set out for Camp 2 with Nick and Dave, the two Sherpas, Jangbo and Pertemba, carrying their personal gear so that they could spend the night there. Most of the Sherpas were using snow-shoes for the first time. Three days had elapsed since the last snowfall and in that time the surface had already formed a slight crust which would have broken under the pressure of a boot, but with snowshoes it remained firm. Nick Estcourt and Dave Bathgate led the way, with the seventeen Sherpas who accompanied them trailing behind, roped together in groups of three. I also went up with Hamish and Dougal to help repair the route and get photographs of the Western Cwm. It was a wondrous sight – the tiny figures of the climbers giving a scale and perspective to the gigantic size of the Cwm. They formed ever-changing patterns as they zig-zagged through the crevasses which stretched across the deep-cut valley like so many moats in some kind of natural fortification. A powder-snow avalanche started as a little puff, high on the steep walls of Nuptse, and then billowed out into a great cloud as it swept down over a couloir and spread across the floor of the Cwm. The cloud of snow particles hovered over the Cwm for a few minutes and then seemed to dissipate in the air, leaving no trace. The avalanche might never have occurred – but of course it had, and we had seen that it went across the line of our proposed route, which was squeezed in towards the right-hand side of the Cwm.

It was only when you started walking that you began to gain a true idea of the gigantic scale of the Western Cwm. At first, the South West Face was hidden coyly behind a subsidiary spur from the West Ridge of Everest, then, as you worked your way up and across to the left-hand side of the Cwm, it came slowly into full sight, foreshortened, massive, the Great Central Gully leading upwards like an arrow, into the guts of the South West Face – the Rock Band which stretches across the wall. The Rock Band looked deceptively short and even more deceptively close to the summit. For Nick and Dave the excitement at the prospect of being the first of the party to set foot on the face was tempered by fatigue, as they forced the route towards what was to be the site of Camp 2. They reached the end of the main crevasse area around mid-day and, looking up the Cwm, the face seemed comparatively close; then, as they started plodding up the long easy slope that led to the centre of the Cwm, they began to realise the vast scale of the place. After an hour's walk they didn't seem to be much closer.

Doug Scott had accompanied them, and he and Nick pushed on towards what had been the site of the German camp that spring. Reaching it at about three o'clock that afternoon, they glanced back and saw that their Sherpas had already made up their minds for them; Pembatharke had stopped in a slight depression about 200m short of their high point, in an area which had been Camp 2 for the International expedition. This was to be the site of Camp 2.

The Sherpas quickly dumped their loads and headed back down the Cwm. They had had a long, hard day. Nick and Dave were left with Pertemba and Jangbo. It must have been a precious moment as they sorted out their gear for the night, and erected two box tents. Once again, they were out in front, four people dwarfed by the immensity of the Western Cwm.

I had planned on their taking just one day to run the rope out to Camp 3, but after our experience of the last few days hardly expected them to make such fast progress. It was a delightful surprise, therefore, the following evening to learn that they had succeeded in reaching their objective. The site of Camp 2 was about half a mile from the foot of the South West Face. Having used snow-shoes to reach the camp, they discovered that once on the face itself, the snow became firm and solid, perfect for crampons. They worked their way across it to the bergschrund which marks the foot of the face proper, and were able to climb it easily, since it was filled with snow. From there, a straightforward snow slope swept up towards the little rock buttress that guarded the site of Camp 3. There was no technical difficulty, it was just a question of front pointing on the hard snow at an angle equivalent to that of a steep hillside in Britain. Dave and Nick made a beautiful, textbook job of the fixed roping, leaving deadmen snow anchors at distances of about a hundred and fifty feet, up the slope all the way to the Rock Buttress, which they reached at 3 p.m. It was here that they found the first signs of previous visitors, in the shape of a few lengths of partially covered rope, and some pitons hammered into cracks. After hammering in their own ceremonial peg, they slid back down their ropes and returned to Camp 2 just in time for the evening radio call at 5 p.m. At last our onslaught seemed to be rolling out according to plan.

The following day, Doug Scott and Mick Burke moved up to Camp 2, accompanied by five Sherpas and myself, while Nick and Dave dropped back to Base Camp for a well-earned rest. It was to be the job of Doug and Mick to establish Camp 3, and then make the route up to the site of Camp 4. I wanted to be at Camp 2, which was already the focal point of the expedition. Here I could keep an eye on the arrival of the flow of supplies up from Camp 1, and at the same time be in touch with Doug and Mike on the face.

For me that day was one of the most satisfying of the expedition up to that point of time. I left Camp 1 late, having been delayed by the necessity to write a report for *The Observer* and wanting to wait for the arrival of mail from Base Camp. As a result I completed the walk from Camp 1 to 2 on my own, and in this solitude could enjoy the euphoria of being in the Western Cwm, surrounded by some of the most magnificent mountain scenery I had ever seen. Behind me, framed by the flanks of Nuptse and the West Ridge of Everest, was Pumo Ri, its summit appearing ever ready to topple down on to the Khumjung Glacier. On either side were the steep retaining walls of the Cwm, grey-brown granite, fluted ice slopes, crested by top-heavy cornices, and in front was the duo of Everest and Lhotse, seeming easy-angled in comparison with the sheer sides of the ravine leading into the upper part of the Western Cwm.

The only signs of man were the tracks in the snow and the bamboo marker wands placed every hundred metres or so. Camp 2 itself was tucked discreetly in a slight depression, invisible until only a hundred metres from it. It was already growing, with four tents and boxes pitched to absorb the fresh arrivals. The following day we all made a carry up to Camp 3 to dig out tent platforms and prepare the camp for Doug and Mick to move into the following day. For me it was to be one of the most testing days of the expedition. Doug and Mick, both fairly lightly loaded, set out first; I followed about half an hour behind them, having made the mistake of trying to carry too much, about 13 kilos. I have always found the height of 6700m (22,000ft) to be critical for me – a height barrier which has to be broken through painfully. The approach to the foot of the face was easy-angled, little more than a walk along a well-defined track, but almost immediately I felt the effects of the altitude. It was not so much a feeling of lack of breath, as a lassitude that stole over my limbs, making each step a separate effort of will. The party behind were rapidly gaining on me and then, even more depressing, some Sherpas who had left half an hour after me stormed past, hardly seeming to notice the altitude. Although still only halfway to the bergschrund, I was reduced to trying to force myself to take just twenty-five paces without a rest; all too often I failed to make even this limited norm, and would collapse over my ice axe, resting for two or three times as long as it had taken to make the previous twenty-five paces, before struggling on again. I had been going quite well the previous day and had hoped that I had, at last, broken through the acclimatisation and fitness barrier. But now I seemed to have slipped right back again. At the bergschrund, and the foot of the fixed ropes, I clipped on with one jumar and started plodding up the slope. By now the others were nearly halfway up – about 120m above me – no distance at all at sea level, but here, at 6850m, they seemed forever unattainable. My progress had been reduced now to ten paces at a time without a rest, and I was finding it difficult to reach even this target, often making only six or seven steps before sinking on to the snow. It is difficult to imagine just how punishing this experience of altitude can be. Each step needs a separate effort of will, and progress is so slow as to be almost imperceptible. The target, in this case the rock buttress guarding Camp 3, never seemed to get any closer; the gap between myself and the others out in front, however, became wider, and before I was a third of the way up, they were already below the buttress, digging out a platform. My own discomfort was now compounded by a constant bombardment of snow blocks which they dislodged in digging out the camp site. I shouted out for them to stop digging until I got out of the danger zone, and slowly plodded on upwards; but it was obvious that I was going to be in the line of fire for at least another hour at my present rate of progress. Mick Burke at last put me out of my misery, shouting down to suggest that I dumped my load and got back down, out of the line of fire. In suggesting this he offered me a let-out that I had thought of adopting, but was loth to do so on the grounds of pride and perhaps the feeling that as leader of the expedition I could not afford to give in. I tried to keep going, but finally collapsed on the snow in a paroxysm of coughing. Able to go no further, I just dumped the load about 60m below the site of the camp and then staggered down the fixed ropes. Even going downhill, I had to stop and rest every 30m or so, and it was all I could do to walk those last few hundred metres over fairly level glacier to the site of Camp 2. I crawled into my tent and dropped into a doze, only waking on the return of the others. They had had a hard day, digging out the platform for Camp 3, and yet they were all in good spirits, and it was strange, that night in spite of my failure to reach the camp, even I felt relaxed and satisfied. I wrote in my diary:

Physical effort is, oddly enough, a great palliative to worry and the nerves. On the surface, for instance, today has been a very unsatisfactory day, and the fact that I failed to reach my objective – I didn't get to Camp 3, and had to come back – doesn't stop me feeling tremendously more relaxed than I did yesterday. All the worries about day-to-day administration seemed expurgated. I suppose the problems are still there, but they don't seem to matter so much and I am concentrating on putting my plan on the mountain into practice.

I think I am certainly in the right place, up here at Camp 2. Even if I'm not going brilliantly well, it doesn't really matter because my job is to direct. This is the real focus of activity. Further back, one would not have this feeling for what is really the 'being' of the expedition – the people who are pushing out in front – in this case, Mick and Doug, who are going out tomorrow. I am simply going to try to keep simmering on, keeping just behind the front pairs, being very careful not to exhaust myself, and even though I know that this height, between 22,000 and 23,000ft [6700–7000m], is a bad height for me (I'm not a brilliant high-altitude goer, there's no doubt about that), I do know that once I get on to oxygen, from Camp 3 onwards, I should be all right. I go very well on oxygen, and I'll be able to move up to Camp 4 to supervise the vital traffic of supplies from Camp 4 to Camp 5.

You've certainly got to be very careful when in this kind of supervising/directing role, that you don't tire yourself too much. For instance, for the four o'clock radio call, I was definitely not totally compos mentis, unable to take in everything as fast as I should because I was so tired. This is something one is going to have to watch more, as one gets higher up the mountain, looking after oneself well so that one can take intelligent decisions.

That same day, nineteen Sherpas carried loads from Camp 1 to Camp 2 while, back at Base Camp, Jimmy Roberts had now arrived and had freed Kelvin to move up to Camp 1. Another arrival at Base Camp was Ken Wilson, editor of *Mountain*. He was a close friend of several members of the team and, in a light-hearted moment during the preparations for the expedition, I had told Ken that if he managed to reach Base Camp at his own expense we would make him welcome. A keen rock-climber, he had done a certain amount of climbing in the Alps, but had no direct experience of expeditioning or high-standard alpinism. He was extremely outspoken, forceful in his views, and of course, through the pages of *Mountain* had considerable influence in the climbing world. I felt, therefore, that it would be good, both for him and for mountaineering in general, if he were able to come out and see how an expedition like ours performs in practice. At the same time, I must confess to having had some doubts, since Ken is splendidly argumentative, and I could not help worrying that he might upset the fine balance of personal relations on which an expedition depends. In the event he was to prove a positive asset. Anyway, he had just arrived at Base Camp and, at this stage, was in no fit state to vent his opinions on anyone, so severely was he affected by the altitude.

On the following day, 5 October, Mick and Doug moved up to Camp 3 to make the route up to Camp 4. This time I succeeded in plodding up to the camp, travelling with a very light load as far as the point where I had dumped my load the previous day. Two Sherpas, Tenzing and Ang Dawa, were going to stay up at Camp 3, whilst the other three, Anu, Ang Phu and Ngati, carried loads and returned to Camp 2. It was on this day that Ang Phu really began to show his determination to do well on the expedition. Not only was he one of the youngest of our high-altitude Sherpas, in some ways he was the least experienced. He had been on the International expedition but had only carried loads as high as Camp 3. He spoke very good English and had been a teacher at one of Ed Hillary's schools before deciding that there was more money to be made as a trekking Sherpa. While working for Jimmy Roberts he had for a time acted as Jimmy's personal servant. We found him to be extremely helpful, going out of his way to look after any of the climbers on the expedition, helping them with their ruck-sacks, bringing them a welcome cup of tea and similar small services, and yet there was nothing obsequious about his approach – one had the feeling that it was from sheer good nature.

I had, however, wondered just how tough he was going to be on the mountain. In the previous few days he had been complaining of severe headaches, and he certainly looked desperately ill. He refused to give in, however. That morning I tried to persuade him to take a day's rest, but he wouldn't hear of it. Then I suggested that at least he took a light load, but no, he was determined to carry as much as anyone else. Once we started, he was obviously walking with difficulty – as tired as I had been the previous day – but he kept plodding on doggedly, until he reached the long slope below the bergschrund leading to the fixed ropes. This was not steep, but the snow was hard, requiring precise use of crampons. Halfway across the slope, the unfortunate Ang Phu tripped and slipped, sliding about 60m back down into the Western Cwm. There was no risk, but it must have been a frightening, humiliating and depressing experience, especially losing all that painfully gained altitude. Many of our Sherpas, and even the climbers, would probably have called it a day, and returned to camp. But not Ang Phu – he slogged, painfully, back up to the track and continued slowly up the line of fixed rope.

That afternoon, as we enlarged the platform for the boxes, wispy clouds chased across the sky, a sign perhaps of yet another change in the weather. Nevertheless, there was a feeling of immense satisfaction as we gazed over the slowly expanding view. From Camp 3 we were tightly blinkered by the great retaining walls of the Western Cwm. At 3 p.m., the view to the south was still barred by the great wall of Nuptse, but to the west we could gaze down the sweep of the Western Cwm, gaining some idea of its scale from the tiny cluster of dots which represented the tents of Camp 2, and the even smaller specks that were our porters carrying loads up from Camp 1. The crevasses, part-covered, looked little more than ripples on the surface of a slow-flowing river, and the sweep of the Cwm led the eye across the hidden void of the Khumjung Glacier to Pumo Ri, whose summit was now very nearly level with us, the great hog's back of Cho Oyu, and the serried ranks of lesser peaks, many of them still unclimbed.

We returned to Camp 2 well content, leaving Doug and Mick ensconced at the high point of the climb so far; but we were to be delayed once again, by a change in the weather. Next morning I woke to find the skin of my little two-man tent forced down towards my face. It had been snowing all night and our camp was nearly engulfed. The South West Face could not be seen, nor, for that matter, could any other mountain. A hundred metres above us a cluster of séracs loomed occasionally out of the gusting snow, but we could have been almost anywhere in the world. There was no question of movement that day – we could only sit out the storm hopeful that it would not delay us too badly. At least it gave time for reflection, reading and letter-writing – the eternal pursuit of all Himalayan climbers. Up at Camp 3, Doug wrote to his wife, Jan. It is a letter which perhaps reveals more of the climber's thought-processes, and how he reacts to an expedition, than even a diary, and I have therefore included it with very few cuts:

6 October, 9.45 a.m.

Hello darling,

Here I am, back at Camp 3, overlooking the Western Cwm and Pumo Ri. The wind is howling outside, and spindrift is pelting the sides of the box more or less continuously – just as it did in that Tunnel tent on Baffin Island with Denis. The box is khaki-coloured and the roof is sagging in with the weight of the snow. I'm here with Mick. He's had a bad night – we most certainly have come up to sleep at 23,000ft too fast, only two weeks since arriving at Base Camp. I'm OK, but Mick's drugged up to his eyeballs on headache and painkillers and sleeping tablets, so he's not much company today. Think I'll go out and rouse the two Sherpas who are in the second box we put up yesterday. It took us five hours to cut into the snow and ice under this bulge of rock. It was like an archaeological dig, bringing up old tents, axes, cylinders, etc., from the German, International and Jap. expeditions. We have two more boxes to put up and also to make the route to 4, but this weather is really going to knock us back, and is what could finish us – the whole face is a mass of spindrift, coming down to here, but then spinning round this little rock step so that to open the box zip means we get covered inside.

Feel guilty lying here, so think I'll go out and put up some more Whillans Boxes. Follow that by dinner of chicken-breast, peas and powder potato and Oxo. Might be able to cheer up Mick, whose headache isn't going away yet; he may have to go down. Still no mail from you in two weeks – pissed off, especially as I'm laying here with nothing else to do but worry about you both. [Jan and his nine-year-old son, Michael.] Look, about me working after Christmas. One or two things you should think about. Most of the expedition lectures will be over by the end of January. I could do my book by half-term, though Easter is more practical. Would it be best for us all if I got a job at half-term (Feb), or after Easter, at a Primary School – yours!!! – or one nearer home? I even feel like getting my hair cut and getting stuck into teaching as a career. I think I'd make a good headmaster! I don't want to come here again – on this face. Tozal Del Malo [a mountain Doug climbed in the Hindu Kush] was far more enjoyable and satisfying at the time. Here I am again a prisoner of my own ambition, very much so, as it's impossible just now to stand up properly outside this tent. We all want to get up and off – Hamish, Dougal, Mick and me, all prepared to rush it out of the way.

Same day, 4 p.m.

Well, I plucked up courage to go outside; the two Sherpas looked really bad, Tenzing and Ang Dawa. So as to enjoy my food and sleep unaided by pills, I got stuck in and dug out another platform, and put up another box with the thing blowing all over the place, with only me to hold it. Anyway, that's one more job done to get me nearer home. The spindrift beyond these canvas walls is terrible, I have to take my glasses off as they steam up. Gave the Sherpas their ration packs, with instructions to make potatoes, etc. Got Mick his oxygen bottle, so that he can take some now, as apart from going down, it's the only way he's going to make it tomorrow up to 4. He's gone off to sleep again, looking like a first-world-war pilot. He's got *The Lord of the Rings* open on his chest; I don't want to read it until I get home to Mike. Apart from wanting to finish the job off, reading it to Mike, it makes me very homesick to even see it.

Seeing as there are no books for me to lose myself in, I'll tell you both about the Sherpas. They are generally a good lot, and any tricks they get up to – well, so would I, if I saw a crowd of Europeans come into their valley, obviously so much richer. So they did go on strike for an extra sleeping bag. But that was sorted out. They are working harder than in the spring, when they had one day on, one day off, for 50p per day, regardless. Now they are working three days and one off. One or two high-altitude Sherpas didn't turn up, so we promoted a cook-boy, Dorjee, who looks about fourteen years old, but is, in fact, eighteen. He looked so proud when he was handed his high-mountain clothes, and even prouder when he came down through the Icefall, having carried a very heavy load of 45lbs. The other Sherpas made sure he got the heaviest load! They don't put up with any softies!

It's getting quite dark in this olive-green hell, as the snow is piling up all round. I'll get dinner ready over a primus gas stove – much better than the Bluet Gaz, especially the double burner that we have down at Base Camp. I'd love to be sat down in our kitchen right now, and have you put some cauliflower-cheese or corn-beef hash, or stew and dumplings, or fresh herrings in front of me. Still, I expect that you're glad for the rest from that. Michael's probably rushing out on a bread butty, to be up on the field. I expect Goose Fair, and then Bonfire Night are all in your minds; if all went well, I could just about make November 5th, but of course there will be weather problems, so it's unfair to make you think of such an early date. I'll get on with the dinner. I love you, love you both.

7 October, 9 a.m.

Well loves, I started getting the dinner ready and Mick said he couldn't eat any, then I heard these horrible groans from next door, and all the time the drifting snowstorm piled up outside the tents. Then I heard the zip frantically open and honk! Both the Sherpas were sick! What a team at the front!! Well, I had my Surprise peas, surprisingly soft and sickly sweet chicken-breast, Oxo and Smash. It took me two hours in the confined space of these boxes. Then I dug out a tin of Nestle's cream and had that with sugar. Too lazy to do apple flakes. Mick had a bad night, and this morning he was coughing blood up from the inside sores in his mouth. He kept taking oxygen, but it didn't help much. He still has a headache. Still no one answering the radio, so I think I'd better get everyone down to Camp 2 – at least they can recover down there, provided we can get through the storm lashing around. I don't like it here! Now the roof is dripping from cooking a brew – all over. My bag is quite wet from the condensation as is Mick's, but he couldn't care less any more – trying to wring some comfort out of an oxygen bottle. Trouble is, Camp 2 won't be much better, we'll have to put tents up in the storm and then I'll have to come back here to do the route to 4 with someone. Main thing is there may be a letter from you, and I can post this and find myself some good books. No other way out but to grin and bear it. Well, hold on, it's 2 p.m.

The Sherpas weren't happy. I looked in their box and there was Ang Dawa. Well, there was a balaclava, covered in spindrift, right by the door and in the darkest far corner there was Tenzing, holding his head. 'Go down, lads,' I said. 'Sahibs go down, OK all go down.' It took three hours to get them ready. Then to take off, down the fixed ropes in white-out conditions. Unable to see out of my steamed-up goggles, so took them off! Like Blind Man's Buff! Snow and air and moving air surfaces were all one, but we got to the bottom of the face with nothing worse than burnt hands from sliding down the rope. Then we had to rope up as one of the Sherpas had fallen off the lower slope and gone a quarter of a mile out of his way! He wasn't hurt, but it shook us all up, and no one wants to walk through up to a quarter of a mile of soft snow. Then we got into the bottom of the Western Cwm, and the snow came up to our waists, wading along very much out of puff, with unseen avalanches pouring over Nuptse, which we felt the wind of. Luckily, we found the marker flags and eventually stumbled into the embryo Advanced Base Camp, half covered in snow.

Chris was there; he had been on his own for three nights, with four Sherpas, and was glad to see us. He gave me your letter and Michael's. Glad you love me – never thought you didn't, really. Anyway, the saga goes on, now in better spirits, as the Sherpas cook us powdered spuds, ham and beans, and eating sweets robbed from ration packs. The snow continues to fall, and there will be no more travel up the Icefall, nor up the Cwm, for a few days. So I can get down to some serious reading and good thoughts about you and Michael. Christ, it's cold here just now, water bottles frozen, and so is this rotten ball-point pen, and now they've sent the dinner in back to front, having cooked the ham in potato powder, not in the ready-made Smash. So I'll make do with KitKat and ship's biscuits.

The in-word here, among the Sherpas, is 'Why not indeed', as Mick hands round fags and they offer each other food and what-not. The 'Goon Show' is on the tape, and Neddy Seagoon is off to find the yeti on the Yorkshire moors! We're sitting in our box, Mick and Chris and me, with a cooking canopy over the front, and all the Sherpas cooking and eating dahl, rice and yak meat. They are chattering together, with the sirdar, Pembatharke, getting all the laughs and others bursting out slapping him on the back and thighs. Strange to see them touch each other the way they do – something we seem to be ashamed of. They certainly don't look effeminate – far from it – tough guys of the mountains with the snow licking round their backs in the candle-light.

8 October, 7.30 a.m.

Morning. The storm seems to have blown itself out, although there are high clouds at 30,000 – an uncontrollable whirlpool of misplaced gases. There's a big breaking of the trail today, some up, some down from 1, 2 and also up to 3. Mick's throat is still bad, and he is now on some strong pills to put him out of his misery. We'll go up to 3 tomorrow, to do the route to 4. Our two Sherpas are still not very happy.

Why on earth do we do it? Doug's feelings would be mirrored by almost every single member of the expedition; the homesickness, worries about letters from our wives, promises that we'll never land ourselves in a similar situation again, and then, a few days after getting back home, most of us are planning the next time. Part of the reason is the shortness of human memory for things unpleasant, part the speed of a change of mood in self or surroundings; the elation of the good days' climbing, when the route is forced out another 300m or so; the impact of a golden sunset; the reward of the ever-expanding scene as we gain height; the satisfaction of facing up to adversity and overcoming it – all are there.

11

The run out to Camp 5

9 October – 14 October

The second storm; only two days of snow, but it set us back four days in our race against the winter winds. It was 9 October before Doug and Mick were able to move back up to Camp 3. The site of the camp was a shambles, with all the loads buried and the boxes sticking out of the snow like three sinking ships, their frames warped and broken, the fabric torn. It was an unpleasant shock, for we had hoped that the Whillans Box would stand up to almost any weight of snow. This had been the case on the South Face of Annapurna but, unfortunately, in an effort to reduce the weight of the box, the manufacturer had reduced the gauge of the aluminium tubing of the frame. In addition, we had specified a Ventile wall material, which was not quite as strong as the canvas used on the boxes for Annapurna. On further inspection of the boxes at Camp 3, it was discovered that two of them were repairable, but one was a total write-off.

While the two Sherpas dug out the platform and patched up the boxes, Doug and Mick set out to start their route up to Camp 4. The way ran out to the left, beneath the rock buttress, across fairly easy-angled snow slopes and over a couple of small rock steps, towards a snowfield leading up into the great couloir that swept down from the centre of the face. It was a fine effort on the part of both of them, but particularly on that of Mick; he had found the trip up to Camp 3 exhausting, making slow, laborious progress. They worked into the dusk, seen from Camp 2 – now in the chill grip of the shadow of Nuptse – two tiny dots against the sunlit snows of the face. The shadows were like the rising tide, for as the sun dropped behind the wall of Nuptse, the shadow crept inexorably up the face and the snows changed from dazzling white, through a rich yellow, to a dusky pink that faded imperceptibly into grey as the sun dropped below the far horizon. The difference between sun and shade was cataclysmic. There was still some warmth in the sun, and if there was no wind you could lounge around without windproofs or down gear, but the moment the sun dropped behind Nuptse the temperature took a nose-dive, down to –10°C, and during the night it was already beginning to drop to –20°.

That evening, Mick and Doug worked until dusk before returning to their Whillans Box, repaired by the Sherpas. Above Camp 2 we always cooked for ourselves, and the food was arranged in two-man day packs. While at Camp 2 and below, we had our Sherpa cooks and the cooking was carried out centrally. It was dark before they had finished melting snow for brews and cooking their supper the next morning they were out of the boxes before the sun struck the face, determined to reach Camp 4 that day. In an effort to avoid the possibility of anyone dropping out from exhaustion before the final push, I had decided that the climbers should use oxygen from Camp 3 onwards. Once you get badly run down at altitude, there is very little opportunity for recovery, since even Base Camp, at 5425m (17,800ft), is situated at too high an altitude for real rest and recuperation.

During the spring expedition Doug had not found it necessary to use oxygen until above Camp 4, and even from there up to Camp 5, the benefit he gained from the set was dubious, since it was faulty for most of the time. He was sceptical on this occasion as to how much good it would do, taking into consideration the weight of the cylinders against the benefit gained from the use of the oxygen, but nonetheless decided to give it a try.

They pulled across the fixed ropes left the previous night, to their high point, and then started to climb the long snow slope that led into the centre of the face. Their two Sherpas, Anu and Ang Phurba, followed, carrying spare reels of rope. Each reel was 90m long, and Mick and Doug took turns to run out the full reel in a single pitch at a time, kicking slowly, laboriously, up the hard snow slope. It was typical of Mick that, after nearly being forced back down to Base Camp by a combination of appalling mouth sores and altitude sickness, he rallied in the face of the challenge, not only of forcing the route out but also of trying to get it on film. Both he and Doug worked through a long trying day. The sun was blazing down out of a brilliant blue sky, but any feeling of warmth was illusory, for a high wind was playing over the upper slopes of the mountain, dislodging the freshly fallen snow and sending it down the Central Couloir in a continuous cascade of fine spindrift which penetrated every chink in their clothing. It got behind goggles, into their mitts and filled the sacks on their pack-frames carrying the oxygen bottles, thus near-doubling their loads. Doug finally abandoned his oxygen set, preferring to climb without its benefit and thus reducing the weight he had to carry by over 9 kilos.

As they gained height, gusts of wind reached down, tearing at their clothing, driving the ice particles, which were as sharp and painful as a thousand minute needles, into their faces. The climbing now became more awkward, over a series of iced rock steps. There was insufficient snow to use the deadman anchors, and even ice pitons were difficult to place. They were on the front points of their crampons, the wind tearing at their clothing, trying to push them back down the slope. Looking down, the Western Cwm was now in deep shadow and its lapping tide was creeping up the slopes of the

South West Face. The two Sherpas were on their way back to the camp, but Mick and Doug kept going into the dusk. Now on their last 90m rope, it came to an end still 20m below the site of the camp. They could see the gleaming corner of one of the platforms sticking tantalisingly out of the snow just above them.

The slope was littered with the flotsam of previous expeditions, tattered fabric, warped alloy poles from the tents and boxes sticking out of the ice – black and yellow from the Japanese attempt, red from the International expedition, and blue from that of the spring. For the first time they caught sight of the white hauserlay nylon rope from the spring attempt, wherever there was a rock step protruding from the snow. Dropping down, they managed to pull some rope, left from the spring attempt, out of the snow, and then, by ripping it through the crust of snow, were able to use it for those last 20m to the site of Camp 4. They found the camp devastated by rockfall since Doug had last been there just five months before; the Japanese platforms, rather like bed-steads dumped on a scrap-heap, were hanging from their anchor points at an angle. The European platforms, however, looked as if they would be usable once they had been dug out, and the mutilated box tents, now little more than distorted skeletons, had been hacked out of the ice and cast down the slope. Given another few months, Everest would have erased this insolent, man-made rubbish from her profile. Mick, tired and cold, turned to race back down the fixed rope to start a brew at Camp 3, but Doug, more reflective, sat amongst the ruins to watch the setting sun:

A moment to myself, for the first time in two months. A place, high in the Himalaya, to watch the quiet evening turn into night – doubly moving after a hard day's climbing. The wind had stopped and the mountains around me were at peace. The sharp line of shadow and sunlight crept up towards me from far below, and then, with a flourish of white bright light, the sun dropped out of sight behind Nuptse. The cold struck into me almost immediately and forced me to scuttle down the fixed ropes, into the steamy warmth of our tent.

In just one and a half days' hard work, Doug and Mick had forced the route to an altitude of 7500m. And things had also been happening down below, for although the making of the route is the most obvious sign of progress, and certainly gives the most dramatic part of the story, it is just one small segment of an expedition. The flow of supplies behind the lead climbers is every bit as important, and can present as much risk and perhaps an even greater physical and mental challenge.

By now, Camp 2 was beginning to resemble an Advanced Base Camp. Dougal and Hamish were ready to move up behind Mick and Doug to push the route on, up to Camp 5, near the foot of the Rock Band. Kelvin, Barney,

Graham and Nick, with a further fifteen Sherpas, had also come up with the big Palace tent and the green cook tent. The dump of supplies was impressive and we were now ready to start ferrying them up the South West Face. But we were also faced with some problems. The Icefall was not nearly as static as we had hoped it would be in the post-monsoon period. Crevasses were opening constantly, and then re-opening, séracs tottering. Dave and Nick had tried to improve the route on their way back up the mountain on 10 October, after their rest at Base Camp, with unfortunate consequences to Dave. He described it in his diary:

Just about sun-up, I enter a very broken section. The first few ladders are OK, but then signs of activity. A crevasse has opened. The two-ladder section spanning it has parted – it was not bolted together. A section hangs either side, connected by a piece of cord. The handrail rope is wire-tight. I wait for Phurkipa and his pals.

'Not possible,' he says. 'Ladders too small; we have no rope.' But there is some rope dangling down on the other side of the crevasse.

'I go, Phurkipa, OK you hold rope.'

Swing down on the ladder, grab for the other one swinging in space, and pull up, breathless – high trapeze act at 20,000ft. The rest is easy. With the extra rope we make a swing ladder bridge.

The next long bridge requires adjusting, and a few cracks dodging. Then I'm back to breaking trail through the spindrift, ice axe probing for the invisible hard stuff below the fluff. Every time I sink to my crutch, having missed the covered path, I have a fit of coughing, and every time I cough I feel as if I've broken a rib.

The last obstacle beyond the big ladder, the violin bridge, lives up to its name – evidence of movement here, and on the rise to Camp 1. Five and a half hours from Base, breaking trail all the way, but it's nice to see Graham again.

11 October 1972

Very cold night, very little sleep. Still got catarrh and my back is a gonner. I was really pleased with myself for all the work I did in the Icefall yesterday, and what do I get for it? – the way I feel, a severely strained back, lower spine. The rope I salvaged from the snow slope was attached to a wooden stake. I tried to pull it out, used all my strength, but obviously the wrong way. Couldn't budge it, so started to dig. The stake was 5ft long. Didn't feel any pain at the time, but later sitting in Graham's tent, cooking the evening meal, I started to ache.

Today has been murder. If I cough I can't straighten; if I lie flat it takes ages to bend again. Meanwhile, I'm missing all the fun up the hill. Today the weather was perfect. Graham did my job, taking the mail up to Camp 2, while I lay in the tent, slowly drying up in the heat; it's a major effort to transfer into Graham's tent to make a brew.

12 October 1972

From the door of my tent I can see it's a beautiful day, so why me? Why do I have to be the one immobilised? I complain too much. Just have to make the most of it when I can move again.

The agonised cry, which any of us in a similar state would have made; but then, the selfless admonishment, so characteristic of Dave. When Graham brought news of Dave's back injury, Barney was desperately worried that he might have slipped a disc, and on 13 October dropped back down to Camp 1, to see how badly injured he was. Barney himself was in a bad way, having cracked a rib from the violence of his bouts of coughing. He was hoping to spend a few days at Camp 1, taking advantage of its slightly lower altitude to recover. Fortunately, he found that Dave had only strained a muscle, and would probably be fit in a few days' time, and commented wryly:

'You're a fitter man than I.'

But he was not to be allowed his rest. On 12 October, Dougal and Hamish, with the Sherpas Pembatharke and Pertemba, had moved up to Camp 4, to build the camp site and start forcing the route up to Camp 5. The following day, four of our Sherpas staying at Camp 3, carried loads up to Camp 4, and on the way down one of them, Ang Dawa, was hit on the mouth by a gas cylinder which must have been dislodged by one of the party at Camp 4. When he got back down to Camp 2 his face was a terrifying sight, covered in blood. I mopped it up gingerly, to find that his upper lip had been split in two by the flange of the falling gas cylinder. It was as if he had been given a hare lip. I cleaned it up as best I could, and tried to put a dressing on it – no easy task on the face. There was nothing more I could do until Barney got back and so I put him to bed with a good dose of painkillers and sleeping tablets. That night, on the evening radio call, I told Barney of the bad news and, even though he was in desperate need of rest, he agreed to return the next morning to patch up Ang Dawa. He must have set out early, for he reached Camp 2 at ten in the morning, his face haggard with pain and fatigue. At every coughing spasm, and they were frequent, he hugged his chest and winced with pain from the cracked rib.

But he wasted no time and turned the untidy Palace tent into a surgery, sterilised his gear and gave Ang Dawa a local anaesthetic. Soon he was stitching away on Ang Dawa's lip, while Ang Dawa, wonderfully stoic, sat motionless, mouth wide open, accepting Barney's ministrations. Once the operation was completed I asked Barney:

'When can we send Ang Dawa back down to Base for convalescence?'

'Convalescence?' said Barney. 'He'll be right as rain in a couple of days. You can keep him up here, and he'll be carrying as if nothing had ever happened to him.'

And Barney was right. Within a week, Ang Dawa's wound had healed completely, there wasn't even a sign of a scar – a tribute to Barney's sewing, and the remarkable healing powers of the Sherpas. This was especially remarkable at that altitude, for any wound takes a long time to heal, and often becomes septic.

This accident emphasised the risks involved on the South West Face. Anyone climbing up to Camp 4 spent some hours in direct line of the camp site and gully above, so that anything dislodged from the camp could easily hit them. At Camp 4, there were no level spaces, and even the ledges cut in the shallow covering of snow quickly filled in with spindrift which became instantly iron hard. You had to use constant vigilance, both to avoid slipping yourself, or dropping anything. Had it been an oxygen cylinder, rather than an empty gas can that had been dropped, Ang Dawa would undoubtedly have been killed.

Up at Camp 4, Dougal and Hamish dug out the platforms left by the European expedition, and erected two of our Ultimate Boxes. These were on a slightly different design from the Whillans Box, were more compact and lighter but, unfortunately, they had one major fault in the design of the corner joints. A hardened steel screw held together the three alloy pins which socketed into the poles of the frame, and this became more brittle in extreme cold. Several broke during the expedition, causing us considerable worry.

At this stage, however, the weather was still clement; hardly a breath of wind brushed the upper part of the face, and on 13 and 14 October, Hamish and Dougal pushed up the Great Central Gulley leading up towards the Rock Band. On their second day they ran out of oxygen about halfway up, having started out with cylinders only half-full. They hung the empty cylinders on the fixed rope, to ensure they could not go tobogganing down the slope on to the camp and the climbers below, and continued without oxygen.

'We were almost glad, afterwards, that we had run out,' commented Dougal. 'It showed us that we, also, could climb without oxygen, like the Sherpas who were carrying our ropes.' Of course, Pembatharke and Pertemba were still going without oxygen.

Two days' work and they had run out the rope to a point just short of the site of Camp 5. Although both were climbing very strongly, they had used up all their stock of fixed rope, and so turned back. It was still only halfway through October, and yet we had now reached a height of approximately 7600m (26,000ft). On the surface we were in a very strong position. The morale of the Sherpas was excellent. In my original planning I had allowed for the Sherpas to do just two carries from Camp 3 to 4, before they returned to Camp 2 for a rest. This was the most they had ever done successfully on either of the two previous expeditions; but Pembatharke, on his way back down to Camp 2, after helping Hamish and Dougal make the route up the gully, volunteered, out of the blue, that the Sherpas would be prepared to make three carries in succession without going back down for a rest. This made a considerable difference to my own logistic planning, for though we had a total of forty Sherpas, there had already been several inroads into our numbers. I had had to keep Sona Hishy back at Base Camp, to supervise all our local purchases; Phurkipa had to stay in the Icefall to supervise and repair the route. There were always a few who were sick, or recovering from illness and, as a result, we never had more than twenty Sherpas at Camp 2 and above. Carrying all the oxygen, food and rope we were going to need was undoubtedly going to cause us some severe problems later on in the expedition.

At this stage we only had twelve 16 kilo loads at Camp 4, of the seventy I had calculated we should need. Camp 5 was not even established, and I had calculated that we should need forty-three 13 kilo loads there. It was no use, therefore, trying to push the route out any further before we had at least built up the stockpile of gear, at both Camp 4 and Camp 5. With this in mind, I had planned to move up to Camp 4 myself, with four Sherpas, and spend four days carrying loads up to Camp 5, before Nick and Dave (provided his back recovered in time), moved back up the mountain to occupy Camp 5 to make the route to Camp 6.

In spite of the two spells of bad weather, we still seemed to be comfortably ahead of schedule, with a good chance of making a summit assault before the start of November. On 14 October, I was ready to move up to Camp 3 on my way to 4. I decided to wait until the load-carriers from Camp 2 arrived, for they were bringing up the mail, and so lazed through the day in the sun, watching through the binoculars as the tiny, ant-like figures of Dougal and Hamish pushed the route up towards Camp 5. It was difficult to imagine that the weather would ever change. There was not a breath of wind in the Western Cwm, not a single plume of spindrift blowing down from the ramparts of Nuptse. The interior of the tents was uncomfortably hot, and outside you only needed a light sweater.

The mail arrived, and with it were some cuttings from the short reports I had written for *The Observer*, and an article by Chris Brasher from the colour supplement, summing up what we were trying to achieve. He ended the article with an extract from Norman Dyhrenfurth's description of his attempt on Lhotse in the autumn of 1956:

The following days were terrible. During the night of 16 October, the storm rose to new heights. It was a miracle that the tents were still standing...what had happened to the weeks of good weather that usually follow the monsoon? One stormy night followed another, the days were no better ... another day passed, and another night straight out of Dante's *Inferno*. In the early morning hours I made up my mind to go down to Camp 2 before losing my sanity in this constant rattling of the tent and the wild howling of the storm ... We had reached the limits of human endurance.

Reading this, in the afternoon sun, it sounded a different mountain from ours, and yet, just two days later, on 16 October 1972, we also were to have our first taste of the post-monsoon Everest winds.

12

Our worst enemy, the wind

15 October – 26 October

The wind, like a raging torrent, cascaded down the Great Central Gully, lapping round the box in which I was lying at Camp 4; it was a river of racing spindrift with lumps of ice and rocks, which had filled the gap between the wall of the box and the snow slope behind, bounding and hammering over the flat roof. Had I been sharing the box with anyone, we would hardly have been able to hear each other speak. There was no question of calling down to the four Sherpas who were in the two boxes just below. Words would have been plucked away in the wind. The only possible means of communication was to get out of the box and visit them personally, a minor expedition in itself with the wind so savage and the situation of Camp 4 so precarious.

The boxes of the Sherpas were perched on an alloy platform left by the Germans. We had also dug out a system of ledges and platforms, but all these were now covered in spindrift, which immediately hardened to the consistency of concrete. It was like living on the pitched roof of a skyscraper. A slip would have been fatal and it was necessary to clip into a network of safety ropes whenever you ventured outside the box.

And yet the previous night it had been possible to relax, once we had dug out a platform and erected my own box tent. There had been no breath of wind, though a bank of high grey cloud did auger a change in the weather. Although desperately tired, at the same time I had been strangely elated to be on my own with four Sherpas, at the highest camp on the climb so far; probably the highest man on earth, for my box was just above that of the Sherpas. That night I had been too tired even to cook and had been touched when there was a call from outside and Ang Phu arrived with a plateful of stew and a mug of tea. I snuggled down into my sleeping bag, still wearing my down suit and all my clothes, ate the meal and then started fiddling with the oxygen equipment. During the day I had used oxygen to reach Camp 4. Though it undoubtedly improved my performance, it had not helped me as much as I had hoped. Part of the reason, perhaps, was that my personal gear weighed in the region of 13 kilos before I added the 7.5 kilo oxygen bottle. The benefit gained from the oxygen, therefore, was in part cancelled out by the extra weight I had to carry. The flow of oxygen had, however, removed that feeling of total lassitude I had experienced on some of my carries up to Camp 3. I had climbed very slowly up to Camp 4, much more slowly than the Sherpas who had not had the benefit of oxygen, but I had, at least, felt in control of my body, had been able to cut down the number of rests, just plodding slowly, one foot in front of the other.

Using oxygen to sleep on at Camp 4 was a questionable subject since we wanted to conserve our supplies on the mountain but, planning to stay there for some days, I decided at least to give it a try. I had brought in a half-empty cylinder for this purpose, attached my reducer valve to it, and then plugged in the little sleeping tube, which bypassed the demand valve and gave a fixed flow of about one litre of oxygen per minute into a light plastic mask. The continuous hiss of oxygen was strangely reassuring, as I cocooned myself in my sleeping bag. Full of food, I felt comfortably warm and sleepy and quickly dropped off into a deep sleep.

At about midnight I awoke to the deafening rattling roar of the wind and spindrift avalanches – the noise was so great I couldn't tell whether the oxygen was flowing or not, fumbled for my torch in the dark, found it, then lay back panting, willing myself to sit up and check the pressure of the oxygen cylinder. At altitude, each separate action takes three times as long as it would lower down, and you tend to think about the simplest task for a long time before actually carrying it out. The cylinder was empty. I didn't want to use another, and anyway there was no question of getting out of the tent in the middle of the night to get one. And so I just lay back in the box and listened to the ice blocks pound down over the roof. It was a frightening experience.

We had brought up a length of chicken wire to Camp 4, on Hamish's advice, to erect an avalanche fence to guard the camp. It had been the task of Dougal and Hamish to erect this before coming back down to Camp 2 for a rest, but somehow they had not got round to it. The weather had been so perfect when they had been up there that probably it had not seemed as necessary as it had been on the spring expedition, when there had been a lot of stonefall; then again, at 7300m everything is such an effort that one inevitably tends to take the easiest way out, and postpone work if possible.

That night, it had been all the Sherpas and I could do to erect the third box, and in the subsequent days that I was at Camp 4, the wind was either too wild for us to even contemplate going out to try to make a fence, or if the weather was good we were fully occupied, digging out the camp or actually making a carry to Camp 5. That night I just lay and listened to the wind hammering the box, praying that nothing big would hit it.

In the morning the wind didn't let up. Just opening the sleeve entrance of the box to dig some snow to melt for a brew was an agonising experience. The spindrift drove into my face and welled into the entrance of the tent, penetrating clothing. I filled a plastic bag with snow, all of which had to be chipped away with an ice axe, for the spindrift formed into a concrete-like mass wherever it settled; find the lighter, light the primus, and then just lie back exhausted, the mind a near blank. It took an hour to melt a panful of water for the first brew of the day. I nibbled some nuts, couldn't be bothered to cook, and listened to the wind; imagined what it would be like struggling against the torrent up towards Camp 5. And the route wasn't even made all the way. Dougal had warned me to be careful of the last length of rope. It was anchored to a very poor rock peg. What would it be like in this wind forcing the route, playing around with risky fixed ropes? Time for another brew; I postponed the decision. And then came the desire to relieve myself – the most dreaded moment of the day. I opened the sleeve entrance a chink, and a gust of spindrift blasted in. The thought of baring my backside to the wind and cold was too much. There is some recompense in having a tent to yourself. I found a plastic bag, and held it carefully. Peeing was a lot easier, we each had a pee bottle and it was just a matter of emptying it afterwards outside the tent, but you had to be careful you didn't let it freeze solid! The temperature inside the box, even with the gas stove going full blast was only –10°C, and once frozen it would have been difficult to thaw it out.

I glanced at my watch – 10.30 a.m. – half the morning gone already and I hadn't even dressed. There was a shout from outside. Gingerly I poked my head out of the sleeve entrance. Ang Phu and Ang Phurba were fully dressed – 'Ready to go, Sahib?' Ang Phu asked.

Feeling a rush of shame that I was not, I thought of the top of the fixed ropes anchored to that uncertain peg, and temporised. 'We wait for hour, see if it gets better.' They shrugged, impassive, and crawled back into their box. I got out *The Lord of the Rings* and slipped away into Tolkien fantasy, the world of Tree Ents, and Isengard, and the terror of the Nazguls, which was nothing to the real, tearing terror of the wind and snow and rocks outside.

An hour went by, but the thunderous torrent of ice and spindrift didn't let up. I didn't even bother to shout out to the Sherpas, but just curled up in my cocoon, put on another brew and started another chapter. And then came a shout from below. A Sherpa had arrived from Camp 3; a sneaking twinge of guilt – if they had fought their way up here, couldn't we have gone to Camp 5? I poked my head out of the box and shouted to him, through the wind, where to put his load of two oxygen bottles. He yelled something about Sahib coming. That made me feel even more guilty, for Kelvin, ever determined, ever willing, was at Camp 3, supervising the build-up of equipment. I had been a little worried about this enthusiasm. He had, of course, less experience of the mountains than any of the others, never having been climbing before the Annapurna South Face expedition. I knew how determined he was, how much he wanted to reach Camp 4 with a load – in a way this was his Everest. And yet at the same time, knowing that he had extended himself to the limit, just to get as high as Camp 3, I was afraid that in trying to reach Camp 4, he could take himself well beyond his limits.

But there was nothing I could do about it. I returned to Tolkein. Then, at about mid-day, there was a shout from below; I poked my head out once again, and there was Kelvin, trying to pull up over the lip of the platform. He looked all in, fumbling helplessly with the fixed rope. I knew that if he tried to unclip his jumar he would, perhaps, slip and fall unprotected.

'Hold it there, Kelvin!' I shouted, and started the cumbersome process of forcing on frozen boots and slipping on my windproof oversuit, before crawling out of the box and swinging down the rope to him.

He was not wearing the hood of his down suit, his head was merely protected by his now iced-up balaclava. Icicles clung to his nose and beard, but the most worrying factor was that he was obviously having difficulty in using his hands. Pulling him up on to the small ledge outside the lower box I said, 'Let's have a look at your hands.' Kelvin pulled off his Dachstein mitts and, as I had feared, his fingers were white right the way down the palm of his hand. He had quite severe frostbite. I'm afraid I laid into him verbally, from a whole mixture of motives, some of which arose from my own sense of guilt, however irrational, that I had not fought my way up to Camp 5; also I had let Kelvin hold the fort at Camp 3, in a position where he could put himself at risk as a result of his lack of experience. It is unlikely that any of the other more experienced members of the team would have got frostbite in similar circumstances. For a start, Kelvin had made the mistake of only using woollen mitts, when he would have been better off with the windproof polar mitts. Even then, he would probably have avoided frostbite if he had noticed his fingers becoming numb, and had stopped to warm them by putting his hand inside his down suit, or just by rubbing them. But he had been fixated by the need to fight his way through to Camp 4, had pushed himself to the limit to get there, not just for his personal satisfaction but primarily to get vital supplies to us. He felt that only by his own personal example could he possibly persuade the Sherpas to make the carry, and this was undoubtedly true.

He was bitterly hurt by my verbal attack and, in retrospect, I regret it, but at the time I also was under stress. Feeling I could not let Kelvin go back down on his own, I wanted to send someone whom I could trust to look after him, and therefore sent him down with Ang Phu, by far the most humane and reliable of our Sherpas. In doing this, I lost another reliable man at Camp 4.

Because we were running short of true high-altitude Sherpas, I had brought up the best of our converted Icefall porters, a broad stocky individual who always had such a wide grin we had nicknamed him Nippon Wide. But he had a grin no longer. Having been affected very badly by the altitude, he was now lying groaning in his sleeping bag. I tried to persuade him to go down with Kelvin, but he muttered that he was too ill to move. And so Kelvin went down with Ang Phu, and reached Camp 2 in the late afternoon, to be treated immediately by Barney.

After being put in a warm sleeping bag with a hot water bottle, he was given a steam inhaler to breathe in hot steam, in order to increase his body temperature quickly. He was then put on oxygen, a bowl of water was warmed up to a temperature of 43°C so that he could immerse his frostbitten fingers and bring back the circulation as fast as possible. This proved an extremely painful process and that night he slept little because of the pain.

The following extracts from Kelvin's diary and letters home written three days later on 19 October from Camp 2 show how he felt:

…So much has happened. Thank God I can still write, even with Barney's Dachstein mitts on.

We're still hemmed in here by a storm which buffets everything. The fact that this safari type tent and some of the others are still standing is a miracle. Outside the full fury of an Arctic gale carries on unceasingly. Awe-inspiring perhaps, but you'd have to be a madman to appreciate it.

I've written to Chris up at 4 to try and explain or justify my carry up there on the 16th. He was pretty annoyed at the time and let fly freely. I wanted to retaliate but didn't have the bloody strength. Anyway it took my mind off the immediate problem. I think frostbite in any circumstances tends to numb the brain as well as the limbs concerned. Physical exhaustion outweighs any thought of potential damage and in any case just standing out on the tiny platform at 4 nearly 25,000ft up in the face of a howling sub-zero blizzard is madness. The whole thing I suppose is madness! Perhaps you've got to put on the right expression of bliss and joy. Some people do, but for me it's like some gigantic minor key composition by Shostakovich where you seem to be falling deeper and deeper into a bottomless pit of despair and suffering. The only difference is that with music it's all in the mind, but here it's a reality – a grim reminder of man's capability to go just so far and yet know that when he ventures past his own defined limit something will happen.

Chris is still up at 4. I don't hold much against him for his outburst. In fact, any leader would have gone to town on me, especially after two days by himself above Camp 3 in appalling conditions. Just to exist there in this storm must be an exercise in survival. It doesn't appear to achieve anything if they can't move forward, but we all know that if he abandons the camp it will be torn to shreds.

I suppose I'll look back on that trip to 4 as the climax of my non-mountaineering career. It was a funny set of circumstances which pressed me to go (in addition to my own personal ego!). That morning (16th) Chris did not come on the radio set. This was unlike him, even though he may have been sleeping. I was especially worried because Camp 4 was crucial to the expedition's comms and in any case Chris – as leader – couldn't do much without being able to keep in touch with other camps. I was fairly certain that his walkie-talkie had broken or that he'd failed to get a good battery connection. In any case I wanted to take up a spare set. Also, we had quite a stockpile of stores at 3 and certain things were running short further up. The Sherpas had specifically requested sugar and the inevitable equal priorities of food packs, oxygen, rope and ironmongery had to be shifted sooner or later – preferably sooner.

I felt OK when we left, although the weather was not good. All four Sherpas at Camp 3 with me reluctantly decided to go up as well. I know they would not have left had I stayed in the tent. As it was, I set out by myself a little ahead of them once I was pretty certain that they would follow. The wind was really howling and unlike the day before there was no sun at all. Even with my windproof suit on I was cold but thought that I would warm up a bit later. It must have been nearly –30°C. I remember that we couldn't cut the corned beef with a knife and we had a breakfast of muesli and coffee. To move out required a lot of will power.

Coming round the corner from the shelter of the rock overhang I had my first real taste of Everest wind. The spindrift was being hurled into my face like someone throwing ice-cold sand. The little traverse into the open had been hard enough for me and being alone I felt extremely insecure. Round the corner it was worse. I couldn't hear a thing and kept on questioning my ability to go on. The trouble was that any forward progress was so slow that even being well wrapped up it was unbelievably cold and unfriendly. No warmth from the sun and visibility so poor that I couldn't see my objective which was some 1500m straight up the face. Even the fixed ropes were steeper than I'd ever been on before. The whole effect was worse than the 3–4 ASFE and this was much higher. Funny, it never occurred to me to set out using oxygen. I wasn't in that class anyway. Perhaps it would have made all the difference.

Anyway, after about two and a half hours my hands and feet started to go numb. Visibility was now only a few yards and even less when the great rollers of spindrift came rumbling down the face like a surfer's wave. It was impossible to look upwards into the driving wind. But occasionally I could just see over to the shoulder of the West Ridge which the American team traversed in '63. We were actually on a sort of vast elongated snow slope about 200m wide with exposed rock on either side. Sometimes small icy outcrops would jut out in the middle of this slope which had been blown hard and jagged like. But there were still patches of deep driven snow and loose blocks of ice.

Below me I could see the four blurred shapes of the Sherpas catching up fast. It was impossible to look right down to the top of the Cwm where the tents of Camp 2 might just have been visible had the weather cleared. I wanted to keep ahead but my body refused to take me forward. Sometimes for five minutes at a time I'd just stand there accepting nature's blows without wanting to fight back. When the rollers came it was like being in the middle of an asteroid belt being bombarded with stone and pieces of ice – some as big as golf balls coming straight at me at 80 mph.

After another half hour of grind up this never ending steep slope I looked down and saw that there were only two Sherpas on the rope – now about 50m below. I couldn't understand this for a while but later realised that the other two had turned back. Heaven knows I wanted to do the same but now the first two Sherpas were right behind me goading me on. They were grumbling and eventually I had to stand aside and let them pass. By this time my right hand was hurting from pain and my bloody camera annoyed me intensely as it swung from side to side dangling from my neck. I wanted to throw it away but equally wanted to try and record on film these incredible conditions which I didn't think anyone else would believe.

You know, I kept thinking that I must be weaker than the others. Doug and Mick, as well as Chris plus some of the Sherpas had all got up to 4 earlier and had made no great song and dance about it. They must have some guts and far more physical and mental determination than I. I really admire them.

Eventually I struggled up to the site of 4. It had taken me nearly five hours. The whole place looked really windswept and deserted like a scene I remember from the film *Scott of the Antarctic*. Everything not actually buried or anchored to the ground was flying horizontally in the wind. The two Sherpas had already dumped their loads and had passed me on their way back down. No word was uttered. Even they looked shattered. But for me, the last two or three lengths of fixed rope was the hardest thing I've ever undertaken. I frankly didn't think I'd make it and especially on the sections where the wind had blown all the snow away from the rock, I doubted my ability to heave up to a firm foothold again or remain in balance as I attempted with more and more difficulty to transfer the karabiner and jumar from one rope to the other. The trouble was that the thumb, index finger and middle finger of the right hand were virtually useless and even the fingers of the left hand which I used to help keep open the ratchet, were all freezing up. The more pressure I used the more useless they became. My feet too were numb and hurting. Also my inexperience in using crampons on the rock sections didn't exactly help! It was all pretty pathetic.

I hadn't ever shouted for help before in my life but this time I was beyond being a hero. Just below the bottom tent I blurted out a plea for assistance and just collapsed in a heap waiting for something to happen. The wind was really ferocious and I could hardly speak. Herzog's words about man not belonging here in his Annapurna book went through my mind vividly. Ang Phu came out of the bottom tent and immediately started to help. He called up to the top tent and I heard him telling other Sherpas to get a brew on. I was hauled up to the top platform and Chris came out. His immediate reaction was hardly cordial. I think he shouted,

'You bloody fool – you've gone and got yourself frostbite, haven't you?' He seemed more annoyed that I'd let the expedition down by writing myself out of the HA action than anything else. This meant of course that he had to give up a Sherpa (Ang Phu) to escort me down. In short I had succeeded in messing up the middle camp's manning plans. He wasn't in the slightest bit interested in my load of sugar, spare radio and Coolite chemical light tubes – which incidentally are proving very good indeed. To Chris I was just an inexperienced fool trying to prove something to myself to the detriment of the expedition as a whole. He almost made me feel that this was in fact the case but, ironically, had his radio worked he evidently was going to say that conditions were so wild at Camp 4 that any carry up from there was out. Equally to carry to 4 was not on! Hardly surprising really when I think of it now. I truly reckon the wind up there was as fierce as the two typhoons I have experienced in Hong Kong. And yet it was rewarding – I knew that.

Getting down to 3 and then on to 2 was not exactly easy, as you can imagine. Without Ang Phu I don't think I could have done it. He was so good and I owe him a lot.

About half past four I staggered in to Advanced Base and was greeted by Barney who immediately went into action. Dougal and Hamish are here as well and have been a great help. Barney is absolutely wonderful. He's had me on oxygen, penicillin, painkillers and hot water treatment, and I know that no one could do more. He is always cheerful, sympathetic and understanding. In many respects I think he's the strongest member of this team.

Next day I looked at Chris's radio. All that was wrong was that the circular dial which you pull out to adjust frequencies had not been pushed back in properly – a five-second job!

… Still the wind rages. It will be this that stops us. Not the mountain or the kit or the climbers. Perhaps if it eases I can go down to Base tomorrow, although trying to get through the Icefall with both hands out of action and no feeling in my feet will be interesting. I think Dougal and Hamish will probably escort/winch me down. I could hardly be in better hands! It's hard to say what the outcome will be. My feet will be OK and the left hand looks only superficial. There's nasty blistering and discolouring but with luck I shouldn't lose too much. At any rate I'm not depressed. I think that at any level the warm feeling of achievement of getting a load to its destination, surpasses the temporary feeling of cold and fatigue. You can feel good even if it hurts …

Back at Camp 4, 1 was already feeling remorse for having been so unsympathetic and wrote Kelvin a letter apologising for biting his head off. At the same time though, I was worried about losing him from the expedition. Ironically, I could afford to lose my support climbers less than the leaders, the immediate problem being that there were no climbers at Camp 3, which needed constant supervision just to keep the boxes from being engulfed in the snow. The Sherpas, left by themselves, tended to huddle inside their boxes until they collapsed on top of them.

In addition, Nippon Wide seemed to have taken a turn for the worse and was lying in the Ultimate Box in a state of semi-coma. I put him on oxygen and at the evening call asked Barney's advice. He recommended a number of drugs, and I persuaded Nippon to take them. He was in such a poor state that he was unable even to eat or drink. It was very noticeable that once the Sherpas did go down with sickness, or became frightened, they had very much less power of resistance or recovery than the European climbers.

The following day it was blowing as hard as ever. There was no question of going up to Camp 5, and it was now becoming increasingly important to get Nippon Wide back down the mountain. At mid-day I succeeded in getting him dressed and sent him down with Anu, just leaving Ang Phurba and myself up at Camp 4. On the way down Anu abandoned Nippon Wide and made tracks for Camp 2, as fast as he could get down. The unfortunate Nippon Wide barely managed to get down to Camp 3, taking a bad fall on the way and as a result got frostbitten hands. He could very easily have died from exposure.

This failure to look after each other was a feature I had noticed before amongst some Sherpas. It was perhaps a symptom, seemingly endemic in the East, of the lack of care for an individual's life created in part, no doubt, by the sheer harshness of day-to-day living. In this particular case, the other Sherpas were as angry as we were at Anu's callousness.

Back at Camp 2, they had tried to force the route up to 3, and I had hoped that Graham would be able to get there to spend the night. The Sherpas, however, had turned back. The conditions in the bottom of the Cwm were nearly as bad as they were on the face, with fresh deep snow covering the track, and spindrift gusting across the foot of the face. That evening one of the five Sherpas staying at Camp 3 dropped back to the lower camp, reporting that one of the three boxes had collapsed under the weight of snow. Four Sherpas were still there, but it seemed unlikely that they would keep the boxes clear of snow without one of the climbers there to help them. That night therefore the party at Camp 2 resolved that Nick and Graham would reach Camp 3 at all costs the next day. Nick described their arrival at Camp 3 in his diary:

It looked as though a bomb had hit it. No sign of gear pile or the two tents at the right-hand end of the ledge. We started digging and dug from 1.30 to 4.30, but the spindrift had set solid and we only succeeded in extracting one Whillans Box.

19/10/72. Wild night – either Graham or I were up every forty-five minutes to clear snow off roof – only spindrift but the amount incredible. Also told Sherpas to do same thing. However, I was very angry when I got up this morning and found that they had not bothered, and that one of the boxes was now even more badly damaged.

Various problems – one working stove between six of us – a lot of snow in our box.

The stove we were using had a damaged burner that was obviously giving off carbon monoxide, but Graham persisted in using it and I nearly passed out. Just after two sips of coffee I puked – unfortunately into the billy which held the rest of the hot water. At least this convinced Graham that I wasn't malingering and I was allowed to have the stove off and the ventilator open.

Various radio calls occupied the morning and at 11.00 we agreed with Chris that two of our Sherpas would carry halfway up, to be met by his four, who would take their loads and the ones abandoned on the 16th, when Kelvin had got frostbite. The other two, Graham and I, would dig out the camp site.

Our Sherpas must be the laziest, thickest four on the entire trip. When the time came, the two that were meant to do the carry disappeared into their tents without saying a word. The others did no digging. The Sherpas in the other Whillans Box attempted to repair it by putting a pole into a small rip in the side. Naturally after three minutes the rip was three feet long …

I am deeply depressed about prospects – it seems this expedition is going the same way of all autumn expeditions – things looked so good, as recently as the 15th.

Later we decided to abandon the other box and sent two Sherpas down with it, with two Sherpas from Camp 4, who also had to go down because their tents had collapsed – things look even worse.

Things also looked bad at Camp 4. One of the Ultimate Boxes had collapsed completely, failing at the corner joints which had already proved to be a weak spot in the design. I had had no choice but to allow Ang Phu and Anu to return to Camp 2, leaving Ang Phurba, Jangbo and myself at Camp 4, to try to sit it out till the weather improved sufficiently for us to establish Camp 5 and make a carry. In my diary I commented: 'It's an absolutely perfect, azure blue sky with a blazing sun. In theory it should give perfect conditions. Looking out over the mountains, mile upon mile of peaks, absolutely clear; very very beautiful, very peaceful, and yet this fiendish wind makes it as harsh a mountain situation as I think I've ever been in.'

It wasn't a continuous wind, but came in gusts. Every now and then there would be a lull, complete silence. You'd think the wind's finished, it's going to be a perfect day – but then there would come a reverberating roar as the next gust hurtled down the slope and engulfed the box.

It was difficult to maintain an overall picture of the expedition from my solitary eyrie at Camp 4. I should probably have been better off with a companion, so that at least I had someone with whom to discuss plans, rather than being dependent exclusively on the radio calls for each step of my planning. As the days went by, my nerves were becoming more and more taut. Merely dealing with the hour-to-hour crises of survival in the camp were enough to stretch me to the limit. And yet I felt I was in the right place, for this was the crucial point for the expedition at that moment; whatever crises developed down below could be solved by the people involved, without affecting the crisis point which the expedition faced forcing supplies up to Camp 5.

That night (19th) Hamish, back in Camp 2, had suggested that we should abandon the face until the weather improved, taking the boxes down and storing them under the platforms to prevent further damage. The tent situation was getting critical with nearly fifty per cent of our tentage written off either by wind or weight of snow. I was loth to agree to this, however, since once we abandoned Camp 4, we could then waste two good days in getting back up, and if we were only to get the odd good day, it seemed essential we should stick it out at the top camp, taking maximum advantage of any break in the weather when, and if, it arrived.

That night I temporised and said: 'Well, let's think about it, and discuss it again tomorrow, there's absolutely nothing we can do about it tonight.'

That night I commented in my diary: 'I have a feeling that once we abandon this camp, we've lost the battle. It all depends on whether this is the average wind direction. If it is, I think we've had it, because we now seem to be in the period of the high autumnal winds and you certainly can't climb the mountain in these conditions.'

With this depressing prediction, I tucked down into my sleeping bag and began to massage my toes to try to get some kind of life back into them. Just going out of the box a few times during the day was enough to freeze toes to such a degree that they never really came back to life, even after a night in the sleeping bag. Although using oxygen helped in this respect, I used as little as possible, and during the six nights I spent at Camp 4 during this stint, only used it twice.

That night was the worst of the lot. The wind built up into a crescendo of violence. I took two sleeping tablets but they had no effect. I just lay, tucked into the inside wall of the box, listening to the thunder of ice blocks rattling across the top of the tent. Nerves stretched to the limit, I was on the point of screaming into the noise-filled opaque void.

By morning I had had enough. At the morning radio call, I agreed with Hamish that it would be best to evacuate the face. Hamish and Dougal were going to return to Base that day, and Mick and Doug would probably do so as well.

Then suddenly I noticed that everything had become silent; there was no wind. I poked my head out of the entrance of the box. It was a brilliant clear day, just as it had been for the last three, but the important factor now was that there was no wind. The sun even seemed to have a little heat in it. Everything was different from what it had seemed early that morning; the nightmarish night was forgotten. This was a day to go up, not down: and so I called out to the Sherpas.

'It's a good day Ang Phurba. We go up.'

They accepted my decision without expression, and by ten o'clock we were ready to make the first carry up to Camp 5. I had decided to go up using oxygen, taking a very light load, so that I could fix the final stage of the route to the site of the camp, while I gave Ang Phurba and Jangbo loads of rope and oxygen cylinders weighing about 16 kilos each.

I set out in front with the two of them close on my heels. In theory, the oxygen set should have reduced the altitude to the equivalent of 5000m, but it certainly didn't seem to be doing this. I was taking a couple of pants for each step and, after a dozen, wanted to take a rest. Perhaps the cold had affected the function of the demand valve. At my first rest, the two Sherpas steadily gained ground on me and stormed past, Ang Phurba making particularly good progress. I shouted out for him to wait at the top of the fixed rope, and warned him that the top peg might be badly placed. He showed no sign of having heard me, but just kept plodding on up the slope, and I had little enough breath to spare to shout after him. That night in my diary I commented:

You just plod on up this endless great wide snow gully. Part of you is wondering why the hell you're doing it – it's absolute misery, one step, then another and then another – the slow monotony of it; yet when you do rest and look round, the view is fantastic. You look down, into the Western Cwm, sweeping down again to this ever widening vista of mountains – Cho Oyu quite close now, only a bit higher than ourselves. Swinging across to the west, Menlungtse, a perfect pyramid; Gaurishankar, round humped, with sheer-seeming walls on every side – these two peaks still unclimbed – and then mile upon mile of other mountains, a lot of them in Tibet. Gosainthan [Shisha Pangma], I think, in the distance, the last 8000m peak to be climbed. This ever-expanding view makes up for all the misery and effort.

You plod on, see the Sherpas getting further and further ahead. By the time I reached Dougal's high point, Ang Phurba had already got out one of the reels of rope he was carrying, and had run it out across to a shoulder on the right, behind which Camp 5 was hidden. By the time I had followed it to the camp, the two Sherpas were already hard at work digging out the camp. An overhanging rock wall gave excellent shelter from any rocks or spindrift from above. A dozen oxygen bottles from the International expedition were left over on one side of the ledge. The Sherpas had already tunnelled down to a part-wrecked tent left by the Germans the previous spring. They offered me some sweets that had been lying there for the last six months;

they could have lain there for a further year or years and would still have been edible.

All the effort and struggle to reach that point was made infinitely worthwhile by the incredible view. We were now level with the summit of Nuptse, on the other side of the Western Cwm, could even glimpse snow peaks on the other side of the long crenellated ridge. It was strange to think that I had stood over there, just eleven years before. At that time I could not have foretold that I should ever be at 8000m on Everest or, for that matter, the course of my life which had led me to this point.

I was content. We had carried two loads up to Camp 5, and that single day of fine weather brought all my optimism back to life. Perhaps we had a chance of reaching the summit after all – just a few more days like this and we could get Camp 5 stocked, and the route run out to the foot of the Rock Band. I set out behind the Sherpas to return to Camp 4, sliding down the fixed ropes, sitting down every 30m or so, both to rest and to watch the sun drop down towards the western horizon, bathing the mountains in a rich yellow glow which slowly turned to orange. The following day the wind was back, but that single day of activity had given us new strength. I was now determined to maintain our toe-hold on the face.

At this stage I still hoped that I should be able to continue to sit it out at Camp 4, pushing Nick and Dave through to Camp 5 as soon as I had managed to do another carry with the Sherpas. But two days went by and we were unable to make any further progress. Ang Phurba had had enough and wanted to go back down, and so I sent him down, replacing him with four fresh Sherpas, Pembatharke, Pertemba, Ang Nima and Ang Phu. Unfortunately, however, Pembatharke was feeling the altitude and Ang Nima complained of headaches. I, too, was reaching the end of my tether – the isolation and the continuous shriek of the wind were beginning to have an effect and I longed to escape, if only for a few days. So I decided that we should have to abandon all hope of getting Camp 5 stocked before Dave and Nick moved up to make the next push forward, and bring them up to Camp 4 to take over from me.

Meanwhile, down below there was no shortage of incident. Dave had made a miraculous recovery from his back injury and had moved up to Camp 3 to join Graham and Nick. Barney, ever faithful, was holding the fort at Camp 2, while Mick and Doug had retreated to Base Camp. There seemed little point in using them to carry loads up to Camp 3, which was well stocked anyway. At Camp 1, Ken Wilson was in charge. It was an important but incredibly dreary role, for Camp 1, though a vital link in our communications, was a depressing place in which to spend any length of time, as uncomfortable as any camp on the mountain, yet with none of the excitement associated with the camps on the face. In addition, the Icefall porters who were looking after Camp 1 spoke practically no English. Ken is a very gregarious person who thrives on argument and discussion, and to put him, in effect, on his own was a refined form of torture. There was a plaintive note in his voice on the radio, when he asked when he was going to be allowed to move up to Camp 2. Nevertheless he did a magnificent job at Camp 1, organising the flow of loads up the mountain and looking after the needs of the Sherpas. There was no doubt that we needed a Camp 1 manager, but I had no one with whom I could replace Ken, and yet it was obviously unfair to keep him there for his stay with the expedition, especially as he had come out to Everest at his own expense to see as much as possible of what we were doing.

I decided, therefore, to risk leaving the camp unsupervised, on the supposition that the Sherpas based there had the comparatively simple task of ferrying everything they received straight through to Camp 2, and allowed Ken to move up to 2, to keep Barney company.

Having made my decision to move back down for a rest, I longed for Dave and Nick's arrival, but this was to be delayed for yet another day. On 22 October, the wind blasted across the face with hardly a break. I could have got down myself, but dared not leave the Sherpas on their own, since almost inevitably, and quite rightly, they would have wanted to go down as well. And so I just sat it out. I commented in my diary:

The wind is the appalling enemy, it is mind-destroying, physically destroying, soul-destroying, and even existing in the tents, which I think are now pretty weather-tight, is still very very hard. This will certainly be the most exacting test I have ever had to face, and I only hope it is one that the others will be able to face.

One worry here is that, having pushed Nick and Dave up to Camp 5, I shall have to push Graham up to here. One problem is his relationship with the Sherpas. He can be very outspoken and could rub them up the wrong way. At the moment it is vital that we keep the Sherpas happy and bend over backwards, just to keep them up here, carrying. Also, how long will he be able to take this kind of wind battering? He might be able to take it better than I – he has less administrative problems, and, I think, is a more phlegmatic kind of person.

Oh, the absolute lethargy of 24,600ft [7500m]. You want to pee and you lie there for a quarter of an hour making up your mind to look for your pee bottle. I've no appetite at all and it's an effort to cook anything for yourself. I suspect it is high time I did go down for a short rest – I think if you try to stay up high the whole time to conduct operations you end up being ineffective in that you are just getting weaker and weaker, more and more lethargic. Part of me wants to stay up here, because this is the focus of events, but I think I really should go down.

And so I waited, longing for a temporary release from Camp 4 and the company of my fellow climbers.

Nick and Dave came up to relieve me on 23 October, yet another brilliant clear day, with the wind tearing out of the empty sky. They came up without using oxygen, engulfed in clouds of spindrift, Nick first, with Dave dragging a little behind him. Nick commented in his diary:

Main worry was my toes, which were numb all the way up to 4. I would stop every thirty steps to wiggle them but it didn't seem to help. Got up in three hours, Dave in about three and a half. Chris seemed pleased to see us. I suspect more because he could now go down, than because of our company. He said he had been furiously spring-cleaning the inside of the box, but it still looked pretty grim to me. Afternoon spent sorting out box. However, it will always be cramped as the upper wall bulges with snow and the lower one overhangs space and you don't like getting too near it.

It had been cramped for one, was even worse for two. During the night, condensation formed an icy armour on the ceiling of the box, above the frost liner; then during the day, with the stove going full blast, it would start to melt, dripping on to the frost liner which provided a supplementary ceiling. Fortunately this was semi-impermeable and would therefore collect little lakes which could be channelled off to the sides. The main problem was storing all one's gear, radio, first-aid kit, spare clothes, cine and still cameras, which had to be hung from the frame of the tent or wedged round the sides. And then there was the food, stove and pans, which took up one corner, it was all too easy to knock over a full pan of soup. You needed relentless self-discipline to keep the box in any kind of order.

I plunged down the fixed ropes in a mere hour and a half, all the way back down to Camp 2, partly in my anxiety to reach semi-civilisation and partly to get the film I had taken, of Nick and Dave arriving at Camp 4, back down to Base Camp that same day. Camp 2 was a different world. Our Sherpa cook thrust a big mug of tea in my hand. You could sit outside; didn't have to watch where you put hands and feet – but most important of all there were people to talk to – Ken had now joined Barney at Camp 2 – Ken full of impressions of Everest, full of enthusiasm; Barney, forever cheerful and helpful, even though he was still having trouble with his chest and in a way had the most mentally exacting and yet least rewarding job on the entire expedition. Holding the fort at Camp 2 entailed directing our Sherpa force in their efforts to supply Camp 4, arguing with them about rest days, keeping records of our bonus schemes, and supervising the camp.

That night, Ken cooked a magnificent three-course dinner over the gas stove and then we lay in our sleeping bags in the comfortable sleeping compartment of the big Palace tent, talking of subjects connected and unconnected with the expedition. Ken is obsessed with climbing, not just from the actual physical process, but the ethics and politics. It was refreshing having a ferocious argument on the use of artificial aids on British rock, in the wild confines of the Western Cwm.

Up at Camp 4, Nick and Dave were not so comfortable. Nick wrote: 'I had a lousy night's sleep – not more than one hour altogether – cold toes, desperately cramped (the floor was shaped for one person, not two) and the continuous howling wind. (At the moment I am reading *Wuthering Heights* – appropriate!)'

The following morning was fine with very little wind. Nick in his diary continued: 'It seemed a warm and pleasant morning though the thermometer outside the tent read –17°C which just shows how we are getting acclimatised to the cold. Just before leaving, a large chunk of ice hit the box and bent part of the frame.'

They were obviously going to be able to make a carry up to Camp 5, but unfortunately they were only to have two Sherpas available to go up. Pembatharke had been steadily deteriorating for the last three days, ever since reaching Camp 4, and it was obvious that he was going to have to return. Ang Nima had also been complaining of headaches and, although he seemed to be fit and strong, insisted on going back down. Maintaining our numbers at Camp 4 had become a real problem and I had no one down at Camp 2 with which to replace them immediately. We had made another change in tactics, since the Sherpas preferred to live at Camp 2, making their carries straight through to 4. They travelled lightly laden up to Camp 3, where Graham was still ensconced, then picked up a load there and pushed on to 4. It made a gruelling day, but they were prepared to do this every other day and of course were very much more comfortable down at Camp 2.

That day, Dave Bathgate decided to stay behind at Camp 4 to receive the Sherpas carrying up from Camp 2 and to sort the camp out while Nick went with the Sherpas up to Camp 5. Nick described the day in his diary.

Pertemba set up a fast pace and the three of us kept close together taking four hours for the trip. I didn't use oxygen but only took one coil of rope. The weather was magnificent – no wind, hardly a cloud in the sky and the view was unbelievable. The greatest moment of all was when I could first look over the Lhotse-Nuptse ridge and see range upon range of peaks stretching on the other side. I am pretty sure I recognised Annapurna away in the distance. It was one of those days when I felt really strong, and thought for a change that we might get up this bloody mountain.

But next day the weather had reverted to normal; the wind was hammering the tent, and, more ominous, a scum of high grey cloud covered the sky. They would have liked to have taken a rest day, but the two Sherpas said that under no circumstances were they prepared to spend another night at Camp 4. They were prepared, however, to make just one more carry up to Camp 5 before going down. And so Dave agreed to go up with them, while Nick rested and did some work on the camp site. Dave also went up without using oxygen, a sterling effort; but conditions were less pleasant than the previous day and by the time he returned to the box his feet were numb with cold. Nick warmed them by putting them in his crutch, using body heat in an effort to get back the circulation, but they remained numb nonetheless.

Everyone on the mountain felt encouraged by their effort. We now had enough gear at Camp 5 for Nick and Dave to take up residence. I was planning to send up a further four Sherpas the next day to help them move up. But as so often happened on this expedition, just as the tide seemed to be turning in our favour, the weather took a hand once again. By dusk, the camp was engulfed in cloud, with the wind tearing at the box. They took Mogadons to try to deaden their senses into sleep in the face of the constant roar of the wind. Dave Bathgate described what happened that night in his diary:

An almighty crash: immediate wakening – everything covered in snow; the bottom end of the Whillans Box torn, the framework broken and sheared through; it must have been a good-sized rock that had hit us. This was taken in, in seconds. I remember Nick saying, 'Well, there she goes.' Both of us trying feverishly to think of what to do, though still half drugged with Mogadon and, anyway, at an altitude of 24,600ft [7500m], constructive thought is difficult.

Eventually Nick sat at the broken end of the box, holding it up with his head. I put boots on over duvet socks and crawled out to inspect the other boxes for possible habitation. It was pitch dark outside, and the beam of my torch hardly cut through the rushing particles of snow. Both boxes had rips or broken zips and were rapidly filling with snow. The temperature was –25°C, and God knows what the strength of the wind was. The only thing I could grab to help with repairs was a shovel, and spare piece of framework. The shovel helped to prop up the damaged corner. Everything was in chaos, but we managed to find some matches, a stove and brew materials – and then, ironically there was a shortage of snow to melt in the cooking pot.

We brewed for two and a half hours, and this raised the temperature in the box to an almost bearable level. Outside the wind was still whistling past, bringing with it a torrent of spindrift and rocks. At 8 a.m. we made radio contact with Camp 2, and Chris agreed that we should abandon Camp 4. He asked whether we could transfer to one of the other boxes, but we told him that they also were damaged and were now part filled with snow. In addition, all our gear was covered in spindrift and we could never have got it effectively dried out.

By 11 a.m. we were ready to go. Down the ropes with numb hands and feet, a river of snow rushing past, ankle-deep. During the big gusts it was total white-out conditions, and if you could manage to open your eyes, you could see black objects rush past. At one point Nick tried to warn me of stonefall. Dozens of rocks, anything from the size of golf balls to that of footballs, whizzed past our ears. We were very lucky not to be hit.

Eventually we got round the rock buttress, to the relative safety of Camp 3, and Graham was waiting for us with gallons of hot drinks. He seemed quite happy at 3 where it was sheltered from the full force of the storm. We left him and clipped on the fixed ropes once again; visibility averaging 50ft, arrived down at the bergschrund safely, and traversed the slope before walking blind for a while. Began to wonder about our chances of finding Camp 2, and chances of survival if we didn't. Then suddenly, during a clear spell, we saw people coming towards us, Barney, Chris and two Sherpas. Our gratitude was indescribable. The Sherpas took over our bags. Everything was laid on at Camp 2.

We were almost as relieved to see them as they were to see us. Even down in the Western Cwm the weather was frighteningly savage. Had they missed Camp 2, they would have had little chance of surviving a night out. Camp 2 was relatively luxurious compared to 4, but it was hardly a holiday camp. The tents were being threatened with destruction from the sheer weight of snow building up around them, and at night one wondered just how long our Palace tent could stand up to the battering of the wind.

Things looked black. We had been forced to abandon Camp 4, and had to face the prospect that all three boxes would probably be destroyed in the storm. Graham was sitting it out on his own at Camp 3, hoping to preserve the box he was living in, at least, and the rest of us were at Camp 2. Communications with Base Camp were broken, both on the Icefall, and the route between Camps 1 and 2.

I could not help wondering whether we had reached the end of our resources, but then put the thought behind me. None of us was prepared to admit defeat.

13

The storm

27 October – 30 October

'Check mate' – another game over, our fifth that day. Barney and I were lying in our sleeping bags in the sleeping compartment of the big Palace tent, which rocked and shook in the wind. The little cassette recorder, kept inside the sleeping bag to warm the batteries, was playing Bach's Orchestral Suite – the music both of us found to be the ideal palliative to taut nerves. We were both relatively warm and comfortable, just as long as the tent stood up. Nick and Dave were in the sleeping compartment beside us, but the living area which filled the rest of the tent was anything but luxurious; spindrift found its way through every single chink, covered the food, piled rucksacks, cooking pots and stoves in its powdery film.

Our cook, Pasang, was crouched over a primus stove, trying to persuade it to work. Muttering imprecations in Nepali, he was pumping furiously, tried to light a match, but the head broke off; he grabbed another and the same happened. By this time the primus had cooled off and the jet of vapour had turned to liquid paraffin – a match smouldered into flame and suddenly the whole tent seemed full of yellow flames. Pasang continued to pump. 'For Christ's sake turn down the pressure,' we shouted. 'You'll burn the tent down if you're not careful.'

Reluctantly, Pasang turned down the pressure and the flames vanished, to be replaced by the pervasive fumes of hot paraffin. The cook's tent had finally been engulfed in the snows that morning and he had been forced to move the communal kitchen, with all its accompanying fumes and mess, into the Palace. This tent had therefore become the communal home for all twenty Sherpas and the four climbers at Camp 2. At night everyone packed into it to eat the evening meal, listen to the radio and talk. With twenty Sherpas and four climbers crammed into the tent, there was hardly room for everyone to sit down but the warmth of close-packed bodies, and the heat from the primus stoves which were burning without a pause throughout the day, raised the temperature to a warm –5°C! We played chess, read and talked. I had left *The Lord of the Rings* up at Camp 4 – it had been too heavy to contemplate carrying it down and then all the way back up again. I'd moved on to *Cider With Rosie* by Laurie Lee – another escapist and rather improbable book for the Western Cwm of Everest. On Nuptse, back in 1961, my main reading had been Apsley Cherry Garrard's *Worst Journey in the World* which told the story of his experiences on Scott's last expedition to Antarctica. Whenever I had thought that life on the mountain was unbearably tough, I just had to read another chapter to realise how much harder it had been for those Antarctic pioneers. On Everest the conditions and stress from cold and wind were probably every bit as bad as those experienced by Cherry Garrard, though of course we did have better equipment and food, and the experience was not so long-drawn-out. We were all looking forward to the end of our ordeal and yet, at the same time, there was real enjoyment in each other's company, in the moments of intense exhilaration caused by the stupendous beauty of the mountains around us, of having made a good carry or, perhaps greatest of all, the thrill of pushing out 50m of the route.

It was in this respect that Barney possibly had the most exacting job of all. He had very little of this type of stimulus, since he was landed at Camp 2 with the nerve-racking job of controlling the Sherpas, keeping a check on the build-up of supplies and administration, all on top of his duties as doctor. He was sparely built before the expedition, but now his face was carved into hollows by the stress of living at over 6400m for a fortnight; he was still coughing, and every single cough caused a stab of pain from his damaged rib. With none of the spur of possibly making a vital section of the route, or the final summit bid, he just had to keep going with only the occasional trip up to Camp 3 to change his horizon. Nevertheless, throughout he remained wonderfully cheerful and kind – a good and very soothing companion.

We started another game of chess, changed the cassette to some Mozart, and tried to ignore the wind outside. There was no movement anywhere on the mountain. Graham, in solitary state, was up at Camp 3, sounding remarkably balanced and content with his lot when contacted on the radio. Barney, Nick, Dave and myself were at Camp 2. Ken Wilson, having made a single trip up to Camp 3, had returned to Base with the comment, 'You're mad – you're all mad. I'm not involved in this expedition, and I'm going to get out of it as fast as I can!' And yet there was no doubt that he had gained a tremendous amount from the experience and had, of course, fulfilled an invaluable role during the lonely week he had held the fort at Camp 1. A gregarious rock-climber, Ken has never had aspirations to being a big expedition man. He was due to leave for home anyway, and did so inspired, and certainly enlightened by his experience, but without regret.

Mick Burke and Doug Scott were at Camp 1, on their way back up the mountain, and the rest of the team was down at Base Camp, which was now being ably run by Jimmy Roberts, assisted by Kelvin Kent and Tony Tighe. Bob Stoodley had also just arrived there. We had paid for his trip out to see us as a recompense for his efforts in raising money in Britain. Having contracted a stomach upset on arrival at Luglha, he never recovered from it, being unable to hold anything down for the entire week he stayed at Base Camp. Consequently, he spent much of the time in his sleeping bag, felt desperately ill throughout, and yet still ranked it as one of the greatest experiences of his life! Beth cared for him, together with all the other convalescents and invalids down at Base, referring the symptoms of each patient to Barney, at Camp 2, for his radio-diagnosis and prescription. Barney finally recommended Bob to start back for civilisation, since he was just wasting away at Base – by the time he got back to England he had lost 9.5 kilos.

Base Camp was certainly a busy place at this stage. Chris Brasher had arrived – he was going to take over my role as expedition writer, sending reports back to *The Observer*. By now the expedition seemed to have turned into a monster with a minute head, in the shape of Graham at Camp 3, a puny body, our team of four climbers and twenty-one Sherpas at Camp 2, and a massive tail sitting at Base Camp. There were several disturbing factors, the most serious being our shortage of tentage. It seemed probable that all the boxes at Camp 4 would be written off, leaving us with hardly any spares. Hamish was designing a special reinforced box which he hoped to prefabricate at Base Camp before it was dismantled and carried up to Camp 4. He had already ordered suitable timber in Namche Bazar. Meanwhile, Dougal and Tony Tighe were on their way to the Base Camp of the French Pumo Ri expedition to see if they had any spare tentage which we could borrow or buy.

Up at Camp 2 I tried to work out our most effective moves once the storm blew itself out. We were now losing tents even at Camp 2 – the kitchen tent, of course, had already foundered, the fly-sheets of the Vango four-man tents were being ripped to bits in the wind and these also were fast vanishing under the snows, in spite of our efforts to keep them dug out. The Palace, miraculously, stood up to the hammering, though at night we were all careful to have our rucksacks packed, ready for a hasty retreat in the event of it blowing away. The constant flapping of the canvas, the all-pervasive spindrift, and the savage wind and snow when you ventured outside to dig out the tent or relieve yourself, were all beginning to drive us to a nervous edge.

And then, on the morning of 28 October, there was an improvement. You could see the top of the Rock Band through swirls of cloud and spindrift. The wind in the bottom of the Western Cwm had dropped, and it looked as if we might be able to re-establish the route between Camps 1 and 2. This had become critical, for we were now low on some foodstocks, particularly tsampa and sugar but, more serious still, we had only 2 gallons (9 litres) of paraffin. To melt all the snow necessary for brews and food for twenty-four people, Pasang had to keep the stoves burning twelve hours a day, using a battery of three primus stoves to melt a single big pot of melt water. At this rate we had barely twenty-four hours' fuel left. Barney had been worried about fuel stocks for some time, but there was a fuel shortage all the way back to Namche Bazar, and a fresh consignment had only just reached Base Camp. At Camp 1 they could only spare two gallons, but this would keep us going for a few days until supplies from Base reached us. Consequently, I resolved to organise a carry from Camp 1 to 2, and hoped that there would be a carry that same day from Base. I sent Dave Bathgate down towards Camp 1 to meet the Sherpas coming up, wading through the thigh-deep snow. At the same time, I told Doug and Mick, who of course were at Camp 1, that they could come up to Camp 2. In retrospect this was a mistake, since though the weather showed signs of improvement, it certainly was not settled, and allowing them to come up to join us meant that Camp 1 was, once again, without a European in charge and take the radio calls. We could possibly have taught Ang Dawa, the Sherpa in charge of the seven porters at Camp 1, to use the radio, but somehow had never thought of it, though later on we were to do just that.

The weather had closed down before Doug and Mick reached us at Camp 2. Once again, it was near white-out conditions and, as dusk fell, the wind built up to a new fury. The Palace tent shook and bent under the force of the wind, and all of us took the precaution, once again, of packing rucksacks preparing for a quick retreat – though where we could have retreated to, I am not at all sure! Nick and Dave, in an effort to build up their stamina, slept on oxygen and as a result slept through the storm.

Next morning it was still gusty but the clouds had at last cleared and the sun was blazing down from a deep blue sky – but any feeling of warmth was illusory. Outside, it was –10°C and even with the stoves going at full fumy blast, the temperature inside the tent never attained freezing point. But the sun was welcome as we crawled out of the tents, shook ourselves and assessed the damage. The camp was almost entirely buried, with the ends of the tents sticking out of the snow like the prows of sinking ships after a U-boat attack on a world war two convoy. We took stock. Banners of spindrift were blowing from the ramparts of Nuptse, forming huge inverted whirlpools over the Western Cwm. It seemed unlikely that the boxes at Camp 4 could have survived their ordeal. I examined the camp through binoculars; it looked as if they were still standing, but it was difficult to assess just how damaged the tents were. Dropping down to Camp 3, I saw no sign of Graham's box – it seemed completely buried by the avalanches of snow which must have poured down the face during the night. What was more worrying, he did not come up on the eight o'clock radio call. This did not mean too much, however, since Graham often overslept the first call of the day. Even so, I was worried, and opening up an hour later was very relieved to hear Graham's voice, still full of sleep, slightly belligerent, very matter-of-fact.

'What's all the fuss about? Slept like a log up here. The box could take any amount of snow and I'd be fine if I didn't have to worry about you buggers down there!'

'Sounds good, Graham. Do you need anything?' I asked. 'We'll try to get up to you today.'

'I'm running a bit low on coffee and biscuits – and could do with a gas lamp – but there's plenty of food up here.'

'We'll try to get them up to you. You've done a great job sitting it out.'

'It's given me plenty of time to think. I've come up with one or two ideas that we can discuss when I get back down.'

'Do you want to come down for a rest?'

'I could do with one. You get a bit tired of a six-foot long box after a time, but I'll be fine until you manage to send someone else up to take over.'

One problem solved, I then got on to Base Camp. As always, Tony Tighe answered the radio. He took all the calls at morning and dusk throughout the expedition, was always calm and cheerful, and very often did an excellent diplomatic job, softening demands for more supplies which came from the mountain to Jimmy, or complaints at a failure to send something up from Base Camp. They also had had a rough night at Base Camp, with tents collapsing under the snow. What was more serious, they were low on food supplies, expecting the latest consignment to arrive that day, but with the snowfall the route was blocked all the way back to Lobuche, and it looked as if it would take some days to force a new trail out, diverting manpower from the equally crucial job of re-establishing the route back up the Icefall.

I wanted to get into communication with Camp 1, to ensure that the Sherpas there had survived the night. From previous experience, we knew that the winds and snowdrifts at this lower camp could be even worse than in the Western Cwm itself.

'Tony, could you tell Hamish and Dougal that I'd like them to force the route up to Camp 1 today. Apart from anything else, we must get some more paraffin up as soon as possible,' I said.

'Could you wait a minute, I'll see what they think.'

A few minutes later – 'Hello, Chris, are you still on the air? Over.'

'Yes, over.'

'I'm afraid they don't think there's much chance of getting up today. The snow's very deep and apparently the Icefall has shifted quite a bit near the top. They reckon it'll take a couple of days to clear the route. They say why not send someone down from your camp?'

'OK fair enough, I'll do that.'

I had no choice but to agree – it had taken two days, earlier on in the expedition, to clear the Icefall after a storm that had been considerably less serious than the most recent one. The question was who to send back. Whoever went down would almost certainly have to stay the night, perhaps longer. It would have been easier had I kept Doug and Mick back at Camp 1, but since I had let them come up the previous day, making the trail afresh practically all the way, it seemed a bit much to send them all the way back again. Nick and Dave, on the other hand, might even benefit from a trip to a slightly lower altitude, especially if these high winds were to persist for several days, holding us down in the Cwm. And so I decided to send them back to Camp 1, knowing full well that they would not be too keen to go.

They agreed without argument, however, and got ready that morning for what was obviously going to be an epic descent. Dave Bathgate described their experience in his diary, immediately after reaching Camp 1.

Only the top third of the green Stormhaven kitchen-tent at Camp 1 protruded from the white expanse of new spindrift. The canvas was taut, and where it disappeared under the snow, a thick layer of ice had formed. The ridge pole, although strengthened by odd sections of metal, sagged alarmingly. All the sleeping tents were buried under 10ft of snow, likewise the expedition gear and food supplies.

Nick and I arrived at this scene of devastation after a four-hour trip down the Cwm from Camp 2. Normally, the journey from 2 to 1 takes an hour, but ploughing through the deep powder, after a four-day Himalayan holocaust, was strenuous work, even with the aid of snow-shoes. Most of the way, only the top few inches of our 6ft marker flags were showing, and there was a half-mile section where they had disappeared altogether. This we put down to a huge powder-snow avalanche from the Nuptse Ridge. The wind often whipped the spindrift into an opaque cloud which blinded us completely, penetrating clothing, stinging our faces, so that we just had to stop in our tracks until it cleared. Our breath froze to our beards and our beards froze to our clothing. It was bitterly cold.

From their past performance, we knew that the Camp 1 Sherpas were a competent bunch, but even so, we could not be certain that they had survived the last storm. The surface area around Camp 1 was flat, and so the snow had drifted evenly to a depth of about 10ft. Nick and I stood on the wind crust and peered down at a Sherpa who was digging out the remains of a Tunnel tent. The orange roof was just visible and the hole was already 4ft deep. Strangely enough, the tent seemed to have retained its shape – a tribute to the robust Tunnel design.

Great clods of hard-packed snow were being tossed by invisible men from several other holes nearby – it was just like an archaeological dig. The Vango tents, which are the conventional triangular shape, were in a much more pitiful condition than the Tunnel tent. They had collapsed, foundered under the pressure of tons of compact snow. Surely, if anyone had been in those tents they would have suffocated. One of the diggers lifted his goggles on to his forehead, and smiled up at us.

'Hallo, Sahib, you want tea?'

It was Ang Dawa, the sirdar of the Camp 1 Sherpas. Our first concern was to ascertain that there had been no casualties and Ang Dawa assured us that his team were all well and in good spirits, but there was much hard digging to be done. It was a terrific boost to our morale to see how well they had coped with the situation and we congratulated them on their survival.

We descended a snow staircase and entered the narrow entrance of the Stormhaven kitchen-tent. At the far end an enormous dixie of water was bubbling on the top of two roaring primus stoves. It was warm in the tent and a pleasant relief to be sheltered from the buffeting of the wind and spindrift, which was still swirling outside. With the rise in temperature, the ice which was caked on our beards and woollen hats melted, and dribbled down our fronts. The steaming mugs of tea warmed our insides, and our hands clasped round the hot cups began to thaw out. We sat on some gear salvaged from the abandoned tents, which was arranged along the sides of the tent, with the Sherpas' personal kit. Ang Dawa told us how, during the worst night of the storm, they all had had to evacuate their tents in favour of the kitchen-tent and how, to save this last refuge from destruction, they had taken turns throughout the night, working in pairs, to keep it clear of snow.

We could imagine how miserable this experience must have been. The spindrift penetrates every nook and cranny of clothing, freezing whilst you are exposed to the cold and the wind, and then melting and soaking everything once you return to the warmth of the tent.

Fortified by the strong tea, we spent the rest of the day uncovering as much equipment as possible and then retired once more to the kitchen-tent, where the Camp 1 cook had been preparing a meal. He served up a special corned beef hash for Nick and myself, which we washed down with scalding sweet tea. There were ten of us, all sitting shoulder to shoulder, knees up to our chins, because all available floor space was taken up with steaming dixies, pans of rice and plates of sempi – the porridge-like dish of tsampa that the Sherpas live on.

At about 8.30 p.m., after everyone had eaten and drunk their fill, Ang Dawa said, 'You sleep here, Sahib.' I had expected to spend the night crouched in my present position. How on earth could we all stretch out in this confined space?

'We do whatever Sherpas do,' I said.

At a word from Ang Dawa, the entire tent erupted into activity. Kitchen and eating gear was polished, clean, large kettles and dixies were stacked inside one another and placed neatly aside, rucksacks were retrieved from behind food packs, and soon plastic-covered foam mattresses were spread out on the icy floor. Next, sleeping bags and all sorts of down equipment began to fill the area, and the floor level seemed to be raised a couple of feet. We joined in all this, and soon ten bodies were securely, warmly covered in down, lying head to toe, side by side, one on top of the other.

Sherpa heads popped up in the most unlikely places, between piles of down. Ang Dawa took the responsible position beside the tent entrance. We all chatted and smoked for about half an hour after we had settled in, as the light from a single kerosene candle flickered across the frost-encrusted canvas roof. Everything was organised. There was nothing to do but to get some sleep.

Back at Camp 2, although our situation was not nearly as uncomfortable as that at Camp 1, we had a much more tense day. It had started that morning, before Nick and Dave set out for Camp 1. A number of Sherpas had been sitting around in the Palace tent and Nick was trying to pack his rucksack, searching for gear in the chaos of kitchen equipment, other people's gear and the general clutter of a camp. Suddenly, he had erupted into a fury that was nearly hysterical.

'Come on, get the hell out of here, all of you – straight away!' he shouted at the Sherpas.

'Nick, for God's sake, calm down,' I said. 'We can't afford to put their backs up. They're only sheltering from the wind. They haven't got a communal tent.'

'Well, how the hell do you expect me to get all my stuff sorted out to go down to Camp 1?' he muttered. But his outburst had subsided. It had had very little to do with the presence of the Sherpas in the tent; it was the sup-pressed nervous tension of four days' hammering by the wind that had burst out, and it was to occur again before the day was out.

Just after Nick and Dave had left, Pasang was struggling with his recalci-trant stoves and allowed one of them to gush flames up to the roof, and throughout the kitchen compartment. This time it was Barney who blew up. He had become increasingly irritated by Pasang's low morale, and the trouble he had been having in keeping the kitchen going during the storm.

'Switch off the kerosene, before you burn the tent down,' we all shouted. Pasang did so but then, in a fury of rage, kicked the fuming stove across the tent smashing it beyond repair in the process. Barney's self-control broke down, and he told Pasang in fluent, and very violent Nepali, exactly what he thought of him. We could not understand it, but the meaning was all too clear!

Half an hour later, I was outside the tent, helping to dig out another buried tent, when I heard a babble of voices build into a crescendo of anger. Normally, I tried to keep out of day-to-day disputes, leaving them to Barney, who could speak the language and was handling all daily administration, but this was obviously something serious. I hurried over to find Barney surrounded by a group of shouting, near-hysterical Sherpas. It looked as if it could easily turn to violence.

'What's happened?' I asked.

'They say I hit Pertemba,' Barney said, looking drawn, near the point of breakdown.

'Did you?'

'Yes, but not on purpose. Pertemba had taken the tarpaulin covering the dump of gear to mend his tent. I was trying to persuade him that we needed it for the gear – if we have another snowfall we could lose a lot of stuff, if it's not covered up. I was explaining this to him, and in gesturing with this bit of tent pole, accidently hit him on the hand. I dropped the pole immediately, and apologised, but you'd think I'd stabbed him for all the fuss he made.'

'He did it on purpose,' Pertemba broke in furiously. 'Doctor Sahib hit me!'

'I saw it – it was on purpose,' shouted Anu. 'Doctor Sahib does not like Sherpas; he shouts at us and is rude to us. He doesn't treat us when we are sick.'

'Look, calm down, all of you,' I shouted over the din. 'Pertemba, Doctor Sahib is the good friend of the Sherpas. He would never hit you, it was a mistake.'

'It wasn't; he did it on purpose,' said Pertemba. His hands were trembling and I could see he was on the point of tears. There was no sense at all in any of the Sherpas. They were in a state of hysteria, created by the hammering we had received in the last four days. All I could do was to try and soothe them and Barney down. I talked for half an hour, trying to bring home to them the wonderful, selfless work Barney had done on their behalf in looking after them when they had been sick or injured, and in running Camp 2 generally. Eventually, they all calmed down, and Pertemba even shook hands with Barney. I felt completely drained by the experience, and was trembling myself when I got back into the big Palace tent.

I suspect we needed that outburst, for that night, when all the Sherpas piled into the Palace tent for the evening meal and chat, there was a feeling of renewed optimism and real friendship. Everyone went out of their way to be pleasant to each other, as if to make up for the fury of the morning. The wind had dropped, and there was hardly a puff of spindrift blown from the summit walls of Nuptse and Lhotse. There was not a cloud in the sky, and as the line of sunlight crept up the South West Face of Everest and the great hanging glacier of Lhotse it turned from a rich yellow to a mellow rose. The sky darkened into the deepest purple and a sickle moon hung poised over the South Col. It was difficult to believe there had ever been a storm and wind, and savage argument in the still, silent dusk. That night

Pasang excelled himself in his cooking and we excelled ourselves in the expression of our appreciation. The unity of the group, so fragile under stress, was restored.

But I could not relax completely. I had to plan our next moves, was beginning to wonder already if I had been over-pessimistic about the progress we could make in the lee of the storm. That night, on the radio, we agreed that Dave and Nick would go down to meet the Sherpas and Dougal, who would try to re-open the route up the Icefall. That day they had only got halfway up, to find that another sérac collapse was endangering the route. Meanwhile, Mick and Doug were going to move up to Camp 3 on their way up to Camp 4, and Graham, who had now been alone for a week, was to return to Camp 2 for a rest.

We all slept well that night, the first quiet night for a fortnight. The next day, Jimmy Roberts reported that the French were making their summit bid on Pumo Ri. We could see them through the binoculars, tiny little black dots moving slowly but surely up the summit snow cone of the mountain, which was only a little higher than our Camp 3. They had completed their objective; we had barely started. This did mean, however, that we should be able to borrow some of the box tents they had with them. Talking it over with Hamish on the mid-day radio call, we agreed that since we could buy at least three box tents from the French, now that they had succeeded and would need them no longer, we could abandon our plans for using his own reinforced home-made box, and concentrate on making progress as fast as possible up the mountain.

It is amazing how quickly pessimism can turn into optimism with a change in the weather. At the height of the storm, although I don't think any of us contemplated giving up our attempt, everything had seemed as black as possible. Camp 4 would be a total write-off, it was going to take several days to resume communications through the Icefall, and at least a week to deploy; and yet, once the storm ended and the sun blazed down once more into the Western Cwm, it all seemed so different. We were full of hope once more. Perhaps the boxes at Camp 4 could be salvaged; perhaps we could start pushing the route out in the next day or so.

Next day, Doug and Mick were due to go up to Camp 3 on their way back up the mountain, while I was going down towards Camp 1 with four of our Sherpas, to meet those sent up by Dave and Nick. In turn they were going to drop down towards Base, to meet the Sherpas coming up. In carrying out this seemingly innocuous task, I had my own narrowest escape on the mountain. The Sherpas were all roped together but, in common with all the climbers, I had not bothered and was stepping off the beaten track from time to time to take pictures of the Sherpas plodding through the snows, silhouetted against the sun which was hanging over the parapets of Nuptse.

We were about halfway down the Western Cwm when I stepped off the track once again and suddenly found myself with my head just below the surface of the snow. It happened too suddenly for me to be frightened, but I realised that I did not dare move or struggle, for fear of disturbing the surrounding snow which held me in place over the hidden crevasse.

'Give me a pull,' I shouted, and the Sherpas edged towards the hole I had made, tossed me a loop of rope and pulled me out. I was landed, like a panting codfish, shaking slightly from the shock of my near escape. I was even more shaken when I looked into the abyss I had uncovered. The crevasse, dark and hell-like, stretched out into black shadows from the tiny hole I had made in its roof. Had the snow not held me, I could have fallen 30m or so. I took a photograph of the hole and we trooped on down the Western Cwm, careful to stay on the track. That moment of inattention, caused by concentrating on photography rather than the route, had very nearly cost me my life. Down we went, to the porters who had come up from Camp 1, full of grins, laden with much-needed food and, even more important, the mail. I shoved the latter in my pack-frame so that I could let Doug and Mick have their letters before they set off for Camp 3.

About halfway back I began to feel the need for a rest. Pausing, I sat on the pack-frame and then, like a small boy looking for Christmas presents, went through the mail to see if I had a letter from my wife, Wendy. There were two; I opened them with frozen fingers, clumsy with cold and excitement, fumbled with the envelope, dropped it and saw it blow away, across trackless snow. With no thought for hidden crevasses, I just dived after the letter, spreadeagled in the snow as I grabbed at it, reached it and then lay there as I read, tearful in my emotion at hearing from home.

Once at Camp 2, there were decisions to make. On the way down and back, I had spent much of the time deciding how I could speed up the run out towards Camp 5 and yet, at the same time, re-adjust the pairing so that each pair would be getting the objective which they had come to accept as their own. I described my predicament in my diary that night:

1 November 1972 – Wednesday.
A right bloody mess I've made – a real cock-up. The problem is, I've sent Nick and Dave, slightly against their wills – or rather, very much against their wills – down to Camp 1 when, in actual fact, it would probably have been wiser to have sent Doug and Mick straight back down even though they had just come up the previous day. The trouble is, by sending Nick and Dave back down, now that the weather's really good, I've got two carefully balanced teams out of sequence. Now that we've got some movement going, the obvious thing is for Mick and Doug to be pushed up to get Camp 4 started. Originally, we agreed that they should do this, and spend two or three days sorting out Camp 4, so that Nick and Dave could move through. But

there shouldn't be three or four days' work – we really need to be pushing out as fast as we possibly can, taking advantage of what good weather we have in the few remaining days before it gets desperately cold.

Doug and Mick went up yesterday with the agreement that they should just spend two or three days, and then come back. But then, last night, Graham came down from Camp 3 bubbling over, obviously having done a lot of thinking, and he put across the very strong point of view that we should be pushing out fast. I had already been thinking of sending up two Sherpas today from Camp 2, straight up to 4, so that Doug and Mick would have their help to speed things up. Graham made me think that we really should send four Sherpas and get the whole camp sorted out so that, ideally, they could make a carry to Camp 5 tomorrow and thus hurry the move up to Camp 5. But, of course, this immediately brings up the problem of Nick and Dave. One way, of course, would be for Doug and Mick to do the route from Camps 5 to 6 and for Nick and Dave to do the Rock Band – they are undoubtedly quite as capable as Doug and Mick – but, and this is a very big 'but' – Doug and Mick have always been promised the Rock Band, and have come to accept it. In addition, although I don't think Doug and Mick are any better mountaineers than Dave and Nick, they might be just that bit more determined – I don't know.

Anyway, it has caused an unholy row, and the most obvious thing now seems to be to get the thing back to its original pattern – to give Dave and Nick the route to Camp 6, and Doug and Mick the actual Rock Band. I pushed around various ways of doing this last night, slightly defensive against Graham urging me to change my plan but, at the same time, feeling that it was necessary and saying so at the seven o'clock call last night.

The problem I was trying to solve was how to get Nick and Dave back into the front, without holding up our advance. It was 1 November, the day that Mick and Doug were to move back up to Camp 4. Having sent four Sherpas up to Camp 4 that same day, I was hoping that on the following day they would be able to make the carry to Camp 5 and the day after that, actually move in. Nick and Dave, however, were only due to reach Camp 2 that day (1 November), having the previous day fulfilled an important task in going down to meet Dougal and Hamish and then transporting the loads by means of an aerial rope-way across the big crevasse immediately below Camp 1. This crevasse had opened up, from being about a metre wide to 15m, in a matter of weeks. Getting back to Camp 2 on 1 November meant that the soonest they could possibly reach Camp 5 would be 4 November, the day after Mick and Doug had reached it. This seemed a sound compromise, for it seemed unlikely that Doug and Mick would be able to run the full route out to Camp 6 in the day they were there by themselves, and this would give Dave and Nick the satisfaction of completing that route as originally planned.

I explained all this on the radio call of the morning of 1 November. Unfortunately, Doug infuriated Nick by making the claim, 'We do want the Rock Band because we've been planning on it, and Mick wants to film it,' a sentiment which was perfectly fair. (In fact, I also wanted Mick to film it.) This, however, made Nick see red; he wrote in his diary: 'This remark made me fume with rage. I switched off the radio in a huff. Fumed all the way up the Cwm and, as a result, did the walk in three and a half hours, in spite of drifting and a not very good path.'

I knew all too well that I was going to have an angry Nick on my hands when he arrived at Camp 2, even though I had tried to restore the original plan. My fears were amply justified. I had taken the precaution of keeping an eye out for him and went down to meet him, getting in the first broadside by apologising for having had to send him down to Camp 1. Nick was literally trembling with rage, feeling that he had been supplanted by Doug and Mick. The root of Nick's indignation was the fact that I had given Doug and Mick the key role in the first place and was now maintaining it, when Nick had every right to feel that he deserved such a role every bit as much. He also pointed out that he had probably made the greatest sacrifice to come on the expedition, having come without pay. In actual fact, this put him in the same position as the rest of us, with the exception of Kelvin. On the other hand, all of us who earned a living partly around climbing would benefit very directly from the expedition.

In the mess tent I was backed up by Barney and Graham, as we cooled Nick down and tried to show him that in reality the original plan had hardly been changed. Even so, I could fully sympathise with his anger, and suspect that I would have felt much the same had I been in his shoes. Dave Bathgate, who arrived at Camp 2 about half an hour after Nick, was much more resigned than his partner, murmuring: 'Well, someone had to go down there – I suppose it might just as well have been us.'

The argument had cleared the air and anyway the objective, combined with our residual friendship, was too strong to disrupt our effort. That night we settled down to our evening meal with a feeling of restored harmony. The weather was perfect; Graham in a single day at Camp 2 had re-organised the camp, sorting out all the loads, putting up a special store tent and creating his own logistic empire. Success, once again, seemed within our grasp.

14

Return to the face

31 October – 7 November

Across the face, the wind gusted at over sixty miles per hour, blowing up clouds of spindrift, blinding the climbers and making any form of work on the wrecked camp site impossible. Mick and Doug had taken four hours to plod up the line of fixed ropes to Camp 4 – ropes which had to be cleared of snow every foot of the way; jumars were perpetually iced up, so that they slipped ineffectively on the ropes. Behind the climbers were fifteen Sherpas, all of whom had come up from Camp 2, to pick up loads stockpiled at 3, to carry them on up to Camp 4. This meant that they climbed 1100m (3600ft) in the day, a truly magnificent effort on their part, and one which they were to repeat on alternate days for the next ten days.

The tension and arguments born from our five storm-bound days were forgotten; we were looking forward once more, full of optimism in spite of the cold and wind, and the lateness of the season.

It was five o'clock in the afternoon before Doug and Mick reached Camp 4. Down in the Western Cwm, Camp 2 had been plunged into shadow for some hours, and the shadow line was already lapping up the face. The Sherpas who had carried loads up to the camp, dumped them wherever they could, tying them to the frames of the platforms, digging out little ledges in the hard snow, and then went whooping down the fixed ropes towards the relative comfort of Camp 2. But Doug and Mick with the two Sherpas Ang Phurba and Anu, who were staying up with them, had a long task in front of them before they could creep into the shelter of the boxes.

From below, the boxes had looked in reasonable shape, slightly mis-shapen but still erect, brightly coloured huts clinging to the slope. On reaching them, however, Mick and Doug discovered that the boxes were filled with spindrift, like snow cubes parcelled in canvas. The frames of two of them had collapsed, and the snow inside had set as hard as concrete, hiding all the stoves and cooking pans left behind when the camp had been abandoned. There was no sign of any of the stores which had been carried up to Camp 4 before the storm; these, also, were concealed under the compacted spindrift. In some ways it was worse than establishing a camp from scratch; poles were bent, sockets jammed with ice, vital pieces missing – and the line of shadow creeping up the face was a tide of darkness that would bring an instant drop in temperature. Fingers and toes were already nipped, but you couldn't hurry; everything had to be systematic; anything dropped was lost for ever. If you slipped, having forgotten to clip on to one of the safety ropes, you'd go all the way down to the bottom of the Cwm.

They dug out the tents, hacking away with the picks of their axes, then clearing the rubble with gloved hands, sifting it for parts of cooking stoves, movie cameras, pots and items of personal equipment. Then they had to re-erect the boxes, manipulating frames to make the canvas fit over them. Six o'clock; time for the radio call. Doug opened up.

'Hello 2, this is 4. Can you hear me? Over.'

'Yes, you're loud and clear, how's it going?'

'Bloody desperate. We still haven't got anywhere to sleep tonight. Must close now; we'll open up in a couple of hours.'

And they went back to digging in the mellow evening sunlight, which gave only the illusion of warmth.

It was dark before they had patched up two boxes for the night – they still had to sort out stoves and cooking pots, collect snow for the evening brew and lie and wait for it to melt. It was ten o'clock at night before they had completed their meal and could curl up in their sleeping bags for a well-earned sleep. Not surprising that they missed the eight o'clock call next morning.

Even though tired from the effort of the previous day, Doug, with two Sherpas, made a carry up to Camp 5, while Mick, with the other two, did his best to dig out all the gear left at Camp 4 before the storm. I was particularly anxious to learn exactly what we had at Camp 4, for my own planning of the build-up to Camp 5. With Doug's carry, we had just enough gear at 5 for him to move up with Mick on the following day, and this is what they did.

And so they had another camp to establish, this time from scratch. A platform had to be dug, tents erected, all in the chilling cold. But at least Camp 5 was a more relaxing place than 4; it was situated in the shelter of an overhanging rock wall, on what must have been a broad rock ledge, covered in snow. While Mick dug out a platform, Doug ranged around taking photographs.

Attempting to get more in the frame of the camera, he stepped back, but still not getting quite enough, stepped back again, over the edge! Unroped, without his axe, it was fortunate that he had removed his gloves to take the pictures. He shot down the fifty-degree slope of hard snow, towards a vertical drop of about 600m leading to the slopes below, a fall which he could never have survived.

With bare hands clawing at the snow, he kicked in with his cramponed boots and somehow, on the very brink of the drop, brought himself to a stop. He was still sufficiently cool to take a unique photograph looking straight down at Camp 4, 450m below, before kicking back up to the ledge!

Mick, digging away at the snow, had been blissfully unaware of this near-fatal accident. That night, they were both badly shaken by the experience, exhausted by the effort of making the camp, and chilled by the bitter cold of Camp 5. Up to this point Doug had fought shy of sleeping tablets, never trusting them, but now, perhaps in a state of shock and because of the savage cold, even inside the tent, he took three, which knocked him out for the night.

Next morning, 5 November, dawned fine, without a breath of wind on the mountain. My build-up seemed to be working out. Nick and Dave had spent the night at Camp 4 and were moving up to 5 to join Mick and Doug; Graham Tiso was moving up to Camp 4 to look after the camp and supervise the Sherpas. I was still at Camp 2, anxious to supervise the build-up from the orchestra stalls, though I was planning to move up to Camp 5 when the route had been established to 6. Things never go completely according to plan, however. I spent most of the morning examining the upper part of the face through binoculars, anxious to see Mick and Doug start out on making the route back across the Great Central Gully towards Camp 6. It was easy to be impatient in the hot sun at Camp 2. It was very different up at Camp 5.

Because of the overhang guarding the camp, the sun did not reach it until two o'clock in the afternoon. Before that time, the camp was held in a vice of cool shadows which made movement outside the tents a refined form of torture; hands inside gloves, feet inside boots and overboots froze in a matter of seconds once outside the shelter of the tent. That morning Doug, having missed the eight o'clock call, finally came up at nine o'clock sounding punch-drunk with cold and altitude; the sleeping pills, also, must have had an effect.

He reported that they had managed to pitch a tent but had got mild frostbite in the process.

'You don't get the sun up here till after two. It's bloody cold at the moment. Your hands and feet freeze even if you go out of the tent for a couple of minutes.'

'Will you get out today?'

'We'll try, but you've no idea how cold it is.'

That had to satisfy me. It seemed a perfect day, not a breath of wind, not a sign of spindrift from the peaks around us. I spent most of the day gazing up at the Great Gully leading up to the Rock Band above Camp 5. To reach the snow rake that led across the base of the Rock Band, they would have to traverse back to the left over the top of the gully, to get beneath a subsidiary rock wall, before traversing back again over the camp and on towards the site of Camp 6. I could see the slow-moving figures of Nick, Dave and two

Sherpas, the latter doing a carry to Camp 5, the former moving up to join Doug and Mick – but there was no sign of movement from Camp 5. As the day wore on, it became increasingly obvious that they were not going to leave camp. I felt all the frustration of the commander sitting in the lush comfort of his headquarters, watching and wanting to drive on the troops in the front line. Not being there myself I was unable to implement my plans, not being fully aware of just how savage were the conditions there. In the last day or so we were becoming aware that we barely had the carrying capacity and drive to make more than one serious attempt at cracking the Rock Band and then making a summit bid.

So far, in keeping with my basic plan I had held Hamish and Dougal back, but could I afford to hold them back as a reserve any longer? I felt that I could not – they were fit, the most experienced pair I had, and raring to go. Whichever pair moved up to Camp 6, they were going to have to move quickly and decisively on the Rock Band, if they were to make a summit assault. A delay at this stage meant that our chances of making such an assault must inevitably recede, for we simply did not have the capability of sustaining the supply of oxygen bottles from Camp 4 to 5, and then to 6. The trouble was that even climbers resting at Camp 5 used up oxygen, for it was essential to sleep on oxygen, not just for sleep itself, but also to retain warmth. The human body without extra oxygen is unable to sustain its warmth at that altitude, no matter how much down gear covers it.

And so I knew that I should have to adapt my plans; use Mick, Doug, Nick and Dave to establish the route to Camp 6, and then supersede Mick and Doug by bringing Hamish and Dougal straight through for the push on the Rock Band. I was under no illusion about the problems that this change in the plan would cause, for I knew that Mick and Doug had set their hearts on having first go at the Rock Band.

That evening at the five o'clock call Doug told me on the radio, 'I'm sorry we didn't get out today. Mick has got bad piles. We're buggered; we're going to have to come down for a rest.'

'Can't you stay up for just a few more days – just to support Nick and Dave in making the route up to Camp 6.'

'It's no good, we're in a really bad way. Both of us have mild frostbite. It's been a hell of a job just getting the camps up. We've had to work into the night. You've no idea how bloody awful conditions are up here. We must have a rest before tackling the Rock Band.'

Then I made a tactical mistake.

'Look, Doug, I'm going to have to push Dougal and Hamish up to try the Rock Band; we just can't afford to keep them in reserve any longer. Can't you keep going for just a few more days to make the route up to 6 and then keep them supported?'

There was a silence for a couple of minutes – Doug was obviously talking it over with Mick, and then Mick's voice came over the radio:

'Up to your old tricks, is it, Chris?' he said.

This was a reference to my decision on the Annapurna South Face expedition to push Don Whillans and Dougal Haston through to the front when the rest of the team seemed to be tiring.

'It's not a question of that,' I said. 'It's simply that you and Doug are obviously tired and that we can't afford to hang around. Dougal and Hamish are the best rested pair and it's time they had a go out in front.'

'But they're not acclimatised,' said Mick. 'If they come straight up here from Camp 1, they're going to have trouble and will probably go no better than us.'

'I'm sorry, Mick, I disagree. They've been once to Camp 5 without trouble and I think they'll do it again. We can carry this argument on when you get back down.'

And so it ended. I didn't relish Doug's and Mick's return when, no doubt, they would present me with the full broadsides of their arguments. That night Nick, who had reached Camp 5 in the late afternoon with Dave, commented in his diary:

Mick and Doug both invalids; I suspect a bit psyched out by cold and altitude. Doug had a headache and Mick, piles. Also their stove kaput. They want to go down tomorrow.

It was a long evening as we had to cook for them as well – very cold (suspect less than –30°C) and there aren't enough foam mats. More to say, but have cold hands.

Next morning Nick was so impressed by the cold that he broke into the eight o'clock call while I was talking to Graham at Camp 4.

'This is Nick at 5, this is Nick at 5, I must come in please, I must come in.'

'OK. Nick, what's the trouble? Over.'

'It's quite incredibly cold up here. You can have no idea how cold it is,' he said. 'We must have more sleeping bags and foams. You need two sleeping bags each and a double thickness of foams. One of the stoves has broken down as well. We must have two stoves to each tent.'

'OK Nick, we'll get these up to you as soon as possible. Can you get out today?'

'Doug and I are going to run the rope out towards the Rock Band, while Mick films us, and Dave sorts out the camp site. We've only got two oxygen sets working at the moment. Doug's has packed up, and one of those we brought up from Camp 4 isn't working properly. Doug and Mick want to come down today after doing their bit of work.'

'OK. Pertemba and Jangbo will join you today. They've got Graham's and my oxygen sets.'

Doug had felt a lot better that morning and was keen to contribute to the day's climbing before coming back down for a rest. Dougal and Hamish also had been influenced by the previous evening's radio call. They had heard Mick's comment about their lack of acclimatisation, and, perhaps partly to prove him wrong, had come storming up to Camp 2 in a mere hour and a half from Camp 1. The previous day they had spent trying to safeguard the route from the Icefall.

There was no wind, but a light veil of cloud hid the top of Everest as we all prepared to sit it out, gazing up, impotent to influence events, at the climbers working from Camp 5.

Nick described the day in his diary:

Woke 5 a.m. when the oxygen ran out, shivered for one and a half hours, and then got up to make a brew; view at sunrise, mind-blowing. Eventually, set off with Doug to make the route. It was very cold for the sun was hidden by cloud clinging to the top of Everest.

We ran out about 600ft [180m] of rope diagonally, back left across to the end of the little Rock Band, at the start of the long rake going back below the Rock Band. Here there were a few old ropes draped across the bare rocks left by the previous expedition. My turn to lead. I climbed the rocks, partly pulling on the ropes, until a few feet up. I must have pulled too hard; a peg came out and I teetered backwards, almost off balance, but somehow managed to lunge into the rock. After that I stopped using the rope and climbed the pitch more or less properly. It was quite hard and the first really technical climbing I had done since the Icefall. It wasn't made any easier by the oxygen kit upsetting my balance and the mask and goggles constantly frosting up. Right at the top the rock became crumbly and I had to make a very precarious mantelshelf on to a ledge covered with ice.

Doug then came up and ran out the next reel of rope all the way to the foot of the Rock Band. I followed but my oxygen gave out when I still had a hundred feet to go (I had started out on a three-quarters full tank). I suppose there wasn't really much point in my struggling up to Doug's high point, but somehow it seemed such a tangible end to the day, to be there at the foot of the Rock Band. There was too the thought, always in the back of my mind, that perhaps I would never ever get any higher. Moreover, having a few pegs with me it seemed logical to leave them at the high point, though that was a justification more than anything else. I just wanted to get there and touch the Rock Band. Without oxygen, every step was an effort – only a hundred feet, yet it never seemed to get any closer; I was shattered when I reached it. That day we had run about 1200ft and reached around 26,700ft [8140m]. Also I had come up from 1900ft in only five days.

I was very tired by the time I got back to Camp 5. Doug had already pushed on down for Camp 2. Graham Tiso was there and said that the temperature that morning at Camp 4 had been –38ºC. That means that our temperature must have been around –45ºC.

Graham had new crampon straps for me and I put them on then and there, while the camp was still in the sun, scared of how cold it would be in the morning. Even so, I nearly got frostbitten fingers in the process, and my fingers were tender all next day.

At about 8 p.m. the Sherpas who have replaced Doug and Mick called me out, asking about how their sleeping oxygen gear worked. I gave them half-an-hour's pep talk and blundered around in the dark looking for the oxygen kit.

It was a very tiring day.

Meanwhile back at Camp 2, Doug and Mick had arrived. That night they accepted my change in plan without comment, though Doug asked several searching questions about my plans for the next few days. Next morning, however, he came into the sleeping compartment I was sharing with Barney.

'Can I talk about our role on the mountain?' he said.

'Yes.'

'Look, I've been looking forward to doing the Rock Band for two and a half months now, and had got it firmly fixed in my mind that I was going to do it. I don't see really why we shouldn't – I don't see that anything's changed. We could go straight up tomorrow.'

'But Doug, if you needed a rest so badly, how can you possibly have had one if you stay down here only a day? It just doesn't make sense.'

'But you've been planning this all along; it's as Mick said, you're up to your old tricks again. In some ways you're no better than Herrligkoffer in the way you're manipulating people.'

And so it went on. Eventually I saw red and suggested that if that was how he felt he should start heading for Kathmandu. Barney just sat there quietly, sympathetic and friendly, the mere presence of him providing a calming influence.

As Doug and I reached a climax to our argument, we temporised, each of us realising that we could not afford to break up the expedition, but more, I think, we both valued the relationship and friendship we had built up over the previous weeks and realised the danger of destroying this. I tried to explain to him how badly we were up against it, and how this now seemed the only course open.

Eventually Doug said, 'Well it'll take a day or so to get used to the idea,' and we left it at that. I felt grateful to him for his acceptance of something about which he obviously still disagreed. Later on that day Mick looked in.

'I disagree with what you've done, but I've had enough of arguments.'

'Thanks, Mick,' I said, 'I appreciate how you feel.'

This had been a real test for the expedition. Whether I had been right or wrong in my decision is immaterial. The important factor was that Doug and Mick, though believing me to be wrong, were able not only to accept my decision but then to give Hamish and Dougal their loyal support. Perhaps most important of all, we remained friends, after having had what could easily have been a bitter row.

Meanwhile, back on the face it was as cold as ever. Graham at Camp 4 was matter-of-fact and cheerful, having made a carry to Camp 5 without using oxygen, admittedly with a nominal load. His main function was just to sit it out at the camp, supervising the Sherpas. Up to this point the Sherpas had two successive carries before returning to Camp 2 for a well-earned rest. We were trying to persuade them to make three. We were getting magnificent help from the Sherpas at this stage of the expedition, both on the 2 to 4 run and the one from Camp 4 to 5.

Up at Camp 5, Dave Bathgate was going to try to force the route out towards Camp 6. That night he wrote in his diary:

Up as early as possible, then start to kit out the Sherpas (Pertemba and Jangbo) with oxygen. They have not used it before; what a place to learn! We wasted almost two hours in the freezing cold, fitting them up before we set out, just after 1.30 in the afternoon. My oxygen set started to pack in (iced up); I managed to fix it so that day I did get a proper flow. At Nick's high point, I decided to run out the old nylon (I think German) rope. It was iced up and tangled but if I hadn't done it others might be reluctant to use it under these conditions. Just as the sun dropped below Nuptse I had run out the nylon and started on the big white reel. It's a clean run on snow all the way up to Camp 6, but it was also very nearly dark. We got back to 5 before total darkness, very cold and tired but Nick had the brew on.

They were cold and tired but they knew the kind of contentment you always gained when out in front. The struggle was simple, rewarding and very positive.

Back at Camp 2, I was grappling with the problems of our supply line. Chris Brasher had arrived the previous day, after a night at Camp 1, bustling with energy.

'It strikes me you've got very little time to make your summit bid. Shouldn't you get Hamish and Dougal up there fast?' he suggested.

'It's not quite as simple as that, Chris,' I replied. 'It's no good having them up at Camp 6 unless they have the wherewithal to actually make some progress with enough oxygen, fixed rope and food to keep them going. At the moment we still haven't even got the route run out.'

The problem was that we could only just sustain four Sherpas at Camp 4 with Graham; in turn, these could barely keep up with the needs of four climbers actually in residence at Camp 5, let alone build up the stockpile of oxygen and fixed rope needed at Camp 6. There seemed only one solution, to build up Camp 5 before sending Hamish and Dougal up, supported by Doug and Mick. And then I thought of a way of speeding up the process at least a little. The Sherpas at Camp 4 should be able to support two climbers at 5, and at the same time, build up enough gear for the two at 5 to start ferrying loads up to Camp 6. And so I made my plan. I hoped that Nick and Dave would complete the route to Camp 6 that day, and I, with the Sherpa Ang Phurba, was going to set out on the journey up the face, to occupy Camp 5 and, I hoped, make the three carries that I calculated would be needed to stock 6, ready for Dougal and Hamish to move in. It would take me three days to reach Camp 5, but in that time the Sherpas at Camp 4 would have further time to stock the camp. What a web of logistics – and yet these have their own fascination. The problem was to implement these plans, forcing one's resolve against the harsh wind, the effects of altitude, and the growing fatigue caused by the two months' struggle.

Back at Camp 5, it was to be Nick's and Dave's big day; for them, in all probability, the end of the expedition. Their goal was not the summit of Everest – just the site of Camp 6. That night, Dave headed his entry in his diary – 'Tuesday 7 November. This is the day of triumph and disaster.'

On this, their third day at Camp 5, they knew their strength and determination were being steadily drained by the bitter cold. Nick wrote in his diary: 'This was to be our big day. All four of us were to make a shit or bust attempt for 6 using the French oxygen. We were set up, and ready to leave at 10 a.m.! Quite an achievement.'

But as so often happens at altitude, there were endless delays. They were planning to use the French oxygen bottles we had brought with us for the final stages on the mountain. We had two types, 170 bottles made by the British firm Luxfer; each weighed 7.5 kilos and had a capacity of around 1200 litres. The French bottles, left over from my Annapurna South Face expedition, weighed only 5.5 kilos, yet carried nearly 1000 litres. Since they had a definite capacity weight ratio advantage, we were hoping to use the latter high on the mountain, where the weight on your back becomes critical. We had a specially designed thread converter, which enabled us to use the French bottles with our American oxygen units. Hamish had tried these out at Base Camp, where they had worked satisfactorily but now, at altitude, perhaps because of the extreme cold, it was impossible to screw the adaptors tight enough either to the French bottles or to the American reducer valves. There was no choice, therefore, but to use what British bottles there were. Unfortunately, there were only three, one of which had a pressure of only 200 psi, when maximum capacity was 3000; another had a pressure of 1800, and the third was full.

By this time, Nick and Dave were both cursing but there was nothing they could do about it except make do with the bottles, for they were still determined to make the push for Camp 6. They explained the problem to the Sherpas who agreed to take one 100m rope each (weighing about 7 kilos a time) without using oxygen, a truly magnificent and very loyal gesture. Dave took the full bottle and Nick took the half-full one, but just as they were ready to set out, Dave began having trouble with his demand valve – it was not functioning properly. They had already lost half the morning; and so Nick set out with Pertemba and Jangbo, leaving Dave to catch up. But Dave's misfortune was not finished. Fingers and mind numbed with cold, he fumbled with his pack-frame, trying to pack it, then dropped it, and watched it toboggan down the slope, out of sight. But he didn't give up – there's a dogged quality in Dave. He improvised a harness for the oxygen bottle and set out after the others. He never caught up with them, however, and continued to experience trouble with the set until it finally packed up altogether. By that time, he was so far behind that he could fulfil no useful function on the climb and therefore decided to return. On the way back he improved the fixed rope, safeguarding some of the long traverses by placing intermediate anchor points, one of them his own axe. As it turned out, it was providential that he did turn back.

Meanwhile, out in front, Nick was making good progress, reaching Dave's high point at about 1 p.m. The view was incredible, for he could now look over the wall of Nuptse at the serried peaks beyond, Ama Dablam, slender and delicate, Kantega more massive and a hundred other mountains he couldn't identify. In the far distance, to the south, mountains merged into the haze of the Indian plains. There was no wind and the sun even seemed to have a touch of warmth in its empty glare.

Uncoiling one of the 100m ropes, he set off round the corner, Pertemba paying it out as he climbed, scrambling over a series of small rocky outcrops that protruded from the snows just below the base of the Rock Band. The Rock Band itself towered above, grey-black slaty rock, steep, seemingly unclimbable at that altitude – it was hard enough crossing comparatively easy snow slopes. Having run out 100m, the rope tugged taut and Nick looked around for somewhere to anchor it. The snow was shallow, a crusty shell over the slate-like rock. He found a rocky encrustation, managed to hammer a rock peg into a crack and tied the end to it.

Whilst the two Sherpas climbed to join him, using the rope as a handrail, he could regain his breath, watch Dave, now far behind, still plodding very very slowly up towards them; then he looked across the snow slope stretching beneath the Rock Band, towards a rocky spur that thrust down from the barrier which barred our way to the summit. That marked the site of Camp 6. Somewhere up there, folded in the angle of the wall, must be the gully which Dougal had assured us led through the Rock Band, a snow-paved gateway through Everest's most formidable obstacle. Nick looked across, but his curiosity was dulled by the sheer fatigue of altitude. His target was Camp 6.

The Sherpas arrived, going strong in spite of the fact that they were without oxygen. Nick set out once again, trailing the second 100m rope behind him. The going was now quite straightforward, across a slope of crisp snow, little more than forty degrees in angle. His cramponed boots bit reassuringly into the snow and it was just a question of plodding slowly, one foot in front of the other. But after only fifty paces, his oxygen ran out, leaving 7 kilos of useless metal on his back. Taking off his pack-frame, he disconnected the cylinder and hurled it down the slope; because of the long traverse, there was no risk of hitting anyone lower down on the mountain. He carried on, immediately feeling much colder because of the lack of oxygen, but at least the pack was lighter.

He climbed a further 100m and was now about halfway across that final slope. He anchored the rope to a snow stake and the two Sherpas followed up. There were now only two ropes left – no point in both of the Sherpas staying, so Nick sent Jangbo back, to start making a brew for Pertemba on his return. Nick tied together the two ropes, one length of 100m and the other 40, and set off once again.

He wrote in his diary:

I was obsessed with the need to reach Camp 6, and didn't notice the time. Eventually, forty feet short of 6, the rope went tight, so assuming I had run out all 470ft, stopped to put in a deadman. I took my rucksack off, to take out the dozen pegs that were in it to leave at the high point. I fumbled and dropped the rucksack, which held my oxygen unit and spare gear, and watched it cartwheeling down the slope out of sight. I very nearly cried, I was so disgusted with my mistake; I'd never dropped anything like that before in all the time I'd been climbing. Then I pulled in the rope so that I could tie it as tautly as possible to the deadman, and fully forty feet came in – it must have been sticking somewhere when I had pulled it before and I could have got all the way to Camp 6 after all. In restrospect, though, it's just as well I didn't, since that last forty feet could easily have taken half an hour, and later on that length of time could have made all the difference between being dead and staying alive.

It was only then that I realised how late it was getting. The sun was dropping below the mountains on the far horizon. I actually said to myself, 'That is an absolutely fantastic view – but you shouldn't be seeing it – not from here anyway.' It's incredible how much colder it gets the moment the sun goes down. And it chose that very moment to start blowing. At first it wasn't too bad, but by the time I had got back to Pertemba, the wind was unbearable. We were having to go back straight into it, and it wasn't in gusts; it was a continuous blast of spindrift; you couldn't open your eyes, couldn't face into it.

Pertemba seemed in a befuddled state from the long wait and the lack of oxygen. I said, 'We'll get down fast now Pertemba,' and led the way down. The descent was a nightmare; it was pitch dark and you were handling the karabiners with totally numb hands. It wouldn't have been so bad if we'd been going straight down, but most of the way back entailed traversing, with long gaps between the anchors. If we'd slipped, we'd have fallen quite a distance before the rope went tight. You couldn't wait for the gusts to die out, for the wind was now continuous, you just rushed on down, completely blind, into the wind. It was a matter of each man for himself; there was nothing we could do for each other. We were both very tired and I must admit I just charged off and left Pertemba behind. I feel a bit guilty now, but at the time if anything had gone wrong I don't think I could have done anything about it anyway; he just came about ten minutes behind. It was fantastically cold, pitch dark, with that howling wind and driving spindrift. God, I was relieved to see the tent, and hear Dave and Jangbo shout 'Hello, hello'. The zip door opened and there was this black hole, through which I just threw myself, crampons and all, and lay down in the dark. I cried in my relief at getting back.

Dave was very relieved to see me. He had spent the last hour holding the box up. A whipcrack of wind had lifted up the floor of the box with him lying on it, and had smashed the frame. After this he had had to hold it up braced across the box. Even so, he had a brew ready for me. We sat there, holding the sides of the tent up; I had a lovely hot drink clutched in my hands, but my hands, not just my fingers, were numb, likewise my feet from my ankles downwards: I was very worried about them. I thawed my hands out, gradually over the course of the evening; I was too cowardly to do it quickly; it's too painful that way.

And then Pertemba got back; that was a relief; I should never have forgiven myself if anything had happened to him. I crawled into the Sherpa tent next door, which was as warm as toast, being a double-skinned Tunnel tent, not a box like ours. We then had our evening pill ceremony; this was a regular feature, in which we gave them sleeping tablet, vitamin tablet, iron tablet, salt tablet, and a headache pill if they needed one. It showed that we were concerned about them, and helped to build up a real friendship. We got very close to those two Sherpas in those few days on the expedition. I felt we had built up a real friendship.

I had a long chat with Pertemba. He made a very relevant remark when he said: 'We nearly died.'

And we bloody well did. If I had been able to pull that extra forty feet of rope through first time off and had actually reached the site of Camp 6 – and I should have done, I was in that kind of mood – we should probably have started down two hours later, and I think under those circumstances we should have been lucky to survive.

But at last they did have some luck. After they had sat up for a couple of hours, holding their box up against the gusting wind, it dropped, then vanished. Using the remainder of Dave's oxygen bottle, they were able to drop off to sleep till next morning.

There was no question of their staying up at Camp 5 to help build up supplies. Next morning Nick's hands and feet were still numb and white. He undoubtedly had frostbite; it was just a question of how bad it was. Dave's feet also were numb. As far as they were concerned the expedition was over, for it was unlikely that either would recover in time to be able to return to the face before its outcome was decided one way or the other.

There is a wind chill scale which gives the effective temperature caused by wind, combined with cold. That previous night the temperature had probably been round about −40°C and the wind had been gusting at anything up to a hundred miles per hour – the special Indian weather forecast had given winds of 220 kilometres per hour over the summit of Everest that night. These conditions are described as 'unbearable' on the wind chill scale.

Nick and Dave had certainly taken themselves beyond normal limits in an effort to make the summit, not for themselves, but to make it possible for two others to move up to Camp 6 for that summit bid. That day had been the equivalent of their own summit push – a very unselfish one, for there was no chance of personal glory or that special satisfaction of standing on the highest point of the mountain. We all owed them our gratitude, and they had earned that personal fulfilment at having completed a task as well as anyone could possibly have done.

15

Building up Camp 6

8 November – 13 November

It was a long road back to Camp 5. I had set out in the early evening from Camp 2 on my way up to Camp 3, the first staging post. We had spent most of the day watching the progress of Nick and the two Sherpas through the binoculars. Down in the comparative luxury of Camp 5, it was difficult to conceive just what it was like up there. The bottom snow slope of the face was now engulfed in grey shadows, with the rocks of the Rock Band and the snows above dyed a rich yellow which faded into pink as dusk fell. That night, as I plodded up the fixed rope, there was no hint of the gale tearing across the slopes above. Here I was protected by the great walls of Nuptse, was still below the cruel winds of the jet-stream which laps round the summit of Everest. The night was needle-cold, but at this altitude there was no wind. At the very time that Nick and Pertemba were fighting for their lives, I was able to sit on the snows, just 1220m below them, enjoying the utter peace of solitude after the previous crowded days. Action is so much easier than direction.

Camp 3 was unoccupied. I was to have the solitary remaining box to myself. Ang Phurba, who was going to join me at Camp 5, was to set out next morning from Camp 2, to make the journey to 4 in a single push. The solitude of that night was a peaceful balm; at Camp 2 there had never been any privacy, with the continuous chatter, and the complicated decisions affecting the course of the expedition which had to be made. Now, for a few hours, I was in a vacuum, out of contact with people. It was pitch dark when I reached the box; I tumbled in with a sense of luxurious satisfaction, fumbled in the dark for a box of matches and eventually found one. Graham, the last tenant, had left everything in immaculate order. I found a candle, struck half a dozen matches before I finally coaxed one into life and lit it. The gentle glow filled the box. The stove alight, I shoved a panful of snow on it and got my sleeping bag out of the pack-frame. Soon I was ensconced, drowsy, listening to the purr of the stove. For me life was good, while 900m above, Nick and Dave were sitting crouched in their box, trying to hold it together against the fury of the wind. Such are the contrasts of Everest!

I met them the next day as I pushed up the fixed ropes on my way to

Camp 4. First were Pertemba and Jangbo, moving quite quickly and precisely, then going much more slowly, sitting down for rests every few yards, Nick and Dave, their faces worn with fatigue, ice clinging to their beards. It was good seeing them. Nick warned me of the conditions I should have to face at Camp 5, but somehow I didn't really take it in; you couldn't until you had experienced it for yourself.

And then on up to Camp 4 – push the jumar forward on the rope, pant into the oxygen mask, take a step forward, step up – slow but rhythmic – blank off the mind, think of anything but Everest. Although very slow, I got there in the end, to see the boxes of Camp 4, brightly coloured in the afternoon sun, clinging to the rocky slope. After passing the debris of the camp, empty tins, tattered pieces of tent, poles sticking out of the ice, I reached camp itself, pulling over the lip of the platform to a mocking laugh from Graham.

'You took your time,' he said.

But he also had a mug of tea ready. I had become accustomed to Graham's hectoring manner by this time, had come to know and like the warmth under his bombastic exterior. Under his command, Camp 4 was beautifully organised. He knew the whereabouts of every single item of kit, had made the box tent as comfortable as possible, with a piece of pole in its middle pushing up the roof, to prevent it sagging. I crawled into the box with him, to be fed with mugs of tea and a magnificent three-course meal of soup, a hooch of fried steak-and-kidney pudding with mashed potato powder, followed by apple flakes washed down with coffee cognac.

Next morning was a brilliant windless day. Graham and I played with the little synch-sound super 8 mm cine camera, trying to make a documentary of what life was like at Camp 4. It was one o'clock in the afternoon before I was ready to set out for Camp 5. This time I threaded my demand valve down inside my one-piece suit, the inlet from the tank coming into the suit through the side pocket slit, and then reaching the mask up the front on the inside of the down suit. I hoped that by keeping the valve warm I should get better performance from the set. This was to prove the case. For the first time at altitude on the mountain, I seemed to be going strongly, didn't feel the need for rest, just put one foot in front of the other, and plodded remorselessly up the Great Central Gully. I seemed to have passed each landmark almost before I expected to see them, reaching the top in just over the hour. As I came to the little red Tunnel tent, Ang Phurba, who had set out earlier, poked his head out, gave me a smile and then thrust out a big mug of tea. It was almost warm in the late afternoon sun and I felt enough spare energy to potter around the camp site, checking oxygen bottles for their pressures, stacking our meagre pile of supplies on the rocky shelf at the back of the ledge holding the Tunnel tent and the ruined box.

That night a deep sense of contentment swept over me as I snuggled into my sleeping bag and listened to the purr of the two gas stoves. Ang Phurba cooked the supper and then I fixed him up with his sleeping oxygen. To sleep on, we had a half tank, which I had used to reach Camp 5, with another half tank to change on to when we ran out halfway through the night. Plastic masks cupped over our faces, the gentle hiss of oxygen was hypnotic, gently lulling us to sleep. We had double sleeping bags at Camp 5, a special Mountain Equipment sleeping bag inside the Fairy Down bag, each one of them normally amply warm enough for any conditions.

I woke up at 3 a.m. to a numbing cold that didn't so much come from the outside as from right inside of me and which then seeped slowly outwards through my limbs. The hiss of oxygen was gone; I lay back for several minutes just summoning up the determination to change cylinders and at last took the plunge, opened the sleeping bag, feeling the cold air rush in – it was probably –40°C outside. After fumbling for the torch, I grabbed the fresh cylinder, fiddled with the valve of the dead bottle with fast numbing fingers and after a struggle changed them over. Reassured by the steady hiss I dropped back into sleep, feeling the life-giving warmth of the oxygen flow through my body.

At about six o'clock, the oxygen ran out once more. I woke up again and lay cold, vacant-minded for a couple of hours. The roof of the tent and the upper parts of our sleeping bags were rimmed with hoar frost, which would melt once we lit the stove. Ang Phurba moved, grunted, then rolled over and lit one of the gas stoves; the frozen cylinder gave off little more than a glimmer. He heated the other stove over it, thawing out the gas until it started burning with a stronger flame, then reversed the process till both stoves were burning strongly. He had filled a pan with snow the previous night, and now we both lay back, dry-mouthed, waiting for the snow to melt, then boil, for the first brew of the day.

At least there was no wind, but even so it was bitterly cold. Nearly eight o'clock, time for the morning radio call – unless you warmed the batteries of the walkie-talkie, the radio wouldn't function at all. I emptied the little pen-light batteries into a frying pan over the stove and heated them up till they were warm to touch, slotted them back into the radio, which I had kept inside my sleeping bag with my cameras and inner boots all night, and shoved the radio back inside my down suit until the time of the radio call. Only with these precautions could we be sure of getting communication with the camps lower down on the mountain. Tony Tighe's voice came through first, very clear and close, though he was 2400m below and about six miles away at Base Camp.

'Hello, Chris, you sound loud and clear, how are you this morning?'

'We're fine today, Tony, there's hardly any wind up here, though it's bloody cold. How're Nick and Dave?'

'They got down last night. Beth's been giving them the full treatment, soaking their feet in hot water, the lot. Dave is OK but Nick has frostbite in two toes. Pertemba and Jangbo are fine.'

'Do you think there's any chance of getting Pertemba and Jangbo back up the hill?'

'I'll ask Jimmy. Pembatharke is a lot better now and is going to go up to Camp 2. He'll be able to keep things going.'

'That sounds great, Tony, well done. Hello Camp 2 are you on the air, over?'

'Hello, Chris, this is Barney, how are things up there?'

'Great, but bloody cold, are you all right at 2?'

'Everyone well, and Sherpa morale good. We're having a big carry to 4 today.'

'Sounds great, Barney; hello 4 are you on the air yet, over?'

Graham's voice, always grumpy in the early morning, came on:

'What are you so bloody cheerful about? It's not civilised this early!'

'Are you making a carry today, Graham?'

'Yes, we'll be able to get four Sherpas up today.'

'That's good, well done!'

At last things seemed to be slotting into place. After the radio call, Ang Phurba and I had another brew in order to postpone the grim moment of crawling out of warm sleeping bags, and start the slow process of dressing. You didn't need to put on any clothes, you had them all on already. It was the footwear that took time. My inner boots, having spent the night at the bottom of my sleeping bag were already warm, I slipped these on while still in my sleeping bag and then started to thaw out the outer leather boots; they were frozen, rigid as steel, icy to the touch. I held them over the gas stove letting the heat go up into the boot. After five minutes they had softened but were still cold to the touch. I forced them on to my feet, tucked the sleeping bag round them in an effort to retain the warmth and started warming up the foam overboots, shoved these on over the boots, then the nylon outer boots. Including my socks, this totalled five layers. Knowing I could delay no longer, I pulled on my windproof outer suit and overmitts and crawled out of the tent. If was now eleven o'clock in the morning. The sun was glaring down, but we were hidden from it, barred from what little heat it gave out by the overhanging rock wall. Within a minute of getting out of the tent, in spite of all precautions, my feet began to feel the cold, and within five minutes were numb, to remain so for the rest of the day. I had to sort the oxygen bottles and the loads we were going to take up to Camp 6 that day, and then crampons, fiddling with the straps with fast-freezing fingers. It was so cold that bare skin stuck to the metal – you had to try to put them on without taking off your windproof mitts.

It was mid-day before Ang Phurba and I were ready to set out. A few days before, safely back at Camp 2, I had been impatient at the slowness of Nick and Dave in setting out from Camp 5; now I knew the reason why. Everything took three times as long as it would have done lower down on the mountain.

We set out across the fixed ropes. We were carrying similar loads of around 16 kilos each. The trouble was, of course, that almost half that load was the oxygen bottle which, by the time we reached Camp 6, would be empty, 7 kilos of useless scrap alloy. My oxygen set seemed to be working well, I could feel the breath of oxygen mixed in air each time I breathed through the mask. Determined to stay out in front this time, I set Ang Phurba firmly behind me. He was always there, close on my heels, a reminder that he was probably fitter than I.

And on we plodded, up to the rock step; tiptoed carefully across the sloping, slabby ledges, leaning out on the rope that led across and away from us, then straight up towards the foot of the Rock Band. Although going slowly, I felt in control of myself, it was just a question of putting one foot in front of the other, ignoring the slowness with which one reached each landmark on the route, ever aware of the incredible expanding vista of mountains stretching ahead. As we crawled above the barrier wall of Nuptse, we could look across to the mountains south of us, as well as the more familiar sight of the peaks in the far far distance to the west.

We had now reached the final section of the route. Nick, single-minded and determined to finish the route in the day, had not had time to make intermediate anchor points. The rope stretched out in single leaps of 90m, stretching across the snowfield below the Rock Band. I had brought up several snow stakes, and now my interest was held by the job of safeguarding the route by placing anchors. In fact my progress was probably slower, but time passed much more easily in my concentration on the simple task I had to complete. Almost without noticing it, I reached Nick's high point, just 15m or so from the rocky spur which dropped down from the foot of the Rock Band. There were a number of ledges set into it, on one of which I should have to find a camp site. At this point I was able to look straight up into the gully which Dougal had described as the way through the Rock Band. He had said that in 1971 it was a straightforward snow gully, but now, looking up, I could see very little snow. Indeed, it barely seemed a gully at all, was more a fissure in the rock wall, narrow, steep, in places overhanging. It looked hard; but then I shut the problem from my mind. I had programmed myself to establish Camp 6, and just completing this simple task was taking all my own resources. The gully was Dougal's problem. It was there, and however difficult, there was nothing I could do about it. Should it prove too difficult in the circumstances, he could always try to find a route round the corner, bypassing the Rock Band.

And so I gave my attention to the more immediate problems of finding a suitable camp site. It all looked very exposed to the wind. Down the side of the spur, underneath each little overhang I could see how the wind had sculpted out hollows from the snow. Eventually I decided that it was unlikely that anywhere at the end of the icefield would be truly protected from the wind; better to choose a site where at least there was plenty of sun to help setting out in the morning.

At last I was going to get a little lead climbing, as I tied on to the end of the rope left dangling by Nick and started to pick my way across towards the rocky spur, kicked steps up a steep little snow slope and then pulled over a rock step. A length of rope, left from the spring expedition, protruded from the snows and was attached to a big boulder on a ledge reaching out to the crest of the spur. It was undoubtedly exposed to the wind, but got plenty of sun and what a situation! Just round the corner we could gaze down on the South Col, over 300m below; immediately across from us was the great mass of Lhotse, its summit only a little higher than the site of Camp 6, and around us was the endless vista of mountains.

I took off my pack and found that I had run out of oxygen – I didn't know for how long. On the other hand, when Ang Phurba arrived he still had three-quarters of a tank left. His set could not have been functioning correctly and yet, in spite of this, he had followed close behind me all the way up. In a way it was a plus, for it meant we had some extra oxygen here at Camp 6.

But time was slipping by; it was now three o'clock in the afternoon and we wanted to get back to Camp 5 well before dusk. We turned round unburdened and set off down the ropes. I stopped every 30m or so, partly to rest, but also to gaze once more over the vista of mountains. Their beauty alone was enough to make up for all the effort and discomfort of the past few weeks.

And so, back to Camp 5. Ang Phurba had already got down and, as I arrived, thrust a steaming mug of lemon tea into my hand. I felt a wave of gratitude for his thoughtfulness. When we had first met Ang Phurba we had no idea of how outstanding a performance he was to produce on the mountain. Slightly built, a bit of a dandy, always elegantly dressed in gear issued by other expeditions, he was a far cry from the simple peasant; it had been difficult to imagine him having the endurance to keep going at altitude and yet he was proving to be one of our most outstanding Sherpas.

That afternoon I felt well content with our performance. There had been hardly a breath of wind all day, and now, bathed by the late sun, Camp 5 was a pleasantly relaxed place to be in. I was anxious to organise our loads for the morning, and was testing the pressures of the oxygen bottles that littered one end of the ledge. I described what happened that night in my diary:

Then I went over to find some full oxygen bottles. All the bottles have been left in an absolute bloody shambles – empties mixed up with full ones. I was testing one of them, to find out whether it was full or empty – enough to go up the next day. It was tied on to a rope, reasonably full, certainly OK for sleeping, and so I tried to get it untied. There was a big pile of other oxygen bottles lying alongside it – not very safe, not very well jammed, and I swung this one up and hit three of them. They cannoned down the slope and there was a tremendous crash as one of them exploded. Camp 5 is almost directly over Camp 4, and I had this horrible vision – Christ, they could have wiped out Camp 4 – I could have killed someone! It was the most agonising thought and Ang Phurba, who had just come out of the tent, shook his head and said, 'Very dangerous, Sahib – very, very dangerous.' He told me that one bottle dropped from Camp 5 on the International expedition had gone straight through one of the tents. I went through absolute agony for about an hour and a half, was unable to raise Camp 4, but Camp 3, occupied by Dougal and Hamish came over the air. It was the five o'clock call. We heard that Graham had had to go down – hit by a stone; it could not have been our oxygen bottles, thank God, because it had happened at about 3.40. Quite honestly though, I think it could well have been a stone that either I or Ang Phurba dislodged on our return from Camp 6, because it was impossible to avoid knocking them down occasionally – they are embedded in the snow. Fortunately, Graham wasn't badly injured, but we didn't yet know whether Camp 4 had been hit. Hamish, who was at Camp 3, said he didn't think it possibly could have been.

Graham had had a narrow escape. The stone had come crashing through the wall of the box, hitting him on his forehead. He was knocked unconscious and does not know for how long he was out. Coming to, he found himself covered in blood, lying inside the box. He called out to the Sherpas, and one of them helped him back down to Camp 2, where Barney was able to stitch his wound. Had the stone hit him on the side of the head, where the skull is very much thinner, he might well have had a fracture.

It could have been a lot worse, but this meant that I had lost yet another climber from the face. That left Dougal and Hamish on their way back up to Camp 5, Mick and Doug still down at Camp 2, and myself. Hamish and Dougal were due to move up to Camp 4 the next day; I should then learn whether Camp 4 had been hit, since, having lost their camp manager, the Sherpas were unlikely to come on to the radio on the morning call.

The wind built up once again, rattling and hammering the tent throughout the night. Next morning Ang Phurba and I began to get ready for another carry. We were both weary from the previous day, but nevertheless determined to make another trip to Camp 6. Already worried about the Sherpa replacement situation, I was going to have to find replacements for Ang Phurba at Camp 5, as well as for the Sherpas at Camp 4 who would be making their second carry that day and, in all probability, would want to go back down. Then there was the problem of the oxygen cylinders, accentuated by the failure of the adaptors for the seventeen French bottles which were sitting at Camp 4 and, of course, on which I had been relying.

That morning, at the nine o'clock call, Mick Burke came up with, 'Look Chris, I'm going to be pessimistic here, to offset your optimism – I just don't think we've got enough oxygen cylinders on the mountain to last beyond 14 November.' We tried to work it out over the radio, but it is not easy to do mental arithmetic at 8000m, one's mind being a little addled by altitude.

Finally, I said, 'Look, Mick, I'll sit down and work things out again and we'll open up in an hour's time.'

I sat down in my sleeping bag, with Ang Phurba watching me impassively, trying to calculate our oxygen consumption. I knew we had one and three-quarter bottles up at the top camp, four cylinders at Camp 5, five were being carried up from Camp 4 that day, four at Camp 4 and so on down the mountain. But when I started trying to work out the rate of consumption at each level of the mountain, a calculation easy enough at sea level, however hard I tried I simply couldn't work it out – the mind was too slow.

Ten o'clock came, and I opened up on the radio.

'Have you worked anything out?' asked Mick.

'Look, I'm still working on it,' I replied. 'We'd better open up again at mid-day.'

I decided to send Ang Phurba on up to Camp 6 by himself, while I tried to work out our logistics. I should have to make my carry to Camp 6 the following day. Ang Phurba, ever loyal, set out without protest and I went back to my figures. Twelve o'clock came, and we talked it over once again on the radio.

Barney suggested that we should try to sleep without using oxygen. Mick agreed that this would be possible. In the meantime we ordered another twenty bottles to be carried up from Base Camp to 1, first thing the next morning, holding back the Sherpas at Camp 1, so that we could push them straight through to Camp 2 on the same day. Mick ended up saying, 'Look, we realise that there isn't a hope in hell's chance of Doug and I having a second attempt on the summit, but even so, we'll do our best to keep going and help Dougal and Hamish.'

That afternoon, as I continued to try to calculate our logistic position, I knew we were up against it and commented in my diary: 'You know, we might pull it off, but by God, if we do, we'll have done it against absolutely every kind of odds that you could possibly imagine.'

Just after one o'clock three Sherpas arrived with loads from Camp 4. This was their second carry to Camp 5, and they said they wanted to go back down for a rest. I used all the inspiration I had in me to persuade them to make just one more carry before going down. They listened impassively and said they'd see how they felt next morning. I felt drained from the emotional effort I had put into trying to inspire them. It was now 1.30 and the sun still had not struck the tent. I had come out without putting on overboots and, as a result, my feet were numb with cold. Back in the tent I lay cold and exhausted until at last the sun lit the nylon fabric and some warmth began to filter into the tent.

A few minutes later Ang Phurba arrived back; he had been very fast, taking under three hours for the round trip, but he looked tired and told me that the wind had been bad on the upper part of the carry. He had shown considerable courage in going up on his own, for the Sherpas prefer company when they're climbing. I prepared a brew for him and he crawled into his sleeping bag.

In spite of the logistic crisis that morning, everything seemed hopeful; it was a beautiful evening, with that rich, rather yellow, mellow glow as the sun went down. I decided to do some filming and got out the little auto-load camera, filming Ang Phurba heating the wireless batteries and preparing a brew. I crawled outside to sort out the loads which had arrived that afternoon, and do some more filming.

And then I needed to relieve myself – and this was my embarrassing, very humiliating downfall. I described it in detail in my diary and I include it here, for I hope it brings home some of the grim, perhaps sordid, and yet in a weird kind of way the funny experiences that are all part of a Himalayan expedition. It is comparatively easy to cope with the dramatic crises, the savage storms, the sheer ice pitch at 7300m, but less easy to cope, day after day, with the basic problems of living at 8000m in sub-zero temperatures.

Now we've got these one-piece down suits; it's not too bad, in fact it's comparatively easy to relieve oneself when wearing the down suit by itself. If, however, you are wearing the down suit and the outer suit, it is absolutely desperate, trying to get the two slits in both suits lined up. Deciding to make it easy for myself, I peeled off the top windproof suit, leaving only the down suit to worry about. Afterwards, without thinking, without looking back, I stood up and shoved my windproof suit back on. Pushing my left hand, which was gloved, through the sleeve, I did not realise anything was wrong – until I poked my hand through the cuff!

I tried to scrape it off – rub it off – but by this time the sun had gone, it was bitterly cold and it had frozen to the consistency of concrete. Poor old Ang Phurba – he's feeling a bit rough anyway, and I said, 'I'm sorry, Ang Phurba – I've made a mistake!' He just buried himself in his sleeping bag and then there was a horrible gasp as he dived for the entrance. And so I took off my down suit as well as the outer suit, and after an attempt to clean them up, shoved them into the collapsed tent next door! I got into my sleeping bag and eventually we dropped off to sleep, though Ang Phurba insisted on having the door open, and it was bloody freezing!

Next morning Ang Phurba woke up and felt ill. I was meant to be doing a carry, while Ang Phurba had said he was going down anyway, and this clinched the deal! It was all I could do – at least he made the breakfast and the morning tea which, I must say, was a nice luxury, while I lay back.

By about 10.30 a.m., Ang Phurba was ready, and he went down. I should have gone up, but Ang Phurba shook his head – he told me that yesterday had been very very cold and conditions very bad. Today seemed much worse – windy all day, but by this time it was 12.15, getting late for a push all the way up to Camp 6 and back, especially thinking about Nick Estcourt's frostbite, and I'm afraid my will power died. I did not think I could do more than two carries anyway, so decided well, let's get the camp sorted out, help Hamish and Dougal, and then I can go up with them tomorrow.

I only hope that when and if Hamish and Dougal turn up, they don't wrinkle up their noses, put me in quarantine and refuse to come anywhere close to me.

Here is your dynamic leader of the British Everest expedition, sitting at 26,000ft [8000m] feeling rather like a social pariah. I wouldn't say I'm feeling sorry for myself, but I don't know – I'm not so much muddled-thinking – my mind in some ways feels quite sharp. I think it's more that you're slow in thinking – very very forgetful; I find it very difficult to master the logistics of our problem. And now I'm just mastering the very simple problem that Ang Phurba has also left all the flipping dirty plates and pans and I'm having a session cleaning these.

The sun's just hit the tent. Life's a lot more bearable now, and when I've done this washing-up, I'm going to get out of the tent and start sorting things out.

And these were my feelings at Camp 5, as I recorded them over a period of twenty-four hours, into the cassette recorder. It's very easy to forget just how you felt, from hour to hour, once you get back to civilisation. One's thought processes are undoubtedly muddled and slow at this altitude – just how slow is only evident when you read back the transcript of recordings made at the time. Hamish and Dougal arrived that evening; it was wonderful seeing them again, having their companionship. Dougal was the first to arrive and I crawled out of the tent to greet him and then started helping him to pitch a new Tunnel tent to replace the box which had collapsed around Nick and Dave. The wind was now scudding round the corner and although the Tunnel tents, which had been designed by Doug Scott, were magnificent once erected, you needed a B.Sc. in engineering to work out how to put them up. Dougal and I did our best, though both of us being far from mechanical by nature, our attempt was a little pathetic. Finally, fingers frozen, we retired to my tent to await Hamish, the expedition engineer. He came up about an hour behind Dougal, having had trouble with his oxygen set, and having been hit on the leg by a stone. He put the finishing touches to their Tunnel tent and then we all gathered in my tent for a communally cooked meal of corned beef hash washed down with coffee cognac. In spite of the cold and wind we were all full of confidence and I felt warmed and cheered by their presence.

We decided that we should set out next morning, Dougal and Hamish to move into Camp 6, myself to carry a load for them. That night, though, the wind blew fiercely. My own tent was pitched securely and was partly protected by that of Hamish and Dougal. Theirs, however, was not nearly as well pitched, and during the night was flapping around to such a degree that most of the time the walls were resting against their faces as if it had been an ordinary bivouac sack. As a result they got practically no sleep. There were other problems as well, as I commented in my diary.

The idea at this stage was to get Dougal and Hamish up to the site of Camp 6. The only problem here was that it became increasingly obvious that we barely had the manpower to do it – we'd only, after all, got three loads up – two loads that Ang Phurba and I had carried, then Ang Phurba's load. Dougal came up with a suggestion that Hamish and he should consolidate today, that Mick and Doug should come up, and then that the five of us should go up to 6 next day, with Dougal and Hamish staying there. This would mean bringing another tent up, however, and I didn't like the idea of this, feeling the fewer people we have up there, the fewer people we have to feed and give oxygen. Therefore I came up with the idea that I should do the carry by myself on the 13th, while Mick and Doug move up to here, and then the next day Mick and Doug should carry Dougal and Hamish into Camp 6. I must say, I'd quite like to have done this myself, but you can't have everything, and this does seem a sensible way of doing it.

And so, I prepared for my own final fling on the mountain, going through the slow, painful process of getting dressed, sorting out my oxygen kit. Unfortunately, the set I had used on my trip with Ang Phurba had belonged to Mick Burke and I had sent it back down the mountain for him to use for his return to Camp 5. This meant I had to use the set which Ang Phurba had been using, one that was suspect anyway. In addition, the mask did not fit sufficiently closely for enough suction to shift the valve, when breathing in. Consequently, a certain amount of precious oxygen was lost round the sides of the mask.

Before I had walked a dozen paces, it was obvious that the mask was only working for part of the time, and I was having to breathe very hard to get any oxygen at all. You could tell when it was working by the sound of the valve opening and closing.

I made my way up the fixed ropes; there was a feeling of exultation in the very lonely emptiness of the world around me – a rope that stretched for ever in front, mountains stretching for an ever-increasing expansive distance as I slowly gained height. The wind hammered and buffeted at my back, as I slowly plodded towards my goal. There was room for fear in the very loneliness of my position, in the demoniac force of the wind that was so much stronger than I; time was slipping by; it was 3.15 and I was still a long way from the rock spur at the end of the icefield; could I get there and all the way back to Camp 5, in time? The oxygen set seemed to have packed in completely but I still had some strength in reserve. I was very very slow, one foot in front of the other, and yet I could keep going without taking rests, felt better than I had done earlier on in the expedition, on my way up to Camp 3.

The sun, low on the horizon, had that warm yellow light that was so meaningless in the constant blast of icy wind. I pulled up over the step, teetered across the narrow rock ledge leading to the little platform I had chosen for Camp 6, and crouched down beneath the slight drift of snow to remove my pack. I had carried up two French oxygen cylinders and a rope, about 18 kilos in weight, too much for that altitude. My pressure-gauge still read 800 psi; it had only been 2400 when I had started, only three-quarters full – so I had used barely half a tank to reach the high point! For well over half the time the set must have been malfunctioning. I felt a faint glow of satisfaction at having forced myself on, but the satisfaction was quickly replaced by doubts about my prospects of getting back down. Could I face into the savage wind, had I sufficient strength for those long traverses?

I started down, blown off track as I stumbled over the long traverse. Pushing myself as hard as I could to reach Camp 5, I could not imagine myself getting all the way down to Camp 4 that night. I was so tired that I cried with exhaustion as I pushed my weary body the last few feet into the camp. Mick and Doug had arrived and had found a snow hole just above the camp. As I came in, Mick poked his head out of a hole in the snow. Doug, matter-of-fact, commented, 'You'd better get a move on if you want to get down to Camp 4.'

Quite obviously, there wasn't any room at Camp 5. Hamish thrust a mug full of soup from out of the tent. I gulped it down, and quickly packed my rucksack with a few belongings; I didn't even need a sleeping bag for these were back at Camp 4.

Fortified by the mug of soup I set off down the Great Central Gully to Camp 4. I was so tired that even going downhill I had to sit down and rest every few feet. And yet, tired as I was, I felt enthralled by the view. The light was beginning to fade from the rocks around me, and the distant peaks were silhouetted against a sky that was gold on the far horizon, merging into a deep red and then an opaque blue-black. For me, whatever the outcome of the expedition, this day had been the climax. The experience, my own peace of mind, having taken myself to the limit and beyond, made everything, all the worries of leadership, stress and discomfort, completely worthwhile.

It was pitch dark by the time I reached Camp 4. I let out a shout, and a cry came back.

'In here, Sahib.' It was Ang Phu. He had cleared the box in readiness for me, had a panful of water heating on the stove and a sleeping bag lying out ready. His thoughtfulness was truly wonderful, bathed me with a warm glow, as I crept into the box, lit a candle and made some lemon drink. I was so tired that I couldn't face cooking or even eating anything. I just curled up in the sleeping bag, wondered if there was a second one anywhere, but had neither strength to search, nor even the energy to find my sleeping tablets. Blowing out the candle, I lay back, feeling icy fingers of cold creeping round my legs, crawling over my body. Even though I had arrived back warm, even slightly sweaty from my exertions, now the cold penetrated everything. I could not take any oxygen and longed for another sleeping bag. Too tired, too cold to sleep, I just lay shivering in the dark – so cold that I shouted out into black space 'I'm cold' but it didn't help. I had not had enough to eat that day, and unless one has taken in enough fuel, especially at that altitude, there is not enough residual warmth in one's body to stay warm, however many layers of down one is covered by. I just lay there waiting for the morning, commenting in my diary next day:

I was very depressed this morning, the 14th, when I felt I had lost control of the expedition. In a way I felt I had lost control of myself, just wanted to be at home, in my own big double bed with my love, under a nice big warm quilt.

There's a hole in this box that I am in at the moment, made by a stone – I think it was the stone that forced Graham to go back down. Spindrift was pouring through it all night and in the morning everything was just covered in spindrift. I was bitterly cold and it was hours before the sun came on to the tent. Life couldn't have been more miserable.

Now though, having been up at nine – then the ten o'clock call – I can look at things more rationally – there's no doubt about it, we've only got about four or five days. We're not in a position to supply our front climbers. We've really pushed Dougal and Hamish out in front a bit too soon, for we can barely keep them supplied – I think everyone is in a mood of 'Let's have done with it'.

The weather forecast, last night, at 9 kilometres, which is just over the top of

Everest, was 'winds of 200 kilometres per hour', and certainly the winds were something like that yesterday. I think the chimney through the Rock Band is very sheltered, but if it is technically difficult it's so bitterly cold that I don't think they're going to be able to really contend with it. But at least we'll be able to get above the high point of the International expedition, I think, and it's just possible we'll be able to climb the Rock Band. I suppose miracles do happen – the miracle could occur, where we could reach the top of Everest. The big problem is supplying this pyramid of oxygen which the lead climbers require to keep going.

Anyway, Dougal and Hamish are getting a French box which is, by far, the best piece of tentage we've got on this expedition, up today, and let's just pray they can have a really good night and tomorrow make some good progress. It will be very very exciting to hear how they've got on tomorrow.

In the meantime things are very very thin here. I've got Jangbo and Pertemba coming up today to Camp 4. Ang Phu is going up to Camp 5. It's going to be very critical, just how tired Mick and Doug are, and whether they can do a carry, because it does need a two-man carry each day, to keep the people out in front supplied. I think we're on a last-ditch, forlorn hope at the moment. I'm going to hold out here, at 4. At least today, I think, I've managed to make my standard of life a little pleasanter than last night and this morning. I also intend to feed myself up, and I think a rest will make all the difference. But it really takes an effort of will to get out of the box and into the cold. It also takes about two hours to get your feet warmed up once again, after you've done it. Your feet get much colder hanging around the camp than they do in a single kind of push or carry.

Anyway, four to five days of this and, success or fail – we can't do any more. Quite honestly, I just want to get home. I think the effort's been worth it – we've had a really fine, great effort, and I think everyone has done their very best and will have taken themselves to their limits, and slightly beyond. But I think the thing we want to do most of all now, all of us, is just get home.

I recorded these comments early in the morning of 14 November, while up at Camp 4. Four hundred and fifty metres above me, Dougal and Hamish were preparing to move up to Camp 6, supported by Mick and Doug. We had been struggling for too long, our resources were too thin, and yet still in the bottom of our hearts we had some hope left.

16

Defeat

14 November – 16 November

14 November. Jimmy Roberts was sitting near the summit of Kalapatar, a small peak which commands a magnificent view of the upper reaches of the south of Everest, above Gorak Shep. He had gone there a few days previously to watch the final stages of the expedition; Kelvin Kent, Nick Estcourt, Dave Bathgate and Graham Tiso, all more or less injured, certainly out of the expedition from a climbing point of view, were convalescing at Base Camp. Tony Tighe and Beth Burke were also there, managing administration. Barney was at Camp 2 and I was sitting it out at Camp 4. Both of us had now been above Base Camp for six weeks, and were desperately tired. Hamish, Dougal, Doug and Mick were at Camp 5. They realised that chances were thin and yet, when I had left them the previous night, morale had been high and we all had felt that, long as the odds were, we still had a chance.

Dougal Haston wrote a description of his experiences in those last two or three days of the expedition, and of that final push towards Camp 6:

Rocked gently by the wind, Hamish and I moved up the familiar highway with its overnight stops at 3 and 4, towards the decision-making at 5. The altitude scarcely seemed to matter. I barely remember the journey as my mind was too full with the problems of the Rock Band and above. Logistics were stretched. Tucked away in my rucksack was a tent sac. I didn't show it to many people and it wasn't in case we got lost between 2 and 5. Slowly, as a positive plan began to appear through the maze of possibilities, a bivouac above the Rock Band became a distinct possibility in any scheme with a chance of success. This wasn't a crazy decision caused by oxygen starvation. We'd talked away many nights at Base Camp on the subject. It's just that a bivouac at 28,000ft [8500m] or above is something you don't consider lightly, or make the decision to attempt easily. You're pushing calculatedly close to the overbalance of the survival seesaw. I'd thrown it out, casually and jokingly, to Doug and Mick and seen their faces assume that funny, vague look that you sometimes see when friends think you've temporarily flipped.

With such thoughts whirling, I moved in an easy, occupied manner into Camp 5, to find Bonington in an occupational sleeping bag. Crawling into the tent, I got the good news that there was a lot of material at the site of Camp 6, then the not-so-good – that we still had to pitch a roof next door for Hamish and I to sleep in. Meanwhile Hamish arrived, muttering about a troublesome oxygen set. It seemed a long and different time since I'd spent so many days there with Whillans in 1971. There was no sitting, watching the evening sun, only a constant roaring, cracking wind projecting spindrift in great clouds throughout the camp. We were still erecting the tent as darkness was falling; fumbling frozen-fingeredly with a good but intricate design system. It was still badly pitched as the final appearance of darkness forced us into Chris's tent for some thaw-out drinks. Hamish and I did pass the night in the new tent – or maybe it passed the night on us. It's all pretty vague. Anyhow, it almost qualified as a bivouac, since the framework collapsed in the night and the wind-cracking roof spent the rest of the time keeping us awake and beating on our heads. No sleep, and a long excavation emergence in the morning put us in no shape to journey towards Camp 6 that day. Chris did a lone carry. Doug and Mick arrived. An incoherently irate Doug fixed his own special brand of tent, with his own special system which was unfortunately only in his head and not in the instruction manual we carried in ours. Mick and I played at snow holing. Hamish fiddled with oxygen. Chris came back and disappeared towards 4, down pointing for ever. Slowly, a plan and order came through and suddenly we were all asleep and organised for the move up on the next day – Hamish and I to occupy 6, Doug and Mick to carry in support.

It was a strange new day as I moved on to the fixed ropes. Sun, yes, but not in the camp, with only the warmth of a gas burner in a banquet hall when eventually reached. I was alone and a good way up the ropes before seeing the others emerge and prepare to follow. On this part there was no exploration for me, only memories of previous struggling, and an awareness of being in much better physical shape than before. Three weeks above 24,000ft [7300m] might be a record for high-altitude holiday camping, but it doesn't do wonders for you physically. Flashes of emaciated effort came back as I moved easily on, upwards. But with all the sense of physical well-being, there were many other not-so-good factors to counteract a light-hearted journey up towards Camp 6.

The wind – always the wind, was viciously asserting its authority. This was no silent journey up a crisp snowfield in the pure high air. I had visions of storms on old trans-Atlantic cutters. The constant banging in your ears would suddenly be intensified with a huge crack, as an extra gust smashed over the West Ridge and pulled at the figures on the ropes. This cracking was at least a warning. The axe was banged in and you crouched and held on. Once I was toppling on a long loose section of fixed rope and went twanging down on to my jumars. Doug told me later that at one point he was caught unprepared, picked up and thrown for a few feet, before clattering on to the ever elastic fixed ropes. I continued quickly, with a mind going almost as quickly as the wind. I had experienced many bad storms, many high winds, but this was a new dimension of wind speed, and it was basically fine weather! The sky, when you could see it through the spindrift, was blue.

I reached the position where the equipment was dumped and at just above that point the wind stopped gusting and moved into continuous movement. Thinking was difficult. I had to turn away and crouch. Two things were blatantly self-evident. There was no way we could attempt to climb on the Rock Band and no way a tent could be pitched. I looked up at the couloir that we had followed before. Another disillusioning surprise. Whillans and I had climbed 100m of it, mainly on snow and easy rock, with the potential continuation also on snow. Now it was bare rock. To my confused head this seemed a total contradiction. The rest of the face had much more snow on it than it had had last spring, but now this part, which should have been filled with snow, had none. Even given the possibility of continuing, which now seemed zero to me, the Band was obviously going to take much more time than even the slowest of our plans had allowed.

Grappling with this thought, I remembered the possibilities of escape on to the relatively easy ground of the South East Ridge. A quick move – out of the face, and round the corner. It was no survival scene. The wind seemed to screw round and blast me on the face. I backed quickly round the corner and the prevailing blast hit me again. A sudden bad thought: I knew that without an oxygen mask I wouldn't have been able to breathe on that particular corner, and just hoped that the cylinder didn't run out at that particular moment. Another thing seemed reasonably certain, the so-called escape route was an escape only into something worse. On the flattish slabby ground, it would have been suicidal to attempt to move. Any gust would have blown one off immediately. Turning back to try to find some kind of shelter, I saw Doug at the top of the ropes. We just muttered a few obvious things. He took some pictures. Hands were turning white, even with double gloves. There was nothing to do but turn around. I jerked my head downwards. He nodded. Setting off down I met Mick. He knew what was happening – there was no real need to say anything. Moving past, I left him with the extremely difficult task of trying to record the scene on film.

Back at Camp 5 I found Hamish, who had turned back because of a faulty oxygen set and, as everyone crowded in to drink tea, we started to talk about the decision made. It was obviously final. Even if the wind had stopped miraculously, we did not have the back-up for another push. And one wind-free day was not enough. That night I put our decision to Chris on the radio.

I knew that something was wrong, for I was in direct radio contact with Jimmy Roberts, six miles away, and 2000m below me at Kalapatar. Through his powerful binoculars he had been able to watch the drama taking place on the long traverse across to the site of Camp 6. It had been like watching a movie with no sound, and just as confusing; although able to pick out the arms and legs of the climbers, it was not possible to identify them. You could barely do this from one metre range, so well-disguised were they by shapeless suits and oxygen masks.

Jimmy had seen and reported the retreat of one figure fairly early in the day, and had then given the fatal news – that the remaining three had also turned back. The weather had now been fine for over a week and, as a result, all the loose spindrift had been blown from the face; yet there were no tell-tale clouds of snow to betray the savage winds. Down at Kalapatar the winter sun blazed hot from a cloudless sky; there was no wind at that level. Up at 4, however, I did at least have some hint of the winds that were being experienced above Camp 5; it was a bitterly cold, blustery day, but I still had some shelter from the great wall of Nuptse. Anyway, it is the top 600m of Everest that juts into the jet-stream blasting with an ever-increasing force through the high airs of the earth.

I knew they were coming back down, that they had not occupied Camp 6 – but why? I surmised that afternoon in my taped diary:

I'm lying here in the gathering gloom (it's about half past five), just waiting for the seven o'clock call, to find out why they didn't establish Camp 6. Can't help being worried that I could have made a mistake. For instance, I know I didn't actually tie down the two parts of the French boxes. Certainly they were there yesterday, but could they have blown away – could *I* have done something wrong which could have prejudiced the expedition? Logically, I don't think so. I think it's more likely that it's just too cold and windy; perhaps they're having trouble with their oxygen sets. But until you know, you can't help being a bit worried.

I think really, this – the whole thing – has become a real battle of attrition and we've all been here too long. We're tired, we're fed up with it, and I think we're all just looking forward to a decision – one way or another. I don't think we've got a chance of getting to the top of Everest – conditions are just too inhuman up there – the human frame cannot cope with hundred-mile-an-hour wind, and a temperature of about –30ºC. When I went up there yesterday afternoon, I don't think I could have erected a tent; I think this might well have been the trouble that Hamish and Dougal got.

And so, Dougal's news on that seven o'clock call wasn't really a surprise. I just accepted their decision straight away, and said, 'Yes, OK, we go down.' I had experienced the wind the previous day, had learned for myself how insufferable it had been. Lower down the mountain they found the decision more difficult to accept. It's strange how quickly the human memory forgets just how savage an experience can be. That night, Nick wrote in his diary: 'My own feeling – emotional I know – is to wish that they had at least spent a night at Camp 6, and tried – somehow. I feel cheated and let down. I know this is stupid; it's partly Base Camp frustration. In some ways it's better, in some ways worse, for the front four. I feel sorry for Chris.'

Jimmy, also, was disappointed. From Kalapatar the climbers looked more like puppets than humans. It was so difficult to appreciate the effect of the wind and cold on the human body and mind. That night I had a feeling of complete peace of mind. We had done our best, had taken ourselves to the limit, and now that it was all over I just longed to clear the mountain safely, and get the hell out of it, back to home.

The front four came back down to Camp 4 that morning, carrying mammoth loads. At the same time, a big party of Sherpas came up from Camp 2 to clear the camp. By evening we were all back down at Camp 2. There was no sense of depression, no regrets – there was almost a feeling of elation, everyone confident that it had been the wind and cold which had beaten us – a wind and cold that I am positive no human being could have struggled against. We were like a pack of schoolboys at boarding school, about to go on holiday after a particularly long and arduous term. The experience had brought us closer together, rather than weakening our bonds of friendship. We had experienced some friction during the course of the expedition; we had had conflicts, but knew these to be inevitable – perhaps essential as a safety-valve to the stresses of such a venture. Every single person on that expedition, Sherpas and climbers alike, had done more than could possibly have been expected of them in the normal course of events. Of the Sherpas, the performance of Ang Phurba, Pertemba, Jangbo and Ang Phu had been exceptional. There was a wonderful feeling of unity, not only between the climbers but also between climbers and Sherpas, and through the throes of the expedition we had emerged as a single close-knit group.

I wanted to clear the mountain as quickly as possible. On 16 November, Dougal, Hamish, Doug and I were setting off from Camp 2 to return to Base. Mick had gone down the previous evening to send film which he had taken at the site of Camp 6 back to Britain, and to prepare our reception from a filming point of view. Chris Brasher had abandoned Camp 2 in the Western Cwm after a couple of days to go to Khumde to complete an interview with Sir Edmund Hillary, but had come rushing back to Base Camp to get the story of our retreat. This was to leave Barney with the unenviable job of holding the fort to the last. He was to have one more night at Camp 2 while the Sherpas stripped it, and was then to drop back down to Camp 1 and then to Base Camp.

We set off at dawn, when the Western Cwm was still in deep shadow, held in the grip of the winter cold. A flurry of vapour was blowing off the summit of Lhotse, sure sign of the ever-present wind. But down in the Cwm, the air was still. I walked down, without regret, very tired yet still marvelling at the incredible architecture of the Western Cwm. The sun, creeping behind the great mass of Everest, lit the upper ramparts of Nuptse then crept above the South Ridge of Everest to throw long shadows down the Cwm itself, emphasising the dark void of crevasses, picking out pinnacles and airy ridges of ice through and over which our route lay.

Camp 1 was rather sad, stripped of all its tents – just the scattered debris of an expedition. Hamish and Dougal were in front. I went down the Icefall with Doug Scott, finding the upper part changed from when I had last seen it six weeks before. Crevasses had opened out, séracs had fallen and the route wound its way through the debris. Strangely, we had little sense of danger, perhaps becoming immune to the feeling after our weeks on the mountain. I spent an hour photographing a particularly spectacular section of the Icefall which, only two hours later, was to collapse – with disastrous results.

We were over halfway down when we met Tony Tighe on his way up the Icefall to meet us. He was tremendously excited at the prospect of getting a glimpse into the Western Cwm. He had spent the last eight weeks at Base Camp fulfilling unexciting but invaluable duties, taking all the radio calls, helping Jimmy Roberts with general administration and the assembly of loads for the mountain. At times he had even taken on the role of diplomat. It is all too easy while on the mountain to resent people having the easy living at Base Camp, to wonder why supplies were not coming up to the front line more quickly; grumbles were passed back to Base Camp all too often over the radio. Tony would soften them down and, in passing them on to Jimmy, would take the sting out of them. In every way he had fulfilled an important role on the expedition through his mature good sense, his kindness and his efficiency. The last day I felt I had to give him some kind of reward for everything he had done for us, knew how much he longed to see into the Western Cwm, to get an inkling of the excitement and struggle we had known and enjoyed all these days. And so I had invited him to come up and meet us.

He was brimming over with happiness when we met him. He had come up with twenty Sherpas who were going to Camp 1 to meet those bringing loads down from Camp 2. Having dropped behind them, being less fit than they, he was now on his own – nothing unusual since the track through the Icefall was clearly marked, and all the crevasses bridged, all difficult sections fixed roped.

We passed him, got back down to Base Camp, to the first wash in six weeks, to mugfuls of tea, to Brasher's debriefing. There was a feeling of the start of the holidays, talk of the meals we were going to have in Kathmandu, dreams of getting home. The afternoon wore on, light-hearted as ever, and then suddenly there was a rising babble of voices amongst the Sherpas. They were obviously worried – they seem to have an almost extra-sensory perception of trouble. Kelvin called me over.

'There's some kind of trouble in the Icefall,' he said.

'What is it?' I asked.

'I'm not sure. They're not at all certain, but seem to think there's been a big collapse.'

Some of the Sherpas were already on their way down, having picked up their loads at Camp 1. A few minutes later Phurkipa arrived and told Kelvin there had been a big collapse in the Icefall just above him. At this stage we could not tell if anyone had been involved – we could see another group on their way down, however. From their position we estimated that they must have been above, or somewhere in the area of the collapse when it occurred. We were all worried about Tony. Phurkipa and he had passed each other, going in their opposite directions just short of the area of collapse and Tony could have had time to get into the danger area. But there was nothing we could do but sit it out and wait.

The large party came in sight; one of them was seen to be wearing a one-piece suit. There was a shout from Mick Burke: 'It's OK – it's Tony!' I felt a wave of relief come over me, unable to stop the tears; Dougal, normally so unemotional, gripped my shoulder and said, 'I couldn't have taken another Annapurna!' (An allusion to Ian Clough's tragic death in the Icefall at the end of the Annapurna South face expedition.) But this is exactly what we were going to have to do. Almost at the moment Mick had called out, someone else shouted, 'It's not Tony – it's Barney – Tony isn't with them!'

We hurried forward to where Barney was coming into the camp with a dozen Sherpas.

'Have you seen any sign of Tony?'

'No.'

'Yet you've come all the way down from Camp 1?'

'Yes, but there's been a hell of a collapse in the Icefall; we had to make a bit of a diversion to get round the debris. I don't think we could have missed him. Was he on his way up?'

'Yes, he was last seen just short of the collapse.'

And so it went on. We were all badly shocked but slowly we pieced together what must have happened. Tony had last been seen by Phurkipa at about mid-day on his way up what we knew as the Ice Pitch ladder. Phurkipa had probably been through the Icefall that year more times than anyone else on the expedition, for he had been in charge of the Icefall Sherpas in the spring, also. He was the last person to see Tony alive.

Meanwhile, another group of six Sherpas had just reached Camp 1, where Barney was supervising the distribution of loads to be carried back down to Base Camp. The Sherpas set off down the top of the Icefall for Base. Barney was still packing loads for the retreat when, just after mid-day, he heard a dull crump from the Icefall. This was followed by a huge cloud of ice particles which boiled up like some gigantic explosion, then hung in the still air for a few minutes before dissipating to leave the Icefall basking, once more, under the cloudless sky. A few minutes later the Sherpas came rushing back. They were hysterical in their panic, but Barney gathered that they had nearly been killed when the ice ridge they had just started to cross had collapsed beneath their feet. More serious, they had left one of their number suspended in mid-air on the fixed rope. Barney reacted immediately, taking with him Pertemba and Jangbo, who had come down from Camp 2 with him. On reaching the area they found that a complete ice ridge, which our route had followed, had collapsed. Fortunately we had always realised that this section was dangerous, being badly undercut beneath, and had therefore put a fixed rope along its length. There was a notice at one end urging everyone to clip on to the rope with their safety sling and fortunately the front Sherpa, Ang Tande, had done so. As he had started out across the ridge it had collapsed beneath his feet, leaving him hanging in mid-air about 20m above the debris. Had the rope pulled its anchor, or had he failed to clip in, there is little doubt that he would have been severely injured, perhaps killed. Even more fortunate was the fact that had the Sherpas been two minutes earlier, or the collapse two minutes later, all of them could have been on the ice ridge and the rope would almost certainly have been pulled from its anchor under their weight.

They had had a miraculous escape, but as we talked to Barney and the Sherpas there was a terrible, growing certainty that Tony had been engulfed in the collapse. The front Sherpa, Ang Tande, had seen no sign of him which meant that Tony must have been in the Trough, just below the ridge.

Barney, having assembled all the Sherpas at Camp 1, had then led them back down to Base, finding a safe way round the disaster area. None of them, of course, had any idea that Tony – or anyone else – had been below them at the time of the sérac fall.

Although there seemed to be little hope, while the faintest vestige remained we could not give up entirely. That afternoon, even though it was getting late, Mick Burke and Dave Bathgate, with four Sherpas, went up the Icefall to investigate the scene of the collapse, reaching the area at about eight o'clock that night.

Eerily lit by moonlight, they could see the Trough filled with huge blocks of ice, the remains of another sérac tower hanging crazily over the scene of disaster, threatening the searchers. They looked and listened, praying that Tony might just have been trapped by one of these huge ice blocks, some of which were as big as houses, and yet somehow miraculously protected. But there was no sound except the occasional creak of the glacier as séracs shifted and ice blocks moved. Mick said afterwards that it was one of the most frightening experiences of his life, for the whole area was obviously ready for a further collapse.

First thing next morning we sent another search party up – Hamish, Doug Scott and a further group of Sherpas. But in the light of the dawn there was no sign of Tony; he had vanished completely under the tons of ice.

And so, we had to face the cruel loss of a very good friend in the very last hours of an expedition which, although unsuccessful in its direct objective, had proved to be a profoundly worthwhile and happy experience. Originally, Dougal had known Tony well, Mick and I had known him only casually, from times spent in Leysin, the rest had come to know him during the course of the expedition; but you get to know a man, come to depend upon him in such circumstances to a degree which would be impossible back in civilisation. We had all come to respect Tony and had built up a series of strong friendships which went a lot deeper than mere acquaintanceship.

As we walked from the Everest Base Camp we fell prey to a whole mixture of emotions; sadness at the loss of a close and respected friend, elation from our experience on the mountain but most of all, unity in the face of the adversity we had faced.

17

Conclusions

We had tried and failed. We knew when we snatched that vacancy in the queue for Everest that we would be fighting against long odds, that chances were thin, but then surely this is part of the challenge of climbing, attempting the seemingly impossible and proving it wrong. There had been some grounds for optimism, the hope that there would be shelter on the face itself, the fact that the Japanese reconnaissance in the autumn of 1969 had made fast easy progress to the foot of the Rock Band and had found it much easier than they did the following spring.

But for us the face had proved impossible. We had been beaten by a combination of high winds and extreme cold. I am confident that no other party could have done much better that autumn, but even this does not mean that the face is impossible in the autumn. Given the right trick of circumstances, a few days of freakish windless weather at the right time, a party could climb the South West Face of Everest at this time of year.

The vicissitudes of the four expeditions which tried and failed on the South West Face could well have masked the greatest problem of all, however, since no expedition – for one reason or another – has reached the foot of the Rock Band in a condition to make a serious attempt to overcome its defences.

In the spring of 1970, the Japanese attempt was undoubtedly half-hearted, with the main effort of the expedition being put into the near certain success of the South Col route. The attempt was finally called off on the grounds of stonefall, though I suspect this to have been no more serious than that experienced by the European expedition of spring, 1972, or even our own expedition. Once again, in the case of the International expedition, the tragedy of Harsh Bahuguna's death, the appalling weather, a high rate of sickness, and friction within the team all contributed to delaying both the initial ascent and build-up on the face, so that finally Whillans and Haston were forced to retreat without really having made any impression on the Rock Band. In the case of the European expedition they did not attempt the Rock Band, but tried to bypass it, traversing round to the right to escape on to the South East Ridge. This offers a comparatively easy way out and it is arguable that Kuen and his team, with a little more determination and in spite of the British contingent's defection, could still have succeeded in reaching the summit by this route. In doing so, however, they would have avoided the challenge presented by the South West Face for up to the foot of the Rock Band the climbing cannot be considered difficult and the escape route, though probably no push-over, could still be climbed quite quickly.

We also were in no fit state to make a sustained attempt on the Rock Band when the time came, having taken too heavy a hammering from the combination of wind and cold. Dougal Haston had described how, on the spring attempt of 1971, they had been able to sit comfortably in the sun, even at Camp 6; there was no question of that in the autumn of 1972. I had never before experienced such a combination of savage wind and intense cold over a sustained period. There was certainly no question of being able to undertake high-standard rock-climbing nor could we have supported a lead pair at Camp 6 in a siege which might have lasted several days in those weather conditions.

Can the South West Face be climbed? I am confident that in the pre-monsoon season it can; the escape route round the side would give an almost certain way to success but in taking this, the real challenge of the South West Face would be evaded. Tackling the South West Face will require a combination of high-standard technical climbing at an altitude higher than almost any other mountain in the world, together with the logistic build-up necessary to support at least two climbers – and ideally, four – at Camp 6, with oxygen, food and equipment.

It is interesting to note that the pattern of failure is very similar to that experienced by pre-war expeditions attempting the first ascent of Everest. Nearly all of these reached a height of around 27,000ft (8230m) to be defeated by the technical difficulties of the Yellow Band and the altitude. Today we can cope with a very much higher standard of difficulty at altitude, thanks to improvements in equipment, but I cannot help wondering whether these improvements are yet sufficient to enable climbers to tackle what, in effect, is a high-standard alpine problem at an altitude of over 8230m. The critical factor is oxygen, both the reliability of the supply and, even more important, the weight of the cylinder. If this weight could be reduced by half, the logistic problem also would be reduced by very nearly the same proportion, making it that much easier to sustain climbers in a siege at altitude. Developments are being made in this direction, particularly with the introduction of a chemical stick oxygen which avoids the need for carrying a heavy cylinder. This type of oxygen works on the principle of igniting a chemical substance which gives off oxygen in its combustion. Unfortunately, however, it also gives off other, noxious gases, as we discovered in the summer of 1972 when investigating the possibility of using it; the system would require a heavy filtration plant to isolate the oxygen. An improvement and reduction in weight of the oxygen system would enable an expedition to reduce the number of Sherpas required to make and maintain the build-up on the face itself, thus easing the problems of the climbers out in front.

Another important factor is the choice of the route itself. Whillans and Haston had adopted the right-hand route up the Rock Band primarily because they had found a convenient site for Camp 5 on the right-hand side of the Great Central Gully. From here it would have been difficult to get back across to the break on the left-hand side of the Rock Band, the line that the Japanese had favoured in 1969 and 1970. This latter line seems to have some distinct advantages. Throughout its length it appears to be a snow and ice gully in photographs taken over a period of years. The gully on the right, on the other hand, seems less reliable. The left-hand gully also has the advantage that it is shorter, being approximately 150m in length, while the right-hand one is probably about 245m. Camp 5 could be situated near the foot of the Rock Band where there seems to be a snow-covered ledge on a small promontory, though even if this were to prove unusable, platforms such as those at Camp 4 could always be constructed. The great advantage of this step would be that Camp 6 would then be above the Rock Band, somewhere on the broad snowfield that stretches back to the right-hand side of the upper part of the face, where an easy-angled snow gully leads to the col between the South Summit and the main summit. The route would be more pleasing aesthetically, for there is not the easy option of an obvious escape off the face and, at the same time, it might prove more practicable.

And so the siege goes on. Is it worth it – worth the expense – worth organising large expeditions (for you would never climb it with a small one) – the discomfort – the possible loss of life – and all the ballyhoo which must inevitably accompany an Everest expedition? I think it is. The South West Face is a major mountaineering challenge which must continue to nag mountaineers until it has been solved, in just the same way that the Walker Spur of the Grandes Jorasses, the North Wall of the Eiger and the North Face of the Matterhorn did mountaineers in Europe before world war two. It is all part of the evolution of mountaineering. Today there is a strong trend in favour of lightweight expeditions, one which all the members of our own team would most certainly support, for there is, without doubt, a greater feeling of adventure and a closer empathy with the mountains when there are only a few other people around. But the only way to climb the South West Face of Everest is with a big expedition – in fact, during the later stages of our expedition we felt anything but over-crowded – each camp being manned by the minimum number of people.

On the question of cost, in my opinion it is impossible to estimate finan-cial worth on any one adventure of man, whether it be reaching the moon, sailing round the world single-handed or climbing the South West Face of Everest. Our expedition cost in the region of £60,000, a sum considerably lower than that spent by many other Everest expeditions. The money was raised from a number of sources – from the media, Rothmans, the general public, the government in the shape of the Sports Council and the Mount Everest Foundation. I believe our sponsors are satisfied that their money was well spent.

Then there is the publicity always surrounding any Everest expedition. This is necessary on two counts, firstly because this is the return our sponsors get for their support and secondly because both the general public and our fellow climbers are interested in what has happened. There is nothing new in this. Pre-war expeditions to Everest were extensively covered by newspapers, carried out lecture tours and excited interest similar to that of today.

Is it worth the risk of life? One could well ask whether any form of climbing is worth such a risk, and in so doing would challenge the very basis of the sport, for an integral part of the game – indeed one of its attractions – is the element of danger, and that very element must on occasions cause loss of life. Himalayan climbing has a greater level of risk than climbing on lower mountains; the climbers take themselves to greater physical limits and the scale of objective danger from weather and avalanche is that much greater, particularly on Everest where, in what must be the most dangerous Icefall in the world, climbers must expose themselves to risk of avalanche over a long period of time. Anyone who climbs on Everest must accept this fact. You reduce the risk factor as far as possible, but you can never eliminate it completely.

And so the challenge of Everest remains, not just that of making a first ascent of its South West Face, but even repeating the well-trodden route to its summit by the South Col. The Italians, with a mammoth-sized expedition, which has also established the controversial precedent of using helicopters to carry some supplies up into the Western Cwm, have concentrated their gigantic effort on climbing Everest by the South Col route. The Spaniards plan to follow the same course in the spring of 1974 and the Japanese Ladies have permission for 1975. Presumably they also will go for the South Col route. The next party going for the South West Face is an expedition organised from the Japanese rock Climbers' Club in the autumn of 1973. It will be interesting to see if they fare any better than we did. A French expedition, led by Pierre Mazeaud, is going to Everest in the autumn of 1974 – presumably for the normal route in the light of Mazeaud's behaviour on the International expedition; the Canadians are going in the autumn of 1975, the British Army in the spring of 1976; French Chamonix Guides, autumn 1976; New Zealanders, spring 1977; South

Koreans, autumn 1977; Austrians, spring 1978 and Dr Herrligkoffer is making a come-back in autumn, 1978. This queue is a tribute to the never-ending fascination of Everest.

And we have made our effort, contributing something to the knowledge of the face, in exactly the same way in which three previous expeditions have done – in the way that subsequent expeditions will do, until one expedition comes up with the right cocktail of planning, timing, determination, weather conditions and a dash of luck. Ask any member of our team, or ask any mountaineer, whether he would like to go to Everest. The answer would almost certainly be 'yes', for a whole gamut of reasons; to finish off a job well started; to work out the complex formula required for success on this immense problem of logistics combined with high-standard technical climbing; to stretch body and will power to the limit; to capture the approbation of his fellow men – a vanity to which almost all of us are prey to some extent. But perhaps the reason above all, is to gaze at that vista of peaks after laboriously crawling, higher and higher, up Everest's South West Face and then, if lucky, to reach the summit, to enjoy that climactic moment when the mountain drops away on every side and you are standing on the highest point on earth.

I – The Team

Chris Bonington, Leader.
Age 38. A photo-journalist living near Manchester. Married with two children. Reached Camp 6, 8320m (27,300ft).

James Roberts, MVO, MBE, MC, Deputy leader.
Age 55. Director of Mountain Travel, Kathmandu. Base Camp, 5425m (17,800ft).

Mick Burke.
Age 32. Film cameraman living in London. Married with one child. Reached Camp 6, 8320m (27,300ft).

Nick Estcourt.
Age 31. Systems Analyst from Manchester. Married with three children. Reached Camp 6, 8320m (27,300ft).

Dougal Haston.
Age 33. Director of International School of Mountaineering in Leysin. Married. Reached Camp 6, 8320m (27,300ft).

Kelvin Kent.
Age 32. Major in the Royal Signals, has served with the Gurkhas and speaks fluent Nepali. Married with one child. Reached Camp 4, 7500m (24,600ft).

Hamish MacInnes.
Age 43. Writer, photographer and equipment designer living in Glencoe. Reached 8077m (26,500ft).

Doug Scott.
Age 32. Schoolteacher from Nottingham. Married with two children. Reached Camp 6, 8320m (27,300ft).

Graham Tiso.
Age 38. Retailer and designer of mountaineering equipment living in Edinburgh. Married with three children. Reached Camp 5, 7925m (26,000ft).

Dave Bathgate.
Age 32. Master-joiner, married, living in Edinburgh. Reached 8138m (26,700ft).

Dr Barney Rosedale.
Age 37. Married with one child. Reached Camp 3, 7010m (23,000ft).

Dr R. B. Subba.
Liaison officer.

Beth Burke.
Base Camp.

Tony Tighe.
Base Camp.

Bob Stoodley.
Chairman of a group of garages in Manchester – Fund Organiser.

Betty Prentice.
Expedition Secretary.

Diana Lister.
Fund Secretary.

II – British Everest High-Altitude Sherpas, 1972:

Jimmy Roberts

	NAME	AGE	VILLAGE	TIMES TO CAMP 5 AND PERFORMANCE
1.	Pembatharke	34	Phorche	Sirdar – once to Camp 5
2.	Sona Hishy	32	Namche	Asst. Sirdar (little H.A. experience) Camp 2
3.	Pasang Namgial	33	Namche	Cook, Camp 2
4.	Phurkipa	45	Namche	Icefall duties
5.	Ang Phurba	27	Khumjung	Five times and Camp 6 twice
6.	Ang Nima	25	Phorche	Three times
7.	Anu	24	Khumjung	Four times
8.	Pertemba	25	Khumjung	Five times and Camp 6 twice
9.	Ang Phu	24	Khumjung	Eight times (!)
10.	Ang Dawa	33	Phorche	Twice
11.	Jangbo	29	Namche	Four times and Camp 6 twice
12.	Tenzing	37	Namche	Three times
13.	Ngati	30	Takto	Camp 4, fairly experienced
14.	Chongrinzing	24	Namche	Camp 4
15.	Pasang Tenzing	39	Khumde	Three times, experienced older man
16.	Tenzing	23	Namche	Five times. New, son of Phurkipa
17.	Mingma Rita	28	Phorche	Three times. Newish
18.	Nima Sange	36	Phorche	Three times. Newish
19.	Nima Rita	33	Phorche	Twice. Newish
20.	Nima Kanchha	24	Jharak	Twice. Newish
21.	Lhakpa Gyalu	22	Phorche	Camp 4. Very young
22.	Mingma	30	Pangboche	Camp 4
23.	Karsang Tile	42	Namche	Camp 4
24.	Nima Tenzing	42	Pangboche	Camp 4

1. *Of the fourteen first selected,* nine carried to Camp 5. Neither the Asst. Sirdar nor Cook went above Camp 2, and Phurkipa was confined to important duties in the Icefall.

2. *System of selection.* Jangbo and Tenzing (12) recommended by 1972 expedition, and also Phurkipa. Remaining seven men were Mountain Travel Sherpas, ex IHE 1971, six having then carried to Camp 5 more than twice and Pertemba also to Camp 6 once. (I). Was on Annapurna South Face, 1970 (5) (6) (7) on Manaslu with Messner in spring 1972. Pertemba reached top camp Annapurna I, north side, 1970. Ang Phu was new, considered too young to go above Camp 2 on IHE.

3. *Ten men added at Base to make twenty-four* (nos (15) to (24) on list). Judging from the villages the Sirdars selected people they knew, only one or two men not being from either Phorche or Namche. However, they did well, all going to Camp 4 and six to Camp 5.

4. In all, out of twenty-four men, fifteen reached Camp 5 and twenty-one reached Camp 4. Of the men who reached Camp 5, three went to Camp 6 as well.

5. About fifty-three Sherpa loads seem to have reached Camp 5, plus those carried by members. On IHE the total was fifty-five – 1972 figure not known, but I don't think more than four or five Sherpas carried to Camp 5 that season.

SOME NOTES ON SHERPA PERFORMANCES ON EVEREST FROM 1924 TO 1972: Jimmy Roberts

The time is the morning of 3 June 1924, the scene, Camp 5 at 25,000ft on the North Side of Mount Everest. It is a crucial morning for the 1924 expedition. Two days before a summit attempt by Mallory and Geoffrey Bruce had petered out when the porters had refused to carry loads beyond Camp 5. Now, Norton and Somervell have, in their turn, reached 5 with four porters and after a bad night the porters are sick and dispirited and unwilling to continue.

In *The Epic of Mount Everest* Sir Francis Younghusband tells the story.

> All having fed, Norton addressed himself to the task. The struggle which now ensued between him and the four porters was essentially a struggle of spirit...Norton...appealed to the imagination...There was no holding a pistol to their heads; no physical force; no threats; nor even bribing by money. He simply painted for the porters a picture of themselves covered with honour and glory and receiving praises from everyone: and he told them how their names would be inscribed in letters of gold in the book which would be written to describe their achievement if only they would carry loads to 27,000 feet.

Three men responded, the fourth was too ill, and Camp 6 was established that day at a record 26,800ft (8168m). However, afterwards, the Mount Everest Committee seems to have run out of funds for buying the necessary gold leaf, as we are asked to turn the black printed names into gold as we read them: Napboo Yishay, Lhakpa Chedi, and Semchumbi.

As a postscript to this story, after the 1953 ascent of the mountain the Himalayan Club instituted a search for Lhakpa Chedi, who was believed to be still alive. He was discovered in Calcutta, working as poor watchman in some obscure factory or storehouse. Small wonder that the modern Sherpa, sometimes described as being 'mercenary', prefers cash to fame, and does not, as some people would like to imagine, risk his life for the fun of the game or out of automatic and unreasoning devotion to his 'Sahibs'.

It is easy enough to write somewhat cynically now, of what one great man wrote of another great man and mountaineer fifty years ago. What is certain is that the transport of three loads to 26,800ft that day of 3 June 1924 did mark a major break-through in Himalayan mountaineering. But I guess it was respect for Norton and Somervell, rather than the promise of fame, which drove the Sherpas upwards and not down, and Younghusband, while emphasising the honour and glory line, does hint at this in a passage I have not quoted. That 'nor even bribing by money' bit reads now like a nasty crack at modern methods, but the modern Sherpa will still respond to a personal appeal from someone he respects and who seems to be doing his best – not necessarily a lead climber, whom he may shrewdly suspect of using his services for selfish ends.

Of course during the fifty years since the 1924 expedition the standard of Sherpa performances on Everest has gone up and up and I have collected together here a few facts and figures and comparisons spaced through the years.

By the end of May 1973 eight Sherpas (some as expedition members but all former porters) had reached the summit of Mount Everest, and one of them, Nawang Gombu, reached it twice. Real fame (and some affluence), the fame and glory said to have been promised on that morning of 3 June twenty years earlier, has come to only one Sherpa, Tenzing. First is first, and one may murmur legiti-mately enough about luck, and being in the right place at the right time. However, in 1953, in the case of Tenzing, there is no doubt that the finger of fate also pointed at the right and most deserving man.

The comparison in progress between the 1924 and the 1953 expedition is not very typical, as in 1953 only three Sherpas (including Tenzing) climbed higher than 26,000ft, whereas in 1924 seven reached Camp 6 at 26,800 (another four having gone up with Mallory and Irvine on 7 June). However in 1953 the top camp was higher and the climbing more difficult: also a much greater number of men reached 26,000ft (the South Col) than on any pre-war expedition. Ten years later during the 1963 American expedition, we find sixteen Sherpas reaching camps on two separate routes above 27,000ft, including one man to the summit. A total of twenty-three men reached the South Col at 26,000ft, but four of these men did the carry three times and eleven men twice, so in all forty-two loads of about 40 lbs. reached the Col. Again in 1965, with the Indians, the number reaching the top camp has increased to twenty and there are more men carrying to the South Col, one man making the trip no less than five times.

Turning to the South West Face we have more precise records of the 1971

(International) and 1972 (British) expeditions. Both expeditions had about the same number – forty – of Sherpas working above Base Camp, of which about twenty to thirty were stationed at or above Camp 2 for work on the face. In general the calibre of the men was better in 1971 than in 1972, although in 1972 the Sherpas had far better co-operation and help from the European members than in 1971. Both expeditions experienced spells of worse than normal weather conditions.

Confining statistics to Camp 5 (at 26,000ft, the equivalent of the South Col) and above: –

In 1971 seventeen men reached Camp 5 or higher, and between them they delivered a total of fifty-five loads to that camp, the best performances being by seven men who carried between 4 and 5 four times each. Two men reached Camp 6 at 27,000, without oxygen.

In 1972 fifteen men reached Camp 5, the total Sherpa loads reaching that camp being fifty-three – much the same figures as in 1971. The best performances were put up by one man who did eight carries, and three who did five each. One man went to Camp 6 twice, and two men helped to make the route to Camp 6.

Comparing the 1963 (American) with the 1971 expedition, of both of which I had personal experience and both of which employed about the same number of Sherpas, it is interesting to note that more loads reached 26,000ft in 1971 than in 1963 although the route was technically more difficult and the weather was far worse in 1971. The conclusion is that once the face route is made and roped (and of course this proviso is important) it is less demanding to carry a load from Camp 2 to 5 on the South West Face than it is to 5 on the South Col. Despite this the Sherpa record on the often criticised 1971 expedition was really very good. Whereas seventeen Sherpas reached Camp 5, only four expedition members made it to that point.

Turning to the matter of 'bribing by money', the principle was built into the strategy of the 1972 expedition, with handsome rewards for reaching the higher camps publicised from the outset. In 1963 and again in 1971 rewards were only introduced towards the end, to maintain the momentum of the carries, and were at best pretty tight-fisted. In 1938 I can remember paying off the Sherpas after a ten-week expedition to Masherbrum in the Karakorum and they received about £10 each. Of course money went further in those days, and also the men had received a small advance of pay before the expedition. But the pay was very little, about ten new pence per day, and all clothing and equipment was taken off the men. Today a high-altitude porter would earn about £50 in pay for a similar expedition, plus possibly £30 or more in rewards, plus about £120 worth of equipment – say £200 in all. Provided he can cash in on the equipment, that is good pay in Nepal, although not high by Western standards, nor expensive for the services rendered by the better men. And of course the second-rate man will receive less in rewards. An increase in rates of pay in the near future is not unlikely. Unfortunately, rich expeditions tend to pile on the 'baksheesh' and incentive money, and thus make things difficult for poorer people who follow them.

The matter of the clothing and equipment has been a bone of contention between expeditions and Sherpas in the past. I have no idea of the policy followed by the pre-war Everest expeditions, but certainly up to about 1948 the men did not expect to keep their clothing and equipment at the end of an expedition. The gifting of equipment, first started by an affluent Swiss expedition coming to India after the war (it was easier to give away the stuff than to take it back to Switzerland), soon caught on, and now there is no surer way of creating poor relations with expedition Sherpas than by short-dealing them (as they think) with inadequate clothing and equipment. In 1963, on the very generously equipped American expedition, sleeping bags were the trouble: in 1971 my expensive advice was followed, and all was well: in 1972 we were in trouble again and although the complaints were soon rectified the need should not have arisen. The irritating aspect of this business, especially to a newcomer to Nepal, is that the complaints may begin before the men have themselves done a stroke of work, and those that start the trouble often turn out to be those who least deserve good equipment.

The porter long ago disappeared from the alpine scene and these days guideless climbers far outnumber those employing guides in Europe and America. However, the conduct of Himalayan expeditions has changed very little in the last fifty years, the routes being climbed or attempted are more difficult but the general strategy employed is the same. Instead of the small compact party doing most of its own carrying, which many of us hoped to see once the giants had been climbed, expeditions have grown bigger and bigger, employing armies of men. For the Sherpas, this is all to the good, and should he tire of expedition life, there is more regular and only slightly less lucrative employment available to him in the trekking and tourist business.

I seem to have strayed from my subject of Sherpa performances on Everest, but I wonder if we have not already seen the most interesting years. No doubt the loads will continue to pile up on the South Col. Climbed fairly and correctly by any route Mount Everest continues to maintain its value, but how long the public will continue to stomach large and costly 'assaults' on the easiest way to the summit, on the lines of the 1973 Italian expedition, remains to be seen.

The South Col route would become exciting once again if the Nepalese authorities could be induced to place a limit on numbers going beyond Base Camp. Fifteen would not be too few – high mountains have been climbed by less – and within this limit it is amusing to work out the optimum composition of the party.

If I suggested one plus fourteen Sherpas I might be accused of being facetious, however five plus ten Sherpas would make a very strong team, and no topping up of numbers with additional 'Icefall Sherpas', and the use of helicopters or light aircraft for dropping supplies would be strictly forbidden. From these rules I must however exclude the 1975 Japanese Ladies Expedition, that year let sheer manpower have its final fling – there will be more than mere loads to shift up the mountain.

Planning Instruction *[Prepared July 1972]*

1. The team and responsibilities

Bonington	Leader and co-ordination in this country.
Roberts	Deputy Leader, organisation in Nepal.
Bathgate	Assistant, equipment.
Burke	Cine and photographic.
Estcourt	Treasurer, insurance details, visas.
Haston	Any work needed on Continent.
Kent	Food and communications – Base Camp Manager.
MacInnes	Oxygen and technical design.
Scott	Equipment.
Tiso	Equipment.
Rosedale	Doctor.

  1 Liaison Officer.
  2 Sirdars.
  7 High-Altitude Sherpas.
30 Icefall Sherpas – with 14 high-altitude conversion kits to make the best 14 Icefall porters into HA Sherpas.
  1 Cook (HA).
  2 Cook-boys.
  4 Mail-runners.

2. Factors affecting choice of timing

(a) *Weather.* The monsoon bad weather can end at any time from the start of September into early October. There is no regular pattern from year to year, but September is often a fine month. In 1971 the weather was good in September, and the Argentinian expedition, which reached Base Camp at the start of September, made rapid progress through the Icefall, but were then hit by bad weather in October. By the time the weather settled in November, they had used up most of their supplies and had lost the ability to keep going. November usually seems to be a fine month, but of course it is getting progressively colder, with shorter days. There is usually a high wind coming from the North East. We should get some protection from this on the face, but could be troubled by spindrift.

The Swiss, in 1952, abandoned their attempt on the summit from the South Col on 26 November, at a height of 26,600ft, where they were beaten back by an icy blast of wind.

Mike Ward reports that a temperature of –40°C has been recorded on the South Col at mid-day in early November, with a wind speed of 30 mph – this would give a very high wind chill factor.

It is obvious that the earlier in the season we can get into position to make a summit assault, the better chance we have of success.

(b) The scale of the logistic problem on the South West Face dictates a relatively slow build-up. To make an effective assault from Camp 6, seventy 30lb loads must go up to Camp 5 – See Note A. Based on these calculations, given perfect weather, it will take approximately twenty-four days to fully stock Camp 5 for the final summit assault.

(c) *Acclimatisation.* It is essential that the team has time to acclimatise at a height of around 12,000ft, working up to 18,000ft before moving up to Base Camp.

(d) *Preparation time.* It is essential that the expedition leaves Britain with the best possible equipment and food correctly and logically packed. The time we have to prepare the expedition is very short, and this must affect the timing of our departure from Britain.

(e) *Transportation problems.* We shall be flying the gear out on a Space Available basis, with BOAC. This means we must let them have the expedition baggage over a space of ten days well before our own departure date.

3. Timings chosen

Bearing the above factors in mind, we shall try to reach Lobuche, the best place for acclimatisation, as early as possible in September, so that we can either have a long period in which to acclimatise if the monsoon is late in breaking up or, in the event of fine weather, make an earlier start on the South West Face, to give us maximum chance of getting high while the weather remains fine.

We shall, therefore, aim to set out on the approach march on the 25 August.

4. Approach march. 25 August to 9 September

The party will consist of the ten climbers, Beth Burke and whatever Sherpa contingent Jimmy has organised to accompany us from Kathmandu. *Jimmy –* could you please advise on this? I estimate we shall need a total of 400 porters. Mike Cheney suggested that it might be a good idea to split the porter force, so that we have a front party with the bulk of the climbers and comparatively few porters, and then a second party, with most of the porters and perhaps two of the climbers – Kelvin plus one other? This could have the advantage that the lighter party could travel quicker, and therefore have longer to acclimatise, and make it easier overall, for finding camp sites. *I leave this entirely to Jimmy.* We could hold back the food needed for Base Camp and Advanced Base, from early October onwards, and have this flown in with Jimmy when he comes out to join us. *Jimmy –* your opinion on this???

5. Acclimatisation period

We shall march straight through to Lobuche and set up acclimatisation camp there. It is impossible to predict how long this period will be, since this will depend on the monsoon. If the weather is settled, an advance party will move up to the site of Base Camp as soon as possible, commensurate with being reasonably acclimatised, to start work on the Icefall – on the other hand, if the monsoon seems to be lingering and the weather is bad, the entire party will remain based on Lobuche, getting what acclimatisation training is possible.

At the same time, the Icefall Sherpas will be sorted out, equipped and given any basic training that seems necessary.

6. The assault

Phase 1: – Making route through Icefall – four to ten days.

Four climbers and four Sherpas and eight Icefall porters with local porters will move up to the site of Base Camp as soon as the weather seems to be settling, to start work on the Icefall. They will make the route fit for porters and warn the main party to set out for Base Camp in time for them to be ready to start ferrying through the Icefall as soon as the route is completed.

Phase 2: – Establishing Advanced Base – eight to ten days. (Manpower available – 49.)

(a) A small advanced party of two climbers and two Sherpas will move up to the site of Camp 2, and then make the route to 3; the two climbers will move up to Camp 3, and make the route to 4.

(b) The Icefall route making party will rest as necessary, and then join the ferrying parties to Camp 2.

(c) The entire party, less the advanced party will be split between Base Camp and Camp 1, to ferry all the food and gear required on the face, to Camp 2.

Phase 3: – Establishing and stocking up to Camp 5. Approximately fifteen days.

(a) The best fourteen Icefall Sherpas will be selected and equipped as HA Sherpas towards the end of Phase 1.

(b) Towards the end of Phase 1, the numbers at Camp 2 will be increased, and as all the gear needed on the face, and at Camp 2, arrives, the carrying force will be deployed as quickly as possible between Camps 2, 3 and 4. We should have thirty men available at Camp 2 and above – eight climbers, eight HA Sherpas and fourteen newly promoted Sherpas. They will be distributed between the three camps, with eight at Camp 4, ten at Camp 3, twelve at Camp 2. This gives a reserve in the lower camps to replace anyone who falls out in a higher camp, but we want to avoid more movement between camps than is strictly necessary.

(c) This leaves two climbers, one HA Sherpa and sixteen Icefall Sherpas who can be used to maintain the day-to-day flow of supplies to Camp 2, and work around Base Camp. At least one of the two climbers represents one that has gone sick. We need one fit and responsible support climber at Camp 1, to keep an eye on the Icefall and flow of supplies. Beth can run Base Camp once Jimmy moves up to Camp 2. If the sickness rate is higher than we predict, the build-up will take longer, but the principle remains the same.

(d) In this Phase, Camp 2 becomes an Advanced Base, is made as comfortable as possible with centralised cooking organised by our HA cook, and as much good, fresh food as possible.

Phase 4: – Climbing the Rock Band – Approximately six days.

(a) Towards the end of Phase 3, a lead pair is filtered up to Camp 5 to make the route to Camp 6. A pair will then move up to Camp 6 and try to force the line through the Rock Band. I shall allow four days for this effort. If they are unable to make any progress on the Rock Band, they will then work round the side and fix rope diagonally up towards the South Ridge.

(b) At the same time, the numbers in Camp 5 will be increased to six. These will ferry up all the food and gear required for the final assault.

(c) Once the lead pair at 6 have completed the route up to Camp 7, ideally in the snow bay at the top of the Rock Band, but should this prove impossible near the crest of the South Ridge, a pair will move up to 6, and from this four, one pair will be selected to move up to 7, supported by the other pair, to make the summit assault.

Phase 5: – First Assault.

(a) The summit assault should be made from the top of the Rock Band. The first assault pair will take enough rope – 600ft to fix awkward sections. This is essential for their retreat and in the event of having to put in a second assault. It is possible that the first assault pair could be so badly delayed by a difficult section that they do not have time to reach the summit in the day. They will have to watch their oxygen very carefully.

(b) At the same time that the assault goes in, it is essential that the pair at Camp 6 do another carry, taking up a further 4 bottles of oxygen, which the assault pair can use on their return to Camp 7, 2 bottles for the night and 2 bottles to get back down the next day. They should use this oxygen as little as possible, since this would be invaluable for a second assault.

Phase 6: – Second Assault.

It is important that we have the ability to make a second assault, ideally, with a fairly rested pair. This will be mounted as soon as possible after the first assault.

Bad Weather: In the event of bad weather, particularly when the team is deployed up to Camps 5 and 6, I shall have the difficult decision of deciding whether to sit it out, using up oxygen, or putting everyone back to Camp 2. In principle, if it means only a short spell of bad weather, it is best to sit it out, using the minimum of oxygen.

Rests: We shall try to avoid people coming back down to rest more than is absolutely essential. It is best for team members to take regular rest days at the camp they happen to be in. I have calculated on an average of 1 in 5 days resting. We must try to keep up the momentum of the deployment on the mountain.

7. Oxygen

(a) *3 to 4.* Climbers to use it for climbing and carrying, if they feel they want it.

(b) *4 to 5.* Climbers use it for carrying and climbing, and occasionally at night if they really feel the need for it. Sherpas carry without it, but can use some at night if necessary.

(c) *5 to 6.* Climbers and Sherpas (if we use them that high) carry and climb with it, and sleep using one bottle between two.

(d) *6 to 7.* Climbers use one bottle a day for climbing or carrying, one bottle each at night.

(e) *7 to top.* The summit pair will spend one night at Camp 7 with a bottle each for sleeping. They will take two bottles each on the summit push. It is vital that the support pair at 6 get a further four bottles up to 7 on the day of the summit push, to be used by the summit pair, if needed, on their way back down. We shall use the French bottles for the summit push, since they have 1000 litres of oxygen in them and therefore have a better capacity weight ratio than the Luxfer bottles.

8. Food

See Note B for detailed food planning.

9. Wireless

As described in my newsletter 2.

10. Tentage

As described in newsletter 2.

NOTE A – WEIGHT STATISTICS

Summit Push

Oxygen	4 bottles – French	48
Regulators	2	2
Pack-frames	2	4
Cine gear	1	4
Rope and iron	500ft	18
		76

76   2 × 38 lb loads

To Camp 7

Oxygen – Sleeping	2 bottles – French	24
Tent	1	6
Foams	2	2
Cooker + Pan + 1 Gas	1	4
Food	2 man-days	4
Personal gear	2	16
Radio	1	2
Oxygen carrying	4 bottles – French	48
		106
		76
		182

182   4 × 45.5 lb loads

Oxygen for return or second ascent	4 bottles – French	48
Oxygen carrying	2 bottles	24
		72
		182
Oxygen bottles – running total = 16		254

To Camp 6

Oxygen – climbing	8 bottles – British	120
– sleeping	14 bottles	210
– spare	4 bottles	60
Boxes	2 × 12 lbs	24
Foams	2	2
Cooking kit	1	2
Gas Cartridges	10 × 1½ lbs	15
Food	16 man-days	40
Rope	2000ft	40
Ironmongery		8
Radio	1	2
Personal gear	2 man	20
Film		8
First Aid kit	1	1
		552
		254
Oxygen bottles – running total = 42		806	33 × 25 lbs loads

To Camp 5

Oxygen – carrying to 6	33 bottles	495
– sleeping	23 bottles	345
– making route	4 bottles	60
– spare	4 bottles	60
Boxes/tunnel tents	3	48
Cooking kits	3	6
Food	40 man-days	100
Radio	1	2
Gas cartridges	20 × 1½ lbs	30
Rope	3000ft	60
Iron		15
Personal gear	4 men	60
Film cassettes etc.		20
First Aid kit	1	1
		1302
		806
Oxygen – running total = 106		2108	70 × 30 lb loads

To Camp 4

Oxygen – carrying	20 bottles	300
– sleeping	20 bottles	300
Rope	2000ft	40
Iron		15
Boxes	4	64

Cooking kits	3	9
Gas cartridges	26	39
Food	50 man-days	125
Personal gear	6 men	60
Radio	1	2
Cine gear		20
Extras		60
First Aid kit	1	1
		1035
		2108

Oxygen – running total = 146   3143   105 × 30 lb loads

To Camp 3

Oxygen	20 bottles	300
Rope	2500ft	50
Iron		15
Boxes	4	64
Cooking kits	3	9
Gas cartridges	40	60
Food	90 man-days	225
Radio	1	2
Personal gear	6	60
Cine gear		20
Extras	1	60
First Aid kit	1	1
		866
		3143

Oxygen – running total = 166   4009   115 × 35 lb loads

To 2 – Initial Stock.

4 Man tents	4	80
Personal gear	8 men	80
Gas cartridges	30	45
Rope	1200ft	22
Ironmongery		30
Food – Mountain	40 man-days	100
Spare oxygen	20	300
Extras		600
Big tents	2	160
Cooking kits	1	60
(including 2 space		1477
heaters)		4009
		5486

140 × 40 lb loads
+ 180 man-days of
food/gas/paraffin
allowance to get above
to Camp 2 at 5 lb man-
day 23 loads.
2–4 man tents + cooking
kit left at 1 = 2 loads.

Grand Total:
165 loads to 2.

This represents the quantity of food to go
to above Camp 2 and all gear to 2 and above.
186 bottles oxygen.
At Base Camp 11 bottles.
Note: Once Camp 2 has been initially established at the end of Phase 2 the 16 Icefall porters, left to service Camp 2, will be sufficient to keep it stocked on day-to-day basis, with fresh food, etc., and at the same time bring up extra cine equipment, personal gear and other items, to convert Camp 2 into an effective Base Camp.

NOTE B – FOOD

1. Quantities
See following breakdown.

2. Approach and Base Camp ration
(a) Allow 1 lb per man-day from England but the effective European ration could be higher than this, since the Sherpas would not want the breakfast foods and some of the other purely European foods.
(b) Put ration from England in twelve man-day boxes so that we can open a fresh one each day.
(c) This can be supplemented by reserve boxes containing such things as de-hydrated meats, egg, vegetables, potato (lots of this) for when we cannot purchase fresh food for one reason or another.
(d) Plan each day's menu to combine the items brought from England – which should be unobtainable in Kathmandu – items bought in Kathmandu, and items that can be purchased on the march, so that each day's menu is varied and interesting.
(e) IT IS VITAL THAT WE EAT WELL ON THE APPROACH MARCH AND AT BASE CAMP.

3. Advanced Base ration
(a) Allow 2 lbs per man-day from England.
(b) Think on lines of eight man-day ration boxes.
(c) The increase in weight from England should be made up with dehydrated meats and some tinned meats, good breakfast foods, and dried vegetables, plenty of mashed potato powder.
(d) Good bulk fillers are important for both Base Camp and Advanced Base. We should be able to get plenty of potatoes in Khumjung, but remember that these will freeze solid on way up to Advanced Base. We might be able to get over this by pre-cooking.
(e) Plan on fresh foods being sent out from Kathmandu – cheeses, salami, good vegetables – once Luglha is open. Liaise with Cheney on this.

(f) Another excellent staple is noodles and all types of pasta – I believe these are obtainable in Kathmandu.

4. Mountain ration

(a) 2½ lb per man-day – GROSS – packed in two man-day packs from England.
(b) Mike's first proposals on right lines, but replace tinned products by dehydrated foods, if possible.
(c) Include effervescent multi-vitamin tablets in each pack. They make a pleasant drink. Talk this over with Barney.
(d) A high-quality box of matches in each pack – remember our troubles on Annapurna?
(e) A slow-burning candle – Price's patent candles – address from Tiso – in every other pack.
(f) Some tissue paper in each pack.
(g) Good cough sweets in each pack – talk to Barney.

5. Packaging

Packaging wants to be light as possible, but must be strong. Make all food loads into 70 lb units, with an outer covering that is *robust, completely waterproof* yet as *light as possible.*

Approach and Base Camp rations. Make up containers of five 12 man-day packs.

Advanced Base ration. Band together two separate containers each containing 2 eight man-day packs. 1 eight man-day pack should weigh 16 lbs, the twin packs with packing will weigh say 34 lbs (right for carrying through Icefall). The complete load will weigh 68 lbs.

Mountain ration. Band together two separate containers, each containing 6 two man-day packs – 1 two man-day pack weighs 5 lbs, the 6 two man-day package will weigh say 32 lbs, the total porter load will weigh 64 lbs.

Individual packing of items. Investigate vac packing, sachets and plastic. We want stuff to be compact as well as light.

6. Research

We haven't much time but check with Services research departments, and contact all the major food firms that make any kind of dehydrated foods. Check with Mike Cheney on foods obtainable in Kathmandu.

7. Marking

Mark all packages and containers clearly.

8. Supplier of Food

I have got one more possible line of getting a single big food complex to take over supply and packing of food. I shall give them till 30 June to make up their minds, then we must go to Andrew Lusk, pay them to do the entire job of getting food together and packing it. Kelvin, you might have to order highly specialised foods – Kendal Mint Cake, some dehydrated food – you could start work on that immediately.

9. Deadline

I want all food packed and ready by the 1 August.

EVEREST SOUTH WEST FACE – 1972

Food Calculations – allowing for 15-day approach march and 70 days at Base Camp
    and above.

Approach March –	12	Europeans	(10 climbers plus Beth + 1 extra)
	12	Nepalis	(9 Sherpas, LO, 2 cook-boys).
	24	For 15 days at	1 lb from England 360 lbs
			3 lbs from Kathmandu 1080 lbs
	360	*man-days*	
Base Camp –	12	Europeans	(10 climbers plus Beth, Extra)
	45	Nepalis	(9 Sherpas, 30 IF Sherpas, LO, 3 kitchen, 2 mail-runners)
	57	For 30 days at	1 lb from England 1710 lbs
			3 lbs from Kathmandu 5130 lbs
	5	Europeans	(Beth, I & II supervisors, 3 sick or visiting)
	17	Nepalis	(10 Sherpas I & II, 2 sick, 2 kitchen, LO, 2 mail)
	22	For 50 days at	1 lb from England 1100 lbs
			1 lb from Kathmandu 1100 lbs
			2 lbs local 2200 lbs
	2810	*man-days*	
Advanced Base	8	climbers, 21 Sherpas for 20 days	
		29 at	2 lbs from England 1160 lbs
			1 lb from Kathmandu 580 lbs
			1 lb local 580 lbs
	4	climbers, 10 Sherpas for 40 days	
		14 at	2 lbs from England 1120 lbs
			1 lb from Kathmandu 560 lbs
			1 lb local 560 lbs
	1140	*man-days*	
Assault Ration –	8	climbers, 14 Sherpas for 40 days	
		22 at	2½ lbs from England 2200 lbs
	880	*man-days*	
		Totals	From England 7650 lbs*
			From Kathmandu 8450 lbs
			Local 3340 lbs
		Porter loads from Kathmandu (first 45 days)	212 loads

Total man-days on Expedition:

Approach	15 × 24 man-days	= 360
Mountain	70 × 56 man-days	= 4265 man-days.
Food allowed for expedition		= 5175 man-days.

*Make up to 8000 lbs with Luxury boxes + dried meat to supplement Base Camp ration.

Equipment: *Graham Tiso*

The manufacturers and suppliers of the equipment we required responded magnificently to our call not only for price concessions but principally for delivery on time. Ordinarily normal delivery times are so extended it would have been impossible to get together such a vast quantity of specialised equipment in eight months let alone eight weeks. The equipment left Britain on time with not one single item missing, proof that in times of crisis people respond. The expedition acknowledges an enormous debt of gratitude to all these people to whom the word 'impossible' did not exist. It may be invidious to single out some for special mention but their response was so outstanding, the risk is worth taking.

Frank Brownlie and Cyril Workman and their assistants at BOAC Cargo Centre, Heathrow, who treated our stores as though they were the most valuable, most fragile, most important goods ever to pass through their hands. No VIP ever had treatment like our stores!

Dave Crooks and Charlie Boyle of LEP Transport Edinburgh who responded to every demand made on them even though on occasions it was only remotely connected with transport and customs clearance.

Mike Devereux of Ashton Containers who designed and produced special waterproof cardboard boxes out of an already overfull pre-holiday production commitment in an incredible seven days.

Alastair Veitch of the Alna Press whose personal attention to our printing and stationery requirements saved Chris Bonington and myself so many valuable hours.

Squadron Leader Simon Baker of RAF Carlisle who refused to be beaten by the problems of packing down suits and foam mats in a vacuum packing machine designed to pack shirts, vests and handkerchiefs.

Black and Edgington Ltd who made specially, at the height of their season, some of the most important of our camping requirements including the tentage which was to perform so well on the mountain.

And lastly, my wife and children who, knowing I was to be away for three months, never complained though I was only to be seen on my way to and from bed for the preceding two months.

We knew that we would have enough problems to cope with even if we had no equipment failure at all. Proven equipment was essential; Everest is not the place to prove new ideas. Doug Scott's recent experience and Bonington's Annapurna knowledge were married to my knowledge of what it was possible to obtain in the short time available and the equipment requirement was drawn up.

The scale of issue of equipment to climbers, high-altitude Sherpas, Icefall Sherpas, cook-boys, mail-runners, the liaison officer and the conversion kit to equip selected Icefall Sherpas to high-altitude standards was drawn up. It was then tossed back and forth between Chris Bonington, Jimmy Roberts and myself until we all agreed. The result is reproduced below. The kit for climbers, high-altitude Sherpas and the liaison officer was packed in personal boxes for issue at Kathmandu, the remainder packed with general equipment for issue on the approach march.

All the equipment was supplied through my own retail organisation and goods for which we had to pay were sold to the expedition at nett cost price. All equipment was assembled and packed in my warehouse in Edinburgh and all my staff worked exceptionally hard, often in their own time, to ensure that the gigantic task of assembling and packing about 10,000 lbs of equipment in eight short weeks was completed on time. Without their help Dave Bathgate and I could never have coped. The expedition in this, as in many other cases, is extremely grateful for the assistance of faceless, nameless helpers.

Personal Equipment – Scale of Issue

		Climbers	HAS	IFS	CK	LO	CB/MR
Windproof suit	Mountain Equipment	1	—	—	—	—	—
Down suit	Mountain Equipment	1	—	—	—	—	—
Ventile anorak	R. L. Harrison & Co. Ltd	—	1	—	1	1	—
Ventile trousers	R. L. Harrison & Co. Ltd	—	1	—	1	1	—
Egger Expedition duvet jackets	ETS Roger Egger	—	1	—	1	1	1
Egger duvet trousers	ETS Roger Egger	—	1	1	1	1	—
Tiklas padded ski jacket	Pindisports Ltd	—	—	1	—	—	1
G.T. zip cagoule	Graham Tiso	1	—	1	—	—	1
Foam-back cagoule	Ultimate Equipment Ltd	—	—	1	—	—	—
Nylon overtrousers	Ultimate Equipment Ltd	—	—	1	—	—	1
Damart suits	Damart Thermawear (Bradford) Ltd	2	2	1	—	2	1
Helly Hansen Polar jackets	Helly Hansen (UK) Ltd	1	1	—	1	1	—
Helly Hansen Polar trousers	Helly Hansen (UK) Ltd	1	1	—	1	1	—
Bukta track suits	Edward R. Buck & Sons Ltd	—	1	1	—	1	—
Clarks Craghopper trousers	H. Pickles & Sons Ltd	—	—	1	—	—	—
Levi jeans	Levi Strauss (UK) Ltd	1	1	—	—	1	1
St Michael sweaters	Marks & Spencers Ltd	2	1	1	—	2	1
Pringle Houston Merino sweaters	Pringle of Scotland	2	—	—	—	—	1
Everest Shetland sweaters	W. Bill Ltd	1	—	—	—	—	1
Summerland sweaters	Jersey Knitwear Co.	1	—	—	—	—	—
Joe Brown shirts	Joe Brown	—	1	—	—	1	—
Viyella shirts	William Hollins & Co. Ltd	2	—	—	—	—	1
Balaclava helmets	Robert Sim of Stewarton	1	1	1	—	1	1
Helly Hansen Polar mitts	Helly Hansen (UK) Ltd	2	2	1	1	1	1
Dachstein mitts	Viktor Derkogner	2	2	—	—	1	—
Miloré silk gloves	Miloré Ltd	2	—	1	—	—	—
Janus mittens	C. & T. Towers	—	—	1	—	—	1

Personal Equipment – Scale of Issue – (continued)

		Climbers	HAS	IFS	CK	LO	CB/MR
Star North Wall stockings	Star Sportswear Ltd	3	3	1	1	3	1
Helly Hansen polar socks	Helly Hansen (UK) Ltd	1	1	–	1	1	–
Down socks	Mountain Equipment	1	1	–	1	–	–
Galibier Makalu boots	Richard Pontvert	1	1	–	1	1	1
Kastinger Nordwand boots	Vango (Scotland) Ltd	–	–	1	1	1	–
Niagara walking boots	A. L. White & Co. Ltd	1	1	–	1	1	–
Morlands sheepskin boots	Morlands of Glastonbury	1	1	–	1	1	–
Millet gaiters	Sacs Millet	1	–	–	–	–	–
Millet overboots	Sacs Millet	1	–	–	–	–	–
Foam overboots	Karrimor Weathertite Products Ltd	1	1	–	1	–	–
Karrimor nylon overboots	Karrimor Weathertite Products Ltd	1	1	1	–	–	1
Stop Tous	J. E. Barlow & Co. Ltd	–	1	1	–	1	1
Aries insoles	E. A. Chamberlain Ltd	2	2	1	1	1	1
Downhill goggles	I. & M. Steiner (1950) Ltd	1	–	–	1	1	1
Folding goggles	I. & M. Steiner (1950) Ltd	2	1	1	1	1	1
Champion goggles	I. & M. Steiner (1950) Ltd	–	1	1	1	1	1
BAO sunglasses	British American Optical Co. Ltd	2	1	–	–	1	–
Fairy Down Polar sleeping bags	Arthur Ellis & Co. Ltd	1	1	–	1	1	1
Dacron Fibrefill sleeping bags	Black & Edgington Ltd/ Du Pont (UK) Ltd	1	–	1	–	–	1
Stuff bags	Tulloch Mountaincraft	3	3	–	2	3	–
Camp Trails Astral pack-frame and bag	Camp Trails	1	–	–	–	–	–
Karrimor Eurotrekker pack-frame and bag	Karrimor Weathertite Products Ltd	–	1	1	–	1	–

Personal Equipment – Scale of Issue – (continued)

		Climbers	HAS	IFS	CK	LO	CB/MR
Inter-Alp Chouinard Frost ice axes	Codega Nicola & Figli snc.	1	1	–	–	–	–
Inter-Alp Cerro Torre ice axes	Codega Nicola & Figli snc.	–	–	1	–	–	–
Chouinard crampons	Salewa	1	1	–	–	–	–
Salewa crampons	Salewa	–	–	1	–	–	–
Whillans harness	Troll Products	1	1	–	–	–	–
Jumars	Robert Lawrie Ltd	2	1	–	1	–	–
Wire brushes for jumars	Myles Brothers	1	1	–	1	–	–
Pile Wonder head torches	Pindisports Ltd	1	1	–	1	1	–
Aluminium water bottles	Martsteller & Killman	1	–	–	–	–	–
Seiko wristwatches	Seiko Time (UK) Ltd	1	–	–	–	–	–
Fero wristwatches	S. B. Schlesinger & Co. Ltd	–	1	–	–	1	–
Ronson Windmaster lighters	Ronson Products Ltd	–	1	–	–	1	–
Feudor stick lighters	R. Barling & Sons Ltd	3	–	–	–	–	–
Swiss Army knife	Swiss Cutlery (London) Ltd	1	1	–	–	1	–
Housewives	Scottish Infantry Depot	1	–	–	–	–	–
Umbrellas	Kathmandu Bazaar	1	–	–	–	–	–
Aiguille extendable sacs	Karrimor Weatherite Products Ltd	–	–	–	–	–	–
Pee bottles	Black & Edgington Ltd	1	–	–	–	–	1

HAS = High Altitude Sherpas
IFS = Icefall Sherpas
CK = Conversion Kit
LO = Liaison Officer
CB/MR = Cook-Boys and Mail-Runners

N.B. Spares are required to cover losses and extra mitts, socks, and goggles should be taken plus a few extras of some other items to cover changes in plan or requirements. For instance, we planned to give the mail-runners the Aiguille Extendable Sacs but found they required bigger ones – we had extra pack-frames and bags and were able to issue these.

NOTES ON PERSONAL EQUIPMENT

Outer clothing must be windproof but must not be so water repellent that condensation occurs on the inside. For climbers a one-piece suit with outer of breathing nylon and lined with Ventile was chosen. Basically the idea worked well but the outer nylon wore badly and a superior quality would have been better. Closer attention to detail points of design and cut would also have been desirable. The pockets were not big enough, were not capable of being fastened securely and the opening of the lower ones was covered by our harnesses. The long front zip should have been capable of opening from the bottom to form a fly. The zip sliders should have had bigger pullers to allow them to be gripped with a gloved hand but a more serious fault was the omission of a hood. The suits were very baggy in the nether regions though our harnesses acted like a corset and held the spare material in place.

For the Sherpas we chose conventional double-texture Ventile anoraks and trousers as they would be of more use to them after the expedition than a one-piece suit. They were totally satisfactory.

Down suits of similar design to the windproof suits were used by climbers. They were very good and had hoods though again detail design could have been better. The nylon was not completely downproof and this caused thin spots and speckled under layers. Egger (Erve) expedition duvet jackets and trousers were given to Sherpas and were much appreciated. A padded ski-jacket was given to Icefall Sherpas, which with the foam-backed cagoule to keep the wind out, heavy serge trousers and nylon overtrousers, provided adequate insulation.

Damart vests and longjohns were worn by everyone for just about all of the time although it is perhaps significant that the two most experienced cold-weather climbers, Bonington and Haston, changed to woollen underwear when it got really cold.

Everyone wore their *polar suits* almost all of the time, and found them excellent. It was felt, however, that they should have had pockets; indeed some members added them themselves.

Although *Dachstein mittens* had previously been thought the best, almost unanimously, *Polar mittens* with nylon outers were found to be superior for swarming up fixed ropes and working around camps. *Miloré silk gloves* are knitted from silk rather than made from a woven fabric and everyone sang their praises.

Down socks are used principally as bed socks but it was felt that the plastic sole transmitted cold and should be replaced with a good insulating material.

Galibier Makalu boots (previously Hivernale) are considered to be the best available. The team felt that one or two detail design changes could be made which would significantly improve the insulating properties of these boots and the factory have responded by making prototypes incorporating changes suggested by us. Although one member enthused about *Millet overboots*, no one else wore them as they have to be permanently fixed to the outer boot and thus preclude the use of the foam overboots. Probably we would have been better to take Chouinard 'Supergators' as they are not a permanent fixture. These would give additional insulation above the sole of the boot and with a nylon overboot with an insulated sole would probably give the best protection against cold for high-altitude climbing.

Nylon overboots are invaluable from Base Camp up, not only for wearing when climbing as an additional insulating and protective layer but also around camp for slipping on over whatever footwear one is wearing in a tent to go outside for a short spell.

Kastinger single boots used by the Icefall Sherpas were supplied big enough to take two or three pairs of socks and proved perfectly adequate up to Advanced Base Camp at 21,800ft. *Morlands* sheepskin boots are welcomed by aching feet after a hot day's walk or a day in the Icefall. They would have been most useful at Camp 2 and we envied the Sherpas who had the foresight to take them this high.

The expensive *'Downhill' goggles* used by the climbers were found to give insufficient protection on their own and an additional spare lens from the *'Champion' goggles* had to be added to cut down glare to an acceptable level. The cheap *folding goggles* however were much appreciated by everyone as disposable adequate protection. It was also found necessary to double up on the lenses in the 'Champion' goggles and undoubtedly the best protection is given by the virtually unbreakable *BAO sunglasses.*

Sleeping bags caused us some concern. We considered that high-quality single bags in conjunction with our down suits would be adequate but the high-altitude Sherpas demanded an inner bag and, as we found when it got colder, they were justified in doing so. Fortunately some members had taken their own personal bags with them and we were able to rush out from Britain some special *Mountain Equipment* bags to supplement our stores. The *Fairy Down* polar bags were too bulky and too heavy, but this was because we had given insufficient thought to their size; they were too big. Had they been the correct dimensions they would have been very good indeed. Probably a good combination would be a very high-quality lightweight, low bulk down bag supplemented by a light synthetic filled bag which could double as a bag for warmer temperatures such as those encountered on the walk in.

Although the experimental *Dacron Fibrefill II sleeping bags* seemed to satisfy the Icefall Sherpas, when the climbers used them doubled up at Base Camp they found them inadequate. Fibrefill II is an experimental sleeping bag filling which theoretically should be much better than any other synthetic filling. It did not perform as well as expected and on return to the UK, investigations showed that the bags were not constructed in such a way as to allow this filling to give optimum insulation.

We chose the *Camp Trails 'Astral' pack-frame* as the 'V' strengthening at the top as opposed to a bar joining the two uprights right at the very top allows the wearer to look up more easily. These frames and bags were completely trouble-free as were the *Karrimor Eurotrekker frames* which carried an astronomical load up the mountain.

We chose the *Chouinard/Frost Bamboo shafted axe* for the high-altitude Sherpas and ourselves as being the best available. As the Icefall Sherpas were likely to do anything with their axes except cut steps we chose *Cerro Torre axes* with high-strength metal shafts. No breakage was incurred in either model in spite of considerable abuse.

The only problem with the new *Chouinard crampons* made by Salewa was with the bar which holds the centre posts; breakages were not uncommon. The fault which caused this has now been rectified at the factory. *The Salewa crampons* basically stood up very well though a vast stock of the serrated bars which joined the front and heel parts was needed as there were two or three breakages a day in the latter part of the expedition. This is possibly due to the crampons being used constantly on ladders and bridges in the Icefall putting an unnatural strain on this part.

The *Whillans harness* was considered indispensable and the only criticism made was that the crutch strap which is now made from 1½" web was more comfortable when it was 1". We understand that there are manufacturing problems in using the 1" web. The *jumars* worked perfectly; no trouble was encountered in slipping on iced ropes. It was found that a single jumar attached with a short length of webbing to the Whillans harness was the easiest way of ascending fixed ropes.

The *Pile Wonder headtorches* were only used on the walk in and around Base Camp. Most of them fell to pieces and were considered to be inadequate for the job.

The *wristwatches* kept excellent time in spite of severe weather conditions. This is important when radio schedules have to be kept.

Lighters are an essential not a luxury. Matches fail to function in the rarified atmosphere of the higher camps and the little 'Stick' lighters are ideal. Provided that they are kept in a warm pocket or warmed for a moment in the hand they work first time even in the coldest conditions.

An *umbrella* serves to keep off the rain on the walk in and the sun once one gets on to the mountain. Definitely another indispensable piece of equipment on a trip such as this.

The *Karrimor Aiguille extendable sacs* were used as day sacs in the Icefall and were satisfactory except that it was found that the harness was set too wide at the top. The factory are taking steps to rectify this failing.

The *pee bottle* was perhaps the most used piece of personal kit. A wide-necked polythene bottle of thirty-five fluid ounces capacity was found adequate for all but the most prolonged stays in one's sleeping bag. It is essential to empty them whilst they are still liquid; a frozen pee bottle was an almost insuperable problem.

CLIMBING GEAR

Quantity	Item	Supplier
5000 M	Edelweiss 8mm tensile rope	M. Teufelberger
150 M	Edelweiss 6mm tensile rope	M. Teufelberger
300 M	Edelweiss 5mm tensile rope	M. Teufelberger
100 M	Edelweiss 4mm tensile rope	M. Teufelberger
12 × 150'	Viking 9mm climbing rope	British Ropes
1000'	Tigers Web R2X 1" Soft	Black & Edgington Ltd
1000'	Tigers Web R2X ½" Soft	Black & Edgington Ltd
300	Bonaiti 12mm alloy karabiners	Guiseppe & F. lli Bonaiti
100	Tubular aluminium snow stakes	Aalco (Glasgow) Ltd
25	Deadmen	Clogwyn Climbing Gear
45	Salewa drive-in ice pitons	Salewa
90	Salewa tubular ice screws	Salewa
30	Stubai ice screws	Stubai
40	Stubai ice pitons	Stubai
100	Chouinard rock pitons	Chouinard
16	Hiebler Prusikers	Salewa
1	Parba bolt kit	Troll Products
24	Troll Etrier steps	Troll Products
1	Avalanche probe	Salewa
20 prs	Snowtread snow-shoes	Sportsman Products Inc
39	Sectional aluminium ladders	Lyte Industries Ltd
100	Marker flags	Ultimate Equipment Ltd
300	Marker canes	Kathmandu Bazaar

NOTES ON CLIMBING GEAR

High tensile strength auxiliary climbing rope is less elastic than a normal climbing rope and was found ideal for fixed ropes. 8mm diameter rope was used up to Camp 6 and from there it was intended to use the 6mm to save weight. The 8mm rope was also cut into sixty-foot lengths as the Sherpas insist on tying themselves together in ropes of three for going up the Icefall and along the Western Cwm. Although it was intended that climbers leading should use 9mm climbing rope single, in practice, they invariably led out on the 8mm rope.

Webbing is used for a wide variety of purposes as are the smaller sizes of rope. Tigers Web was found to be satisfactory provided that the ends were taped after the knot had been tied otherwise it was found that the knot worked loose.

After a typing error, which resulted in our taking 5000ft of rope instead of 5000m, had been rectified we found that our supplies of rope and webbing were just adequate. All the rope intended for use as fixed rope was taken on 100-metre drums which eased running out problems.

Tubular aluminium snow stakes and *deadmen* were used as snow anchors. A considerable quantity was used in the Icefall, for fixing ropes, bridges and ladders and because of this we had to manufacture a further supply of deadmen for use on the mountain. We could have used 200 snow stakes and 50 deadmen. The tubular aluminium stakes were also invaluable for anchoring tents in soft snow. Stakes were taken in 18", 24" and 30" lengths and the longest ones were easily the best. We could well have taken the whole lot in that length.

Ice pitons were used more for anchoring ladders and bridges in the Icefall than on the face itself and we had more than enough. Very few rock pitons were needed though if we had gone on to the Rock Band undoubtedly more would have been used.

The *Hiebler Prusikers* were taken in case we experienced problems with jumars on iced-up ropes but were not needed. *The Parba bolt kit, Etrier steps* and the *avalanche probe* were not used.

Our *Snowtread* snow-shoes were used after heavy snowfalls on the journeys between Camps 1 and 2 up the Western Cwm. They certainly speeded the progress of the person wearing them but were not very satisfactory in compacting a trail.

Aluminium ladders are essential for bridging and surmounting ice cliffs in the Icefall. They must be very strong as they are subjected to considerable pressures due to the changing nature of the Icefall. They must fit together easily and should have only a minimal sag when made up into 25ft lengths. The ones we took were excellent in every respect.

The small triangular nylon *marker flags* we took were excellent but we did not have anything like enough and had to improvise by sticking tape on top of the canes. A marker cane on its own is not easily seen. A flag is essential and we should have had three hundred.

TENTAGE ETC.

2	Black's Safari Regent tents	Black & Edgington Ltd
3	Black's Stormhaven tents	Black & Edgington Ltd
5	Black's Scott tunnel tents	Black & Edgington Ltd
2	Black's Itisa Senior tents	Black & Edgington Ltd
6	Karrimor Whillans Boxes	Karrimor Weathertite Products
8	Ultimate Everest Boxes	Ultimate Equipment Ltd
1	Ultimate Assault tent	Ultimate Equipment Ltd
4	North Face tents	The North Face
1	Powderhorn tent	Powderhorn Mountaineering
6	Vango Force 10 Mark 5 tents	Vango (Scotland) Ltd
56	Open Cell foam mats	Kay Metzler
100	Karrimats	Expanded Rubber and Plastic
100	Aluminium tent pegs	Aalco (Glasgow) Ltd
20	Snow brushes	Myles Brothers

NOTES ON TENTAGE

Good tentage on a long expedition is essential as morale must suffer if a group of people are living in cramped unsatisfactory conditions.

We found the large *Black's Safari Regent* family camping tents ideal for our communal living tent at Base Camp and Camp 2. They both comfortably withstood the foulest weather the mountain threw at them except when one was pitched at Camp 1 with only two climbers in residence. This tent collapsed due to the weight of snow on it as the occupants could not shovel it off fast enough. It was soon re-erected and continued to perform perfectly both at Camp 1 and later at Camp 2. The main zips on the doors of both tents eventually failed allowing spindrift to enter during storms. Spindrift also came in through gaps round the edges of the windows but these were easily sealed with adhesive tape. The tents were quite remarkably stable and we experienced no other problems with them whatsoever.

The *Black's Stormhaven* tents were used as cook tents at Camps 1 and 2, the Camp 1 tent surviving the whole of the expedition in spite of the tremendous weight of snow which accumulated at this camp. The Camp 2 tent survived most of the time but eventually succumbed to the final storm. It was buried right up to ridge height.

Black's special double-skin nylon *tunnel tents* designed by Doug Scott eventually proved to be the strongest most reliable tents we had. The layer of air trapped between the two skins gave welcome insulation when it got really cold and more than compensated for the consequent lack of space inside the tent as compared to our boxes. The joints on the fibreglass wands which more than doubled the diameter of the wand for a short length made it difficult to pitch and strike the tents. Once they were up they could withstand the most severe weather.

Black's Itisa Senior Tents were used on the walk in and at Base Camp. They were perfectly satisfactory until a heavy snowfall weighed down the flysheet to such an extent that the pole poked its way through the top. This would appear to be a failing in this single pole design of tent as the *Powderhorn Tent* which is of similar design also suffered in this way.

The *Karrimor Whillans Boxes* which have previously performed so well in the most adverse weather conditions were just not capable of withstanding autumnal Everest weather. The principal fault was that the framework bent and broke. The poles were different from those used on tents supplied to previous expeditions but Karrimor understood from the manufacturer that they were of equal strength. We proved to our cost that this was not the case and Karrimor are now reverting to poles which are to the original specification.

A less serious failing was that the Ventile material used on the sides and ends of the boxes was insufficiently strong. We had arranged for this material to be supplied by the manufacturers, Ashton Brothers, and had unwittingly used medium-weight Ventile instead of heavyweight. We proved that a really strong material is needed to withstand the inevitable nicks and gashes it gets from axes, crampons and other sharp objects.

A minor but niggling fault was that the zipped door started to open from the bottom which was a nuisance when snow was piled high against it. It would be much better if a double-ended slider zip were used so that one could open the door from the top under these conditions and clear the snow away to prevent it all falling into the tent.

We found the boxes to be rather short, so short that the tallest members could not comfortably stretch out in them. We think the body of the box should be not less than seven feet and a storage bay should be built in so that rucksacks can be taken inside rather than left out to get buried in the snow.

We chose to take some *Ultimate Everest Boxes* as they were considerably lighter than the Whillans Box. We carefully checked the design and construction with the manufacturer before deciding to use them but unfortunately did not realise a number of their failings. The box is lower than the Whillans and the lack of head-room made them most uncomfortable to live in. We also felt that they should be substantially longer to give room for kit storage.

Condensation was also a problem with these boxes. The ends, unlike the Whillans, are made from waterproof nylon and we found that heavy condensation occurred here causing considerable problems.

In an attempt to strengthen the framework we added an upright halfway along the longitudinal members. This upright had conventional tent pole spikes at each end and located into holes in the top and bottom longitudinal poles. Elementary physics would have told us that this pole served practically no useful function without a complementary pole between the two upper longitudinal members at roof height. Boxes tend to collapse due to the weight of snow piling up on the roof. The Ultimate Boxes did have fibreglass wands tensioned between these two upright members forming an arch but after a small amount of snow had landed on the roof, they soon flipped and served no purpose whatsoever. The holes drilled in the longitudinal members to take the upright brace in fact formed weak spots in these poles and they often bent or broke at this point. We felt that these additional bracing members halfway along longitudinal poles were basically a good idea but they should be fixed with clips so as not to weaken the framework.

An interesting lightweight design of three-way corner piece was evolved for the Ultimate Boxes but this involved the use of a high tensile steel screw which became very brittle at low temperatures. They snapped with very little provocation. The zips on the door of the Ultimate Box suffered from the same failing as those on the Whillans Box.

It can be very cold inside a single-skin tent when the temperature outside drops to −35°C. Karrimor and Ultimate Equipment Boxes are both single skin, take a lot of warming up and lose heat quickly. Some form of double-skin boxes would undoubtedly be much more comfortable to live in when it is really cold.

Whereas the Whillans Box is erected by first assembling the framework and then throwing the tent fabric over it, the Ultimate Box is designed to be erected by one or two people sitting in the tent fabric itself. This seemed to be a very good idea as the people erecting the box were protected from the elements. It works well on a peaceful Scottish lawn on a summer's afternoon but in an autumnal blizzard in the dark, twenty-five thousand feet up Everest it proved an almost insuperable problem. The Whillans Box was definitely found to be much easier to erect under adverse conditions.

The *Ultimate Assault tent* was a special lightweight design A-frame tent intended to be used at our projected Camp 7. In fact it never went above Base Camp but the basic concept seemed to be very good as Edward Whymper proved many years ago.

We had no particular function in mind for the little nylon *North Face tents* which are conventional A-frame tents with an American pattern (i.e. not down to earth and not bell ended) flysheet. Due to our problems with tentage they were used both at Base Camp and Camp 2 for the whole of the expedition and stood up fantastically well. Although the flysheets eventually were torn to shreds up at Camp 2 and a few poles got broken, the tents were most useful to us.

The *Vango Force Ten Mark 5 tents* were exactly as supplied on the domestic market except that for lightness we took nylon flysheets and had a snow valance fitted. Their ease of pitching and roominess when up was much appreciated and they performed extremely well right up to Camp 2 for the whole length of the expedition. The nylon flysheets tended to get nicked when being dug out after a snow storm and the nicks gradually worked themselves into tears which finally destroyed most of the flysheets. The tents however were still in use right at the very end. We think that it would have been worth having the heavier more robust cotton flysheets.

All our troubles seemed to centre on our tents. This was partly our fault in placing too great an emphasis on weight and giving insufficient thought to design and partly because we met far more inclement weather on the mountain than we envisaged.

We realise now that it is much better to take one tent which may be a full porter load but will last for the duration rather than try to economise by taking a tent which may be only three-quarters of a porter load and have to replace it as it has failed to withstand the conditions. Tent failure probably caused more changes of plan than any other single factor and had it not been for the fortunate fact that we were able to purchase four French box tents from the Pumo Ri expedition it is questionable whether we would have had sufficient tentage to get as high as we did. Undoubtedly, the rule is take tents which will stand up to the conditions, which are easy to erect in atrocious weather, which are comfortable to live in for prolonged spells and pay little heed to the weight factor.

We took comfortable open cell *foam mats* for use on the walk in and at Base Camp and closed cell *Karrimats* for use higher up the mountain. Although we took a considerable number of both types we still did not have enough. This is partly because we suspect the Sherpas tended to 'acquire' them but also because we found that one Karrimat was just not thick enough to give adequate insulation in the very cold conditions. Two were acceptable and three definitely more comfortable. It is important to match the number of mats taken to the tent space available, not to members of the expedition. Members do not want to carry mats around with them; they should belong to the tent.

Comfort is important, the open cell mats were very popular even though they did get rather damp due to condensation building up on the underside.

We took V-section *aluminium tent pegs* about 12" long but found these were of little use in the deep soft snow. The snow stakes referred to under Climbing Equipment and marker canes were used wherever possible to anchor tents.

Snow brushes, ordinary little hand brushes, are invaluable for sweeping the snow under the groundsheet or out of the tent, and every tent above Base Camp should be equipped with one.

COOKING EQUIPMENT

2	Primus gas double burner stoves	Bahco Tools Ltd
12	Primus gas single burner stoves	Bahco Tools Ltd
252	Primus 2202 gas cartridges	Calor Gas Ltd
8	Optimus paraffin pressure stoves	AB Optimus Ltd
14	Nester sets cooking pans	I. & M. Steiner (1950) Ltd
50	Knife, fork and spoon sets	I. & M. Steiner (1950) Ltd
50	Spare spoons	I. & M. Steiner (1950) Ltd
100	Plastic plates	Scot Thomas & Co. Ltd
100	Large plastic mugs	Sea Span
2	Large pressure cookers	Myles Brothers
4	Standard pressure cookers	Prestige Group Ltd
60	Baby can openers	Black & Edgington Ltd
60	Meta bar 20s	Black & Edgington Ltd
50	Pot scourers	Myles Brothers
2 sets	Kitchen knives	Swiss Cutlery (London) Ltd
300	Kitchen towels	Strentex Fabrics Ltd
1000	Kitchen wipes	Strentex Fabrics Ltd
2	Trigano 6 tables	Black & Edgington Ltd
12	Trigano folding chairs	Black & Edgington Ltd
2	Cooking shelters 27' × 20'	Tulloch Mountaincraft
	Other kitchen equipment	Kathmandu Bazaar

HEATING AND LIGHTING

8	Primus gas lanterns	Bahco Tools Ltd
2	Primus gas heaters	Bahco Tools Ltd
4	Optimus paraffin pressure lanterns	AB Optimus Ltd
1000	Coolite chemical lights	Baxter Fell Products Ltd
	Candles	Kathmandu Bazaar
96	Ever Ready batteries	Brown Brothers
4	Hurricane lamps	Black & Edgington Ltd

NOTES ON COOKING EQUIPMENT, HEATING AND LIGHTING

Although cooking up to and including Camp 2 was done by Sherpas we found it useful to have a gas stove in each of the communal living tents for quick brews and snacks. The *Primus gas double burner stove* working off disposable cartridges proved ideal for this purpose. The Sherpas cooked on wood up to Base Camp and thereafter used *Optimus paraffin pressure stoves.*

The Sherpas are not economical in their use of paraffin, heat or hot water. The stoves we had stood up to Sherpa abuse remarkably well but a good supply of spare parts is needed and double the quantity of stoves would undoubtedly have been useful. The Sherpas burn the stoves for twelve to eighteen hours per day usually melting water for a multitude of purposes. Furnaces, paraffin pressure stoves with four, six or eight burner heads, would certainly have speeded up the process of reducing enormous dixies of snow to boiling water.

For cooking above Camp 2 single burner *Primus Gas stoves* were used and by and large these worked extremely well. A little difficulty was encountered with the regulating valve on the burners at and above 25,000ft and occasionally the self-sealing device on the cartridge failed to work when a partly used can of gas was removed from the stove for some reason. These failings have been brought to the notice of the manufacturers and are now almost certainly eliminated.

Knives, forks, spoons, plates and *mugs* tend to get lost and we found that two or three of each per person on the expedition was about the right quantity to take.

Pressure cookers are invaluable for cooking rice and meat. Amazingly the Sherpas know how to use them.

Tables and chairs are important trappings of civilisation which must be taken. Another two tables of the type we took would have been useful. No trouble was experienced with them but the chairs all collapsed in one way or another on the walk in and we would have been better taking a stronger model.

The Sherpas use the *cooking shelters*, large heavyweight waterproof nylon sheets 27' × 20', to form small huts by building walls to fill the gap between the eaves and the ground. Although two were adequate another one could well have been useful.

The *Optimus paraffin pressure lamps* were used to light the kitchen shelters and communal tents. On occasions they objected to local impure paraffin but generally worked well. A large supply of spare mantles is needed, something approaching two per lamp per week.

The *Primus gas lanterns* working on disposable cartridges were used in the sleeping compartments of the communal tents and also for lighting individual members' tents up to Camp 4. They worked extremely well and though the mantles seemed more durable than the ones on the paraffin lamps a good supply of spares is necessary.

Coolite is a device comprising of a phial approximately 6" long and 1" in diameter containing a chemical, inside which is a small capsule with another chemical. While the inner capsule is unbroken the chemicals are inert but when the inner capsule is discharged by bending the outer phial almost in half the two chemicals can mix and give off a greenish glow. At normal temperatures this glow is just sufficient to read by and gives quite good lighting in a tent, but at low temperatures the chemical reaction slows down and light intensity diminishes. At normal temperatures the light intensity is fairly constant for about three hours whilst at low temperatures it continues at a much lower level for a considerably longer period. Coolites would be useful on some expeditions but not under the conditions we encountered on Everest.

MISCELLANEOUS EQUIPMENT

4	Lightweight tarpaulins 12' × 12'	Tulloch Mountaincraft
4	Heavyweight tarpaulins 12' × 12'	Tulloch Mountaincraft
12	Large aluminium shovels	George Wolfe & Son Ltd
25	Kit bags	Laurence Corner
1500	Polythene bags	British Visqueen Ltd
500	Polythene sheets 6' × 6'	British Visqueen Ltd
12 tins	Suppletect	Stephens Belting Co. Ltd
100 prs	Miraclaces	Stephens Belting Co. Ltd
24 tins	Dubbin	Caswell & Co. Ltd
12 tins	Boot polish	Caswell & Co. Ltd
12	Boot brushes	Myles Brothers
1	Sony TC 95 cassette recorder	Sony (UK) Ltd
4	Sony TC 40 cassette recorders	Sony (UK) Ltd
96	Mallory MN 1400 batteries	Mallory Batteries Ltd
300	Mallory RM 502 batteries	Mallory Batteries Ltd
300	Mallory MN 1500 batteries	Mallory Batteries Ltd
100	TDK blank cassettes	Peter Bowthorpe & Associates Ltd
30	Pre-recorded cassettes	EMI Ltd
30	Penguin paperbacks	Penguin Books Ltd
5	Silva No. 3 compasses	B. J. Ward Ltd
2	110 lb spring balances	Salter Industrial Measurement Ltd
6	40 lb spring balances	Salter Industrial Measurement Ltd
100	Aluminium tube containers	Metal Box Co. Ltd
3	Alarm clocks	Andrew & Co.
2 prs	Binoculars	Butterworth (Edinburgh) Ltd
200	Waterproof cardboard boxes	Ashton Containers Ltd
26	Personal boxes	WCB Containers Ltd
	Waterproof Vinyl tape	Samuel Jones & Co. Ltd
	2" self-adhesive fabric tape	T. J. Smith & Nephew Ltd
100	Yale locks	Eaton Corporation
2	Thermometers	James Scientific Instruments
2	Altimeters	Royal Geographical Society
1	Anemometer	Royal Geographical Society
60,000	Rothmans 'Pall Mall' cigarettes	Rothmans of Pall Mall
6	Boxes for repair kit, stationery etc.	WCB Containers Ltd
	Stationery requirements	Alna Press
	Comprehensive repair kit	
	Games	

Note: The nylon for cooking shelters, tarpaulins and stuff bags was supplied by Crepe Weavers and was Neoprene coated by British Vita Ltd.

NOTES ON MISCELLANEOUS

Tarpaulins are most useful, not only for keeping rain and snow off the loads stacked at camps but also for locating the bottom of load buried in snow. The heavyweight tarpaulins gave great service up to and including Camp 2 and the lighter-weight versions made from two-ounce ripstop nylon were used higher up the mountain.

The small *avalanche shovels* manufactured by climbing gear manufacturers are quite inadequate to cope with the immense volume of snow encountered on a large Himalayan mountain. We used full-sized shovels with blades made of high-strength aluminium alloy and with 21" shafts. They all survived the whole expedition and were invaluable.

Kit bags and large polythene waste bags are most useful for assembling and keeping together porter loads. We had three hundred of the polythene waste bags amongst our fifteen hundred assorted polythene bags. Of the other sizes, the larger ones were found to be more useful than the small ones.

The *six-foot square polythene sheets* were used to protect our porters and their loads from the monsoon rain on the walk in. They performed very well after we had persuaded the porters to use them and were eventually useful for protecting the undersides of tents and for a variety of other purposes at Base Camp.

We found that because conditions were so dry on the mountain very little boot dressing was required though most of our high-altitude boots had a good coating of '*Suppletect*' before they left Britain and a further one or two coats during the course of the expedition. No trouble due to the leather of boot uppers freezing was experienced. The Icefall porters diligently '*dubbined*' their boots with considerable regularity. It seems wise to issue each Sherpa with his own tin of dubbin; they are most reluctant to share!

The *Sony TC 95 cassette recorder* was used as a source of music during the whole of the expedition and performed faultlessly. The smaller *TC 40 recorders* were used as personal recorders and served not only as a music source higher up the mountain but also as an excellent means of keeping a diary. Some trouble was encountered with these in getting the batteries to connect properly, but this was the fault of the batteries and not the tape recorders. For some unknown reason, *Mallory cells* apparently differ very slightly in size from conventional batteries and it is often difficult to get them to make contact. When the batteries do work, they last for a very considerable time provided that one takes the trouble to keep them warm.

We were concerned that we might have trouble with the tape in the blank *cassettes* getting brittle and breaking. In spite of the intense cold no trouble of any kind was experienced and very high quality recordings were made. A good selection of *pre-recorded cassettes* and a good library is essential to while away the time one is stuck in camp in storm conditions. It is interesting to record that the 'pop' music fanatics became more and more interested in classical music the higher they went up the mountain!

Fortunately we were never out in white-out conditions and did not have to use our *compasses*. Fortunately, because it is almost certain that the compasses would not have worked. The needle points to magnetic north ignoring the curvature of the earth. This means that in the southern hemisphere and regions close to the Equator the needle dips so as to point in a direct straight line to the north pole and the other end of the needle has to be weighted for use in these areas to compensate.

Spring balances are required to check the weight of porter and Sherpa loads and although the Sherpas never argued about the weight they were asked to carry, it is as well to ensure that one is not overloading them. The smaller forty-pound spring balances were used higher up the mountain; the larger ones were kept at Base Camp.

The problem of finding something in which to pack our equipment proved more of a problem than getting the equipment itself. A porter will carry sixty-five pounds and obviously it is important to have loads weighing as close to that figure as is possible. We decided to have really good boxes for our own personal kit and for the high-altitude Sherpas' kit. These were made from a fibre-board material with metal strengthening, and had a removable lid which could be locked by straps and padlocks. They worked very well, lasting the whole expedition and they were eventually used to crate our remaining kit for the return to Britain. The only disadvantage was weight; they weighed eighteen pounds which is a severe weight penalty when a porter will only carry sixty-five pounds.

For our other equipment we felt that a lighter box was essential and set a maximum weight for the box on its own of eight pounds. The box had to be waterproof as it would have to withstand up to twenty-one days' monsoon rain without disintegrating and had to be adjustable for size as obviously not every sixty-five pound load was going to occupy the same volume. Eventually we discovered Ashton Containers who produced a cardboard with a layer of polythene bonded to both sides. As this material was used for making fish boxes we reckoned that it would be satisfactory for our purpose. In practice, although some deterioration occurred on corners where the polythene rubbed off, our loads made it to Base Camp without any mishaps.

A very comprehensive *repair kit* was taken and as well as the usual spare parts for stoves and crampons we took a full range of hand tools. Grips, pliers, hand-wrenches and hacksaws were probably the most used tools and a good quantity of maleable wire and bootlace nylon was also found useful.

Liar dice, packs of cards and 'Scrabble' proved very popular, but we probably could have done with a wider variety of games.

Oxygen: *Hamish MacInnes*

On the 1922 British Everest expedition, George Finch and Geoffrey Bruce used the first oxygen cylinders on the world's highest mountain. Porters had taken the cylinders to their camp on the North West Ridge, at a height of 25,000ft. Here they spent two nights before a summit bid. They reached a height of 27,300ft (8320m) before giving up.

Since 1922 there have been great advances in oxygen equipment for high-altitude climbing and the diluter-demand system has emerged as the best all-round equipment, though even this, due to the extreme conditions experienced on the 1973 British Everest South West Face expedition, gave trouble.

In the intervening years several other systems were tried. The closed-circuit set had been used both on Mount Everest in 1953 and an improved version later on Kangchenjunga. Though this system gives the best possible utilisation of a given supply of oxygen, the equipment is bulky and is also complex mechanically. A carbon dioxide absorbant is used, which must be renewed as well as the oxygen supply, thus the logistic problems are doubled. There is the further difficulty in that should the oxygen supply fail when the equipment is in use, the percentage of oxygen in the circulating gas can fall below that in the ambient air, without the wearer being aware of it. The set, with mask and tubing and with one soda lime canister weighs approximately 19 lbs. The canister would last as long as an 800-litre oxygen cylinder, which is an additional 11 lbs, filled (French cylinder).

Obviously, such a system is heavy as well as complicated, and it is seldom considered now for high-altitude work on mountains, though it has proved both reliable and good for lunar astronauts.

Thomas Hornbein designed a system which was very successful on the 1963 American Mount Everest expedition. It comprises a face mask, designed so that a variable quantity of manually regulated oxygen is delivered to the oro-nasal region of the mask at each breath. There is a manual regulation of the flow rate from 1–4 litres per minute. One of the disadvantages of the system is the restriction imposed by this regulation, for the system tends to be wasteful of oxygen at the lower respiratory rates and deficient at the high rates. The regulator is set prior to the day's climbing, but can be adjusted at any time by moving the regulator. On the other hand, the equipment is relatively simple and does not give a great deal of trouble.

The White Mountain Research Station of the University of California, Berkeley, were asked in 1969 to help design oxygen breathing apparatus for use on the 1971 International expedition which was going to attempt the South West Face of Everest. Dr F. Duane Blume was appointed Oxygen Officer of this expedition and he was mainly responsible for the development of the diluter-demand oxygen system for mountaineering.

This system is widely used in aviation and works on the principle that when the individual inspires he also draws ambient air into his mask through an orifice in the regulator, as well as pure oxygen from a cylinder through a demand valve in the regulator. The regulator as used for aviation purposes was altered to give four clip-stop ambient-air orifices in place of the original aneroid valve as this was not sensitive enough for mountaineering purposes. The four settings correspond to approximately 2000ft increments from 22,000ft to 30,000ft.

We used two types of oxygen cylinders with the diluter-demand equipment. The first was a British cylinder, specially made for the expedition by Luxfer Ltd, Colwick Industrial Estate, Nottingham, and this weighed 12.3 lbs empty and had a capacity of 1000 litres. It was painted blue, as this colour stands out clearly and it also absorbs relatively little heat by radiation. It was fitted with the standard American valve for the diluter-demand system. These proved excellent.

The other cylinders used were French, also made from aluminium alloy, painted yellow, with a capacity of 800 litres and weighing 9 lbs when empty. As these were fitted with the standard French valves, adaptors were made for us by Sabre Safety Ltd, Ash Road, Aldershot, who also supplied British face masks which we used for medical purposes. Some leakage occurred with the French valves.

The cylinders were filled by the British Oxygen Company with an American Specification Aviation Oxygen, with a dew point of 6 vpm. The complete oxygen system comprised the oxygen cylinder, a pressure reducer with pressure gauge attached, a length of high-pressure tubing, the diluter-demand regulator and a length of flexible, corrugated tubing integral with the face mask. A further orifice on the pressure reducer is used for the connection to the plastic sleeping mask, which supplies oxygen at a rate of one litre per minute, which was found to be adequate by all members of the expedition.

Our normal, everyday pack-frames were adapted to carry one British bottle inside, or two French. This was done by having each frame fitted with two straps inside the pack container for holding the cylinder(s) in a rigid, upright position. Other equipment could be carried with the cylinder(s) inside the pack.

The cylinders were charged at a pressure of 3000 psi, and the modified Robertshaw on-off reducer gave a gas pressure reduction to 60–70 psi at its outlet. The mask for this equipment is the standard military A-14 oxygen mask assembly, which weighs 14 oz. (Sierra Engineering Co.) It is made of silicone rubber and has a reliable performance in cold conditions. The mask is readily crushable in place with a gloved hand, to free ice from the exhaust valve and ports. However, on our expedition, the build-up of ice in the mask on occasions was so great that this was not always successful. The total weight of the system when using a filled French bottle, with adaptor, was 13.8 lbs (6 kilos).

Despite the success of this equipment on the 1971 International expedition, we did experience major drawbacks during the post-monsoon attempt, which may be attributed to the severe conditions encountered. Trouble was experienced mainly at the demand valve, and though we made a point of having this enclosed within our eiderdown suits, freezing still occurred in certain instances. Two of these were replaced by spares during the expedition, and several changes of components were made between various sets to obtain better results. At the end of the expedition it was found that only one set gave what we felt to be a satisfactory performance. There were at least three occasions when complete blockage was experienced and the masks had to be removed. To combat spindrift, a further small 'mask' was made to fit over the inlet of the demand valve, and this proved to be quite success-ful. We also experienced leakage from the adaptors for the French cylinders and had to utilise 'home-made' rubber seals to prevent this.

Communications: *Major Kelvin Kent*

On an expedition such as Everest a failure to communicate would be disastrous. A great deal of thought therefore went into the planning requirement and selection of equipment than in certain other spheres. In our case the requirements were broken down into four categories: –

1. A main supply route or line of communication from Kathmandu to Base Camp.
2. A radio rear link from Base Camp to the Sherpa town of Namche Bazar where limited facilities existed.
3. A solid communication link up the Icefall to Advanced Base.
4. A good working radio net from Advanced Base up the face using very light-weight small walkie-talkies.

The Line of Communication

The main supply route was fairly obvious; a small air strip exists at Luglha in the Dudh Kosi valley about a day's walk down from Namche Bazar. This was the key to fast physical carrying of mail, TV film and vital supplies from Kathmandu to Base Camp. Aircraft came in every day except for very bad weather, and we hired a local man to act as agent on the airfield. He held incoming mail for us and received out-going film and mail from the mail-runner for putting on the next plane. Similarly in Kathmandu, we used the kind services of Miss Elizabeth Hawley (Tiger Tops Office) for mail and film and Mr Mike Cheney (Mountain Travel Office) for sup-plies and press reports. This arrangement worked very well as both parties did the same for us on Annapurna in 1970 and really knew the form – especially on the aircraft movements as they control much of the available space themselves!

From Luglha to Base Camp the only effective way to ensure prompt up and down delivery of mail, film and press reports etc., is to engage mail-runners. We decided on four men whose sole task was to run between these two places carrying the absolute minimum of personal equipment. We had to kit them out for the job and paid them a flat rate (50p per day) plus a small road allowance whilst actually running. Each man had a torch and a spare set of batteries for night work.

Fuel (firewood and kerosene) and fresh food was contracted out to people in Sherpa villages round Namche, and the contractors sent up their own Sherpas and Sherpanis to carry the produce up. Sometimes yaks were used. These could carry the equivalent of three loads right through to Base if conditions were good: other-wise the yaks got as far as they could, and the herdsmen ferried the goods on to Base.

Radio

The plan catered for fourteen radios including one to be set up en route at Namche Bazar. My own tasks involved rather more than just the communications, and therefore I requested the Gurkha Signal Regiment in Hong Kong to release a capable operator to help me establish the various links. They readily agreed to this and sent Sgt Bartaman Limbu, a tough hardworking NCO with whom I had served previously, to assist in the packing, testing and setting-up phases. He met the expedition in Kathmandu and left about five weeks later having completed his job methodically and expertly.

The communication diagram shows in detail the relative locations and types of sets, and below are listed the actual models.

1. *Rear Link (Base to Namche Bazar)*
   Racal Squadcal – HF
   Mode: SSB
   Frequency: 4.1 MHz
   Antenna: Half Wave Dipole
   Output: 5 watts
   Power Supply: 14 'D' cells or 18v supply
   Weight: 18 lbs complete with case, ancillaries and batteries.
2. *Icefall Net (Base – Camp 1 – Advance Base)*
   Racal Telecal – VHF
   Mode: Narrow Band FM
   Frequency: 40–50 MHz
   Antenna: Telescopic Rod
   Output: 1 watt
   Power Supply: 8 'C' cells or 12v supply
   Weight: 3.7 lbs with batteries.
3. *Upper Camp Net (Advance Base to Camp 6)*
   Philips Handy Talkie – VHF
   Mode: Phase modulation
   Frequency: 47–57 MHz
   Antenna: Folding springblade
   Output: 400 MW
   Power Supply: 6 Penlight batteries or 9v supply
   Weight: 2.2 lbs including batteries.
4. *Radio Receivers (All India Weather Forecasts and World News)*
   Hacker Helmsman
   Bush VTR 178.
5. *Batteries*
   All radios were powered by MN 1300, 1400 and 1500 cold weather
   cells specially prepared by Mallory Batteries Ltd.

Conclusion

At no time was the operational or administrative planning held up through lack of communications forwards or rearwards. Unlike some of the previous Everest expeditions good communications, using the powerful Racal Telecals, were obtained through the Icefall and Western Cwm especially between Base Camp and Camp 2 (Advanced Base) which were by no means in line of sight and separated by at least 4½ miles. Further up, also, excellent clear communications were possible with the very light easy to operate Philips Handy Talkie which also provided a listen-in facility at Base Camp. Rearwards the well-proven Racal Squadcal produced a good voice signal over the difficult 18-mile distance with a group of 23,000ft mountains in between. It is significant that all sets, including the two excellent Hacker and Bush receivers, worked well on normal size Mallory batteries. No re-charging facility or engine was therefore necessary.

This time we chose the right sets for the right job. The overall result was successful and a tribute to the manufacturers' equipment. To withstand the rough handling of a 3-week monsoon approach march and then be subjected to conditions varying from scorching tropical heat (which could warp the side of hard plastic casings) to the intense cold of −40°C with gale force winds and driven snow is an advertisement in itself. I was very pleased.

Food: *Major Kelvin Kent*

Time Problems

Pre-packed food in cardboard boxes formed half of the total expedition airfreight to Kathmandu. With local purchased supplements in Nepal something over eight tons was consumed altogether. It's not surprising therefore that food is the most talked-about topic of conversation on a large expedition. It becomes an outlet for grumbling and a natural source of discontent under conditions of stress. Everyone knows what they want, but I don't think any ration yet designed has been able to please all of the people all of the time.

The job of organising the food was passed to me seven weeks before we were due to leave. This was nobody's fault, but it did mean that the majority of the items had to be obtained off the shelf and paid for. Normally, with any six months' preparation time, it would have been feasible to get eighty per cent of all contents supplied on a free basis by the larger catering concerns. As it was, we were extremely pushed to reach our deadline date for sorting and packing using Sainsbury and Tesco items of immediate availability. With helpful suggestions from Chris, Hamish, Nick, and my wife we set about producing the menu lists. We had about ten frantic days.

For packing I went straight to Andrew Lusk & Co. Ltd, whose experience, helpful advice, and friendly co-operation made the whole thing a realistic proposition. To achieve this they had to work overtime for nearly three weeks including weekends in order to get everything to BOAC Air Cargo at Heathrow by the beginning of August – the deadline date for airfreight.

The Requirement

First we had to agree on the menus. An endless chain of visits to supermarkets, testing, tabulating, and weight calculations followed. The idea was to produce three different rations each with four menus based on predetermined figures for man-day intakes. These were to include the total Sherpa and Nepali strength (over sixty in all). Various other factors, too, had to be taken into account in the light of previous experience and based on Chris's instructions and preliminary calculations. It is easier to tabulate these: –

1. Each food ration pack to be made up into a strong, well-sealed full approach porter load. (Ideal maximum, 70 lbs)
2. Breakdown ration packs (inside the main porter load) to be packed in strong, double-layer water resistant containers, suitable for Icefall carrying. (Ideal maximum, 38 lbs)

3. Approach march and Base Camp rations to be designed in 12 man-day packs, ideally at 1 lb per man-day (to be supplemented by 2 lbs per man-day of local food).

4. Advanced Base ration to be 8 man-day packs, ideally at 2 lbs per man-day (to be supplemented by 1 lb per man-day of local food).

5. HA (Mountain Ration) to be 2½ lbs per man in 2 man-day packs, not to weigh more than 5 lbs in separate sealed water-resistant bags. This ration to be a fully self-contained unit.

6. Weight to be kept to a minimum.

7. Budget to be watched carefully.

8. Items to be available now.

9. Menus to be interesting and easy to prepare.

Always Questionable?

For composition I examined the Annapurna ration, the British TransAmericas expedition ration, Mike Thompson's valuable original homework on the subject, and various other guides. Outweighing all of this is basic common sense. The ideal theoretical food ration is far removed from practical circumstance where *palatability*, combined with an intense dislike for certain strong-smelling items at altitude is more important than the stereotype medical 3000 calories-per-man-day approach. However good or appetising something looks on paper, it's no use if no one will eat it. Indeed, many of the mouthwatering luxuries end up being thrown away.

To achieve the bulk required within the weight allocated to food, it was necessary to rely heavily on dehydrated items in the packs and known availability of local rice, potatoes, dhal, onions, maize, ghi, sempi, tsampa, maida (flour) and cooking oil obtainable above Namche Bazar. Never will dehydrated meat or vegetables be as good as tinned items, but there is little alternative in the circumstances. Luckily our Batchelor's items were acceptable to most people despite inevitable monotony after a few weeks. The Cadbury's 'Appletree' fruit flake desserts were especially good value. But the tinned fruit, salmon, corned beef, good old digestive biscuits, and shortbread won the most praise. Tinned pears provide virtually no nutritious energy, but the sacrifice of weight for something popular and easily digestible is worth it.

Having got out the provisional menu lists, Andrew Lusks worked flat out on procurement and breakdown. Much was fairly straightforward, but the breakdown from bulk catering containers to one and two ounce packets was niggly and time-consuming. A few headaches occurred over the procurement of margarine in one-ounce metal tubes. Stuffing it all up those painted toothpaste tubes must have been a devil of a job!

Other odds and ends which we included were cough sweets, candles, loo paper, good matches, and Kleenex tissues. But everything added to weight, and when a basic pack was weighed prior to packing, it was discovered that the combined weight was as much as twenty per cent more than previously worked out. This is partly because a one-pound cake does not take into account the tin; likewise everything else that is in a tin, jar, or wrapping.

Containers

Another problem was that of outer containers suitable for porterage. Perhaps this is not so important in the dry season, but our loads were to be heaved, dropped, dragged, and humped across half of Nepal in monsoon conditions. We thought of plastic or fibreglass containers and even light plywood boxes, but the cheapest of these would have put another thousand pounds on the bill (both ways). The solution arrived at was good solid cardboard with waterproof paper covering and really strong binding. As it turned out only a minute percentage of food was spoilt or lost through bad or undurable packing, despite the approach march man and yak handling.

Whilst Lusks were clearing their factory floor at Barking, I was hunting around for other 'goodies' which we thought would be advantageous to the main ration, provided we could get the items out as separate airfreight to Kathmandu. The following was obtained in addition to the ordinary rations: –

One container of lemonade powder Two containers of medical throat tablets/ leftovers Two containers of Coburg ham One container of kitchen cloths (like J cloths)	Expedition purchase. Expedition airfreight.
Three containers of Bauschpeck bacon	Supplied free. Expedition airfreight.
Four containers of Kelloggs' Rise and Shine fruit drinks (mixed flavours) Eight containers of Pattersons Scottish Shortbread and Griddle Oat Cake biscuits Four containers of Fortnum & Mason luxury hampers Two containers of Chivers jams, marmalades and honey in minipots	Supplied and airfreighted to Kathmandu by the firms concerned.

The above items proved essential and extremely popular with everyone. The meat was specially smoked and cured and lasted well.

Altogether the UK food despatched cost £4000 and required 158 porters to get it to Base Camp. In addition a further 350 loads of local purchase supplement was purchased at the beginning and throughout the expedition at a further cost of £1500. Most of this was consumed by the Sherpas who wouldn't touch the dehydrated food unless absolutely necessary. They were nevertheless quick to raid the packs for tinned meats, fish, and biscuits.

Here are the menus:

APPROACH MARCH AND BASE CAMP RATION

12 man-days, 1 lb per man-day with 2 lbs local supplement. Four packs (Menus A, B, C and D) to one approach march porter load.

Menu A (60):

1 × 13 oz carton	Alpen Swiss Cereal
1 × 1 lb tin	Nestlés Full Cream Milk Powder
2 packs	Flat Toilet Tissue
1 × 14½ oz pack	Batchelor's Scotch Broth
1 × 9 oz pack	Batchelor's Dried Cabbage
1 × 15 oz pack	Batchelor's Farmhouse Stew
1 × 8 oz tin	Egg Powder
1 × 8 oz tin	Blue Band Margarine
12 bars	Mars Bars
2 × 7 oz pkts	Garibaldi Biscuits
1 × 4 oz pkt	Tea
1 × 8 oz tin	Nescafé
2 × 1 lb tins	Fruit Salad
1 packet	Kleenex
6 boxes	Brymay Safety Matches
2	Can Openers
2	Jiffy Lemons

Menu B (60):

1 × 8 oz pkt	'Redibrek' Instant Porridge
1 × 1 lb tin	Nestlés Full Cream Milk Powder
2 packs	Flat Toilet Tissue
1 × 1 lb jar	Strawberry Jam
1 × 11½ oz pack	Batchelor's Minestrone Soup Powder
1 × 16½ oz pack	Batchelor's Savoury Mince
1 × 11½ oz pack	Batchelor's Carrot Strips
4 packs	Cadbury Smash Potato
1 × 1½ lb tin	Dundee Cake
1 × 8 oz tin	Blue Band Margarine
12 strips	Dextrasol
12 small bars	Cadbury's Fruit & Nut
2 × 7 oz pkts	Garibaldi Biscuits
3 pkts	Cadbury's 'Appletree' Blackberry & Apple
1 pkt	Kleenex
6 boxes	Brymay Safety Matches
2	Can Openers
2	Jiffy Lemons

Menu C (60):

1 × 13 oz pkt	Alpen Swiss Cereal
1 × 1 lb tin	Nestlés Full Cream Milk Powder
2 packs	Flat Toilet Tissue
1 × 13 oz pack	Batchelor's Beef and Tomato Soup
1 × 8 oz tin	Egg Powder
1 × 14 oz pack	Batchelor's Chicken Oriental
3 packs	Cadbury's Smash Potato
2 × 4 oz packs	Batchelor's Peas
1 × 8 oz tin	Blue Band Margarine
1 × 1½ lb tin	Dundee Cake
12 strips	Dextrasol
12 bars	Crunchie
2 × 7 oz pkts	Garibaldi Biscuits
1 × 1 lb tube	Austrian Smoked Cheese
3 pkts	Cadbury's 'Appletree' Apple
5 × 4 oz tins	Nestlés Cream
1 pkt	Kleenex
6 boxes	Brymay Safety Matches
2	Can Openers
2	Jiffy Lemons

Menu D (60):

1 × 8 oz pkt	'Redibrek' Instant Porridge
3 × 3 oz pkts	Cadbury's Smash
1 × 1 lb tin	Nestlés Full Cream Milk Powder
1 × 1 lb jar	Apricot Jam
2 packs	Flat Toilet Tissue
1 × 10 oz pack	Batchelor's Clear Vegetable Soup
4 × 3½ oz packs	Kraft Dairylea Cheese
1 × 16½ oz pack	Batchelor's Minced Beef
1 × 13½ oz pack	Batchelor's Mixed Vegetables
1 × 8 oz tin	Blue Band Margarine
1 × 4 oz pkt	Tea
1 × 8 oz tin	Nescafé
2 × 8 oz pkts	Chocolate Biscuits
12 strips	Dextrasol
12 bars	Mars Bars
3 packets	Cadbury's 'Appletree' Orange
5 × 4 oz tins	Nestlés Cream
1 pkt	Kleenex
6 boxes	Brymay Safety Matches
2	Can Openers
2	Jiffy Lemons

ADVANCED BASE RATION

Eight man-days, 2 lbs per man-day with 1 lb local supplement. Four packs (Menus A, B, C and D) to one approach march porter load.

Menu A (36):

4 × 2½ oz pkts	Alpen Swiss Cereal
1 × 1 lb pkt	Granulated Sugar
1 pack	Flat Toilet Tissues
4 boxes	Brymay Safety Matches
4 × 1 pint pkts	Maggi Tomato Soup
2 × 7 oz pkts	Digestive Biscuits
8 small bars	Cadbury's Dairy Milk Chocolate
8 bars	Mars Bars
8 strips	Dextrasol
8 pkts	Spangles
4 × 4 oz ctns	Smarties
12 cubes	Oxo
2 × 8 oz tins	Sardines in Oil
1 × 8 oz pkt	Raisins
1 × 8 oz pkt	Sultanas
4 × 2½ oz pkts	Batchelor's Beef Granules
4 × 2 oz pkts	Batchelor's Mixed Vegetables
2 × 1 oz pkts	Knorr Onion Sauce Mix
1 × 8 oz tin	Ovaltine
1 × 4 oz bag	Orangeade Crystals
1 × 8 oz tin	Nescafé
1 × 1 pint pkt	Jelly Crystals
1 × 1 lb tube	Austrian Smoked Cheese
2 × 8 oz tins	Red Salmon
2 × 8 oz tins	Milac Milk Powder
3 pkts	Cadbury's 'Appletree' Blackberry & Apple
4 × 1 oz tubes	Margarine
2	Can Openers
4 pkts	Mac Cough Sweets
2	Jiffy Lemons

Menu B (36):

1 × 8 oz pkt	'Redibrek' Instant Porridge
1 × 1 lb bag	Granulated Sugar
1 pack	Flat Toilet Tissues
4 boxes	Brymay Safety Matches
4 × 1 pint pkts	Maggi Minestrone Soup
2 × 7 oz pkts	Digestive Biscuits
16 tubes	Polo Mints
1 × 6 oz pkt	Kendal Mint Cake
8 small bars	Cadbury's Fruit & Nut
8 bars	Crunchie

1 × 8 oz pkt	Sultanas
1 × 8 oz pkt	Raisins
8 strips	Dextrasol
4 × 2½ oz pkts	Batchelor's Beef Granules
4 × 2 oz pkts	Batchelor's Surprise Peas
3 pkts	Cadbury's Smash Potato
1 × 11 oz jar	Branston Pickle
1 × 8 oz tin	Nescafé
1 × 4 oz pkt	Cocoa
1 × 4 oz bag	Orangeade Crystals
2 × 1 lb tins	Fruit Salad
2 × 4 oz tins	Nestlés Cream
1 × 1 lb	Fruit Cake
1 × 8 oz tin	Milac Milk Powder
3 × 3½ oz boxes	Kraft Dairylea Cheese
4 × 1 oz tubes	Margarine
2	Can Openers
4 pkts	Mac Cough Sweets
2	Jiffy Lemons

Menu C (36):

4 × 2½ oz pkts	Alpen Swiss Cereal
1 × 1 lb pkt	Granulated Sugar
1 pack	Flat Toilet Tissues
4 boxes	Brymay Safety Matches
4 × 1 pint pkts	Maggi Asparagus Soup
2 × 7 oz pkts	Digestive Biscuits
8 bars	KitKat
8 bars	Bounty
8 pkts	Spangles
16 tubes	Polo
12 cubes	Oxo
2 × 7 oz tins	Tuna
2 × 8 oz tins	Sardines in Olive Oil
1 × 1 lb tin	Heinz Vegetable Salad
8 strips	Dextrasol
4 × 2½ oz pkts	Batchelor's Curry Granules
4 × 2 oz pkts	Batchelor's Surprise French Beans
1 × 1 lb	Fruit Cake
1 × 8 oz tin	Milac Milk Powder
2 × 11 oz tins	Mandarin Oranges
1 × 8 oz tin	Nescafé
1 × 4 oz pkt	Horlicks
1 × 4 oz bag	Lemonade Crystals
4 × 1 oz tubes	Margarine
2	Can Openers
2	Jiffy Lemons

Menu D (36):

1 × 10 oz pkt	Shredded Wheat
1 × 1 lb pkt	Granulated Sugar
4 boxes	Brymay Safety Matches
4 × 1 pint pkts	Maggi Vegetable Soup
2 × 7 oz pkts	Digestive Biscuits
8 small bars	Cadbury's Fruit & Nut
2 × 7 oz pkts	Glacier Mints
4 × 4 oz ctns	Smarties
4 × 2 oz pkts	Nuts & Raisins
12 cubes	Oxo
2 × 1 pint pkts	Jelly Crystals
2 × 4 oz tins	Nestlés Cream
8 strips	Dextrasol
1 × 1 lb	Fruit Cake
2 × 7 oz tins	Rob Roy Kipper Fillets
2 packets	Cadbury Smash Potato
1 × 1 lb tin	Heinz Baked Beans
4 × 2 oz pkts	Surprise Peas
2 × 1 oz pkts	Knorr Savoury White Sauce Mix
1 × 8 oz tin	Nescafé
8 × ½ oz sachets	Suchard Drinking Chocolate
1 × 4 oz bag	Lemonade Crystals
1 × 16 oz tube	Austrian Smoked Cheese
3 pkts	Cadbury's 'Appletree' Apple
4 × 1 oz tubes	Margarine
2	Can Openers
4 pkts	Mac Cough Sweets
2	Jiffy Lemons

HA (MOUTAIN RATION)

2 man-days, 2½ lbs per man-day. Self-contained. Six packs to each sub-container with two sub-containers making up one approach march porter load.

Menu A (111):

3 × 2½ oz pkts	Alpen Swiss Cereal
1 × 6 oz bag	Granulated Sugar
30 sachets	Marvel Milk Powder
2 × ¼ oz tubes	Salt
1 × 2 oz bag	Dried Egg
4 sachets	Nescafé
4	Tea Bags
4 sachets	Suchard Drinking Chocolate
6 cubes	Oxo
1 × 2 oz bag	Orangeade Crystals
2 strips	Dextrasol

1 × 1 pint pkt	Maggi Vegetable Soup
1 × 3 oz pkt	Kendal Mint Cake
2 bars	Mars
2 × 1¼ oz bars	Mapleton Fruit & Nut Bar
2 pkts	Spangles
1	White Candle
2 boxes	Brymay Safety Matches
2 × 10's pkts	Flat Toilet Tissues (Kleenex Pocket)
2 × 10's pkts	Kleenex Pocket Tissues
1 × 1 oz tube	Margarine
1 × 1 lb tin	Steak & Kidney Pudding
1 × 2 oz pkt	Surprise Peas
1 × 3 oz	Austrian Smoked Cheese
8 oz k pack (6 slices)	Sliced Fruit Cake
2	Can Openers
2 pkts	Mac Cough Sweets
1	Jiffy Lemon

Menu B (111):

1 × 3 oz bag	'Redibrek' Instant Porridge
1 × 6 oz bag	Granulated Sugar
30 sachets	Marvel Milk Powder
2 × ¼ oz tubes	Salt
1 × 2 oz bag	Dried Egg
4 sachets	Nescafé
4	Tea Bags
4 sachets	Ovaltine
6 cubes	Oxo
1 × 2 oz bag	Lemonade
2 strips	Dextrasol
1 × 1 pint pkt	Maggi Chicken Soup
1 × 3 oz bag	Fudge Pieces
2 small bars	Cadbury's Fruit & Nut Chocolate
2 × 1¼ oz bars	Mapleton Fruit & Nut Bar
2 tubes	Polo Mints
1	White Candle
2 boxes	Brymay Safety Matches
2 × 10's pkts	Flat Toilet Tissue (Kleenex Pocket)
2 × 10's pkts	Kleenex Pocket Tissues
1	Jiffy Lemon
1 × 1 lb tin	Ye Olde Oak Ham
1 × 2 oz pkt	Surprise French Beans
1 pkt	Cadbury's Smash
1 × 4 oz tin	Red Salmon
1 × 3 oz pkt	Ration Biscuits
1 × 2¼ oz jar	Meat Paste
1 × 3½ oz pkt	Kraft Dairylea Cheese
2	Can Openers
2 pkts	Mac Cough Sweets

Menu C (111):

3 × 2½ oz pkts	Alpen Swiss Cereal
1 × 6 oz bag	Granulated Sugar
30 sachets	Marvel Milk Powder
2 × ¼ oz tubes	Salt
1 × 2 oz bag	Egg Powder
4 sachets	Nescafé
4	Tea Bags
4 sachets	Ovaltine
6	Oxo Cubes
1 × 2 oz bag	Orangeade Crystals
2 strips	Dextrasol
1 × 1 pint pkt	Maggi Mushroom Soup
1 × 3 oz pkt	Kendal Mint Cake
2 bars	KitKat
2 × 1¼ oz bars	Mapleton Fruit & Nut Bars
2 pkts	Spangles
2 bars	Fry's Chocolate Cream
1	White Candle
2 boxes	Brymay Safety Matches
2 × 10's pkts	Flat Toilet Tissues (Kleenex Pocket)
2 × 10's pkts	Kleenex Pocket Tissues
1 × 1 oz tube	Margarine
1 × 12 oz tin	Armour Corned Beef
1 × 2 oz pkt	Batchelor's Dried Mixed Vegetables
1 pkt	Cadbury's Smash
1 pkt	Cadbury's 'Appletree' Blackberry & Apple
1 × 4 oz tin	Nestlés Cream
2	Can Openers
2 pkts	Mac Cough Sweets
1	Jiffy Lemon

Menu D (111):

1 × 3 oz bag	'Redibrek' Instant Porridge
1 × 6 oz bag	Granulated Sugar
30 sachets	Marvel Dried Milk
2 × ¼ oz tubes	Salt
1 × 2 oz bag	Egg Powder
4 sachets	Nescafé
4	Tea Bags
4 sachets	Suchard Drinking Chocolate
6 cubes	Oxo
1 × 2 oz bag	Lemonade Crystals
2 strips	Dextrasol
1 × 1 pint pkt	Maggi Minestrone Soup
2 bars	Mars Bars
2 × 1¼ oz bars	Mapleton Fruit & Nut Bars
2 pkts	Spangles

6 × 10 gram pkts	Brazil Nuts
2 tubes	Polo Mints
1	White Candle
2 boxes	Brymay Safety Matches
2 × 10's pkts	Flat Toilet Tissues (Kleenex Pocket)
2 × 10's pkts	Kleenex Pocket Tissues
1 × 1 oz tube	Margarine
4 × 3¼ oz tin	Chicken Breasts/jelly
1 pkt	Cadbury's Smash
1 × 2 oz pkt	Surprise Peas
6 oz k pack (4 slices)	Sliced Fruit Cake
1 pkt	Cadbury's 'Appletree' Apple
1	Jiffy Lemon
1 × 4 oz tin	Nestlés Cream
2	Can Openers
2 pkts	Mac Cough Sweets

In the light of (further) experience

Not enough tinned meat foods. Too many sweets and chocolates. Cut out most of the Dextrasols. Include more powdered milk, sugar, and digestive biscuits – especially chocolate ones. Make sure that things can be heated sufficiently at high altitude. For example the steak and kidney pudding was taking over an hour to get warm and edible. Put in a few Army-type Irish stews.

The Coburg ham and Bauschpeck bacon was great in the higher camps as well as further down. Well worth the effort of getting it.

Alpen was an excellent cereal, but shredded wheat was also popular as a change. Porridge, too, would not have gone amiss. Tinned fruit is worth its weight. Put in more.

One last fairly obvious observation. Dehydrated foods require water, and melted snow and ice require more utensils and a lot more fuel.

Conclusion

The basic idea of food rations packed in containers to cater for different conditions, local produce availability and cooking methods on a defined man-day pack basis, is a good one. However, the pre-packed ration pack, even if supplemented with local fresh produce, will inevitably become monotonous however good its contents. It is therefore vital to include beforehand or pre-arrange locally (not possible in most cases) an adequate stock of protein-giving extras. These, plus a few luxury items, can be successfully made up into 'goodie parcels' and their distribution to camps reasonably controlled.

The general reaction to our rations with their twelve different menus was 'quite good'. Everyone got to Base Camp with no weight loss, and I didn't see any cases of malnutrition after twelve weeks. Of course it could have been better. In fact, given unlimited weight, bulk, and financial budget I suppose we could have designed an excellent ration in fifteen seconds: 500 Fortnum and Mason hampers! Even so, a lot would still depend on the resourcefulness, ingenuity, and dogged determination of the unfortunate cook. Above Advanced Base it is not what you feel like eating so much as whether you feel like getting the cooker going and producing more than a brew – if that.

Medical Notes: *Dr Barney Rosedale*

Preparations

The expedition members were widely scattered before we started, so most of the medical preparations were made by letter. All members were asked to have their haemoglobin estimated, their urine fully tested and their chests X-rayed. Tuberculosis is a severe risk in Nepal, and everyone was advised to ensure that they had some resistance to this disease by means of Mantoux testing and to accept BCG vaccination if the test showed it to be necessary. A dental check, treatment of piles, and attention to athlete's foot or troublesome toenails were recommended.

Lastly, a record was compiled for each member of his blood group, and serious diseases, operations or injuries he had had, any sensitivity to drugs and whether his appendix was still in.

Vaccination was carried out against smallpox and cholera (for both of which valid international certificates are required) and against polio, tetanus and typhoid (TAB). Infectious hepatitis is an appreciable risk to visitors to Nepal: injections of gamma-globulin give excellent levels of protection for about three months and were given to everyone soon after our arrival in Kathmandu. Although malaria is now very well controlled throughout most of Nepal, weekly Daraprim tablets were used to protect the team during the monsoon approach march.

Drugs and equipment were gathered together in UK and these were then repacked into personal kits, which accompanied each team member both on the approach march and on the mountain, rather larger camp kits, my medical box and emergency resuscitation kit and reserve stores of dressing and drugs.

The Approach March

This 200-mile amble runs through fairly well populated hills between 4000 and 12,000ft and was completed in monsoon conditions of high temperatures and very high humidity. The main hazards of this period were gut and skin infections, and the vital rules were to treat (clean, dry and dress) all skin lesions, however trivial, and to regard all water, however limpid its source, as infected. All drinking water was treated with Halazone tablets, but tea, boiled milk or water and yoghurt (dhai) needed no treatment.

Leeches were a considerable nuisance since the bites tend to become infected. Liberal use of ordinary insect repellent cream (e.g. Sketofax) will effectively deter them, but in such sweaty conditions the cream needs to be reapplied two or three times a day, and to boots and socks as well as exposed skin.

Sunburn is a problem on this route at other times of the year, but not in the monsoon. However, exertion in these hot, damp, conditions can produce enough sweating to deplete the body's salt resources, so salt tablets should be available. It is probably simpler though to encourage expedition members to take extra salt with their meals, and, to ensure an adequate fluid intake it is similarly simpler to ask each member to ensure that they are drinking enough fluid to pass dilute urine, rather than insist on an arbitrary number of pints a day.

Porters were treated at the end of the day's march and the commonest problems were infected skin conditions, joint pains, dysentery, intestinal parasites and chest infections. A good deal of simple dentistry was done. The few cases of tuberculosis encountered were encouraged to go to their nearest hospital. In general we declined to treat the villagers in the areas we went through: transient treatment by passing trekkers does far more harm than good and can destroy confidence in their own developing medical services.

Throughout the approach march the only troublesome problems among the members were two cases of infected heel blisters and one of moderately severe diarrhoea.

Acclimatisation

In the context of mountain expeditions this process really means becoming physically adapted to living at high altitudes and failure to adapt entails the risk of some degree of acute mountain sickness. This disease affects some people and not others, and youth or fitness are no protection against it. It may affect people at any altitude over 10,000ft but the symptoms may not develop for one to four days after reaching the critical altitude.

The first sign, often not noticed, is passage of reduced amounts of urine: in fact susceptible climbers are retaining fluid in their bodies, and this excess fluid can affect the function of the lungs (high-altitude pulmonary oedema) or the brain (high-altitude cerebral oedema), or occasionally both.

Early symptoms are headache, nausea, loss of appetite and vomiting. Where pulmonary oedema predominates, breathlessness, cyanosis (seen as a blue discoloration of the lips, tongue and mucous membranes due to the low oxygen content of the blood) and chest pains occur. With cerebral oedema, giddiness, insomnia or nightmares, increasing confusion and personality changes are seen and the vision may be blurred. Both forms may proceed to coma and death, sometimes within hours.

Failure to recognise this syndrome, or confusing it with pneumonia, migraine or heart attack has in recent years led to many unnecessary deaths in the Himalaya among trekkers and mountaineers.

It is caused by going too high too fast. It is now possible to fly from Kathmandu to high air strips at the edge of the Himalaya, and a fit mountaineer going fast from such a landing strip to a Base Camp on the glaciers at 16,000 to 18,000ft is in mortal danger. The crux of prevention is to avoid a fast ascent over 10,000ft, ideally allowing about a week for each 3000ft above this height.

It is just as important that anyone suffering from any of the early symptoms should not be induced to go higher until he is feeling well again and is passing at least a litre of urine a day, and if things are not improving within two days he should waste no time in going down.

Diuretic drugs, which increase the output of urine have been shown to have some protective effect. Acetazolamide (Diamox 250 mg three times daily) appears to be the best drug for this purpose, but it should not be used without good reason or for more than a week without medical advice, and extra drinking water and salt may be required during periods of exertion while on treatment. The more rapid acting Frusemide (Lasix) is probably best kept for treatment of the established disease. These severe cases also require oxygen by mask, injections of morphine and sometimes corticosteroids in the form of hydrocortisone or betamethazone, but above all the definitive treatment of acute mountain sickness is the valleys: arrangements must be started to get the patient down without delay.

This expedition had little trouble from this problem: although several members had headaches or poor appetites early on above 16,000ft, the long walk in had given us a chance to acclimatise gently and we found that rest for a day or two allowed us to go on to further camps without any trouble.

A few points about this problem: very few climbers seem to meet an altitude barrier above which they cannot go however slowly they acclimatise. This is rare, and climbers going to the Himalaya for the first time and concerned about how well they will go at altitude may need reassurance in the early stages of the expedition. Women climbers can be affected by mountain sickness just as well as men. They should be advised not to take the Pill while at altitude and may require diuretic treatment in the pre-menstrual period. Sherpas are not immune, but the altitude at which symptoms start is much higher than for Westerners.

Medical Problems on the Mountain

The main hazards at Base Camp and above were intense cold, very low humidity, and injury. Some attention to hygiene is still required: neglected wounds heal poorly at altitude and it is important to ensure that the drinking water sources whether snow banks or, at Base Camp, glacier streams, are well away, up stream, and down wind, from the 'shitting areas' which must be both defined and enforced. All climbers should be encouraged to maintain a good fluid intake and to ensure that they are passing dilute urine. We found a screw-top plastic urine bottle an invaluable piece of equipment for everyone above Base Camp.

Food: the importance of a really palatable diet with a high proportion of fresh food cannot be too highly stressed. Iron and vitamin tablets were available to all members both on the approach march and on the mountain, the former to prevent depletion of body iron stores by the increase in blood cells formed at altitude, the latter mainly for psychological reasons.

Rescue arrangements: when climbing was in progress on the face inflatable fracture splints were kept at a camp on the face, resuscitation and minor surgical equipment with me at Camp 2, with a sledge stretcher for evacuation down the Cwm and Icefall. Evacuation from Base Camp would be by helicopter to Kathmandu or by stretcher to Khumde Hospital depending on the nature of the emergency. In addition each pair of lead climbers carried morphine and Dexedrine, the latter to be employed only in an emergency to get down to safety and in fact never used. Each climber's personal kit also included a local anaesthetic eye drop for use in case of acute snow blindness to enable him to see well enough to reach camp for further treatment.

Two climbers required stitching for deep cuts of the face caused by falling stones: both were done at Camp 2 and healed well. Fortunately no emergency evacuation was called for on this expedition.

Frostbite: deep frostbite must be distinguished from two other conditions, frostnip (superficial frostbite) and frostnumb. In frostnip, exposed patches of skin become white and doughy, commonly on the checks, nose or ears and without the climber noticing it. It is thus important for the climber to keep an eye on his companion and warn him of early changes (the 'buddy' system). Frostnip will recover if the part is gently warmed by the heat from a hand, and then covered up. Like frostbite, it should never be rubbed.

Frostnumb is a loss of sensation commonly in the toes and fingers, occurring in those living continuously in conditions of extreme cold for prolonged periods. There is no blistering or loss of tissue and the condition recovers slowly within three months of return to warmer conditions.

True frostbite occurs when body heat loss is excessive and the core temperature is threatened: the problem is not just a cold hand or foot, but a generally chilled body losing heat faster than it is forming it. This is why an injured climber, who cannot maintain his heat production by active movements, and one who is shocked or panicking and thus losing excess heat, is at particular risk of frostbite. To reduce the heat loss from the most exposed parts (generally the hands and feet), spasm of small arteries cuts off the blood supply and the affected tissues freeze: the toes or fingers go numb, white and hard.

Left as it is, this frozen tissue may remain capable of some recovery for several days. But pressure, injury or rubbing will mechanically grind up the cells and destroy any possibility of their recovery. This established frostbite is best left cold and untreated, apart from measures to prevent any pressure or injury, until the climber can be brought to a centre where his body heat can be raised, the hands or feet be thawed out, and continued warmth be supplied.

This initial treatment was carried out at Camp 2: the climber was first warmed up with hot drinks and extra sleeping bags. Oxygen was given (it would be advantageous to warm and humidify the oxygen by bubbling it through very hot water on its way to the mask), and when the patient felt better, the hands or feet were suspended for half an hour in a large can of water kept at 42°C. After that he was kept warm, treated with an antibiotic, and evacuated down the mountain as soon as possible. Even in a mild case some blistering and blackening will occur, but of the four people frostbitten during the expedition only one suffered any residual tissue loss. When the frostbite is very extensive or severe, the use of low molecular weight dextran or rapid evacuation for treatment with hyperbaric oxygen should be considered after initial re-thawing.

The use of vasodilator drugs such as Ronicol remains controversial. It seems likely that they have no place in prevention of frostbite, and are only justified during the thawing process once the core temperature is restored, when whisky is a more satisfactory alternative anyway.

Other problems: cough and sore throat, caused by cold, dry air, seem to be an inescapable part of Himalayan climbing. Vast amounts of cough sweets and lozenges are required to help, but not overcome, this problem. Two climbers suffered from cough fractures. An old-fashioned steam inhaler was found well worth taking. There is scope for developing a light heat exchange system for prewarming and humidifying inhaled air or oxygen and conserving heat loss from the lungs.

Diarrhoea was not a common problem on the mountain but an urgent one when it occurred. The 'Everest cocktail' of 2 teaspoons kaolin powder, 3 Lomotil tablets, 30 mg codeine phosphate and 4–5 drops of tincture of morphine taken at night was justified under these circumstances and nearly always successful. Piles have been a source of much trouble and disablement on Himalayan expeditions, and all members were equipped with Anusol suppositories though only one needed them. Early attention to constipation will reduce the danger.

Snow blindness affected two Sherpas who went into the Icefall without goggles: this acute conjunctivitis responds to treatment with homatropine eye drops twice daily, antibiotic eye ointment, and avoidance of bright light for two or three days.

A few climbers found difficulty in sleeping at altitude, but fewer than might have been expected considering the cold and wind. Nitrazepam (Mogadon) seemed adequate and reliable, certainly superior to barbiturates whose action and side effects at altitude are unpredictable.

Personal and Camp Kits

Personal medical kits were packed in Tupperware boxes which fit into a rucksack side pocket. They contained Fortral tablets (strong painkillers), codeine tablets, Lomotil tablets, sleeping pills (usually Mogadon), and suppositories for piles, each in a sealing plastic bag with instructions for use. There was also a selection of small wound dressings, antiseptic skin cream, lip salve, insect repellent and Lorexane shampoo (useful for lice), throat tablets, a tube of water-sterilising tablets, local anaesthetic eye drops (for snow blindness first aid), sunburn cream, and a bandage with safety pin. In addition, tins of footpowder were issued to each climber, and morphine and tablets of Dexedrine were carried by lead climbers on the face.

The camp kits, packed in rather larger Tupperware boxes, contained replacement stocks of most of the personal kit items but also small stocks of antibiotics (Amoxil and Septrin), Lasix, salt, vitamin and iron tablets, antibiotic eye ointments, homatropine and local anaesthetic eye drops, ear drops, an anti-congestant nasal spray, Valium tablets and aluminium hydroxide tablets, various dressings, bandages, elastoplast, scissors and a scalpel.

Health can make or break any expedition. Medical preparedness and proper drugs and equipment are clearly essential, but it is as well to remember that an expedition's health is related fairly closely to its morale which in turn depends on factors like the leadership, equipment, weather and the compatibility of its members under stress. The team member responsible for medical arrangements, whether a doctor or not, can contribute to morale by considering these principles:–

1. Employ a maximum of preventive medicine beforehand, and a minimum of interference on the mountain.
2. Keep the hygiene rules to a simple minimum: a few basic rules are more likely to be observed than lists of complex and marginal instructions.
3. Make sure the medical packs contain only what is likely to be needed, that they are well understood by those who use them, and that they are in the right place at the right time.
4. Avoid unnecessary research procedures and long discussions of potential medical hazards: in fact maintain a low medical profile.

I should like to thank Dr Peter Steele who not only helped me with preparations but also gave a great deal of valuable advice about all aspects of mountain medicine from his experiences on the 1971 International Himalayan expedition; Dr John Dickenson of the Shanta Bhawan Hospital, Kathmandu who advised on acute mountain sickness and more; and Dr Lindsay Strang, a staunch back-up to the expedition from his hospital in Khumde.

I – Film: *Mick Burke*

Following the successful Annapurna filming we decided to follow basically the same format for Everest, namely, that we would try to sell newsreel and film rights in one package.

ITN, blackmailed by Don Horobin and David Nicholas, bought the newsreel rights. They in turn persuaded Jeremy Isaacs and John Edwards to buy the film rights for Thames Television.

Hopefully we would return film to Britain whilst we were on the mountain. ITN sent Alan Hankinson out to Kathmandu to fix up arrangements there so that the film would pass through quickly and safely.

We would be using Ektachrome EF 7242 having a daylight ASA rating of 80. It isn't the ideal film for mountains but it did have the advantage that it could be processed at ITN within an hour of arriving in London. We had the film in 50' 8mm cassettes, 50' cassettes for the 16mm Autoload cameras, 100' daylight spools for the Bell & Howell 70DR camera and 400' rolls for the Arriflex.

In total we had eight cine cameras. For interviews we had an Arriflex ST. It was used on either an Arriflex slip head tripod or on a special ITN shoulder mount. The Arriflex went as far as Camp 2. It was left in Camp 2 with the Telestigmat lens so that Barney could film people working on the face. Above Camp 2 I used a Bell & Howell 70DR. We also had four Bell & Howell Autoload cameras and then a Bell & Howell 442 Filmosound camera and a Kodak XL33 camera.

The Arriflex had a 12–120mm Angenieux zoom lens plus a set of Taylor Hobson lenses. The Bell & Howell 70DR had 1" and 2" Taylor Hobson lenses and an Angenieux 10mm lens. The Autoloads all had Angenieux 10mm lenses and one of them which was a twin turret Autoload also had a Taylor Hobson 1" lens. The Bell & Howell had a 11–35mm zoom and the Kodak XL33 had a 9mm fixed lens. I also had a 300mm Telestigmat lens for use on the Arriflex.

The Arriflex was used with a Bell & Howell Filmosound Cassette Recorder which had been modified to record a pulse from the Arriflex. Camp 2 was the highest we used this channel but the Bell & Howell 8mm used with its own filmosound recorder was used at Camp 5 at 26,000ft. We also had two Nagra SN Recorders. As we were unable to sync. them up to any of the cameras they were used purely to record wild track. They also were used up to Camp 5.

I had a lot of problems with filters due to the extreme cold. Luckily the Tiffen filters held up on the zoom and BDB were able to make some of their Filtran filters up at short notice. For light meters I used my own Gossen Luna Six. For the Arriflex I had six nickel cadmium batteries. These were sent back in rotation to

Kathmandu for re-charging. I had no trouble with them apart from them losing power sooner than they would at sea level. All the tape recorders were powered by Mallory cells and gave very little trouble. Our contacts for shipping our film back to Britain were built on our experiences from Annapurna. In practice we were able to get film from the mountain to London within four days.

Fortunately the only problems we had were minor ones. A battery shorting out, a battery cable with a loose connection and a main spring breaking on one of the Autoloads. The first two mendable, the third, well we had a spare. Apart from these minor problems, the only other problem was persuading tall climbers not to put cameras outside at nights to give a little more room. I did spend quite a lot of the time at the higher camps with some piece or other of filming equipment inside my sleeping bag. It was my experience that in these very cold temperatures anything that was left outside at night was unlikely to work until it had had forty-eight hours inside a sleeping bag. I tried wherever possible not to take equipment, especially lenses, outside until the sun had made an appearance. This way I didn't have too many problems with lenses getting condensation between the elements. If I had to go outside whilst it was still very cold, I would try to introduce the lenses gradually to the cold. On the occasion when I did get condensation inside the lens, five or ten minutes holding a chamois leather to the front element would usually shift it. The light as we expected was very bright. Even with an 85 ND 06 filter, the aperture under bright sunlight was usually f8–11. Even when it was cloudy it normally opened up only one stop. To try to cut out some of the camera shake one normally gets on mountains I used wherever possible a shoulder mount which camera maintenance department at ITN made.

Using the Lunasix exposure meter I generally relied on incident light readings. In mountains one constantly gets misleading readings from either the snow or the sky. To get accurate readings one has to use a little bit of common sense. If one takes a general incident light reading faces and objects will tend to be underexposed, due to the greater influence that the snow and sky have on the meter. It is as well to slightly overexpose the snow. (I used to overexpose ¼–⅓ of a stop, generally.) However, on landscapes the snow and sky very quickly go wishy-washy, so one has to be very careful.

Back in London the film was viewed and edited by ITN and they made up their news items as soon as they received the film. It was then passed on to Thames where John Edwards and Trevor Waite started to knock it into shape for the 'This Week' programme. The idea was that it would be transmitted as soon as possible after we had either succeeded or failed on the mountain. In actual fact it was transmitted one week after we had turned back from Camp 6.

In total we shot about 18,000ft of film and recorded about fifteen hours of tape. This has now been edited into approximately twenty news items of around three minutes each, a half-hour film for Thames, a second half-hour film for Rothmans, one of our sponsors and a six-minute film which Rothmans hope to release to cinemas in their Great Achievements series.

II – Still Photography: *Doug Scott*

There are two lessons that the high-altitude climber learns; one, to conserve his strength by an economy of movement and the other, to compose his mind by avoiding complicated technicalities. Old hands, like Dougal Haston and Hamish MacInnes, know better than to fiddle with filters, light meters and camera lenses high on the South West Face of Mount Everest. Dougal, especially, has never had that compulsion to use his camera in the mountains. In this age of intense visual communication it is in some ways refreshing to find climbers who are not consumed with the burning need to capture on film every passing moment of a climb, and one can respect their point of view.

In Victorian times such 'vulgarities' as illustrations were usually left to the 'gutter press' as they were thought to 'encourage mental laziness which could lead to moral collapse'. In order to put over a message, there is no doubt that photographs do not demand the same intellectual effort as does the written word. This combination of Victorian snobbery and puritanism, as well as simple economics, was a feature of mountaineering publications, books and journals, up until the last war. Now, however, they become even more pictorial and glossy, and magazine editors in particular have an insatiable appetite for photographs to portray climbing events graphically.

Expedition leaders must badger their teams to use their cameras constantly, so that their sponsors are provided with adequate material. This is essential, since without the sponsors, the expedition would probably not be possible.

Apart from having the opportunity of seeing one's photographs 'in print' there was for all of us a natural wish to keep a personal photographic record of our visit to Everest. There was no holding back from taking photographs, fearing we might run short of film, since Kodak had supplied copious amounts to meet all our needs. They generously supplied:

300 rolls Kodachrome II	(A.S.A./25)
20 rolls High Speed Ektachrome	(A.S.A./160)
100 rolls Panatomic X	(A.S.A./30)
20 rolls TRI X	(A.S.A./400)

It was reassuring to know that all our pooled, exposed film was going back to the Expedition Secretary, Betty Prentice, and Wendy Bonington who between them sent the film for processing and then stamped every transparency with the photographer's name. This tedious job was only relieved for them by the opportunity to 'have a look' at our progress from the picture content. Wendy was also meticulous in sending out reports to each of us as to the quality of each slide. From her remarks we were able to make belated adjustments when necessary. The black and white material was extremely well processed by *The Observer* and all our printing was carried out by Marshall & Company of Nottingham. They produced high-standard prints at very short notice and gave us an excellent service.

Kodachrome II was far and away the most popular and effective colour film used on the expedition. It was fast enough to help produce sharp, lively results in the bright light prevailing on the mountain. Some high-speed Ektachrome was used on the approach march, to help with the dull monsoon conditions through the foothills. This was also a useful film at Base Camp whenever we wished to indulge in moonlit or fireside photography.

Exposure:

Most of the team used inbuilt exposure meters. On the mountain we tended to shoot at 250 at f8–f11–f16, depending on whether the foreground was rock or snow or mixed ground. The relatively fast speed helped to compensate for camera shake, due to rapid breathing and strong winds – always a feature of this expedition. One problem on the mountain was in trying to preserve something of the texture of the snow and, at the same time, attempting to show subject detail. If the faces of one's companions were in shadow then their features were usually lost. In this respect, the dark-skinned Sherpas gave noticeably poorer results, photographically, than the pale faces of the European members.

It was always a wise precaution to bracket exposures. With plenty of film available, it only required personal discipline to do this.

Camera Equipment:

The majority of the expedition members used Pentax equipment, generously supplied by Rank Photographic, through the kind offices of Peter Railton their Marketing Manager. Kelvin Kent, Mick Burke and Nick Estcourt had all used Pentax equipment on the Annapurna South Face expedition. The author of this section had also used Pentax equipment on the European Mount Everest expedition.

For the actual climbing, a good combination of lenses was the interchangeable 28mm and 85mm Takuma lenses on two Spotmatic bodies. Providing the coloured filter is removed at the appropriate time, this equipment allows for both a full range of colour and black and white photography.

Useful extras were the 400mm lens for long-range photographs from Base Camp into the Icefall, and from Camp 2 on to the face. A 35mm lens was found to be best for picking out detail from a range of subject matter, whilst the 85mm was a useful lens for portraiture.

In the Western Cwm a 17mm lens was used occasionally for special effects although, as Nick Estcourt suggested, a full panoramic view might best be achieved with a fish-eye lens placed on the floor of the Cwm.

Although none of the Pentax equipment had been winterised, none of it failed in the sub-zero temperatures. Chris Bonington used two Leica M2 cameras and two Nikon cameras. They all functioned perfectly well throughout the expedition. Ken Wilson, when he visited the expedition, used a 2¼ square camera. His Mamiyaflex Professional achieved good results throughout his short stay. His second camera was a Leica M2.

As a precaution against the SLR mechanism freezing, Bonington and I used Rollei 35 cameras from Camp 5 to Camp 6 at 27,300ft. Whilst using two Rollei 35s at the site of Camp 6, one of the author's cameras froze up. This was in temperatures of −40°C and in winds of over 100 mph. Unfortunately, that particular camera had been left out of its leather case and outside the duvet suit, for over five minutes. The film was removed back in Britain after our return.

The Rollei 35 is, nevertheless, a very useful expedition camera, being so compact and simple to operate and with the excellent 40mm Zeiss lens gives very crisp definition.

One problem with changing from through-the-lens viewing to a camera with side viewing, is that it is so easy to let thick woollen mitts partly or wholly obscure the lens. Several potentially good photographs were lost at Camp 6 because of this. Those members who used only Rollei 35 cameras took good care not to allow this to happen – Graham Tiso and Dougal Haston both achieved good results below Camp 4.

The expedition coincided with the launching by Kodak of their new, revolutionary Pocket Instamatic range of cameras. On some expeditions climbers have been reluctant to carry camera equipment when the combination of bad weather and altitude has caused them to abandon all but the barest essentials in their carrying loads. The tiny, lightweight, easy to use Pocket Instamatic was an obvious choice for the lead climbers who would be making a summit bid. Kodak, therefore, generously supplied the expedition with this range of cameras and Hamish MacInnes used one all the way up the Face, to an altitude of approximately 26,500ft. The results were excellent and since they are so small and compact could be carried in our inside pockets and, as a result, did not freeze up.

Results:

The best results, as one might expect from the law of averages, were produced by those photographers who ran most film through their cameras. On the approach march several subjects were left for someone else to cover who, in turn, also left them for someone else, with the result that leeches, for instance, were not very well covered; neither was the full range of wild flowers covered.

In the Icefall, which lends itself to spectacular climbing photography, good results were obtained by all the team – even Dougal distinguishing himself by having an excellent Icefall picture appear on the front page of *The Observer* newspaper!

Although results while lead climbing on the face itself were comparatively few, they were probably better than those from previous expeditions. Because we were able to judge from previous photographs where the best camera positions were likely to be we were able to improve on previous photographic performance.

Twice our efforts nearly ended in disaster – when Chris stepped back, into a hidden crevasse in the Western Cwm when photographing his Sherpas, and when I stepped off the face whilst photographing Mick Burke at Camp 5; I slipped down 30ft before luckily stopping myself. Both times we were able to extricate ourselves from the misadventure.

We all had days off from photography when it seemed inappropriate to let the camera interfere with the climbing experience. Thus few photographs were taken by actual lead climbers whilst pushing the fixed ropes up the mountain side. When there are only one or two days' lead climbing for each member, out of a three-month expedition then perhaps he may be forgiven for wanting to climb rather than to mix it with photography.

EVEREST
THE HARD WAY

To Mick Burke and Mingma Nuru

Contents

Foreword

by Lord Hunt of Llanvair Waterdine, CBE, DSO

In December 1972 I greeted Chris Bonington and his team at a reception on their return from his previous attempt on the South West Face, from which they had been turned back at 27,300ft [8320m], and at the very limits of human endurance, by the combined effects of low temperatures and high wind at very high altitude. 'Never again,' was his verdict.

I knew how he felt. Many years before, in the winter of 1937, with my wife and Reggie Cooke, I had taken part in a light expedition during the months of October to December to the eastern surroundings of Kangchenjunga, third highest mountain in the world. One of our purposes was to try out climbing conditions during the long clear spell at the beginning of winter, so as to prove whether that period might offer a better chance to climb Everest than the usually favoured but brief opportunity before the monsoon brings heavy snowfalls to the South East Himalaya. We had some successes, including a 23,500ft [7160m] peak; and we pushed a reconnaissance on Kangchenjunga to within a few hundred feet of its North Col, from which a ridge leads to the summit. But an indelible memory had been the bitter cold and a terrifying wind – especially that wind. Yet looking through my diaries, I find that I wrote later: 'Taken all round, I feel that it is unwise to generalise as a result of this experience, and that it is most desirable to visit Everest in the post-monsoon period.'

So it came as no surprise when Chris phoned me in September 1973 to tell me that a Canadian expedition had cancelled their permit to attempt Everest in the autumn of 1975, and said he was keen to have another go. What did I think? Of course I agreed, and I meant it. Maybe the chances of success would not be much greater than before – I gave the odds at evens – but we both knew that some day that face would be climbed by someone. The urge to be that somebody was irresistible and with all the experience he had gained, Chris just had to try again.

There were certain lessons from the last attempt by which he was determined to profit. One of these was to start earlier and be off the mountain before life was made intolerable. But this meant beginning the climb before the monsoon ended; there would still be masses of snow on the mountain and fresh snow would be falling from time to time. I agreed with that proposition, too, despite its snags. On our way up the Zemu Glacier in 1937 we had met a German party on their way down flushed with triumph after climbing Siniolchu, a beautiful and very difficult peak, during September, in spite of the difficult snow conditions. Even more impressive had been the astonishing skill and endurance of an earlier German party led by Paul Bauer which, during more than two months of continuous hard climbing between July and September 1931, had forced their way up the North East Spur of Kangchenjunga, living in ice caves, to reach a height of 25,260ft [7700m]. They were finally defeated by an avalanche-prone snow slope just below the crest of the main North Ridge, whence the route to the summit appeared to be relatively straightforward.

So one of the problems attaching to Bonington's choice of that earlier period was the danger of avalanches. This point was tragically brought home to us again a year after our telephone conversation when, while we were attending the centenary celebrations of the French Alpine Club at Chamonix, the leader of a French expedition on Everest and five Sherpas were swept to their deaths down a couloir leading to the West Ridge.

Reading this book, that word 'avalanche' looms large. An avalanche badly damaged Camp 4; a much bigger one wrought havoc in the Advanced Base Camp at the foot of the face; smaller snow slides, some of them serious enough to carry climbers out of their steps, were an almost daily occurrence on the great steep slopes between the high camps. That the climbers pressed on, taking calculated risks, without loss of life from this danger, speaks worlds for the new equipment they used, for their mastery of modern techniques, sheer determination – and a large slice of luck; there were some very narrow escapes.

As for equipment, there is no doubt that it played an important role. I will mention only the matter of the expedition tents. Watching members of the team, armed with improbable climbing weapons – spanners, laboriously piecing together the steel framework of a MacInnes box tent on a gentle grassy slope above the waters of Windermere on a sunny morning last summer, I found it hard to imagine the same operation being performed on a slope of ice tilted at 50 degrees, at 25,000ft on Everest, with the temperature well below zero centigrade. Yet it was done, not once but at every one of the four camps on the face. Those boxes, products of the inventive genius of Hamish MacInnes, were further proof of the foresight of the team; credit is also due to the inventor of their prototype, Don Whillans, whose own performance on earlier attempts by this route had made such a great contribution to the final result. The robustness of these tents, with the relative comfort and protection they provided, was an important factor in success.

On techniques, the extensive use of fixed ropes, up and down which all the climbers, attached by jumar clamps, can slide with security and relative ease once the leading climber has forced a passage, is the most revolutionary change in climbing big mountain faces during the past twenty years. It played an important part in all the onslaughts on the South West Face of Everest, and but for its skilful use last September several climbers would have been carried away by avalanches. But I think that all members of the party would concede (with the exception of the person I allude to) that the supreme example of climbing technique, applied with exceptional determination, was Nick Estcourt's superb lead, without the normal safeguards or oxygen at 27,000ft [8230m], up the rickety, outward-leaning ramp of snow-covered rubble which led from the gully in the Rock Band up to the Upper Snowfield. This must be one of the greatest leads in climbing history, comparable, at least in its psychological effect, with the original lead across the Hinterstösser Traverse or the exit gully above the Spider, on the North Face of the Eiger.

I would like to say more about determination, for the urge to press on pervades the whole of this story. The will to get up Everest must be there in large measure in every Everest climber before he sets out, if he is to reach the top. It is a necessary reserve of inner strength which, if – and only if – it is in abundant supply at the foot of the mountain, may just about see him through – perhaps ebbing slightly all the time. It is a peculiarly personal thing, for which the word 'ambition' in its conventional sense is quite inadequate to explain the motive power needed for this kind of high endeavour. But no one reading those graphic passages from the diaries of the summit climbers, floundering and flailing their agonising way in deep, incoherent snow up the couloir below the South Summit, can question that it was this matter of will, reinforced by confidence, that carried Dougal Haston and Doug Scott to the crest. It was this same will alone, flickering through a bitter night, which made it possible for them to return and tell their story to the world.

Everest imposes enormous emotional strains on the climber, which are an inescapable consequence of his determination and will; and those tensions are movingly conveyed to the reader of this book. Upon no one was the stress so great and so prolonged as on the leader of the expedition. His was the original decision to make the bid; his the choice of companions, the general strategy, the supervision of the whole complex plan and its unfolding on Everest. His was the responsibility for the lives of more than seventy men, exposed to risks of many kinds and for a considerable time: from crevasses and séracs in the Icefall; from the labyrinth of monstrous hidden chasms in the Western Cwm; from avalanches on the face and the sudden onset of bad weather on the summit ridge. On the leader would be heaped the chorus of criticism – even obloquy – from some climbers and many members of the public if this expensive venture were to prove to be yet another failure.

Chris Bonington is such an effective writer partly because he writes himself, his doubts and fears, his irritations and rejoicings, into the story. We can feel his edginess as the effects of mental stress, physical exhaustion and oxygen lack during eight days and nights spent at and above Camp 5. Through his perceptive understanding of his fellow climbers, and by the inclusion of excerpts from their own accounts, we experience their moods, too. Nothing moved me more than Bonington's tears when Dougal's radio message from Camp 6 on the morning of 25 September announced success – and their safe return; and the unashamed weeping of Pete Boardman, youngest member of the team, when he staggered into that same camp after his own triumph and ordeal, with its accompanying tragedy of the loss of Mick Burke.

But when all has been said about equipment, climbing techniques and the individual qualities of the climbers, my final word must be about the team as a whole and their interaction one with another during this epic enterprise. For me, this is the most fascinating aspect of the story. Much has been written in praise of small light expeditions, in condemnation of large ones. I share with most other climbers a strong preference for going to the mountains with a few close friends: some of my happiest memories derive from expeditions of this nature. But where the objectives are diverse, or when the scale of the undertaking demands larger numbers, there is also much reward to be enjoyed from its complexity, with many members playing different roles to produce a combined result. The satisfaction may come from the fact that unison in these circumstances is that much harder to achieve and, if it can be made to work, the experience can be exhilarating. I can say about this team that the quality of their achievement lies not only in the fact that they reached their objective; not only in some brilliant climbing, nor the perfect timing of the plan, which avoided the worst onslaught of the elements. It is to be found in the manner of the doing by the very individualistic members working as a team, in accepting their various parts, tempering their disappointments and being such a happy united band.

The British triumph on the South West Face is the culmination of a succession of attempts to solve this problem during the past five years: an international expedition in 1971; a European expedition in the spring of 1972, followed by Bonington's first attempt that autumn. And both before and after these three efforts came climbers from Japan: in the autumn of 1969, the spring of 1970 and finally the autumn of 1973. To all of these, but especially to the Japanese, much credit should be given for their contribution to the eventual British success.

This book is entitled *Everest the Hard Way*. Undoubtedly, the South West Face is a very difficult and arduous climb. Some day, no doubt, climbers will have so far improved their performances that this climb will be classified in a lower order of difficulty; such is the way of progress. Meanwhile, let nobody suppose that Everest by any other way, including our route in 1953, is an easy mountain; it is not. And at all times it is dangerous, as the sad toll of life in the Icefall, the Western Cwm and on the Lhotse Face bears witness. Whenever the wind is blowing strongly it is impossible to move along the summit ridges, and that means on most days in the year.

And it is well that this should be the case, for man should be humble before the greatest works of nature.

JOHN HUNT
Henley on Thames

Author's note

So many people have helped make this book possible, for a start the huge number of individuals and organisations who helped get the expedition under way. Without these, of course there would be no book. I hope we have mentioned everyone, expressing our appreciation, either in the text or the appendices. I should like to express our very special gratitude however to Barclays Bank International for underwriting the expedition, for without this support it is unlikely that it would ever have taken place. We are particularly grateful to the chairman, Anthony Tuke, whose ultimate decision it was, and to Alan Tritton, who sat on our Committee of Management and looked after our interests throughout the expedition.

I should like to give my special thanks to all the members of the climbing team, who not only gave me their utmost support and friendship throughout the climb, but also made available to me their diaries, letters home and, in several instances, original writing of their experience on the expedition. They gave me a wealth of superb material from which to select what I hope represents a balanced, living account of an expedition, not just from my point of view, but also from the viewpoint of many other members of the team, recreating the day-to-day emotions, fears, enjoyment and stress of a group of climbers on Everest.

I should also like to thank the many helpers who remain in the background but without whom I should never have managed to write this book within my deadline; Margaret Body, my editor at Hodder and Stoughton, who has constantly helped me with encouragement, balanced advice and judicious editing; Ronnie Richards and an old friend of mine, David Hellings, for their painstaking proof-reading and helpful suggestions; Betty Prentice, who not only typed most of the manuscript but also did some very useful initial editing; my secretary, Louise Wilson, who helped close the expedition down, completed one of the appendices and protected me from the outside world whilst I struggled with the book; my wife, Wendy, who looked affer all the expedition transparencies and made the basic picture selection for the book; George Greenfield, the expedition literary agent, for his support and sound advice.

Finally I should like to thank John Hunt, both for writing the foreword to this book, and for providing me with inspiration and an example to follow from studying his leadership of the 1953 Everest expedition which provides a blueprint for organising any major venture, and for the kind support and advice he has given me at every stage.

CHRISTIAN BONINGTON

1

A second chance

After we gave up our attempt on the South West Face of Everest in November 1972, 1 remember saying to Chris Brasher who had come out to Base Camp to report our story for *The Observer*: 'Climbing is all about gambling. It's not about sure things. It's about challenging the impossible. I think we have found that the South West Face of Everest in the post-monsoon period is impossible!' Rash words for, of course, the story of mountaineering has proven time and again that there is no such thing as impossible – although, I think, we could be allowed this self-indulgence immediately after our beating.

Only two days before, on 14 November, I had been lying in my hoar-frost encrusted sleeping bag in the battered box tent of Camp 4, at about 7500m on the South West Face. The wind was hammering at the walls, driving small spurts of spindrift through the many rents caused by stones dislodged from the face above. Outside there was a brilliant blue sky and a sun that blazed without warmth. From out of this void had come the wind, tearing and probing at tent and climber.

Somewhere above, Dougal Haston, Hamish MacInnes, Doug Scott and Mick Burke were pulling across the line of fixed ropes towards Camp 6. The wind was so strong that it had lifted Doug, a big thirteen-stoner, bodily from his steps and hurled him down; only the fixed rope saved him. I had had some inkling what it was like, for the previous day I had made a solitary carry up to the site of Camp 6 – even then the wind had been buffeting hard and I had wondered just how they were going to be able to erect the box tent in those conditions.

But there had been nothing I could do but wait. Jimmy Roberts, my deputy leader, was far below, camped on Kalapatar, the rocky hummock of 5500m that rises above the Khumbu Glacier forming a perfect dress-circle from which to view climbers on the upper part of the South West Face of Everest. He had a walkie-talkie with him and throughout the day reported on the tiny black dots which were making their slow progress across the snow slopes below the Rock Band. One had turned back early but then, having reached the site of Camp 6, the remaining three turned back. For some reason Dougal Haston and Hamish MacInnes had decided not to stay at the camp as originally planned and I could only guess that, because of the strength of the wind, they had been unable to erect their box tent. There was no way of knowing for certain until they got back to their tents at Camp 5 and made the seven o'clock call that night. Night fell quickly but then the time crept by slowly until, at last, I could switch on the radio.

I got Dougal. They had pressed on to the site of Camp 6, but as I had suspected, they had been unable to get the tent up and even if they had, there is little they could have done. The gully ahead had been swept clear of snow, and the rock could not be climbed in that intense wind and cold. They were coming down the next day. And so I started to arrange our retreat from the mountain; all the Sherpas at Camp 2 to come up to Camp 4 the next day to pick up loads; the Nepalese Foreign Office to be informed.

It was all so terse and matter-of-fact but after switching off the radio I could not stop myself crying in the solitude of that small dark tent. We had tried so hard but in those last few days I suspect that all of us had realised that there was no chance of success, although none of us was prepared to admit openly to defeat. It was too late in the season; the winds of Everest were reaching over a hundred miles per hour; the temperature was dropping as low as −40°C. We were all much too tired and our equipment was in tatters.

We returned to Britain with a mixture of emotions. There was sadness at the loss of Tony Tighe, a young Australian who had helped us at Base Camp during the expedition and who had been killed by the collapse of a sérac wall on the last day of the evacuation of the mountain. This was mingled with satisfaction at having taken ourselves beyond limits that we had previously thought possible and feelings of heightened friendship and respect for each other cemented by the experience. There were memories of fearsome nights in Camp 4 with the wind hammering at the box tent, bringing stones from the Rock Band above thundering over the roof as one huddled against the inner side of the tent and wondered when it would be crushed. But there had been moments as well which made all the struggle and suffering worthwhile. I shall never forget my solitary trip to Camp 6 on the penultimate day of the expedition as I plodded laboriously up the line of fixed rope. My oxygen system was only working for part of the time but as I slowly gained height, creeping above the confines of the Western Cwm − higher at that moment than any other person on the surface of the earth − the very effort I had made and the loneliness of my position made the ever-expanding vista of mountains seem even more beautiful.

Before leaving Kathmandu at the end of November 1972, I had already filed an application for another attempt on the South West Face in the next available spring slot. This was a slightly hopeless gesture since the mountain was now fully booked, autumn and spring, until 1979. The Nepalese only allowed one expedition on the mountain at a time, and such is the popularity of Everest that it becomes booked up years in advance. There are two periods in which the mountain is considered climbable – spring and autumn. The former season, undoubtedly, has much to recommend it; there is less wind, particularly at altitude but, most important of all, squeezed as it is between the end of winter and the arrival of the monsoon (sometime at the end of May or the beginning of June) an expedition starts at Base Camp at the coldest period of the season and then enjoys relatively warmer weather as it progresses up the mountain, having the warmest possible period just before making a summit bid. On the other hand, in the autumn the climbing period is slotted between the end of the monsoon, around the middle of September, and the arrival of the winter winds and cold which we had found, to our cost, come in mid-October, giving an uncomfortably short period of tolerable weather in which to climb the mountain.

It seemed highly probable that the South West Face would be climbed before we could have another chance at it, even though a fair proportion of the expeditions that had booked Everest were not planning to attempt the South West Face. There did seem to be one hope, however, for the Army Mountaineering Association had the booking for the spring 1976 slot; by themselves they were not strong enough to tackle the South West Face and had no plans for doing so. During the previous few years the Army had organised a number of successful expeditions to the Himalaya, climbing both Tirich Mir and Annapurna from the north side. I had been a regular soldier and was a founder member of the Army Mountaineering Association; this seemed an excellent opportunity to persuade the Army to incorporate three or four strong civilian climbers, such as Haston or Scott, and try the South West Face at what appeared to be the best time of year for such an attempt. I was prepared to take on the role of climbing leader under the overall leadership of an active soldier, feeling that in this way the expedition could have been fully cohesive and that the civilian members could have fitted in.

I went down to Warminster to see Major General Brockbank, who was Chairman of the Army Mountaineering Association, and put my plan across. He did not like the idea and turned it down. I can sympathise with his thinking for there were obviously several problems. The Army Mountaineering Association naturally wanted to maintain its own identity and, although I was an ex-member, there was the possibility that my own reputation as a mountaineer could have engulfed them. Success could have been portrayed by the press as that of myself and the talented civilian climbers who had been brought in, rather than of the team as a whole. There could also have been personality problems inevitably created by bringing two groups of climbers together for reasons of convenience rather than selecting a team from scratch. I would, nevertheless, have been prepared to take this risk and make it work, since this seemed the only chance we had of reaching Everest.

In the spring of 1973, Guido Monzino – the Italian millionaire who had relinquished the autumn 1972 booking, thus allowing us our chance – organised a massive expedition to repeat the South Col route. This expedition used two helicopters, hoping to ferry gear up the Icefall and even into the Western Cwm. This was a controversial step since the Icefall and lower part of the mountain are an integral part of the climb and the use of aircraft to solve logistic problems seemed an unpleasant erosion of the climbing ethic. Monzino could have argued that it is preferable to use an aircraft rather than risk the lives of the Sherpas who carry the brunt of the risk ferrying loads in the Icefall and Western Cwm but, in the event, this argument was proved specious. The helicopters, at altitude, could not manage a sufficiently effective pay-load to eliminate the use of the Sherpas and were used instead for ferrying members of the climbing team up and down the mountain for their rest periods. In the end, fate took a hand – one of the helicopters crashed, fortunately without any injury to the occupants, and this ended a very expensive experiment. Our objection to the use of helicopters on Everest is on aesthetic grounds, for one of the beauties of the Western Cwm is its majestic silence; both the sound and sight of a helicopter chattering up the Cwm would be an unpleasant, if not unbearable intrusion. In spite of these problems, the Italians were successful, placing eight men on the summit of Everest by the original South East Ridge route.

In the autumn of 1973 came the next serious onslaught on to the South West Face, with the biggest expedition so far; thirty-six Japanese climbers, sixty-two Sherpas and a twelve-man Base Camp group. The expedition was organised by the Japanese Rock Climbers' Club. They started earlier than we had done, with an eight-man advance party going out to Kathmandu in early April, sending part of their gear by light plane to Luglha, the air strip in the Dudh Kosi valley just below Namche Bazar. They brought the rest of their gear out with them in mid-July which meant that they had to carry it through the worst of the monsoon rains to Sola Khumbu.

They established their Base Camp on 25 August and at first made excellent progress, following the same route as ourselves in 1972. They were hit by a savage seven-day storm at the beginning of October, just after they had reached the site of Camp 5 at 8000m (26,000ft). Sadly, they lost Jangbo, one of their best Sherpas, who had also been with us in 1972, in an avalanche on the lower part of the face. Influenced by this tragedy and the deterioration of the weather, they resolved to turn their main effort to an attempt on the South Col route. Two of the party, Ishiguro and Kato, reached the summit of Everest in a single push from the South Col on 26 October. They had to bivouac on the way down and suffered from frostbite. This was the first post-monsoon ascent of Everest and a magnificent achievement, but the South West Face remained unclimbed. The Japanese had not abandoned the attempt on the face when they turned to the South Col, but on 28 October, after two other members of the expedition had reached the site of Camp 6 on the face, they decided to call off the expedition.

Back in England I followed the Japanese progress as closely as sparse newspaper reports and intermittent letters from friends in Kathmandu would allow. In some ways I should have been quite relieved had the Japanese succeeded, since this would have removed the nagging problem, enabling myself and other British climbers to get on with our more modest but nonetheless satisfying schemes. It did seem fairly unlikely, anyway, that the South West Face would still be unclimbed in 1979 – the next date there was a free booking – and so that autumn I was already immersed in other plans. In the spring of 1974, Doug Scott, Dougal Haston, Martin Boysen and I were going to Changabang, a shapely rock peak of 6900m (22,700ft) in the Garhwal Himalaya. I had also applied for permission to attempt the Trango Tower, a magnificent rock spire off the Baltoro Glacier in the Karakorum for the summer of 1975.

And then, one morning in early December 1973, a cable arrived from Kathmandu. It was from Mike Cheney, who helps to run a trekking business called Mountain Travel. It was founded by Jimmy Roberts, who had been the leader of the first Himalayan expedition to Annapurna II in 1960, had given me advice and help in the intervening years, and had been deputy leader in our 1972 attempt. Mike had always been the back-room boy, doing all the donkey work of arranging documentation, booking porters, helping our gear through Customs, but had never actually been a full member of an expedition. He had also always kept me very well informed of happenings in Nepal.

The cable read: 'Canadians cancelled for autumn 1975 stop Do you want to apply Reply urgent Cheney.'

Suddenly all my nicely laid plans were upset; I had another chance of going for the South West Face but at the wrong time of year. We had already found that it was too cold and windy to climb the South West Face in the autumn. The Japanese had also failed but at least that had shown that a man could reach the summit of Everest in late October by the South Col route and that he could even survive a bivouac within 300m of the summit, admittedly at the price of severe frostbite.

It took me several days to decide. If I were to attempt the South West Face again I felt strongly that it should be in the spring rather than in the autumn. The memories of the bitter wind and cold of the autumn, the problems of leadership and organisation, the worries of finding the money to pay for it were all too fresh. Could I go through all this again for what might be little more than a forlorn hope of success? Every consideration of reason and common sense said 'Don't go!'

But the fact that Everest is the highest mountain in the world, the variety of mountaineering challenges it presents, the richness of its history, combine to make it difficult for any mountaineer to resist. And for me it had a special magnetism. I had been there before and failed, and in the end I knew that I could not let pass the opportunity to go to Everest again, even if an attempt on the South West Face seemed impractical.

One challenge that intrigued me was the possibility of organising a lightweight expedition to climb Everest by the original South Col route, employing no Sherpas and moving up the mountain as a self-contained unit of twelve climbers. I had pursued the same line of thought before committing myself to the South West Face in 1972, from similar motives of worry about the practical feasibility of a full-scale attempt on the South West Face. I talked to Doug Scott, Dougal Haston and Graham Tiso about my plans. All three had been with me in 1972. Doug and Dougal were noncommittal but Graham, who had organised all the equipment for my first Everest expedition, was positively enthusiastic about the scheme. All too well he knew the problems of assembling the equipment necessary for a major expedition. He had put in a brilliant performance as a support climber on our 1972 trip, reaching 8000m without using oxygen and staying at altitude as long as anyone on the expedition; the thought of taking part in a small compact expedition, where he could even have the opportunity of reaching the summit of Everest, obviously appealed to him.

Through the winter of 1973–4, Mike Cheney pushed our cause in Kathmandu and I did what I could from this country, enlisting the help of the Foreign Office and any other contacts I could think of. But Everest filled only a small part of my mind for I was busy planning our expedition to Changabang which we hoped to climb with a group of Indian mountaineers. At the same time Wendy and I were in the throes of moving from suburban Manchester to a small cottage on the northern side of the Lake District.

I had lived in the Lake District from 1962–8 but then found myself getting more involved in photo-journalism than in climbing, with all my work coming from London. The move to Manchester was rather an unsatisfactory compromise between staying in the Lakes and moving all the way down to London. I very much doubt, however, if I could have organised my first two expeditions – to the South Face of Annapurna in 1970 and Everest in 1972 – from the Lake District. At that stage I needed the amenities provided by a large city, near the centre of the country. We bought a small cottage in the Lake District for weekends and holidays and, in the spring of 1973, whilst lying in the garden one day, relaxing from the stress of closing down the 1972 expedition and writing its book, I suddenly realised how important was this quiet peace and beauty. My life was now much more closely involved with climbing and expeditions and it seemed ridiculous to live in a place whose sole advantage was that it was easy to get away from and fairly accessible to London. And so we started the long, laborious task of making our cottage large enough to take not only a family, but also act as a place of work where I could organise my expeditions and write. Thus, that spring of 1974, Everest only occupied part of my mind.

When I set out for Changabang at the end of April the cottage still wasn't finished and I left Wendy and the children ensconced in a small caravan at the bottom of our field. We had reached Delhi and Doug Scott, Dougal Haston and I were staying at the Indian Officers' Club before setting out on the final stage of our journey to the Garhwal Himalaya when the telegram arrived. We had permission for Everest in the autumn of 1975.

2

It's the South West Face

Doug Scott came into my room later on that morning. He told me that he and Dougal had been talking about the opportunity that had been given us and suggested that I might reconsider my decision to make a lightweight push by the South Col route. He asked me how we'd all feel if we arrived in the Western Cwm and conditions seemed suitable for an attempt on the South West Face, and yet by the very nature and size of the expedition we were forced to pursue our plan for making a lightweight push by the South Col. We should always be aware of the South West Face towering above us with its intriguing unknowns of the Rock Band and the upper stretches of the mountain. This was the real challenge and until it had been met and overcome any other route or style in climbing could only be a second best.

I shared their feelings, but knew all too well that it was I that would have to spend the next year putting together the strong expedition that we should need to give us the slightest chance of success, with all its accompanying problems of raising funds, co-ordinating another large team and taking the ultimate responsibility for all our decisions and acts. This time we would have over a year to make our preparations and anyway, here in Delhi, on the way to another mountain, the romance of the challenge was stronger than my own practical doubts or memories of the months of worry and hard work which the last expedition had brought with it.

Even so, I was cautious in my reply, insisting that we must first find a single sponsor who could cover the cost. We had only just succeeded in raising sufficient funds in 1972 from several different sources, and most of my energies had been spent in fund-raising instead of planning how best to climb the mountain. It was obvious that to have any chance of success we were now going to need an even stronger and therefore more expensive expedition. We should also have to take into account the effects of inflation and the fact that many companies and certainly the entire media were feeling the pinch of the economic crisis. In other words, we needed more money, but there was less of it around.

We left Delhi that night for a rackety journey in the back of an open truck, across the moonlit Indian plains, on our way to the Garhwal Himalaya. On the approach march to Changabang, and even on the mountain itself, we often talked of Everest, analysing the reasons for our failure in 1972 and looking for the means of improving our chances in our next attempt. The key problems were the cold and high winds of the post-monsoon period. Somehow we had to get into position to make a summit bid before the arrival of the winds which seem to come at any time from early to mid-October. An obvious way would be to start earlier, but here one was limited by the monsoon, which continues until towards the end of September. By starting too early in the monsoon, however, quite apart from delays caused by bad weather, there would also be much greater danger from avalanche. The critical question, therefore, was just how early in the monsoon did one dare start? The Japanese had reported fine mornings followed by snow most afternoons when they established their Base Camp on 25 August. This, therefore – three weeks earlier than we had started in 1972 – seemed a reasonable target to aim for.

Having established Base Camp early, the next essential would be greater speed in climbing the mountain. Inevitably this meant a larger team would be required to give greater carrying power. In 1972 with eleven climbers and forty Sherpas, there had been several occasions when we had had to delay our advance on the mountain in order to build up supplies at one of the camps. Once again I had to find a balance between a sufficiently large team to ensure that we could maintain our speed up the mountain and yet, at the same time, avoid becoming unwieldy. We needed better tentage which could stand up to the high winds, the heavy snowfall and the stones that raked the face. By the end of the previous expedition, hardly a tent remained undamaged and we had even had to cadge some box tents from a neighbouring expedition.

Finally, and perhaps most important of all, we needed to find a better route. The feature which had defeated all expeditions so far was the Rock Band. In the autumn of 1969 the Japanese had for the first time reached the foot of this wall of sheer rock stretching across the face, its base around the 8230m (27,000ft) mark. They approached it at the left-hand end where a deep-cut gully seemed almost to lead off the face and a narrow chimney stretched up more towards its centre. They favoured this chimney as the best line when they returned in the spring of 1970 with a very strong expedition, but failed to climb the South West Face partially because there was practically no snow covering the rocks immediately below the Rock Band, thus making it difficult to establish Camp 5. Also, as a result of the scarcity of snow, there was heavy stonefall. Another reason for their failure was probably their decision to attempt two routes at the same time. It is all too easy to concentrate on the easier option once the going becomes rough on the other and the Japanese, turning back below the Rock Band, then climbed Everest by the South Col route.

The International expedition made their attempt the following spring. Although weaker in numbers than the Japanese expedition, they also went for two routes – the South West Face and a direct route up the West Ridge of Everest. This was over-ambitious and many of the arguments which bedevilled this expedition resulted from the almost inevitable abandonment of one of the routes, in this instance the West Ridge. Don Whillans and Dougal Haston, who were out in front on the face for almost the entire climb, found similar problems to those the Japanese had faced the previous year. They used the tent platforms constructed by the Japanese at Camp 4 but, above it, also having failed to find a suitable camp site on the left-hand side of the Rock Band, they were attracted towards the right by a well-protected ledge in the upper part of the Great Central Gully. This channelled them on to a long snow rake which stretched across the foot of the Rock Band towards the right-hand end of the face. Here they established their sixth camp at a height of 8320m (27,300ft), just below a chimney that seemed to lead to the top of the Rock Band. But by this time they had been at altitude for too long, their supplies had thinned down to a trickle and they were forced to retreat.

The following spring Don Whillans, with Doug Scott and Hamish MacInnes joined Dr Karl Herrligkoffer's European Everest expedition. This time they concentrated on the South West Face as a single objective, but the expedition was poorly equipped and disunited from the start with the large Austro-German group distrusting the British element. Don Whillans had recommended bypassing the Rock Band by skirting its right-hand corner and crossing the relatively easy slopes towards the South East Ridge just below the South Summit. The British party withdrew from the expedition when it became evident that they were not even going to be given the chance of making a second ascent once a German pair had made the first summit bid. Felix Kuen and Adolf Huber did reach the top camp but after a night there were driven back down, having done little more than look round the corner.

In our turn, in 1972, I had planned on making a determined attempt on the right-hand chimney, since Dougal had assured me that it had been filled with snow in the spring of 1971. In the event, the snow had been blown away. More serious, however, the chimney did not even lead to the Upper Snowfield which had an exit up a gully leading to the South Summit; on close examination it could be seen to lead on to the crest of a buttress between the South West Face and the South Face, leaving a lot of hard climbing before reaching the summit.

It is surprising that the Japanese, in 1973, followed the same line as ourselves and previous expeditions, particularly since the first Japanese expedition had been confident that there was a route through the Rock Band over on the left. They had decided, however, that the Rock Band was too difficult for a first ascent and favoured the tactics of the German expedition, bypassing the band on the right, with a seventh camp on the way across to the South East Ridge – or even perhaps on the ridge itself. In fact, they were unable to establish their sixth camp.

Whilst planning the autumn 1972 trip, I had come to the conclusion that it would be impractical to think of a seventh camp on Everest since it would inevitably place too heavy a burden on the lines of supply. It is advisable to sleep on oxygen and, of course, to use it for climbing and load-carrying from about 7770m upwards to ensure that the team can maintain their effort to the top on a mountain as high as Everest. Camp 5 is at around 8000m and it seemed possible to service only one camp above this point, however strong the expedition.

Examination of our own performance in 1972, and that of all the other expeditions to the face, seemed to show that the right-hand route was a blind alley. Both Doug Scott and I were very attracted to the deep-cut gully which appeared to penetrate the left-hand side of the Rock Band. You could not see all the way into the back of it, but a tongue of snow led into it and there seemed a good chance that this could continue a good way up. The problem might be to find an escape from the gully out on to the Upper Snowfield, but it was thought likely that the difficult climbing would be for a comparatively short section.

Another advantage of attempting the Rock Band from the left was that we should be able to tackle it from Camp 5, ensuring that our lines of communication would be that much shorter, with the climbers sleeping lower and, therefore, going more strongly. If successful, we should be able to have our Camp 6 above the Rock Band – admittedly, with a long traverse across the Upper Snowfield to the foot of the South Summit gully – but this seemed acceptable since the main difficulties would then be over. Most important of all, the successful ascent of the Rock Band would provide a considerable morale boost to the team. I suspect one of the reasons for a retreat had been the demoralising realisation that, in spite of having reached 8300m and establishing Camp 6, the hard climbing was still in front.

By the time we returned to Britain, heartened by our success on Changabang, I had mapped out the general principles for our new approach. I still had to find our single sponsor, however, and that looked as though it could be difficult. The day after we got back I went to see my literary agent, George Greenfield, to present him with the problem. He knew all about my lightweight Everest project and was confident that he could raise the money for this without too much trouble, for it would only have cost about £12,000. Now I wanted to raise over £100,000. He winced as I told him of the change, but after I described the discussions that Doug, Dougal and I had had during the Changabang expedition, I succeeded in convincing George that we had a chance. The next problem was to find our single sponsor. George suggested that we might approach Barclays Bank, especially as we had a mutual friend, Alan Tritton, who was a director.

George arranged an appointment and I prepared a paper on why I thought we had a chance this time and the probable cost of the expedition. A week later we were ushered into Alan Tritton's office in Pall Mall. He was sympathetic but non-committal. He had to put it in front of his Board. I sat it out for a fortnight, living in the confusion of a small caravan at the bottom of our field as the builders still worked on the cottage. Now – back in Britain – the prospect of master-minding yet another huge expedition was terrifying. It was hard enough writing an article to help pay for our Changabang trip, sorting out all the pictures and supervising the alterations to the cottage. Why the hell did I have to complicate everything!

And then I learnt that we were over the first hurdle. Barclays were prepared to sponsor the expedition. In taking this bold step they made our effort on the South West Face possible, for I suspect that there were very few, if any, other major companies which would have given this level of support. Although Barclays had sponsored other sporting activities in the past, usually through their International arm, they had never undertaken such a major commitment. In effect, they were going to underwrite the expedition for, although their sponsorship was given on the strength of the budget I submitted, they were accepting the responsibility of having to foot the balance if I went seriously over budget.

For me, it removed the greatest worry that any expedition leader can have. Now I could concentrate on organising the expedition, secure in the knowledge that we could select the very best possible equipment, that we would not have to take second-best, just to save money.

I shall always be grateful to Alan Tritton for putting our case to the Board of Barclays Bank International with the conviction and enthusiasm necessary to get their support. In the final analysis, however, it was Anthony Tuke, the Chairman, who had to give his consent. Over the last few years I have approached many organisations for help in equipping or organising climbing ventures and have become increasingly convinced that very rarely is this support given for purely commercial reasons. In almost every case, the potential sponsor or supplier has had his imagination caught by the venture in question, has decided he would like to back it and then, and only then, has he started to try to justify it to himself and his board in commercial terms.

Barclays' support for the expedition was announced on 18 October 1974, at a press conference at their Head Office. I suspect they were slightly shaken by one aspect of the response by some of the media and their customers. Although many acclaimed their initiative, a number of people asked how they could possibly justify spending so much money on a point-less venture, which seemed to have little chance of success, at a time of grave economic crisis. Even the mountaineering press questioned the wisdom of the expedition.

Ken Wilson, who edits *Mountain,* and had been with us for a short time in 1972 helping to look after Camp 1 and then staying at Camp 2, felt he had to question the viability of the forthcoming attempt, writing in an editorial:

Does the forthcoming Everest South West Face Expedition stand any chance of success? This is a question that many British climbers are asking themselves, as Chris Bonington and his wealthy sponsors, Barclays Bank Limited, crank that whole tedious media bandwaggon back into action after a two year break...

There are however a number of ancillary considerations that should be given greater weight on this occasion. Many people in the climbing world and a growing sector of the press are becoming increasingly sceptical about the value of the project. Is such a route really worth the expenditure of £100,000 and should climbers remain so completely oblivious of this point when the country and indeed the world are in such dire economic straits? To state that the money could not be diverted elsewhere is to avoid the issue. The fact is that involvement in such an extravagant project at this time of austerity lays the expedition, and indeed the entire climbing world, open to the charge of irresponsibility and frivolity in relation to the world about them...

A successful conclusion (a remote possibility) would please everybody, but a more likely outcome would be an embarrassing rehash of the 1972 affair with a few hundred feet gained and some ticklish explaining to be done to an increasingly sceptical press.

A Member of Parliament, Mr John Lee, Labour Member for Handsworth, even announced he was going to ask a question in the House. 'I have great admiration for mountaineers,' he said, 'but frankly, the banks surely have better things than that to finance at the moment – like the regeneration of our economy for instance.'

Perhaps most daunting of all for Barclays International was a flood of letters from angry customers who had, perhaps, just been refused over-drafts, asking how the bank could justify refusing them when they had just given a mountaineering expedition so much money.

Alan Tritton remained splendidly imperturbable – at any rate to all the expedition members – and continued to give us unstinting support. We got on with the business of organising the expedition, but the questions needed answering. After the 1972 expedition I had been shaken, even hurt, by the criticism of a number of mountaineers whose opinion I respect, both of the value of the route and the size of the expedition we had used to tackle it.

For instance, David Cox, an ex-President of the Alpine Club, in a review he wrote of our 1972 attempt, expressed his regret that we had abandoned the concept of a lightweight push by the South Col for a siege of the face.

The fundamental question was whether the South West Face could be considered a worthwhile objective. I think it was. There is a natural evolution from attempting a mountain by its easiest route; on Everest, the South Col and South East Ridge; then tackling other perhaps harder facets such as the North Ridge or the West Ridge and then, finally, the steep walls embraced by the ridges. This same evolution has taken place in the Alps on the Matterhorn and the Eiger, and on every other mountain and the steps forward on to harder ground were often accompanied by controversy over new techniques used or risks taken. The South West Face of Everest was not 'The Ultimate Challenge' of mountaineering (the title used for the American edition of our 1972 book) – there is no such thing, for no sooner is one 'last great problem' solved, than another is found. It was, nevertheless, an intriguing problem which would continue to nag mountaineers until it was solved and man – perhaps especially, climbing man, being a very competitive creature – would be even more attracted to it, the more his fellows failed to solve it. It is this very instinct of enquiry linked with competitiveness which has accounted for much of man's progress, as well, of course, as his aggressiveness.

There was no doubt in my mind about the worth of the route; inevitably I did wonder about the means we were going to use to climb it. My own philosophy is that one should use the minimum force or number of climbers necessary to give some chance of success. Lito Tejada Flores has explored these ideas in a magnificent article called 'Games Climbers Play', first published in an American magazine called *Ascent* and subsequently reproduced in *Mountain*. He has taken the various types of climbing, from bouldering, through short rock climbs to alpine face climbing and Himalayan mountaineering, and examined the various unwritten rules which climbers have imposed upon themselves to maintain the element of uncertainty that is such an important feature of the sport. In other words, there would be neither risk nor uncertainty of success if one used a top rope on a short but difficult boulder problem in Derbyshire, or used pitons for aid on all the difficult sections on a rock climb in North Wales. These self-imposed rules change in time, usually becoming more rigorous as the sport develops and frontiers of the unknown become more limited. A large number of rock climbs in Britain and the Alps which were first climbed using pitons for aid have since been ascended completely free, using only what the natural rock offers. This is not necessarily a reflection on the pioneers who originally climbed the route, but merely a mark of the development of climbing skills and changing ethics.

In the Himalaya there has been a growing trend towards very lightweight expeditions tackling increasingly difficult problems, often using an alpine-style approach, abandoning the concept of set camps, high-altitude porters and fixed ropes, for a continuous movement up the mountain, carrying everything on the backs of the party and bivouacking each night. This is an exciting and very satisfying concept – one which Haston, Scott, Boysen and I followed on Changabang in 1974. Another pleasing feature of this approach is that the entire team can go to the summit together, thus all share in the climax of the expedition.

On the South West Face of Everest, however, there could be no question of such an approach. In a way, one of its most pleasing features as a problem was that no matter what steps we took in our attempt to solve it – size of team, improved equipment, better food – our chances of success still seemed very thin. I found the sheer immensity of the problem fascinating. To be successful on any kind of major climb, whatever the size of party, requires meticulous planning. This in no way diminishes the essential romance of the adventure – indeed, it heightens it – for any venture can turn sour very quickly if the basic planning is faulty. Everest South West Face needed a whole set of new concepts in planning, equipment and timing to give any chance of success at all. Perhaps I am a frustrated Field Marshal, my passion for war games and my early military career providing a clue in this direction, but I both enjoyed, and at times was frightened by, the scale of the responsibility I had undertaken – to form a sound plan and then to make it work in practice in terms of people, the wind, the cold and the thin air of the upper slopes of Everest. This was every bit as intriguing as tackling a smaller mountain with a more compact team.

It could be argued that we should have waited, or even allowed some future generation with improved equipment, or longer necks, to make a lightweight push straight up the face. I have a feeling, however, that if each generation just sat back, abandoning the challenge of the moment to the people of the future, we would never make any progress at all. In the climbing sense, though this probably also applies to the entire range of human discovery, each generation blunders forward, using the resources and concepts it has at its disposal to make an advance which at the time seems supremely difficult but which, in the course of time, could appear comparatively easy.

The team members were certainly satisfied that the South West Face was a worthwhile objective and there is little doubt that very few mountaineers anywhere in the world would have turned down an invitation to join an expedition to attempt it. If uncertainty of success is one of the prime attributes of an unsolved problem, the face certainly rated very highly. None of the team gave more than a fifty-fifty chance of success and some of them – especially at the beginning – gave us no chance at all, yet could not resist the invitation to join. Their attitude mirrored that of the majority of mountaineers.

But could we justify spending so much money on the venture? As climbers without large amounts of money of our own, we have to justify our financial needs to the people we ask for sponsorship. I had succeeded in covering the cost of my expeditions in the past through the sale of magazine articles, the expedition book and film rights. The Annapurna South Face Expedition, which was fully sponsored by the Mount Everest Foundation, actually made a profit which was then recycled back into the Foundation funds for use in helping other expeditions. But Everest was a bigger proposition altogether and there was no prospect of financing this expedition on the same basis. If we were to go ahead we needed an outside sponsor.

Barclays' decision to back us, inspired though it no doubt was by enthusiasm for what we were attempting, was based nevertheless on a commercial judgment. We were not receiving charitable help; Barclays Bank International backed us from their advertising budget in order to help promote their name and identity. They were certain to have a huge number of mentions in the press and, of course, provided we were successful, would show that they knew how to back a good investment which brought prestige not only to themselves but to the entire country. At this stage, when we had barely started to organise the expedition, however, it was a very bold step for it was becoming equally obvious that, should we fail, they could pick up a great deal of counter-publicity. But this was the chance they were prepared to take. Only they, at the end of the expedition, could say whether their association with it had been worthwhile.

£100,000 is a lot of money by mountaineering standards, but set against the magnitude of the problem we were tackling, the size of the team we needed, the quantity of specialised equipment required, our budget becomes quite modest. But £100,000 is still a lot of money. There is no commercial value in climbing a mountain, and no simple answer to the question of whether such expenditure can be justified. In the end, this is something about which we must each make up our own minds. I do know, however, that we gave many people a great deal of enjoyment – and perhaps even a little inspiration as well – as they followed our story in the newspapers and on television.

3

Picking the team

Even before the press launch of the expedition I had put in a great deal of work, deciding on the basic plan on the mountain and, from this, determining the strength of the team and our programme over the next year. These were the foundations of the expedition; get these wrong and the entire edifice could collapse later on. It was only after completing this initial work that I finalised the selection of the team.

In a series of conversations whilst climbing Changabang, we had already determined our basic strategy and it was almost inevitable that Martin Boysen, Doug Scott and Dougal Haston should become members of the team. I had known Dougal since 1966, when we had both taken part in the first ascent of the Eiger Direct with John Harlin, a brilliant American climber whose meteoric climbing career tragically ended when a fixed rope was cut by a falling stone. Since that time Dougal and I had made a number of winter ascents in the Alps together; he had been with me on the South Face of Annapurna, when he reached the summit with Don Whillans, and had also taken a leading part in the 1972 Everest expedition. He knew the South West Face well, for he had been there in 1971, as a member of Norman Dyhrenfurth's ill-fated International expedition. With Don Whillans, Dougal had been out in front most of the time and had, of course, selected the right-hand line crossing below the Rock Band as the ideal route through this barrier.

I never came to know Dougal closely – I doubt if anyone ever could, he had so strong a reserve – but throughout our years of climbing together he has proved a loyal friend, always giving me a quiet support on expeditions. With a finely developed mountain sense and considerable determination, he seemed to know exactly what he wanted from life and quietly, but resolutely pursued his own course.

I had known Doug Scott for a much shorter period and, although having met him on the climbing scene from time to time and given a few lectures at Nottingham for his local climbing club, in which he has always taken a very active part, we had never climbed together before our autumn attempt on the face. He had already been to Everest once that year, with Dr Herrligkoffer's European expedition. Out of the 1972 expedition had grown a friendship which had been further strengthened by our experience on Changabang. Doug and Dougal formed an interesting contrast. Dougal was self-contained, with a carefully ordered mind, developed perhaps in the years spent at Edinburgh University studying philosophy, his mind reflecting his appearance, clean-shaven, casually but carefully dressed, economical in thought, effort and movement. Doug, on the other hand, was a great shaggy bear with shoulder-length hair, beard and eyes that peer through wire-framed spectacles. His dress, and at times his thoughts, were untidy, though his creative capacity every bit as strong as Dougal's — less disciplined, perhaps, but more broadly based, for as well as being a good writer Doug was a superb photographer. Like the traditional picture of the bear, he had a latent strength and violence in his make-up but, at the same time, was very lovable, with a warm emotional spontaneity. I have never known anyone with such an appetite for climbing. For instance, in the early part of 1972 he went climbing in the Alps, then took part in the European Everest expedition in the spring, went to Baffin Island in the summer and joined me on Everest in the autumn. He had been away from home for over three-quarters of the year.

Martin Boysen, the fourth member of our Changabang team, was another obvious choice for Everest. He was one of my oldest climbing friends; we had both started in the same climbing area, on Kentish sandstone, and had known each other from the early sixties, when Martin had just left school and had already become the climbing star of south-east England. He went on to Manchester University, chosen because of its proximity to the crags, and quickly emerged as an outstanding rock-climber. He might not have had the single-minded drive of Haston or Scott, but he had a broader love of the mountains, born from a passionate interest in their fauna and flora which led him to study botany at university. His was a complex personality, combining the competitiveness and ego-drive of most successful climbers or sportsmen hidden beneath an easy-going, indolent exterior. He was with me on the South Face of Annapurna, sacrificing his own chances of going for the summit in the work he did in support of the lead climbers at a crucial stage of the expedition. I had invited him to join us on Everest in 1972 but his wife, Maggie, had been pregnant at the time and he had therefore reluctantly refused.

Graham Tiso and Nick Estcourt were already involved in my plans for a lightweight push on the mountain. Nick Estcourt was one of the few top-class climbers I knew who combined a considerable talent for climbing with one for organisation. By profession a computer programmer, he brought a well-trained analytical mind to bear on every mountaineering problem, often coming up with sounder solutions than climbers like Doug Scott or Dougal Haston who, perhaps, had greater élan and drive. Both on Annapurna South Face and to an even greater extent on Everest in 1972 he fulfilled important roles. In the latter expedition he kept our accounts straight as treasurer and led some of the key sections of the route almost all the way to our high point at 8320m, just short of the site of Camp 6 below the right-hand chimney through the Rock Band. Nick Estcourt welcomed my change from a lightweight push to a full-scale attempt on the South West Face, but Graham Tiso had different feelings.

Having organised all the equipment in 1972, he knew the vast amount of work entailed by another full-scale attempt. A canny, forceful businessman, he ran a very successful climbing shop in Edinburgh and was used to working out the odds dispassionately. Viewed with cold logic, our chances of success to him did not seem great. He did not feel inclined to put in all the grinding, repetitive effort of getting our equipment together for a trip which seemed to have little chance of success and in which his role would have been identical to the one he had fulfilled in 1972. Then, he had worked magnificently in support, staying at Camp 4 for a long period and carrying up to Camp 5 without the use of oxygen. He had been enthusiastic about my lightweight push, for this might have given him a chance of going for the summit. Graham would not claim to be a brilliant mountaineer but he had sound judgment and, in 1972, had shown that he also had a fine pair of lungs. When he decided against coming with us I was seriously disturbed, for good administrators who can also climb are in much shorter supply than brilliant mountaineers.

Now I had a nucleus of five whom I had invited to join the expedition. In my initial planning I had decided a stronger team would be needed to fulfil the lead climbing role and also the support. In 1972, with six good climbers who took turns out in front, and five, including myself, in support, we had been desperately short-handed. I juggled numbers around and finally decided on sixteen, with eight lead climbers and eight in support. Later, we were to increase this number to eighteen.

The next place to look was obviously amongst the other members of the 1972 expedition. Hamish MacInnes was natural choice for deputy leader. He was one of my oldest friends; we had first climbed together in 1953, when I was a young lad on my first winter climbing trip to Scotland. We had met up with Hamish and climbed with him, making the first winter ascent of Agag's Groove on the Buachaille Etive Mor. My more experienced companion had then returned home and Hamish, also on his own, decided to use me, a young novice at winter mountaineering, as a portable belay on a couple of hard winter first ascents – one of them on Raven's Gully, which retains its reputation even today. We went off to climb together in the Alps, making an abortive attempt on the Eiger North Wall in 1957, for my first alpine climb, and climbing the South West Pillar of the Petit Dru. Hamish, at forty-six, five years older than myself, was an immensely experienced, very sound mountaineer who had made his life in Glencoe and become a world expert on mountain rescue. This would be his third trip to the South West Face, for he had been on Dr Herrligkoffer's expedition as well as my own. He accepted my invitation with some reservation, being doubtful about our chances of success, but unable to resist going to Everest once again.

Mick Burke's reaction was much the same, at first. He did not think we had much chance but could not resist the challenge. When asked why he was going to Everest again, he said: 'I don't think the whole business allows much choice. If you've been once and you didn't get to the top then, when the opportunity comes again, although you might not want to go, you don't really have a choice – you've got to go. I mean, just think how ropey you'd feel if someone got to the top this time and you weren't mixed up in it. It's as straightforward as that.'

Mick's role, however, was not entirely simple, for besides being an ambitious and forceful mountaineer, he had become a professional cameraman and was now working full-time for the BBC. I asked him whether he wanted to come along as a member of the climbing team or to concentrate on being a cameraman and, presumably, be paid for doing so. After quite a bit of thought he decided he would like to be a full member of the team and then film as much as he could at altitude. This was a very similar role to the one he had held both on the South Face of Annapurna and on Everest in 1972 when he had taken a cine camera to our high point on the last day of the expedition.

I also asked Kelvin Kent who had been with me in 1970 and 1972, running Base Camp and organising the porters. A serving officer in the Army, he had been with the Gurkha Signals and, as a result, spoke fluent Nepali. His military career had by now reached a crucial stage, however, and he decided he had better sit this one out.

I could easily understand the decision of the support climbers not to go on another trip to the South West Face. They have all the hard work and very little of the exhilaration of making the route out in front. As a result, even if we were successful, their own experience would be very similar to what it had been in 1972. The lead climbers, on the other hand, had the lure of the summit and, even if they failed to get there themselves, the prospect of making the route over new ground. I was surprised, therefore, when Dave Bathgate decided against another trip. He had played an important part in 1972 when, with Nick Estcourt, he had made the route out to Camp 6. In doing so they had accepted a role which gave them very little chance of making a summit bid and, in effect, were setting it up for the other lead climbers. Dave was one of the least selfish people I knew. A climber of considerable ability, his very modesty and lack of push had stopped him achieving the reputation of some of his peers. He was doubtful of our chances of success, suspecting perhaps that he might find himself in a subsidiary role and, anyway, had plans for a smaller peak and smaller expedition.

As our medical officer in 1972, Barney Rosedale had been ideal. Although not a hard climber, he had spent two years in Nepal working in a hospital. His entire medical career had been in out-of-the-way places where he had had to take the full responsibility for medical decisions, even doing simple operations without the back-up of specialists. His maturity, rich sense of humour and work in managing Camp 2 in addition to his medical responsibilities, had been a tremendous source of strength to me. He was now practising in Marlborough, his wife had just had her second child and, as I suspected, the unrelenting responsibility of doctor to an Everest expedition was something he wanted to undertake only once. He therefore regretfully declined my invitation. It was going to be difficult to find anyone to live up to his precedent but, in the event, we did.

Charlie Clarke, the very antithesis of Barney Rosedale, was a keen expedition climber in his own right, having undertaken several expeditions to the Nepal Himalaya and the Kishtwar range in Kashmir. On first meeting he seemed almost too smooth – well dressed, with almost boyish good looks and an elegant house in Islington – very much the public-school product. On getting to know him, however, his enthusiasm proved to be backed by a steady strength of character and on the mountain, in spite of his strong interest in the climbing, he always placed his medical responsibilities to the fore as a reliable and very dependable doctor. He described his own reaction to the expedition shortly after I had invited him to join us.

This isn't my style of expedition at all. Previously, I've been on small trips, often without much serious climbing. I'm coming firstly because I've never been to the Everest region, and I've always wanted to, and secondly the lure of the big mountain is absolutely enormous. Though I could turn down most other expeditions without too much heart-searching, I'm sure I could never turn down a chance to go to Everest.

Strangely, it isn't the face that worries me so much, but I often wake at night and worry about the Icefall; I suppose it's the thought of the vast number of people having to go through it the whole time. In fact, most expeditions – however careful they've been – either lose somebody or come very close to doing so. I must say, I think we've the best chance of anybody of getting up the face. We seem to have the right size of party and, what is most important, we have people who are not prima donnas making up a substantial part of the team.

There was no shortage of advice concerning potential team members and probably very few climbers would have refused an invitation. To me, at this stage, the most important choice was not that of the lead climbers but of the right person to organise all our equipment now that Graham Tiso had decided against coming with us. I certainly wanted someone in the equipment business, who would have the right contacts and a businesslike, organised way of tackling the mammoth task which was going to confront him. Then I remembered that an old friend of mine, Dave Clarke, who ran a climbing shop in Leeds, had written just before the 1972 expedition, volunteering his services as an unpaid Sherpa.

Dave Clarke had been on an expedition to South Patagonia in 1962, primarily to carry out a geological survey. The leader of this team and two of its members had later invited Don Whillans, Ian Clough and myself to join them on a climbing venture to tackle the most challenging peak of the range, the Central Tower of Paine. Dave was just starting work as a civil engineer at that time and therefore had to stand down from this expedition. We had met again when he came to the Lake District to build a bridge by Backbarrow in 1964. The lure of the Lakes was strong and he accepted a job as quarry manager in Coniston but in 1967 he moved on to open a climbing shop in Leeds. We had climbed together on several occasions in the Lake District and, in 1968, had both been involved in an attempt to canoe down the upper reaches of the River Inn in Switzerland, Dave acting as support party with myself photographing the venture for the *Daily Telegraph Magazine*. We succeeded in snatching a climb on the 3000ft high Laliderer Wall in the Karwendelgebirge in Austria on the way out.

Dave was the only person I could think of who had all the qualifications for collecting the equipment. He was a hard worker, a perfectionist in everything he did and yet, at the same time, had a warm sense of humour and a real consideration for the people with whom he was working. When he accepted my invitation, however, I doubt whether he realised just what he was letting himself in for. No more did I, for the scale of this expedition was so much greater than anything I had organised previously. Nevertheless he fully justified the confidence we put in him, and it was a great relief that I had found the ideal person for this formidable task.

Mike Thompson was another old friend. We had been at Sandhurst and done a lot of climbing together over the years. On the South Face of Annapurna he was a support climber and had organised the food. His career as an anthropologist had been at a critical stage when I had invited him to join us on Everest in 1972 and he had decided not to come. He could not resist the invitation this time, however, and once again took on the task of food organiser.

I talked to Mike about the role he expected to fill on the expedition, and he commented:

It's easy for me, in a sense, because I'm going along as a supporter anyway. One says to oneself, 'I won't think too much about anything else – just get on with the job in hand, acting as a supporter and keeping an eye on the food.' It all happens naturally; you just get on with that and if other opportunities present themselves that's a bonus. It's ideal, really, because in a support role nobody is expecting anything more of you. On the other hand, if you're expected to reach the top and you do no more than carry two loads to one of the lower camps, that's a disappointment.

Now I started to look round for another support climber, one I hoped would be able to help me with some of the organisation prior to setting out on the expedition. I had asked other members of the team for suggestions and one name came up from two very different quarters – that of Ronnie Richards. Doug Scott had met Ronnie in the Pamirs during the summer of 1974, when they had both attended an International Mountaineering Camp organised by the Russians. His steady endurance as a mountaineer, his quiet modesty and the fact that he obviously knew how to organise himself, had impressed Doug.

'We didn't think much of him at first,' he said. 'I suppose he was too much of the public-school type, but when we got to know him, we realised he was a good bloke.'

A recommendation also came from Graham Tiso, who has climbed Pik Lenin (23,400ft) in the Pamirs with Ronnie, that he was a first-class, steady, well-organised mountaineer. There was also the extra advantage that he was living at home with his parents in Keswick, close enough to me to be of immediate help. He came over to see me and I took to him immediately, inviting him on the spot.

Another vital gap to be filled was the job of Base Camp manager and organiser in Nepal. In 1972, Jimmy Roberts had been deputy leader, looking after the recruitment of all our Sherpas. His last job with the Army had been that of military attaché in Kathmandu and, on retirement when he had started his very successful trekking firm, Mountain Travel, he used Sherpas to run the treks. As a result, he had on his books some of the best high-altitude porters available. They were all devoted to Jimmy and this had been a tremendous help to us in 1972.

Jimmy's director was Mike Cheney, who had done so much of the background organising of the 1972 expedition. An arthritic hip had been giving Jimmy an increasing amount of trouble over the previous two years and so it seemed wise to give Mike his chance. I asked him to act as 'Our Man in Nepal' while Jimmy Roberts continued to give us his help and advice.

Mike was not a climber, but would run Base Camp and I felt we needed another fluent Nepali-speaker to look after our Advanced Base Camp in the

Western Cwm. It is all too easy to have unnecessary misunderstandings between climbers and Sherpas simply through lack of communication. I left this selection to Mike Cheney who suggested Adrian Gordon, an ex-Gurkha Captain who had recently left the Army and was now working with the Gurkha Resettlement Scheme in Nepal.

With my full allocation of support climbers, there were still two places to fill amongst the lead climbers. The problem here was one of over-abundance – there were so many good climbers to choose from. I was aware of the criticism in the climbing world that only Bonington's cronies had any chance of getting on a Bonington expedition. There was, of course, some truth in this since one naturally tends to ask people one already knows and of whose performance and compatibility one has first-hand knowledge. At the same time, though, I wanted to broaden the membership of the expedition, but to achieve this through the recommendations of the other members.

Paul Braithwaite, better known in climbing circles as 'Tut', had had, in the last few years, an outstanding alpine record, making a number of impressive first British ascents. He had also had some expedition experience in Baffin Island with Doug Scott and then, at greater altitude, in the Pamirs when he reached the summit of Pik Lenin, also with Doug. He had been to art college but gave it up to become a freelance decorator, finding that this gave him the freedom and money to climb when he wanted. On meeting him, it was difficult to believe that he had the endurance to climb at altitude – he has a slight build which is emphasised somehow by his wispy moustache and long, straggly hair.

There seemed to be a multitude of possibilities for the eighth place and yet, when one started analysing the mountaineering background, experience at altitude and general compatibility of candidates, it quickly thinned out. Tut Braithwaite, Doug Scott and I had gone for a quick trip to the Alps and it was during this holiday that Tut suggested the name of Pete Boardman as a talented young climber who would get on with the other team members. He was only twenty-three, but already had experience of one very successful expedition to the Hindu Kush, when he had made bold, alpine-style ascents of the North Faces of the Koh-i-Mondi and Koh-i-Khaaik. Now he was working as a mountaineering instructor at Glenmore Lodge, the Scottish National Mountaineering Centre in the Cairngorms. I had never met him, and so asked him to come down for a weekend in the Lake District, and was immediately impressed by his quiet maturity. I invited him to join us, at the end of the weekend.

There was just one more place to fill to bring my team up to sixteen. We had agreed to take along a representative of Barclays Bank and since we needed another support climber, this should obviously be the same person.

At this stage I was getting suggestions from a dozen different quarters. Ken Wilson phoned me at least once a week with unsolicited advice: 'You've got no sense of politics,' he'd say. 'Your team just isn't representational. You want some of the lads in it from the Welsh scene. Who on earth has heard of Richards or this fellow Gordon.'

I tried to explain that I was trying to build up a compatible team, not a political party.

I was still juggling names when Graham Tiso rang me one night.

'You must have Allen Fyffe,' he told me. 'I can't think how you've missed him out! He's as good as anyone on ice, went really well on Dhaulagiri and would fit well into your team.'

From my high regard for Graham's judgment and knowing Allen slightly, having met him in Glencoe several times over the years, I decided – perhaps impulsively – to invite him to join the expedition. In doing so, I undoubtedly complicated things for myself. Allen was very definitely a lead climber and this gave an uneven number, unless I included myself or another member of the team in this category. We now had seventeen members, including the Barclays representative, Mike Rhodes, an easy-going, enthusiastic rock-climber from Bradford.

By this time there was also a Committee of Management, chaired by Lord Hunt. Sir Jack Longland, who had been on Everest before the war, Ian McNaught-Davis and Charles Wylie were members. I shall always be grateful for their advice and support. Doug Scott was also on the committee, to represent the feelings of the expedition members. At one of their early meetings Sir Jack Longland suggested that with such a large team it might be advisable to have a second doctor. The good sense of this was immediately apparent; I had already received a letter from Jim Duff, a young doctor who was working in Nepal on the Trans-Nepal Highway as medical officer. A friend of Doug Scott and Mick Burke, both of whom gave him a strong recommendation, he seemed ideal and I invited him. This, then, completed the team. In subsequent months I often worried that I might have made the team too large and wondered how on earth I could control them all on the mountain. I had also agreed to taking with us a BBC team of four and Keith Richardson of the *Sunday Times*. But there was little time for reflection in those seven hectic months before despatching our gear to Nepal.

One of my most critical decisions was the date on which to establish Base Camp and start the climb. The monsoon, which brings warm, very wet weather to the foothills and heavy snowfall to the mountains, ends around late September, usually with a violent storm that heralds settled, sunny weather. With this, however, come the constant high winds and bitter cold of the autumn that had defeated our 1972 attempt. I wanted to be in a position to establish our top camp and make a summit bid before the arrival of these winds. This would mean climbing through the monsoon, with the accompanying risk of bad weather and of avalanches. Hitherto the usual practice for autumn expeditions had been to start after the monsoon was over, though some pre-war expeditions had climbed through the monsoon.

The report of the 1973 Japanese expedition, however, was encouraging. They had established their base camp on 25 August and enjoyed surprisingly settled weather until early October and the arrival of the end of monsoon storm, after which the high winds had constantly plagued them. Up to this date, they had had fine mornings, but snowfall almost every afternoon. Most important of all, there was practically no wind.

I wondered whether to start the climb even earlier than the Japanese, but finally decided against it; I felt that the earlier one started in August, the warmer it would be during the day, and the greater the avalanche risk. I decided therefore to follow the example of the Japanese and establish Base Camp around 25 August. On this basis I planned for the team to leave Britain on 29 July, allowing us just over three weeks to get ourselves organised in Kathmandu and make the approach march.

The key problem then was how to get the gear out. In this respect, Mike Cheney had recommended that we send it out before the arrival of the monsoon, reaching Kathmandu by early May, so that it could be flown from there to Luglha, the air strip just a day's carry from the Sherpa villages below Everest. This would avoid the problems involved in carrying all the expedition gear overland, through the monsoon, when rivers are swollen and it is almost impossible to keep loads dry. There were three ways of getting the gear to Kathmandu – by air, by sea or overland. The former was undoubtedly the easiest and most reliable. It was also prohibitively expensive as we estimated there would be at least 20 tons of food and equipment. Having sent the expedition gear out by sea for the Annapurna South Face expedition in 1970, we had very nearly failed before setting foot on the mountain as a result. Engine failure had caused the ship carrying our gear to be nearly two months late in arriving. I was attracted, therefore, to the idea of sending the gear overland since, even if a truck broke down on the way, we could still do something about it, even if it meant sending a reserve truck. If the gear is at the bottom of the hold on a cargo ship, on the other hand, it is completely outside one's control. The only thing to do is to wait for it to be unloaded.

Someone was needed to organise the overland transport and I approached Bob Stoodley, a friend who is chairman of a large garage group in Manchester and had helped raise funds for our 1972 trip. He seemed ideally suited for the job and flung himself into it with enthusiasm, persuaded Godfrey Davis to hire us – at an almost nominal rent – two 16 ton Ford lorries and coped with the complex tangle of paperwork required to send commercial vehicles from London to Kathmandu. Ronnie Richards took on the job of communications and helped Bob Stoodley with the documentation.

To reach Nepal by early May, the very latest Bob could afford to leave Britain was early April. This meant we would have to have everything ready and packed in Leeds in time for loading. The story of the problems and work involved is told in the relevant appendices, but this represented an Everest in itself!

Mike Thompson had to feed over a hundred people for a period of twelve weeks with three types of ration, for Base Camp, Advanced Base and the face itself, with variety built into each type of ration. He went about the task with characteristic ingenuity and economy of effort, completing the job so efficiently that there was a tendency to underestimate its magnitude.

There is no doubt, though, that the job of organising the equipment was probably the most complex of any expedition to have left Britain. Dave Clarke had to equip not only the eighteen climbers, but a BBC film team of four, a *Sunday Times* reporter, thirty-eight high-altitude porters, thirty Icefall porters and various Base Camp personnel. There were the problems of getting all the correct boot and clothing sizes, ensuring that there were sufficient reserves and steering a number of prototypes through their development. In this respect he was helped by Hamish MacInnes who not only organised our oxygen system but also designed a completely new series of very strong box tents for use at Base and Advanced Base Camps, on the face and for the summit camp. In 1972 our tentage had not been strong enough to withstand the wind, avalanches or stonefalls. These were probably the strongest tentage ever designed for an expedition and are described in Appendix 5. It was interesting to see how his attitude to the expedition developed from initial pessimism to growing optimism and then very real enthusiasm as a result of both his involvement and the confidence he had in the equipment he had designed.

I shall never forget that week in Leeds when, in a chilly dusty warehouse we packed the myriad of gear required for a major expedition. At first glance it was difficult to believe it could all be fitted into two trucks. Not only did we have to pack it, we also had to keep an accurate record of the contents of each box. I wanted to pack it all into loads which would either be left at Kathmandu, sent through to Khumde, a Sherpa village near the foot of Everest to be opened on our arrival, or carried straight through to Base Camp. Each load had to be weather-proofed, fragile items packed safely and then, to make life even more complicated, each load had to weigh roughly 27 kilos, the standard weight for a porter, as well as fitting into our two standard-size boxes.

We worked for eighteen hours a day, helped by a group of volunteer Scouts. Bob Stoodley brought the two vehicles over on 6 April and we spent two days loading them. We only just managed to fit everything on board, thanks to careful packing by Bob, his secretary, his four teenage children and the drivers, but each truck was 2 tons over weight, rolling to a frightening degree on the easiest bend. Another night spent by my long-suffering secretary, Louise Wilson, typing the manifests and we were able to collapse, thankfully, the first phase of the expedition over. The bulk of the gear and food was now on its way to Kathmandu.

Bob Stoodley had with him Ronnie Richards and three professional drivers, Alan Riley, Allen Evans and John O'Neill. They drove night and day, with only three scheduled night stops at Ankara, Tehran and New Delhi, making the 7000 mile journey in twenty-four days, a remarkable achievement considering the size of the vehicle and the degree of overloading.

I couldn't resist remarking to Dave, just after the gear had left Britain, 'Well, if it's all hijacked on the way out, you'll still have more time to replace it than we had to organise the whole expedition in 1972!'

Dave did not think this was funny. On the contrary it brought out a very real fear that I had, that in choosing this overland route we were taking risks not just of hijack but also of accidents. At least we had plenty of time in hand, though; if the worst happened and the gear was delayed for some reason – for anything up to eight weeks – we should still have been able to hire porters and carry it from Kathmandu to Base Camp when we flew out at the end of July. Even so I was immensely relieved to get Bob's telegram that they had arrived safely in Kathmandu.

The vehicles reached Kathmandu on 3 May and were unloaded in Mike Cheney's garden. The next three weeks were spent in shuttling the loads to the airport, waiting for the right kind of weather to fly the planes to Luglha and, from there, ferrying them by Sherpa porter to the home of Nima, one of the Mountain Travel sirdars who had agreed to store everything in his house in Khumde.

Mike Cheney was employing several new approaches; instead of controlling everything himself he had come to an agreement with the Sherpa Co-operative (which he had recently helped to form) to pay them 5.50 rupees per kilo of baggage from Kathmandu to Khumde, leaving them responsible for the contracts with the light aircraft, organisation and payment of porters from Luglha to Khumde. It was more than just a modern, more effective way of doing things, it was also a demonstration of trust in both the integrity and – more to the point – the management ability of our key

Sherpas. This was to prove one of the corner stones of the eventual success of the expedition.

Jimmy Roberts had suggested Pertemba as sirdar, or head Sherpa, of the expedition. Although he had been one of our outstanding high-altitude porters in 1972, he was still very young at the age of twenty-six for such a responsibility. I had been very impressed not only by his performance but also by his personality, however, and was very happy to agree to Jimmy's suggestion. The deputy sirdar, Ang Phu, was a year younger than Pertemba and had also put up a good performance in 1972. Like Pertemba, he was typical of an emerging generation of Sherpa, educated at one of the schools founded by Sir Edmund Hillary and accustomed to Western ways.

Mike, having consulted his Sherpas closely throughout the planning phase of the expedition, wrote to me on one occasion:

The Sherpa Co-operative (which includes Mountain Travel staff and Sherpas as well as expedition Sherpas) should be treated as full partners in support of the expedition. I now hold regular meetings with Dawa Norbu (head of the Co-op), Pertemba and Lhakpa Thondup (to be Base Camp sirdar) and discuss everything with them. I trust them in the same way that you trust Nick, Dave, Ronnie, etc.

This is something new and very valuable. To a large extent it looks after the security of gear problem. The staff of the Sherpa Co-op are looking after the gear of *their* expedition, not just the gear of a lot of foreign climbers.

In spite of bad weather which sometimes prevented flights to Luglha, the Sherpa Co-operative completed the airlift of our stores by early June. Everything was crammed into Nima's house.

It was good to have our last-minute rush three months before we were due to set out for Kathmandu in the luxurious comfort of an Air India 747. Inevitably, a few items had not been delivered on time and there were lots of loose ends to tie up, but the bulk of the organisational work had been carried out. This gave most of us time to relax a little before the expedition. Doug Scott, with his insatiable appetite for climbing, went off to the Karakorum to climb in the Biafo region, Ronnie Richards joined him from Kathmandu; Martin Boysen went to the Trango Tower; Tut Braithwaite went off to the Alps and had a very successful season.

With time to concentrate on some detailed expedition planning, I endeavoured to work out the exact logistic pattern we might encounter on the mountain. Ian McNaught-Davis, an old friend and member of our Committee of Management, ran a computer firm in London and he made available Stephen Taylor, one of his programmers, to write a program to help plan our logistics. Quickly, I discovered that it was impossible to get the computer to do it all for you; rather, it represented a quick check on one's own planning ideas, telling whether the logistic plan would work or not. We made a climbing game in which I gave the order for movement and load-carrying, and the computer would swiftly calculate the finish at the end of each day. We played this through three times but always reached a logistic bottleneck around Camp 4. As a result of this, I developed a formula for planning the most effective distribution of manpower in the early and mid stages of the expedition, which seemed to solve the problem. Not only did this work so well that we followed it almost exactly in practice, but also – when we changed the siting of our camps in the later stages of the expedition – I found I was able to adapt mentally to the changing situation quickly, even at 7770m. I prepared a programme for the climb which would, in theory, enable us to make a summit bid towards the end of September. At the end of July 1975, however, when we flew out to Kathmandu, I did not dare believe that we could possibly achieve these targets; there were so many unknown factors; the weather, performance of the Sherpas, the state of the snow, our own ability to acclimatise in a very fast ascent.

On the eve of departure, even our best friends gave us no more than an even chance of success – these were the odds quoted by John Hunt at our press conference. Some members of the team felt even this to be optimistic.

4

The approach march

2 August – 16 August 1975

The path winding up the hill past small mud houses, under the spreading branches of the peepul tree, was just the same as it had been three years before; it was just as humid, just as hot with the sun glaring through billowing clouds, which would shed their load of monsoon rain well before dusk.

The start of another Everest expedition approach march; the ride in Land-Rovers from Kathmandu to Lamosangu, along the winding Chinese-built road; the seeming chaos of the start with cursing Sherpas distributing loads to a mob of porters; three or four local photographers from the news agencies darting about getting pictures of each other, of the porters, of the gear; pictures that could be transposed with those of so many other expeditions.

It was the same, and yet unique. Those of us who had been there before were three years older, had learnt more about ourselves and each other; for the rest it had the freshness of a new adventure about to start. There was excited anticipation, tempered I suspect in every case by some apprehension.

Just before leaving England our doctor, Charlie Clarke, had written in his diary:

There is, of course, that awful empty fear, with so many men passing through the Icefall for so long, how can we avoid a serious accident and even a fatality or two. I know we can probably take no real precautions; selfishly I pray that it won't be me, but I have got myself into the position that I am prepared to take the small risk – no more work, no more Ruth, no more little Rebecca; tears, anger, hardship, widow, fatherless child – these are very horrid things to think about. To justify them is easy by saying, 'Well, I've always climbed and I've always accepted the risk of a fatal accident – Ruth knew it before we married,' and so on. It just doesn't bear thinking about too much. Even though I have just walked over to see little Rebecca in bed, I know that I really do want to go, I know that I will actually enjoy myself for a large part of our trip in Nepal, it doesn't stop me being frightened. What I wish for is what it could be worth in terms of that lovely feeling as we turn our backs on Base Camp for the last time and walk back to safety. I want men to do these things and I want one of those men to be me, second-hand isn't any good and I just hope all is well because I really think we deserve it.

The expedition no longer seemed quite so big and unmanageable, for we were walking into Sola Khumbu in two separate parties. All twenty-three of us would have been too many to pack into one of our mess tents at a single sitting and we should even have had trouble in finding enough space at the camp sites on the way to pitch everyone's tent. Mike Cheney was going to look after our first party, which consisted of Nick Estcourt, Dougal Haston, Allen Fyffe, Dave Clarke, Ronnie Richards, Charlie Clarke and myself. The complete BBC team had wanted to travel together with us, so that they could get used to each other as a team within our team, but, unfortunately, Ned Kelly, the co-producer had fallen sick in Kathmandu and as a result had to wait for the second party. We therefore had with us Chris Ralling, the producer, Ian Stuart the cameraman, Arthur Chesterman the sound man, and Mick Burke, who was fulfilling his two roles as full team member and BBC high-altitude cameraman. We also had with our first party Keith Richardson, the *Sunday Times* reporter, and our liaison officer, Lieutenant Gurung. We could just fit round our camp tables in the mess tent each night and, because of this, could start to become a cohesive group.

Dividing the party had worried me, however. The second group had been due to leave a day behind us but on the evening of our first day out I learned over the Racal HF radio we carried with us, that they were going to be delayed at least another day.

That night I commented in the tape-diary I kept throughout the expedition:

The news that they haven't set out is a bit disturbing because I definitely don't want the groups too separated. It's always a problem separating at all, because all kinds of implications are read into how I divide the groups and, of course, I haven't taken the names of the members of the groups out of a hat. I have tried to break up really close pairings; for instance, Pete Boardman and Allen Fyffe know each other very well, and it seems a good idea to break them up, so that they have a chance to get to know other members of the team. I suppose also there's a feeling of the possibility of a strong, small clique developing, which might have ideas of its own that could conflict with mine; it's not a bad idea to try to avoid this as well. I think this is most unlikely ever to occur, though. But, there is no doubt about it that a second group, especially if it's two or three days behind us, is going to feel slightly more uncertain of itself, just because it is so far behind; and therefore it could become more defensive in its discussions and thinking, when it eventually joins us. The other real danger, if it's about three days behind us, is that they could find it difficult to catch up with us on the Icefall because I certainly am not going to delay for the second group. I'm going to push through as fast as I possibly can.

Chris Ralling, who travelled for a time with each group, was able to observe their different character objectively, writing in his diary:

It's interesting, what a different character Group B has to Group A. I've dropped back to Group B now, so that I can do the sound with Ian because Ned is still two or three days behind us until he gets better. In Group A Chris Bonington more or less sets the tone and they are all rather keen to get on with the climbing; in the evening they play cards like mad; you can see chess, pontoon and poker all going on at the same table. Group B are much more relaxed; they stop at every chang house they can find for hours at a time and when the evening comes no one wants to play cards at all, they just want to go out and find yet another chang house. They are a more amusing group but I think Chris will be well advised to mix the two up quite soon. Probably it'll happen automatically when we get to Base Camp.

To Pete Boardman everything about the walk in was a fresh experience, as he recorded in his diary:

Not at all like the monsoon I imagined. A clear sunny hot day, umbrellas up to keep us in the shade. Much tea drunk, much sweated out and a little shed as fairly undiluted urine…A day of fireflies, lizards, leeches, swallows, kestrels, vultures, kingfishers, crickets, grasshoppers and other noisy insects, of water-buffalo, goats and carefully nurtured cows, of chortens passed on the left-hand side, of gompas, prayerflags, chang and rakshi. We round a corner and there is the British Raj in all its glory neatly lined up erected tents, crowds kept at a distance and we sit down at tables in the mess tent and are brought steaming kettles full of tea. For a mountaineer surely a Bonington Everest expedition is one of the last great imperial experiences that life can offer.

8 p.m. and an early night. One of the great things about this trip is the relaxed atmosphere it had lent to it by it being such a gathering of hard and experienced travellers. The Hindu Kush trip [Pete's only other Himalayan expedition, made whilst an undergraduate at Nottingham University] was such a trip in the dark and we never met anyone who had been there before or could make it any easier for us. But being on an Everest expedition you meet more people. Mike Thompson, Ned Kelly, Hamish MacInnes, Adrian Gordon, Doug Scott; they've been all over the world and tell good travellers' tales about their experiences. This evening we ate chicken and heard all about lions, tigers, elephants and spiders; of Africa, South America and the Himalaya; all of vital fascination. I am the cub in the wolf pack and sit in the background on the edge of the light, listening to the stories as they are related; but also I am the camera with its shutter open, quite passive, recording, not thinking. The time for evaluation comes later I suppose. Tut and I share a joke, 'I'm not here to criticise. I'm here to learn.'

Yet at the back of my mind lies a worry I haven't climbed with any of them and as they all seem to know each other and each other's relative abilities, I sometimes feel I have yet to prove myself so that I can talk with ease and confidence like I do to somebody I have climbed with over a longer period.

11.45 p.m. The dreams before the seriousness of Everest; so distant and yet such an undercurrent. Tut and Doug confessed with gallows humour 'I keep getting stranded above the Rock Band' and 'Dougal got severe frostbite last night' …

8 August. 1 slowly gain confidence within the group, but am daunted into a fawning chameleon by the background experience and anecdotal powers of the others.

9 August. After eating a bizarre meal of chicken, potato and spaghetti to the dramatic background of Beethoven's Fifth we discuss penal reform and then the new dance, doing the Hillary Step to the music of the Rock Band; Bonehead on trumpet, Mick Burke on skive, Hamish on fiddle.

Expeditions are good spacers – time and distance for weighing and evaluating life back home as well as beginning to understand somewhere new.

Everyone read a great deal, paperbacks being passed around the team. Reading tastes varied from light thrillers, through the classics to historical works. I titillated myself with *Couples* by John Updike and then studied the *Origins of the Second World War*, with A. J. P. Taylor. Conversation was also varied, rarely sexual or bawdy, very often political and inevitably quite a bit about climbing in general, but comparatively rarely about the climb we were about to tackle. Our own group had a broad spectrum of political opinion, from Keith Richardson, the *Sunday Times* correspondent, who was prospective conservative candidate for Hemel Hempstead, to Mick Burke who was a strong socialist.

The routine of a Himalayan approach march is always much the same. This one was particularly relaxing because of the superb organisation master-minded by Mike Cheney. Once again he had delegated all the authority to the Sherpas who were looking after us, in our case to Pertemba, our sirdar, who supervised the porters, loads and setting up of the camp each night, and to Purna, our cook, who fed us better than I have ever before experienced on a Himalayan expedition. Purna was a great character; he was Mike Cheney's personal cook and protégé and had been with him for several years, ever since Mike had been working on a tea plantation near Darjeeling. One night he had been driving into the town and a group of youngsters had hitched a lift. He had been impressed by the appearance and brightness of one of them and had offered him a job as cook-boy. Purna had accepted and has been with Mike ever since. He can neither read nor write and has the additional disadvantage of being only half Sherpa. His mother was Tamang. In spite of this, through his powerful personality he has captured the respect of the Sherpas and on the expedition was a natural leader who automatically became the major domo of every ceremony.

Thanks to Pertemba and Purna, we climbers had nothing to do but pack our rucksacks each morning and walk on to the next stopping point. The day started at about 6 a.m. with a cheerful 'Chiya, Sahib', from Changpa, our cook-boy, and a plastic mug full of tea would be thrust through the entrance of the tent. By the time one had wakened fully and downed the tea, a little group of Sherpas and porters would be standing round, ready to take one's load and collapse the tent. It was necessary only to pack a porter load and day sack and amble over to the mess tent, which on a fine morning would already have been taken down, to have breakfast of porridge, cereal, sausages, fried potatoes and egg, washed down with more tea. By the time breakfast was over our overnight home would have vanished, the porters would be on their way and it just remained for us to pick up a rucksack and stroll along in their wake, overtaking them through the day for they were carrying anything up to 30 kilos, whilst none of us carried much more than 9.

Pete Boardman couldn't help being worried by the contrast, commenting:

I sense a tinge of guilt about this expedition. Nobody ever thinks that it is right that a foreign power subjugates another; and so it is that I feel guilty about being waited on by the Sherpas and having all the appendages and contrivances of the Western world carried on the backs of a string of Tamang porters; sunglasses and 'Vaponas' for keeping out insects, changes of socks, tables and foam mattresses...

The porters have a smell like the Afghans, that drifts to my nose as I stumble up the trail amongst them – a mixture of sweat and woodsmoke. I expect Europeans have a smell too; apparently the Chinese think we smell like corpses.

The only ones amongst us who had to work hard were the BBC team, for Chris Ralling wanted to film the approach. He was a big man of forty-six, over six feet in height, who had made a series of very successful dramatised television documentaries of the discovery of the Nile and, just before our expedition, on slavery. I had immediately taken to him when I first met him in London some months before. He had a combination of a strong person-ality and considerable sensitivity; the quiet self-confidence that fulfilled creative ability can give. His role in making a documentary of our expedi-tion and at the same time becoming an integral part of the team, which was necessary if their venture was to succeed, was not easy and it is a tribute to the personalities of both Chris Ralling and Ned Kelly that they were indeed so successful. I also found in Chris a useful confidant with whom I could talk over some of my problems, with the certainty that the confidence would be respected. I could talk to him in a way that I could never have talked with the members of the expedition, even though some of them were among my oldest friends, because they were too closely involved.

On the approach Chris Ralling tried to set up one or two filmed sequences each day. He was very aware of the dangers of irritating the team members so that once we got on the mountain he might lose some of their co-operation. But, at the same time, making any kind of film takes a lot of work and inevitably sequences have to be set up and repeated. Even with the comparatively little filming that he did on the approach there was some grumbling within the team. It also meant that he and his film crew had to rush ahead each morning, set themselves up with their cameras and sound recording gear, film us as we passed and then, if they wanted another sequence, overtake us and set up yet again. And we just wandered from tea house to tea house, very rarely in a group, sometimes two or three climbers together, but as often, each climber on his own, travelling at his own pace, wrapped in his own thoughts. Jim Duff, our doctor with the second party, caught the mood in his diary:

9 August. Clear dawn. Up at 5.15 and away up the trail – not going so well up 3500 feet of ascent – at least it was shady. Walking along behind Doug and Pete listening to their conversation. Thread of thought much less choppy in this one foot after the other routine of sweat, tired calves and broken breathing. Spent a quarter of an hour drinking tea at the top of the pass. Small boy with thrush. Then on up to a non-view; cloud gathered as we arrived. Large collection of mani walls – two tea shops; chang, tea and talk. Tenzing off laughing into the mist to fetch cheese from the Jiri cheese factory. Easily downhill to camp to pass a deserted gompa. The Lama died last year. Two beautiful stupas and more chang next door. Caught up with Doug bargaining for a musical instrument with four strings and a horse's head.

So into camp by mid-day. Very hot – and after breakfast and camp erection spent three hours playing with ulcers and abscesses. Washing games to start with! What's the point of treating abscesses if you don't dress them every day. Sherpa with a sprained knee, elastic bandage. Porter with a sprained ankle.

A chicken being chopped. An American comes in from the wet and talks about Carolina and medicine.

Chicken and chips followed by apple and Nestle's milk. So to bed after a windy shit. Spent a lot of time in unstructured thought, roaming the byways of past and present. A bad habit and waste of time.

> Walking up and down
> Through sun-drenched valleys
> Unfolding
> Small houses

Smaller people
Green
Vibrant green

Trees and rice
Shot through by sun
Rain green.

A porter
Bent below his load
Box or cooking pot
Snow shoes
Medicine
Bare feet
Tense muscles
A stop, a whistling sigh,
Drink of water
Cigarette of course
Fourteen or forty
In ragged shorts
When all the world is on your back
Smoke on.

But Jim was also aware of the stratification of our small society, where the pecking order was unstated but very important. A little diagram immediately after the lines quoted above shows this awareness.

There are three distinct groups:

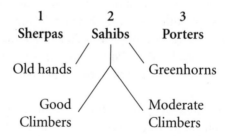

I spent much of my time on the walk balancing out these groups in my mind. Before leaving Britain, I had planned out the expedition in terms of numbers and logistics, was armed with a batch of graphs and diagrams arrived at by a series of formulae taking into account the likelihood of bad weather, the number of days' rest I expected climbers or Sherpas would need, the kind of loads they could carry at different heights and the need, based on hard experience, for a contingency margin against the unexpected. These were the foundation but they were meaningless unless I could fit them to the people with me. Now, with part of the team around me, in the reality of the Nepalese foothills, much of my waking thoughts were directed to this problem, fitting real people, each with his own personality into an overall plan. I had to take into account how different individuals got on together, what kind of role on the expedition they expected, the balance of each particular team.

In 1972 I had gone through the same thought process and resolved on giving everyone a clear role in advance all the way to the summit bid. Climbing Everest using siege tactics is like a ponderous game of leap-frog, each group out in front, usually a foursome, making the route from one camp to the next and then retiring for a rest, thus enabling the lead climbers to remain sufficiently fresh to contend with the challenge of the final 600m of the mountain and at the same time to maintain the momentum of the ascent. I had had three teams, each of two climbers and two Sherpas. I had given Nick Estcourt and Dave Bathgate the invidious job of making the route from Camp 5 to Camp 6, Doug Scott and Mick Burke the task of climbing the Rock Band and putting in the first summit bid, Dougal Haston and Hamish MacInnes, that of making the second summit bid. The advantage of this approach was that once everyone had accepted their role, they automatically made the best of it and since everyone knew their position, in theory there would be much less stress and manoeuvring for a favourable position to have a chance of making a summit bid. In practice, however, it did not work out so well, since it presupposed that everything would go to plan, a most unlikely eventuality on a mountain the size of Everest. Having given team members a role expectancy they inevitably become very possessive about it, and one of the few serious rows we had in 1972 was when I was forced to give Hamish MacInnes and Dougal Haston the role I had promised Doug Scott and Mick Burke. The same problem had arisen on Annapurna in 1970.

This time, therefore, I resolved to avoid committing myself to giving individuals a specific role within a climbing team any earlier than absolutely necessary. But because of the leap-frog principle, the initial grouping of team members could determine their position on the mountain in the final vital stages, thus affecting the logical choice of the summit pair. I consequently spent many hours, as I walked up and down the winding paths of the foothills, fitting together the different combinations of lead climbers and also trying to formulate my own response to the challenge of leadership of this tremendously talented strong-willed group of mountaineers. My thinking changed and developed with the days. This time, however, I managed to keep most of my thoughts to myself. In the past I have often made life difficult both for myself and my team by thinking out aloud, plunging into speech when thoughts have only been part formed. This has inevitably led to what has seemed like changes of mind, upsetting everyone concerned.

One obviously wanted to have at least one experienced person with each of the three lead teams to make quite sure there were no stupid mistakes about siting camps, or other delays. One also wanted to have each group fairly equal in ability. And there were bound to be some groups who would be used in a support role in the later stages of the climb, but who wouldn't be involved in a summit push. But nothing was certain. Everything depended on the weather and it would be a matter of seeing that whichever group was in a position to make a summit bid had a pair fully capable of doing it.

In the end I decided to delay making a decision on the composition of the three lead teams until our two groups had been reunited and we had climbed the Icefall. I also wanted a chance to sound out the old hands – Nick Estcourt, Dougal Haston, Mick Burke and Hamish MacInnes – in a way that didn't commit me, so that I could get their feelings on how they would like to be split up. On 5 August I commented:

Nobody ever really feels like having a formal discussion and certainly nobody offered any criticism, constructive or otherwise, at the one formal meeting we have had so far. In the evenings people much prefer to play liar dice, read a book, joke or what have you. I think this is a lot healthier; the fewer meetings I can get away with the better. Obviously we need a few but I prefer to keep them to a minimum, getting the feel of what's going on, and getting my own ideas across by just infor-mal chatting.

Had a bit of this yesterday with Dave Clarke. I walked quite a long way with him and we were able to discuss informally how we were going to sort out all the gear and its distribution to the Sherpas once we reach Khumde.

I don't think there's any danger of us ever having leadership by committee. Of course, though, if there is a strong consensus against what I say, this is going to emerge in a troublesome sense later on and I think this is where I've got to be very receptive to the feelings of the team so that I can effectively sell them my ideas and make them feel and believe that these are ideas they have taken part in forming. At the same time I must draw ideas from their combined experience and not be afraid to change my own plans if other suggestions seem better. I don't think the old mil-itary style of leadership can possibly work.

I also talked round their potential roles on the climb to Dougal Haston, Nick Estcourt and Mick Burke, on the way to Khumde. After our arrival I recorded their reactions in my tape-diary:

Their various attitudes are quite interesting. Dougal's approach is undoubtedly that of a prima donna; he reckons that he wants to get to the top, that he deserves the top and that he's certainly the best person to go there. I'm inclined to agree with him. At the same time, though, one must be very aware that forcing the Rock Band, pushing the route out above it, might be just as exacting and every bit as vital. I don't think Dougal, if I ever put him in a position where he was forcing above the Rock Band, would agree to drop back and let someone else go for the top.

Anyway, we talked round his role and the one that I had seen for him was one that he's happy to fit in with, establishing Camp 4 and pushing the route out towards Camp 5, as a member of my third lead climbing party, with Hamish MacInnes and two of the others whom I have still not decided upon.

We swapped round some names. Dougal did raise the point – wouldn't it be ideal if he and Doug Scott were paired up. I countered this though, with the fact that I couldn't possibly put the strongest pair together right at the beginning, both from a morale point of view and also because I wanted to even out the abilities of each of my lead climbing teams. At this stage I think it unlikely that Doug and Dougal will end up climbing together; I think I'd rather use them in successive summit bids, to ensure that a second attempt is as strong as the first.

I also talked to Nick Estcourt. He's a bit uncertain of himself in many ways, can be obsessive over small things, but in many ways, the big important ones, is very unselfish. Nick just said, 'I leave it entirely to you, Chris; you know I'll do anything you ask me to do.' It's great having this kind of support but I can't help worrying that perhaps I end up taking advantage of him, using him for a key role on the way up the climb that I know requires a highly developed sense of social responsibility.

I talked to Mick Burke as well. Last expedition he was much more tense because he hadn't got his own role in life clear. This time he's more relaxed, largely I suspect because he has a secure career with the BBC and even more important his role in the expedition is secure in that whatever happens he's the star of the BBC team; he's got everything to gain and very little to lose. Mick said, 'Just play it along as you see best; I'll fit in with whatever you want.' He then grinned and said, 'You've got one hell of a job; I don't envy you one little bit.'

I still had to talk with Hamish MacInnes and Doug Scott, but my plans were now becoming more formalised. For me the latter stages of the approach march to Khumde were a nightmare. I had begun to suffer from some kind of bug and plodded from one camp site to the next racked with fever and dysentery. I went for three days without being able to hold down any food, and began to worry that this might seriously affect my endurance on the mountain itself.

I wasn't the only one who was sick. In the second party Ned Kelly was desperately weak from something he had contracted in Kathmandu and had to be carried by horse for much of the way. Hamish was also slow to recover from the infection he had picked up in Kathmandu. Most worrying of all, however, was the health of Mike Cheney. He had been in hospital only a few weeks before our arrival as a result of an allergy to penicillin. He had looked very frail when we met him in Kathmandu, but was determined to set out with us. Each day he started several hours before us, but was always the last in to camp, often getting in after dark. He never complained even though it was obvious that he was in considerable pain for much of the time. Charlie Clarke commented in his diary on 6 August:

Mike is toiling along, looking very very grey and ill, with severe girdle pains at mid-abdomen. Very worrying – what he is describing is hideously like spinal cord compression but there is no cough or strain pain. I haven't examined him because he hasn't really asked for advice – I think he is really best left his own way at present. Even if this is his last trip, is there a better way to go?

I sometimes wonder if perhaps I missed some of the fresh beauty of the approach march through my preoccupation with the climb ahead. To the members of the team who were making it for the first time, and who had no such responsibility, it undoubtedly had a special impact which is captured in the pages of Charlie's diary.

Kharikhola – 11 August 1975: At last we have reached the Dudh Kosi; how the scale of the country has changed from the little Beatrix Potter valleys and re-entrants to the vast sweeps of the ridges of the Dudh Kosi. No wonder there is the highest mountain in the world at the top of it.

Kharikhola is a horrid little place with people and relics of tea shops. 'You can buy bread and biscuits here', says one sign. But it's still remarkable to me that this main route through Nepal to Khumbu is still so unspoilt.

I wonder what the life-cycle of a leech is?

I still worry about the dangers of the Icefall. Enormous avalanches sweeping down off Nuptse; tottering ice towers just waiting for me personally; or the horror of being off-route in mist and hearing the groaning of avalanches and séracs. I have other fantasies about going to the top, but these will shortly be dashed when I find how unpleasant it is.

The bridge below Namche – 13 August 1975: There is something very special about this valley which still entrances me, entrances us travellers as though we were the first to come here. The majestic scale is impossible to capture on film and it is only by having to walk up the Dudh Kosi that one realises how enormous it all is. Each little side valley is as large as most main Himalayan valleys and each ridge or re-entrant takes an age to cross.

A delightful chang session with potatoes at lunchtime, marred only by the recurring political arguments about the state of the nation – I do wish I had something original to say about it all, but it does bore me.

Here in camp I watched, I made certain I saw, the slaughter of our dinner – a large, black goat. I've never seen an execution before and one is certainly enough. The squealing creature was dragged over a tree trunk and then with a single blow of a kukri, the head was severed and leapt forward on the rope around the neck, followed by two jets of blood. I was very nearly sick and thought how tenuously the whole of our individual lives is held together. I think about death a lot – not my own particularly – but the practical aspects of what we'll have to do. It's rather like being at war, this expedition, with the Sherpas as our mercenaries. I think many of us are scared, but no one will bring himself to discuss it – Chris just turned off it a few days ago. It's so odd how Ian Clough and Tony Tighe are talked about as though they're still around, and morbidly fascinating to hear Nick discussing Dougal's floppy hat as the one Tony used to wear. I like Dougal very much, in a quiet sort of way. I wonder what he thinks about all the time. Mick has curious effect. Talkative, funny, aggressive. I think he is very anxious about everything and this is his reaction to it. I've never really seen him in this setting before and at home he is very much quieter.

So, to Khumde tomorrow and the action really starts. I realise how important it is to have a reasonably long approach on an expedition of this size. Everyone seemed fairly unfit and enough of us were newcomers to need a substantial settling-in period.

I do wonder how enjoyable this expedition will be and, unlike others, I don't think I must look for too much individual pleasure. It will be a collective thing probably, as Mick said, irrelevant of the outcome, 'It doesn't seem to alter your joy at the end of an expedition whether or not you've climbed the mountain.'

We reached Khumde on 14 August, just twelve days after leaving Kathmandu. Dave Clarke and Ronnie Richards had pressed on a day ahead to start unpacking the gear and by the time we reached the village, the tents were already up and piles of boxes neatly covered by tarpaulins were scattered over the small field in which we were to camp.

Khumde and Khumjung are two Sherpa villages, 3800m above sea level, lying in a shallow valley, cradled by the craggy slopes of Khumbui Yul Lha, a 5760m peak that towers above the villages to their north, and the carelessly flung arm of a tree-clad, bouldered ridge line that clutches the little valley on its southern side. To reach it, we walked through one of the most perfect natural rock gardens I have ever seen. The leaves of the trees were already touched by autumn and varied from a dusty green, through shades of yellow to rusty red. The ground was carpeted by an array of exquisite flowers, shrubs and mosses that nestled into the crannies of boulders, some of which were as big as houses. The mist clung to the top of the ridge and hid the high mountains around us, somehow increasing the romance and feel of excited anticipation that we all felt.

At first glance Khumde had not changed at all since 1961, when I first visited it. But then a second look showed differences. Most of the houses still have the traditional slate roofs, and are two-storeyed, with small deep-cut windows. The smoke from the open cooking fire in the corner of the single first-floor living chamber finds its way out through the windows and chinks in the roof. There are very few houses that have chimneys. One house in Khumjung was different; it had a bright green corrugated iron roof and big glass windows. It looked like a badly designed detached house on a modern housing estate and was completely out of character in the village. It was a symbol of the growing affluence of the Sherpa people; an affluence born from the developing tourist trade and expeditions like our own. It was owned by Ang Tsering, the chairman of the village panchayat, or council. He had been the sirdar of our expedition to Nuptse in 1961 and had since taken part in many major expeditions.

There are other signs of change as well. At the top of the village of Khumde is the hospital built by Ed Hillary; between the two villages is the school which was also opened by Hillary, though is now entirely run by the Nepalese. Hillary more than anyone has helped the Sherpas to help themselves, in starting schools and hospitals, in building bridges, in financing scholarships to secondary schools and universities in Kathmandu and India. External influences are also growing. The Japanese have built a hotel on the crest of the low ridge dividing Khumjung from Namche Bazar. Just below it at Syangboche they have carved out of the hillside an air strip which Pilatus Porter aircraft can land on. As a result the tourists, who otherwise could never have walked from Luglha, the other air strip, can now be carried straight in to a height of over 3650m (12,000ft). We met some of them in the lounge of the Everest View Hotel. They belonged to a tour party from the Mid West of the United States. They were all over sixty, and two of them had needed oxygen on the walk up from the air strip. One lady, dreadfully pale, had a bottle of oxygen beside her and was clutching a mask to her mouth. They were there for only two days and so far had only had a glimpse of Mount Everest. Not one of them had felt up to walking down to the village or through the flower-filled woods around the hotel. Apparently no one has yet died from altitude sickness at the hotel but one can't help wondering when will be the first casualty. For an elderly person to fly up to this altitude is a risky business.

A young American girl who had been there several days and who had visited Tengpoche and some of the neighbouring villages commented, 'What a pity these places have got to change. I suppose they'll have electric lights soon.'

This attitude highlights the problem of a place which wants to acquire modern amenities without losing too much of the pattern of life that both renders the place attractive to the outsider and, much more important, represents a stable and very balanced society. Running water, sewage systems and electricity make life both easier and pleasanter, but are all too often accompanied by many of the evils of modern development. The Sherpas, however, are very adaptable and have a background that should enable them to adopt what they want of Western ways. They are not a primitive people; living as they do on the watershed of the Himalaya in a region that is barely fertile enough to support them, they have always depended on trade to make a living. The Sherpa menfolk have always travelled far into Tibet and down into lowland Nepal and India on their trading ventures. They were already settled in Darjeeling in the twenties when the early Everest expeditions set out for Tibet and were therefore natural candidates for high-altitude porters. Today, more and more Westerners are coming into their home country, bringing with them all the problems as well as benefits of a fast expanding tourist economy. The trails are littered with rubbish; the rate of deforestation is being increased, the Sherpas are having to import more rice and basic foods into Khumbu to help feed the visitors. At the same time, the brighter Sherpas and the families who already have wealth are making a lot of money, whilst the less adaptable are probably only slightly benefiting, thus exaggerating the extremes of wealth and poverty within the villages. It is the development of tourism and trekking rather than that of mountaineering expeditions that is pushing on these changes. Each season many thousands of trekkers throng the trails, while even a massive Everest expedition only involves thirty or so outsiders at the very most.

Very few of the menfolk in Khumde wear traditional dress. Most of them have expedition clothing, breeches, anoraks, down jackets in various stages of decrepitude. The women on the other hand still wear the traditional Sherpa dress of long sleeveless tunic of plain dark material, livened by a gaily striped apron and coloured blouse. Very few wore the traditional Tibetan boots, most having plimsolls or basketball boots. The children were just as dirty, just as inquisitive and just as cheerful. It was a time of meeting with old friends, all of whom had bottles of chang, the Sherpa rice beer, to offer us. There was Ang Pema, with his round moon face, who had been cook-boy on my first ever expedition to Annapurna II, who had come with me to the summit of Nuptse in 1961 and who had been cook on Annapurna South Face in 1970. There was Pasang Kami, as dapper and smart as ever, very much the modern Sherpa. He had been our sirdar on Annapurna South Face, but now preferred the trekking game. He looked, and was, a successful businessman, with his smart guide's peaked cap and horn-rimmed spectacles. He spoke fluent English, had been to California and Europe, owned a restaurant in Namche Bazar. There was Kanchha, who had carried an incredible double load of 27 kilos on Annapurna, who had always been so willing. He was the same as ever, grinning through broken teeth. Somehow he hadn't made the grade, was hoping to carry a load for us to Base Camp, and said, without regret or jealousy, 'I'm just a poor Sherpa. I have no yaks, only a little land.'

It was good to see so many old friends. We did no work that night, and went to bed befuddled with chang and talk.

5

From Khumde to Base Camp

17 August – 25 August 1975

The gentle limbo of the approach was over; there were boxes and piles of gear everywhere, piled high round the field, cramming our big Camp 2 box tents and lying stacked beneath tarpaulins. Dave, millboard under his arm, had a permanent worried frown as he juggled sleeping bags, boots, pen-knives, down suits and the thirty or so other items of personal issue amongst the eighty Sherpas and twenty-five Europeans. Everyone, suddenly avaricious, was looking across at other people's kit.

We had been at work for two days when the second party arrived. We had become used to each other and had felt a small, compact team that was easily managed. Dave had taken complete charge and we all, including myself, did what he asked in making up the individual issues. But then the second party, happily drunk from a series of reunions in Namche Bazar, had straggled in and suddenly I realised just how large a party we were. We could not even all fit into a single mess tent, but needed two. The camp became a teeming village; effective communication was difficult. You needed a meeting to ensure that everyone knew what was going on. I think everyone was slightly appalled by our unwieldy size and it was emphasised by the way each group tended to maintain its own identity, sitting for the most part in different mess tents, accustomed to relaxing in different ways. Each night the gambling school played poker, whilst the second party talked or wandered off to find more chang.

In spite of the frantic rush and the almost inevitable shortfalls on a few items of kit, we had achieved a lot in those few days. Traditionally, an expedition makes a leisured progress to Base Camp, pausing for the odd week to acclimatise to the altitude and organise itself. I have never believed in this approach, preferring to instil a sense of urgency in the party from the very beginning. In 1975 this was accentuated by the settled nature of the weather. Although it rained each afternoon, the mornings were clear and still – ideal weather for getting started on the Everest Icefall. I resolved, therefore, to send Nick Estcourt and Dougal Haston ahead on 17 August to find a site for Base Camp and make a first reconnaissance of the Icefall. The first party would then set out on the 18th to move straight on up to Base Camp, with the second party following on the 19th. Although I proposed to set up an acclimatisation camp at Gorak Shep, a short day's walk from Base Camp, I only wanted to use it for the team members who felt in need of a few extra days' acclimatisation. In this way I hoped to get Base Camp established as soon as possible. I also had the chance of talking to Hamish and Doug Scott about their roles on the expedition. In my diary I described the conversation:

Had a long talk with Hamish where I laid out my ideas and plans, and discussed the composition of the lead teams on the face. I definitely want Hamish to set up the boxes at Camp 4. 1 think that is one of the most important moves on the expedition, for unless this camp is secure, we won't be able to keep up the flow of supplies on the face. With a bit of luck he will also be able to site Camp 5 and make sure that's all right. It's really good having his advice and support – he's so wonderfully relaxed about it all and yet, at the same time, very canny.

I also talked to Doug. Doug was very reasonable. I think he likes the idea of having a crack at the Rock Band and would even take on one of the genuinely sacrificial roles – for instance, forcing the route across the Upper Icefields, as close to the South Summit as possible, thus putting it on a plate for the next pair through. He just commented: 'There's no point getting uptight about it. You never know – the weather might close in and anything could happen to change the role you think you're going to get.' I think he really means it and that means that he will be relaxed. I must say, he is one of the biggest, most unselfish people I have got amongst the lead climbers.

I still couldn't help worrying about the size of the team. Being big meant we had the reserves we might need, but there were going to be a lot of people sitting around at times, and there's nothing like idleness for making people discontented. This was something I realised I was going to have to watch.

Although the team was so big, at Khumde there was certainly no shortage of work for everyone. Hamish was checking the oxygen cylinders and producing a new invention daily, developing a special rucksack for the lead climbers to use with their oxygen, modifying the platforms, helping team members fit their oxygen masks. Mike Thompson was sorting out the distribution of ration boxes, Adrian Gordon was helping Mike Cheney, and the BBC team were filming, while at the same time trying to get some climbing gear for themselves.

It was a relief to set out for the final stage of our walk to Base Camp, to break away from the big expedition and to form, once again, into two compact parties. Charlie Clarke and I set off together, picking our way along the narrow footpaths that wind through the little drystone-walled fields of the villages of Khumjung and Khumde. It was easy to identify our Sherpas, for most of them were wearing red T-shirts stamped with the legend 'British Everest Expedition'. They were also getting ready to leave home. Charlie described a ceremony we witnessed on our way through Khumjung:

We saw a touching, solemn scene of a Sherpa parting with his family: the sacrificial fire of juniper, his wife and three children standing round – the silent prayer that he would return to them. A soldier leaving for the wars, pointless wars, wars he is fighting for someone else. How happy I shall be if we return safe with as many as left Khumde.

And we wandered down past the last mani wall below the village, along the narrow path skirting the precipitous slopes above the Dudh Kosi, past a deserted village, terraced fields lying barren and untended, past stunted pine trees and big succulent blue-black cones which oozed resin. A lammergeier cruised above on great outstretched wings; cumulo-nimbus clouds towered above Ama Dablam, engulfing its shapely spire, ready for the afternoon storm.

It was easy to forget the size of the expedition, even the ever-present problem of logistics, people, their vulnerable egos, dreams and expectations. Charlie and I crossed the Dudh Kosi, feet thudding on the worn boards of a cantilever bridge, jostling with a small herd of yaks which were being driven unladen to Pheriche, ready to act as beasts of burden. The area panchayat, or council, had decreed that we could not use yaks before Pheriche for fear that they might damage the crop of grass that lay, ready to mow, on every available flat space in the villages and surrounding fields.

We paused for chang at the little tea house at the foot of the long hill that led up to Tengpoche and then shouldered rucksacks and wafted in an alcoholic haze to the monastery. That night we stopped at Makyong, the other side of the hill just below the Tengpoche monastery. Our porters, most of them women ranging in age from thirteen to seventy, were camped in the open in the woods around us, huddled through the night round little camp fires, wrapped in a few dirty old blankets. They seemed to regard their work almost as a holiday, flirting with the lads, talking and singing far into the night. The lucky ones shared a tent with our high-altitude porters.

The following morning, in the dawn, we walked back up, under the dripping rhododendron trees, to the monastery to receive the blessing of the Head Lama and to present him with the expedition's offering towards the upkeep of the monastery. We were ushered into his reception room where he was sitting, clad in saffron robe, quiet and impassive. The Sherpas made three ritual bows, each time touching the floor with their foreheads in a gymnastic, flowing movement which had a strange grace, before bowing their heads to receive the Lama's scarf. We made our namaste greeting and then sat round the room, making stilted conversation with the help of Mike Cheney as interpreter.

The Lama gave us the same advice as he had given in 1972: 'If you work together and do not argue amongst yourselves, you have a chance of climbing the mountain.'

Outside, the ceremony was repeated in the courtyard of the monastery for the benefit of the BBC. Patiently, the Head Lama did as he was asked, his little group of lamas standing to either side of him at the head of the steps leading to the great double doors of the temple as I walked up and said my little piece. Even though the cameras were turning and the ceremony had been specially set up, I found it strangely moving. Charlie was less sure, writing that night:

A ceremonial hand-over of 2000 rupees to the High Lama (the Second Incarnation). Film, flash, majesty. The ascetic mysticism of those remote monasteries always seems a thin covering of an empty world. Can there really be all that learning, wisdom and religious thought practised by these monks who fought and giggled in the courtyard. I suppose my disbelief in God makes it very hard for me to accept. Then on to Pheriche. How fabulous is this glacial plain with swirling mists and jangling yaks. Dusty, hooded shadows collecting firewood in the fog, the yak looking out of nowhere. This is like Central Asia.

Pheriche is a summer village, where a few crops are grown and now, with the growing number of trekkers, it has also become a trekkers' stopping-place with four or five Sherpa hotels which are little more than single-storeyed shacks, stocked with food bought from expeditions and offering some floor space for anyone who wants to stay the night. The most modern of these 'hotels' was owned by Nima, one of the youngest Mountain Travel sirdars. He had been with us on the South Face of Annapurna but had then decided that the life of a high-altitude porter was altogether too risky. Now he worked as a trekking sirdar but was also a freewheeling entrepreneur, owning a small herd of yaks and this hotel, which his wife would look after through the trekking season. He even had bottles of beer and cans of German lager.

Sitting on a rough bench in the single room of the hotel, it was interesting to see the Sherpas together. We had with us two of my former sirdars, Pasang Kami from Annapurna and Pembatharke who had been sirdar on Everest in 1972. Both were providing yaks and helping to organise the porters in the carry to Base Camp. There seemed to be no resentment of Pertemba, who had the job of sirdar this time, even though he was so much younger than either of them. He was assured and dynamic; they were friendly and helpful. They were all united in a struggle with the local panchayat which had just decreed that no yaks were to be used in the carry to Base Camp. This was aimed at the yak-owners, of whom several were expedition Sherpas who could make a fair amount of money carrying double loads of gear on their strings of yaks. The idea behind the panchayat decision was that the money should be spread amongst the ordinary Sherpas – at first glance a very fair principle. Pertemba argued, however, that they could not recruit sufficient local porters to carry our gear and that therefore we needed as many yaks as they could get.

The problem was further complicated by the fact that Ang Phu was, at the same time, trying to negotiate a divorce from his wife with the panchayat, and was worried that a conflict between the expedition and local council would delay a settlement of his own personal problems. We were fortunate in having Mike Cheney with us, for he counselled us to leave the Sherpas to sort it out amongst themselves and not to become involved. That night, Pertemba raced down to Pangpoche to argue with the panchayat and the following morning returned with the news that they had agreed to the yaks being used, provided no one supplied more than four of his own yaks. I suspect that the Sherpas paid little more than lip-service to this proviso.

And so we walked towards our mountain in three easy – almost lazy – mornings, up the flower-jewelled slopes below the snout of the Khumbu Glacier to Lobuche, on to Gorak Shep, over the tumbled boulders of the base of the Changri Nup Glacier and, on the 22nd, we walked up the Khumbu Glacier itself to the site of Base Camp.

Our Sherpas had cut out of the ice a track for the yaks. Base Camp was as bleak as ever, the rubbish of the Japanese Ladies' expedition strewing the rocks just below the site that Nick and Dougal had chosen. There was no more grass, no flowers, not even any moss; dusty granite blocks covered the ice and an occasional grinding groan reminded us that we were on a slow-moving glacier. Wet snow gusted down as the porters trailed in, dropping their loads in careless piles. Young Sherpanis giggled and made eyes at us as we tried to photograph them. A couple of yaks stampeded, trampling over our personal boxes. We sorted out the boxes into ordered piles. Pertemba and some of the Sherpas had erected a tarpaulin shelter and were paying off a shouting crowd of Sherpas and Sherpanis. Purna was building the cook-shelter, other Sherpas and climbers were levelling spaces for their tents.

That day, Dougal Haston and Nick Estcourt were already up in the Icefall, making the first reconnaissance. It was 22 August, three days earlier than I had scheduled the establishment of Base Camp. We were starting on the right note in our race against the autumnal winds and cold. We had a total of 300 loads at Base Camp and the second party were at Gorak Shep, ready to follow on. Pete Boardman was among those who arrived next day. His first impression of Base Camp was of a cold humourless place, with the freshly scarred unwelcoming character of a working quarry.

It was Pete who recorded an early impression of Allen Fyffe and Mick Burke.

Allen shared a tent with Mick on the walk in and I think they got on very well. Allen sometimes appears a bit distant and dour partly because he is rather shy, but he has a very shrewd sense of humour that glows in Mick's company here at Base Camp. I think they feel an affinity for each other both being on the small side. They share a tent next door to Keith Richardson who owns one of those tiny computerised watches, on which, if you press the right button the time and date lights up in red lettering. One night Allen and Mick were in bed when Allen said, 'Well, I think I'll get some kip. I won't stay up to watch the date change on my watch tonight.' Mick said, 'I'll tell you what, if we go next door we can watch it in colour.'

In the next three days the rest of the climbing team arrived and the vast bulk of our loads was carried up to Base. No longer did we feel such an unwieldy expedition. There was too much to do, and barely enough people to undertake all the tasks in hand. Each day a group went up into the Icefall to push the route out towards its top. Back at Base Camp, there were crampons to fit to boots, all the face boxes to be erected then dismantled and made up into manageable loads, the Sherpas issue to complete of karabiners and lengths of nylon tape for clipping into the fixed ropes on the way up. There were boots which didn't fit and had to be exchanged. Dave Clarke worked for twelve hours a day, a perpetual worried frown on his face. Members of the climbing team were doing a morning's work in the Icefall and then coming back to Base Camp to spend the rest of the day helping with the hundred different administrative chores. Each day caravans of yaks and Sherpanis carried loads up from Gorak Shep.

The morning of the 24th dawned warm and cloudy. Dougal Haston and Nick Estcourt had intended to go into the Icefall, but decided against it. This was one of the hazards of tackling the mountain during the monsoon. It snowed most afternoons, but usually cleared during the night, with a hard frost that helped to consolidate the snow. We always set out in the early hours of the morning before dawn, in order to get back down from the Icefall before mid-day, when the fierce heat of the sun softened the snow and brought down huge avalanches. On the occasions that it did not freeze during the night, we had to stay put in our camp the following day and wait for the next night that it did freeze.

We resigned ourselves to a day of administrative chores. I had settled down in one of the big box tents with Dougal, Hamish and Ronnie Richards to alter the Sherpas' crampons. We had ordered a size too big for most of them and to get them to fit their boots we had to shorten the arm linking the heel piece to the main set of spikes. Hamish was the expert at this rough engineering, whilst the rest of us riveted on the straps and altered the screw on sections. It was about 10.30 when Pertemba came into the tent and told me that I was wanted for a ceremony to consecrate the Base Camp altar. This was the first time any of us had heard about it. Slightly mystified, I followed him out to find all the Sherpas assembled round a pile of stones which had been built up into a simple altar. Purna was the self-appointed master of ceremonies and thrust into my hand a tray on which was balanced a bottle of local rum and around which was heaped rice and tsampa smeared with margarine. A ceremonial scarf was placed around my neck and another around the bottle of rum. Phurkipa was chanting a prayer from a tattered book of Tibetan script whilst the rest of the Sherpas were shouting and laughing. The entire ceremony was typical of the Sherpa temperament, light-hearted yet very serious, all at the same time. The Sherpas were throwing handfuls of rice and tsampa over Pertemba, myself and each other; laughter and muttered prayers mingled, whilst I clutched my top-heavy tray, fearful that the bottle of rum might topple over. I imagined that this would have been a terrible omen.

A fire of juniper shrubs had been lit on the altar and its aromatic smoke swirled into a grey sky dusted with snowflakes. Other members of the team had gathered around to watch the spectacle, but were yelled at to get to one side. No one was allowed to come between the altar and Sagarmatha (the Nepalese name for Everest), to whose guardian gods the offering was being made.

A flag pole, decked with prayerflags, the expedition flag and that of the BBC Television show 'Blue Peter' was pushed and heaved into position on the altar; Pertemba then placed his offering on to the altar and I followed suit, making, at Pertemba's bidding, a namaste, bowing with hands held in prayer to the altar and Sagarmatha. Phurkipa's chant rose to a climax and the rest of the Sherpas shouted, laughed and yelled, hurling fusillades of tsampa over everyone. I felt tears in my eyes as I walked over to the others and secretly prayed that our Sherpas would be protected through the expedition.

Every morning before setting out into the Icefall, the juniper fire was lit and each Sherpa made an offering of a little tsampa or rice on the altar. On the way through the Icefall many of them muttered prayers, particularly in the danger areas threatened by avalanches. The ceremony over, we had to come to terms with an increasingly worrying problem.

The previous evening it had been reported that one of the porters who had set out that day from Gorak Shep had failed to return. He was a young deaf and dumb lad called Mingma. At that stage none of the Sherpas was worried, thinking that perhaps he'd missed the path on his way back and had spent the night out. The following morning, however, he still hadn't turned up and it was obvious that something could perhaps be wrong;

being deaf and dumb, if he had only strayed a little distance from the path and had sprained an ankle, he would have had no means of calling attention to himself. Perhaps because he was particularly vulnerable this young lad had a rather special relationship with the expedition. I had noticed him at Khumde, bare-chested under an old torn plastic motorcycle jacket, his intelligent face often wearing an anxious grin. As long as he was with us we were responsible for his safety, but being intelligent, and yet unable to make himself understood, he was rather unpredictable. The Sherpas seemed to feel the same and were quite happy to let him go his own way.

Doug Scott, however, felt more involved, for he had first befriended the boy in 1972 when he and Don Whillans and Hamish MacInnes had stayed with Mingma's family in Pheriche. Now he saw quite a bit of the lad on the walk in, on one occasion even helping him with his load. At Gorak Shep Doug and Tut Braithwaite had climbed to Kalapatar, a 5486m shoulder of Pumo Ri which gives wonderful views of the Khumbu Glacier and the Everest massif, and they had taken Mingma along to help carry some of the heavy camera equipment, which had meant extra money for the boy.

By the time Doug and Tut got back down from Kalapatar, most of the porters had already left for Base Camp. Doug asked Ang Phu if he could find a load for Mingma so that he also could earn a day's wage for the carry. Ang Phu agreed and Mingma set off just behind some yaks that were being driven across the glacier. There was a constant coming and going of the yaks and Sherpanis along the trail across the glacier. This was the last time he was seen alive.

Gazing over the rocky wilderness of the Khumbu Glacier, I was appalled by the extent of the area we should have to cover in our search. I divided the team into six parties of climbers and Sherpas, each equipped with a walkie-talkie. The occasional figure that came into view, a tiny dot in the vast expanse, only emphasised the magnitude of our task. Dougal Haston wandered over the lower limits of the Icefall, Tut Braithwaite was in among the ice fins and ridges just below it. Charlie Clarke scoured the rocky debris below Base Camp. Doug, because he was the last person to employ the boy, had an unwarranted sense of guilt, records what happened next:

We took a section each and fanned out down the valley, all in radio contact with Base Camp. I felt very much alone with my three Sherpas and grieved that the lad, unable to shout, might be trapped under moraine debris or a fallen sérac. I scrambled along like a madman until Adrian [Gordon] reported sighting clothing and then a body in a stream.

I went down to him, lifted Mingma out of the icy stream and put him on the side. His face was just like it had been around camp, set firm, withdrawn into his silent world. I sobbed uncontrollably for him.

Chris appeared, having run the two miles down from Base and put his arms around me and wept. He spoke of Conrad, his first child who had been drowned whilst playing by himself on the banks of a stream in Scotland. He was able to put the situation in another light, one of accident and not of fault – and yet how can I absolve myself? I don't think I ever can. Adrian also showed compassion, pointing out that I had brightened up his life for this short spell and how bleak would have been his prospects for the future. On our return to camp, the ever-pragmatic Mick Burke pointed out that the Sherpas were not unduly troubled because they could shrug it off with a thought that his time had come and he had gone to a better life. I hope I can finally accept it as they did.

Next day we pressed on. Yet I could not help asking myself, once again, whether these climbs were worth the loss of life that so often accompanied them. I have no answer. People die climbing in Britain too, and few outdoor sports are entirely without some element of risk. But a climber can assess the risks, and can accept or reject them. Mingma was not a climber, and can have had no thought of danger. His death was an accident which might have happened at any time, but he was carrying for us, and we are responsible.

And yet everything went on; the drive to climb the mountain was as great as it ever had been and on this expedition there would be good moments, happy moments, wonderful moments and perhaps there would be some very sad moments as well. We could only pray that there would be no more accidents.

6

The Icefall

22 August – 27 August 1975

The Icefall, gateway to Everest from the south, is also one of the most dangerous sections of the route. It is a frozen cataract, the solid river of ice being broken up into huge blocks which are thrust inexorably downwards by the force of the glacier slowly flowing down the Western Cwm. One can never make a route that is completely safe through the Everest Icefall, but merely try to avoid as many of the dangers as possible. Inevitably though there are places where the route must go under a tower or ice wall which sooner or later is going to collapse. One can only rationalise the risk; the fact that one is only in the danger area for a few minutes at the most, whilst the tower will stand for weeks, or even months before it falls. The trouble of course is that climbers and Sherpas were moving through the Icefall daily for however long the expedition was going to last. We had learnt to our cost in 1972, when Tony Tighe was killed on the last day of the expedition, just how random the risk could be.

We had already completed two days' work in the Icefall before Mingma's death. On 22 August, the day the main party reached Base Camp, Dougal Haston and Nick Estcourt succeeded in climbing halfway up and on their return reported that it seemed as safe as it ever could be. On 23 August Allen Fyffe, Ronnie Richards, Mick Burke, Arthur Chesterman and I went into the Icefall to consolidate the route. Dougal and Nick had left no ladders or ropes in place and our aim on 23 August was to build a road through the Icefall as well as to press the route beyond their high point. For this purpose eleven Sherpas, led by Phurkipa our Icefall sirdar, were going with us, carrying fixed rope, bamboo markers and ladders. Phurkipa, now in his fifties, was the oldest member of the team and our most experienced Sherpa. Having probably been through the Everest Icefall more often than any man alive, he had become an Icefall specialist. In both the spring and autumn expeditions of 1972 he had taken charge of the Icefall Sherpas, earning the title of 'road-mender' for his efforts in repairing the route and building bridges over crevasses. He was to have the same job this time.

Setting out just after dawn, we followed the tracks made by Dougal and Nick. For half a mile the route weaved round piles of rubble and low ice ridges, on the way to the foot of the Icefall. Some of the Sherpas had set out earlier and we overtook them where the angle began to increase; they were putting on their crampons and seemed to be having some kind of argument, with Phurkipa talking very vehemently and pointing over to the right. Quickly I gathered that he did not like the route to the Icefall chosen by Nick and Dougal. I could see his point. The existing route, although certainly the easiest and most direct – going straight to the foot of the Icefall – crossed the glacier immediately below the Lho Lha pass into Tibet and the great Western Shoulder of Everest, both slopes being the spawning ground for huge avalanches. Phurkipa preferred to make a long dog-leg to the right to avoid this risk. I was happy to follow him. After all, it was the Sherpas who would be going through the Icefall most often and it seemed only right, therefore, that the ultimate choice of approach should be left to them.

We met the tracks of the reconnaissance party at the foot of the Icefall itself and followed them up, placing marker flags at close intervals, anchoring in fixed rope wherever it seemed necessary and bridging the few crevasses which were not covered. After all the months of theorising and the past three weeks' walking, it was profoundly satisfying work and by nine o'clock that morning we had reached Nick and Dougal's high point, just below 5790m (19,000ft). So far the route had been both straightforward and very safe; it ran up an ice spur on the left-hand side of the Icefall and was not threatened by any dangerous sérac towers.

Now we were venturing into the centre area, where the Icefall flattens out for a short section, just before its final climb into the Western Cwm. This is one of the most unstable sections, being prone to cataclysmic ice-quakes caused by the pressure of ice from above. Mick Burke and Arthur Chesterman had come along to film, and here they set up a short climbing sequence with Allen Fyffe leading out up a snow slope above the previous pair's high point. It was indicative of Mick's divided loyalties between filming and climbing that, as soon as he had completed his stint of filming, he abandoned his camera and joined Allen and myself in pushing out the route into a region of unstable ice blocks, lavishly covered in snow. The crevasses seemed deeper than they had been in 1972 and we had to advance very cautiously to find a route through them.

The sun had by now struck the glacier and within a matter of minutes it was like an inferno, its dazzling light reflected by the snow around us; the air temperature was in the seventies. Everest is a place of extremes, of violent changes from bitter cold to blazing heat, sapping one's energy and changing hard frozen snow to a soft morass in a matter of minutes.

Although having climbed not yet a 100m beyond the previous day's high point, we were well content with our progress. Not only had we made a little new ground, we had also consolidated our route, ready for the next thrust forward into the upper reaches of the Icefall.

The next day had brought tragedy and had been spent searching the Khumbu Glacier for Mingma, but on the 25th we returned to the Icefall. By the time I got up, Nick Estcourt and Pete Boardman were already high ahead, two tiny black dots dwarfed by the towers of snow-clad ice which, in their turn, were dominated by the soaring walls of Nuptse and the West Ridge of Everest. Dougal, also having set out that morning, in the dark had stepped on to an ice-covered glacier pool and fallen through into the icy water, up to his waist. He had had no choice but to return to Base Camp.

Hamish MacInnes and Mike Thompson, with twelve Sherpas carrying ladders and rope, had also gone into the Icefall to consolidate the route pushed forward by the leading group. Hamish, in spite of suffering from severe dysentery, put in a fine morning's work, laddering the section immediately beyond the high point reached by Mick Burke, Allen Fyffe and myself on the 23rd. The ladders were in 6ft (1.8m) sections which could be bolted together to form a ladder of any desired length. These were used either to scale ice walls, or as bridges over crevasses.

Climbing the Icefall is a cross between a medieval assault on a fortress and crossing a dangerous minefield. The first time through, everything seems to be full of lurking threats, of toppling séracs and hidden chasms, but once a trail has been broken, with all the obstacles laddered, one can quickly be lulled into a dangerous illusion of security, for the risk is always there, as we had learned so tragically in 1972, right at the end of the expedition.

Nick and Pete, out in front, were savouring all the fresh joy of discovery as they picked their way up a long shallow ice valley and then tackled a line of ice walls that barred their way across the Icefall. Pete Boardman, telling the story, said:

Route finding through the Icefall has a very creative feeling – plodding through guttering gateways of ice, looking in all directions for the snow bridge that will not collapse, moving on the horizontal, backwards and forwards as a team, a roped entity, to find the way – not only for us but for the future.

Such is the power of the media myth-making machine, I have lurking thoughts that all the Big Names gain superhuman qualities when they set foot on a big mountain. But Nick Estcourt gasps with the altitude just as I do. It's just Nick and me, and now I feel I'm doing something I understand. I enjoy climbing with Nick; he treats me with respect and encouragement – always willing to hand over the lead, give praise where it's due.

We arrived at the foot of a short overhanging ice wall – 'It's your turn,' said Nick. 'I led the one lower down!'

I started front pointing, straight up it. It was overhanging and towards the top, about 20ft up, it domed out with softer snow. I rested on my terrordactyl (a special ice hammer designed by Hamish MacInnes) and got Nick to pass up his axe. I clipped the terrordactyl in as a runner then attacked the top, but my arms felt drained and fingers were opening so I left one axe firmly embedded at my high point and came down to rest on the terrordactyl. Suddenly, I found myself in an undignified heap, gasping and wheezing in the snow next to Nick. Feeling a bit ridiculous, with a small cut on my forehead, a distant quote from an American guide book drifted into my head: 'A climber is like a bull, wandering around tormented and confused who, when he sees the red flag of a cliff, all he can do is charge!'

Nick took over and I learnt a lot watching him lead the pitch. He seemed to pace his breathing as he carefully cut steps and handholds all the way up so that he could gain the maximum rest. Slowly, he moved over the top – but at least he did stop there for five minutes, unable to speak and feeling ill!

We had been watching their progress through our binoculars back at Base Camp and had been slightly perturbed to see that they were following a shallow valley that led up towards the left-hand side of the Icefall. This looked a certain channel for any major avalanches from the West Ridge of Everest. A few minutes after they got back, hot, tired but jubilant from their morning's climb, a huge avalanche curled down the flanks at the West Ridge into the shallow valley that they had just ascended, a cloud of powder snow hiding their tracks. We were all badly shaken by the threat, but Nick Estcourt – ever rational – pointed out that the three avalanches were more visually impressive than truly dangerous, for the tracks were still there, once the snow cloud had drifted away; he reaffirmed the relative safety of the route which Pete and he had pioneered. I temporised and left the choice of line the following day to Dougal Haston and Doug Scott.

Our minds were taken away from the threat of avalanche by the arrival of Martin Boysen. His expedition to the Trango Tower had lasted longer than he had anticipated, and he had only got back to Britain on the same day that we had flown to Kathmandu. I had left him a note advising him to make sure he gave himself sufficient rest before joining us, but at the same time urged him to try to catch us up before we were fully embarked on the climb. Naturally, I had been worried about his late arrival, whether he would be too tired or stale, coming straight off one expedition to join another.

His wife, Maggie, had arranged to go on holiday camping in the French Riviera and so he joined her there for a fortnight and then flew out to Kathmandu arriving on 12 August. He had hoped to get a light plane to Luglha but the monsoon was still active and so he had to walk, making the journey to Base Camp in the very fast time of ten days. He looked lean, fit and pleasantly relaxed as he strolled into camp just before lunch. It was very good to see him and he quickly became absorbed into the life of the expedition.

Each day I had to make a difficult decision – to stay put, because the weather was too warm or there was too much snow, or to push on with the day's work. We were racing against time but under no circumstances did I want to risk another accident. On 26 August, having set reveille at 2 a.m., I woke automatically just before our early-morning call, to find it was snowing lightly and that we were in a dense mist. I decided to delay the decision to move, dropped off into a light sleep to wake at 3 a.m. The mist had cleared and it was freezing hard. The sky, jet black, was encrusted in stars that shone with the brilliance only seen amongst the mountains. Rolling out of my sleeping bag, I went down to wake Changpa, the cook-boy. The fire in the corner of the cook tent was still smouldering, a huge kettle already filled with water.

The previous night we had heard a great commotion in the cook tent, which was also the meeting place of the senior Sherpas. Purna, forever the natural leader, was organising the funding of the Sherpas' end-of-expedition party. Each Sherpa had to pay a certain amount into the kitty for every Sherpani he had slept with on the approach march. This was a sure way of making plenty of money, for very quickly the Sherpas were having to pay for their boasts of sexual prowess.

Now, in the quiet of the dawn, Changpa was hunched over the cook fire, waking the smouldering embers into a blaze. The other cook-boys were still fast asleep, wrapped in their sleeping bags. I felt a warm feeling of satisfaction in just being there, and one of anticipation for the day in front of us. Doug and Dougal were going to press on ahead, to try to extend the route all the way to the top of the Icefall whilst I, with Allen Fyffe, Ronnie Richards, Mike Rhodes and Charlie Clarke – with sixteen Sherpas carrying ladders and rope – was going to consolidate the route behind them. The Sherpas had made up their loads the previous night and now, in the glimmering of the early dawn, were starting out in little groups, placing their offerings on the altar and muttering prayers as they plodded up the well-worn trail.

That day I got no further than the middle of the Icefall, into a region we named the 'Egg Shells', because of the complexity of the crevasses and the seeming fragility of the blades of ice which were holding up a roof of snow. We had to fix an almost continuous track of ladders and fixed rope to ensure that if the entire area collapsed, any climbers or Sherpas passing through at the time would have a chance of survival through being clipped into the line of rope.

Whilst fixing the ladders in place we very nearly lost Mike Rhodes, the Barclays Bank nominee. This was the first time he had ever been in an icefall of this complexity. I called him back to help Ronnie Richards bridge a particularly wide hidden crevasse. Automatically, he should have clipped into the safety rope we had already stretched over the snow, but through inexperience it never occurred to him. Walking across the innocent-seeming snow towards Ronnie, he suddenly dropped through, up to his shoulders, only saving himself by flinging his arms out to either side. We pulled him back and cautiously gazed down the hole he had made. It was like looking down into the nave of St Paul's Cathedral from the top of the dome! The crevasse looked at least 60m deep, vanishing into blue-black shadows which opened out into a giant abyss. I think I was even more shaken than Mike by his narrow escape, and told him: 'For Christ's sake, always clip on to the rope if there is one. We bloody nearly lost you just now.'

By this time the sun had crept over the West Ridge of Everest and was pounding down on to the Icefall. We had fixed roped and laddered the entire middle section and had run out of ladders. I wanted to get the Sherpas back before the mid-day avalanches and so we turned back in the enervating heat, to skid and slide back to Base.

The previous evening I had paired Doug Scott with Dougal Haston. At this stage I had no particular thought of putting them together for a summit bid and their pairing was largely a matter of temporary convenience. Doug described his reaction:

Every decision Chris made from start to finish was scrutinised minutely. This was only natural with such a close-knit bunch, where everyone would be affected in some way or another. When Chris paired me with Dougal I was conscious that I was with someone special, for everyone knew that Dougal was summit material. Then I wondered what Tut Braithwaite would think of this arrangement, for only recently I had spoken to Tut about Chris's intimation that he wanted me to lead the Rock Band and I had asked Tut if he fancied doing it with me. Now, here I was, out of the blue, paired with the star of our show. All I could do was to go along with the flow and see what turned up next. There was no telling at that stage of the game and no point in thinking it was Dougal and me for the top.

After a 4 a.m. breakfast I left Purna's kitchen; following marker flags I stumbled and clattered across the moraine to the snow path winding up and round Icefall hummocks. I noted my heavy breathing with some concern but comforted myself that I was going better than in 1972. I knew, however, that I was in for the usual 'little bit of suffering' of acclimatisation. Dougal came by, gliding along the trail effortlessly, whereas I sweated and staggered in his wake – perhaps in a week's time I would move with the same economy as he.

We rested at the avalanche debris that had scoured Nick's route and veered right through knee-deep virgin snow, sharing leads to the base of a 200ft ice cliff. I led up to mid-height and Dougal came through to lead the steeper top section. By now, Pumo Ri was all lit up behind us in a bright, white show of light, in complete contrast to the cold, dark Icefall. As Dougal led up, he had to chop off slender icicles that tinkled down past my stance, he then traversed right, on hands and knees, along an ice shelf just below the top cornice.

Our concentration was interrupted by shouts from below. Mick Burke and Arthur Chesterman had arrived to film the climbing. It wasn't the place for Dougal to hang around and so he continued inching his way across and up through the cornice, much to Mick's annoyance, for he had had no chance to set up his hefty camera gear. Dougal climbed on to the top of the ice cliff and disappeared way back to belay. I scrambled up, listened to Mick's light-hearted abuse and gave him as good as I got. We always did this whenever we were together.

'Why did you let him lead it?' he asked.

'Because he's better than me,' I shouted down, for want of a better answer.

'You're not doing very well, are you?' he said, as I squirmed my way along the gangway shelf and out on to the top.

'Cheeky little sod,' I said to Dougal, who was oblivious to such jibes. 'Seeing as how you got up too late to film, you may as well make yourself useful and ladder this section,' I yelled down, sarcastically.

We left Mick, Arthur and their Sherpas to the difficult task of anchoring ladders to the vertical and slightly impending ice cliff. The sun was now skimming across the snow, bringing life and colour to the dead cold ice. Mushrooms of fresh snow sparked like cushions of sequins; ice walls glinted back the light from their wind-scalloped surfaces and icicles everywhere hung down, twinkling light, as we moved along. It was good to be back. We moved faster, knowing that the day would be hot and the powdered snow would turn into a mire.

By 10 a.m. we had scrambled across the last of the crevasses and up the remaining snow slope to the top of the Icefall; we found ourselves at the entrance to the Western Cwm. As luck would have it, we had arrived at a perfect place for Camp 1. It was a flattish area, completely surrounded by crevasses that would absorb the biggest avalanches which might topple down from Nuptse on the right and Everest on the left. We left our rope fixed from the site and slid down to meet the climbers and Sherpas, everywhere laddering up the route.

Back at Base Camp, there were plenty of problems to be solved. That afternoon, I had a meeting with Pertemba, Ang Phu, Adrian Gordon and Mike Cheney, to decide on the loads the Sherpas would carry and the numbers of rest days they would need at different heights, the payment of bonuses and other incentives to ensure maximum co-operation. We already had an excellent spirit between climbers and Sherpas. They were happy with their equipment and impressed by the organisation of the expedition. They certainly seemed to believe that we were going to succeed this time. I wanted to make certain, however, that they also felt that they were going to reap the rewards of this success.

I promised a generous bonus scheme, therefore, where Sherpas were to receive 50 rupees (£2), for each carry from Camp 2 through to Camp 4, 100 rupees for every carry from Camp 4 to 5, and 200 rupees for a carry from Camp 5 to 6 – this, in addition to their daily pay of 30 rupees. I promised also an additional baksheesh, to be divided amongst the entire Sherpa team, of £1000 over and above the standard baksheesh of approximately ten per cent of their total regular wage if the expedition proved successful. This might sound very mercenary, but then it must be remembered that in helping the expedition in return for payment, the Sherpas are no different from any other employees on a daily wage, though – in common with an ordinary factory-worker in Britain – they need more than just money to command their enthusiasm as well as obedience. They need to feel that the job is worth doing; they need to develop friendship with their employers and to feel that their efforts are fully recognised. In this respect Pertemba and Ang Phu were especially important, for I was employing them as managers in the very fullest sense of the word. I consulted Pertemba at each step, occasionally irritating my lead climbers by accepting Pertemba's advice on what he felt the Sherpas could do, or even on route selection, in preference to their own. He was left entirely to his own judgment on the choice of individual Sherpas for different roles.

I offered both Pertemba and Ang Phu some very real incentives to make the expedition successful, promising each of them a trip to England in the event of success, and promising Pertemba that I would try to get at least one Sherpa (which in all probability would be him) to the summit. Very strongly, I felt that we owed the Sherpas the opportunity of putting one of their number on top. Admittedly, they were getting their material rewards in return for helping us but then, in many instances, so would the members of the team. If anything, the Sherpas took greater risks than we did and certainly tended to work harder, having only one rest day in four below Camp 2, whilst the climbers usually rested every other day. They too deserved to share in the ultimate satisfaction of standing on the top of Everest.

It was this feeling of sharing, and the care that every single member of the climbing team took for the Sherpas working for us, that was as important as the money we paid them in creating the spirit of co-operation which contributed so much to our success.

I was getting increasingly worried about the route through the Western Cwm. Climbing this early through the monsoon increased the risks of avalanche, and it was beginning to look as if the Western Cwm could be even more dangerous than the Icefall. I resolved, therefore, to send Dougal

Haston, Doug Scott, Hamish MacInnes and Allen Fyffe, with Mick Burke to film them, up to Camp 1 as soon as the route through the Icefall was secured. This still left the question of how I was going to deploy the climbers on the face, and the next two days were spent in finalising this, talking it over with Hamish MacInnes and one or two of my old hands.

On 27 August we consolidated the route up to the site of Camp 1, Nick Estcourt, Pete Boardman, Tut Braithwaite, Ronnie Richards, Jim Duff and seventeen Sherpas moving up, into the Icefall. One of the advantages of having such a big team was that it could be split into small working groups, each bridging a section of the route, all at the same time. Back at Base we could follow them through our binoculars as the long line of dots snaked its way across to the far right of the Icefall and then disappeared completely into what seemed a narrow corridor leading back to the left. Dougal was convinced they had taken the wrong route, and we were all getting rather heated about their incompetence when, suddenly, a little figure appeared at the top of a massive square-cut tower at the very head of the Icefall. Whichever route they had chosen, they had reached Camp 1 and, more important, had marked and consolidated the route.

We had climbed the Icefall in just five days, had consolidated the route on the sixth and would be ready to move into Camp 1 on the seventh. So far, so good; we were ahead of schedule, but I was still worried about the Western Cwm. The weather pattern was as settled as we had hoped, with clear mornings every day, but the snow build-up was considerable and the avalanches across the Cwm from the walls of Nuptse and the West Ridge of Everest were frightening.

7

The Western Cwm

28 August – 1 September 1975

There were queues of Sherpas at every ladder, sixty-eight people in the Icefall that morning, plodding up through the gloom of the pre-dawn, shouts and laughter mingling with the muttered prayers of the fearful or very religious. Charlie Clarke caught the excitement in his diary:

28 August. The day we established Camp 1. A swift 3 a.m. start in mist, though with the brilliance of a moon still bright enough to march by. A crisp route, reasonably safe, and for once I felt terrific.

Up at Camp 1 by 7 a.m. and back down by 9.30 to an enormous breakfast. Chris Bonington, Keith Richardson, Adrian Gordon and I set off together, Keith going very poorly from the word go, slow, breathless, vomiting. It was clear that he was still very unacclimatised and privately I wonder whether he will ever become properly fit. Adrian going well, but diarrhoea defeated him. I felt strong and confident, having left behind my fears of several days ago.

The Western Cwm was everything I had not expected. It should have been straight, wide, vast. Instead, it was so narrow with the walls of Nuptse and the West Shoulder barely making room for it; certainly the route through this defile is hardly attractive.

I, also, enjoyed that early-morning climb through the Icefall, was able to revel in being able to carry a 13 kilo load without undue fatigue, talked and joked with the Sherpas who were resting as I passed. I tried to remember names, asked them about previous expeditions; some had been with me in 1972, others had been to Everest three, four or even five times with various expeditions. Some youngsters were there for the first time. I felt an ebullient love for this whole massive enterprise, this group of people who, although with widely differing motives, were so united in a common purpose. As I passed one group I yelled out 'Likpadello' (a Sherpa sexual boast). My remark was received with roars of laughter and accompanying calls of 'Likpadello' and other sallies in the Sherpa language.

That morning there was a great atmosphere of dynamic unified movement. But there were also worries. A particularly bad pile-up of climbers and Sherpas occurred as they waited to climb the big sérac wall by a series of ladders. The entire sérac was dangerous. You could see where it was beginning to peel away. Shouting and yelling at the Sherpas to stay well back, I resolved to work out a programme for a staggered start so that we could, in future, keep the groups of Sherpas climbing the Icefall more separated.

The site of Camp 1 was on top of a huge ice block, poised on the very brink of the start of the Icefall. Eventually it would be thrust over the brink, but it looked as though it would survive the expedition, and was out of the line of avalanches that could come down from either wall of the Western Cwm. It was further protected by a deep moat, described by a broad crevasse that barred the way into the Cwm.

Leaving the little force who were going to push the route into the Cwm, I dropped down to the ladders on the sérac wall. Phurkipa was already there and we spent an exhausting but satisfying hour making improvements, joining together four more sections of ladders, to engineer the route up the wall clear of a potential collapse. In spite of all this work, I was still able to get back to Base Camp by 11 a.m., and collapsed into my sleeping bag for a couple of hours' sleep before getting up to lunch and the next crisis of the day. This one was rather different from the normal.

The one person on the team who had not become completely accepted was Keith Richardson, the *Sunday Times* correspondent. He was a big slightly clumsy man who, one felt, had almost cultivated a blunt Yorkshire manner as a protective shell. We had climbed together many years before, when I had spent a short period working in London and he was a junior reporter with the *Financial Times*. He had stayed with the business world and, at the time of the expedition, was Industrial Editor of the *Sunday Times Business News*. Impressed by his balanced reporting of industrial problems, I had felt that a fresh approach to climbing reporting could be interesting. Although I got on well with him myself, I had been worried by the very defensive stance he had adopted in not being prepared to show the expedition members what he had written before sending his reports back to England. Perhaps this was unwise, since he could have allowed people to see his copy with the proviso that he had the final say on what went out under his name, but he was not prepared to do this. Several members of the team had complained to me about his approach and I decided, therefore, to bring it out into the open, and raised the topic at lunchtime.

Nick Estcourt advanced a very rational argument in favour of Keith showing us his copy, making it quite clear that we would not expect, or want, any kind of power of veto. In this way, we could at least ensure that what went out was correct, free from the errors which any observer, however expert, could easily make. Keith countered this with the argument that he would feel inhibited in what he wrote, if he had to show it to everyone, and that this could lead to even more acrimony. I tried to remain neutral but felt obliged to back Keith up, emphasising that once we had elected to take a journalist with us, we had to respect his professional judgment and accept his methods of reporting. I could sympathise with Keith, having been the journalist of the Blue Nile expedition of 1968, and knew something of the problems. In that instance, however, I had followed a policy of showing the expedition the reports I was sending back.

His attitude had undoubtedly antagonised most of the rest of the team and, in doing so, he was making it harder for himself to gain the confidence of individual members. Charlie Clarke commented:

In the end it will be Keith's loss, I know; he seems to make no effort to penetrate the fascinating lives of the individual members and, in his words, 'stands back from the expedition'. It would be so nice if he was a member of the expedition who could share the joys and arguments and the tragedies.

It is possible that, through working with the rest of us, carrying loads into the Western Cwm and high on to the face, he might slowly have relaxed his stance and become a member of the team. Sadly, this was not to be the case, as Charlie described in his diary:

On the 29th, the day after Keith's speech, I felt he was not very well and asked to see him in the evening to look at his retinae. In chatting, it transpired that he really had deteriorated over the week at Base. 'Disproportionately breathless' is the key to it all. His respiration has never settled to that regular compensation for either exercise or altitude. He has puffed and panted up small, low hills – was very unfit (but no more than me) at the beginning – and now puffs on minimal exertion. It's so easy to miss this. There were no abnormal signs in the chest, though his blood pressure was a little high, at 140 over 100. I could see a flame haemorrhage at three o'clock in the left fundus, but the discs were flat. Clearly, he was in incipient pulmonary oedema, and with his horrid, hacking, unproductive cough, I worried about what to do. I had not really expected this confrontation with serious illness at all and had no prefixed remedy for its management. Slowly, it became abundantly obvious that he must go down at the earliest opportunity and, in his present state, that a doctor should go with him. Pheriche seemed the only place to aim for.

I struggled with the emergency oxygen and couldn't get it together until it seemed midnight but it was only 9.30 p.m. I hardly slept. I was worried about the case, faintly annoyed that I hadn't jumped on it earlier, but a little proud that I had done so at all.

A foul night, sleepless almost completely, but as Mum says 'the best thing to do is lie still', so I did. Big breakfast at 2.30 a.m., then another at 7.15, and we were off with Pemba Tsering, the smiling kitchen boy, two porters and one Mountain

Travel sirdar. The descent to Gorak Shep, three hours, was anguish with frequent stops and Keith gulping the oxygen I was carrying. It was clear that he was moderately anoxic when his colour changed for pink, and equally clear that he would only have had to have been slightly worse to have needed a stretcher. For this, our thanks. He improved gradually, but steadily, throughout the descent and, even though exhausted, he was good and didn't stop too often. We were down by four. I was very, very tired myself and had been carrying a good 50lb all the way. Still, we were down and we were happy.

The problem of the day is what to advise. Keith is Cheyne-Stokesing now – or at least his respiratory pattern is very irregular. Clearly, a good look in his fundi is essential to make sure there is no macular haemorrhage. However, I really do feel that if anything happened on a re-ascent I would be very much to blame. Reluctantly, I spelt out the news and, in an odd way, he seemed relieved. He said he had half thought it all along. We wrote our letters, packed and were away by two for Tengpoche.

At about 3.30, past Pangpoche, we met the returning Pertemba. [Pertemba had been down to Khumde to buy more ladders.] Keith was going well – it seemed clear that my job was done. Three hours' march to Khumde on the following day; he really should be fine by then.

So, back the weary way to Pheriche and a ribald chang session – a delicious dinner of spud and buckwheat curry, flavoured with chives and curd and two bottles of beer. I'll take one up for Chris tomorrow.

I had been tremendously impressed by the way Charlie had handled the crisis, both in taking the action he did and in so willingly volunteering to accompany Keith down to Tengpoche. This brought home to us how fortunate we were in having two doctors, for I should have been very unhappy at the prospect of losing my only doctor, even on a temporary basis.

The strain of taking an active part in the climbing, as well as coping with all the administrative problems of the expedition was beginning to tell. At the end of a session in the Icefall, carrying a load and improving sections of ladder or fixed rope, one felt like spending the rest of the day relaxing. Things were getting easier, however, with the organisational structure sorting itself out – largely due to the work of Dave Clarke, Adrian Gordon and Mike Cheney.

By now, Dave was going from strength to strength. At the beginning, with the pressure and horror of getting everyone kitted out in correctly fitting gear, and the discovery that he was short of some items, he had been rather tense. Now he was very relaxed, pleased with the really superb job he had done. Dave, Mike and Adrian were sorting out the equipment and everyone was getting stuck in to all the work that needed to be done. I felt that there was not a single slacker in the team.

But I still had to finalise the composition of my three lead climbing teams. Juggling names, I played just about every permutation possible, wondering whether it would ever work out right. In combining each team it was essential also to bear in mind the role each would play on the mountain. Group 1 would be making the route from Camp 2 to 3 – not a particularly interesting or exciting job, but one which would put them into the logistical position of going up to Camp 5 eventually. Group 3 would establish Camp 4 and make the route to Camp 5. Group 2, who would have the long push from Camp 3 to 4, could then be in a position of finishing off the Rock Band later on – or perhaps even pushing the route across above it.

It was on the afternoon of the 28th that I finally made my decision. Doug Scott and Mick Burke were obvious choices for the 2 to 3 run – Doug to force it, Mick to film it. They also got on well together. Nick Estcourt seemed ideal for 3 to 4, a long, interesting stretch which he could get his teeth into, making him available for some of the vital work towards the top. It occurred to me that Nick and Tut Braithwaite would complement each other; Nick, very conscientious but sometimes tense and anxious, Tut, easy-going but, at the same time, very ambitious with a tremendous appetite for hard climbing. I knew Dougal and Hamish were happy about their proposed role in putting up Camp 4 and pushing the route to 5, thus putting Dougal in a good position for the summit while Hamish could ensure that the platform boxes at Camp 4 were really secure.

For sheer skill in climbing there was no one to touch Martin Boysen and I should have liked him to have had a go at the Rock Band. Not the most methodical of souls, the logical place for him would have been with Doug or Nick, but he had only just caught up with us and seemed in need of a rest. I decided, therefore, to send him up to Camp 4. This left Pete Boardman with the third party, and Ronnie Richards and Allen Fyffe in the first.

Finally, I felt it would be sensible to use two Sherpas in the run from Camp 3 to 4. It was one of the longest stretches and the Sherpas would probably be able to carry better loads than the climbers, without oxygen.

These were the combinations I announced at lunchtime the following day. Meanwhile Doug Scott, Dougal Haston, Hamish MacInnes, Mick Burke, Allen Fyffe, Arthur Chesterman and Mike Rhodes were up at Camp 1, ready to force the route through the Western Cwm. I had decided to send Mike Rhodes up to the camp so that he could act as camp manager, receiving and sorting the thirty or forty loads which would arrive each day through the Icefall, leaving the others free to force the route. Allen described their arrival at the site of Camp 1 in his diary on the night of the 28th:

Got here, sat about for a time and then put up one of the big box tents which will be permanent here. It was worth working, just to get out of the sun. We then lay in the box and had a couple of brews, when the Sherpas who are going to stay up here arrived after a late start. They got their own bell tent and cook area organised.

Doug had one of his tunnel tents up, so Mick and I, with Arthur, helped him put up another. Hamish and Dougal immediately installed themselves in the big box and didn't move. Eventually, it turned out that I was in a tunnel, as was Arthur. Mick and Doug indulged in a bit of squabbling, but both settled in the box. There seems a real division here as to the 'old timers' who know the score, and the new mugs, like me, who get left working alone if they are not quick enough!

This kind of situation was probably inevitable; the important thing was that it never got out of hand, never provided more irritation than the odd healthy grumble.

The following day Doug Scott and Dougal Haston went forward to find a route through the labyrinth of crevasses that barred the way up the lower part of the Western Cwm, while the rest of the group, under the supervision of Hamish MacInnes, concentrated on the initial part of the route. It was here that Hamish really came into his own, applying all his skill in engineering and his enthusiasm for building complex structures. He writes:

It was Dougal who told me there was the daddy of all crevasses just past Camp 1. He and Nick Estcourt had just come down from there and assured me it was 30ft across and no way round. 'You'll be able to use some of that fiendish gear you've been working on,' Dougal said cheerfully. Everybody seemed to be finding the prospect entertaining, and Mick Burke was determined to film the bridge-making episode. When I saw the pleasant little Rubicon we were going to have to span, I wasn't overjoyed myself, and suggested, in vain of course, that Mick wait until it was finished.

Next morning Ang Phu had already started sorting out equipment by the time we emerged from the super box after breakfast. The scene resembled the siege of Troy – ladders, ropes and stakes littered the snow. Sherpas enjoy constructing things and have an amazing aptitude for mechanical innovations, so building a burra bridge appealed to them enormously, and I found that they had to be restrained in their zeal, as one 6ft section after another was bolted together with haphazard abandon.

Mick already had his camera going, but Allen Fyffe and I soon forgot him as we became absorbed in the task on hand. There were two deadmen anchors secured on our side of the crevasse. Looking over the lip, there was a vertical 30ft drop to a shaky snow bridge which connected with the far bank at a lower level. I suggested to Allen that he nip across and field the ladder when we lowered it. The ladder had by now grown to about 40ft. 'I always like to volunteer for these less dangerous ploys, Hamish,' he spoke resignedly, and disappeared from view, crossing the tremulous snow bridge with the celerity of an Aberdonian avoiding a charity collector. When he was safely over I threw him one end of a coil of corlene rope and attached the other to the ladder. While Allen fixed more deadmen belays on his side of the crevasse, I was bolting on three ladder sections at right angles to the centre of the main span, using special triangular alloy plates for the purpose, and baffling the Sherpas completely. When I fixed tensioning ropes from each end of the main spanning ladder and over the top of the upright sections, even Ang Phu began to lose faith. I assured him I was merely bringing some science to Icefall thinking and told him to find two more 6ft lengths and send one over to Allen. They would act as doormats at either end of the bridge and prevent it sinking into the ice.

Ten minutes later the bridge was ready to lower into position, but first it had to be raised upright. This was accomplished by the combined manpower of fifteen Sherpas, aided by several guy ropes. One end was placed close to the lip of the crevasse and the structure was lowered slowly, drawbridge fashion, down to Allen who guided it with the corlene tail rope. We brought it to rest with the right-angled section uppermost and the main span bowed downwards by the tension of the double ropes from the bridge ends.

'Hey, MacInnes,' Mick Burke had stopped filming for a moment, 'how the hell can we get across that contraption? That other ladder in the middle is blocking the bloody way.' Another one who didn't appreciate Icefall science. I bade him have patience, while I mustered the Sherpas for the last move. The whole shooting match was then rotated on its major axis, so that the right-angled section now hung below and the main span rested, snugly tensioned, over the crevasse. We lashed the bridge ends and rigged parallel ropes from the four deadmen, one on either side of the ladder, and finally tied off short lengths of cord from the ropes down to the ladder rungs to form a handrail cum safety net. The bridge was complete.

We called it the Ballachulish Bridge, in honour of the bridge over Loch Leven that had nearly been completed near Hamish's home in Glencoe. There was one difference between the two bridges, however. Hamish built his in a day, keeping well up to schedule, whilst the Ballachulish Road Bridge was then a full year over deadline!

It took Doug and Dougal just three days to make their way to the site of Camp 2. The initial stretch was much more complex than it had been in 1972, with a network of wide deep crevasses. They had hoped to keep to the middle of the glacier all the way up, to avoid the risk of avalanches from the flanks, but about halfway up the centre is barred by a series of broad crevasses and they were forced into the Nuptse flank. We were running out of ladders, even though we had brought out half as many again as we had used in 1972, and Pertemba had already been sent back to Khumde to purchase more, some of which were ones salvaged by the Sherpas from the Icefall in 1972. We were also rescuing as many ladders as possible left by other expeditions both from the Western Cwm and the Icefall itself. Allen Fyffe describes digging one out:

Took us about four hours, but after a lot of hard digging ended up with about 40ft of Japanese ladder. It was a three-section job, and we must have dug about 25ft of it out of an overhanging sérac face. The contrast between sun and shade is enormous. Down in the crevasse, digging out the ladder, it was like an ice box and I was cold even in my orange jacket, windsuit and silk underwear. But then the sun crept round the shoulder and my cold hole suddenly became an oven. The heat is incredible.

Whilst my lead party were pushing out the route up the Western Cwm, between thirty and forty Sherpas were shuttling loads to Camp 1 through the Icefall each day. Dave Clarke and his helpers were doing a magnificent job, packing and listing the loads as they left Base Camp. One of the most awkward problems was that of the MacInnes face boxes, which had a dozen different parts ranging from tiny wing bolts to the complex frames and special flooring of honeycombed plastic. These had to be made up into easily-carriable loads of 13 kilos each, so that they could go straight to their destinations on the South West Face without having to be unpacked. Mike Thompson, with characteristic thoroughness, had solved this problem

Ronnie Richards moved up to Camp 1 on 30 August. In a letter home he caught the romantic beauty of the Icefall and Western Cwm in his first impression:

Ghostly white, sugar mountains clustered round the other side of Base – Pumo Ri, Lingtren, their exquisite summit slopes contrasting with the debris-coated avalanche slopes of their lower flanks, associated with the gigantic rumbling fusillades which alarmed, excited, and then caused little comment.

As the dawn approached, the sky changed from deep blue-grey to a lighter shade and the grey-white summits became golden, ribs of rock and ridges casting deep black shadows. The gold turned to yellow, extending further down and soon the mountains reflected a dazzling white. By mid-day, mist and cloud would usually creep in and snow or sleet could be expected.

Arthur and I followed Hamish and his band, bound for higher up the Cwm. As we walked up the Cwm, the valley sweeping round to the left became visible. First Lhotse and the massive Lhotse Face presented themselves more fully than can be seen from Camp 1; an emphatic full stop to a remarkable valley. On the right the huge expanse of buttress, snow and rib that goes to the top of Nuptse was a constant companion; and then the South Col of Everest came into view and finally a ridge going up and up to the summit of Everest itself, so often obscured by lesser mountains. A spiral of windblown snow was pluming from its summit and the South West Face was now fully visible, falling continuously to the Western Cwm. The sun was up and we had no more work now, so wandered back to our camp.

Closer acquaintance with the Western Cwm revealed other aspects, not all of them romantic cinerama. September the first was spent resting at Camp 1, which was no loss since there was a bright mist and sleet all day, with very mild conditions; a possible trigger to avalanches from Nuptse. In fact, rumbling avalanches were heard all day, and it was good to know that the camp site was so safe; as long as Hamish's contention was ignored, that the camp site, perched on the brink of the Icefall where the Western Cwm starts its dive downwards, had moved 4ft in the night. This was a parting shot as he, Dougal and ten Sherpas disappeared towards Base for a rest. We reckon it's his ladder (the massive cradle by Camp 1) which has sunk 4ft, due to traffic and soft snow, and not to the crevasse widening that amount – but professional pride is reluctant to admit that. Others say that Camp 1 is only held from a downward shuffle by old Japanese ropes tautly spanning the last crevasse.

Doug Scott and Dougal Haston reached the site of Camp 2 on 31 August. That night, on the radio, Doug asked to talk to me.

'We've found a safer site than last time; it's further up the Cwm, on a rounded hummock which should keep it clear of any avalanches. It won't be so far to walk to the foot of the face, either. There's another thing – we think we've found a better and more direct route up the lower part of the face which'll bypass the old Camp 3. We'd like you to have a look at it when you come up.'

I instinctively liked the idea, for, as Doug pointed out, it would give us an almost completely fresh route up the face, but that night I began to think about it and decided to ask Nick Estcourt to come up a day early, so that he could join in the discussion on the proposed route change. I have always had a great deal of respect for his mountaineering judgment.

We were still well ahead of schedule, with 150 loads now dumped at Camp 1. Dougal and Hamish were on their way back to Base Camp for a rest, while Doug Scott, Mick Burke, Ronnie Richards and Allen Fyffe were to move up to Camp 2 to start work on the face itself.

It was tremendously satisfying to leave Base Camp on 1 September and set off for Camp 1, in my own case knowing that this was probably the last time I would see Base Camp until the end of the expedition. I went up with Nick Estcourt and Adrian Gordon, who would take over the camp from Mike Rhodes. Camp 1 was now a small village, with the big Camp 2 box which the old hands had promptly seized, the bell tent for the Sherpas, and a scattering of smaller tents and boxes round it. Our stockpile of gear and food had reached impressive proportions and it had been all Mike Rhodes could do just to keep it neatly stacked, digging it out each day after the afternoon snowfall. I helped the Sherpas put up another bell tent, erected a tunnel tent for myself and settled down for the rest of the day.

It had started clouding over early that morning and now we were in a brilliant white rain-soaked mist. If it didn't freeze that night, there'd be no way we could go up the Western Cwm next day. It must have been conditions like these that destroyed the expedition of Chamonix Guides who attempted to make a route up the West Ridge of Everest, starting from just above Base Camp, in the autumn of 1974. Two of their camps on the flanks of the West Ridge had been swept by a huge avalanche, with the tragic loss of the expedition leader and five Sherpas.

I was longing to get up to the site of Camp 2, longing to look at the route and then face that tremendously exciting, important decision – should we take the left-hand route, or stick to the original one? Temperamentally, without having seen it, the new one appealed to me, and I had a great deal of confidence in Doug and Dougal's judgment. In the meantime, we had superb morale at Camp 1; the Sherpas were singing in the tent next door, and I could hear the lads talking in the big box tent. I felt supremely content to be there, and proud to have the team I had.

8

Avalanches and debate

2 September – 6 September 1975

The high-pitched call of the alarm buzzed me into wakefulness at 2 a.m. on the morning of 2 September. I lay for a couple of minutes, snuggled in my sleeping bag, nerving myself to open the tent door. Rain had been pattering down on to the tent roof when I dropped off to sleep the previous night but now it was still and silent with the moonlight filtering through the thin walls. I looked out to see the steep walled canyon of the Western Cwm glimmering under its myriad of stars set in an opaque black sky; fog crystals, like tiny fireflies, danced in the light of the moon.

I switched on the radio for we had agreed to have a two o'clock call to Base Camp to decide whether the Icefall was safe enough for the Sherpas. The weather now seemed settled and so I gave the go ahead to Dave Clarke down at Base. This was always a nerve-racking decision, for if an accident had occurred after I had declared the route safe, I should always have felt guilty. The trouble was that one could not possibly be a hundred per cent certain the route was ever safe; it was just a case of balancing relative risks.

I then crawled out of the tent and walked over the crisp hard snow to the Sherpas' bell tent to wake our cook; it was difficult to find him for there were twelve Sherpas crammed into the tent, lying like a heap of dark slugs in a careless pile. After prodding at a few heads buried in sleeping bags, I found the one that I thought was that of Kanchha, our cook, told him to start breakfast and returned to my tent. I lay back in my sleeping bag and started to think out the problems of the next few days. We were maintaining our momentum on the mountain, but just keeping track of the huge mass of supplies was now a major problem. Adrian had to ensure that it flowed in the right order from Camp 1 to 2, so that we had everything we needed for the initial stages on the face. I anticipated the first sight of the face as we walked up the Western Cwm, wondered whether the new line might work, and then thoughts and plans merged into a deep sleep and it was daylight when I next woke to the call of 'Chiya, Sahib'.

I looked at my watch; it was 5.30. Why the hell was it so late; surely the cook couldn't have taken three and a half hours to make a cup of tea. I was worried about getting up to Camp 2 and back to Camp 1 before the great powder-snow avalanches started trundling down the steep flanks of

Nuptse. I rushed out of the tent in a nervous rage to ask Kanchha why he had been so long, only to discover that the Sherpa I had woken in the night hadn't been Kanchha at all and must have rolled over and gone back to sleep. There was nothing more I could do, but try to get everyone off as fast as possible and by 6.30 we had set out from camp. In my haste, I was one of the first to start and found myself breaking the trail, plodding the zig-zag route through the initial network of crevasses. Twenty minutes' walking and I was still only a hundred metres in a direct line from the camp, so intricate was the route.

I was quite relieved when Doug Scott and Nick Estcourt caught me up. They were deep in discussion over the relative merits of the routes they had picked through the Icefall. I decided that if they had enough breath to talk they might just as well break trail, and stood aside to let them pass. I was going slowly, definitely feeling the altitude, but at the same time was able to enjoy the walk as I plodded on with a load of ropes on my back. That day we had with us eighteen Sherpas, forming a long snaking tail winding back along the track up the Cwm. The path took us inexorably towards the walls of Nuptse. The debris of a huge wet snow avalanche had spilt over it, covering the marker flags for a stretch of over a hundred metres. Anyone caught in the holocaust would have had little chance of survival.

And then the face came into view. I made this an excuse to sit down and rest, examining the lower slopes for the proposed new line. It was obvious enough, working its way up a series of snow arêtes on the left-hand side of the face, just opposite the site of Camp 2. It was much more direct, and therefore would probably be much quicker. It was also more open to avalanche risk.

After the dog-leg which crept under the flanks of Nuptse, the track swung into the centre of the Cwm and stretched, long and steady, up a shallow depression towards the site of Camp 2. I met Nick Estcourt on his way back down. He didn't like the new line at all.

A few minutes later I reached Camp 2 to find Doug, Ronnie, Allen and Mick Burke who were going to stay the night already erecting one of the big box tents. I had intended to return that night to Camp 1, partially to ensure that the flow of loads was being organised correctly and partially because I preferred to keep out of the way of my lead climbers so that they could make their own tactical decisions without any kind of interference from me. By this time, however, I was worried about the proposed new line on the lower part of the face, was still quite attracted to it, but wanted to have a much closer look before committing myself to one line or another. I therefore decided to stay the night, borrowing a down suit from someone and having my gear sent up the next day.

That night I squeezed in between Mick Burke and Doug Scott and shivered through the dark hours. The face was hidden in cloud in the dawn and we therefore decided to delay a reconnaissance till the following day.

But the weather didn't improve and we spent another day around the camp. There was a continuous rumble of avalanches, a kind of shooshing thunder, like a distant train rushing through a tunnel. It would have been suicidal to have tried to get through from Camp 1 to 2. I felt my policy was being borne out, for though the avalanche risk was high, by being careful in siting the camps we could sit out the storms, free from avalanche threat. We just had to make sure there was enough food and fuel at each camp.

That day there had been some activity in the Icefall below Camp 1. The crevasse a short way below the camp had opened out and the Sherpas coming up the Icefall that day had dumped their loads below it. Hamish had come up with some ladders to rebuild the bridge over it. Nick Estcourt had also dropped down below the camp to give a hand.

On the morning of the 5th, I set my alarm for 3.45, woke up and called Camp 1 for the pre-arranged call at 4 a.m., but got no reply. Cursing them for oversleeping, I dropped off to sleep only to wake up again at 7.30 that morning. Adrian must have just missed me at 4 a.m. and had been calling on the quarter hour ever since. Unfortunately he had let the Sherpas set off at about 5.30, a decision that both Nick at Camp 1 and I at 2 were unhappy about. In fact Nick, on waking, had raced after them to bring them back, before they got into the dangerous bottleneck, but had been unable to head them off. He had then followed them up to find out what had gone wrong with the communications at our camp.

We still hadn't set foot on the face and had spent the entire morning gazing at the lower slopes arguing the pros and cons of the two routes.

I must confess I was uncertain which was the best choice, but the argument was tending in favour of the new direct route, when a series of good sized avalanches came straight down it. This seemed a fairly conclusive argument against the route but even then we didn't reach a final decision. Nick, who had arrived about one o'clock, the one person consistently against the left-hand line, pointed out how it was in the natural fall line of avalanches from the Great Central Gully, while the right-hand route worked its way up to one side of all the avalanche runnels. Mick and, to a lesser degree, Doug argued for the left-hand line, pointing out how we could easily lose all our fixed ropes on the original route to the right whenever it snowed heavily. But everyone, almost imperceptibly, came back to the original right-hand route and we finally settled on it.

Looking back at the argument that night I wondered about my own role as leader. Perhaps I should have been more positive, but I wasn't, and I think the way we all changed our points of view and argued round the problem to reach a democratic decision was, in this particular case, the best way we could have done it. We were very closely united by a decision that everyone helped to make. Many months later I was bemused to discover how our consultations had looked to other members of the party. Doug Scott recollects:

Chris suddenly ended the debate with 'We'll go the old way; I've made my decision.' It wasn't exactly democratic. He had listened to us rather like a prime minister might consult his civil servants before making his decisions. But here it worked and we were all relieved that a decision had been made.

Doug is a passionate believer in a climbing democracy where all decisions are made through group discussion. What he perhaps isn't fully aware of is how strong his own personality is, and how often it is his decision that is adopted. At the same time, though, he understood my side of the problem and always gave me the fullest support, even when perhaps he was unhappy about the way I had gone about it.

The discussion had dragged on through the afternoon. We still had to sort out climbing gear for the following morning and store the loads that had come up that day. We spent the rest of the afternoon doing this and then, in the early evening, I decided to pick up the flags that Doug had placed the previous day to mark our proposed direct route. I wandered along the tracks he had left towards the face. It was a tantalisingly short way to the foot of the wall; little more than a quarter of an hour's walk with hardly any height to gain, but sitting by the flag, with the face soaring above me, I did not regret our decision. It looked rather grim and evil, shoals of black rock sticking out from the snow. A powder-snow avalanche boiled over a rocky outcrop and poured down on to one of the avalanche cones, a grim warning of more to come. I turned back without regret and plodded back towards the camp.

We didn't have any Sherpas with us and while I had been away Doug had prepared a magnificent high tea of sausages, mashed potatoes and peas. Afterwards he decided to go up and mark the route to the foot of the bergschrund and set out clutching a handful of flags. We were all relieved that the decision had been made and that we were going to push forward once more the following morning.

Earlier in the day I had sensed some tension in Doug. He had been rather quiet and moody, almost pointedly seeming to exclude me from the plans for the next day. He and Mick Burke were going to push out the route to Camp 3 and I had suggested that Nick and I might go along to give them a hand. What I didn't realise properly at first was that Mick saw this innocent offer as a threat. He felt that I was interfering with their freedom to be a climbing group out in front on their own, making their own decisions and, for that short time, being autonomous within a huge expedition. For Doug, my policy of keeping roles fluid was slightly worrying. He wrote:

From my own personal point of view I must admit to having been at that time uneasy about my overall role on the trip. For I was now teamed up with two climbers who had no previous experience of Everest and with Mick who was primarily there to film. I kept quiet about my restlessness, as Chris was so wound up with more important problems, and I continued to hope that weather, route and team fitness would determine mine and, in fact, everyone's role. I knew anyway from previous experience that Chris, whose actions were dictated by the overall strategy, often seemed mercurial at a personal level, for he would swop and change his job allocations frequently. We did, however, talk out the making of the route to Camp 3 and, in fact, as it turned out, Nick decided not to go up, but to rest, and Chris himself said he merely fancied a day out load-carrying in support. I felt really mean for having been so possessive about our bit. It was just what he needed, a day out front to enable him to clear his head of all the logistical problems and other worries.

That evening I walked a short distance from the camp, just to be alone. In a way my role, I realised, was similar to that of an admiral in a flagship who has to be terribly careful not to interfere with the tactical day-to-day decisions of the ship's captain.

Escaping from my fellow team members, I was able to savour the mountains. From where I sat I could just see one tent, a soft ruddy glow from the lamp inside somehow emphasising the beauty of the great cirque of ice around us, which was so peaceful and yet held such menace. The threat was lurking the whole time and yet the beauty and challenge of the place were as fresh as they had ever been.

It froze hard that night and we set out in the dark, following the tracks Doug had made the previous evening. I took with me a heavy load of ropes and deadmen. These are small alloy plates which are dug into the snow and act rather like a fluke anchor, digging deeper the harder they are pulled. I didn't bother to bring my crampons because I only intended to go to the foot of the bergschrund so that I could leave the others to the job of making the route and get back to start planning the push up the face itself. The route swung far into the centre of the Cwm, to keep it well away from the threat of avalanches from the face, and then took the slope of fresh avalanche debris at the bottom of the face as direct as possible, to reduce the period we should be exposed to the risk to as short a time as possible. An old rope and some wire emerged from the ice in the bergschrund as a reminder of the 1973 Japanese attempt. Doug had already tied a rope round his waist and was somewhere up above, cramponing up the hard frozen snow. Mick Burke was scouting round for an easier way over the bergschrund itself.

Well content, I heaved up the fixed rope on to the start of the face, dropped my load at the first belay point and wandered back down in the cool shadows of the dawn. I was going much more strongly than I had done in 1972, when it had been all I could do to reach the foot of the face on my first attempt. This time I felt I had plenty in reserve.

Doug continued up the long slope stretching towards Camp 3; it was at a steady angle of around 45 degrees, with a covering of 12in of soft, unstable snow on top of ice. This was where we started the continuous line of fixed rope that I hoped would stretch as close as possible to the foot of the South Summit gully, prior to the summit bid. At this stage the angle was still easy, the climbing technically simple, but any kind of movement at around 7000m (23,000ft) is slow and cumbersome. Going very strongly for the altitude, Doug led out all the way. He used the method we were to follow for the rest of the climb, tying on one of the 8mm non-stretch terylene ropes, which we had unwound from large drums the night before, to make up coils of approximately 60m (200ft) each. He then led on up the snow slope, belayed by Ronnie Richards or Allen Fyffe, while Mick Burke filmed them at work. He plodded up the long slope, kicking cramponed boots into the soft snow, digging in ice axe and terrordactyl; five steps, pause for breath, another five, and on it went to the end of the rope. Doug then anchored the rope, securing it to a special type of ice piton called a wart hog.

The other members of the team then climbed up the rope, that had now been fixed, using their jumar clamps to fix on to the rope. The clamp easily slides up the rope, but, working on the ratchet principle, bites into the rope, as soon as it is pulled on, giving the climber both security and a handle to grasp, as he plods up the slope. Whilst leading, even up an easy snow slope, there is the thrill of pioneering that engulfs fatigue, but climbing the fixed ropes is a slow monotonous business, of making targets, ten steps without a rest, and all too often failing to meet them, sinking back on to the safety line from jumar to harness at the seventh or eighth step just short of the magic ten. And then another rope-length to run out, another rope to follow up.

They climbed the 365m to the foot of the rocky buttress that guards the site of Camp 3. From there the view began to open out, with Pumo Ri jutting out of the swelling tide of cloud at the end of the Western Cwm, framed by the fluted walls of Nuptse and the steep slopes of the West Ridge of Everest. Camp 2 was little more than a cluster of dots, dark against the brilliant snow; the trail up the Western Cwm wound, serpentlike, through the crevasse systems from Camp 1, and beyond Camp 2 towards the face. Even smaller dots, moving imperceptibly, marked the teeming activity that was bringing our supplies to the foot of the face. The scale of the Cwm was so vast. Those dots were so minute against its gigantic scale, so vulnerable to the huge billowing powder-snow avalanches that swept from either wall, seemingly at any time of day or night. It was a sight that was unbelievably beautiful, peaceful, yet full of menace to us tiny humans who did not belong there; whose fate seemed of so little consequence amongst these massive changeless mountains.

But we were full of confidence, poised ready for the fast push up the South West Face to the foot of the Rock Band, still ahead of schedule. It was 6 September, Tut Braithwaite had joined Nick Estcourt at Camp 2. Martin Boysen and Pete Boardman had also moved up with six Sherpas and a cook to relieve us from the chore of doing our own cooking. At Camp 1 Adrian Gordon had everything under control. Whatever I asked him, however infuriating the request, he remained imperturbable. Down at Base Camp Dave Clarke had very nearly finished all the loads that were needed on the mountain and was ready to leave the day-to-day supervision of the start of our supply line to Mike Cheney.

9

A new site for Camp 4

7 September – 10 September 1975

Tut Braithwaite and Nick Estcourt were going to move up to Camp 3 the following morning on 7 September to start pushing the route out towards Camp 4. That night Tut experienced the doubts and worry that nearly always precede a major climb. This was to be his first time on the South West Face itself. That day he had watched the avalanches pour down the Great Central Gully and the rocks on either side, had decided that the entire face was dangerous and yet at the same time was keyed up and excited at the thought of being out in front, making the route. He wrote:

Evening apprehension and morning lethargy soon wore off. Felt good; don't think I'll ever get used to those nights; Nick right on my heels, reassuring, Chris following with Pertemba and his Sherpa team. First fixed rope; clipped into it, pulled over the bergschrund. I had at last set foot on the face, and then the silence was broken by what was to become a familiar cry from Nick, 'I've simply got to have a shit' – one of the two things that Nick takes great delight in telling you, the other being when he has just had one.

I carried on, moving quickly up the endless line of fixed ropes. Occasionally, momentum was broken by the odd section of rope which had been frozen into the snow during the night and pulled free under my body weight; I slipped back down for what felt like a lifetime, though usually it was only a few feet. Looking back down I could see Nick, Chris and the Sherpas follow up behind me; across to the right was the South Col. This really was the South West Face; finally the short traverse to the site of Camp 3. It was still early with the sun high over Nuptse. Nick and I decided to carry on and push some ropes out towards Camp 4.

How much rope should we take? always a problem. I was excited and wanted to get to grips with the face above, possibly to convince myself that I was strong enough to break the trail in the tiring and unpredictable snow conditions. I thought, if I can prove it to myself today, I might at least get some sleep tonight.

I led off, traversing under the shattered rocky buttress that protected Camp 3, out towards the centre of the face; ran out the 150ft [45m] length of rope, but couldn't find a crack in the rock in which to hammer in a piton; the snow was too unstable to put in a snow anchor, so yelled to Nick to tie on another length of rope and just carried on. I would stay on the surface of the crusty snow for a few feet but would then go crashing through into the deep powder, up to my knees or even deeper. Finally found a rock spur where I could belay. I had made my first contribution to the expedition, 300ft of rope fixed in place.

Nick Estcourt and Tut Braithwaite worked through the morning, taking turns to lead each pitch, slowly running out the lifeline of rope towards the Great Gully that split the centre of the face. As they worked, they could see the dazzling line of sunlight slowly work its way down and across the face of Lhotse as the sun, still hidden by the South East Buttress, crept up into a cloudless sky. They were still in the shadowed cool, until the sun reached the crest of the buttress, then within moments they were exposed to its full strength-draining force. Their progress reduced to a spasmodic crawl, they turned back to Camp 3 where Pertemba, the six Sherpas and I had been busy digging out the site and erecting two face boxes.

It was like an archaeological dig, for we quickly began to unearth the relics left by the 1973 Japanese expedition. There was a complete tent that had obviously been left pitched; it had filled up with snow which in the subsequent two years had turned to ice. Embedded in it was some food and various belongings – an old anorak, a down boot, an ice axe, an oxygen mask and various bits of climbing paraphernalia. It was as if the tent had been left for the day and its occupants had never returned. I wondered what interpretation an archaeologist discovering the tent in a thousand years' time might make. More to the point, we were all interested to see if the Japanese food was still edible. There were little plastic bags of seaweed, boiled sweets and tins of fruit, all of which provided a welcome change from our diet and which proved perfectly edible. We hacked through the relics of the Japanese expedition, salvaging as much as possible, and then came across the ruins of one of our 1972 box tents. No doubt, had we dug deep enough we should also have found reminders of all the previous expeditions. By this time the sun had come round to us and we took progressively longer rests between digging and erecting the tent. Tut and Nick returned and we left them and two Sherpas ensconced in their new home and went back down the fixed ropes. The snow below the camp was now an ugly sight, littered with the newly excavated rubbish, but I was able to console myself with the thought that it would soon be covered by the afternoon snowfall.

Back at Camp 2, we whiled away the hot afternoon discussing the problem of where to put Camp 4. The site used by all the previous expeditions was exposed to avalanche and stonefall from the Rock Band. This was the reason why Hamish had designed such a strong box tent, but it seemed preferable to find some way of avoiding the dangerous camp site altogether. Hamish suggested that perhaps Dougal and he might go up to the old site of Camp 4 with one of the lightweight summit assault tents to try to find a better spot. We talked around the problem but didn't come to any conclusion. I was tired anyway from my day's work at Camp 3 and went to bed early.

I often woke up in the early hours of the morning and would mull over the problems of the moment. This was one such morning and an idea, which was to change the entire logistic balance of the expedition, began to germinate. So far, each expedition had followed its predecessor in siting Camp 4 and had then accepted not only the inherent danger of its situation but also the fact that it was in the wrong place logistically in relation to the other camps. The trouble was that Camp 3 was much too low, too short a day from Camp 2, and Camp 4 was too high. In 1972, the Sherpas had preferred to stay at Camp 2 and then every other day had done a very long day's carry up to Camp 4, a height gain of 900m (2950ft) from 6600m (21,650ft) to 7500m (24,600ft). The climbers had been unable to manage this and had always staged at Camp 3 on the way up. This is what we were planning to do this time. I had always been a little unhappy however about the principle of the Sherpas obviously undertaking a very much harder carry than the climbers.

The solution suddenly occurred to me. Bring the site of Camp 4 much lower, to a point just 300m (1000ft) above our existing Camp 3. There was a convenient spur running down from the retaining buttress of the Great Central Gully that looked as if it would give the new camp site some protection from avalanches and at the same time would be a reasonable day's carry for climbers and Sherpas alike from Camp 2. Hamish was immediately enthusiastic, as was Dougal when he returned from a long solitary walk up the Western Cwm to try and spy out the route through the Rock Band. I then put the idea to Pertemba, for his reaction was the most important of all, and he was also in favour.

We could see Nick Estcourt and Tut Braithwaite, two tiny dots on the face, making slow but very steady progress. That morning of 8 September they had already passed the proposed site of Camp 4 so I decided to let them have another day, pushing the route out as far as they could into the Great Central Gully. They would then drop straight back to Camp 2, so that Hamish and Dougal could move up into Camp 3 that night ready to move into Camp 4.

I spent the morning making the detailed logistic calculations that the change of site for Camp 4 made necessary. I had to discuss with Pertemba the number of carries without a rest day he thought the Sherpas would be able to make. We decided on two carries and then one day off; much better than if we had had Camp 4 in its original position. I then had to explain the change of plan over the radio to the rest of the team at Camp 1 and Base

Camp, in a mammoth radio call. Charlie Clarke described his reaction to my activity in his diary.

Chris is in a state of hyper mania at Camp 2 in the Western Cwm, drawing charts of stores, oxygen, men, being uncontrollably effusive down the radio and Mick has christened him the 'Mad Mahdi'. He is desperate that the master plan unfolds smoothly and above all that the route from Base to Camp 2 is safe, for it is here that the Sherpas go alone and much can go wrong.

He really is a great leader in spite of all the criticism levelled at him. Nobody else has the personality to command us and deep down we respect him. I have a very good relationship with him particularly as I, thank God, am not in the raffle – i.e. the great decision of who goes to the top. This sadly alienates him from most of the lead climbers. Even a little is enough and it's just beginning to show itself. No splits, no factions, no nastiness, but it's all there in their hearts.

This was written by Charlie just after Mick Burke, Doug Scott and the rest of the first lead party had got back down to Base Camp. For all our mutual reassurances at Camp 2 it was inevitable that tensions should remain on an expedition as large as this, with so much at stake, particularly as the climb progressed and small groups became scattered in different camps up the mountain. Members of the team, and for that matter I myself, needed to express worries and fears either to each other or, in my case, to the confidence of my tape-diary. These, with the odd outburst, provided the vital escape valves that enabled us to go on working together in amazing harmony through the expedition. Certainly, that sunny day of 8 September, there was a feeling of relaxed excitement as we discussed the implications of the decision to change the site of Camp 4.

Up on the face, Tut Braithwaite, Nick Estcourt and the two Sherpas were absorbed by the challenge of making the route up into the Great Central Gully. Tut describes it:

Strange that I should be climbing with Nick; we both live in the Manchester area and I must have known him for about ten years, yet it was this expedition that brought us together to climb for the first time. I remember it very well; Orion Face, Ben Nevis, March 1975. Nick, whilst tackling a pitch in the upper section, dislodged a large piece of ice which came smashing down into my face and broke five of my front teeth. He did apologise, but what impressed me in those dazed and painful hours that followed, he never suggested retreating; kept on insisting that it cost too much these days to drive to Scotland and not get at least one big route done per day. I remember at the time thinking, well if he feels like this about £10 and a couple of days, there would be no stopping him on Everest.

We left camp at about 6.30 and an hour later reached the previous day's high point. We'd decided against using oxygen. I started off, conditions desperate, heading slightly leftwards into the centre of the face. Constant streams of avalanche poured down on either side of us. I was feeling extremely fit but at the same time incredibly nervous, even to the point of constantly telling Nick not to pull too hard on the fixed rope, afraid he might at any moment drag out the very insecure deadman anchor belays. At every step above I was frightened the 3in crust of wind slab would break away, taking all four of us with it. After six or seven rope-lengths, sharing the lead and the tension all the way, we at last reached the rock step that had beckoned to us all the way up. We littered it with rock pitons, at last feeling secure. I remember saying to Nick, what a pity it was so low, since it would make a good site for Camp 4.

In fact this was the site that I had planned that night. Tut and Nick succeeded in pushing the route out a further three pitches before the enervating strength of the sun drove them back to their camp. They spent the rest of the day dozing and cooking in their tent, and that night, for the first time, Tut took a sleeping tablet. He described the result in his diary.

September 9. Woke feeling terrible; I'd tried a sleeping tablet, never again. It was to be my first day on oxygen. Nick in his normal very precise informative way, was explaining every detail of the equipment, and all I wanted to do was to stay in my sleeping bag. I had wanted to make that last day out in front really count, but there was no chance, I felt so sick. Started off very slowly, feeling depressed at the thought of wasting one of those precious days out in front, disappointed for the expedition, but even more for myself personally.

Nick came steaming past, then the two Sherpas, and they weren't even using oxygen. God, was I sick. I finally caught up with Nick at our high point and had to offer him the lead all the way. He jumped at the chance, commenting, 'You should try sleeping pills more often.'

Streams of avalanches a constant reminder of the danger of leaving the descent too late; we finally started back down after reaching a point a couple of hundred feet below and to the right of the 1972 site of Camp 4. The actual climbing at this stage on Everest isn't technically difficult or even interesting, but the big overriding factor is that it is on Everest. My thoughts are constantly in the upper section of the face, the Rock Band, the unknown section above, and, dare I even dream it, the summit itself.

Tackling this lower section in its present condition is what I imagine the trenches were like in 1914. Throw yourselves at it for a few days, then drop back and let another bugger have a go. I feel satisfied with our performance these last few days and pleased that by chance or design I've teamed up with Nick.

It is sometimes difficult to conceive how many different things were going on at different levels of the mountain, all at the same time; each incident of vital importance to the expedition as a whole and to the individuals concerned. The same morning that Nick and Tut pushed up towards the old site of Camp 4, whilst Hamish and Dougal made their leisured way to Camp 3, I had to deal with a minor, but potentially serious, crisis lower down on the mountain.

On the night of 7 to 8 September it had snowed heavily with a fall of 45cm at Camp 1 and even more at Base. The morning was clear however and at the four o'clock early morning call I told Adrian to send the Sherpas up the Cwm. I decided however to break trail for them by dropping down to meet them. Mike Thompson very kindly volunteered to join me and we left Camp 2 at about 6 a.m. wading down through the deep fresh snow, picking our way from one almost submerged marker flag to the next. It was exhilarating walking down in the crisp cool of the morning, good to get away from the crowds and pressing decisions of Advanced Base for a few hours, to give oneself a simple, almost mindless role.

But this wasn't to be. It never was. As we dropped further down the Western Cwm, I became increasingly worried for there was no sign of the Sherpa party from Camp 1. We reached the bend in the Cwm, where the route was forced into the side. Still no sign, and it was now nearly 7.30 in the morning, the sun already loosening the heavy piled new snow on Nuptse. We hurried along the track where it curved into the side, uncomfortably aware of the proximity of the avalanche-prone slope. It was all very well, going down, for you could run, but on the way up, weighed down by an 18 kilo load, you could do no more than plod, and hope that no avalanche came your way.

Still no sign of the carrying party. We dropped down into the crevassed area, zig-zagging away from the threatening wall of Nuptse, and then, in the distance, seemingly only just beyond Camp 1, I saw the vanguard of our Sherpa carrying party. By this time I was in a fine rage, raced down to meet them, and asked Ang Phu, who was in charge, what the hell he thought he was doing starting out so late. Back in the decision-making game. It was now eight o'clock; it would take them three hours to reach Camp 2 and then they had to get back. I decided to call the carry off and told them to stack their loads and return to Camp 1. The Sherpas were sceptical; Ang Phu obviously thought I was being a bit of an old woman. An avalanche, the first of the morning, curled down from the upper ramparts of Nuptse, reinforcing my decision. I raced on down to Camp 1, running all the way to try to catch the eight o'clock radio call before it came to an end, but arrived just too late.

Camp 1 now had the BBC team in residence. Mike Thompson and I lazed the rest of the day, planning to return to Advanced Base the following morning, and retired to a tent on the edge of the camp quite early. I had dropped off into a deep sleep, when suddenly I woke to the feel of an icy wet powder on the small portion of my face that protruded from my sleeping bag. It was pitch dark, but I was vaguely conscious of being shaken, someone, presumably Mike, struggling to get out of the tent, and a flood of powder snow pouring in. Mike shouted something about avalanche, but I just snuggled deeper into my warm sleeping bag, clinging to comforting sleep. He had been unlucky in being awake at the time, had heard the giant swoosh of the avalanche coming down, struggled out of his sleeping bag and had dived for the door, hoping to get to safety, wherever that might have been. At the same time he had shaken me to give me a chance to escape. As a result he got covered in the powder snow, which poured into the tent and had filled his sleeping bag. What we had been hit by was the snow-laden air blast that is driven in front of a large avalanche, though that night we couldn't see its extent. At least none of the tents had been damaged and no one at Camp 1 was hurt. Mike spent a bitterly cold shivery night in his snow-plastered clothes, eventually moving into the big box tent to find a spare dry sleeping bag.

The following morning of 10 September dawned fine and at the early morning call I decided that it was probably safe enough to make a carry up to Camp 2 and for the Icefall Sherpas to make a carry to Camp 1, on the assumption that the worst of the avalanches had already been spent. Mike and I made an early start from Camp 1, to get up to our Advanced Base well before the sun hit the Cwm, so that the Sherpas could get back safely. Down at Base, they were less happy about the order to do a carry up the Icefall. They also had been hit by the windblast of the avalanche, and they were worried about the state the Icefall might be. On a show of hands they decided it would be wiser to send a lightweight repair party, headed by Phurkipa, to reconnoitre the damage and declare whether the route was safe. This was undoubtedly the wisest decision, and one that I was relieved had been taken when I heard of their step on the afternoon call. I was fortunate in having a group of highly experienced mountaineers in the team who were fully capable of taking their own decisions, and on the occasions when I made a directive by radio which seemed impractical to the party at the camp concerned, they would assess the situation for themselves, obviously discuss it with me if this was practical, but if it wasn't, take action accordingly. In the event, no further avalanches swept the Icefall that day, but a huge avalanche had earlier come pouring down the feature we had given the name 'Death Valley', crushing and collapsing the broken crevasse region at its foot. As a result a section needed re-laddering and a new line had to be made alongside the valley. It was just as well we had not sent in heavily laden porters that day.

By the time that Dave Clarke, who had come up from Base, and Jim Duff, Mike Thompson and I reached Camp 2, Martin Boysen and Pete Boardman had followed Hamish and Dougal to Camp 3. The following day, on 11 September, they were going to move up to Camp 4.

Up the Great Central Gully

10 September – 15 September 1975

One of the problems of having sufficient lead climbers in the expedition to cope with a sustained siege of the Rock Band was maintaining their interest and morale whilst they waited for their turn out in front. In this respect the support climbers were more fortunate. They had administrative responsibilities and were able to gain a satisfaction from helping to carry loads that the lead climbers seemed unable to share. Back at Camp 2, just before taking his turn in the lead Martin Boysen had been very depressed:

It's such a large expedition, I just don't feel the necessary sense of involvement. It really doesn't matter if I'm here or not. I have done sweet Fanny Adams apart from dragging my unwilling body up and down the Icefall. Worse, it's dangerous, menaced by avalanches and I just don't feel like sticking my neck out for something I just don't feel wound up with.

And yet on the following morning, 10 September:

Amazing how one day's depression dissolves into happiness. At Camp 2 I was at my lowest ebb, yet next day walking up the Western Cwm with Pete I felt lighthearted and gloriously happy for the first time. The morning was so magically beautiful, the Cwm swathed in boiling mists, Everest in dark blue shadow, Nuptse emerging diamond white, a hundred ice crests gleaming.

They spent the night at Camp 3 and the next morning on 11 September set out for the site of Camp 4. Pertemba and I with twelve Sherpas had already left Camp 2 with loads of box tents, food, fixed rope-climbing hardware for the push into the Great Central Gully. The Sherpas pulled ahead of me without any trouble, but I kept plodding – slow but steady up the long line of fixed rope. Martin had waited for me at Camp 3 and it was good to see him relaxed and happy. We set out together for the new camp, being hit by the sun before we were halfway up the big snow slope that led across to the base of the Great Central Gully. The heat was immediately oppressive and our upwards progress slowed to a crawl. Dougal Haston, Hamish MacInnes and Pete Boardman had already reached the site of the camp and were hacking out their platforms. It didn't look quite as well protected as it had through our binoculars from below. They were digging their way into a shallow snow arête, which we hoped would divide any avalanches from the very considerable broken snow slope above and protect the camp from the worst of their force. The powder-snow avalanches had already carved out channels, down which a torrent of snow was pouring. This was the first time that the complete MacInnes box, with its platforms, special floor of plastic honeycomb sandwiched between plywood and bullet-proofed tarpaulins, was to be tried out. Hamish was in his element, spanner in hand, erecting one of the boxes.

Martin digging a platform just below, observed slightly caustically:

Pete sits above acting as Hamish's bolt boy. Dougal squats impassively under the rocks. Pete calls incessantly, 'Martin could you secure my rucksack? Martin could you bring my camera up? Martin...' I told him to stop pissing about, expecting me to run around for him, and come down to help dig out our platform. Am I being unreasonable to be so shirty? I know I am being a bit grumpy, but why should I feel so annoyed? Perhaps it's because Pete is so young, too easily managed by the old stagers. He's such a dreamy bugger and can appear to be so damned helpless. But I like his company and, as for climbing, he's as tough and determined as anyone.

Eventually the boxes were erected and the foursome settled down to the afternoon routine of brewing tea and cooking the evening meal, our own high-altitude rations being titivated with some Japanese tinned food collected from Camp 3.

The following morning Martin Boysen and Pete Boardman, the two newcomers to Everest, were to go out on their own, while Dougal Haston and Hamish MacInnes were going to improve the camp site. They set out at 6 a.m., jumaring up the line of fixed ropes left in place by Tut Braithwaite and Nick Estcourt. They had decided against using oxygen but were going quite strongly up to the high point about 230m above their camp.

Martin Boysen led out up the first pitch, revelling in the experience of lead climbing: 'The climbing was of a low order of technical difficulty but at least I had to think, make decisions, test the bite of crampons, search for belays, not just jumar up a pre-existing rope.'

He led out two rope-lengths and allowed Pete Boardman to take over, heading towards the site of earlier expeditions' Camp 4 which was marked by a few crushed aluminium tubes sticking out of the snow. A length of rope, probably left from the 1973 Japanese expedition, was lying clear of the snow and Pete was able to use it, pulling on it very carefully for fear it was no longer anchored at its top. They reached the site of the former Camp 4 and returned well pleased with their day's work, to find a third box erected with reinforcements in the shape of two of our strongest Sherpas, Ang Phurba and Tenzing, who is the son of Phurkipa. That day eleven Sherpas, accompanied by Mike Thompson, had made a carry up to Camp 4, bringing up a good stock of rope, deadmen, more boxes and oxygen cylinders.

The carrying party had returned, leaving the four climbers and two Sherpas to their own devices for the afternoon. Pete Boardman commented in his diary:

Hamish has designed quite a dramatic loo and produces the auto load (film camera) as I squat. Martin yells at one of the Sherpas, a bit too seriously I think, because they seem to have more yellow foam mattresses than we have; he's also irritated when he sees yet another piece of gear that I have, that he's missed out on through arriving late. But we have a pleasant lunch of mashed potato, peas and roast lamb, followed by fried slices of Christmas pudding with cream. Martin seems to have slotted me light-heartedly as Bramhall middle class. Hamish is friendly and cheerful but Dougal is ever distant.

They were shaken out of their feeling of well-being that evening when a big powder-snow avalanche swept over the camp. Hamish MacInnes describes what it felt like:

I don't know what the time was when we woke up, but we woke with a start! The whole box was vibrating in sympathy with the motion of snow not so very far away: the face was avalanching. Suddenly there was a thud. The box shook violently. The overhanging rock hadn't been such good protection after all. For an instant Dougal and I feared we might follow the debris down the face. A short time later we were hit by a further salvo. Martin and Peter, some 6ft below, were receiving the avalanche second-hand, so to speak, but this was obviously enough to make them perturbed – it was sufficient to make me terrified. The thought of hurtling down the South West Face in a box was not a pleasant prospect, even if the structure did rejoice in the name of its designer/occupant.

Darkness seemed reluctant to leave next morning, but at long last an anaemic dawn spilled from the heights and we peered out cautiously. All was much the same as before, though the camp scene did look a bit snowswept. Despite the fact that the Sherpa village of Namche Bazar is itself precariously perched on a hillside, one 'street' above the next, Ang Phurba and Tenzing, who were occupying a third box, didn't seem too cheerful that morning. Neither was I, for that matter, and I didn't voice any bubbling enthusiasm for blazing a trail to Camp 5. The snow appeared to be in a critical condition. But Dougal and I donned our oxygen equipment and struggled resolutely out into a day reminiscent of the damp Scottish Highlands. Martin and Peter were to follow later.

The rope rose directly above the camp over a steep step. Dougal went first. I turned on my oxygen cylinder, pulled the face mask in place, and took a deep breath. At least I tried to, but there was no oxygen. As the person responsible for the oxygen equipment, I felt unfairly singled out, as in 1972, in possessing a faulty set. Despite coaxing, it refused to work so finally, in disgust, I threw it into the box and set off without it.

I was making good time; Dougal was only a short way ahead. Looking down on the two boxes, snuggled into the slope like Oxo cubes, I could see Ang Phurba and Tenzing coming up, several rope-lengths behind. Dougal had traversed left towards the rope which led over to the main gully from the upper face. I was ascending in a shallow runnel, but due to ice on the rope, my jumar clamps were not holding too well.

Then I heard a swoosh like a quiet fast-moving car above me. The avalanche overtook me and I was engulfed in a maelstrom of snow particles. It was like breathing fine white smoke. I could feel it crowding my lungs and sensed the agonising horror of a drowning man. In the last instant before I was hit, I had managed to wrap the rope round my left hand to prevent the jumar sliding down the rope, with the result that my arm was now being stretched unmercifully by the force of the avalanche. I was passing out as the avalanche stopped just as suddenly as it had commenced. I retched distressfully for a good fifteen minutes. My bladder had released involuntarily – not that this mattered, since I was stuffed, inside and out, with powder snow. Even my boots, encased in double gaiters, were filled with the stuff.

Eventually my breathing reverted to an approximation of that cacophony more usually associated with the bagpipes being tuned, and I made an unsteady descent. I was totally numbed by the experience and felt an excruciating pain in my chest. A short way down I encountered the Sherpas but was unable to speak to them and staggered past, clutching the rope.

Martin and Peter were standing outside their box when I appeared above them on the slope. I must have looked a wild sight: I had lost a crampon and was swaying dangerously. I explained what had happened as best I could, and crawled into my box. Eventually I extracted the snow which had penetrated to my skin, took oxygen and Martin brought me a mug of tea.

It was the Sherpas' rest day, for they had made carries in the two previous days up to Camp 4. I was very anxious to maintain the momentum and therefore we had a big climbers' carry that day. Doug was the first to set out with a heavy load of rope and some of his own personal gear. He was accompanied by Pertemba, who, even though he was due for a rest, volunteered to help us. They were both going very strongly and pulled out far ahead of Ronnie and myself, who plodded up at a much slower, rate. Allen Fyffe and Jim Duff were bringing up the rear.

The last 30m or so, in the full strength of the sun, was particularly exhausting and our progress had slowed down to a crawl. Doug and Martin's gesture in dropping down to meet us, to carry our loads the last few metres, was specially welcome. Allen Fyffe reached Camp 4 about an hour later, keeping going through the heat of the day, through sheer perseverance and will power, but he was obviously finding the going very hard. Jim Duff had also tried a carry but was forced to return just beyond Camp 3. It was unfortunate that he was carrying the mail for the occupants of Camp 4.

Dougal Haston, Pete Boardman and the two Sherpas got back just after we reached the camp. They had only been able to run out a single length of rope beyond the previous day's high point, having found that they had left all the snow anchors behind. It had been a day of mishaps, but I was not unduly perturbed for our forward progress was now outstripping our ability to maintain the flow of supplies to sustain further progress. It also seemed probable that the next morning they should be able to get most of the way to the site of Camp 5, though at this stage we were not at all sure of where this was going to be.

On the morning of 14 September they made an early start. Pete Boardman woke up at 3.15, called the others and started melting snow for the first brew for Martin Boysen and himself. After having two brews and some Ready-brek, they started the slow cumbersome business of getting ready for the day. They had most of their clothes on already, but had to squeeze their feet into the three layers of footwear, inner boots, the main leather outer, then the Neoprene overboots and finally their crampons. This time Martin ensured that his oxygen was functioning correctly and was the first to get away. Dougal followed, and Pete Boardman and the two Sherpas were only a short way behind. Hamish MacInnes tried to follow them, using a fresh oxygen system that we had brought up, but even with oxygen he was dangerously breathless and weak. Extremely worried about the state of his lungs, he reluctantly turned round and dropped back down to Camp 2. The others pressed on towards their previous day's high point. Dougal reached it first, and while he sorted out the ropes for the day's climbing, pondered about the climb ahead.

What we wanted was a site for Camp 5. We had thought the left side of the couloir would be best but there was a suspicious amount of avalanche activity there. We were already a long way up from the present 4. The Sherpas' optimum function-ability had to be taken into consideration. Also we had to be reasonably close to the Rock Band. The old 5 was too high and too far right. It was then that I began thinking of the ledges on the right where the couloir begins to fan out. I had seen them many times, knew they existed, but had never regarded them with an eye to a camp, as they weren't of any use on the old right-hand route with its prevailing camp settings. But this time maybe? The other two arrived and progress continued steadily with everyone and everything functioning well. Near the top of the narrows there was only one 300ft section of fixed rope left and the sun had caught us. Martin, oxygen finished, descended. I continued in the lead with Pete, carrying strongly and steadily behind. The last piece of fixed rope was like the last piece of a successful jigsaw. I turned a corner and there were some good ledges on the right, sheltered by overhangs. Ahead a long snow slope led up to the Rock Band couloir. I reckoned we had found our Camp 5 site.

Pete Boardman also had enjoyed his day out in front, writing:

Going well on oxygen as long as I keep on plodding and don't try any major bursts of effort that make me gasp too furiously. Soft slides pour down either side of our rib of snow. The channel on our left is continually moving, giving that uncertain feeling one gets in a railway carriage when the train next to one starts moving. It's a strange sensation to plod upwards, the only sound one's own breathing and the thump of the oxygen valve. So much of this expedition is self-preservation, keeping warm and fed, pacing oneself, looking after one's fingers and toes. Today cold toes as usual and Dougal good to follow, despite his self-congratulatory air … Back to Camp 4 and warm toes in the sunshine and at last some letters from home – pleasant to read in the late morning sun and strange to think that I'm at Camp 4 on Everest.

Back at Camp 2 we had been able to watch their progress through binoculars. That afternoon at the two o'clock call, Dougal told me of his thinking behind siting Camp 5 on the side of the gully. It made excellent sense. They had now completed their task and were coming back down for a rest. We were in a position to establish Camp 5 in another two days, but the difficult question was who should establish it? I had originally thought of sending Ronnie Richards and Allen Fyffe up to get the camp built and the route started towards the Rock Band, so that then Doug Scott, Mick Burke, Nick Estcourt and Tut Braithwaite could have moved up to force the left-hand couloir.

Unfortunately, however, Allen did not seem sufficiently acclimatised to move up to Camp 4. He had only just managed to stagger there the previous day. Ronnie was going reasonably well, at about the same rate as myself, but he lacked experience of this kind of climbing. I talked over the problem with Doug Scott. He was obviously worried about going up to Camp 5 too early, especially when it was obviously going to be a very long haul, just to the foot of the Rock Band, on which he had set his own sights. Therefore I decided to go up to Camp 5 myself, get it securely established, start the route out towards the Rock Band and then probably stay there to co-ordinate the flow of supplies for the assault itself.

In this I was breaking one of the rules I had originally set myself, that I should try to be in the camp immediately behind the lead climbers, to keep an eye on their problems without getting involved in tactical decisions. In this instance, however, I felt justified in going out in front. We had changed so much from our original plan, I no longer thought I had the feel of the problem, found it difficult to visualise the site of camps or the distances involved. Another factor was that Camp 5 was obviously going to be a crucial camp site and I wanted to ensure that it was securely established. Dave Clarke at Camp 2 and Adrian Gordon at Camp 1 had the day-to-day running of the camps and movement of porters well under control, so it seemed that I should be able to run the expedition for a short time from the front, while getting Camp 5 established, and even supervise the final stages of the expedition from this position. Also, I must confess, I was itching to have a little session out in front, actually making the route. I decided there-fore to move up to Camp 4 with Ronnie Richards and six Sherpas the following day, 15 September.

Pete Boardman and Martin Boysen with Ang Phurba and Tenzing, dropped back to Camp 2 that day, but Dougal Haston had an urge to be alone for a change and elected to spend the night at Camp 4, observing:

I settled comfortably into my sleeping bag, stove melting snow, and read some letters. Drifting, dreaming, and sifting thoughts about our progress to date and to come, the hours meandered gently onwards until the sun settled down, leaving a stronger than usual night wind. Taking a quick look outside I found that it had started snowing. This was not unusual, and I didn't give it too much thought. Slowly I worked my way through the evening meal and about nine o'clock drifted into a dream-filled sleep. My dreams were pleasant but I kept waking into an almost awake state. As the snowfall continued the avalanches started pouring down the central couloir which was one of the reasons for taking Camp 4 out of the couloir. My present box had been erected on as safe a site as we could find but, of course, it is not possible to be one hundred per cent certain of anything in the mountains.

My home was under a rock – I drifted back to sleep again, only to be awakened a few minutes later by big avalanches going past on the other side. A faint glimmer-ing of unease crept into my mind as I worked out where it had come from. It couldn't possibly have come from the couloir, I calculated. From where then? Thinking back to my previous times high on the face, the conclusion seemed to be that it came from the snow slope going up on the rightward route to the old Camp 6. That also meant that the snow was building up to heavier than normal propor-tions. Next thing all calculating fled from my head as there was a loud whistling and rushing noise and a few seconds later a great bang on the side wall of the box smashed me in a tangled heap against the other side of the tent. For one instant I felt completely disorientated and vulnerable. Was I still attached to the slope or rolling down towards the bergschrund? Then a glad realisation of being all right as stability and the movement of body and limbs was established.

There wasn't much fear – vulnerability being the predominant emotion as I'd stripped off most of my clothes in one of our very warm sleeping bags. Groping, I remembered a lighter in my rucksack pocket which was still under my head. The ensuing flame didn't reveal an optimistic sight. A huge bulge in the inner wall showed where the avalanche hadn't managed to escape down the slope. All the equipment was mixed up. First thoughts were to get dressed and get off down the ropes as quickly as possible – a straight panic reaction. Movement and getting away from the scene of an accident is often the first thing that comes to mind in situations like this. It almost goes as far as to be instinctive. Then rational processes started again, working it out clinically. I reckoned that I'd be safer sitting in the tent than on the exposed slopes below. Working also on the optimistic premise that it was still a safe site, that it had been a freak avalanche and it was unlikely to hit the same spot again.

Having decided to do this I stuck my head out the entrance. It wasn't an encouraging scene but it proved one thing. I'd been fortunate in my choice of box. The one opposite was wrecked. There wouldn't have been any survival for its occupants. It was 2 a.m. and the rest of my night consisted of sitting fully clothed, with boots, overboots and crampons on as well, inside my sleeping bag waiting for another one. It didn't happen. The snow stopped and at first light I was quickly sliding down the ropes and telling an upcoming Chris the not-so-glad news.

11

Camp 5

15 September – 19 September 1975

I plodded on up the ropes full of forebodings, out of the still shadows into the glare of the sun that was slanting across the lower snowfields of the face from above the South East Ridge. I was out in front, Ronnie Richards a rope-length behind; a puff of snow appeared on the rocks far above, snow crystals glittering in the sun. The puff spread into a boiling cloud, seeming to stretch across the entire wall. There was no sound and, but for memories of Hamish's experience, or the story that Dougal had just told me, it wouldn't even have seemed menacing. I took a couple of photographs of the approaching avalanche, noticed Ronnie huddling into the snow, and then quickly, now fearful, turned my own back to the coming onslaught, tried to burrow my chin into the collar of my silk polo neck to stop the snow flooding down my throat. A wind whipped round me, I was in a turbulent blizzard, the snow plucking me from my stance. And then, as suddenly as it had enveloped me, it was gone.

I had been on the very edge of the avalanche. Ronnie had had slightly rougher treatment and was looking like a snowman as he shook himself clear of the snow. I was most worried, however, about our Sherpas, who had set out from Camp 2 after us, and who, when we had last seen them, had just been starting up the line of fixed ropes below Camp 3. Unless they had reached the shelter of the rock buttress they could have been in the direct path of the avalanche. I was immensely relieved, shortly after reaching Camp 4, to see them coming up round the corner. They had reached the shelter of the buttress just in time, and the huge avalanche had come pouring over their heads. They were obviously shaken by their experience, but could still raise a smile and were fully prepared to spend the night at Camp 4.

Camp 4 was a mess with tents and gear submerged in snow. It was easy to see why the damage had occurred. We had brought with us special tarpaulins of reinforced nylon that are used for the construction of bullet-proof jackets. We were hoping that these would provide protection against both stonefall and avalanches. To be effective, however, they needed to be pegged out in the slope above the box they were protecting, so that they would act as a chute, carrying the snow over the roof of the box.

Unfortunately, Hamish and Dougal had only draped the tarpaulins over the boxes, with the result that the snow had built up against the walls, crushing them inwards, and, in the case of the box on the outside of the spur, actually buckling the frame. On clearing the snow away, however, we saw the damage was not quite as bad as it had seemed to Dougal in the early hours. A conventional tent or box would undoubtedly have been flattened, but the frame of Hamish's box was so strong that it had been bent inwards but had not collapsed completely and had there been any occupants that night, they would almost certainly have survived, but might well have had a few bruises.

Even so, the damage was worrying and we spent the rest of the day digging out the boxes, uncovering the stockpile of gear, excavating new platforms and erecting two further box tents. We placed one above and one below the two that were already erected immediately underneath the little rock outcrop that had saved Dougal the night before. It was hard work at 7225m (23,700ft), and even when the boxes were up, the day's work was not over. I was determined to establish Camp 5 the next day, on the 16th. This meant sorting out the necessary loads. Dougal had told me that there seemed a good snow build-up at the site he had chosen and so I decided to risk leaving behind the platform; the face box still represented three loads. We also needed rope and snow anchors for fixing the route beyond, oxygen bottles, not only for climbing with during the day, but for sleeping and, of course, some food and cooking gear. The frames of the boxes were all tangled together, and Ronnie Richards, ever methodical, patiently sorted them out into their separate sets. By this time the sun was dropping down below the West Ridge of Nuptse, bathing the face in a rich yellow glow that had little warmth in it. We had made up our six loads for the next day, were about to start cooking our evening meal, when Mingma, one of our Sherpas, poked his head into the box and told us that Dorje, one of our youngest Sherpas, was feeling sick and had a bad headache. He had been our cook-boy in 1972, always wore a happy smile and was immensely willing, but now, when I slid down the steep alleyway between the tents to see him, he was lying grey-faced in his sleeping bag, very sorry for himself. I dosed him with codeine and a sleeping tablet, but it seemed most unlikely that he would be able to undertake a carry the following morning. We had stretched our carrying resources to the limit already and now in the gathering dark I had to try to reduce our loads by one. I flung out the summit box, which we had decided to take, just in case we couldn't find a snow slope deep enough to fit in one of the standard face boxes; I also redistributed some of the ropes and gas cylinders, before swinging up to our own box. One could never relax at Camp 4; one had to be sure to clip into one of the safety lines at all times, the slope was so steep.

By the time I got back into the tent, Ronnie had prepared a meal of soup, followed by corned beef hash. We gorged ourselves happily, tired but very content at the end of a long yet satisfying day. Camp 4 seemed firmly established, and I was confident that any snow slides that did come during the night would shoot straight over the roofs of the boxes.

I dropped quickly into a deep sleep, no need for sleeping tablets, and woke up at about three in the morning. I have always been a natural early riser. Though the sleeping bag was snug and warm, the panful of water we had left ready the previous night was now frozen solid. Even so, it would melt much faster than snow, and give very much more water. The trouble with snow is that it takes several panfuls to produce a full pan of boiling liquid.

I lit the gas stove and lay back savouring the moments of idleness before we started the day, feeling deliciously liberated from the administrative and organisational worries of the expedition. Today Ronnie and I would step on to new ground, even if it was only the 15m or so that led to the camp site that Dougal had noticed.

The water started to boil and I dropped in the tea bags, stirred in a dozen cubes of sugar and thrust a mug of tea at Ronnie who was just creeping into protesting wakefulness. We nibbled some biscuits and jam, crawled out of our sleeping bags, completed dressing and were ready to set out by 5 a.m. Ronnie and I were using oxygen, the Sherpas were climbing without. I had often worried whether this was really fair, but on this occasion I certainly didn't. Ronnie and I had been working on the camp and sorting out loads till late the previous night. Once we reached Camp 5, we should have to dig out a platform and erect a box. I should also have to continue running the expedition. The Sherpas on the other hand had no responsibility, were given a load, carried it up to the camp in question and could then return to their sleeping bags and have a good rest. We had agreed with Pertemba that the Sherpas would stay at Camp 4 for four days at a time and in that time each should make three carries, before returning to Camp 2 for a further two days of complete rest. This gave us a reasonable continuity for this vital carry.

That morning Ronnie and I followed the line of fixed rope alongside the raging torrent of powder snow that came pouring down a deep-cut channel in the centre of the gully. I had never seen anything quite like it before. Using oxygen it was possible to take about thirty steps at a time without a rest, even though I had about 18 kilos on my back, with all my personal gear, a rope and my oxygen cylinder.

It was about nine o'clock when I reached Dougal's high point; an empty oxygen cylinder was attached to the ice axe he had left in place as an anchor. It was just round a bend in the gully, and the little gully he had noticed was a mere 30m away. It was ideal for our purpose. I tied the rope to my harness and set out; it was just a question of kicking into deep soft snow, thrusting my ice axe into its full length; no technical difficulty at all, but immensely exciting. I kicked my way into the base of the little gully, probed with an avalanche probe we had brought up, to find a good site, wondered whether to follow the gully up on to the crest of the buttress to get us even further out of the fall line of avalanches, but abandoned the idea when I found how steep and unstable the snow was, and dropped back down to the base of the gully. It was sheltered from the wind and avalanches, but also looked as if it might be sheltered from the sun; it seemed the safest spot. I buried a deadman, attached the rope to it, and called Ronnie and the Sherpas, who were patiently waiting below, to come and join me. Camp 5 was nearly established.

Nearly, but not quite; once the Sherpas had dumped their loads and left us on our own, in all probability the highest men on earth that 16 September (the same date incidentally that we had reached Base Camp in 1972) we still had to dig out a platform for the box. It took us the rest of the morning, with frequent rests, to erect a box. By about half past one, we were able to lay out the foam mats, get out our sleeping bags and really relax. It was time for a brew; our mouths were parched dry and furry from breathing in the cold dry oxygen air mixture on the way up. The sun had now crept round the buttress above me and had been hammering on our backs as we had finished erecting the box. I searched through one of the kit bags, found the gas stove and some spare cartridges, but there was no sign of the cooking pan, plates, mugs or eating utensils. I was sure I had packed them, searched our rucksacks, but still no sign, and suddenly I realised what had happened. In redistributing them the previous night I had left them behind at Camp 4.

It might seem a very minor inconvenience to be without cooking and eating utensils, but in fact it was quite serious, for one needs a large pan to melt sufficient snow to make a good brew. At altitude dehydration is one of the principal debilitating factors and experts recommend a liquid consumption of at least 4 litres a day. Ronnie rummaged through our high-altitude packs but the only remotely suitable container he could find was a corned beef tin. We filled the tin with snow, perched it on top of the stove and waited, mouths dry with thirst for the drink, but the tin was the wrong shape and most of the flame was wasted to either side. Ten minutes later there was a dessert spoonful of dirty water in the bottom of the tin; I added more snow, another ten minutes; added some more snow still, and after half an hour we had a quarter of a pint of water to share between us. I grabbed the tin, burnt myself and dropped it. The precious water trickled over my sleeping bag. We tried again, and after an hour had had a small drink each, barely sufficient to moisten our throats. It was now nearly two o'clock, time for the afternoon call, vital not only to get a pan and mugs sent up the next morning, but also to keep in touch with the rest of the expedition, to be able to monitor the flow of supplies up the mountain.

The radio crackled into life; two o'clock came and I called up Camp 4. Mike Thompson was moving up that day to take charge. There was no reply; I then tried all the other camps in turn, still no reply. And then Camp 2 came on the air, called Camp 4 and they started a long discussion on the following day's carry. I waited, frustrated at not being able to get into the wireless conversation, wanting to assume control and make my requirements known. There was a pause and I quickly called Camp 4 again, no reply; then Base Camp came on the air, talking to Camp 2. At last Camp 2 called me. I replied, but they couldn't hear me, and suddenly I realised the awful truth. For some reason, the wireless set was not transmitting. I could hear everything but was unable to communicate with anyone. By this time I'd lost my temper and had begun to bang the damned radio in an effort to make it work. It didn't respond to treatment, and I continued an impotent listener to the pulsing life of the expedition.

Ronnie had been watching me with quiet amusement and at the end of the call, when everyone had closed down, suggested he try to repair it. He spent the rest of the afternoon fiddling with the radio and miraculously by the time of the four o'clock call he had succeeded in repairing the switch which he had discovered was faulty. To make it work one had to poke a finger or pencil into the hole where the switch had been, press a spring with just the right degree of force and you could send a message.

I forgot my irritation and the constant nagging thirst in my relief and in the late afternoon call was able to order the gear we needed for the following morning. Our kitchen kit came top of the list, but then I had to juggle priorities on whether to get up as much climbing gear and rope as possible to run the route out, or to bring up another box tent to start building up the camp. I decided on the latter, since this was my main object in coming up to the front. In addition, with just two of us at Camp 5 we were going to use three bottles of oxygen a day, two for climbing and one for sleeping. In pushing the route out so fast we were now going to stretch our carrying capacity to the limit. I also had to check that the right sequence of supplies was flowing up to Camp 4 from Camp 2, to ensure that we had the tentage and oxygen reserves we were going to need for forcing the Rock Band. I also asked Doug Scott and Mick Burke to set out for Camp 4 the following morning so that they could join us at Camp 5 on the 18th, by which time I hoped to be near the foot of the Rock Band.

After the radio call we spent a couple of hours brewing small quantities of water that barely moistened our throats, before settling down for the night. This was the first time we were to sleep on oxygen. We each had small plastic masks which were joined by a T-junction to a tube that plugged straight into the reducer valve on top of one of the oxygen bottles. This gave a steady flow of one litre per minute. Although the mask quickly became wet and clammy, giving a claustrophobic feeling, the benefit from the oxygen through the night was considerable, helping one to sleep and stay warm; but even more important, enabling one to build up the necessary reserves for the following day's climbing. The low hiss of the cylinder, as well as being strangely comforting, was also a sign that the system was working. We used, as far as possible, bottles that had already been part emptied to save the full ones for use during the day; this meant that we had to change bottles during the night, never a pleasant task.

I woke as usual at about 3 a.m. and started brewing up in our corned-beef tin. I was determined to get in a morning's climbing. The slope, covered in a uniform blanket of snow, seemed to stretch interminably up to the left-hand gully, which we hoped would take us through the Rock Band. We were going to have to run out many rope-lengths just to reach the foot of the Band. Would we need another camp at the foot of the gully for our assault on the Rock Band? Could we sustain such a camp, and then place yet another above? These were just some of the questions I asked myself that morning. I took the lead, kicking into the crisp snow with cramponed boots, crossing diagonally left towards the base of the gully, still some hundreds of metres away. A buttress of black rock thrust out of the snow; should we go to the left or right of it? I decided on the right-hand side, and started kicking straight upwards. The snow was getting softer and I was going through to the rock underneath; the angle steepened, the snow thinned; there was barely enough to take my weight; there certainly wasn't enough snow for a deadman. I swept it away, hoping to find a crack in the rock for a piton, but it was smooth and compact, all sloping downwards in a series of tiny ledges. I teetered on in my blinkered world, encased in oxygen mask and goggles, feeling more and more insecure as I ran out more rope above Ronnie. At last I came to a deeper patch of snow, put in a deadman and brought him up to me; I set out on another rope-length. The snow got steadily thinner – I more anxious. You're meant to be co-ordinating this bloody expedition, Bonington, not playing silly buggers on dicy snow, I told myself. Looking upwards, rocks, like treacherous reefs, protruded from the snow. I looked across to the left and realised I'd taken the wrong line; I should have traversed. You don't waste height and effort willingly at 8000m, but I had no choice. I hated the thought of trying to reverse what I had just climbed; on the way up it had simply been a question of stepping delicately, but going down, I couldn't see where I was putting my feet, the oxygen mask got in the way. I had no sense of touch; there were too many layers between toes and rock thinly covered by snow.

By the time I got back to Ronnie, I was panting even harder than I had on the way up. And we had another pitch to reverse.

At last we were on the right route, but had wasted two hours; the dazzling line of sunlight had crept down the long slope and now blasted down on us. As we only had just under 200 metres of rope we had brought with us that morning, and no more would be coming up that day, I decided to abandon our effort and return to camp. We could devote the rest of the day to digging out another platform and erecting a second box, ready to run out the remaining rope the following day.

Mike Thompson with five Sherpas did a carry from Camp 4 that day, bringing up another face box and some more oxygen; I was anxious to build up a reasonable stockpile for when we increased the population of Camp 5, to get Camp 6 established. Most welcome of all, they brought up a cooking pot so that Ronnie and I could quench our thirsts for the first time in thirty-six hours.

I had made a mistake in not asking for any rope to be sent up, since we only had 180m at our high point and none at the camp. Doug Scott and Mick Burke were coming up the next day, and I asked Doug if he could set out early and try to get some rope to us before seven o'clock, so that we could run out as much as possible that day. It took him longer than he anticipated to reach us, however, and there was still no sign of him at seven. I was impatient to start before the sun hit the gully and therefore set out before his arrival. We ran out what rope we had all too quickly. By traversing across into the centre of the gully we found deep compact snow and were able to make fast progress. There was still a long way to go from our high point to the foot of the Rock Band. Doug had reached the camp a short time after we set out and by the time we got back Mick Burke had also arrived and they were digging out a platform for our third box. It was grand to see them, and the slight tension Doug and I had experienced at Camp 2 now vanished. We were four climbers out in front with a common aim and purpose, to reach the Rock Band, and at this level could reach our decisions together; it was just like being on a climb in the Alps or a small trip on bigger mountains. My own co-ordinating role was not obtrusive within the small group we had at our top camp.

Two Sherpas and Jim Duff had set out from Camp 4 to make a carry; the Sherpas arrived but there was no sign of Jim. I volunteered to go down and pick up his load, thinking that he was probably just round the corner of the gully a hundred metres or so below the camp. I got there, but there was no sign of him. I started down the fixed rope and dropped about a 300m before I saw him sitting in the snow just above the old site of Camp 4. He seemed in a dream, slurring his words slightly, showing no sign of wanting to go up or down. He had been using oxygen on the way up, but it is possible that it hadn't been functioning correctly. I was anxious to start back up the fixed ropes for I had a 300m climb in front of me and had come down without any oxygen. It was a lovely windless afternoon and I assumed that Jim would be all right just sliding down the fixed ropes without a load. I therefore told him to start down as soon as he had had a rest and started the long ascent back up to Camp 5. I was pleased at how strongly I was going, was able to take about fifty steps at a time without a rest. I glanced back occasionally at Jim, but he was motionless, still sitting in the snow.

I got back to camp just before the afternoon call and was very worried to hear that Jim still hadn't returned to Camp 4. Tut Braithwaite and Nick Estcourt, who had moved up to the camp that morning, went out to see what was wrong and found him lying semi-conscious a hundred metres below where I had left him. He had taken his crampons off and as a result had been sliding out of control down the ropes until he had collapsed completely. It took them a further two and a half hours to get him back to Camp 4, where they poured hot drinks down him, put him into a sleeping bag with a couple of stoves going full blast in the tent. It is frightening just how narrow are the margins of life and death at altitude. When I had left him he had seemed a little groggy, but perfectly capable of getting back down, and yet, had the weather been less than perfect, it is possible that Jim could have died from exposure before Tut and Nick managed to get him back to the tent.

It hadn't been planned for him to stay at Camp 4. He had gone up on a day carry on the 17th to find that one of the Sherpas was suffering from altitude sickness and needed to go back down. He therefore decided to stay the night to take the Sherpa's place in the carry the next morning, knowing how short of supplies we were at Camp 5. He didn't have a sleeping bag and spent a bitterly cold night in the partly collapsed box with only a down suit to keep him warm. This probably weakened him for the carry that day. He returned to Camp 2 the following morning. Fortunately he suffered from no after-effects and had had the satisfaction of climbing as high as he was capable on the South West Face. I resolved, however, to be very careful with the less experienced members of the team.

Only four loads had reached us on the 18th and as a result we were still short of rope and had only just enough oxygen for the four of us to set out the following day. We were going to have a strong carry on the 19th however for I had brought eight fresh Sherpas up to Camp 4. This meant their sleeping three to a face box which was only designed for two. I had consulted Pertemba about this step and he had just grinned and said Sherpas like sleeping close together. This attitude was a token of the enthusiastic support we were getting from them. We wanted to take up as much rope as possible on the 19th to enable us to reach the foot of the Rock Band. I therefore decided to wait at Camp 5 for the arrival of the Sherpas from below so that I could carry a full load of rope, while the other three could load up with what we had already got.

Doug Scott set out from the camp at about 6 a.m., quickly reached the end of the fixed rope that I had put out the previous day and, supported by Ronnie Richards, began kicking up a long snow arête that led straight up towards the Rock Band. Mick Burke had left just behind them, but was obviously having some kind of trouble with his oxygen set, frequently stopping, taking his mask off and fiddling with the set. He was carrying some spare rope and the cine camera and was hoping to film the first piton being hammered into the Rock Band.

By the time the first Sherpa reached the camp, the sun was already glaring on to the long snow slope leading up to the Rock Band. It was going to be hard work catching up with the others. I loaded 180m of rope and some deadmen snow anchors into my sack and started off. I was pleased to find that I was going strongly and quickly caught up with Mick Burke who told me that his oxygen system had packed in completely. There was no question of him going on, so he gave me another rope to carry and dropped back down to the camp, while I continued up the line of fixed ropes. The snow was soft and deep, giving Doug, out in front, desperately hard work, while I had the benefit of the tracks that he had made and Ronnie had consolidated. I finally caught up with Ronnie about 180m below the base of the Rock Band. He was paying the rope out to Doug about 60m above. I moved through, once Doug had belayed, and took another load of rope up to him, belaying him as he kicked up the last snow slope before the Rock Band.

It was a good feeling, looking down the long slope back to Camp 5, Ronnie coming up towards me, Mick very nearly back at the camp, the Sherpa who had brought me the load of rope still by the boxes and then, looking down into the still shadowed gully below, ten tiny figures strung out along the line of fixed rope, a visual demonstration of our momentum up the mountain. Below them was the Western Cwm, patterned with crevasses; Camp 2, little more than a collection of micro dots dwarfed by the immensity of the mountains around it. We were too far above to pick out the porters carrying loads from Camp 1. At the end of the Cwm, the summit of Pumo Ri was now 900m below; we were level with the top of Cho Oyu, massive and rounded at 8153m (26,750ft). As we gained height the view had expanded; we could just see over the containing wall of Nuptse, could gaze far to the west at Gaurishankar and Menlungtse, two mountains that were still inviolate. Memories of 1972; I was looking across and down at that bitterly cold windswept site of Camp 5; the long traverse below the

Rock Band to its right-hand end was in full view; we were very nearly at the same level as our high point three years before. But it was all so different; we were so much earlier, had more climbers and Sherpas, the gear was so much better.

A shout from above, the bell-like ring of the first piton being hammered into the Rock Band. A few minutes later I plodded up the rope to join Doug. 'Do you want to go on through and lead the next pitch, youth?' he asked, as I reached him.

We were now close to the mouth of the left-hand gully, but were barred from it by a snow-clad buttress that jutted down from the wall of the Rock Band. As I set out towards it, a powder-snow avalanche billowed from out of the jaws of the gully. I couldn't help wondering how we should have fared if we had been halfway up it. There would have been no way of avoiding it and the weight of snow pouring through its narrow confines would have been like the waters of a great river squeezed through a narrow gorge. But there was no time for fears and I kicked on, excited to be in the lead, only just below the Rock Band, ran out my 60m length of rope and belayed to a rock spur on the edge of a subsidiary gully which was also an avalanche chute, carrying great lumps of ice, dislodged by the probing rays of the sun from the rocks above.

Doug was about to follow me but found that he had run out of oxygen; Ronnie still had some in his cylinder and with characteristic selflessness, offered to give Doug his cylinder, so that Doug could have the chance of leading the final pitch into the base of the left-hand gully. Doug crossed the shallow gully and climbed a steep little snow wall on the other side, to the crest of the arête just short of the gully. It was obviously going to be awkward and as Doug had finished Ronnie's bottle of oxygen and we were very nearly out of rope, we decided to return to camp. It had been a good day with 426m of rope run out. Although we had not been able to see into the gully I had my confidence boosted by the sheer momentum of our progress that we should force the Rock Band.

Nick Estcourt and Tut Braithwaite had already pitched another box tent when we returned. Mike Thompson and eight Sherpas had made another big carry to the camp that day and had waited for us to return to learn of the progress we had made. As they set off down, Mike received as fine an accolade as anyone could have on an expedition, when one of the Sherpas turned to him and said, 'Now you are a real Sherpa. You carry as much as we do and go just as fast.' Mike had not used oxygen for either of his two carries up to Camp 5.

Ronnie was now feeling quite tired and therefore decided to go back down with Mike and the Sherpas. I wanted to stay at 5 until the Rock Band had been climbed. I had allowed myself the personal ambition of making the carry to put the summit pair in their top camp. I could then feel that I had done everything possible to give them a chance of success, and then, of course, it would be entirely in their hands.

I had been giving a lot of thought to the summit push and had already changed some of my original ideas. While we had been making our first steps on the face I had decided that it would be wise to ensure that the first summit bid was as strong as possible; we might not get a second chance. In this respect I felt that Doug Scott and Dougal Haston probably were the strongest pair. They seemed to get on well together, were very experienced and determined, and for each this was the third visit to the South West Face. Our progress had been so fast, however, that I now had them out of phase. Doug was here at Camp 5 while Dougal was still at Camp 2. It would have been logical for Doug to climb the Rock Band with Nick and Tut, and then for Dougal to move through with one of the other lead climbers to make the summit bid, but I was not happy about such a concept. Hamish was still badly weakened by his experience in the avalanche and had not gone above Camp 2; Allen Fyffe was having difficulty in acclimatising and was still moving very slowly and painfully up to the altitude of Camp 4. Pete Boardman, although his performance so far was excellent, was untried and had never climbed with Dougal before the expedition. I was worried that Martin Boysen, a strong contender, might still be run down as a result of his Trango Tower trip. I decided therefore to bring Dougal straight up to Camp 5, which he would reach in two days, on the assumption that by that time we should have forced the Rock Band and be ready to establish Camp 6.

I spent the rest of the afternoon working out the complex logistics that the proposed assault dictated, to ensure we should have enough oxygen, rope and tentage, not only for our daily consumption, but for the summit bid as well. To do this I had to take into account the stockpile already at Camp 4, the number of Sherpas and climbers at each camp, and when they were due for rests, which in the case of Camp 4 meant a complete turnover of Sherpas. I felt surprisingly fresh but took the odd whiff of oxygen to clear my brain. Our supply situation was very tight. To get Dougal and Doug into position at Camp 6 with enough oxygen and fixed rope, not only to make the summit bid but also to spend a day running a line of fixed rope across the Upper Icefield towards the South Summit gully, we were going to need a carrying party of six. This would mean eight climbers and Sherpas stopping at Camp 5, which in turn would mean four oxygen bottles consumed for sleeping and a further eight used on the move up to the top camp. The day before we made this move, I had to ensure that there had been brought up from Camp 4, the assault box, camp kit, rations, 300m of fixed rope, and three bottles of oxygen for the push above the Rock Band.

On the day they ran out the fixed rope I should have to send up a further five bottles of oxygen and more rope for the summit bid itself. It was obvious that they were going to need two oxygen bottles when they went for the top.

I also had to work out our plans for the ascent of the Rock Band. Tut Braithwaite and Nick Estcourt, supported by Mick Burke and myself would go into the left-hand gully and try to force our way to the top. I thought that this would probably take two days, by which time Dougal would have reached Camp 5. It was asking a lot of Nick and Tut, for in solving the problem that had defeated all four previous expeditions they would be giving the summit to Doug Scott and Dougal Haston.

Doug offered to come up the following day, the 20th, to give a hand. I declined however, for I felt that not only would he need the rest, but that the Rock Band should be left exclusively to Tut and Nick, as some consolation for not making the first summit bid. I had made another departure from my original plan in deciding to give the summit pair the job of putting the fixed rope out across the Upper Snowfield. I had originally thought of another pair undertaking this task. It seemed too much, however, to ask anyone to go up to the top camp, get to within a hundred metres or so of the South Summit gully and then come back down and so I had decided to combine the task of running out the route and making the first summit bid, even though this meant a hard day's work and an extra night at 8320m (27,000ft), before the most exacting day of all.

I only just managed to make all my plans before the four o'clock call. I was uncomfortably aware that I had not had time to work out any subsequent bids, even though the climbers resting at Camp 2 would undoubtedly be getting anxious about their chances for the summit. Our progress had been so fast that I now had a surfeit of reserve climbers all justifiably anxious to take their part in the final drama. All I could do was to promise them that I would work out the logistics of subsequent ascents the following afternoon.

I then settled down for the night. We had just discovered we had only four oxygen sleeping sets and I therefore decided I would have to do without oxygen that night, since I had a tent to myself; I took the occasional breath from my climbing mask, but it did not do much to help me. To gain the maximum benefit from a demand system you have to breathe hard. Even so I dropped off into a light sleep and dozed through the night.

12

Through the Rock Band

20 September

The oxygen cylinder that Tut Braithwaite and Nick Estcourt were using for sleeping, ran out at about 2 a.m. They lay half awake for a time, just willing each other to start making a brew, and finally Nick won the contest; Tut was thirstier and got his arm out of the sleeping bag to light the stove. Getting ready in the morning is a slow process. It took them three hours to have a couple of brews, nibble some chocolate and get dressed, setting out from camp just after half past five. Mick Burke and I could afford to be more leisured in our approach, for once again we were short of rope and were going to have to await the arrival of two Sherpas setting out early from Camp 4 with enough rope, we hoped, to reach the top of the Rock Band. As a result the sun was already on the slope when we set out.

I felt bad from the very start that day. I suspect it was partially the result of spending a night without any sleeping oxygen, but also of general fatigue, for this was my fourth day at Camp 5, and I had been on the go without a day's rest for six days. I felt as if I hadn't slept at all. Mick Burke, who had a heavy load of film gear in addition to a couple of ropes, was going just a little more slowly than I. The sun hammered down as we slogged up the endless slope, but at least we had well-trodden steps. The tracks we had made the previous day had filled in during the night but Nick and Tut had rebroken the trail and by this time had reached our high point of the previous day. It was like the first climb of the day on any crag in Britain; the ritual to decide who should lead the first pitch. Tut had hidden a small piece of rock in the palm of one hand, had held out his clenched fists and told Nick to guess which hand. Nick had guessed wrong. Tut led.

By the time I caught up with them Tut was out of sight round the corner. There was a hammering of a piton, scuffling in the snow, but no movement at all. I was tired and petulant and asked Tut what the hell he was doing. We'd never get up the Rock Band, if he couldn't even get into the foot of the gully. Tut ignored me; probably didn't even hear. The climbing was the most difficult we had yet encountered, with insubstantial snow lying over steep smooth rock. There were hardly any piton cracks and insufficient snow for a deadman anchor. It would have been awkward at any altitude, but at nearly 8230m, encased in high-altitude clothing with an oxygen mask clamped over the face, it was desperate.

Cramponed boots slithered on the sloping rock holds, there was nothing for his glove-encased hands. He stuck his axe into the snow, but it just tore through the loosely coagulated powder. He managed to hammer a long ice piton a couple of inches into a crack, clipped into it, and then, taking rope tension from Nick, leant across from one small spur to the next, his balance thrown out by the weight of his rucksack holding oxygen cylinder and spare rope. He reached a haven of balance, panting hard into the set, paused for breath, and then continued the delicate traverse, using three more pitons for protection and aid. This was real climbing; fatigue and altitude, the grinding plods up lines of fixed rope were all forgotten in the riveted concentration of negotiating those few metres. The angle began to ease, the snow deepened, he was in the flared-out funnel leading to the dark gash of the left-hand gully. He buried a snow anchor, fastened the rope and called Nick up to join him. I followed.

Nick led out the next pitch into the mouth of the gully. It was about 3.5m wide, with sheer inescapable rock walls towering on either side. The floor of the gully was covered in deep compact snow, sweeping smoothly at an angle of about fifty degrees to a snowclad overhanging bulge which probably covered a rock jammed between the gully walls. Above this first barrier, it stretched up to a point where the gully curved slightly and seemed to open out, for the upper part was lit by sunlight. A small spindrift avalanche curled down the right-hand retaining wall. It wasn't big enough to be dangerous, but it made me feel very vulnerable. We were in a trap; there was no shelter from any big avalanches that might pour down that gully.

In the bottom of the gully we were in deep shade. Nick had run out of oxygen, taken off his mask and abandoned the bottle, but was determined to keep going. It was now Tut's turn to lead and he kicked up the even slope leading to the jammed rock about 15m above. He describes what happened next.

On the right there appeared to be a ledge with a possible belay but there were no cracks for pitons and the ledge turned out to be little more than a sloping shelf. I'd run out of rope but managed to pull a spare one out of my sack, tied on and then threw the tangle down to Nick 50ft below, with the idea that he could sort out the tangle whilst I negotiated the overhang.

By this time Chris had caught up with us and had started to untangle the rope, muttering abuse about inefficiency and how stupid it had been to just throw the rope down, without first untangling it. He didn't realise that this was an arrangement that Nick and I had already worked out to save time. Chris insisted that I shouldn't move till he'd sorted out the mess. An understanding glance from Nick, but we both kept quiet until he had it sorted out some dozen curses later.

I placed an angle piton on the right and wriggled up the groove between the rock and the wall behind, my oxygen bottle catching on every protrusion, boots kicking in thin air. At last, panting hard, I was above it. The gully narrowed and steepened; excellent snow conditions made the next section almost enjoyable. Above me were huge overhangs, with powder snow streaming down over them, from either side of the gully. How the hell were we going to get out?

I managed to find a good piton belay, and Nick, moving slowly but with great determination, followed up the rope. I set out again and soon the gully widened. I had to see what there was round the corner, but had now run out of rope. I tied on to my last rope, dropped the slack to Nick and carried on for another 60ft; then at last I could see out to the right. There seemed to be a gangway leading up to some snow ledges. Too tired even to tell the others I just kept going until a small rocky step stopped me. It looked easier on the right and I edged my way over, stepped carefully up sloping little rock ledges, nothing much for the hands. I was excited at the prospects offered by the gangway, and totally involved in the climbing. Suddenly my oxygen ran out. I don't think I shall ever forget the feeling of suffocation as I ripped the mask away from my face. I was on the brink of falling, beginning to panic, felt a warm trickle run down my leg. God, what's happening? Scrabbled up the rock arête until at last I reached some firm snow. I collapsed, exhausted. I had no runners out and was over a 100ft above Nick; I'd have had it if I'd fallen. I just dug my axe into the snow and hung on to it till I got my breath back; got a grip of myself. I then got my rucksack off, took the oxygen bottle out, shoved that in the snow and belayed on to it.

Tut had reached a spot where the gully widened out into a small amphitheatre. The main arm of the gully continued up to the left, but a ramp forked out to the right, beneath an impending wall of yellow rock. This seemed to lead out above the Rock Band. Nick, ever courageous, followed up the rope to join Tut. He had almost become accustomed to going without oxygen, and said later that he had felt like a 105-year-old war veteran and had paced himself accordingly.

Tut had stopped about 6m below the bottom of the ramp. Nick led on through to the beginning of the rocks, brought Tut up to him, but then was determined to have his full fair share of leading even though it meant tackling what was obviously going to be a difficult piece of climbing without oxygen. At least he wasn't going to be blinkered by the mask and encumbered by the rucksack containing the bottle. The first metres were quite straightforward; the ramp sloped off gently and had a reasonable covering of snow; but after 6m, it tapered into nothing, forcing Nick into the impending wall, which, in turn, forced him out of balance. The snow was thin and insubstantial over steep, hideously loose rock. There was nothing for his feet, no holds for his hands. The snow was too soft to use his ice axe. His entire weight was now resting on his left arm which he had jammed behind a boss of snow that had formed between the impending wall above and what was left of the ramp.

Somehow he had to get in a piton. He tried to clear the snow away with his other hand, but the rock was either smooth and compact or, on the ramp itself, little more than rubble, cemented together by snow.

I was getting desperate; goggles all misted up, panting helplessly. I somehow managed to clear some of the snow behind the boss, using my fingers, while my arm still held my weight. I was losing strength fast. I think the others thought I was about to fall off, but whatever happened I wasn't going to give up. If I had, and let Tut do it, I'd have kicked myself for years.

Anyway, I found a crack that was about an inch wide, fumbled for a piton that was the right size. It was hanging on my harness behind my back, couldn't see it, didn't have any sense of feel with my gloves. Somehow got an angle peg that was the right size, eased it behind the boss and shoved it into the crack. I then had to get out my hammer, had a desperate struggle to pull it out of my holster. It had jammed somehow, but I couldn't see how. I got it out at last and managed to tap in the piton.

It was obviously useless, but if you pulled it, in just one direction, it was safe. I managed to lean out on it a little bit, walked my feet up, jammed my other arm behind the boss, reached up, dug into the snow and found something, I'm not sure what, and just kept going. It was still hard and there was nothing secure to hold on to or stand on. It was a question of just keeping going.

I now came out into the sun, and the snow was even softer, no longer holding the rocks together. I just had to keep going. I couldn't possibly have got back even if I'd wanted to. Another 6m, and I found a decent crack, got a good peg in and brought Tut up. Given the conditions it was the hardest pitch I've ever led.

In leading it, Nick had solved the problem of the Rock Band and had led the most difficult pitch on the South West Face of Everest. We had been waiting, cold and anxious, down below. Tut followed Nick up, jumaring up the rope, while Mick Burke and I started back down the fixed ropes. That day the pair in front pushed on another 12m, on to a snow spur that seemed to lead up on to the Upper Snowfield. We dropped down tired but jubilant. Nick and Tut had cracked the Rock Band.

13

Poised for the top

21 September – 22 September 1975

The return to Camp 5 seemed even further, even more arduous, than the way up. I stopped for a rest every few metres, slid down the ropes on my backside wherever possible and had to force myself to take each step on the last traverse back to the camp. It was five o'clock, time for the evening call, but I was too tired to think, let alone talk, and asked Doug Scott to take it. With a bit of luck I would come round in an hour's time, and asked him to arrange a later call. It was all I could do to dump my pack-frame, pull off my boots and collapse into my sleeping bag. The others were just as tired.

Ang Phurba had moved up to Camp 5 that day and was sleeping in my tent. He brewed up endless mugfuls of tea through the evening to slake my thirst. Between gulps of hot tea, I dozed and from time to time tried to force my addled brain to come to grips with the problem, not only of ensuring we had everything we needed for the summit bid but also for subsequent ascents.

Six o'clock came all too fast however, and I hadn't managed to plan out anything further than our requirements for the following day. Dougal Haston, Mike Thompson, Pertemba and Tenzing were to move up to Camp 5 next morning. Dave Clarke was going to take over the running of Camp 4 from Mike and had already moved up so that Mike could put him in the picture. Pete Boardman seemed an obvious potential candidate for one of the summit bids after that of Doug and Dougal. So I asked him also to go up to Camp 4, not fully appreciating how the others at Camp 2 would interpret my action. At the end of the call, Martin came up on the radio and asked if I had any plans for him; all I could do was ask him to wait patiently till the next day, the 21st, when I hoped to plan the subsequent ascents in detail.

I spent much of the night trying to balance out different permutations of climbers. I had originally planned on just one subsequent ascent; back in England even this seemed optimistic, but our progress had been so fast that for some days it had seemed we might be able to have a series of ascents as long as the weather lasted. The obvious choices for the second ascent were Tut Braithwaite and Nick Estcourt. They were here at Camp 5, had shown that they were fully capable of making a fast safe summit bid and had opened the way for Doug and Dougal. We had discussed the second summit bid and I had told them that they would be making it, but now I began to worry about the wider implications of what I had said. I was all too aware of how frustrated the lead climbers sitting it out at Camp 2 must be. If I allowed Nick and Tut to stay up at Camp 5 for the second summit bid, I should be excluding the rest of the team from all further involvement in the climb as they waited their turns in the queue for the summit. I therefore reluctantly decided I should have to break the news to Nick and Tut that I wanted them to return to Camp 2, to go to the back of the queue, and let some of the others have their turn.

I then began to think of the ascents themselves. I definitely wanted to include at least one Sherpa in the subsequent ascents. Quite apart from having promised Pertemba that I would try to get a Sherpa up, they had done so much to help us, entered so much into the spirit of the expedition that I felt it only fair that they shared in the summit experience. But that meant one less place for the climbers.

It then occurred to me that we might be able to support a party of four at Camp 6. This would mean that we could avoid a long-drawn-out series of summit bids and, in two further bids, get another eight to the top. Quite apart from the extra tent, this meant at least ten bottles of oxygen, five loads to be carried up to 6 for each four-man summit bid. I began to work on it in the early hours of the morning. We had to get all that oxygen and a bit of food up to Camp 5, then on to Camp 6. We had to do this with the Sherpas and climbers we had available, allowing them sufficient rest days and the necessary changeovers at both Camps 4 and 5. How many carries would anyone be able to make from Camp 5 to 6? This carry was obviously going to be long and arduous. But by breakfast I had worked out that it was logistically feasible. It was now a matter of fitting names to the eight places for the two subsequent bids. Tut and Nick were going to be in the third summit bid, and I climbed up to their tent to break the news. They took it marvellously well, even though it must have been infuriating to have to give up all that height, in dropping back to Camp 2, only to come back up again in six days' time.

I then started to work out the other possible places. A couple of days earlier, Hamish had told me over the radio that he was going to drop back down to Camp 1, whose ice island seemed on the point of sliding down the Icefall. Hamish was going to see if we needed to resite the camp. I knew that he was still suffering from the after-effects of the powder-snow avalanche and assumed that he would not be sufficiently fit to make a summit bid. Allen Fyffe also seemed out of the running. He had acclimatised very slowly and had not yet managed to get above Camp 4. Of the lead climbers, this left Mick Burke with me at Camp 5, Pete Boardman, who was now at Camp

4, Martin Boysen and Ronnie Richards at Camp 2. Mick had been moving slightly more slowly than I on the fixed ropes, but he was cheerful and seemed able to pace himself well. In addition he had consistently been carrying heavy loads, determined not only to fulfil his filming commitment as the BBC high-altitude cameraman, but also to contribute to the climbing of the mountain as a climber. I very much wanted it to be a good film and to give Mick as much scope as possible. I therefore decided to put him into the second summit party. Martin and Pete were two other obvious candidates, so I included them and brought it up to four with the inclusion of a Sherpa. On this score I consulted Pertemba, telling him that I would like to put a Sherpa into both the second and third summit bids. He nominated himself for the second ascent and Ang Phurba for the third team. That left just one place on the third ascent, with three possible candidates, Mike Thompson, Ronnie Richards and myself.

The lure of the summit; I couldn't resist it, but would I be fit enough? The third summit team wouldn't move up to Camp 6 until 27 September. It was now the 21st and I had already been up for a week. But I felt fine, rationalised that this was the best place for me to stay until everyone was ready to come down from the mountain. But what about Mike or Ronnie? Would they want to go for the summit? I rationalised once again that my experience was greater than theirs. In those final days of the expedition I think we were all in a state of euphoria, were rather like a group of men suddenly offered the chance of a limitless fortune, were looking at each other assessing each other's share.

I announced the results of my logistic planning at the two o'clock radio call. Martin Boysen recollects the impact at Camp 2.

We waited tensed with expectation and ambition. Hamish took the call and Chris came over loud and clear in the warm air of the afternoon.

'I've decided after a lot of thought ...' Wait for it, I listened only for the names not the justifications ... 'Mick, Martin, Pete and Pertemba ...' Thank God for that. 'Tut, Nick, Ang Phurba ...' I had no further interest in listening; I had been given my chance and now I looked at the others. Poor Allen, his face hardened with disappointment as the names poured out, but not his own. The radio stopped and everyone departed quietly with their own hopes, ambitions and disappointments.

Back at Camp 5, we were absorbed in our preparations for the morrow, sorting out the loads, ensuring that Doug and Dougal would have everything they needed to push the route out above the Rock Band. The four o'clock call came with more logistic details, last-minute demands of gear to be brought up to the camp the following morning. I discovered there was a critical lack of oxygen bottles for our summit attempts and had to arrange for a midnight carry from Base Camp, for it to get up the mountain in time. Pertemba then had to deploy his Sherpas and spent half an hour on the radio talking to Camp 4, Camp 2 and Base. As the wireless closed down he told me that Charlie wanted to talk to me privately at seven o'clock that night. I waited, intrigued, slightly worried to hear what he had to tell me.

Seven o'clock came. Nobody else would be listening out on any of the radios littered up and down the mountain. Charlie's voice came over the air from Camp 2. He asked me to reconsider my decision to stay on at Camp 5 and take part in the third summit bid, pointed out the length of time that I had been living above 7600m (25,000ft), the fact that my voice was often slurred over the radio, that my calls that day had sometimes been muddled. He also made the point that I was getting out of contact with the situation on the rest of the mountain, my eyes just focused on establishing the top camp and making the summit.

He also told me that he had come to this conclusion without consulting any of the others and was approaching me in his capacity as expedition doctor. It certainly made sense, even brought out some of the doubts that had lurked in the back of my mind. I agreed to think it over, and then Charlie told me that Hamish would also like to talk to me. There was a pause, and then Hamish's clipped Scots voice crackled through the speaker. 'I've decided to go home, Chris.' I was staggered, but he went on to tell me that he was still feeling the after-effects of his experience in the avalanche and was worried about the state of his lungs. I could understand how he felt and accepted his decision. We were all sorry to see Hamish forced to leave when a successful outcome seemed so close. He had done so much to help achieve it, in designing the face boxes and the assault box in which Dougal and Doug were comfortably ensconced 600m above me, in building our bridges in the Icefall and Western Cwm and in setting up Camp 4; most of all though for his quiet sense of humour and canny judgment that had helped us along throughout the expedition.

Once the wireless was switched off, I began to consider my course of action. I had undoubtedly become divorced from the rest of the team down below; I didn't feel, however, that I was suffering from anoxia, or had been muddled in my thinking. I doubt if I could have worked out our plan for the next week any quicker or better had I been down at Camp 2; in fact it would have been much more difficult there, for it was only by moving up to Camp 5 that I had been able to get a full understanding of the problems involved and what we were all capable of in terms of load-carrying and lengths of stay at the various camps. At the same time, though, I had undoubtedly become obsessive in my drive for the summit, an obsession which I suspect was necessary to build the essential urgency for the summit bid. Combined with this obsessiveness, however, I had just, and only just, managed to make logistic sense. We had the supplies we needed at Camp 5 and the ability to sustain the subsequent summit bids. Charlie Clarke had brought home to me that I was being unwise in putting myself into that third summit team, for by then, if I stayed at Camp 5, I should have been there for nearly a fortnight, much too long a stay at that altitude under any circumstances, let alone prior to trying to reach the summit of Everest. I decided therefore to hand over to Ronnie Richards, who would be better rested than I and certainly deserved the chance. Mike Thompson had decided to go down for a rest after making a tiring carry. I flirted with the thought that perhaps Allen Fyffe, Dave Clarke, Mike Thompson and I could make a fourth summit bid, and with these thoughts dropped off to sleep.

The following morning, 22 September, eight of us set out for Camp 6. Dougal and Doug left first, for they were going to have to complete the route from the top of the ramp on to the Upper Icefield where they hoped to find a suitable camp site. Ang Phurba, probably the strongest and most talented of all the Sherpas, followed close on their heels, dressed in ski pants and sweater, his oxygen set and mask looking incongruous with such attire. Pertemba and Tenzing went at a slightly more leisured rate, while Mike Thompson, Mick Burke and I brought up the rear.

The chapter that follows belongs to Dougal Haston and Doug Scott, and I leave them to tell their story between them.

14

The summit

23 September – 25 September 1975

DOUG SCOTT   I caught Dougal up at the bottom of the Rock Band and carried on up into the foot of the gully. I cleared the rope of ice as I jumared up, conscious of the struggle that Tut must have had, firstly traversing into the gully and then clambering over a giant snow-covered chock stone halfway up. I noted the new perspective with interest, for the ropes led through a huge gash – a veritable Devil's Kitchen of a chasm 90m (300ft) deep into the rocks, whereas the rest of Everest had been wide slopes and broad open valleys. At the top of the gully I followed Nick's rope out and up steeply right. I clipped on to the rope, using it as a safety rail, rather than pulling on it directly with my jumars, for he had warned me that the rope was anchored to pegs of dubious quality. It was awkward climbing with a framed rucksack, especially as the straps kept slipping on crucial hard sections. Nick had done a first-class job leading it without oxygen. I was glad to get to his high point and hammer in extra pegs.

Ang Phurba came up the rope next, for Dougal had stopped lower down to adjust his crampons which kept falling off his sponge overboots and also to disentangle the remains of Nick's rope. Ang Phurba belayed me with all the confidence of a regular alpine climber. I think he is the most natural climber I have ever met amongst the Sherpas. After only 9m of difficult climbing I tied off the rope and Ang Phurba came up to me. I stood there exhausted from having climbed a vertical 3m block with too much clothing and too heavy a sack. From there I led out 75m of rope to a site for Camp 6. Ang Phurba came up and we both kicked out a small notch in a ridge of snow which could be enlarged to take our summit box tent. Dougal came up with his crampons swinging from his waist.

DOUGAL HASTON   I hauled on to the proposed site of Camp 6. Straight away my energy and upward urges came rushing back – there ahead in reality was the way we'd been hypothetically tracing for so long with fingers on photographs and making us forget everything else was the fact it looked feasible. There was a steepish-looking rock pitch just ahead, but after it seemed like unbroken snow slopes to the couloir. It looked as if progress was inevitable as long as the others were successful in their carry. Ang

Phurba kept muttering about a camp site further up under some rocks, but this looked like wasted effort to us, as the traverse line started logically from where we were at the moment. Diplomatically we told him that we were staying there, it being mainly Doug's and my concern, as we were going to have to occupy the camp, and he started off down leaving his valuable load. We began digging in spells, without oxygen, but using some to regain strength during the rests.

Mike, Chris and Mick arrived one after the other looking tired, as well they should be. Carrying heavy loads at over 8200m (27,000ft) is no easy occupation.

DOUG SCOTT Theirs had been a magnificent carry, especially Chris who had now been at Camp 5 and above for eight days, and also Mick who was carrying a dead weight of cine equipment. He had been at Camp 5 for five days, and Pertemba had worked hard practically every day of the expedition carrying heavy loads and encouraging his Sherpas. While Mike Thompson, who had never been above 7000m (23,000ft) before, had arrived carrying a heavy sack with apparent ease at 8230m (27,300ft). We sat there talking confidently in the late afternoon sun. There was a strong bond of companionship as there had been all the way up the face. One by one they departed for Camp 5 and they left us with the bare essentials to make this last step to the top of our route and perhaps the summit itself. I yelled our thanks down to Mike as they were sliding back down the rope. He must have known his chances of making a summit bid were slim yet he replied, 'Just you get up, that's all the reward I need.' And that's how it had been from start to finish with all members of the team. It had taken the combined effort of forty Sherpas, and sixteen climbers, together with Chris's planning, to get the two of us into this position. We knew how lucky we were being the representatives of such a team and to be given the chance to put the finishing touches to all our efforts. Finally Mick left, having run all the film he had through the cameras. Dougal and I were left alone to dig out a more substantial platform and to erect the two-man summit tent. We were working without oxygen and took frequent rests to recover, but also to look across the Upper Snowfield leading up to the South Summit couloir. After the tent was up Dougal got inside to prepare the evening meal, whilst I pottered about outside stowing away equipment in a little ice cave and tying empty oxygen bottles around the tent to weight it down. They hung in festoons on either side of the snow arête. Finally I bundled rope and oxygen bottles into our sacks for the following morning and dived into the tent to join Dougal.

DOUGAL HASTON Inside, we worked on plans for the next day. We had

500m (1640ft) of rope for fixing along the traverse and hoped to do that, then come back to 6 and make our big push the day after.

I was higher on Everest than I'd ever been before, yet thoughts of the summit were still far away in the thinking and hoping process. It had all seemed so near before in 1971 and 1972: euphoric nights at Camps 5 and 6 when progress had seemed good and one tended to skip the difficult parts with visions of oneself standing at the top of the South West Face, then reality shattering the dreams in progressive phases as realisation of certain failure burst the bubble. There had been an inevitability about both previous failures, but still carrying a lot of disappointment. Failure you must accept but that does not make it any easier, especially on a project like the South West Face where so much thinking, will power and straight physical effort are necessary to get to the higher points. This time it seemed better. We were above the Rock Band and the ground ahead looked climbable, but I kept a rigid limit on my thoughts, contemplating possible progress along the traverse to the exit couloir, nothing more. If that proved possible then I would allow for further up-type thinking.

Our physical situation felt comfortable. Maybe that is a reflection of the degree of progress that we have made in our adaptation to altitude. Many the story we had read or been told about assault camps on the world's highest peak. No one ever seemed to spend a comfortable night at Camp 6 on the South Col route. Their nights seemed to be compounded of sleeplessness, discomfort and thirst. Here there was none of that. The situation was very bearable. We weren't stretched personally, didn't even feel tired or uncomfortable, despite a long day. The stove brewed the hours away – tea, lemon drinks and even a full-scale meal with meat and mashed potatoes. Each was deep into his own thoughts with only one slightly urgent communal reaction as a change of oxygen cylinder went wrong and the gas stove roared into white heat. Order was restored before an explosion, with Doug fixing the leak at the same time as I turned off the stove. Emergency over, we laughed, conjuring visions of the reaction at Camp 2 as Camp 6 exploded like a successfully attacked missile target. It would have been a new reason for failure!

Thereafter sleep claimed its way and I moved gently into another world of tangled dreams, eased by a gentle flow of oxygen. The night was only disturbed by a light wind rocking our box and a changing of sleeping cylinders. One would need to be a good or very exhausted sleeper to sleep through a cylinder running out. From a gentle warm comfort one suddenly feels cold, uneasy and very awake. Just after midnight and the changeover, we gave up sleeping and started the long task of preparing for the morning's work.

Shortly after first light I moved out into blue and white dawn to continue the upward way, leaving Doug wrapped in all the down in the tent mouth, cameras and belays set up for action. There was a rock step lurking ahead that had seemed reasonably close in the setting afternoon sun of the previous day. Now in the clear first light a truer perspective was established, as I kept on thrusting into the deep powdered fifty-degree slope, sliding sideways like a crab out of its element reaching for an object that didn't seem to come any closer. A hundred metres (330ft) of this progress it was, before I could finally fix a piton and eye the rock step. It wasn't long, 7 or 8 metres, but looked difficult enough. Downward sloping, steep slabs with a layer of powder. Interesting work. Grade 5 at this height. Much concentration and three more pitons saw a delicate rightwards exit and back, temporarily thankful, into deep snow to finish the rope-length and finally give Doug the signal to move.

DOUG SCOTT   I traversed across on his rope and up the difficult rocks to his stance. I led out another 120m (400ft) over much easier ground, parallel with the top of the Rock Band. We gradually warmed to the task and began to enjoy our position. After all the months of dreaming, here we were cutting across that Upper Snowfield. Dougal led out the next reel of rope.

DOUGAL HASTON   The conditions and climbing difficulty began to change again. Kicking through with crampons there was now no ice beneath. Rock slabs only which have never been renowned for their adherence to front points. A few tentative movements up, down, sideways proved it existed all around. It seemed the time for a tension traverse. But on what? The rock was shattered loose and worse – no cracks. Scraping away a large area, a small movable flake appeared. It would have to do. Tapping in the beginnings of an angle, which seemed to be OK to pull on it not for a fall, I started tensioning across to an inviting-looking snow lump. Thoughts flashed through my mind of a similar traverse nine years before, near the top of the Eiger Direct. There it would have been all over with a slip and suddenly, working it out, things didn't look too good here, if you cared to think in those directions. Not only didn't I care to, I also didn't dare to think of full consequences and chasing the dangerous thoughts away concentrated on tiptoeing progress. Slowly the limit of tension was reached and feet were on some vaguely adhering snow. It would have to do for the present, were my thoughts as I let go the rope and looked around. A couple of probes with the axe brought nothing but a sense of commitment.

'No man is an island,' it is said. I felt very close to a realisation of the contrary of this, standing on that semi-secure snow step in the midst of a sea of insecurity. But there was no racing adrenalin only the cold clinical thought of years of experience. About 5 metres away the snow appeared to deepen. It would have to be another tension traverse. Long periods of excavation found no cracks. Tugs on the rope and impatient shouting from Doug. Communication at altitude is bad in awkward situations. One has to take off the oxygen mask to shout. Then when one tries to do this the throat is so dry and painful that nothing comes out. Hoping that Doug would keep his cool I carried on looking for a piton placement. A reasonable-looking crack came to light and two pitons linked up meant the game could go on. This time I felt I could put more bearing weight on the anchor. Just as well. Twice the tension limit failed and there was the skidding movement backwards on the scraping slabs. But a third try and a long reach saw me in deep good snow, sucking oxygen violently. The way ahead relented, looking reasonable. My voice gained enough momentum to shout to Doug and soon he was on his way. Following is usually monotone – sliding along on jumars. This one was not so. I could almost see the gleam in Doug's eyes shining through his layers of glasses as he pulled out the first tension piton with his fingers.

'Nasty stuff, youth.'

I had to agree as he passed on through.

DOUG SCOTT   I continued across further, using up one of our two climbing ropes, before dropping down slightly to belay. We had probably come too high, for there was easier snow below the rocks that led right up towards the South Summit couloir. However, avalanches were still cascading down the mountain, so we climbed up to the rocks in an effort to find good peg anchors for the fixed ropes. We didn't want to return the next day to find them hanging over the Rock Band. Dougal led a short section on easy snow, then all the rope was run out and we turned back for camp.

I sat in the snow to take photographs and watched the sun go down over Gaurishankar. What a place to be! I could look straight down and see Camp 2 1800m (6000ft) down. There were people moving about between tents, obviously preparing to camp for the night. Mounds of equipment were being covered with tarpaulins, one or two wandered out to the crevasse toilet, others stood about in small groups before diving into their tents for the night. A line of shadow crept up the face to Camp 4 by the time I was back to our tent. I again sorted out loads and pushed in oxygen bottles for the night, whilst Dougal melted down snow for the evening meal.

We discovered over the radio that only Lhakpa Dorje had made the carry to Camp 6 that day. He had managed to bring up vital supplies of oxygen but, unfortunately, the food, cine camera and still film we needed had not arrived. Anyway they were not essential, so we could still make our bid for the summit next day. There was also no more rope in camp, but I think we were both secretly relieved about this. Chris had always insisted that whoever made the first summit bid should lay down as much fixed rope as possible so that if that first attempt failed the effort would not be wasted. This made good sense, but it did take a lot of effort up there and we all longed for the time when we could cut loose from the fixed ropes. It was a perfect evening with no wind at all as we sat looking out of the tent doorway supping mugs of tea. Finally the sun was gone from our tent and lit up only the upper snows, golden turning red, before all the mountain was in shadow. We zipped up the tent door and built up quite a fug of warm air heating up water for corned beef hash.

DOUGAL HASTON   Five hundred metres (1640ft) of committing ground was a good day's work on any point of the mountain. The fact that it was all above 8200m (26,900ft) made our performance-level high and, more to the point, we hadn't exhausted ourselves in doing it. This was crucial because deterioration is rapid at such altitudes. Over tea we discussed what to take next day. I still reckoned deep down on the possibility of a bivouac. Doug seemed reluctant to admit to the straight fact, but didn't disagree when I mentioned packing a tent sac and stove. The packs weren't going to be light. Two oxygen cylinders each would be needed for the undoubtedly long day, plus three 50m ropes, also various pitons and karabiners. Even if a bivouac was contemplated we couldn't pack a sleeping bag. This would have been pushing weight too much. The bivouac idea was only for an emergency and we would have hastened that emergency by slowing ourselves down through too much weight – so we tried to avoid the possibility by going as lightly as possible. The only extra I allowed myself was a pair of down socks, reckoning they could be invaluable for warming very cold or even frostbitten feet and hands. There was no sense of drama that evening. Not even any unusual conversation. We radioed down and told those at Camp 2 what we were doing, ate the rest of our food and fell asleep.

DOUG SCOTT   About one in the morning we awoke to a rising wind. It was buffeting the tent, shaking it about and pelting it with spindrift, snow and ice chips. I lay there wondering what the morning would bring, for if the wind increased in violence we should surely not be able to move. At about 2.30 we began slowly to wind ourselves up for the climb. We put a brew on and heated up the remains of the corned beef hash for breakfast. The wind speed was decreasing slightly as we put on our frozen boots and zipped up our suits. Dougal chose his duvet suit, whilst I took only my windproofs, hoping to move faster and easier without the restriction of tightly packed feathers around my legs. I had never got round to sorting out a duvet suit that fitted me properly.

Because of the intense cold it was essential to put on crampons, harnesses, even the rucksack and oxygen system in the warmth of the tent. Just after 3.30 we emerged to get straight on to the ropes and away to the end. It was a blustery morning, difficult in the dark and miserable in the cold. It was one of those mornings when you keep going because he does and he, no doubt, because you do. By the time we had passed the end of the fixed ropes the sun popped up from behind the South Summit and we awoke to the new day. It was exhilarating to part company with our safety line, for that is after all what fixed ropes are. They facilitate troop movements, but at the same time they do detract from the adventure of the climb. Now at last we were committed and it felt good to be out on our own.

DOUGAL HASTON   There's something surrealistic about being alone high on Everest at this hour. No end to the strange beauty of the experience. Alone, enclosed in a mask with the harsh rattle of your breathing echoing in your ears. Already far in the west behind Cho Oyu a few pale strands of the day and ahead and all around a deep midnight blue with the South Summit sharply, whitely, defined in my line of vision and the always predawn wind picking up stray runnels of spindrift and swirling them gently, but not malignantly, around me. Movement was relaxed and easy. Passing by yesterday's tension points only a brief flash of them came into memory. They were stored for future remembrances, but the today mind was geared for more to come. Not geared with any sense of nervousness or foreboding just happily relaxed, waiting – anticipating. Signs of life on the rope behind indicated that Doug was following apace and I waited at yesterday's abandoned oxygen cylinders as he came up with the sun, almost haloed in silhouette, uncountable peaks as his background. But no saint this.

'All right, youth?' in a flat Nottingham accent.

'Yeah, yourself?'

A nod and the appearance of a camera for sunrise pictures answered this question, so I tied on the rope and started breaking new ground. The entrance to the couloir wasn't particularly good, but there again it was not outstandingly bad by Himalayan standards, merely knee-deep powder snow with the occasional make-you-think hard patch where there was no snow base on the rock. On the last part before entering the couloir proper there was a longish section of this where we just climbed together relying on each other's ability, rope trailing in between, there being no belays to speak of.

The rope-length before the rock step changed into beautiful, hard front pointing snow ice but the pleasure suddenly seemed to diminish. Leading, my progress started to get slower. By now the signs were well known. I knew it wasn't me. One just doesn't degenerate so quickly. Oxygen again. It seemed early for a cylinder to run out. Forcing it, I reached a stance beneath the rock step. Rucksack off. Check cylinder gauge first. Still plenty left. That's got to be bad. It must be the system. Doug comes up. We both start investigating. Over an hour we played with it. No avail. Strangely enough I felt quite calm and resigned about everything. I say strangely, because if the system had proved irrepairable then our summit chance would have been ruined. There was only a quiet cloud of disappointment creeping over our heads. Doug decided to try extreme unction. 'Let's take it apart piece by piece, kid. There's nothing to lose.' I merely nodded as he started prising apart the jubilee clip which held the tube on to the mouthpiece. At last something positive – a lump of ice was securely blocked in the junction. Carving it out with a knife, we tentatively stuck the two points together again, then shut off the flow so we could register oxygen being used. A couple of hard sucks on the mask – that was it. I could breathe freely again.

Doug started out on the rock step, leaving me contemplating the escape we'd just had. I was still thinking very calmly about it, but could just about start to imagine what my feelings of disgust would have been like down below if we'd been turned back by mechanical failure. Self-failure you have to accept, bitter though it can be. Defeat by bad weather also, but to be turned back by failure of a humanly constructed system would have left a mental scar. But now it was upward thinking again. Idly, but carefully, I watched Doug. He was climbing well. Slowly, relaxed, putting in the odd piton for protection. Only his strange masked and hump-backed appearance gave any indication that he was climbing hard rock at 8500m (28,000ft).

DOUG SCOTT   At first I worked my way across from Dougal's stance easily in deep soft snow, but then it steepened and thinned out until it was all a veneer covering the yellow amorphous rock underneath. I went up quite steeply for 9m, hoping the front points of my crampons were dug well into the sandy rock underneath the snow. I managed to get in three pegs in a cluster, hoping that one of them might hold, should I fall off. However, the next 9m were less steep and the snow lay thicker, which was fortunate seeing as I had run out of oxygen. I reached a stance about 30m above Dougal and with heaving lungs I started to anchor off the rope. I pounded in the last of our rock pegs and yelled down to Dougal to come up. Whilst he was prusiking up the rope I took photographs and changed over to my remaining full bottle of oxygen. I left the empty bottle tied on the pegs.

We were now into the South Summit couloir and a way seemed clear to the top of the South West Face. We led another rope-length each and stopped for a chat about the route. Dougal's sporting instincts came to the fore – he fancied a direct gully straight up to the Hillary Step. I wasn't keen on account of the soft snow, so he shrugged his shoulders and continued off towards the South Summit. I don't know whether the direct way would have been any less strenuous, but from now on the route to the South Summit became increasingly difficult.

DOUGAL HASTON   The South West Face wasn't going to relax its opposition one little bit. That became very evident as I ploughed into the first rope-length above the rock step. I had met many bad types of snow conditions in eighteen years of climbing. Chris and I had once been shoulder deep retreating from a winter attempt on a new line on the North Face of the Grandes Jorasses. The snow in the couloir wasn't that deep, but it seemed much worse to handle. In the Alps we had been retreating, now we were trying to make progress. Progress? The word seemed almost laughable as I moved more and more slowly. A first step and in up to the waist. Attempts to move upward only resulted in a deeper sinking motion. Time for new techniques: steps up, sink in, then start clearing away the slope in front like some breast-stroking snow plough and eventually you pack enough together to be able to move a little further and sink in only to your knees. Two work-loaded rope-lengths like this brought us to the choice of going leftwards on the more direct line I had suggested to Doug in an earlier moment of somewhat undisciplined thinking. By now my head was in control again and I scarcely gave it a glance, thinking that at the current rate of progress we'd be lucky to make even the South Summit.

It seemed that conditions would have to improve but they didn't. The slope steepened to sixty degrees and I swung rightwards, heading for a rock step in an attempt to get out of this treadmill of nature. No relief for us. The snow stayed the same, but not only was it steeper, we were now on open wind-blown slopes and there was a hard breakable crust. Classic wind slab avalanche conditions. In some kind of maniacal cold anger I ploughed on. There was no point in stopping for belays. There weren't any possibilities. I had a rhythm, so kept the evil stroking upwards with Doug tight on my heels. Two feet in a hole, I'd bang the slope to shatter the crust, push away the debris, move up, sink in. Thigh. Sweep away. Knees. Gain a metre. Then repeat the process. It was useful having Doug right behind, as sometimes, when it was particularly difficult to make progress, he was able to stick two hands in my back to stop me sliding backwards. Hours were flashing like minutes, but it was still upward gain.

DOUG SCOTT   I took over the awful work just as it was beginning to ease off. I clambered over some rocks poking out of the snow and noticed that there was a cave between the rocks and the névé ice – a good bivvy for later perhaps. Just before the South Summit I rested whilst Dougal came up. I continued round the South Summit rock whilst Dougal got his breath. I was crawling on all fours with the wind blowing up spindrift snow all around. I collapsed into a belay position just below the frontier ridge and took in the rope as Dougal came up my tracks. After a few minutes' rest we both stood up and climbed on to the ridge and there before us was Tibet.

After all those months spent in the Western Cwm over this and two other expeditions now at last we could look out of the Cwm to the world beyond – the rolling brown lands of Tibet in the north and north east, to Kangchenjunga and just below us Makalu and Chomo Lonzo. Neither of us said much, we just stood there absorbed in the scene.

DOUGAL HASTON   The wind was going round the South Summit like a mad maypole. The face was finished, successfully climbed, but there was no calm to give much thought to rejoicing. It should have been a moment for elation but wasn't. Certainly we'd climbed the face but neither of us wanted to stop there. The summit was beckoning.

Often in the Alps it seems fine to complete one's route and not go to the summit, but in the Himalaya it's somewhat different. An expedition is not regarded as being totally successful unless the top is reached. Everything was known to us about the way ahead. This was the South East Ridge, the original Hillary/Tenzing route of 1953. It was reckoned to be mainly snow, without too much technical difficulty. But snow on the ridge similar to the snow in the couloir would provide a greater obstacle to progress than any technical difficulties. There were dilemmas hanging around and question marks on all plans.

My head was considering sitting in the tent sac until sunset or later, then climbing the ridge when it would be, theoretically, frozen hard. Doug saw the logic of this thinking but obviously wasn't too happy about it. No other suggestions were forthcoming from his direction, however, so I got into the tent sac, got the stove going to give our thinking power a boost with some hot water. Doug began scooping a shallow snow cave in the side of the cornice, showing that he hadn't totally rejected the idea. The hot water passing over our raw, damaged throat linings brought our slide into lethargic pessimism to a sharp halt.

Swinging his pack on to his back Doug croaked, 'Look after the rope. I'm going to at least try a rope-length to sample conditions. If it's too bad we'll bivouac. If not we carry on as far as possible.'

I couldn't find any fault with this reasoning, so grabbed the rope as he disappeared back into Nepal. The way it was going quickly through my hands augured well. Reaching the end Doug gave a 'come on' signal. Following quickly I realised that there were now summit possibilities in the wind. Conditions were by no means excellent, but relative to those in the couloir they merited the title reasonable. There was no need to say anything as I reached Doug. He just stepped aside, changed the rope around and I continued. Savage, wonderful country. On the left the South West Face dropped away steeply, to the right wild curving cornices pointed the way to Tibet. Much care was needed but there was a certain elation in our movements. The Hillary Step appeared, unlike any photograph we had seen. No rock step this year, just a break in the continuity of the snow ridge. Seventy degrees of steepness and 24m (80ft) of length. It was my turn to explore again. Conditions reverted to bad, but by now I'd become so inured to the technique that even the extra ten degrees didn't present too much problem.

DOUG SCOTT   As I belayed Dougal up the Hillary Step it gradually dawned upon me that we were going to reach the summit of Big E. I took another photograph of Dougal and wound on the film to find that it was finished. I didn't think I had any more film in my rucksack, for I had left film and spare gloves with the bivvy sheet and stove at the South Summit. I took off my oxygen mask and rucksack and put them on the ridge in front of me. I was sat astride it, one leg in Nepal the other in Tibet. I hoped Dougal's steps would hold, for I could think of no other place to put his rope than between my teeth as I rummaged around in my sack. I found a cassette of colour film that had somehow got left behind several days before. The cold was intense and the brittle film kept breaking off. The wind was strong and blew the snow Dougal was sending down the Nepalese side right back into the air and over into Tibet. I fitted the film into the camera and followed him up. This was the place where Ed Hillary had chimneyed his way up the crevasse between the rock and the ice. Now with all the monsoon snow on the mountain it was well banked up, but with snow the consistency of sugar it looked decidedly difficult.

A wide whaleback ridge ran up the last 275m (900ft). It was just a matter of trail-breaking. Sometimes the crust would hold for a few steps and then suddenly we would be stumbling around as it broke through to our knees. All the way along we were fully aware of the enormous monsoon cornices, overhanging the 3000m (10,000ft) East Face of Everest. We therefore kept well to the left.

It was whilst trail-breaking on this last section that I noticed my mind seemed to be operating in two parts, one external to my head. In my head I referred to the external part somewhere over my left shoulder. I rationalised the situation with it making reference to it about not going too far right in the area of the cornice, and it would urge me to keep well to the left. Whenever I stumbled through the crust it suggested that I slowed down and picked my way through more carefully. In general it seemed to give me confidence and seemed such a natural phenomenon that I hardly gave it a second thought at the time. Dougal took over the trail-breaking and headed up the final slope to the top – and a red flag flying there. The snow improved and he slackened his pace to let me come alongside. We then walked up side by side the last few paces to the top, arriving there together.

All the world lay before us. That summit was everything and more that a summit should be. My usually reticent partner became expansive, his face broke out into a broad happy smile and we stood there hugging each other and thumping each other's backs. The implications of reaching the highest mountain in the world surely had some bearings on our feelings, I'm sure they did on mine, but I can't say that it was that strong. I can't say either that I felt any relief that the struggle was over. In fact, in some ways it seemed a shame that it was, for we had been fully programmed and now we had to switch off and go back into reverse. But not yet, for the view was so staggering, the disappearing sun so full of colour that the setting held us in awe. I was absorbed by the brown hills of Tibet. They only looked like hills from our lofty summit. They were really high mountains, some of them 7300m (24,000ft) high, but with hardly any snow to indicate their importance. I could see silver threads of rivers meandering down between them, flowing north and west to bigger rivers which might have included the Tsang Po. Towards the east Kangchenjunga caught the setting sun, although around to the south clouds boiled down in the Nepalese valleys and far down behind a vast front of black cloud was advancing towards us from the plains of India. It flickered lightning ominously. There was no rush though, for it would be a long time coming over Everest – time to pick out the north side route – the Rongbuk Glacier, the East Rongbuk Glacier and Changtse in between. There was the North Col, and the place Odell was standing when he last saw Mallory and Irvine climbing up towards him. Wonder if they made it? Their route was hidden by the convex slope – no sign of them, edge out a bit further – no nothing. Not with all the monsoon snow, my external mind pointed out.

The only sign of anyone was the flag, it was some time before I got round to looking at it. It was an unwelcome intrusion and there had been more to do than look at man-made objects. Still, you couldn't help but look at it, seeing as how it was a tripod and pole nearly 1.5m high with a rosary of red ribbons attached to the top. Take a photograph. Ah, yes! Dougal ought to get some of me. He hadn't taken a single photograph on the whole trip. 'Here you are, youth. Take a snap for my mother.' I passed him my camera. 'Better take another one, your glove's in front of the lens. Now a black and white one.' He's never been keen on photography, but he obliged.

DOUGAL HASTON   We were sampling a unique moment in our lives.

Down and over into the brown plains of Tibet a purple shadow of Everest was projected for what must have been something like 200 miles. On these north and east sides there was a sense of wildness and remoteness, almost untouchability. Miraculous events seemed to be taking place in the region of the sun. One moment it seemed to dip behind a cloud layer lying a little above the horizon. End Game – thought we. But then the cloud dropped faster than the sun and out it came again. Three times in all. I began to feel like Saul on the road to Damascus. More materially, right in front of me was an aluminium survey pole with a strip of red canvas attached. The Japanese ladies in the spring hadn't mentioned leaving or seeing anything. Puzzlement for a moment. Then the only answer. There had been a Chinese ascent of the North Ridge claimed, just after the Japanese ascent. Some doubt, however, had been cast on the validity of this, due to the summit pictures lacking the detail associated with previous summit shots. It was good to have the ultimate proof in front of us. Having to play the doubt game in climbing is never a pleasant experience.

Slowly creeping into the euphoria came one very insistent thought as the sun finally won its race with the clouds and slid over the edge. The thought? Well, we were after all on the top of the world but it was still a long way back to Camp 6 and it was going to be dark very soon and then what would we do? We knew we could get back to the South Summit in the half light. On the previous nights there had been a very bright moon and it seemed reasonable to assume we could retrace our steps down the face if this came out. If it didn't, as a last resort we could bivouac. That after all was the reason for bringing the tent sac. I'd always reckoned a bivouac possible at such altitude, but that doesn't mean to say I looked upon the project with a great degree of enthusiasm. We finally turned our backs to the summit and set off down.

Our tracks were already freezing up, making the going reasonable. An abseil got rid of the Hillary Step with the rope left in place. Moving together we were soon back at our little cave. Much cloud activity didn't bode well for the appearance of a moon. The oxygen cylinders dribbled out their last drops of usefulness and became mere burdens. Standing vaguely waiting for some light to happen, it was good to take off the tanks and mask. Lighter feeling but not lighter headed. Slowly, as it clouded over, the choices were gradually cut down. We decided to have a look at the possibility of a descent in the dark, knowing the up-trail to be deep and maybe now frozen, but a tentative 15m grope on the South West Face side of the ridge into the strong night wind with fingers and toes going solid finally slammed all the alternative choices to a bivouac out of mind. Dropping back to the sheltered side I told Doug the news. There was nothing really to say. He started enlarging the hole.

DOUG SCOTT   Dougal melted snow on the stove once again whilst I continued digging into the hillside. After we had had a few sips of warm water, Dougal joined me and we quickly enlarged the snow cave, digging away with our ice axes, pushing the loose snow out through the entrance. By nine o'clock it was big enough to lie down in, we pushed out more snow against the entrance and reduced it to a narrow slit. We were now out of the wind, which was fortunate, as already our oxygen bottles were empty, or our sets had refused to function. The little stove, too, was soon used up. So there we lay on top of our rucksacks and the bivvy sheet, wishing perhaps we had given more thought to the possibility of bivouacking, for we had no food and no sleeping bags. I was wearing only the clothes that I had climbed up in, a silk vest, a wool jumper, a nylon pile suit and my wind suit. I don't think we were ever worried about surviving for we had read of other climbers who had spent the night out on Everest without much gear, although lower down. However they had all subsequently had some fingers and toes cut off. What worried us was the quality of survival and we brought all the strength of our dulled listless minds to bear upon that. I shivered uncontrollably and took off my gloves, boots and socks to rub life back into my extremities for hours at a time. We were so wrapped up in our own personal miseries that we hardly noticed each other, though at one point Dougal unzipped the front of his duvet suit and kindly allowed me to put my bare left foot under his right arm pit and my other at his crutch which seemed to help. Without oxygen there didn't seem to be any internal heat being created, so I mostly sat and rubbed and rubbed my fingers and toes. This was no time for sleep. It needed the utmost vigilance to concentrate on survival, keeping my boots upright out of the snow, keeping the snow off my bare hands and feet, warming my socks against my stomach, keeping my head from brushing snow off the roof of the cave. The temperature was probably −30°C. It was so cold that at first when I left a sock on my rucksack the foot of the sock went as stiff as a board. Most of the night I dug away at the cave just to keep warm, hacking away at the back with the ice axe into the hard snow and pushing it out through the doorway. By the dawn it was to be big enough to sleep five people lying down!

Our minds started to wander with the stress and the lack of sleep and oxygen. Dougal quite clearly spoke out to Dave Clarke. He had quite a long and involved conversation with him. I found myself talking to my feet. I personalised them to such an extent that they were two separate beings needing help. The left one was very slow to warm up and, after conversations with the right one, we decided I had better concentrate on rubbing it hard. And all the time my external mind was putting its spoke in as well.

DOUGAL HASTON   I was locked in suffering silence except for the occasional quiet conversation with Dave Clarke. Hallucination or dream? It seemed comforting and occasionally directed my mind away from the cold. That stopped and then it was a retreat so far into silence that I seemed to be going to sleep. Shaking awake I decided to stay this way. We'd heard too many tales of people in survival situations falling asleep and not waking up. It seemed as if we'd both come to this conclusion and Doug's incoherent speech served to keep both awake. There was no escaping the cold. Every position was tried. Holding together, feet in each other's armpits, rubbing, moving around the hole constantly, exercising arms. Just no way to catch a vestige of warmth. But during all this the hours were passing. I don't think anything we did or said that night was very rational or planned. Suffering from lack of oxygen, cold, tiredness but with a terrible will to get through the night all our survival instincts came right up front. These and our wills saw the night to a successful end.

First light came and we were able to start the process of preparing for downward movement. Checks showed an ability to stand up and move. Extremities had slight numbness, but no frostbite. Kidney pains were locking us in an almost bent-in-two position. Boots were difficult to get on. I gave up my frozen inner boots and used duvet boots as a replacement. The sun came up, but with no hope of getting any warmth to our bodies. Movement was the only way and soon we were across the cornice, saying adieu to Tibet and starting off back down the face. The warmth of movement was almost orgasmic in its intensity as the blood started recirculating. Aware of the possibilities of lack of oxygen hallucinations and their potentially dire effects we kept a wary eye on each other as we belayed down the first few pitches.

DOUG SCOTT We had not slept or eaten for nearly thirty hours, we had actually spent the night out in China, and we had done it at 8750m (28,700ft) without oxygen. Eventually we made the fixed rope and at 9 a.m. fell into our sleeping bags at Camp 6. I put the stove on and looked around for something to eat and came across the radio. We had been so absorbed in surviving the night and the descent that at times it had all seemed so much like a dream, just the two of us and no one else in the world to share the cold swirling snow. The radio brought us back to reality, it crackled into life. Answering voices – Chris concerned, relieved – happy with the success. Put on a good voice I thought, don't want to sound slurred, although I felt it. 'No, I don't think we are frostbitten,' I said, for by then our fingers and toes were tingling.

The quality of survival had been good.

15

Success and tragedy

25 September – 26 September 1975

Back at Camp 2, we had followed the progress of Doug and Dougal through our binoculars and the 600mm lens of the camera. They were tiny black dots, whose spidery arms and legs were just visible in the eye piece. On the 24th we first picked them out near the end of their traverse across the line of rope they had fixed the previous day. They were making good progress, for it was only nine o'clock in the morning and they were already at the foot of the gully leading up to the South Summit. They vanished into it and the hours through the day began to drag out, with someone every few minutes taking a look through the binoculars at the head of the gully. Surely we must have somehow missed them as they came out of the gully. Perhaps they had gone on to the other side of the ridge.

It was four o'clock. Nick Estcourt was gazing through the 600mm lens. He let out a shout. He had seen someone at the top of the gully; we crowded around, impatiently waiting our turn to look. Surely they're on their way down. They must be. And then the realisation came that they were on their way up, they should make the summit, but at that time of day a night bivouac was going to be inevitable. I don't think any of us slept well that night or really relaxed until the following morning we saw the two tiny figures crawl back across the long traverse to Camp 6. Then there was the joyous call that they were home, that they'd made the summit, and had no more than frost nip as their payment for the highest bivouac that has ever been undertaken and one of the boldest bids that has ever been made on the summit of Everest. There was a feeling throughout the expedition of undiluted joy; I couldn't help crying as I ended my wireless conversation with Doug. Dougal could hardly talk; his throat was so parched and sore.

They were on their way down, but the second party was already on its way up. Martin Boysen, Pete Boardman, Mick Burke and Pertemba had set out from Camp 5 that morning, prepared either for a summit bid or a semi-rescue operation if Dougal and Doug were in a bad way. The momentary euphoria soon wore off; I was going to have to sit through two more summit bids, powerless to do anything but wait and hope that nothing went wrong. I knew all too well that the next few days, until all eight climbers returned safely, were going to be hell. I sat at Camp 2, tensed and anxious, waiting for the two o'clock call, when I should learn that my second summit party were ensconsed at Camp 6. They had with them two Sherpas, Lhakpa Dorje and Mingma, who were going to carry up the vital bottles of oxygen for their bid.

It was Martin who came on to the air. He told me that Mick had not yet arrived and that Lhakpa Dorje had also failed to make it. Only Mingma had reached them. As a result they had only enough oxygen for Pete, Pertemba and Martin, for their summit bid the following day. They were therefore going to have to tell Mick that he would have to stand down, particularly as he seemed the slowest of the four; they had been at the site of Camp 6 for over two hours and there was still no sign of him.

I think I had been quietly worrying about Mick, in the very back of my mind. When I had decided to drop out of the third summit bid and return to Camp 2 I put it to Mick that he also had been up at Camp 5 for some time. (He had arrived with Doug on the 18th and so by the morning of the 23rd, when I dropped back, he had been there for six nights compared to my eight. By the 25th, however, on his way up to Camp 6 he had been up there for eight nights as well.) He had replied that he felt he was still going well and that he would be able to get a good rest in the next few days. I knew how determined he was, how savagely disappointed he would be, if having told him he could take part in the second summit bid, I changed the decision, and so I had let him stay.

But now my anxiety, triggered by Martin's, burst out with all the violence of suppressed tension. I told him very strongly that under no circumstances did I want Mick to go for the summit next day. I wanted him to come back down. Martin was shaken by the violence of my reaction and after he went off the air I realised I was perhaps ordering the impossible. Once climbers have got to the top camp on Everest they are very much on their own. Up to that point, they are members of a team, dependent on each other and the overall control of a leader, but the summit bid was different. This was a climbing situation that you might get on a smaller expedition or in the Alps. It was their lives, in their own hands, and only they could decide upon their course of action. We kept the radio open and I had told Martin that Mick was to call me as soon as he reached camp.

It was an unenviable message that Martin, as spokesman of the trio at Camp 6, had to give Mick. Lhakpa Dorje was the first to arrive and gave him a confused story that he had been delayed because of oxygen failure. Mick reached the camp a short time later. Martin heard the fixed rope stretch and rattle and had gone out to help Mick up the last few metres, grabbed his rucksack, and was immediately impressed by how heavy it was. Mick was his old chirpy self, explained that he had sorted out some of the fixed ropes below the Rock Band, something that I had asked him to do; he had then overtaken Lhakpa Dorje, to find that his oxygen set had failed. He had stopped him going back, had waited for Mingma to return from carrying his load up to Camp 6 and had then exchanged Mingma's good set for Lhakpa's unserviceable one so that Lhakpa could complete the carry to Camp 6. All this had taken time.

Confronted with Mick's explanation, the decision they had taken to leave him behind no longer seemed tenable, especially since they had subsequently discovered a further two bottles of oxygen buried in the snow. When told that I wanted to talk to him on the radio to tell him to come back down, he commented, 'Chris can get stuffed.'

I was sitting in my tent, the walkie-talkie radio turned on, trying to write a letter, when Mick's voice called me from Camp 6. He sounded guarded, potentially aggressive as he said he believed I wanted a word with him. I explained that I was worried about his slowness and the fact that he had been high on the mountain for such a long time. He countered this with the explanation of why he had taken so long. There was no point in having a confrontation by radio, so I asked him to put me on to Martin. It was up to them to decide whether they wanted to take Mick on the summit bid. Martin, obviously embarrassed and worried, said that Mick seemed to be going sufficiently strongly and that they didn't see how they could leave him out from the summit push. All I could do was exhort them to stick together and that if anyone did retreat, that they should all return.

In retrospect, even this exhortation was fairly meaningless in the reality of the situation. A line of fixed rope, followed by tracks, stretched towards the summit of Everest just 450m (1475ft) above. I was asking too much. They talked it over that night and agreed that if anyone was going so slowly that he might jeopardise their chances of reaching the summit, he should turn back, before reaching the end of the fixed rope.

They were ready to start at 4.30 the following morning. It was an ominous dawn. Although there was no wind, a thin high haze covered the western horizon and a tide of cloud was fast lapping up the valley bottoms, filling the Western Cwm below them and creeping up the face itself. The weather seemed on the point of change and they all realised that they were going to have to move fast to avoid a bivouac.

Martin Boysen, ever impatient, was away first, Pete Boardman was next, closely followed by Pertemba, and Mick Burke brought up the rear. It is almost impossible to stay together while climbing a fixed rope, for each person is individually clipped into it, travelling at his own speed, and high on Everest is cocooned behind mask and goggles.

Martin suffered an early and bitter setback when his oxygen set packed up and he lost a crampon, this misfortune effectively putting him out of the summit bid; the others overtook him and despairingly he retreated to the tent.

I crawled inside and howled with anguish, frustration and self-pity. Later the sun crept round, but a strong breeze sprang up. I poked my head out and scanned the gully. Two tiny specks were visible, one just below the summit ridge. I wondered where Mick was and eventually spied him at the bottom of the gully as the two figures above reached the crest. It was only 11 a.m. – they were doing well. I closed the door. I could hardly bear to watch.

Pete Boardman and Pertemba had made good progress, climbing unroped beyond the end of the fixed ropes along the track leading to the foot of the South Summit gully and then on up to its top. Although some of the tracks had been filled in by wind-driven spindrift, the snow was much better consolidated than it had been two days before. Pete had glanced back once or twice, had seen a distant figure on the traverse across the Upper Snowfield but had assumed that this was Martin or Mick sitting watching them and that they both would return to camp.

On reaching the South Summit, Pertemba had trouble with his oxygen, when his set jammed. The problem was similar to the one that had beset Dougal and they spent an hour fiddling with it before they managed to clear 5cm of ice blocking the airflow. Even so, they were still making excellent time, changed their oxygen bottles and forged on towards the summit, roped up, but climbing together.

The cloud had now crept up the face, engulfing them in a thin mist. The wind was rising steadily, but visibility was still quite reasonable. They could see the line of tracks snaking up the South East Ridge in front of them and felt comfortably in control of the situation.

They reached the top at about ten past one, a very fast time indeed, even allowing for the tracks left by the first summit pair. They were not rewarded by the magnificent view that Doug and Dougal had enjoyed, for they were still enclosed in fine wind-driven mist, the Chinese maypole, the only sign that they were standing on the highest point on earth. Pete was wearing a specially decorated T-shirt presented to him by the Mynydd Mountaineering Club in honour of the occasion. It was like a medieval knight's surcoat worn over his down suit of armour. Pertemba took out a Nepalese flag, which they attached to the Chinese emblem. They took photographs of each other and Pete addressed the world on a miniature tape recorder: 'Hello, here is the first bit of recorded sound from the summit of Mount Everest. Would you like to say a word to the viewers, Pertemba?' A muffled sound followed, due to Pertemba still being encased in his oxygen mask, but when asked if he was tired, there came a very firm 'No'. Pete then went on to outline briefly the details of their ascent and the weather conditions and signed off with the cheerful comment, 'Well, I can't see a Barclays Bank branch anywhere.' In this totally relaxed mood they ate some chocolate and mint cake, and then set off down. They still had plenty of time; it was barely 1.40.

They had not gone more than a few hundred metres when to their utter amazement a figure began to take shape through the mist. Pete Boardman tells what happened next:

Mick was sitting on the snow only a few hundred yards down an easy angled snow slope from the summit. He congratulated us and said he wanted to film us on a bump on the ridge and pretend it was the summit, but I told him about the Chinese maypole. Then he asked us to go back to the summit with him. I agreed reluctantly and he, sensing my reluctance, changed his mind and said he'd go up and film it and then come straight down after us. He borrowed Pertemba's camera to take some stills on the top and we walked back 50ft and then walked past him whilst he filmed us. I took a couple of pictures of him. He had the 'Blue Peter' flag and an Autoload camera with him. He asked us to wait for him by the big rock on the South Summit where Pertemba and I had dumped our first oxygen cylinders and some rope and film on the way up. I told him that Pertemba was wanting to move roped with me – so he should catch us up fairly quickly. I said, 'See you soon,' and we moved back down the ridge to the South Summit.

After they parted company the weather began to deteriorate fast. Pete and Pertemba continued down to wait with increasing apprehension:

All the winds of Asia seemed to be trying to blow us from the ridge. A decision was needed. It was four in the afternoon and the skies were already darkening around the South Summit of Everest. I threw my iced and useless snow goggles away into the whiteness and tried, clumsily mitted, to clear the ice from my eyelashes. I bowed my head into the spindrift and tried to peer along the ridge. Mick should have met us at least three-quarters of an hour before. We had been waiting for nearly one and a half hours. There was no sign of Doug and Dougal's bivouac site. The sky and cornices and whirling snow merged together, visibility was reduced to 10ft and all tracks were obliterated. Pertemba and I huddled next to the rock of the South Summit where Mick had asked us to wait for him. Pertemba said he could not feel his toes or fingers and mine, too, were nailed with cold. I thought of Mick wearing his glasses and blinded by spindrift, negotiating the short length of fixed rope on the Hillary Step, the fragile 1ft windslab on the Nepal side and the cornices on the Tibetan side of the ridge. I thought of our own predicament, with the 800ft [245m] of the South Summit gully – guarded by a 60ft rock step halfway – to descend, and then half of the 2000ft [600m] great traverse above the Rock Band to cross before reaching the end of the fixed ropes that extended across from Camp 6.

It had taken Doug and Dougal three hours in the dawn sunshine after their bivouac to reach Camp 6 – but we now had only an hour of light left. At 28,700ft [8750m] the boundary between a controlled and an uncontrolled situation is narrow and we had crossed that boundary within minutes – a strong wind and sun shining through clouds had turned into a violent blizzard of driving snow.

A decision was needed. I pointed at my watch and said, 'We'll wait ten more minutes.' Pertemba agreed. That helped us – it shifted some responsibility to the watch. I fumbled in my sack and pulled out our stove to leave behind. The time was up. At first we went the wrong way, too far towards the South Col. About 150ft [45m] down we traversed back until we found what we thought was the South Summit gully. There was a momentary lessening in the blizzard, and I looked up to see the rock of the South Summit. There was still no sign of Mick and it was now about half past four. The decision had been made and now we had to fight for our own lives and think downwards. The early afternoon had drifted into approaching night and our success was turning into tragedy.

Pertemba is not a technical climber, not used to moving away from fixed ropes or in bad conditions. At first he was slow. For three pitches I kicked down furiously, placed a deadman and virtually pulled him down in the sliding, blowing powder snow. But Pertemba is strong and adaptable. He began to move faster and soon we were able to move together. Were we in the gully? I felt panic surge inside. Then I saw twin rocks in the snow that I recognised from the morning. We descended diagonally from there and in the dusk saw Doug's oxygen cylinder that marked the top of the fixed rope over the rock step. We abseiled down to the end of the rope and tied a spare rope we had to the end and descended the other 150ft. From there we descended down and across for 1000ft towards the end of the fixed ropes. As soon as we started the traverse we were covered by a powder-snow avalanche from the summit slopes. Fortunately our oxygen cylinders were still functioning and we could breathe. We threaded our way blindly across the thin runnels of ice and snow that covered the sloping rocks. I felt a brush of snow on my head and looked up to see another big avalanche coming, channelled, straight at me. I looked across. Pertemba was crouched to hold my fall, and was whipping in the rope between us tight to my waist. I smashed my axe into the ice and hung on. The surging snow buffeted over and around me for minutes. Then it stopped. Pertemba had held; the axe had stayed in the ice. We moved on. It was a miracle that we found the end of the fixed ropes in the dark marked by two oxygen cylinders sticking out of the snow. On the fixed rope Pertemba slowed down and I pulled him mercilessly until he shouted that one of his crampons had fallen off. The rope between us snagged and, in flicking it free, I tumbled over a 15ft rock step to be held on the fixed rope. At one point a section of the rope had been swept away. At half past seven we stumbled into the summit boxes at Camp 6. Martin was there and I burst into tears.

16

Clearing the mountain

27 September – 30 September 1975

Back at Camp 2 we had waited, helpless, through the day. In the early morning we had glimpsed two figures, probably Pete and Pertemba, near the foot of the South Summit gully and were filled with hope for a fast safe ascent, but then the cloud had rolled over us and all we could see through the occasional break were banners of spindrift being blown from the top of the Rock Band and the South East Ridge.

After two o'clock we kept the radio permanently open, could detect the growing anxiety in Martin's voice whenever he called us, as the wind hammering his little tent rose through the afternoon. It became dark, and there was still no sign of them. We were all sitting, tensed and silent round the piled boxes of the mess tent at Camp 2; the only sounds, the wind howling across the face above us and the crackle and buzz of the radio. A severe storm had broken and a bivouac would be an even more serious business than it had been for Doug and Dougal.

And then at seven o'clock Martin's voice came through. There was a momentary glimmer of relief; they were back. But our hopes were quickly dashed by the agony in his voice as he told us that only Pete and Pertemba had returned and that Pete would tell me what had happened.

None of us could believe that Mick was dead; he'd stagger back along the ropes in an hour or so's time; he'd bivouac, and return to Camp 6 the following morning; the same irrepressible cocky Mick whom we'd known for so many years on so many climbs. But as the night dragged out, the fury of the storm increased; it raged throughout the following day, and as the hours crept by our hopes began to vanish, to be replaced with anxiety not only for Mick but for the safety of the three now pinned down, tired and exhausted at the end of the Upper Snowfield, with only a limited quantity of food and oxygen, exposed to the full force of the powder-snow avalanches that were pouring down from the summit rocks. Pete had arrived back first at the tent, and Pertemba, still tied to Pete, took over half an hour just to crawl the last 30m and also tumble into the small tent occupied by Martin. He took off their crampons and forced a brew down them, before shifting them to the other tent, since he had organised his own as the camp kitchen. Pete's feet were numb and he was afraid they were frostbitten, while Pertemba just lay in his sleeping bag suffering from snow blindness and in the last stages of exhaustion. Pete had got him back only just in time.

Martin will never forget the next thirty-six hours.

The night and following day is a permanent scar on my memory, a tender wound, painfully healed but all too easily broken open again. Two nights and a day are not, in themselves a long period of time, yet every hour of waiting seemed stretched to infinity. At first I could hardly accept Mick's death; I clung to slender hope, but with each passing hour all hope disappeared, torn and blown away by the raging winds and blizzard.

I had hoped to go back up the ropes with a working oxygen set, to look for Mick, perhaps to go to the top, but the next morning crushed any such plan. The wind still gusted and tore at the boxes, the air was full of eye stinging spindrift and I emerged outside but briefly to dig furiously at the torrent of snow that was engulfing the tents, intent on squeezing us out like pips from a lemon. Pete and Pertemba's box was already badly deformed, a low white hump out of which an arm occasionally stretched to accept tea, soup and porridge.

Conversation was impossible in the shrieking wind and muffled tents; even if it hadn't been, there was nothing to say. I sat in my box and brewed up. The stove would no longer work without some more air, but if I opened the door more than a chink the spindrift came flooding in.

A wave of panic, claustrophobia overcomes me. I'm incarcerated in an airless little tent; I can't even sit it out here without oxygen. What the hell do we do when it runs out? 'Martin, could you possibly find us another bottle of oxygen?' It's Pete. I cook for them, dig for them, find oxygen for them; I'm their bloody nurse maid.

Still it's time to dig snow off their tents again and have a look outside. I can only stand a few moments at a time as the spindrift blasts my face. I dig frantically until exhausted and then throw myself into the little green grotto, rest a few moments, and out again. Metal hits metal; at last an oxygen bottle emerges from under the accumulated snows. Back to my tent and try to warm up. Snow gradually drifting in, hands and feet icy cold. Every time outside chills me deeper and it takes longer to warm up back in my sleeping bag. Another brew and take full stock. A couple of oxygen cylinders, two tea bags, two gas cartridges and a packet of soup; that's it. We can manage for a few days, but what if the storm continues? Oh Christ, please let's get out.

Time for a radio call – Thank God. We never appreciated the wretched thing before. Chris comes on the air, calm, soothing: 'Just hold out for a little; Nick, Tut and Ronnie are in support at Camp 5 ... try to conserve fuel ... the storm can't last much longer ... there's no need to worry.'

Worry – I'm beyond worry. Mick's dead ... Poor Beth and little Sarah. Oh God, emptiness, loss. If only my oxygen had worked; not even the consolation of the summit; self-pity, anger ... I'm getting out of this hole somehow.

'Want a brew, Pete?'

'Thanks, mate.'

'Well, it's the last, there's bugger all else.'

Darkness came and with it, another night of doubt. Would the storm just carry on, tents collapse, the fuel and oxygen run out?

I woke up; an unnatural calm prevailed. The wind had died; we were saved. A sudden wave of emotion overwhelmed me; I cried bitterly, for Mick, for myself, for everything.

It was the morning of 28 September. In the last twenty-four hours we had been shown how puny and fragile were our carefully laid plans, logistic build-up and human strength against the power of wind and snow. Mick was dead and every camp was threatened. We had been forced to evacuate Camp 1 on the afternoon of the 26th; its occupants had felt the ice island shift beneath their feet, in its inexorable slide down into the Icefall. This, in effect, cut our line of supply with Base Camp, but we reckoned that we had enough supplies at Camp 2 for the last few days of the expedition.

As the storm raged through the day of the 27th, we also abandoned all hope of Mick's survival. Dougal and Doug, who had seen how badly corniced and how narrow was the ridge leading down from the foot of the Hillary Step, felt that it would have been all too easy for him to have walked over the edge in the white-out conditions that must have beset him on his descent. If he had stopped for the night, hoping to get back down to the end of the fixed rope the following morning of the 27th, he could not possibly have moved that day, and there was no way he could have survived two nights at that altitude without food, shelter or oxygen, even if he had dug a snow hole.

I was getting increasingly worried about the safety of the rest of the team. Nick, Ronnie, Ang Phurba and Tut at Camp 5 seemed safe enough, tucked away in the small gully that was guarded by a rock buttress above, but they reported huge powder-snow avalanches pouring in a constant torrent down the Great Central Gully. There was no question of movement either up or down until these ceased.

Camp 4, however, was in a more exposed situation, only partially protected by the slender snow arête above it. I was frightened of the huge build-up of snow that was probably forming on the snowfields above the camp. Even though they had now spread tarpaulin sheets over all the boxes, the memory of the avalanche that had damaged one of them when the camp was established made me wonder what might happen if the whole slope slid away.

At five o'clock, therefore, on the afternoon of the 27th I told Adrian Gordon, who was in charge of Camp 4, to abandon the camp and bring down the six Sherpas who were manning it. Very shortly we were involved in another crisis. The Sherpas raced down the fixed ropes and got back to Camp 2 just before dark. Adrian had delayed a little, ensuring that the camp was left secure, and moved more slowly because he was less experienced; this was the first time he had been on the face. As a result, he was caught in the dark. His head torch failed; he couldn't see where he was going, took a wrong turn following some old rope that had been left by the Japanese, and eventually decided he had better stay where he was. By this time it was nine o'clock at night and the storm was raging unabated. We sent some Sherpas back to see what had happened to him, but they had gone up without any jumar clamps. Very courageously Ang Phu had climbed a full rope-length hand over hand, but could see no sign of him and was forced to return. Increasingly worried, I set out from Camp 2 with Dave Clarke, Mike Rhodes and another group of Sherpas armed with survival gear, Thermos flasks of hot tea and jumar clamps. It was past ten that night when eventually Mike Rhodes and I reached Adrian halfway up the fixed ropes to the site of Camp 3. He was characteristically calm, in fact had just decided to feel his way back up the rope to the site of Camp 3 and dig himself a snow hole for the night. At the same time, though, he was desperately tired. It is quite possible that if we hadn't reached him, he could have collapsed and died from exposure. It took him a long time to walk back to Camp 2, but he steadfastly refused to take any help, courageously stumbled fifty paces or so, paused for a few minutes, and then stumbled on once again. Our tracks had been covered in the short time between walking out and returning and, without the marker flags placed every 30m or so, we should have been lost in the maze of crevasses that barred the way back to the camp. We only saw the light of the camp when we got within fifty paces of the first tent, the wind-driven snow was so dense.

It was midnight before we all got to bed. I dropped off into a deep sleep, only to wake dimly to the sound of someone shouting my name. It was Charlie Clarke, who describes what happened in his diary:

Shortly before 4 a.m. there was a deafening roar and in the moment of wakening I felt myself turning, lifted and pitched for a few seconds. It was immediately obvious that we had been hit by a large avalanche and I thought to myself, 'Yes, I'm alive and I can breathe.' The tent zip was very near to my hand and I was out into the still icy night in seconds. Chris Ralling's tent was completely flattened, while the BBC super box which stood beside ours was no longer there. Eventually I realised that the twisted mass of metal and canvas was both our tent and theirs – containing in all, Doug and Dougal, Ned and Ian, Arthur and myself. Sherpas peeped from the remains, grinning, still warm in their sleeping bags. I walked round. No one was hurt or missing. Several tents had remained unscathed, among them Chris Bonington's face box.

I wandered over to it and woke him up, told him the rest of the camp was flat. 'Anyone dead?' he asked. I replied that all was well and he crashed back into drugged sleep. We wandered about, re-orientating ourselves. 'Looters will be shot,' shouted someone. We all seemed in a jovial mood, wholly unfrightened by the episode which had seemed so sudden yet so short-lived.

Within minutes the kitchen was re-erected and the good Kanchha was making tea – always so necessary in accidents. The remarkable thing was how coolly we took it all. None of the sick shaky feeling or even relief that it was all over. It seemed as if it was just another chapter in the struggle to get off the mountain safely.

It dawned into a brilliant clear still morning. There was no question of mounting a search for Mick or another summit bid. He couldn't possibly be alive. I wanted to clear the mountain, which had a dangerous quantity of snow on it, as quickly as possible. I told the party at Camp 5 to wait for the arrival of Pete, Pertemba and Martin and then to accompany them back to Camp 2. I had decided to abandon everything that they couldn't carry down with them. I was not prepared to take any further risks just to rescue pieces of equipment, however valuable.

That morning of 28 September, they had crawled out of the two battered little tents at Camp 6, and crammed their frozen sleeping bags into their rucksacks. Pete Boardman almost dreaded the return.

I felt isolated from my friends lower down the mountain by a decision and experience I could not share. We looked across the traverse and up the gully to the South Summit, but there was no sign of Mick. We turned and began the long repetitive ritual of clipping and unclipping the piton brake and safety loop and abseiling rope-length after rope-length, 6000ft [1830m] down to the Western Cwm.

As we emerged from the foot of the gully through the Rock Band we could see tiny figures outside the three boxes of Camp 5, 1000ft below us. It took a long time to reach them for many of the anchors on the fixed rope had been swept away. Ronnie, Nick, Tut and Ang Phurba were waiting for us and helped us down into the living air and warmth of the Western Cwm and the reassuring faces of Camp 2.

'Everest is not a private affair; it belongs to many men.' That afternoon I was in front of a camera, explaining what had happened. But now friends were all around me. Dougal, usually so distant and undemonstrative, had walked out in the mid-day heat of the Western Cwm to meet me, Doug had tenderly taken off my boots, Chris had reassured me. It was good to hear about other people's experiences, and all the individual traits I had noticed in others in the last few months seemed refreshingly evident – Tut, strutting about like a starved turkey, Ronnie hoovering the table, Doug his hair still at half-mast, Charlie dressed in his red underwear.

The following morning we turned our backs on the South West Face of

Everest and headed down the Western Cwm, in a long straggling line of climbers and Sherpas, bowed under monstrous loads of up to 36 kilos. We were trying to clear the Cwm in just two carries. Adrian Gordon and Allen Fyffe had volunteered to stay behind just one more day and the bulk of our Sherpas returned to Camp 2 after carrying their loads down to the head of the Icefall, while most of the climbers and the Sherpas who had been working in the upper camps, continued down to Base. Adrian, Allen and the remaining Sherpas were able to clear the Western Cwm the following day and that high valley once more was left empty of life, except for a few goraks (huge, crow-like birds) who were scavenging the last of the food left in our rubbish dump, before it was covered for ever more by the snows.

I didn't relax until the last man came down the Icefall on 30 September. That night the Sherpas had a party to celebrate the successful outcome of the expedition and the safe return of all their numbers. They lit a huge bonfire and danced round it, late into the night, arms linked, chanting out their songs, swaying in and out, to the brink of the flames and out into the dark, throwing great shadows on to the tents and snow behind us. Plastic jerry cans of chang were passed round; we were offered mugfuls of throat-searing rakshi, tried our hand at dancing and contributed a few noisy and very tuneless chorus songs. There was plenty of laughter and shouting, but there were moments of reflection as well.

I know that I and, I suspect, most other members of the team, would have followed the same course as Mick, in similar circumstances. In pressing on alone he took a climber's calculated risk, in principle similar to the ones one often takes on British hills, the Alps or other mountains of the Himalaya. He balanced in his mind the risks of going on by himself in the face of deteriorating weather, with the knowledge that there were fixed ropes on all the awkward sections and a line of tracks stretching away before him. Although he was travelling more slowly than Pertemba and Pete Boardman, he was still making good progress and always had plenty of time before dark to return to Camp 6. Had the weather not deteriorated into white-out conditions so quickly, I am convinced he would have caught up with Pete Boardman and Pertemba on the South Summit. Sadly, his calculations didn't work out.

We were rather like the mourners after the funeral; glad to be alive, getting on with our own lives, the memory of Mick held with sadness and regret, yet accepted as an act that had happened; one of the risks of our climbing game.

Is there a self-centred selfishness in this attitude? For those of us who are happily married and have children, there must be or we should not have carried on our life of climbing aware, as we are, of the risks involved. In our own single-minded drive and love for the mountains, we hope that the fatal accident will never happen to us, are frightened to contemplate the cruel long-lasting sorrow suffered by the widows, parents and children – an endless tunnel that for them must never seem to end.

Our doubts and sorrow were mixed with a feeling of satisfaction at having taken part in a successful, demanding, yet very happy expedition. Inevitably there had been moments of tension and misunderstanding within the team, but these had been very few and had been quickly dispelled with frank words. Our friendship and respect for each other had been heightened rather than weakened.

In our race to beat the winter winds and cold, we had climbed the mountain in thirty-three exacting, exhilarating days after arriving at Base Camp. Everyone had stretched himself to his limit. Each of us had known moments of immense personal fulfilment, of self-revelation or just simple wonder at the beauty and scale of the mountain itself and the ever-expanding view to be gained from it.

The South West Face of Everest was a major landmark in all our climbing lives, one that had taken up so much of our mental and physical energy in the months of preparation, planning and finally of climbing, but already we were beginning to talk of future objectives in the Karakorum, Garhwal, Nepal, in Alaska or Patagonia. There are so many mountains in the world, many of them still unclimbed, all with unclimbed facets, ridges or faces.

There is no question of anticlimax in tackling smaller peaks than Everest, for simply by reducing the size of the team one can maintain the level of challenge that is the essence of climbing. Each problem, whether it be a granite spire in the Karakorum, a great unclimbed snow face in the Nepal Himalaya or a complex ridge in the Garhwal, has its own special mystery and appeal.

One of the joys of mountaineering in this fast shrinking world is that mountaineers for many generations to come will still be able to discover untrodden corners in the greater mountain ranges of the earth. We, however, shall always feel fortunate and privileged to have been able to unravel the complex problems that were presented by the world's highest and steepest mountain face.

Members of the expedition and a diary of events

The Team

Chris Bonington, Leader.
Aged 41. Married with two children. Writer and photographer, living in Lake District. 1st ascent Annapurna II (26,041ft) in Nepal, 1960. 1st ascent Nuptse (25,850ft), third peak of Everest, in 1961. 1st ascent Central Pillar of Frêney, Mont Blanc, 1961. 1st British ascent of North Wall of Eiger, 1962. 1st ascent Central Tower of Paine, Patagonia, 1963. 1st ascent Old Man of Hoy, 1966. Leader Annapurna South Face expedition, 1970. Leader British Everest expedition, 1972. 1st ascent Brammah (21,036ft) in Kashmir, 1973. 1st ascent Changabang in Garhwal Himalaya, 1974. Fellow of Royal Geographical Society.

Hamish MacInnes, Deputy Leader.
Aged 44. Equipment designer, writer and photographer living in Glencoe. Has climbed extensively in Scotland, the European Alps, New Zealand, Caucasus and the Himalaya with many new routes to his credit. Member of the spring 1972 European Everest expedition and autumn 1972 British Everest expedition. 1st ascent of the Prow of Roraima in Guyana, 1973. World authority in mountain rescue. Secretary Scottish Mountain Rescue Committee.

Peter Boardman.
Aged 24. National Officer British Mountaineering Council. North Face of Matterhorn and 5 first British ascents in the Western Alps including the North Face Direct of the Olan and the North Faces of the Nesthorn and the Lauterbrunnen Breitborn. 1st ascents of North Faces of Koh-i-Mondi and Koh-i-Khaaik in the Central Hindu Kush, 1972. 1st ascent of the South Face of Mount Dan Beard in the Central Alaska Range, 1974. Expedition to Caucasus, 1975.

Martin Boysen, Assistant Food.
Aged 32. Married with one child. Schoolteacher living in Manchester. 2nd ascent South Face of the Fou, one of the most difficult rock routes in the Alps. 1st ascent of the West Face of the Pic Sans Nom, near Mont Blanc, 1967. Member of the 1967 Cerro Torre expedition; 1970 Annapurna South Face expedition. 1st ascent Point Innominata in Patagonia, 1974. 1st ascent Changabang, 1974.

Paul Braithwaite, Assistant Equipment.
Aged 28. Decorator living in Oldham. 1st British ascent of Croz Spur on the

Grandes Jorasses, Couzy Pillar of the Droites, Grand Pilier d'Angle on Mont Blanc, expedition to Caucasus. 1st ascent E. Pillar Asgard in Baffin Island, 1972. Expedition to Baffin Island 1973. 1st ascent Point Innominata in Patagonia, 1974. 1st ascent S.E. Spur of Pik Lenin in the Pamirs, 1974.

Mick Burke, Mountain Cameraman.
Aged 32. Film cameraman living in London. Married with one child. Cerro Torre expedition. North Face of Matterhorn in winter. 1st British ascent of the Nose of El Capitan in Yosemite, 1968. Member of Annapurna South Face expedition, 1970 and of British Everest expedition in 1972. President Alpine Climbing Group.

Mike Cheney, Base Camp Manager.
Aged 46. Director of Mountain Travel, Kathmandu. Extensive trekking experience in Nepal.

Charles Clarke, Expedition Doctor.
Aged 31. Married with one child. Registrar in Neurology, Middlesex Hospital London. Six Himalayan expeditions, including 1st ascent Swargarohini in Garhwal Himalaya 1974.

Dave Clarke, Equipment Organiser.
Aged 37. Married with two children. Proprietor of Centresport, a climbing shop in Leeds. Expedition to Paine area of South Patagonia, 1961.

Jim Duff, 2nd Expedition Doctor.
Aged 28. Qualified physiologist with medical experience in Nepal. 14 years' climbing experience including the Great Troll Wall in Norway.

Nick Estcourt, Treasurer and Insurance.
Aged 31. Married with three children. Systems analyst from Manchester. 2nd ascent South Face of the Fou. 1st ascent of the West Face of the Pic Sans Nom, 1967. Member of Annapurna South Face expedition 1970 and British Everest expedition 1972. 1st ascent Brammah in Kashmir, 1973.

Allen Fyffe.
Aged 28. Climbing instructor at Glenmore Lodge in Cairngorms. 1st British ascent of North Face Direct of Les Droites. 1st winter ascent of Central Spur of North Face of Les Courtes. North Face of Eiger. Member of the British Dhaulagiri expedition, 1973. Over 40 first ascents in Scotland, summer and winter.

Adrian Gordon, Advanced Base Manager.
Aged 28. Administrative officer in British Gurkha Ex-Servicemen's Reintegration Training Scheme in Nepal. A fluent Nepali speaker with extensive trekking experience.

Dougal Haston.
Aged 32. Married. Director of International School of Mountaineering in Leysin. 1st

ascent Eiger Direct, one of the most difficult climbs in Alps, 1966. Winter ascent of North Face of Matterhorn. Cerro Torre expedition. Member of Annapurna South Face expedition, reaching its summit. Member of International Everest expedition, 1971 and British Everest expedition, 1972. 1st ascent Changabang, 1974.

Mike Rhodes.
Aged 27. Married with three children. Clerk with Barclays Bank International in Bradford. Member of Barclays Bank Climbing Club with extensive climbing experience in Britain, the Alps and the Dolomites.

Ronnie Richards, Transport and Communications.
Aged 29. Chemist living in the Lake District. Extensive alpine experience. West Ridge of Pik Lenin, Pamirs, 1974.

Doug Scott, Assistant Equipment.
Aged 33. Married with two children. Teacher, writer and photographer living in Nottingham. Atlas mountains, 1962, Tibesti Mountains in Sahara 1965, Cilo Dag Mountains in Turkey in 1966, Hindu Kush with 1st ascent of South Face Koh-i-Bandaka (22,500ft), 1967. 1st British ascent Salathé Wall in Yosemite, 1970. European Everest expedition, spring 1972. 1st ascent E. Pillar of Mount Asgard, Baffin, summer 1972, British Everest expedition, autumn 1972. 1st ascent Changabang, 1974. 1st ascent S.E. Spur Pik Lenin. 1974. Member training committee of BMC, FRGS.

Mike Thompson, Food Organiser.
Aged 37. Married with two children. Anthropologist living in London. Expedition to Indrasan in Kangra Himalaya. Member of Annapurna South Face expedition, 1970, and of Roraima expedition, 1973.

Lt Mohan Pratap Gurung, of the Royal Nepalese Army, Liaison Officer.

Gurkha Signallers

L/C Jai Kumar Rai.
Cpl Prembahadur Thapa.

BBC team

Arthur Chesterman, Sound Recordist.
Aged 33. Married with one child. Sound recordist with the BBC. Very experienced technician in mountain environment. Was sound recordist on International Everest expedition, 1971.

Ned Kelly, Film Producer.
Aged 40. Married and living in Bristol. BBC film producer of natural history and

mountaineering films. Very experienced in mountain photography with four previous visits to Nepal, including filming of International Everest expedition, 1971.
Producer of award-winning Alplamayo film, 1966.

Chris Ralling, Film Producer.
Aged 46. Married with one child. Producer of television documentary films. Also
experienced climber and ski mountaineer.

Ian Stuart, Film Cameraman.
Aged 43. Married with three children. BBC film cameraman with considerable
experience of mountain and expedition photography, including International
Everest expedition, 1971.

Sunday Times correspondent

Keith Richardson.
Aged 38. Married with three children. Journalist of considerable experience. Also
mountaineer who has taken part in climbs in the Alps, and an expedition to Arctic
Norway.

Transport

Bob Stoodley, Overland Transport Organiser.
Aged 51. Married with five children. Chairman and Managing Director of
Manchester Garages Limited. British Everest expedition, 1972.

Allen Evans, Driver.
Aged 23. Married and living in Manchester.

John O'Neill, Driver.
Aged 28. Single and living in Manchester.

Alan Riley, Driver.
Aged 27. Born in Kenya, but living in Worcestershire. Not married.

Committee of Management

Chairman:	The Rt Hon. the Lord Hunt, CBE, DSO, DCL, Ll.D
	Sir Jack Longland
	Ian McNaught-Davis
	Alan Tritton
	Lt Col. Charles Wylie
	Chris Bonington, CBE
	Doug Scott

Louise Wilson, Expedition Secretary.

High-altitude porters

NAME	AGE	VILLAGE	HIGHEST CAMP CARRIED TO
Pertemba Sherpa (Head Sirdar)	27	Khumjung	Camp 6
Ang Phu Sherpa (2nd Sirdar)	26	Khumjung	
Ang Phurba 'I' Sherpa	29	Khumjung (4 times)	Camp 6
Lhakpa Dorje Sherpa	22	Khumjung	Camp 6
Mingma Sherpa	23	Khumjung	Camp 6
'Young' Tenzing Sherpa	24	Namche Bazar	Camp 6
Pasang Tenzing Sherpa	40	Khumde	Camp 6
Phutsering Sherpa	32	Khumjung	Camp 5
Ang Nuru Sherpa	30	Phortse	Camp 5
'Long' Tenzing Sherpa	36	Namche Bazar	Camp 5
Lhakpa Gyalu Sherpa	26	Phortse	
Nawang Tenzing Sherpa	26	Namche Bazar	Camp 5
Sundhare Sherpa*	22	Pangpoche	Camp 5
Pasang Gyalzen Sherpa*	20	Phortse	Camp 4
Mingma Gyalzen Sherpa	24	Phortse	Camp 5
'Small' Tenzing Sherpa	25	Namche Bazar	
Urken Dorje Sherpa	34	Ghat	Camp 5
Sonam Jangbo Sherpa	35	Pangpoche	Camp 5
Lhakpa Gyalzen Sherpa	28	Pangpoche	Camp 5
Pasang Wangchup Sherpa*	21	Namche Bazar	Camp 4
Dorje Sherpa	21	Drokkharka	Camp 5
Ang Phurba 'II' Sherpa	35	Chermading	Camp 5
Ang Lhakpa Sherpa	35	Khumjung	
Dawa Gyalzen Sherpa*	23	Khamche	Camp 5
Mingma Nuru Sherpa*	24	Thame	Camp 4
Pasang Namgyal Sherpa	38	Namche Bazar	Camp 5
Ang Nima Sherpa	37	Namche Bazar	
Nima Kanchha Sherpa	28	Jarok	Camp 5
Dawa Norbu Sherpa	39	Thame	
Pema Tham Jen Sherpa	28	Thame	
Nima Tsering Sherpa	42	Rolwaling	
Phurtenzing Sherpa	38	Thame	Camp 5
Nimachiri Lhawa Sherpa	39	Khumjung	

BBC team's high-altitude porters

NAME	AGE	VILLAGE	HIGHEST CAMP CARRIED TO
Jagatman Tamang (BBC Sirdar)	33	Temal	
Pemba Lama	26	Junbesi	Camp 4
Pasang Temba Sherpa	36	Khumjung	Camp 4
Chowang Rinzi Sherpa	27	Namche Bazar	Camp 4
Sona Sherpa	36	Khumde	Camp 4
Gyalzen Sherpa	33	Phortse	Camp 2
Pema Tsering*	30	Darjeeling	Camp 2
Saila Tamang*	40	Temal	Camp 2

Icefall porters

NAME	AGE	VILLAGE
Phurkipa Sherpa (Icefall Sirdar)	54	Namche Bazar
Ang Tenzing Sherpa	38	Thomde
Changpa Sherpa*	31	Namche Bazar
Gyane Sherpa	29	Namche Bazar
Temba Sherpa*	28	Khumjung
Sangke Sherpa	20	Namche Bazar
Nimanuru Sherpa*	20	Khumjung
Ang Dali Sherpa*	23	Khumde
Ang Pasang Sherpa*	22	Phortse
Mingma Dorje Sherpa*	34	Namche Bazar
Phuri Sherpa*	28	Solu
Pasang Sherpa*	27	Solu
Dawa Sherpa	20	Namche Bazar
Ang Pemba Sherpa	28	Thomde
Nima Dorje Sherpa*	21	Phakding
Ang Nima Sherpa	27	Khumde
Sonam Gyalzen Sherpa	28	Phortse
Pasang Kipa Sherpa	38	Rolwaling
Gyalzen Sherpa	25	Chhulemd
Sontemba Sherpa	32	Phulungtokpa
Ang Dorje Sherpa	29	Rolwaling
Thawa Gyalzen Sherpa	30	Pangboche
Nawang Yonden Sherpa*	31	Surke
Phutharke Sherpa	29	Yulajung
Nuru Jangbo Sherpa	29	Lomjo
Tsering Phenjo Sherpa	25	Namche Bazar

* Indicates a man on his first expedition.

Base Camp staff / Cook staff

NAME	POSITION	AGE	VILLAGE
Lhakpa Thondup Sherpa	Base Camp Sirdar	25	Khumjung
Purna Sherpa	Base Camp Head Cook	32	Darjeeling & Kathmandu
Pasang Tendi Sherpa	Base Camp 2nd Cook	33	Khumjung
Kanchha Sherpa	Camp 2 Cook	29	Chhabel
Wangchu Gyalu Sherpa	Base Camp Sherpa Cook	48	Khumde
Sona Sherpa	Kitchen boy	42	Namche Bazar
Changpa Sherpa	Kitchen boy	21	Temal
Dome Sherpa	Kitchen boy	22	Namche Bazar
Ang Dawa Sherpa	Mail-runner	48	Namche Bazar
Tashi Sherpa	Mail-runner	26	Namche Bazar
Tendi Sherpa	Mail-runner	19	Khumde
Athutup Sherpa	Mail-runner	46	Khumjung
Damai Singh	Mail-runner	24	Temal
Pema Sherpa	Mail-runner	18	Chawa Khorye

A Diary of Events

May 1974

Permission for Everest was granted to Bonington.

18 December

Barclays announced their support for the expedition. Without it the expedition could not have taken place.

9 April 1975

The expedition gear is sent overland in two Ford D 1614 standard box vans, loaned by Godfrey Davis, carrying 24 tons of food and equipment. The lorries were driven by Bob Stoodley, our Transport Organiser, and three professional drivers. They were accompanied by Ronnie Richards, a member of the climbing team.

3 May

The lorries reached Kathmandu.

9 May to 10 June

Gear was airfreighted from Kathmandu to the air strip at Luglha and then carried by porters to Khumde where it was stored.

29 July

The team left Britain by an Air India 747 en route for Kathmandu.

2 August

The first party left Kathmandu as planned, travelling by Land-Rover to Lamosangu and then starting the walk. The weather was surprisingly good for monsoon conditions with fine sunny mornings and afternoon rain.

The journey was completed in thirteen days and the party arrived in Khumde on 14 August.

4 August

The second party left Kathmandu, reaching Khumde on 16 August.

17 August

Nick Estcourt and Dougal Haston with four Sherpas set out from Khumde as an advanced party to site Base Camp.

18 August

The first main party set out from Khumde with 200 porters for Base Camp, followed by a second party on the 19th.

The remainder of the expedition gear was ferried up over the succeeding ten days.

21 August

Nick Estcourt and Dougal Haston reached and sited Base Camp at a height of 17,800ft, accompanied by the Icefall sirdar, Phurkipa, and four Sherpas.

22 August

Base Camp was reached by Chris Bonington, Mick Burke, Charles Clarke, Arthur Chesterman, Allen Fyffe and Ronnie Richards. This party included sixteen high-altitude Sherpas and thirteen Icefall Sherpas with 300 loads carried by porters and yaks. Base Camp could be considered established on this date.

Nick Estcourt and Dougal Haston made a recce of the Icefall reaching a height of approximately 19,000ft.

23 August

Bonington, Fyffe, Burke, Chesterman and Richards with twelve Sherpas consolidated the route made by Estcourt and Haston and pushed on for a further few hundred feet up the Icefall. The middle section of the route through the Icefall seemed more complex than it was in 1972, with a series of lateral crevasses.

The second party arrived at Base Camp, consisting of Peter Boardman, Mike Cheney, Hamish MacInnes, Dave Clarke, Mike Thompson, Chris Ralling and Ian Stuart with fourteen high-altitude and twelve Icefall Sherpas.

25 August

A strong party continued to make progress in the Icefall. Martin Boysen reached Base Camp after his delayed arrival at Kathmandu.

26 August

Haston and Scott reached the site of Camp 1 and time was spent in improving the Icefall route with ladders and fixed rope.

28 August

Camp 1 was established when MacInnes, Haston, Scott and Fyffe as lead climbers moved into the camp. Accompanying them were Mike Rhodes as camp manager, Mick Burke and Arthur Chesterman, filming, and ten Sherpas.

2 September

Camp 2 was established at a height of 21,700ft. The Western Cwm was forced by the four lead climbers supported by six Sherpas.

6 September

The South West Face was first stood on by Scott, Burke, Fyffe and Richards who reached the site of Camp 3, fixing ropes along the route.

7 September

Braithwaite and Estcourt move into Camp 3 and push route out towards Great Central Gully.

8 September

Bonington decided to drop the proposed site of Camp 4 to about 800ft above Camp 3. This was the last point giving real protection from avalanches or stonefall from above.

11 September

MacInnes, Boysen and Boardman moved up to Camp 4.

By this time the expedition was well ahead of schedule.

17 September

Bonington and Richards established Camp 5 at 25,500ft.

18 September

Scott and Burke move up to Camp 5.

19 September

Scott, Bonington and Richards run rope out to foot of Rock Band.

20 September

Estcourt and Braithwaite, supported by Burke and Bonington, solved the problem of scaling the 1000ft high Rock Band, the major obstacle on the South West Face. They found a ramp that led out of the deep-cut left-hand gully towards the top of the Band.

22 September

Haston and Scott completed the ascent of the Rock Band and moved into Camp 6, loads being carried by three Sherpas, Bonington, Burke and Thompson.

23 September

Haston and Scott prepared for the first assault of the summit, running 1500ft of fixed rope across the Upper Snowfield towards the South Summit gully. There was one difficult rock pitch that required five pitons to surmount.

24 September

Doug Scott and Dougal Haston set out from Camp 6 at 3 a.m. They made good progress to the foot of the gully leading up to the South Summit, which they reached at 1 p.m. Doug Scott led a difficult rock step of about 60ft which was thinly covered in snow. This was time-consuming and then the gully itself proved very laborious, being filled with deep soft snow.

It was already 3 p.m. when they reached the South Summit. They had a brew here and dug a small snow hollow for a bivouac before setting out for the summit, which they reached at 6 p.m. They found there the Chinese flag with some red bunting on a 4ft pole, clear proof of the Chinese ascent pre-monsoon 1975. It was a magnificent sunset and Doug took some magnificent photographs.

They then returned to the site of their bivouac and had what Doug described as the coldest bivouac of his life. They did have a bivvy stove with them. As this bivouac was actually on the South Summit it must be the highest in history. They only suffered frostnipped toes and fingers.

25 September

They left the bivouac at 6 a.m. and were back at Camp 6, at a height of approximately 27,300ft, at 9 a.m. The second assault party were already on their way up and, of course, would have acted as a back-up team had Dougal and Doug needed help. There was ample oxygen in the top camp.

26 September

A second attempt to reach the summit was made by Boysen, Burke, Boardman and Sherpa Pertemba. The party set out at 4.30 in the morning from Camp 6. Boysen was forced to turn back at about 5.30 after his oxygen failed and a crampon fell off. At this point Boardman and Pertemba were ahead and continued to the summit of Everest which they reached at approximately 1.10 p.m. On their way down, a short distance from the top, they were surprised to meet Burke. He was in good spirits and continued to the summit, whilst Boardman and Pertemba made their way down towards the South Summit where they had agreed to wait for Burke. They waited for over an hour during which time the weather deteriorated seriously into white-out conditions and a violent gale. Their own position was now critical. Boardman therefore took the agonising decision to continue down. They only just managed to get back to their camp, an hour after dark. The storm raged throughout the next day making any kind of movement impossible. There was therefore no question of making any kind of further search for Mick Burke and on 28 September, in the interest of safety, the mountain was cleared.

30 September

All expedition back in Base Camp.

11 October

All expedition back in Kathmandu to prepare for the journey back to Britain.

17 October

Expedition fly into London.

Logistics *by Chris Bonington*

Logistics and planning may seem the very antithesis of the romantic adventure that mountaineering undoubtedly is. Without careful planning, however, even the smallest two-man trip may fail through lack of food or equipment at the right place at the right time and the romance will quickly turn sour. Personally I have found the planning of an expedition, particularly one as complex as Everest, an intriguing intellectual exercise. These notes are designed to show the course of my thinking in planning our attempt on the South West Face of Everest, but they would be relevant to the planning of any siege-style mountaineering expedition, where a series of camps, linked by fixed rope, are set up.

FIRST STEP

The way I set about it was to start with the summit bid, and then to work back down to determine the number of camps, amount of fixed rope, tentage and other supplies I was going to need. This also indicated the ideal size of team for the climb in hand. At this stage it is also possible to make an initial assessment of the consumption of food and oxygen in the higher camps, but as one gets further down the mountain this becomes too complex and one needs a separate set of calculations.

I have listed in Annexe A the quantities of equipment I assessed we needed from Camp 6 back down to Camp 1. This provided the foundation of my planning for our rate of progress up the mountain and my deployment of the climbers and Sherpas at my disposal. Annexe A also sets out the basic approach to the climb.

DEPLOYMENT ON MOUNTAIN

I had now worked out the weight and quantity of non-consumable supplies (items such as tents, cooking stoves, rope and medical kits, that would stay at each camp or in place on the mountain once they had been carried there). I also calculated the reserves of consumable items such as food/fuel and oxygen to be held at each camp. All this weighed 8785 lbs (251 35 lb loads) and had to be carried from Base Camp to the appropriate camp on the mountain. The simplest way would have been to shift the lot from one camp to the next using all our carrying power to do it, only moving up as each stage was completed. This course, however, would have been slow and cumbersome, since this would have involved moving all our gear up to our highest point before moving on up to the next camp. This in effect would mean that the speed of our advance would be determined by the build-up of supplies and not by the pace set by our lead climbers.

The solution was to move no more supplies into each camp than was necessary to sustain the advance; this made it possible to ensure that the lead climbers were never held up for lack of supplies. To achieve this ideal, however, was not easy, for it meant calculating exactly what supplies would be needed at each camp at any time and then ensuring that we had sufficient carrying power, and that it was correctly deployed.

The rate at which we could carry gear up the mountain, assuming a given number of carriers, depended on four factors:

1 The number of rest days required.
2 The effective payload that could be carried by climbers and Sherpas at different heights.
3 An estimate of failures to make carries because of sickness, misunderstandings, etc.
4 The weather – this was something that one couldn't predict. I therefore worked out the best possible rate of progress and ensured we had sufficient reserves at each camp so that we could sit out periods of bad weather.

The estimates I worked out are shown below:

PLANNING FACTORS – Reproduced from the original Planning Document before the expedition

1 REST RATES

a Sherpas

Base to 3	1 day in 4.
2 to 4	1 day in 2.
4 to 5	Last time we only managed to keep the Sherpas at 4 for two days, during which they made two carries, then returning to 2. To keep 6 Sherpas at 4 this would mean one would need 18 altogether, the other 12 resting or moving.
	This time, with a better Camp 4, I hope to keep the Sherpas up for 4 days, one of which would be resting. They would then return to 2 and have three days' rest before returning. This would mean we should only need 12 Sherpas for the 2 to 4 carry.
5 to 6	Probably not more than 2 carries in succession without a rest – will have to play by ear. They would use oxygen.

b Climbers

Base to 3	Allow every other day.
2 to 4	It is unlikely that the climbers would manage this carry – we might

be able to use carries for a 3 to 4 carry once again on an every other day principle.

4 to 5   Every other day. Last time several members of the team made this carry without oxygen – a definite plus.

5 to 6   Same as Sherpas. At this height the climbers probably have the edge on the Sherpas.

2 LOADS

a Sherpas

Base to 3	35 lbs (Camp 2 food boxes 38 lbs, which they should manage)
2 to 4	30 lbs
4 to 5	30 lbs
5 to 6	20 lbs

b Climbers

Base to 3	24 lbs (.66 load)
3 to 4	20 lbs
4 to 5	20 lbs ⎫
5 to 6	20 lbs ⎭ using oxygen to bring it to 32 lbs

These weights are based on what happened last time. If climbers can manage more without smashing themselves this will obviously be a good plus. All climbers carry their personal gear from camp to camp which almost certainly will be more than the above.

3 FAILURE TO MAKE CARRIES

This is very difficult to assess, since it can depend on sickness, lack of morale or alternative use of people. In any day's carry I have reckoned on the following percentage of loads not being taken to their destination –

Base to 3   10%   2 to 4   20%   4 to 5   40%

FORMULA FOR MOVEMENT UP MOUNTAIN

Using the above information I now had to work out the most effective way of deploying our carrying power, in the first instance to place in the appropriate camp all the non-consumable items and then to ensure that the expedition's daily consumption was met. There were two major consumable items – food/fuel – which could be considered together, and above Camp 4 oxygen for both climbing and sleeping.

Having done this I was ready to calculate our rate of progress and deployment on the climb. In the early stages the vital factor was the problem of clearing firstly

Base Camp and then Camp 1 of all the non-consumable items and reserves of food/fuel and oxygen, sufficiently quickly so that I could move the bulk of my thirty-four high-altitude porters up to Camp 2, to start relaying our gear up the face. With fifty-seven Sherpas and climbers at Camp 2 and above, I had calculated I needed a minimum of twelve carries a day to Camp 2 just to keep them supplied with food/fuel and oxygen (to keep my oxygen reserve at 2 at the desired level as bottles were taken out of it, up the face). My calculations are shown as follows:

Day 0: At Base – 17 climbers, 60 Sherpas, 2 cook staff – independent 12 BBC team 251/35 lb loads to go to 1 and above plus daily consumption.
Day 1: 'A' team plus four Sherpas move to 1.
Day 1 to Day 3:

Available Manpower				Effective Loads
Climbers/ Sherpas ×	Rest Days ×	Sherpa Loads ×	No. of days available to carry	
15 (Cl.)	.50	.66	3	15
54 (Sh.)	.75		3	121

$$136 \text{ less } 10\%^* = 123 \text{ loads}$$
$$- \underline{\quad 4} \text{ loads (consumed)}$$
$$119$$
$$- \underline{\quad 48} \text{ loads stay at 1}$$
$$\underline{71} \text{ loads to go on}$$

Calculation of food/fuel consumed at
1 and above for Day 4 on: 45 people × 5 lbs   = 7 loads per day
Time taken to clear base with 30
Sherpas at Base: 251–119   = 132 loads to be shifted from Base =
30 (Sh.) .75   = 23 loads per day
less 10%* =   20 loads
$$- \underline{\quad 7} \text{ loads consumed at 1}$$
13 loads per day with
stockpile to go on

Therefore it will take 11 days to clear Base Camp of all non-consumable items and consumable remains.

Day 5 to 7 from 1:

10 (Cl.)	.50	.66	3	10
28 (Sh.)	.75		3	63

$$73 \text{ less } 10\%^* = 66 \text{ loads}$$
$$- \quad 2 \text{ loads consumed}$$
$$\text{at 2}$$
$$\underline{64} \text{ loads to go on}$$

Day 8 to 12 from 1:
  5 (Cl.)
  from Day
  9 on

| 5 (Cl.) | .50 | .66 | 5 | 8 |
| 28 (Sh.) | .75 | | 5 | 90 |

                       95 less 10%* =   88 loads
                                    −   11 loads consumed
                                         at 2
                                      77 loads to go on
                                   141 loads accumu-
                                       lated at 2

---

* Inefficiency factor

Daily consumption at 1 and above, including
BBC team – 71 people   =   11 loads food/fuel
                                           1 load film stock
                                        12 loads per day

Daily consumption at 2 and above, including
BBC team – 41 people   =   6 loads food/fuel
                                           1 load film stock
                                         7 loads per day

Day 13 to 15 from 1 to 2
Holding consumption rate plus a bit more taken up with
the many things I can't have accounted for, from Mick's
false teeth to a forgotten pair of boots.

Day 16 to 22 from 1
Time taken to shift 66 loads to Camp 2 to clear 1:
204 − 138 = 66 loads. After consumption at 1, 10 loads
per day
                                   7 days to shift

Movement chart – predicted

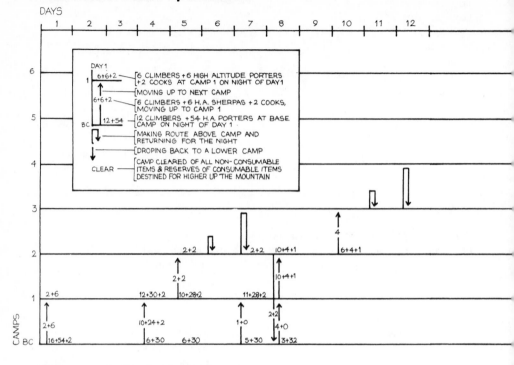

Movement chart – actual

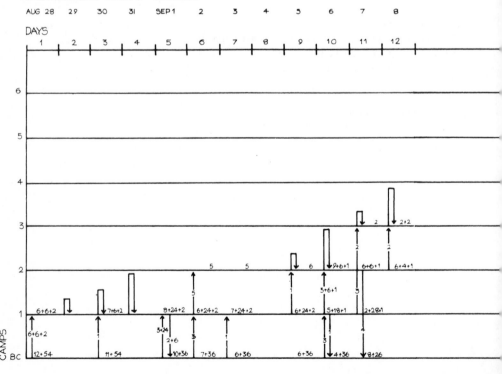

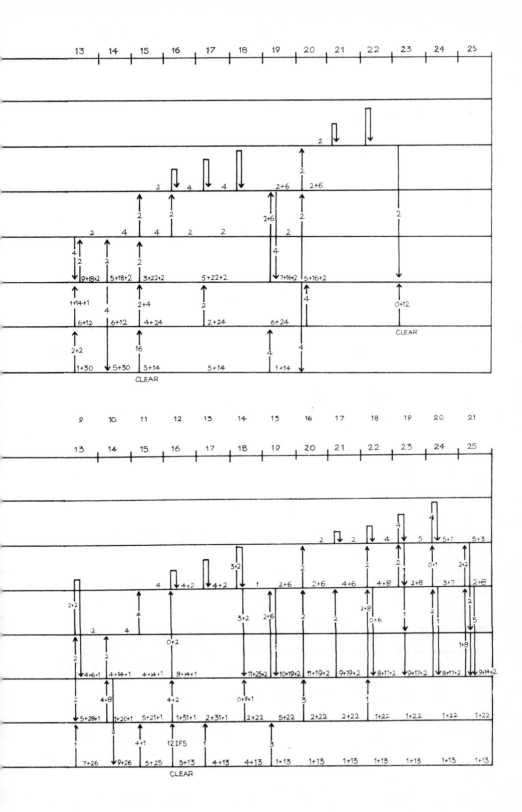

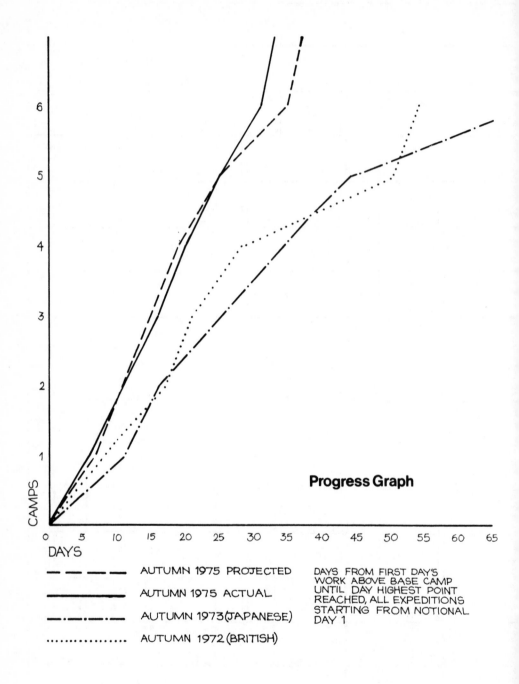

Progress Graph

CAMPS

DAYS

— — — — AUTUMN 1975 PROJECTED

———————— AUTUMN 1975 ACTUAL

—·—·—·— AUTUMN 1973 (JAPANESE)

··············· AUTUMN 1972 (BRITISH)

DAYS FROM FIRST DAY'S WORK ABOVE BASE CAMP UNTIL DAY HIGHEST POINT REACHED, ALL EXPEDITIONS STARTING FROM NOTIONAL DAY 1

These calculations gave me the most effective initial strategy for shifting all the gear we needed from Base to Camp 2. We followed it very closely on the mountain as comparison of the predicted and the actual movement charts, below, will show.

Above Camp 2 we altered our plans a great deal, changing the sites of Camps 4 and 5, introducing the concept of two tents at Camp 6 for the second and third summit bid, allowing four men to take part in each bid. I was able to cope with these changes even in the rarified atmosphere of Camp 5, because of the depth of planning and thinking earlier on. You can always change and modify a plan, but without one, you have nothing on which a change can be based.

Our rate of progress up the mountain was also very close to what I had predicted. This, of course, was greatly helped by the fact that the weather was kinder to us than to either the Japanese in autumn 1973, or us in autumn 1972, being settled right up to the storm that terminated the expedition, with sunny, windless mornings and snow most afternoons. This weather pattern had been indicated by a rainfall analysis I had made from the different sources that were available.

In my innocence I had originally imagined that the computer would be able to tell me how to plan the expedition, an illusion which I suspect is shared by most laymen. Whilst planning our 1972 expedition, Ian McNaught-Davis, a climbing friend of mine and managing director of Comshare, had suggested that we might like to use one of his computers to help in planning. Because the expedition had been organised in such a rush, we had been unable to make full use of this facility; it had, however, shown me its value as a means, not so much of finding the perfect logistic answer, but one of checking out one's own planning thinking.

In the spring of 1975 Ian McNaught-Davis once again offered his help making available one of his programmers, Stephen Taylor, and through the spring and early summer we played out a series of computer games, simulating the movement of men and supplies up the mountain. We never actually reached the top, since we always seemed to get stuck in a logistic bottleneck round about the time that Camp 4 was established, the reason being that I was moving my men and supplies by intuition rather than by logic based on a clearcut formula. I only created the formula described above after three abortive attempts. Stephen Taylor now describes his approach to the computing problem.

WRITING AND WORKING THE PROGRAMME
by STEPHEN TAYLOR

Initially, the problem seemed quite daunting, and far removed from my usual fare of business and OR models. Closer inspection revealed the critical similarity: despite the fact that the problem involved climbers and Sherpas, and tents and whatever else, I could consider the whole thing as a problem in stock control. I had seven camps on the mountain, and men and equipment to put in them, plus some rules governing how I might move them around. All my model had to do was to accept instructions regarding the movements, check that the rules weren't being broken, and keep track of where everybody and everything went, including the food, which disappeared.

We managed to break the equipment into four categories: tentage; food and gas cartridges; oxygen cylinders; and climbing gear.

These four categories had to be treated differently. Tentage determined how many people could sleep in a camp. The food and gas cartridges were consumed at a reasonably predictable rate, which depended upon altitude. The same went for the oxygen cylinders except that the rate was different, and they didn't start to be used until Camp 5. The climbing gear was mostly hammered into the mountain, but without an adequate supply in the highest established camp, the lead climbers would have been stranded. Every member of the expedition was allowed a limited allowance of personal baggage, which was kept with him wherever he went, but we didn't have to account for this in the model: every time someone moved camp, he didn't carry anything other than his bedroll. We expected that only European climbers would need to use oxygen at Camp 4. All these rules had to be built into the model.

The model was constructed around five system arrays. These were:

1. MOVE – this array held the current day's orders, i.e. the proposed movements of men and materials both up and down the mountain.
2. POSITION – this array held details of the numbers of men and weights of equipment of different categories for each of the seven camps.
3. NPOSITION – a 'working' array which held the results of performing the moves held in MOVE in the situation described in POSITION. The program validated this position and checked back with the user before saving the old POSITION and overwriting it with NPOSITION.
4. HISTORY – this was a 3-D matrix which consisted of successive POSITIONs laminated together to form a 'history' of the stock positions on the mountain.
5. STRATEGY – similar to HISTORY, this matrix consisted of successive layers of the MOVE arrays.

At the end of a 'run' we were able to have the HISTORY and STRATEGY arrays printed out, and these constituted a plan for the assault.

In accordance with the current dogma of system design and programming, I took as structured an approach to implementing the model as the limitations of APL would permit. The main features of the model were the seven APL functions START, CONTINUE, ORDERS, PROJECT, CHANGE, SAVE and DISPLAY.

Briefly, the effect of each function was as follows:

1. START – initialises the system variables for the beginning of the expedition, putting correct supplies in Base Camp (Camp 0). After initialisation, it called ORDERS.

2. CONTINUE – similar to START, but continued work on previously defined HISTORY and STRATEGY arrays, allowing the user to take up a plan where he had left it.

3. ORDERS – this function handled and prompted for instructions from the user, and built them up into the MOVE matrix, displaying the final MOVE array, and calling CHANGE if the user was dissatisfied with what he had asked for.

4. CHANGE – an editing function which handled changes to be made to the MOVE array.

5. PROJECT – this function calculated the results of making the moves described in MOVE on the position as described by POSITION. It stored the result in NPOSITION, and checked for mistakes, issuing warnings, and invoked CHANGE if errors were found, or if the user was dissatisfied with the results of his instructions. This was an iterative function to the extent that the user could continue to modify and 'project' the results of his orders until he reached the position that he wanted.

6. SAVE – a simple function that laminated MOVE and POSITION on to STRATEGY and HISTORY respectively, overwrote POSITION with NPOSITION, and reset MOVE and NPOSITION at zero.

7 DISPLAY – a utility function to print the system matrices. Having been passed a matrix as its argument, it determines from the size of the matrix whether it is MOVE, STRATEGY, HISTORY, or POSITION/NPOSITION, and prints the array using an appropriate format. Although all the supplies were stored in the system as weights, DISPLAY, by reference to a number of tables within the workspace, was able to show weight of oxygen as so many bottles, weight of food as so many man/days (it varied with height …) and so on. It was an enormous help during development of the model to be able to print out (intelligibly!) any of the system arrays with a single command, as for instance 'DISPLAY POSITION'.

RUNNING THE MODEL

Ideally, I should have disappeared into a hole in the ground sometime in the spring of 1975, and emerged after a suitably short period with a fully documented and tested model to hand over to Chris, who would then be freely and easily able to play with it until he had evolved his Master Strategy.

Often as we were working on the model, I was debugging and reprogramming as we went along; something that is only really feasible to my knowledge in APL. There were many times that the entire program seemed to be held together with string and recycled chewing-gum; but the overall soundness of the structured approach held up and allowed me to extricate myself from some very messy situations. An immeasurable help was the compactness of the APL code – the seven main functions comprised no more than 150 lines of code – and the amenability of the APL interpreter to my amending the program in the middle of its execution.

I had originally visited Chris Bonington in March to discuss the model, and I returned with a trial version in April for three days. On this occasion, I took with me a portable computer terminal, which I was able to use via the telephone. Time was getting short and subsequent sessions were held by telephone, late at night, with me sitting at a terminal in the basement of Comshare's London office, and Chris doing all the hard work up in Cumbria.

I'd like to emphasise that last point. Once the model had been written, the hard work really became his department. I would be sitting at the terminal 'driving', with a book in my lap, and Chris would telephone me with his proposals for the next moves. I'd type them in, and read back to him the results. I could then go back to my book, while Chris struggled with the next set of moves. As a model, the program in no way solved his problem – it served as a tool for discussing it, handling the very tedious and involved calculations concerning weight allowances, food reserves, and gear and food consumption.

And so the work went on, usually late into the night and small hours, exploring Chris's ideas and strategies, and trying to identify critical points, phases in the climb which were very sensitive to variation. It was during this period when I was acting as a chauffeur that I carried out the second part of the study.

By the green glow of a terminal screen, about midnight on a May night, I shuffled the seventy-eight cards of the Waite Tarot deck, and spread them out in the Grand Cross reading to see what could be read of the expedition's future. The prognosis was excellent, with strong indications of success based on the united efforts of a balanced team, and fame at the end. For the interested, some of the details were:

Significator	The Fool
Beneath him	Two of Swords
Crowning	Three of Pentacles
Covering	Ace of Swords
Tenth card	The Sun
Ninth card	Ace of Pentacles

The final plan, as used on Everest, was never tested on the computer model before the expedition left; and I think that this gives a clue to the real benefits of the study. Chris handed me a copy of the Final Solution just before he left, announcing blithely that he'd reconsidered his plans and had come up with a new one. Momentarily, I was appalled. Was he going to reject the results of all the work that we had done?

In fact not. The Final Solution was very much, I think, the child of the work that Chris had put into the study. The process of exploring and testing his ideas on the logistical problems had yielded the insights into the problem that we had originally been aiming for, and as a result of this he was able to construct the strategy that was so successfully employed, confident in his ability to modify it in action. My biggest thrill of the expedition was a card from the mountain reporting that Camp 4 had been established at the same time that Base Camp was cleared – a point which had been established as critical. My personal satisfaction at the end came from the realisation that Chris had been able to use his resources so that the climbing problems were not unnecessarily complicated by logistical ones; and in doing so had managed to take the biggest expedition by the hardest route in the shortest time – to the top of Everest.

ANNEXE A: OUTLINE PLAN OF THE MOUNTAIN (prepared August 1974)

1. Team strength to go to Camp 2 and above
   14 climbers (European)
   2 climbers (European) based on Camp 2
   2 climbers (European) based on Base Camp
   26 Sherpas shared between Camp 1 and Base
   34 Sherpas available for Camp 2 and above

2. Forcing the Icefall
It is impossible to determine when we can start climbing the Icefall. This depends on the pattern of weather during the monsoon. We should be in a position, however, to start work on the Icefall from 25 August. It should not take longer than 5 days.

3. Making route to Rock Band, once Icefall has been climbed
We shall have 3 parties of 4 climbers each who will take turns in making the route up to Camp 5.
   Party A makes the route from Camp 1–3
   Party B makes the route from Camp 3–4
   Party C makes the route from Camp 4–5
We push the route out as quickly as we can – avoiding any delays.

4. Build-up of supplies to Rock Band
This build-up is made as fast as possible by Sherpas and climbers not involved in lead climbing, Sherpas and climbers moving up to high camps in such a way as to enable the forward momentum to be kept up – in other words, Advanced Base is built up at the same time as supplies are shifted from it up the face.

5. Carrying policy on face
Camp 3 is used solely as a staging post. Sherpas prefer to carry straight through to 4 from 2 and have a rest day in between. In autumn 1972 very few Sherpas did more than two carries from 2 to 5 without coming down for a rest at 2. We shall make 4 a much more comfortable place in the hope of getting at least three carries from

Sherpas. We should try to maintain 2 climbers and 6 Sherpas at Camp 4 while building up Camp 5 and 6. There will be space for 4 climbers at Camp 5.

6. Forcing Rock Band

It is impossible to tell how long this will take. We want to start work on the Rock Band as quickly as possible. In the first instance, therefore, a pair will go up – then a foursome – to work on it.

7. Fixed roping above 6

This will be carried out by four climbers operating from 5, once the Rock Band has been fixed roped, using 1000ft of 7mm rope, which should reach most of the way across the traverse.

8. Establishing Camp 6

Camp 6 will then be established by climbers and Sherpas making one carry and on the following day the summiters supported by two moving into the camp.

9. Resting

Climbers can rest at either Base or 2. If there is to be a prolonged rest it is best for climbers to return to Base.

10. Oxygen policy

Sherpas do not use oxygen till Camp 5 and above. Climbers do not use oxygen until Camp 4 and above. It is not necessary to use oxygen at Camp 4 for sleeping, but there is enough there for anyone in a bad way to use it.

11. Tentage Plan

Camp 6	1 assault box	Sleeps 2
Camp 5	2 face boxes with platforms and reinforced nylon covers	Sleeps 4
Camp 4	4 face boxes with platforms and covers	Sleeps 8
Camp 3	2 boxes (for staging)	Sleeps 4
Camp 2	4 super boxes	Stores, mess kitchen, but can be used for sleeping in emergency
	4 face boxes	Sleeps 8
	8 Vango tents	Sleeps 24
	4 tunnel tents	Sleeps 8
		40
Camp 1	2 super boxes	Sleeps 16
	2 Vango tents	Sleeps 4
		20
Base	2 super boxes	
	3 big bell tents	
	3 cook-shelters	
	10 Vango tents	

		Weight/ lbs	Oxygen	Gas	Food
ABOVE CAMP 6					
1st assault	4 bottles oxygen	48	4		
	120m 7 mm climbing rope	8			
	Karabiners & pegs/stakes	5			
	Pack	3			
	Oxygen system	3			
	Bivvy sack	1			
	Movie camera & magazine	5			
	Still camera	3			
	2 × 38 lb loads	76	4	–	–
2nd assault	Same as above				
	2 × 38 lb loads	76	4	–	–
TO CAMP 6					
For 1st	Assault box	30			
assault	Camp kit, inc. stove etc.	5			
	2 man-days food	5			2
	4 carts gas	3		4	
	1 bottle oxygen	12	1		
	2 men's personal gear	30			
	Radio & batteries	3			
		88	1	4	2
For 2nd	2 man-days food	5			2
assault	4 carts gas	3		4	
	2 men's personal gear	30			
	1 bottle oxygen	12	1		
		50	1	4	2
	TOTALS TO CAMP 6:	290	10	8	4

Payload for 1st assault, allowing 20 lbs per man:
   8 loads
Payload for 2nd assault, allowing 21 lbs per man:
   6 loads

TOTAL LOADS TO CAMP 6
= 14 loads

		Weight/ lbs	Oxygen	Gas	Food
CAMP 5–6					
Fixing 6+	3 × 120 metres 7mm rope (972ft)	24			
from 5	10 snow stakes	10			
	16 karabiners	3			
	4 deadmen	4			
	4 bottles oxygen	48	4		
		89	4		

		Weight/ lbs	Oxygen	Gas	Food
	4 men carrying 22 lbs each				
Fixing 5	3 × 200 metre 8mm ropes	78			
to 6	600ft 9mm climbing rope	20			
	Assorted ironware	20			
	5 × 4 man-days 20 btls oxygen	240	20		
	8 man-days carry for 1st assault				
	8 bottles oxygen	96	8		
	4 man-days carry 2nd assault				
	4 bottles oxygen	48	4		
		502	32		
AT CAMP 5					
4 men					
8 × 4 man-days	2 face boxes with platforms	200			
work	2 camp kits plus foams	40			
4 × 4 man-days	48 man-days food 3 lbs	144			48
reserve	96 carts gas	60		96	
48 man-days	Sleeping oxygen & spare – 24	288	24		
	Radio & batteries	12			
	Medical kit	6			
	Film stock and cameras	60			
		810	24	96	48
Less personal gear – 20 lbs each					
	RUNNING TOTAL TO 5	1685	70	104	52
	Payload of 30 lbs – 56 loads				
CAMP 4–5	4 × 200 metre 8mm ropes	104			
	Ironware	20			
	32 climber trips with oxygen				
	– 32 bottles	384	32		
		508	32		
AT CAMP 4	4 face boxes with platforms	400			
	4 tent kits	20			
6 Sherpas	140 man-days food	420			140
2 climbers	280 carts gas	175		280	
60 man-day	Radio & batteries	16			
carry	Medical kit	10			
80 man-day	Spare oxygen (16)	192	16		
rest	Film cameras and stock	90			
		1323	16	280	140
	RUNNING TOTALS TO 4	3516	118	384	192
	Payload of 30 lbs – 118 loads				
CAMP 3–4	8 × 200 metre 8mm		208		
	Assorted ironware		20		
		228			

		Weight/ lbs	Oxygen	Gas	Food
AT CAMP 3					
Used as staging	2 boxes	120			
post –	2 camp kits	40			
Sherpas carry	Radio & batteries	10			
from 2	Medical kit	6			
	40 man-days food	120			40
	80 carts fuel	50		80	
		346		80	40
	RUNNING TOTAL THROUGH 3	4090	118	464	232
	Payload of 30 lbs – 137 loads				
CAMP 2–3	2 × 200 metres 8mm rope	52			
	Assorted ironware	15			
		67			

With bad weather there could be greater delays, demanding more food and fuel.

		Weight/ lbs	Oxygen	Gas	Food
AT CAMP 2	4 super boxes	480			
	8 Vango tents	240			
	4 face boxes	240			
	4 tunnel tents	80			
	4 lightweight tarps	40			
	Medical kit	80			
	Kitchen kit	80			
	Lighting	20			
	Radios & batteries	50			
	Office	40			
	Tool kit	40			
	Extras	300			
	Spare oxygen (25)	300	25		
	560 man-days reserve				
	Camp 2 food (4 lbs)	2240			
	560 man-days reserve				
	kerosene	600			
	80 man days reserve				
	mountain rations	240			80
	160 reserve carts	100		160	
		5170	25	160	80
	Allow 40 lbs per man				
	personal gear going to 2 –				
	50 men	2000			
	RUNNING TOTALS TO 2	11,327	143	624	312
	Payload of 35 lbs – 324 loads				

(I have not allowed for day-to-day servicing of food and fuel – allow an average population of 42 consuming 5 lbs per day of food and fuel = 210 lbs per day – 6 loads)

		Weight/ lbs	Oxygen	Gas	Food
CAMP 1–2	Marker poles (200)	200			
	8 ladders	160			
	3 × 200 metres 8mm rope	78			
	Assorted ironware	20			
		458			
AT CAMP 1	2 super boxes	240			
	2 Vango tents	60			
	Kitchen kit	40			
	70 man-days reserve fuel/food	350			
	Radio & batteries	20			
	360 man-days food/fuel to feed men carrying to				
	2–5 lbs	1800			
		2510			
	RUNNING TOTAL TO 1	14,295			
	Payload of 35 lbs – 409 loads				

ANNEXE B: WEIGHT DISTRIBUTION

A. NON-CONSUMABLE

1. *Ropes and fixings*

To camp	Net weight to camp	Accumulative
Camp 6	32	32
Camp 5	159	191
Camp 4	124	315
Camp 3	228	543
Camp 2	67	610
Camp 1	458	1068

2. *Tentage and camp gear*

Camp 6	48	48
Camp 5	318	366
Camp 4	506	872
Camp 3	176	1048
Camp 2	1690	2738
Camp 1	360	3090

B. RESERVES – *Consumable items at camps when fully established.*

1. *Oxygen*

Camp 6	10 bottles	120	120
Camp 5	12 bottles	144	264
Camp 4	16 bottles	192	456
Camp 2	32 bottles	384	840
Camp 1	4 bottles	48	888

Oxygen used in initial run out from 4 to 5 and then in movement of climbers from 4 to 5, can be drawn from reserve, which will automatically be topped up allowance for basic consumption.

2. Food/fuel

For Camps 1 and 2 this represents 4 lbs food plus 1 lb kerosene.

For Camps 3 to 6 this represents 3 lbs food plus 1 lb Camping Gaz.

Camp 6	2 m/d	8	8
Camp 5	20 m/d	80	88
Camp 4	42 m/d	168	256
Camp 3	7 m/d	28	284
Camp 2	530 m/d	2650	2934*
Camp 1	160 m/d	800	3734

265 man/days mountain ration and 318 man/days Camp 2 ration – because of different weights there is a discrepancy in no. of man/days at 2.

* To be divided into a third mountain and two thirds Camp 2 rations.

C. TOTAL WEIGHTS AT CAMPS

		Lbs	Loads/lbs
Camp 6	208	208	11/20
Camp 5	701	909	31/30
Camp 4	990	1899	64/30
Camp 3	432	2331	67/35
Camp 2	4791	7122	204/35
Camp 1	1666	8788	251/35

CONSUMPTION RATE WHEN CAMP 5 IS FULLY OCCUPIED

	Daily Consumption										
Camp	Cl.	Sh.	Cks.	BBC + HA Sh.	Total	Items	Wt. per unit	Wt. each Camp	Loads at each Camp	Acc. Wt.	Acc. Loads
5	4	–	–	–	4	6 btls oxygen	12	72			
						4 man-days ff	4	16			
						Film bats		10			
								98	3 × 30	98	3 × 30
4	2	6	–	–	8	1 btl. oxygen	12	12			
						8 man-days ff*	4	32			
								44	–	142	8 × 30
2	7	28	2	8	45	45 day ff	5	225			
						1 load film		35			
								260	8 × 35	402	12 × 35
1	2	12		2	16	16 man-day ff	5	80	2 + × 35	482	14 × 35
Base	4 + 2	14	10	2	32						

*BBC team responsible for getting film up to Camp 4 from 2 with their 4 HA Sherpas.

ACKNOWLEDGEMENT TO SUPPLIERS

We were able to organise the expedition with the help of a very small administrative staff, thanks to the hard work of the secretaries of the organisers, many of whom carried out the work in addition to their normal jobs without any extra pay, and also to a high level of automation in my own small office.

Organisation in Nepal *by Mike Cheney*

In organising the expedition arrangements in Nepal I was helped by Lt Col. Jimmy Roberts, owner of our trekking and mountaineering agency, Mountain Travel, and also by my own very experienced staff at Mountain Travel, Mr Dawa Norbu Sherpa of the Sherpa Co-operative Trekking (P) Ltd and Sirdar Pertemba Sherpa.

My five main tasks were to obtain import licences for the expedition equipment and stores, and liaise with the various Nepalese government departments; to meet the expedition's two trucks on arrival at the border and clear them through Customs; to have all the stores and equipment flown to Luglha and stored safely in Khumde before the monsoon; to recruit the Sherpa team of eighty high-altitude and Icefall porters; and to make all the arrangements for the approach march.

As well as the import licences, special government permits had to be obtained to operate wireless sets from Base Camp to Namche Bazar, as well as on the mountain. The expedition was the first to make full use of the Nepal Meteorological Service for weather forecasts, instead of getting forecasts from India. Weather reports were received daily at 5 p.m. for the following twenty-four hours together with the outlook for the day after. The weather reports were sent by wireless from Kathmandu to the Syangboche Meteorological Station, from Syangboche the reports were relayed to Base Camp on the expedition's own radio, installed at the Namche Bazar Police Post. To assist the Meteorological Department reports on the weather at Base Camp were sent to Kathmandu by wireless twice a day at 8 a.m. and 12 noon.

RECRUITMENT OF SHERPA TEAM

As early as July 1974 Chris Bonington was anxious to have Pertemba as sirdar for the expedition: Pertemba was not so sure he wanted the job at that point, but agreed in principle.

In December 1974 selection of the Sherpa team started in all seriousness. Colonel Roberts and I selected a hard core from Mountain Travel staff Sherpas, Ang Phu as assistant to Pertemba, Lhakpa Thondup as Base Camp sirdar, Purna Sherpa, my personal cook-bearer for sixteen years, as Base Camp cook, together with some twelve regular Mountain Travel employees as high-altitude porters, Icefall porters and Base Camp/Camp 2 staff. Phurkipa was selected for Icefall sirdar, an older man with more experience of the Icefall than any other Sherpa or climber.

Between December 1974 and July 1975 the lists for thirty-four high-altitude porters and twenty-six Icefall porters were completed from the many volunteers.

There were many young Sherpas from villages outside Khumbu anxious to join the expedition, also Tamangs, usually employed as low-altitude porters, who were anxious to prove that they were as good as Sherpas as high-altitude porters. The final selection of the high-altitude porter team rested with Pertemba and Ang Phu. The final team selected reflected the combination of experience, strength of character and youthfulness of Sirdar Pertemba who used his authority in the matter of selection to very good effect. His team was a good mix of experienced men from previous South West Face expeditions, experienced young Icefall porters, nearly all in their twenties, being given a chance to go high for the first time, and a few keen young men on their first expedition. Similarly the Icefall team consisted of approximately half old hands, some selected on arrival in Khumbu in August, and half keen young men who had failed to make the high-altitude team.

The Base Camp staff, cooks and kitchen boys who would remain at Base Camp or Camp 2, were selected by Purna and Lhakpa Thondup. The mail-runners, also, were a combination of youth and keenness and past experience. The express mail team were two youngsters, one Sherpa, Tendi, and one Tamang, Damai Singh Lama. Their best time was eighteen days from Base Camp to Kathmandu and back to Base Camp – sixteen days actually on the move for the approximately 240-mile round journey.

After the expedition Sherpa team had been largely completed the BBC film team came up in May 1975 with a requirement of their own. They wanted a Sherpa team of eight, two of whom were to be high-altitude porters to go above Camp 2, and during the approach march they wished to be semi-independent, able to camp separately, if necessary. Jagatman Lama, a Tamang, was selected as their sirdar and another Tamang, Saila, was a camera porter. Saila had worked with Ned Kelly as a camera porter on previous filming projects in Nepal.

The total Sherpa team of eighty-two was completed by the inclusion of two Gurkha serving soldiers as signalmen to operate the main Squadcal radios between Base Camp and Namche Bazar. The two men selected by HQ Brigade of Gurkhas for service with the expedition were Cpl Prembahadur Thapa 6GR and L/C Jaikumar Rai 7GR. L/C Jaikumar had served with the Army Nuptse expedition in the spring of 1975 and both men were to go with the Army Everest expedition in the spring of 1976.

We had hoped to employ more Tamangs in the team, but this went against the grain with the Sherpas, on the grounds that Tamangs were unproven as high-altitude and Icefall porters and there were plenty of proven Sherpas available, especially as the expedition was the only one in the Khumbu area at the time. Four Tamangs were, in fact, employed by the expedition and worked in perfect harmony with the Sherpas.

In accordance with Nepalese regulations, our Sherpas and Liaison Officer were insured. Cover was obtained in the UK. In addition, due to the very large sum (£6000) to be paid in compensation on the death of any Sherpa killed during the expedition, I introduced for the first time a Form of Will to be completed by all Sherpas employed by the expedition so that the compensation payable on their death should go to relatives of their own choice. The Will Form was prepared by Messrs Robson and Morrow Auditors to Mountain Travel and was accepted as an authorised legal document by the Solicitor General of the Government of Nepal.

Transport *by Ronnie Richards and Bob Stoodley*

When it became evident in November 1974 that the expedition gear was going to need to be transported overland to Kathmandu, the Transport Section was soon immersed in what was almost an expedition of its own. Bob Stoodley, who is chairman of Manchester Garages, was able to enlist the assistance of Diana Lister in dealing with many hundreds of letters and documents required. It is comparatively straightforward to obtain a cheap lorry or van and just set out with fairly minimal preparations, as is done by many small expeditions. To transport over 20 tons introduces complications, however.

Bob had first of all to identify and obtain suitable vehicles. A camel train of small trucks seemed extravagant where two elephantine ones would suffice, but these would then require drivers of professional standard. One truck would come straight back empty, while the other would stay in Kathmandu and bring back gear at the end of the expedition. We were fortunate that Cecil Redfern, chairman of Godfrey Davis, agreed to make two 16-ton Ford D 1614 lorries available on very generous terms for hire somewhat outside their customary area. The lorries each had a separate 1700 cu. ft van container capable of carrying 10 tons and were adapted for the journey by Manchester Garages. A sleeper cab, complete with cupboards, light and signal to the driver below was built on top of each driving cab so that we could sleep while on the move and drive fairly continuously. Side lockers were constructed below the container chassis to store food, spares, tools and anything needed for the journey. Extra fuel tanks, a tow bar and other refinements were also added. Total cargo volume was about 2200 cu. ft per lorry.

Three experienced and qualified HGV drivers were then contacted who were willing and able to tackle this sort of journey. Allen Evans and John O'Neill were lorry drivers for a subsidiary of Manchester Garages, had been in the Army together and had travelled overseas. Alan Riley originally came from Kenya, knew Mike Cheney and was contemplating starting an overland trucking service to Nepal. Our trip would be a useful reconnaissance. (On seeing the problems facing a commercial operation further east, particularly crossing India, the idea was shelved.) Ronnie Richards was also part of the overland team as navigator and occasional driver, since he had done the journey before and would then help with the further transport of gear in Nepal. Bob Stoodley's experience in maintaining as well as driving large vehicles filled the crucial role of mechanic.

The other main problem was documentation to cover both vehicles and their contents. We would be carrying a large quantity and high value of goods and all the tedious paper work would have to be in order for each of the twenty-two Customs posts crossed and up to the strict commercial requirements. Expeditions carrying a fraction of our cargo have been known to experience delays or difficulties at some frontier through inadequate documentation. On our scale we seemed unlikely to get through by the usual ploy of waving an expedition leaflet and making impromptu explanations.

In addition to standard considerations of insurance and visas, countries en route require assurance that vehicles and valuable goods in transit are not going to be sold or offloaded and this is given in the form of bank guarantees or deposits. Vehicle carnets are a familiar requirement for many countries and easily obtainable from the AA. For the journey out we decided to follow the example of most international lorry traffic and registered as a haulage company with the Freight Haulage Association so that we could use the TIR system. Basically this is an arrangement where a company can lodge a single guarantee with a central organisation in Geneva who issue via local agents certificates of approval for vehicles and a contents carnet which must be completed and then endorsed by Customs. The one set of documents is valid across Europe, Turkey and Iran. For the return journey we would only have a small cargo of little value and could bumble back in a less professional expedition fashion.

As we were operating to a tight time schedule, we also contacted foreign embassies in London and British embassies abroad in countries where border delays were probable or uncertainties prevailed. Letters of introduction were often valuable and some borders had even been given advance notice which accelerated our clearance considerably. A few days at least were probably saved by these efforts, since there were the inevitable officials who otherwise made difficulties over minor regulations or discrepancies. Our deadline departure date of 9 April put pressure on Dave Clarke getting equipment together in time, but it was the latest we could delay in order to reach Kathmandu by early May and then secure enough flights to the Khumbu so that everything could be stored in Khumde before the monsoon came.

Weeks of work were compressed into a few intense days in Leeds before departure. All the oxygen and equipment had to be packed into hundreds of boxes and comprehensively listed; lorries had to be carefully loaded and detailed manifests compiled with dozens of copies. A final task, classifying and coding each of our hundreds of items for government export statistics was waived at the last moment, although we did register items which might be re-imported.

JOURNEY DATA

MILEAGE		FRONTIERS AND SOME MAIN TOWNS	NIGHT STOPS
CUMULATIVE	STAGE	ON ROUTE	
		LONDON	Dep. 9 April
	73	UK – Belgium	
		Zeebrugge	
	158	Belgium/Germany	
	405	Munich (via Brussels, Nürnberg)	
	79	Germany/Austria	10/11 April
	191	Graz (via Radstadt)	
	31	Austria/Yugoslavia	
	324	Belgrade	
	212	Yugoslavia/Bulgaria	
	38	Sofia	
	201	Bulgaria/Turkey	
	159	Istanbul	
2153	282	Ankara	14/15 April
	278	Sivas	
	285	Erzurum	
	201	Turkey/Iran	
	189	Tabriz	
3514	408	Tehran	18/20 April
	626	Mashhad (via Sari)	
	150	Iran/Afghanistan	21/22 April
	83	Herat	22/23 April
	350	Kandahar	
5041	318	Kabul	
	155	Afghanistan/Pakistan	24/25 April
	139	Rawalpindi	
	171	Lahore	
	17	Pakistan/India	
5820	297	Delhi	27/28 April
	304	Kanpur (via Agra)	
	197	Benares	
	390	Raxaul (India)/Birganj (Nepal)	1/2 May
6835	124	KATHMANDU	Arr. 3 May

Notes:

1. The lorries covered a total of 6996 miles due to various detours.
2. Three of the indicated night stops were scheduled, the other five were incurred at frontiers. About fifty hours were actually spent waiting for Customs formalities to be settled.
3. On the return journey, the shorter and easier route via Gorakhpur (208m to Kanpur) was taken and this now links up with both main Nepalese entry points. The road via Nautanwa/Bhairawa and Pokhara (Gorakhpur–Kathmandu 292m) was less difficult but Import clearance and collection of deposits had to be done at Birganj (Gorakhpur–Kathmandu over new Gandak bridge 261m).
4. The empty lorry returning in May took only 19 days to cover the 6624 miles. In November the partially filled lorry took 27 days, due to border delays.
5. Our 6.2 litre lorries each averaged 9.5 mpg and a fuel cost of 3p/mile. Diesel fuel costs ranged from 70p/gallon in Germany to 6p/gallon in Iran!

Equipment *by Dave Clarke*

The reader who has reached this point in the book should already know the story of how and why we attempted to climb Everest the Hard Way. This appendix is therefore directed firstly to those who would like to know just what equipment is necessary to climb on the highest mountain in the world and secondly to those who would like to benefit from my involvement in order to organise equipment for their own expeditions in the future. For readers in the first category I hope the following few pages of tables and notes will give you all the information you require, and for the second category I should start off by advising you, very firmly, not to say yes if you should ever be asked to organise equipment for an Everest expedition! But for those who, like me, find the lure irresistible, let me add that you will need a very sympathetic set of friends, family and firm to help you through the months of preparation and winding up as well as the actual climb. I was lucky to have all three and would like to thank them for making my involvement possible.

I was also very grateful to have from the beginning, the list of gear prepared by Graham Tiso who was responsible for the equipment on the 1972 trip. There were also in the 1975 team, six climbers who had been on Everest before and they were only too willing to pass on to me their experience and advice. Everest is no place to try out new ideas and equipment development rather than innovation is the only way to secure maximum performance which can be relied on. Despite the formidable financial backing Chris had organised with Barclays Bank, we still needed a great deal of support from manufacturers and suppliers both in cash form and also in design time. Most important from my point of view was to secure help from those firms who were prepared to spend time in producing equipment to our design specifications. The trade did respond very generously to the challenge and I can only hope that materials and techniques developed during the manufacture of our equipment will benefit the general climber in much the same way that rally testing results in safer motoring for the general public. We spent almost four months developing equipment and two months manufacturing the finished results before delivering to our packing centre in Leeds. The accumulated twenty-four tons of equipment and food were listed and packed into well over a thousand boxes before loading into the two sixteen-ton trucks which were to take them overland to Kathmandu.

Chris had gambled that by going earlier in the year we would enjoy better weather than on his previous expedition and that by using a larger team our build-up time would also be improved. His forecast was right, with the result that equipment designed for the worst conditions was never subjected to really extreme weather. Put simply, this meant that in the event we were over-equipped but this proved to be a big physical and psychological advantage. It meant that at all times climbers could choose a clothing combination best suited to their own temperament or temperature needs and the resulting comfort meant maximum performance.

It must be obvious that our climbing success was due, not only to our own efforts but also to the accumulated experience of all previous climbs on the mountain and in the same way the successful performance of our equipment would not have been possible without the knowledge gained on those attempts. One can only hope therefore that, by recording the details of our own equipment and experiences, these will in turn serve future expeditions to climb more safely and efficiently in the high mountains of the world.

SCALE OF ISSUE

It might seem, to the non-climber, that all members of an expedition should be issued with the same clothing and equipment but there are two main reasons why this is not so. One purely physical and the other largely political.

When the expedition is fully deployed on the mountain, porters and climbers operate all the way from the relatively sheltered small town that is Base Camp up to the unbelievably exposed and vulnerable Camp 6 and the equipment they require is correspondingly varied. The political reason for varying the equipment is due to the fact that over the years the clothing issue to porters has become a very real part of the bargain struck when they agree to join the team. When the issue is first made it is quite a tense time as they inspect clothing, first to assess its resale value at the end of the trip and only secondly, I suspect, to see whether it is capable of keeping them warm on the mountain. So one has to establish an accurate social pecking order and here, as I was such a novice in Sherpa affairs, we were fortunate to have as our Base Camp organiser Mike Cheney who lives and works in Nepal. He was able to point out the subtle differences between say a mail-runner employed by the BBC team and the runners working for the expedition proper. Altogether we had fourteen different classifications and the following table shows our eventual distribution. The issue was made in Khumde, four days' march from Base Camp and it needed four days to complete. So near their own homes it was very tempting for a Sherpa to take brand new equipment away and store it in his house, so as to sell it unused later on. We were concerned that all members should be clothed as well and as warmly as possible and asked Pertemba, the Sherpa sirdar, to address all the assembled team before we finally left for the climb to impress on them that we expected to see all the clothing on the mountain on their backs, not in their rucksacks.

In addition to the 24 tons of equipment and food sent out by trucks from England in the spring, Mike Cheney in Kathmandu had gathered together a fair amount of cooking gear, fuel and tentage as well as a good deal of fresh food for the walk in and for Base Camp. So the final weight we had to handle was almost 30 tons and the approximate breakdown is shown below.

Personal Equipment	4.00 tons
Climbing Equipment	1.00
Tentage Equipment	2.00
Cooking Equipment	0.75
Miscellaneous	1.50
Fuel	2.00
Oxygen and Packing	1.50
Food and Packing	13.00
General Packing and Plastic	3.00

Well over a thousand boxes were packed and weighed and their contents recorded with values in three currencies before loading into the two trucks at Leeds before Customs officials sealed them and released them for the 7000 mile trip to Nepal. Life for me was governed by endless lists and those which follow summarise the work we had put into the design and preparation of our equipment. They also record the suppliers without whose help and support the whole thing would have been impossible.

All the food as it was so vulnerable was packed by professionals and only sent to Leeds for final loading into the trucks but the equipment was packed by a few of the expedition team and a great number of Boy Scouts who gave a lot of their time voluntarily and cheerfully. We owe them a great deal, and I'd like to thank John Jeffrey and his friends in the 19th NW Leeds troop and Andrew Carter, together with all the members of his troop. As volume was as critical as weight for the overland journey, we are also grateful to the RAF, Carlisle, for vacuum packing all our bulky down equipment and foam mattresses.

PERSONAL EQUIPMENT

The complete equipment issue to climbers and high-altitude Sherpas was intended to cover all requirements on the expedition. This ranged from the waterproof clothing and boots needed for the walk in, which was made in full monsoon conditions, to the five layer protective system designed to cope with the extremes of wind and cold which we expected on the face later on in the expedition. The first layer of this system was an excellent two-piece silk undersuit. It was very light and although it was only envisaged as a cold-weather garment, we soon found that it provided first-class protection from the burning sun during the day. Although there were no gloves with the suit, socks and balaclavas in the same material were used. The socks were not very popular and climbers seemed to prefer the more familiar feel of wool but the balaclavas were universally popular either on their own or as an underhood to the brushed wool variety used by climbers the world over.

The second layer was a suit in thermolactyl fibre, better known by the name of the manufacturer, Damart Thermawear. Although the 'double force' material from which our suits were made is normally only available in white, a special batch of navy suits were made for us and balaclavas and gloves from the same material. It was not possible to spend time altering the basic design of the hood which was far from perfect. This was a great pity as I feel sure the relatively windproof material could well have been better than the more open weave of the wool version. Without doubt, however, the gloves made from 'double force' were excellent and all climbers preferred them to the silk gloves normally used as inners to wool or fibrepile overmitts. Especially useful when handling cameras and karabiners, they were also quite adequate when jumaring in all but the coldest conditions. Each climber had three pairs and this proved more than adequate as the material did not wear out as fast as we had feared.

On top of the Damart suit we used a Polyester fibre pile suit made up to our design by Javlin, from material supplied by Glenoit in Leeds. Following a design originally used by an Army expedition, improvements were made to the general shaping as well as collar design and the size and placing of four pockets on the front opening jacket. A full-length fly zip reaching to the back waistband was inserted in the trousers to ensure that nature's demands could be adequately met. Sherpa climbers who expected to be issued with a duvet only were initially doubtful about this material which they had not seen before. It soon became something of a uniform when they discovered how warm and comfortable the jackets were and the only complaints were from photographers who despaired of the overwhelming orange colour presented to the cameras.

The fourth and last layer of insulation was the one-piece down suit developed over several expeditions from the original designed by Don Whillans in the sixties. All the suits were made to measure by Mountain Equipment, who were responsible for all the down gear on the expedition and are arguably the best down equipment manufacturers in the world. Pete Hutchinson worked very hard to meet our requirements and the down suits were filled with twenty-five per cent more down than normal. New pocket flaps were designed and pockets were carefully placed to avoid the climbing harnesses. The legs of the suit were filled differentially to make walking easier and a complicated system of Velcro and zip closures worked out to ensure maximum versatility. The suit shell is 2oz ripstop nylon which feels very fragile but suffered no damage on the climb. In such a case, however, the material is very easily repaired with the self-adhesive repair strips we took with us.

As the final layer, an outer windsuit is essential; this protects the more vulnerable down suit from crampons and general abrasion as well as preventing the wind carrying away valuable heat held in the four layers of insulating clothing. In effect a sophisticated boiler suit, our one-piece outer windsuits were made with a 2oz ripstop nylon outer shell and lined with a medium-weight Ventile. As the climb went so quickly and the weather remained relatively warm, three or four of the climbers removed the Ventile lining, prepared to accept the loss of warmth and increase in condensation because of the weight saving and a possible improvement in ease of movement. In the event this proved a good move but had the climb gone on into October, as expected, the double suit would have been invaluable.

All high-altitude Sherpas, although equipped to the same general standard as the climbers, prefer two-piece rather than the one-piece suits issued to the team. This is largely due to the fact that separate jacket and trousers have a better resale value when the expedition is over, but in the better weather we experienced on the trip, they were probably more versatile than the single oversuit. Mountain Equipment Snowline duvet, breeches and down boots were standard issue for them and the Ventile oversuits made by Harrison's were front opening, self-lined jackets with single, one-size overtrousers. These commercially available suits made to an American specification have an unusually generous hood with wired visor and could not be faulted for design or performance.

Single Snowline sleeping bags were issued to Base Camp personnel and Icefall Sherpas but all expedition members above Camp 2 were given double sleeping bags. The standard Everest bag from Mountain Equipment was lengthened and widened to accommodate an inner mummy bag and a climber in down clothing. The inner was not cut differentially but was made intentionally over size so that the excess material would fill up the air pockets normally left round a sleeping body. In practice nobody needed to sleep in a down suit as the double bag easily coped with the minimum recorded temperature of −30°C. As all oversuits had attached hoods, very little extra protection was needed for the head and the silk or wool balaclavas were quite adequate for the job. For finer weather, or photographic requirements or merely to satisfy nationalistic fervour, all climbers were issued with a Union Jack wool hat.

At the other extremity, feet require far more protection and altogether six items of footwear were needed to meet the varied needs of the expedition climbers.

We used a standard pair of training shoes for camp and some excellent flexible boots from Hawkins, called Astronaut Hikers, for the actual walk in. These boots have a good leather upper and a very light cellular sole with a standard Vibram pattern. We all found them very comfortable and there was very little blistering. Our feet stayed remarkably dry even though we were walking a lot of the time along paths which were two or three inches deep in monsoon rain.

On the mountain all the expedition members were supplied with sheepskin boots as a general purpose camp boot and a pair of sheepskin socks for use in tents or inside specially developed Neoprene overboots. Icefall Sherpas were given a variety of alpine standard single climbing boots, but climbers and high-altitude Sherpas were all supplied with the Galibier double boot model called Makalu. We had considered three other types, some of which were considerably cheaper, but over the years the French boot had been used successfully by almost all of the team and in the end it was universally accepted to be the only boot we could really risk.

The boot is normally supplied with one pair of felt and one pair of fur inners, but the felt alternative is not adequate for Everest conditions, whereas the two pairs of fur inner boots are ideal.

To act as a combined gaiter and outer insulating layer we developed a 5mm Neoprene overboot which had a smooth nylon outer skin and nylon towelling inner. The boot was like a giant front opening sock and was stretched over the double boot. The sole gave insulation under the boot and despite our fears that the material was not strong enough, no collapses occurred and holes made by crampon spikes could be quickly and easily repaired. We added a non-slip sole to some of these overboots as we thought extra reinforcing would be necessary when walking round camp or to prevent the bars of crampons tearing through the material. This was not necessary, but an added sophistication which would have been worthwhile was the addition of a snowproof closure at the top of the boot and this is now incorporated in the latest development model.

Standard pattern 8oz gaiters were issued to Sherpas working in Base Camp and the Icefall but a nylon Karrimor overboot, insulated with 3mm closed cell foam was given to high-altitude Sherpas. These proved too stiff and awkward to wear with crampons and eventually spare Neoprene overboots intended as reserves for the climbing team had to be issued in their place.

Hands also require a number of differing mitts to cope with the very varied conditions experienced throughout the trip. The basic high-altitude provision for climbers and Sherpas alike was split between the classic Dachstein wool mitts and a specially developed fibre pile gauntlet. The Dachsteins were, predictably, very good but some interesting alternatives from Allan Austin in Bradford and Millar in London were equally acceptable and with further development could be even better. The fibre pile gauntlets were lined with the same Glenoit material used in our undersuits and covered with a nylon outer. A 4oz, bright orange nylon front (for strength) was reinforced with leather and the back was made from 2oz material. The long gauntlet was elasticated and wide enough to fit snugly over the padded arm of the down suit. The silk or Damart inners already mentioned were used in conjunction with the overmitts.

Finally a number of industrial insulated leather working gloves, normally used by cold storage operators, were given to the Base Camp personnel. They were very much appreciated when handling boxes, yaks or moving stones to build tent platforms.

Jeans were given to all Sherpas and although a lot of them were worn on the expedition the issue is really considered to be part of their wages for use afterwards and as a result the preferred styling owed more to fashion than function.

Except for the highly successful special lettered 'Everest Expedition' T-shirts and matching hats given to the Sherpa team, the remaining clothing was all basically the 'wool wear'.

Almost 500 pairs of long stockings from different sources were distributed but a particular mention could be made of the all-wool specials made up for the climbers by Star Sportswear in Wakefield, as they were quite luxurious.

A wide variety of sweaters were used, ranging from some hard wearing, heavy-weight Guernseys to the superlightweight Shetlands and Merino sweaters worn mainly as underwear on the mountain but also as smart casuals at the post-expedition receptions.

Some very good Viyella shirts, made by King's of Maidstone, proved long enough and warm enough to satisfy our climbing specifications even though they were originally designed for sailors, and as they wore extremely well there seems no doubt that they will survive many more expeditions in the future.

Two final pieces of clothing originally intended for the Icefall Sherpas only, complete the softwear provision on the expedition. The first was a really luxurious padded two-piece suit made for us by Tenson in Sweden. Using an already well proven thigh-length jacket as the starting point, we designed a pair of matching bib and brace overtrousers to complete the suit. Delighted with the result, Tenson generously supplied the climbing team as well as the twenty-six Icefall Sherpas and although, as intended, the suits were never really used above Camp 1 by the Sherpas, several climbers took the overtrousers to Camp 2. The second item was breeches and we had three quite different styles and materials on the trip. Breeches for the Icefall Sherpas were made from a tweed by Craghoppers in Hebden Bridge and their reputation for warmth and strength was once more demonstrated. Harris Meyer in Leeds had provided some very smart made-to-measure breeches in ski-pant material for the climbers and they, although professing a reluctance to wear such elegant attire on an actual climb, were impressed with the warmth and snow shedding properties of the material.

For the walk in, Hoyle's, who are another Hebden Bridge manufacturing concern, supplied special lightweight moleskin breeches for the team. The cut and material made them very popular and they were worn a lot in the early part of the expedition.

Good protection from wind and cold is essential on Everest but complete protection for eyes is vital and we were very lucky to obtain the support of the French firm Bollé through their British organisation. The firm had spent a lot of time developing a complete range of glasses and goggles for the recent Chamonix Guides expedition to Everest and we were able to take advantage of their experience when deciding on our requirements. All climbers and high-altitude Sherpas were issued with four pairs of large goggles each fitted with two colours of non-mist lenses as well as two pairs of mirror lens, high-altitude glasses. Hundreds of another smaller goggle were taken for Base Camp personnel, mail-runners and Icefall Sherpas but this was false economy. Small goggles restrict vision and, more importantly, suffer greatly from condensation and we should have provided the bigger no mist goggles to all personnel, even though they were more expensive.

Technically the climbing on Everest is not of a high standard but even using fixed ropes requires a certain amount of hardwear and each of the face team were issued with a pair of jumars as well as a Whillans climbing harness from Troll with a slightly narrower crutch strap. This recommendation came from the 1972 expedition as several members on that trip had suffered soreness where the wider strap compressed all the down in the oversuits to a lumpy abrasion.

Each harness was provided with holsters which were used or rejected according to personal prejudices. Sherpas were issued with standard, fairly long ash-shafted Stubai axes and climbers were asked to bring their own particular preferences as the only issue was a terrordactyl hammer which we thought might be an appropriate tool in the Icefall. Everyone on the expedition was supplied with a pair of the new Clog adjustable crampons but because they were new, all the climbing team insisted on taking Salewa adjustables as well. Reaction to the Clog crampon varied from initial outspoken criticism, to an easy acceptance of the new model, felt to be as good as the better known German lightweight. On the mountain most of the trouble in fact came at the fitting stage rather than in use, although in many cases the Neoprene retaining straps cracked after only very short usage.

Everything on an Everest trip, once Kathmandu has been left behind, is carried on backs and consequently we spent a lot of thought trying to design the best but simplest range of rucksacks which would meet all our load-carrying requirements.

Most people, on the walk in, carried light loads in a Karrimor Lofoten which is a medium-size frameless rucksack intended for use in the Icefall later on. Sherpa load-carriers were given a specially strengthened non-welded pack-frame, the Euro-trekker, with carrying belt and a sack with no frills, pockets or zips. The high-altitude climbers were supplied with a light-welded orienteer pack-frame complete with modified Randonneur sack to accommodate three oxygen cylinders in locating tubes and a pocket for the demand valve of the oxygen breathing set. Top lid pockets were all deepened so that cameras and accessories could easily be accommodated, and all zips everywhere were fitted with giant tape pullers so that pockets could still be opened even when wearing heavy mitts. We had very little trouble with the hundred and fifty rucksacks which were all provided by Karrimor.

A small addition to our carrying capacity was possible due to the stuff bags provided. These were made in nylon, once again by Karrimor, and were like miniature kit bags, just large enough to hold a sleeping bag or duvet. Small but vital items of equipment like water bottles, lighters, Swiss pocket knives, whistles and plastic insoles were distributed as well as a few housewives. Originally the source of a great deal of ribald expectation, the name housewife is one given to any small collection of useful repair materials such as needle and thread, buttons and string.

For the walk in, rain or sun, an umbrella is an essential luxury and the same might be said of a plastic pee bottle which can make all the difference to climbers in need in a stormbound face box.

Two other items to comfort the walker during the approach march are a plentiful supply of paper underwear and a sponge mattress. Not everybody agrees about the first, but all would about the second and despite the difficulty in keeping them dry, good thick sponge mattresses are very welcome in the early part of any expedition.

Early morning starts are never ever enjoyable but they are not even possible without good illumination and we were provided with a range of very good torches from Saft. Small disposable pocket torches were probably the most useful and we should have taken more. Six big hand lanterns were issued to the cook and hospital tents, as well as headlamps to each climber. The Saft headlamp gave an excellent light but was rather heavy and the switch mechanism could be turned on accidentally in a rucksack. We used Saft high-power batteries in all these lights, although we were using Mallory batteries in radios and tape recorders.

It was felt politically desirable to issue Sherpas working in the Icefall with a crash helmet and we had taken a limited number of Galibier lightweights for that reason. In fact the main danger of the Icefall, collapsing séracs, can hardly be countered with a crash helmet no matter how good and a much more appropriate place to use them is on the face itself. Here small but fast moving pieces of ice and stone are continually falling, putting climbers in danger and it is always wise to use head protection, preferably lightweight, and the Galibier model was ideal for our needs.

To provide all the expedition members with a watch each may seem something of a perk, but in order to successfully co-ordinate the movements of 100 men and 10 tons of equipment on the mountain, it is essential to use a system of radio calls to relay instructions. Obviously these calls have to be made at pre-arranged times and it is essential, if the programme is to work, that the radio exchanges are on time. The fact that climbers and Sherpas alike all have a synchronised watch is very desirable and in our case was only made possible by ACC Swiss Time who provided a range of Certina watches to match the relative needs of all the team.

SCALE OF ISSUE		Climbers and four man BBC TV team	Expedition and BBC high-altitude Sherpas	Camp 2 cooks	Base Camp staff	Expedition and BBC Icefall Sherpas	Mail-runners	Base Camp cook-boys	Signallers	Sunday Times Correspondent
	DESCRIPTION	22	39	2	3	29	4	4	2	1
1	Windsuits	1								
2	Ventile oversuit		1	1	1					
3	Nylon oversuit	1			1	1	1	1	1	1
4	Down suit	1								1
5	Duvet and down trousers		1	1	1			1		
6	Double sleeping bags	1	1	1	1					1
7	Single sleeping bag					1	1	1	1	
8	Down socks	1	1	1	1			1		1
9	Nylon pile suits	1	1	1	1	1	1	1	1	1

10	Tenson-padded suit	1				1				
11	Overmitts and gloves	4	2	2	2	2	1	1	1	2
12	Inner gloves	3	1	1						1
13	Breeches	2				1		1		
14	Damart undersuits	1	1	1	1	1	1	1	1	1
15	Silk undersuits	1								
16	Jeans	1	1	1	1		1	1	1	1
17	Sweaters – heavyweight	1	1	1	1	1		1		1
18	Sweaters – lightweight	1	1	1	1				1	1
19	Wool undersuit	1								
20	Viyella shirt	1	1	1	1					1
21	Balaclava	3	2	2	2	1	1	1	1	2
22	Stockings	4	4	4	4	3	2	2	2	2
23	Double boots	1	1	1						1
24	Single boots				1	1	1	1	1	
25	Walking boots	2	1	1	1					2
26	Sheepskin boots	1	1	1	1			1	1	1
27	Gaiters	1	1	1	1	1				1
28	Nylon overboots		1	1	1			1	1	1
29	Neoprene overboots	1								
30	Goggles	6	4	3	3	3	1	1	1	4
31	Sunglasses	3	2	1	1	1		1	1	2
32	Stuff bags	3	2	2	2	1				2
33	Pack-frames	1	1	1	1	1	1	1	1	1
34	Pack sacks	1	1	1	1	1	1	1	1	1
35	Ice axes		1	1		1				1
36	Crampons	2	1	1		1				1
37	Climbing harness	1	1							1
38	Jumars	1	1							
39	Headlamp	1	1	1						
40	Water bottle	1	1	1	1	1			1	1
41	Wristwatch	1								
42	Wristwatch		1	1	1					
43	Wristwatch					1		1		
44	Gas lighter	2	1	2	2	1		2		1
45	Pocket knife	1	1	1	1					
46	Housewife	1								
47	Umbrellas	1								
48	Paper underwear	4								4
49	Pee bottle	1	1	1						
50	Whistle	1	1	1	1					1
51	Expedition T-shirt		1	1	1	1	1	1	1	

52	Climbing helmet		1			1				
53	Hand torches	2	1	2	2	1		1	1	1
54	Frameless rucksack	1								1
55	Insoles	1								1
56	Sponge mattress	1	1	1	1	1		1	1	1
57	Sheepskin socks	1								

Note: In addition equipment was issued to the five drivers who drove our two lorries overland to Kathmandu.

CLIMBING EQUIPMENT

The first time most of us saw all the expedition equipment assembled in one place was at the Sherpa village of Khumde just before it was issued to all the team members. It looked an enormous amount, but completely lost amongst the boxes of down gear, food, and fuel, the actual climbing gear – the hardware that is – looked such a small heap I wondered whether I had made a mistake and forgotten some vital equipment. In fact I had everything we needed, but the fact is on a non-technical climb like the South West Face the only things needed in real quantities are rope, ladders, oxygen and effort.

As weight, in logistical terms, is the key factor controlling the speed of our build-up the attraction of Polypropylene ropes was obvious. Ropes in this material are only two-thirds of the weight of nylon ropes, strength for strength, and we spent a lot of time discussing this and other advantages of the rope before we decided that its big drawback – rapid deterioration under ultraviolet radiation – was too big a risk to take. We had to provide rope to cover three areas of activity – the fixed ropes and safety line in the Icefall; fixed ropes on the face; and climbing ropes for teams operating in either situation. All the climbing and fixed ropes on the face were provided by Bridon Fibres and all fixed rope in the Icefall was specially made for us only a couple of days before we left by a Leeds ropeworks – Synthetic Ropes and Cordage.

Climbing rope: 9mm Dynaflex provided in 90m lengths. This was cut in two and issued to all Icefall Sherpas who preferred to be roped together, usually three or four to a length, although a few ropes were reserved for climbers operating in the Rock Band. Normal climbing technique was to lead out on Polypropylene or Super Braidline, tying off to deadmen at intervals, leaving the resulting fixed rope for load-carrying Sherpas to follow using jumars.

8mm Super Braidline: This was a terylene rope with no weight, strength, or abrasion resistant advantages over nylon, but the one great difference is a comparative lack of stretch and as a fixed rope on the face it proved ideal. Carried to Camp 2 in 200m reels, it was cut into more manageable 50m lengths and fixed in that form.

7mm Dynaflex: In order to protect a possible retreat in bad weather across the exposed traverse above the Rock Band, we had always planned the provision of a fixed rope as far as possible across the Upper Snowfield from Camp 6. Although not as strong as the 8mm Braidline, this rope was considerably lighter – a point of great advantage at that altitude and very much appreciated by Doug Scott and Dougal Haston when they placed it on the day before their successful summit bid.

We also took limited quantities of 4mm Kernmantel rope as well as ⅝" and 1" tape to cut up into slings and tie-offs when required.

10mm Polypropylene: This was all pink and used only in the Icefall. The colour coding was very useful as Sherpas tend to use any rope that is handy but this obvious identification made it easy to make sure that ropes were only used in the appropriate situation. The rope was very light but not easy to knot, and a careful watch was necessary to make sure that anchorages and hand lines remained safe.

4mm Polypropylene: Made to the same specification as the rope used as handrails, lifelines and braces, the smaller diameter rope was used for tarpaulin ties, guy lines, pack-frame lashing and general security everywhere. Needless to say we didn't take nearly enough and double quantities would be nearer the mark.

For anchors in the snow to secure fixed ropes, tents or ladder bridges we took deadmen, snow stakes and ice pitons but as there was so much new soft snow on the mountain, only the deadmen were really useful and we soon used all our supplies. The snow stakes, which had been invaluable in the harder snow of Bonington's 1972 expedition, were useless in the normal position, so we taped and tied them together before burying them as emergency deadmen and they proved very successful in their modified role.

Although we often seemed short of karabiners, a purge in the camps and a keener look at the often extravagant methods of rope-fixing usually produced sufficient supplies to meet demands from the lead climbers at the front. A small selection of rock pegs was taken and a few used, but the bolt kits and avalanche probes, thankfully, were not.

We also provided snow-shoes and short touring skis in case it was ever necessary to make an emergency trip between Camps 1 and 2. Luckily this too was never necessary, although I had one or two short outings from Camp 1 just to enjoy the experience of skiing at that altitude. The snow saws were not used much, although I think more use could have been made of them. Sherpas cut snow blocks for melting, deepened the floor of the cook tent to give more headroom and a wall was made between store tents as a windbreak, but there was certainly more potential for their use.

Marker flags are essential in good and bad weather on a big route like Everest to ensure that Sherpas follow the selected route safely and we used 18" long luminous orange nylon flags tied off to 8' long bamboo canes bought in Nepal.

LADDERS, HEAT BOXES AND THE STRETCHER (by Hamish MacInnes)

The 6' aluminium alloy bolt-together ladder sections, as used on our 1972 expedition, were excellent. The only addition to the design was a suggestion to Dr Mathews, of Lyte Industries – who made them for us – to supply triangular plates which could bolt on to the ladder sections and enable further ladders to be attached at right angles. High tensile wire could be tensioned from the spanning ladder ends over the end of the ladder placed at right angles. The 'bridge' would then be slung with the 'stuck on' ladder underneath. This enabled us to span larger crevasses and, in practice, it worked well. I had made up also several handrails which were ostensibly ice-fall belay tubes (again, 1¼" aluminium alloy) with ⅞₆" holes at the bottom end. Long bolts, fixed through the ⅞₆" holes, and also through the tubular rungs of the ladder, made upright supports of these tubes. A handline could be attached to their tops to safeguard crossing.

Work on heat boxes was done both by me and by Leeds Polytechnic to produce a form of container inside which a small butane gas stove could operate with the minimum of heat loss. Various experiments were made with not very favourable results. Eventually, we made up several titanium boxes insulated with Ceramic Fibre, a highly efficient insulating material manufactured by Morgan Refactories Ltd. Although they were taken out to Everest with us it was not necessary to use them, thanks to the success of a propane/butane gas mixture.

A special compact lightweight stretcher was taken out for use on the expedition. It was a tubular, capsule type which I had developed for helicopter rescue work, but which also has mountain rescue application. It weighs 23 lbs and fits in a carrying bag which doubles when extended as a casualty bag, size: 3' 2" × 20" × 3". It has rucksack-type carrying straps with helicopter lift wires attached.

	CLIMBING EQUIPMENT DESCRIPTION	QUANTITIES
1	9mm climbing rope	2000m
2	8mm Super Braidline	4000m
3	7mm climbing rope	1000m
4	4mm tensile rope	500m
5	1" soft tape	300m
6	⅝" soft tape	150m
7	screwgate alloy karabiners	70
8	non-screw alloy karabiners	400
9	tubular snow stakes 30"	200
10	deadmen snow anchor	100
11	drive-in ice pitons	20
12	tubular ice pitons	75
13	standard ice pitons	75
14	rock pitons	100

15	bolt kits	2
16	snow-shoes	10
17	skis	12
18	aluminium ladder	60
19	marker flags	600
20	avalanche probes	10
21	snow saws	8
22	ski sticks	60
23	Polypropylene rope	3000m

TENTAGE: MACINNES BOXES (by Hamish MacInnes)

There is no better incentive for design than to suffer the shortcomings of poor equipment. During our post-monsoon attempt on the South West Face of Everest in 1972, we found that the tentage and boxes were inadequate for the conditions prevailing at that time of year. It was therefore with considerable determination that I tackled the problem of having boxes constructed which would give some degree of comfort in that inhospitable environment.

Initially, I thought of making up only two types: a large 'Super box' for use up to Camp 2, to accommodate three climbers in comfort in an inner vestibule, with a similar spacious floor area for equipment and cooking. The other box, now known as the MacInnes box, was specifically designed for the face: extremely strong and utilising, where necessary, a special built-in platform with legs capable of siting the box on a level plane, even on very steep slopes.

Due to the fact that the MacInnes boxes emerged in their final design as mini-fortresses it was deemed necessary to have a lightweight, easy to erect, 'Summit box' and so this last member of the Everest stable was created.

For both the super and MacInnes boxes, 1¼" o.d. fully heat-treated alcan aluminium alloy was used for the frames and pressed steel Clinch joints utilised as they are both strong and light. Tube sections were interconnected, using male and female sliding-fit joints, each end individually machined by expanding parallel reamer so that very close tolerances were achieved. Manufacture of the frames was carried out by J. & T. Lawrie of Clydebank. Both the super box and the MacInnes 2-man box use interchangeable 6' tube lengths but, in the case of the MacInnes box, these are in three 2' long interconnecting sections fitted with internal shock cord for rapid assembly. All other parts of the MacInnes boxes are similarly fitted with this elasticated cord to expedite erection in difficult situations and minimise the danger of losing individual tubes.

All internal fixed male tubes for pole connection were riveted with Tucker rivets, as were the Clinch joints. All boxes had high tensile wires supplied by British Ropes Ltd, criss-cross on roof and wall sections for stiffening frames, and stainless steel Gibb turnbuckles were used initially for tensioning them. Later, sections of rope

The MacInnes super box

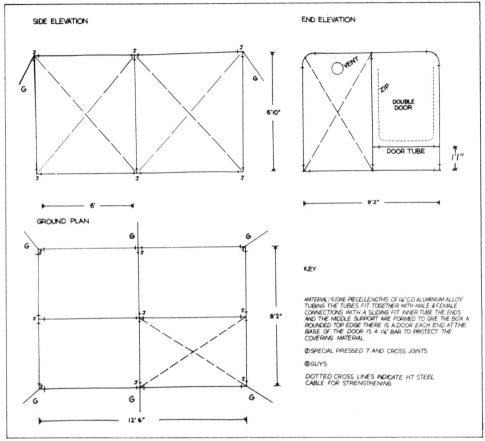

SIDE ELEVATION

END ELEVATION

6'10"

6'

GROUND PLAN

8'2"

12'6"

VENT

DOUBLE DOOR

ZIP

DOOR TUBE

1'1"

8'2"

KEY

MATERIAL: 6 (ONE PIECE) LENGTHS OF 1¼" O.D ALUMINIUM ALLOY TUBING THE TUBES FIT TOGETHER WITH MALE & FEMALE CONNECTIONS WITH A SLIDING FIT INNER TUBE THE ENDS AND THE MIDDLE SUPPORT ARE FORMED TO GIVE THE BOX A ROUNDED TOP EDGE THERE IS A DOOR EACH END AT THE BASE OF THE DOOR IS A 1¼" BAR TO PROTECT THE COVERING MATERIAL.

Ⓙ SPECIAL PRESSED T AND CROSS JOINTS

Ⓖ GUYS

DOTTED CROSS LINES INDICATE HT STEEL CABLE FOR STRENGTHENING

were used for securing the wires; nylon rope proved quite adequate for this, and on super boxes several coils of solid wire were used also, cut on site for the purpose. The completed super box weighs 124 lbs, including the inner vestibule.

To aid fitting the box covers, the frames are angled inwards; this also reduces wind resistance. Not only had the face boxes to be erected in difficult situations, they had also to be proof from falling stones, high winds and, to a limited degree, avalanche proof. On the 1972 expedition we had stones coming right through the walls of the boxes so, to prevent this happening again, I experimented using a titanium mesh as an outer covering for roof and rear wall. Due to the expense of titanium mesh, I tried aluminium Expamet instead. Later, after discussing the matter with an ICI representative, a 'bullet proof' cloth was finally selected; used in three layers, it proved excellent and easy to handle.

On my two previous expeditions to the South West Face, we had used separate platforms for the face boxes but this seemed unnecessary extra weight. I therefore consulted the British Aircraft Corporation and their Materials Design Section

The MacInnes face box

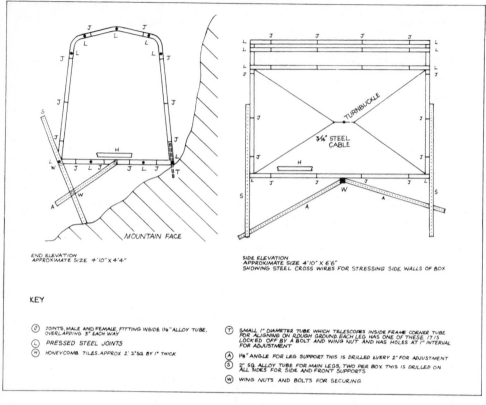

END ELEVATION
APPROXIMATE SIZE 4'10" X 4'4"

SIDE ELEVATION
APPROXIMATE SIZE 4'10" X 6'6"
SHOWING STEEL CROSS WIRES FOR STRESSING SIDE WALLS OF BOX

KEY

(J) JOINTS, MALE AND FEMALE, FITTING INSIDE 1½" ALLOY TUBE, OVERLAPPING 3" EACH WAY

(L) PRESSED STEEL JOINTS

(H) HONEYCOMB TILES. APPROX 2' 2"SQ BY 1" THICK

(T) SMALL 1" DIAMETER TUBE WHICH TELESCOPES INSIDE FRAME CORNER TUBE FOR ALIGNING ON ROUGH GROUND. EACH LEG HAS ONE OF THESE. IT IS LOCKED OFF BY A BOLT AND WING NUT AND HAS HOLES AT 1" INTERVAL FOR ADJUSTMENT

(A) 1½" ANGLE FOR LEG SUPPORT THIS IS DRILLED EVERY 2" FOR ADJUSTMENT

(S) 2" SQ. ALLOY TUBE FOR MAIN LEGS, TWO PER BOX THIS IS DRILLED ON ALL SIDES FOR SIDE AND FRONT SUPPORTS

(W) WING NUTS AND BOLTS FOR SECURING

suggested a plastic honeycomb material sandwiched between two layers of thin balsa wood as the optimum platform material for the boxes. We therefore had 'tiles' made up for the floor of the boxes; fitted internally, they rested on the two lower frame longitudinal box members and on two further 1¼" o.d. tubes running parallel to them, close to the centre of the box. As the floor proved to be rather flexible with the eight tiles in place, I had to introduce T-section alloy which fitted between tiles and rested transversely across the floor members. This floor/platform system proved adequate and gave the best possible insulation/rigidity. The outer cover of the box laced underneath the platform.

The legs of the MacInnes box are of square section aluminium alloy, drilled at 2" intervals on all four faces to give 1" intervals of adjustment. They have drilled adjustable angle braces from the outer, lower longitudinal frame member, and from each of the two lower end frame members the legs are held in position by the four angle alloy braces which can be fixed either below or above the horizontal, depending on terrain. The leg braces also help to support the box platform. The square section platform legs attach to the corner of the box with HT bolts and wing nuts. A short 1" diameter tube is located inside each of the four upright frame corner tubes of the box at the bottom. On the mountainside of the box they are telescopic and can be locked off to give variable lengths on uneven ground. On the outer aspect of the box, the square platform legs bolt to these short extension tubes.

The box outer cover has small sleeve extensions for making spindrift seals over the attachments to the box frame. The 'bullet-proof' protective cover is fitted over the roof and rear of the box and tied off to the platform legs to the rear with nylon cord. The boxes can be anchored to the face at any convenient point of the platform, or by the legs, or from tape loops fitted to the outer cover. Pre-cut, closed cell foam was used for insulation of floor, walls, and roof, and a 1 oz inner cotton liner can be clipped to the frame once the box is erected. This liner, in all three boxes, is fitted with storage pockets. The final weight of the MacInnes box, less platform, is 66 lbs. It can, of course, be used with or without the platform.

The summit box is formed basically from two rectangular aluminium alloy sections, crossed at each end to form an X. All the 1" o.d. tubing is fitted with internal shock cord for rapid assembly and the two rectangles are permanently bolted together. The theory is that the bundle of short sections of tubing, when shaken out, springs together to form the frame. It is then inserted into the cover which has a fully zipped floor (i.e. zipped round three sides). The frame is then forced out to form the X construction which tensions the cover. Finally, the floor is zipped up. This box proved very rigid, light (weight approximately 16½ lbs, plus inner), and easy to erect. Its design is such that, if required, it can actually hang from piton belays (a clip is located at the centre of each X for this purpose) and special wide banding strips are attached to reinforce the floor. Criss-cross thin, stainless steel

The MacInnes summit box

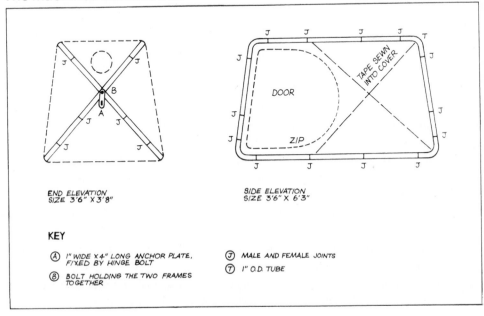

END ELEVATION
SIZE 3'6" X 3'8"

SIDE ELEVATION
SIZE 3'6" X 6'3"

KEY

Ⓐ 1" WIDE X 4" LONG ANCHOR PLATE, FIXED BY HINGE BOLT

Ⓑ BOLT HOLDING THE TWO FRAMES TOGETHER

Ⓙ MALE AND FEMALE JOINTS

Ⓣ 1" O.D. TUBE

wire is used for bracing walls and floor where necessary. For Everest, the box was supplied only with side stainless steel bracing wires.

I chose BM Coatings, Belflex 40, 1.7 oz, for the outer cover of the summit box, as this offered the necessary strength/weight ratio; the inner was made from artificial silk. Only two summit boxes were manufactured and, as with the other box frames, the prototype was made in Glencoe. One box cover and inner was sewn by the Greenock Sail and Tent Company; the other by Karrimor Ltd. As only green Belflex was obtainable initially, fluorescent crosses were stitched on to the outer cover for locating the box in poor visibility. The summit box cover was painstakingly constructed, using tape reinforcing and zig-zag stitching. At each corner a doubled tape was used to attach a nylon line guy. Each of the four guys led from the top corner to the bottom corner of the box and the ends were tied off with a Tarbuck knot for quick adjustment. A single-sleeve ventilator was located at the door end of the box.

AUXILIARY TENTAGE

On a recent Anglo-Indian trip to Changabang, Chris Bonington had been very impressed by the performance of a bell tent made by the Indian Ordnance factory, and Major Han Alhuwalia (who was responsible for these tents) kindly offered to supply the expedition with four similar ones. They were extremely heavy and not popular with the climbing team, but the Sherpas seemed to enjoy the warm dark interior and preferred them to our own larger, lighter super boxes. Three of the tents stayed at Base, but the fourth went to Camp 1 where it was eventually lost during an amazing night when the whole tent sank into the ground as a previously unsuspected crevasse opened up. No one was hurt but, needless to say, it was never occupied again.

We used a number of Vango Mark Five tents for the walk in and at Base as two-man general purpose living tents. But later, as it became obvious that we could develop Camp 2 as an advanced base, several of the tents were moved to the Western Cwm where they performed very well until an avalanche swept through the camp and destroyed five of them completely, along with two of the big super boxes. The tents were virtually unaltered commercially available models and I only added a third set of A poles to strengthen the ridge and also took the precaution of fitting a nylon snow valance and protective panel at the foot of the flysheet.

We had, in addition, four Scott tunnel tents, taken as emergency lightweights, and two simple nylon bivouac sacs which were taken by both summit teams. In fact, when Doug Scott and Dougal Haston were forced into the highest ever recorded bivouac they were able to dig a snow hole and use the bivouac sac as a groundsheet to sleep on rather than in!

Sleeping on snow means floor insulation is essential and the 9mm sheets of Karrimat already well known to most climbers performed excellently. At Camp 2 those Sherpas and climbers who had also brought up the open cell foam mattresses used originally for the walk in slept in real comfort. On the face Karrimats were also used as roof insulation in an attempt to cut down the condensation which is unavoidable when cooking is done inside.

Other essential items for the efficient running or erection of camps on the face in particular were shovels, brushes and tarpaulins. The aluminium shovels were the size normally seen on roadsweepers' carts but they were very light and one soon appreciated that size is essential if platforms are to be dug quickly – a job that takes an age if the only available tools are ice axes. The brushes are not for tent-proud occupants to keep things looking tidy but are used to brush out snow brought in on boots and clothing or blown-in spindrift. If this isn't done the warmth inside the tent soon melts the snow and dampens clothing and spirits alike.

Although recommended strongly by Graham Tiso, the 1972 expedition equipment organiser, I hadn't realised how valuable is the provision of a good supply of tarpaulins. Luckily we had a good deal of nylon on the roll given to us by BM Coatings. This was sent out to Nepal and made up in Kathmandu into a variety of sheet sizes. Simply reinforced at the edges and corners and fitted with eyelets at regular centres, these sheets served in turn as tents, temporary cook-shelters, covered store areas between tents, emergency flysheets, groundsheets, and as covers over and under equipment boxes stored outside. It is so easy to lose equipment left accidentally outside when snow falls and covers everything. Underneath a generous cover it is easy to find and clear the snow away, and if my turn comes to advise future organisers I would urge them not to forget these apparently unimportant additions to their tent lists.

A number of tents were actually destroyed during the climb and even more had to be abandoned as camps were evacuated in the aftermath of the storm which finished the expedition. Nevertheless, we were able to bring some back with us and these have now been given to the British Mountaineering Council to form the beginnings of the new expedition equipment pool. The three bell tents have been loaned to the British Army spring '76 attempt on Everest by the South Col route and will return to the pool in the summer.

	TENTAGE – DESCRIPTION	QUANTITIES
1	Base Camp bell tents	4
2	Super boxes	7
3	Force ten Mk. 5	25
4	Scott tunnel tents	4
5	Face boxes	12
6	Karrimats	200
7	tent brushes	30
8	cook-shelters	3
9	store tarpaulins	12
10	hypothermia bags	6

11	snow shovels	12
12	Summit boxes	2
13	bivouac sacs	2

COOKING EQUIPMENT

There seems little doubt that as a general recommendation paraffin stoves are far and away the most reliable and economical heat source where large numbers have to be catered for and we used a variety of large domestic stoves up to Camp 2. The main drawback of these stoves however, apart from weight, is that locally available kerosene is invariably contaminated. We took the very necessary precaution of taking over 200 gallons of specially filtered fuel from this country and used this exclusively above Base Camp where the effects of breakdowns and blockages are far harder to deal with. Supplementary local fuel was restricted, where possible, to Base and only used after filtering, in theory anyway, by the Sherpa cooks. On the face during the climb, we used gas stoves with disposable cartridges, as this is easily the most efficient way of carrying fuel on the mountain. The cleanliness of the fuel together with the ease of lighting and absence of noxious fumes, all important in a small tent, make this choice almost inevitable. However, this method also has one serious disadvantage. All small stoves use butane as fuel and this is quite susceptible to temperature changes, not volatile at all at −5°C, a condition quite common on Everest. Propane is a much better gas to use at lower temperatures, but unfortunately British Specifications do not allow high-pressure fuels to be contained in the lightweight disposable cartridges we required. Luckily we were able to purchase from a French expedition in the Himalaya 500 cylinders of a fifty-fifty propane-butane mix and we used this exclusively and with great success on the face.

Both Hamish MacInnes and I had spent a great deal of time, along with designers and friends in general research, attempting to develop a cooking unit which would improve performance and efficiency. It is very easy to improve performance by protection from wind, but this is never really a problem on Everest, as all cooking is done inside tents. In the end, despite all our work with insulation and double walls, internal flues and textured surfaces, we were unable to make any appreciable savings and even at 28,000ft on the mountain, apart from special fuel, we were cooking on the standard picnicker's lightweight stove and billy, used by hundreds of hikers every weekend at altitudes nearer sea level than the summit of Everest. Certainly a great endorsement of their performance.

For a single burner gas stove we used the Standard Bluet S200 with stabiliser, no modifications except the use of special fuel.

We took 100 per cent in 7oz disposable cartridges. In practice, although performance is badly affected by low temperature, if the containers were kept inside there was little problem in getting the stove to light and the rapid rise in temperature within the tent when they were running soon raised performance to normal levels.

The propane-butane mix ensured maximum performance from the start and would have been essential if the worst weather conditions for which we had prepared had developed. Fortunately we completed the climb so rapidly that in common with most of our equipment they were never subjected to the expected extreme conditions and we always had performance in hand.

The Mammoth Optimus No. 3 Domestic single burner stoves gave us very little trouble and the replacement of a few washers and nipples was a small effort in return for their reliable performance, often burning nonstop from 2 a.m. to 10 p.m., only pausing for fuel refils. We did not take with us the very heavy cast iron hob provided with the stove and had no trouble balancing even the biggest pans which were almost two feet in diameter.

We also took a number of smaller paraffin stoves as lightweight emergency stoves if the gas cookers proved unsatisfactory, but those were never used. In addition we provided some industrial heaters, a formidable stove with four burner heads, intended for snow melting. They performed well, but I had omitted to provide a decent stand for the billies which is not provided as standard with this model. Consequently they were never used very much, but were never missed as the No. 3 stoves performed so well.

I had hoped to develop a constant feed system direct from the fuel containers, as this would do away with the tricky job of constant refilling and relighting. In the event, there wasn't enough time, but it will be a worthwhile development for some future expedition and another equipment organiser.

Most of the really big 5-gallon snow melting and cooking pans were bought in Kathmandu market where they are well made and cheap, although we took lightweight nesting sets from this country and included them in camp kits for the face. Standard lightweight knife, fork and spoon sets were also taken, together with an unbelievable number of spare spoons as these seem to disappear after every meal, along with the one pint plastic mugs which were also constantly in short supply.

Stoves and lights were preheated with Meta paste which seemed better and certainly more efficient to use than the solid type. It was lit by matches, which were included in every camp kit, or with small butane lighters issued personally to every climber and Sherpa.

Most of the general kitchen supplies were bought in Nepal but we included in equipment sent out from England, nylon and metal pan scrubs, the invaluable can opener made by Morfed and kitchen knives from Swiss Cutlery, as well as candles, washing-up bowls, fuel funnels, axes, plates and a huge supply of very useful paper towels. With a great deal of rice and potatoes to cook, the provision of pressure cookers not only makes sense but is essential as the fuel they save far outweighs the relatively small disadvantage of bulk and weight. They were used in all major camps and at Camp 2 the rice and tsampa were precooked before sending up to Sherpa climbers on the face, saving time and fuel where it was most needed.

We also took a number of Thermos flasks ranging in size from one pint drink size to almost three pint food containers and used with a little forethought these too saved time, effort and valuable fuel at Camp 2 and above.

Finally, it is worth writing a few words about what seems a luxury item, folding tables and chairs. If climbers are to perform well on the mountain, it is essential that they eat and rest as well as possible in camp and the benefits of a well set-up mess tent in the big camps should not need explanation, only emphasising. The provision of decent, robust chairs and tables, although nothing like as glamorous as the supply of climbing hardware, nevertheless played a real part in ensuring our success.

	COOK, HEAT & LIGHT – DESCRIPTION	QUANTITIES
1	double burner gas stove	2
2	single burner gas stove	28
3	gas cartridges	1000
4	paraffin stoves	25
5	nesting sets	28
6	KFS sets	100
	spare spoons	200
7	gas lanterns	20
8	plastic one pint mugs	200
9	pressure cookers	10
10	gas heaters	4
11	can openers	200
12	Meta paste	100
13	pan scourers	60
14	Thermos flasks	20
15	paper kitchen towels	800
16	paraffin lanterns	16
17	folding tables	20
18	folding chairs	30
19	kitchen knives	6
20	multi-burner stoves	8
21	candles	200
22	batteries	800
23	hurricane lamps	4
24	kerosene (galls)	250

Material Suppliers: Although all our gas equipment was manufactured by Camping Gaz, we were unable to obtain support directly from them and all the equipment was supplied through Tentequip of Ossett. At the last minute we were still short of a number of small items for this section and were helped greatly by Institution

Supplies of Leeds who at very short notice made good our shortfalls and in the same way Countess Gravina was responsible for presenting the expedition with an enormous pressure cooker to supplement the standard size models already provided by Prestige.

Although the specially filtered kerosene was obtained through Rockoil it was sent to Nepal in special 'Paracans' from Harcostar.

MISCELLANEOUS

Under a heading like this one usually finds all the little unimportant bits forgotten until the last minute. In our case, however, there are several most important items and their inclusion here is only because they cannot really be covered by the other classifications.

Packing materials, for example, includes the indispensable heavy duck kit bags which were issued to each climber and high-altitude Sherpas for general packaging. Bigger bags were used, with plastic liners, to store rice, sugar, and flour in both base camps. Almost 2000 assorted plastic bags in different sizes and gauges were taken although the bigger 500 gauge ones were the most useful. Big 10' × 4' lightweight sheets were essential as personal cover for Sherpas, under groundsheets for tents, and to keep snow off equipment stored outside. Each climber had his own issue personal box which was lockable and could be left at Base while he was on the mountain, but we had in addition thirty special fibre boxes to store and protect more vulnerable equipment like medical supplies, batteries, and radio equipment.

All equipment otherwise was sent out from England and stored during the expedition in waxed cardboard boxes made especially for us and overprinted with the expedition title and numbered for easy identification. All joints, edges, and corners were sealed and protected with extremely strong waterproof 2" tape before banding with nylon strapping. This banding was particularly important when the contents were heavy, like the oxygen bottles, and it is essential to stop any possible movement within the box which could easily damage the cylinder or burst the container.

The other equipment needed to handle the boxes was a good range of scales to weigh contents during preparation in England and also to make sure that porter loads are correct. Too little in each load soon adds up to a big reduction in carrying power and too much results, understandably, in complaints and trouble from Sherpas who have contracted to carry fixed weight loads. Generally speaking this was 60 lbs on the walk in and a 40 lb maximum above Base Camp.

Lastly, two large, comprehensive tool boxes were prepared covering every need from needle and thread and hand cleaner to riveting tool and wrenches.

For entertainment a compendium of games and books is essential, although on this trip only cards and dice were played with regularity. Dice, chess and Scrabble were also played, but basically anything that needed time or brainwork couldn't be sustained and the short-term excitement of gambling was understandably the most popular.

As a background to our evenings of eating and cards a couple of tape recorders were provided and a very mixed bag of tapes taken in an attempt to satisfy musical tastes ranging from heavy rock to grand opera.

Two smaller recorders were also used to record diaries and other conversations as well as a secondary music source. All four were winterised by National Panasonic and played faultlessly during our time on the mountain. The two smaller machines had already had a battering in the overland lorry trip so had been from extremes of heat and dust to cold, and snow, and I cannot think of a more rigorous proof of their reliability.

Two other machines specially prepared for the trip were the portable Remington typewriters. They were in constant use during the walk in, at Base Camp, and later Chris Bonington used one at Camp 2 for report preparation, sharing it with Hamish MacInnes who was busily trying to finish his latest novel in between days on the face. The two typewriters were carried in special boxes – mini-offices really – complete with paper, envelopes, biros, and all the other equipment needed to control and record on paper the progress of the climb.

	MISCELLANEOUS EQUIPMENT – DESCRIPTION	QUANTITIES
1	repair kits (tools)	2
2	games collection	2
3	portable offices	2
4	kit bags	100
5	assorted poly bags & sheets	1200
6	boot polish & dubbin	50
7	boot oils (suppletect)	36
8	miraclaces	50
9	yale locks	100
10	low temperature thermometer	2
11	boot brushes	20
12	cassette recorders	4
13	Thommen altimeters	2
14	batteries	1200
15	Anemometer	2
16	binding machine	2
17	blank cassettes	100
18	pre-recorded cassettes	30
19	paperbacks	80
20	compasses	8
21	spring balances	8
22	metal box containers	100

23	alarm clocks	6
24	binoculars	2
25	packing boxes	400
26	personal & special boxes	40
27	adhesive tape	600
28	toothpaste, shampoo & soap	400

CONCLUSION

It took a short six months of very hard work to get our equipment designed, manufactured and despatched before the expedition proper began. The route was climbed in record time and we were back in England almost a month sooner than we expected, but nobody, I suspect, had any idea even then that our post-expedition commitment would be so great. For me it has taken a period of six embarrassing months to complete reports and provide pictures for over 150 suppliers to the trip. I had promised all of them material which would make it possible to develop the advertising potential their support deserved, but the mammoth job of looking for appropriate material in the 15,000 transparencies we took was bound to take time. In addition, we had to attend an incredible number of receptions and lectures, all of them most enjoyable but all of them time-consuming and this may be the best place to thank them all for their help in the first instance and their understanding and patience in the months since our return. I should also like to add my thanks to my administration team, secretaries, June Slater, Maureen Fernehough, and all the Centresport staff for all their hard work.

On the expedition my time of greatest pleasure was the few days spent at Camp 4 because there at last I was an active part of the climbing effort, in a fantastic camp, but most important of all I was free of the equipment organiser's title. In that unglamorous role one is inevitably preoccupied with impersonal lists of equipment and loading schedules, with little time to relax and enjoy people rather than packing. One eventually resents the situation but it seems to go with the job and one has to look for satisfaction to the successful maintenance of equipment flowing up and down the mountain and feel that it all really does help to put the team on top.

So my lasting memory of the expedition will not be of data under control and successfully co-ordinated but it will be of golden sunsets seen from Camp 4 and the warm sound of Sherpa laughter from the tent next door.

Oxygen Equipment *by Hamish MacInnes*

The oxygen apparatus is probably the most important single item of equipment for high-altitude climbing. George Finch and Geoffrey Bruce were the first climbers to use oxygen cylinders on Everest. Sherpas carried them to their camp at 25,000ft on the North East Ridge in 1922. The climbers reached 27,300ft (8320m) before admitting defeat. During the intervening years, several other systems were tried out. On the first successful ascent of Everest, in 1953, both open and closed-circuit sets were used. Though the closed-circuit set gives the best possible utilisation of a given supply of oxygen, the equipment is bulky and complex. A soda lime canister is used to absorb the expired carbon dioxide and allows the exhaled oxygen to return to a breathing bag. Direction of flow is ensured by two non-return valves. Oxygen which is used by the climber is replaced from an oxygen cylinder. An improved version of the 1953 Everest closed-circuit equipment was used on Kangchenjunga. There is a further disadvantage in that, should the oxygen supply fail for some reason whilst the equipment is in use, the percentage of oxygen in the circulating gas can fall below that in the ambient air without the user being aware of the fact. The set, with one soda lime canister, weighs approximately 19 lbs. The canister lasts as long as an 800-litre oxygen cylinder, which is an extra 11.6 lbs. Though this system has proved to be reliable, it is heavy and seldom considered for high-altitude mountaineering, though it is used by astronauts.

We considered the various types of equipment available for the 1975 expedition with particular care. During the 1972 South West Face expedition we had experienced considerable trouble with the diluter-demand system developed by Dr F. Duane Blume and the Robertshaw Company of the USA. A post-mortem on the sets, which we returned to the company after the expedition, revealed that a valve had been left in place in error at the end of the corrugated mask hose. This stopped the oxygen flow when the mask froze up – which happened frequently. It was a dangerous fault, as it was often difficult to remove the face mask quickly, when the blockage occurred, whilst wearing two pairs of gloves. Later, we were told that the valves should have been removed by the suppliers of the masks for the special requirements of high-altitude climbing, as opposed to high-altitude flying for which they were originally designed. We were assured that it would not happen again.

I was still in favour of a simple constant flow system such as the Hornbein equipment which comprises a face mask with a manually controlled variable oxygen supply to the oro-nasal region of the mask. The flow rate can be varied from between 1–4 litres per minute. The system tends to be wasteful of oxygen at the lower respiratory rates and deficient at the high rates but, on the other hand, there is not much that can go wrong with it.

Chris Bonington wrote to Tom Hornbein for his advice in the matter and was informed that, in Hornbein's opinion, the Blume/Robertshaw system was superior. So we decided in favour of the latter, despite our previous ill-luck with the system. Dr Duane Blume had been appointed the Oxygen Officer for the International Everest expedition in 1971 and he was largely responsible for the development of the diluter-demand system. Similar equipment is used widely in aviation; it works on the principle that, when one inspires, ambient air is also drawn into the mask via a port in the regulator together with pure oxygen from the cylinder in a ruck-sack on the climber's back. The regulator is a modified aviation type, altered to give four ambient-air orifices in place of the original aneroid valve. This aneroid valve was not sensitive enough for high-altitude climbing purposes. Each setting is equal to increments of 2000ft from 22,000 to 30,000ft.

Earlier, I had gone into the possibility of using cartridges of solid oxygen but, although this system is excellent for emergency oxygen supplies in aircraft, it proved to be too expensive and the replenishment cartridge of too short a life for high-altitude climbing.

The question of cylinders for the oxygen was my next problem, and Captain Henry Day who had been working on a similar problem for the British Army Everest expedition recommended Reynolds Tubes. When I contacted Stan Gould, Manager of Research and Development, I found that he had designed a cylinder which was, at 7½lbs, one of the lightest ever produced. The cylinders which we had used in 1972 had a capacity of 1000 litres which was just too much for the average day's climbing. 800 litres, we felt, would be just about right and, in retrospect, this estimate still holds good. The cylinders were manufactured from HE 15TF alumini-um alloy; overall length: 25", and width: 4". The working pressure was 3300 lbs/ins^2; the burst pressure 9500 lbs/ins^2.

The cylinders were filled with oxygen of a dew point of 6 vpm. The cylinder valves were made by Sherwood Selpac, type TV-5441, and these proved excellent; no leakage was observed from any of the cylinders. Burst discs on several cylinders blew whilst they were being transported in one of the two expedition trucks. This was due to excessive heat and in fact the burst discs fulfilled their function in blowing at approximately 5000 lbs/ins^2.

I studied the possibility of overwrapping cylinders with glass fibre and also with a different material Kevlar 49. Overwrapping steel cylinders with wire had been practised for a number of years and such cylinders were used by the successful Kangchenjunga expedition, manufactured by the Chesterfield Tube Company, an associate of Reynolds. Glass fibre overwrapping is a more recent innovation and, to date, Kevlar 49 has not yet been used for this purpose. Mr M. E. Humphries, of IMI Engineering looked into the possibility of using Kevlar 49 but unfortunately, due to the lack of time, the testing programme could not be carried out. Perhaps on some future expedition the spherical container with Kevlar overwrapping will provide the ideal oxygen container?

The diluter-demand system which we eventually used is made up from the following components: the oxygen cylinder, with a pressure reducer and pressure gauge attached which fits on to the cylinder valve a length of high-pressure tubing leading from it to the diluter-demand regulator; and a shorter section of flexible corrugated tubing which links it to the face mask. A further orifice on the pressure reducer is fitted to a plastic medical-type mask for use whilst sleeping. Oxygen for sleeping purposes is supplied to two people via a small T manifold at a flow rate of one litre per minute which, by experience, we have found to be quite adequate. The weight of the complete system with one filled cylinder is 30.1 lb.

In conjunction with Karrimor and Graham Tiso, Karrimor's pack-frame was adapted to carry the oxygen cylinders and other equipment within the sack. Two small pockets inside the bottom of the sack allowed the base of cylinders to be located and strap ties at the top ensured that they were held in position. An aperture was made from the main compartment of the sack to the inside of a side pocket on the left-hand side of the pack-frame to take the high-pressure hose. The demand valve was located within this pocket, the side wall of which was made from a breathing material. In fact the pocket was a spindrift filter. A short sleeve allowed the end of the corrugated mask hose to connect with the demand valve. When the pack-frame was worn, the corrugated mask hose led from under the left armpit to the climber's face. I had the hose lengthened specifically for this purpose.

The face mask was a standard military one: the A-14. It weighs 14 ozs and is made by the Sierra Engineering Company. Manufactured from silicone rubber, it gives a reliable performance in cold environments. It is readily crushable in place with a gloved hand – to free ice from the ports and exhaust valve. However, one of the summit parties found that more drastic treatment had to be used for clearing an ice blockage.

Two types of helmet were used for holding the face masks in place. One was the white flying helmet loaned to us by the Swiss Foundation for Alpine Research which we had also used in 1972. The other was an ex-RAF flying helmet supplied to us by Victor Lawrence Supplies, London. Both proved excellent.

Our experiences with the Blume/Robertshaw system on the 1975 expedition were unsatisfactory. Of the eighteen sets supplied to the expedition, only five eventually worked, and several of these were not 100 per cent. Almost without exception, the faults were due to defective demand valves. Even under normal conditions, with no abuse whatsoever to the equipment, failure would occur. The equipment was, moreover, subjected to much less arduous conditions than on the 1972 post-monsoon attempt; the temperatures on this most recent expedition were considerably higher.

It is worth noting that the Japanese did considerable research on high-altitude oxygen equipment and several interesting design aspects emerged. An economiser which fits into the climber's helmet proved successful. This economiser consists of a polythylene bag designed to accumulate the quantity of oxygen needed during inhalation; the internal capacity is 2.8 litres. In the earlier systems the economising bag was housed within a light alloy box. Two valves were used: the inhalation valve, and the outer air inhalation valve. During inhalation both valves opened simultaneously and a mixture of oxygen and outer air passed through the hose into the mask. During exhalation both valves closed. Oxygen was supplied from the cylinder via a reducing valve to the economiser bag. The reason for not adopting a helmet type economiser for our expedition was that the economiser box was always awkward – located either on the pack-frame, or 'fixed' somewhere more convenient to the climber. There are several other advantages in the helmet-mounted economiser, one being that the inhaled oxygen is slightly warmed before inhalation; another is that the economiser is out of the way and very close to the face mask. This equipment was tested in temperatures of −50°C. The face mask developed for the helmet-economiser system was the H mask and a great deal of work was put into this design, but it was moulded for the Japanese face and not suitable for our physiognomy.

For the purpose of attempting the South West Face of Everest, the Japanese perfected a system of piping oxygen from the second man to the leader, thereby obviating the need for the leader to carry the cylinder whilst lead climbing. They experimented with 40m long hoses of an internal diameter of 6mm. When the oxygen was put out from the cylinder pressure reducer at 3 litres per minute, there was only a reduction of 7 per cent at the other end; therefore, by slightly boosting the input flow, a normal supply could be obtained by the lead climber. Another interesting fact emerging from this experiment was that the hose was found to be strong enough to support a climber weighing 70kg. Perhaps when the South West Face 'Super Direct' is finally made, this will be the oxygen system to be used.

Food *by Mike Thompson*

The letter in the unmistakable Bonington scrawl, once deciphered, read: 'How about coming on the coldest holiday of your life? P.S. Will you do the food?'

In fact, as it turned out it wasn't *that* cold: but then it wasn't much of a holiday either. 'Doing the food' is a fairly thankless task and the famous dictum, 'The most important thing about food is that there should be some,' whilst undoubtedly true, is not the only requirement for satisfaction and success.

During my military days in Malaya an Australian vet attached to the regiment in lieu of a padre pronounced, with that antipodean knack for bibulous vulgarity combined with deep philosophical intuition: 'There's only two things that matter in life – your belly and what's on the end of it.' On Everest life is even simpler – there is just your belly; for whatever might have been on the end of it has become, at best, vestigial. In consequence food, far from being simply a fuel, becomes the central mystery of existence; the sole remnant of culture and repository of meaning; the metaphor within which all dissatisfaction is expressed.

Only too aware of this, I took the earliest opportunity of consulting that most fluent expressor of dissatisfaction, Mick Burke. With disarming candour he confessed that for him food presented no problems: 'For breakfast, bacon, eggs, mushrooms and fried bread, tea and toast. For lunch, fish and chips. For supper, meat and potato pie and chips.' And that, in a nutshell, is the whole problem: to get as close as possible, with non-perishable foodstuffs, with severe weight restrictions and with primitive cooking facilities, to this ideal diet. But this is only the start of the problem, for there are likely to be as many ideal diets as there are members of the expedition. Of course, if the entire expedition had been recruited from Wigan they would have shared Mick's tastes, but unfortunately other criteria governed the selection of the team and, as its geographically and socially diverse membership grew towards twenty (not to mention the eighty Sherpas and *their* ideal diets), the chances of my satisfying even a small proportion rapidly faded. Denied the opportunity of selecting the members to suit the food, I decided that I could at least satisfy one person, so I chose the food that *I* liked. I took the precaution of sending each member a list of likely items and the sorts of menus they could provide and asked for their objections and suggestions. Nick Estcourt imposed his usual veto on peanut butter, Doug Scott revealed his cravings for granola and French nougat and Chris Bonington urged 'lots of really hot pickles and chutneys', but otherwise the response was slight, so, interpreting apathy as approval, I set to work on the detailed planning.

People often say to me: 'I suppose you start off with a target number of calories and certain ratios of fat, carbohydrate and protein, and then try to achieve these within the minimum weight.' In fact, I do no such thing. I am an anthropologist not a nutritionist and I start off with the *idea* of a meal, and of a day punctuated and made meaningful by a series of meals, and of a succession of days distinguished one from another by different series of meals. A typical starting point would be an outline of a day's eating such as this:

BREAKFAST:	Tea
	Porridge, brown sugar, milk
	Biscuits, margarine, honey
	More tea
DURING DAY:	Chocolate (Roast almond)
	Spangles
	Nuts and raisins
	Brew of hot fruit juice on return
	(Possibility of something more substantial if staying in the camp during the day, e.g. tomato soup and digestive biscuits.)
EVENING MEAL:	Tea
	Irish stew, mashed potatoes, peas
	Christmas pudding and cream
	Coffee, whisky, chocolate

It is this sort of menu that generates the ration packs for use on the face itself, but most food is consumed at Base Camp or in the Western Cwm and is prepared by Sherpa cooks catering for as many as twenty people. At Base Camp and during the approach march it is a good idea to have as much fresh food as possible and quite a lot of fresh food can be incorporated even at Camp 2 (for instance, we had fresh meat and spinach and even fresh(ish) salad with olive oil and lemon juice at 22,000ft). The Sherpas, of course, like to include as much fresh and familiar food in their diet as possible.

In view of these differences in camp size, in cooking arrangements and in access to local and fresh food, it seemed a good idea to have three different types of ration: 'Base and Approach', 'Advanced Base', and 'Face' – an arrangement that neatly fitted in with the changes in load weight on the mountain (60 lbs to Base Camp, 40 lbs to Camp 2 and 30 lbs on the face).

In deference to the Sherpa preference for local produce the 'Base and Approach' rations were subdivided into 'Climber' and 'Sherpa', the climbers getting 1½ lbs per man-day (and about 2½ lbs local purchase) and the Sherpas 1 lb per man-day (and about 3 lbs local purchase). The weight allowance for Advanced Base (Camp 1 and Camp 2) was a generous 2½ lbs per man-day (and about 1½ lbs of local purchase). For the face, the rations were broken down into 4 man-day packs each weighing 8½ lbs which gives just over 2 lbs per man per day (which though probably not enough to support life indefinitely is as much, if not more, than anyone managed to eat).

At this stage the planning of the food became intricately involved with Chris's overall planning: the weights, once decided upon, had to be adhered to scrupulously or else the meticulously planned movements of loads and personnel would be thrown out and the narrow logistic margins exceeded. Also I needed to know how many mouths there would be to feed (always a varying, and usually increasing, quantity in the early stages of planning) and where those mouths were likely to be situated on the mountain. Eventually, I obtained three figures: estimated number of man-days above Camp 2, between Base Camp and Camp 2, at Base Camp and below. These I then biased slightly in favour of face and Advanced Base (since one can eat face rations at Base but not vice versa), multiplied by the weights of food allowed per man-day at the different altitudes, divided by the load weights at the different altitudes, and, assuming the arithmetic was right, I then knew how many boxes of food we would have to take: 480 boxes totalling approximately 11 tons.

The next straightforward but laborious task was to compile a shopping list (149 items including 110,988 tea bags and 96 plastic lemons) and then take it down the road to Liptons the Grocers. Allied Suppliers, of which Liptons are the retail outlets, had kindly agreed to provide those items which they themselves produced (under the Liptons and Sunshine labels) at cost, and to obtain all the other items on the list and to gather them all together in one place. In all, fifty-eight separate suppliers were involved and Gordon Lambert of Allied Suppliers had the appalling job of dealing with them all and of persuading them to provide the items free or at a much reduced cost. It is a measure of his success and hard work that the final cost was some £2000 below budget.

I am very proud of the fact that in organising the food I wrote only two letters but this statistic obscures a lot of leg-work and endless telephone calls. For instance, the dried egg was only obtained after the personal intervention of Sir Geoffrey de Freitas and the cans of cooking oil were, I believe, stealthily diverted from supplies destined for the Royal Household (thank you, Prince Philip). Green's of Brighton queried our order for ninety-six packets of instant pancake mix. Had we, they wondered, left out a decimal point? If not, we would have enough pancakes to pave a footpath all the way to the summit of Everest. The order *was* right and the pancakes were a great success – quite fluffy and not at all like paving stones. In some cases we were asking quite small firms for large quantities of expensive items. The director of Rowland Smith Limited who had received an order for a vast quantity of Ye Olde Oak Hams and Ye Olde Oak Chickens telephoned to ask just what sort of publicity he could hope for in return for helping us. Would I, he asked, guarantee to mention Ye Olde Oak by name in the book? Gambling everything, I said 'Yes.' 'All right,' he said, 'you've got the lot, free.' (Well, there you are Mr Smith, you've got what I promised you, three times over!)

Pitt and Scott who did the packing specialise in fine art removals. Indeed, it is often said of them that they have made the packing of art an art form in itself. They adopted the same reverential attitude to our humble provisions, treating bottles of soy sauce as if they were from the Tang Dynasty and handling jars of Branston Pickle as if they were Henry Moore bronzes.

Not only was the food going to be transported overland to Kathmandu and then handled and mishandled again and again by both yaks and humans, but it had to survive the heat and humidity of the monsoon while stored in Nima Tsering's house in Khumde. The tins would present no problems but such items as cereals, biscuits, chocolate, Christmas puddings and cheese were just as they come off the supermarket shelf in flimsy cardboard and cellophane wrappings. In the hope of retarding their inevitable decay, each water-proofed fibre-board box had a sealable plastic-coated liner; a precaution that really paid off for, apart from the occasional exploding drum of parmesan cheese and some compost-grown muesli that completed its ecological cycle before it could be eaten, these perishable items were still in remarkably good condition at the end of their ordeal. The boxes were wrapped in a tough bitumen sandwich paper and all the seams and folds covered with plastic tape. With heavy symbolism, the boxes were colour-coded: green tape for the pastoral safety of Base Camp, red tape for the dangers of the face, and yellow for the bit in between. Once wrapped there was no way of telling the menu of a box and this was quite deliberate. The inconvenience of occasionally having the same menu two days running is nothing compared with the ill-feeling generated by those in the lower camps consuming the more favoured boxes and passing on the unpopular ones, which is what inevitably happens if the boxes are labelled.

As it happened, there were enough leftovers to keep the Thompson family in steak and kidney puddings for several months *and* to make up nineteen extra boxes for the approach march. Finally, a few boxes of overs were made up for 'Base and Approach' and for 'Advanced Base', and some 'Kitchen boxes' containing items for stocking the kitchens, such as cooking oil, curry powder, baking powder and dried garlic which were provided for Base Camp and Camp 2.

RATION LISTS

RATION TYPE	COLOUR CODE	PACKAGING UNITS AND WEIGHTS		NUMBER OF BOXES		
Face rations	Red	4 man-day packs each 8½ lbs (menus A, B, C)	3 to a box (one of each menu A, B, C). Each box weight 30 lbs	165 × 4 man-day packs = 54 × 3 pack boxes	20" × 12" × 8" (pack in double poly bags)	Small
Advanced Base rations	Yellow	16 man-day packs. Each 40 lbs (6 menus A, B, C, D, E, F)		44 of each menu A, B, C, D, E, F, giving total 266	20" × 12" × 12"	Medium

Base and Approach (Climber)	Green (Marked) 'Climber')	40 man-day packs. Each 60 lbs (3 menus A, B, C)	13 of each menu A, B, C giving total 39	25" × 12" × 12"	Large
Base and Approach (Sherpa)	Green (Marked) 'Sherpa')	60 man-day packs. Each 60 lbs (3 menus A, B, C)	20 of each menu A, B, C giving total 60	25" × 12" × 12"	Large
Advanced Base (Kitchen)	Yellow (Marked 'Kitchen')	Each box approx. 40 lbs	12	20" × 12" × 12"	Medium
Base and Approach (Kitchen)	Green (Marked 'Kitchen')	Each box approx. 60 lbs	12	25" × 12" × 12"	Large
Overs (Base and Approach)	Green (Marked 'Overs')	Each box approx. 60 lbs	13	25" × 12" × 12"	Large
Overs (Advanced Base)	Yellow (Marked 'Overs')	Each box approx. 40 lbs	5	20" × 12" × 12"	Medium
Walk in rations	Pitt & Scott Tape (Marked 'Keep in Kathmandu')	30 man-day packs. Each 60 lbs	19	25" × 12" × 12"	Large

FACE RATIONS

Typical 4 Man-Day Pack Menu

Sugar (cube)	1 box	Vitamin tablets	1 strip (4 tablets)
Coffee Mate	6 sachets	Salt	2 drums
Nescafé	6 sachets	Margarine	2 tube × 1 oz
Tea	12 tea bags	Tin opener	1
Rise 'n Shine fruit drink (lemon)	1 packet	Readibrek (instant porridge)	8 oz bag
Stock cubes	4 cubes	Irish Stew	2 × 16 oz tins
Soup (Mushroom)	2 packets	Smash (dehydrated potato)	2 × 6 oz packets
Mint cake	4 × 3 oz bars	Surprise peas	1 × 2 oz packets
Chocolate (Roast almond)	4 × 2 oz bars	High fat biscuits	2 × 3 oz packets
Nougat	4 × 2 oz packets	Xmas Pudding	2 × 8 oz packets
Candle	1	Cream	1 × 4 oz tin
Matches	2 boxes	Choc. digestive biscuits	1 × 8 oz packet
Tissues	½ box	Honey	2 × 1 oz pots

ADVANCED BASE RATIONS

Typical 16 Man-Day Pack Menu

Porridge	1 × 12 oz packet	Stock cubes	3 packets of 6
Marvel milk	2 × 7 oz tins	Ovaltine	1 × 8 oz tin
Sugar (cube)	4 × 16 oz boxes	Irish stew	6 × 16 oz tins
Sugar (soft brown)	2 × 16 oz packets	Mango chutney	1 × 10 oz jar
Baconburgers	4 × 10 oz tins	Shortbread	3 × 7 oz packets
High fat biscuits	10 × 3 oz packets	Honey	2 × 12 oz tubes
Milk chocolate	16 × 1¾ oz bars	Kitchen roll	1 packet
Nuts & raisins	16 × 2 oz packets	Toilet roll	1 doublet
Pilchards in tomato sauce	3 × 14 oz tins	Safety matches	4 boxes
Tea bags	1 × box of 72	Salt	1 × 1 lb 8 oz packet
Nescafé	1 × 4 oz tin	Ham	1 × 16 oz tin

BASE AND APPROACH (CLIMBER) RATIONS

Typical 40 Man-Day Pack Menu

Porridge or muesli	5 lbs	Irish stew	7 × 16 oz tins
Marvel milk	4 × 7 oz tins	Marmalade	2 × 16 oz jars
Condensed milk	3 × 16 oz tins	Fruit cake (Dundee)	3 × 2 lb tins
Dehydrated egg	1 × 32 oz tin	Chocolate Garibaldi biscuits	2 × 4½ oz packets
Plain chocolate	40 × 1¾ oz bars	Kitchen roll	2 packets
Spangles	40 × 1 oz packets	Toilet paper	2 doublets
Tea	2 × 8 oz packets	Safety matches	8 boxes
Real coffee	1 × 16 oz packet	Margarine	1 × 16 oz tin
Packet soups (2 kinds)	2 × 1 gal.	Salt	1 × 1 lb 8 oz

BASE AND APPROACH (SHERPA) RATIONS

Typical 60 Man-Day Pack Menu

Marvel milk	6 × 7 oz tins	Tuna fish	12 × 8 oz tins
Condensed milk	4 × 16 oz tins	Salmon	6 × 16 oz tins
Crunchie bars	60 × 1¾ oz packets	Margarine	3 × 16 oz tins
Tea	3 × 4 oz tins	Kitchen roll	3 packets
Choc. digestive biscuits	12 × 16 oz packets	Safety matches	12 boxes
Jam (strawberry)	5 × 1 lb jars	Salt	1 × 1 lb 8 oz

KITCHEN BOXES: ADVANCED BASE

Olive oil	1 × 1 litre bottle	Plastic lemons	4
Cooking oil (Mazola)	1 × 1 gal. can	Mango pickle	1 jar
Jellies	6 assorted	Lime pickle	1 jar
Dehydrated onion flakes	1 packet	Branston pickle	1 jar
Dehydrated garlic	¼ packet	Marmite	2 jars
Curry powder	1 × 16 oz tin	Baking powder	1 tin
Chilli powder	¼ packet	Soy sauce	1 bottle
Mixed spice	3 tins	Marmite	2 oz jar
Instant batter mix	8 × 7 packets	Hunzana cake	2 × 2 lb tins
Golden syrup	1 × 2 lb tin		

KITCHEN BOXES: BASE AND APPROACH

Olive oil	}	2 × 1 gal. oil *or* 1 × 1 gal. oil +	Bamboo pickle	1 jar
Cooking oil		2 × 1 lit. bottle	Branston pickle	1 jar
Jellies	9 assorted		Marmite	1 jar
Dehydrated onion flakes		2 packets	Baking powder	1 tin
Dehydrated garlic		¼ tub	Dried yeast	3 packets
Curry powder		2 × 1 lb tins	Chilli sauce	1 bottle
Chilli powder		¼ tub	Soy sauce	3 bottles
Mixed spice		3 tins	Marmite	8 oz jar
Instant pancake mix		8 × 7 oz packets	Marmite	2 oz jar
Golden syrup		1 × 2 lb tin	Margarine	2 × 16 oz tins
Plastic lemons		4	Salt	1 × 1½ lb packet
Mango pickle		1 jar	Apple dice	2 × 1 lb packet
Lime pickle		1 jar	Hunzana cake	2 × 2 lb tins

WALK IN RATIONS: 30 MAN-DAY PACKS

Cereal (muesli or porridge)	5 lbs	Soup	3 × 1 gal. packets
Milk (Marvel and condensed)	4 tins	Pancake mix	1 × 7 oz packet
Dehydrated egg	1 × 2 lb tin	Apple dice	1 × 16 oz packet
Tea	1 × 72 box tea bags	Salt	1 × 1½ lb packet
Sugar	6 × 16 oz boxes	Margarine	1 × 1 lb tin
Rise 'n Shine	6 packets	Cream	2 × 4 oz tins
Stock cubes	6 boxes of 6	Fish, various	
Peanuts/nuts and raisins/cashews	48 × 2 oz	Ham	
packets		Sausages	
Spangles/Starburst	6 × 5 packs	Chilli con carne	
Jam	2 × 1 lb jar	Irish stew	} Total of 15 lbs
Toilet paper	1 doublet	Butter beans	
Scotties (tissues)	1 box	Beans and sausage	
Matches	2 boxes; 1 box lifeboat	Spam	

Communications *by Ronnie Richards*

On a large expedition good communications are essential, since many unforeseeable circumstances occur which require concerted action over a distance in a short time. In contrast to a small expedition, the team is more widely scattered and the problems of co-ordinating and implementing best courses of action are much more complex. In addition, there needs to be provision for getting messages and materials from and to the outside world.

No one on the team was a radio expert but we were able to draw on the experience of the 1972 expedition when Kelvin Kent had organised communications. This alleviated the main problem of identifying a system of radio equipment which was both technically suitable for the different types of link required and would also stand up to the usage and cold. Since the equipment used in 1972 had performed so well, there seemed no reason to change and the suppliers generously made sets available.

There were three functions requiring different types of radio:

1. The Rear Link, connecting the main Sherpa village of Namche Bazar with Base Camp and Camp 2, demanded short-wave transceivers having adequate power and range to transmit over terrain including 23,000ft mountains. For security reasons, the set in Namche had to be housed in the Police Post and any radio messages for Kathmandu relayed on the Nepalese Police net and not our own (our import licence required separate clearance and a permit for the use of radio transmitters).

The Police Radio was out of action much of the time, however, but we were able to pass messages via Syangboche air strip, just above Namche, whom we also supplied with meteorological data in return for special weather forecasts relayed from Kathmandu. The British Army had kindly loaned us two Gurkha Signallers who operated the short-wave sets at Base and Namche. This was a great help.

2. The Icefall net connected Base Camp, Camp 1 and Camp 2 which were non 'line of sight' and so needed higher power VHF sets than those used in the face. These sets were also for use in case of accident in the Icefall etc. where lightness and power might be necessary.

3. The face net connected Camp 2 with camps on the face which were all nearly line of sight, allowing a lighter walkie-talkie VHF set to be used. One frequency common to nets 2 and 3 permitted interchangeability.

DETAILS OF RADIO SETS

1. *Rear Link* (Base to Namche Bazar)
   Racal Squadcal-HF. Mode: SSB/AM. Frequency: 4.2–4.5 MHz (2 channels). Antenna:

Half Wave Dipole or Rod. Output: 5 watts. Power supply: 14 'D' cells or 18v supply. Weight: 18 lbs complete with case, ancillaries and batteries. No. of sets: 3.

2. *Icefall Net* (Base to Camp 1 to Advanced Base)
   Racal Telecal-VHF. Mode: Narrow Band FM. Frequency: 40–50 MHz – (2 channels). Antenna: Telescopic Rod. Output: 1 watt. Power supply: 8 'C' cells or 12v supply. Weight: 3.7 lbs with batteries. No. of sets: 3.

3. *Upper Camp Net* (Advanced Base to Camp 6)
   Philips Handy Talkie (Type MC203) – VHF. Mode: Phase Modulation. Frequency: 47–57 MHz – (6 channels). Antenna: Folding springblade. Output: 400 MW. Power supply: 6 Penlight batteries or 9v supply. Weight: 2.2 lbs including batteries. No. of sets: 8.

4. *Radio Receivers:* Hacker Super Sovereign. Bush VTR 178.

5. *Batteries:* all radios were powered by MN 1300, 1400 and 1500 cells from Mallory Batteries Limited.

The short-wave sets used for the rear link performed well, but for communications on the mountain with Base Camp it was found more convenient to use the light walkie-talkies and relay any messages, if necessary, through Camp 1. Direct communications, particularly from high camps, were often surprisingly good. All types of set developed some faults, mainly in transmission, but we fortunately had sufficient overlap or spare capacity.

Since the air strips at Syangboche and Luglha (one or two days by mail-runner from Base Camp) did not operate during the monsoon period, mail, press and film dispatches had to be sent back by mail-runner all the way to Kathmandu, where they were as ever efficiently dealt with by Elizabeth Hawley, our press agent. Six mail-runners, operating in pairs, were used for the 300 mile round trip and achieved a quickest return within 18 days. Requirements of firewood and fresh food were contracted out to Sherpas and supplies were regularly brought up to Base Camp by yak.

Photography

Still Photography by Doug Scott

On Everest in autumn 1975 there was no excuse for not having complete photographic coverage of our expedition. The weather was mainly favourable and every member of the team was well equipped to take photographs.

We were all issued with the Olympus OM1 body and 75–150mm zoom lens. We also had the choice of any other lens. Most of us chose either the 28mm or the 35mm wide-angle lens. There were also two spare bodies for the real enthusiast plus a plethora of lenses from two macro 50mm lenses up to a 600mm telephoto. The camera bodies were ninety-five per cent reliable. The only faults were two broken light meters, one stuck shutter and three ASA rating discs fell off. Considering there were twenty bodies altogether in use, and used pretty well continuously for two and a half months, this was a good performance. The 28mm lens seemed particularly sharp and the team had no complaints about other lenses either.

We were obliged not to use our own cameras as Olympus had generously supplied all the equipment at a hundred per cent discount. However for the approach march I was able to use a Pentax 6 × 7 camera with a wide-angle f 3.5/55 lens, standard f 2.4 105 lens and a telephoto f 4/400 lens. Whilst the quality of definition was excellent, I found that the combination of never having handled a large-format camera before, plus its weight, rather counted against the interest of my results. I shot far more 35mm film but, even accounting for the law of averages, these results tended to be of most value. No other cameras were used for colour photography.

Some of us carried battered Rollei 35 cameras for black and white. I took one, made in West Germany, to the summit and was well satisfied with the sharp results. I kept a 2 × 2 red filter over the lens at all times mainly because I was too lazy to change it.

Film was also generously supplied free of charge. Kodak gave us the following film.

600 rolls (36 exposure)	Kodachrome 25
100 rolls (20 exposure)	High Speed Ektachrome
100 rolls	Tri X
200 rolls	Panatomic X
100 rolls	Ektachrome X
A small quantity	2¼" square format film

Bob Stoodley was given the loan of an XL330 movie camera +20 cartridges of

Kodachrome II Super 8 movie film for the journey with the lorries.

I also had a similar range of film for my 6 × 7 camera.

The Kodachrome 25 film was by far and away the most popular. The results achieved were superb. One feature that was extremely useful in the often contrasting condition of light and shade was this film's ability to pick out detail in the shadow, whilst allowing full exposure to be given to the lighter areas. In this respect it does seem to be an improvement upon the old Kodachrome II.

The high speed Ektachrome was either a poor film or we could not handle it properly, for the results it gave were very disappointing.

The Panatomic X black and white film proved once again very successful, especially in the bright light condition often prevailing.

PERSONAL CONSIDERATIONS

Despite the unstinted help given by Kodak and Olympus the higher we climbed the less we photographed. Masses of good photographs were taken on the walk in through the Himalayan foothills and there were some superb results from the Icefall and the Western Cwm, but there was much less from the face itself where photography became very much a subordinate activity among the lead climbers. Apart from this, it was not unusual to experience −35°C of frost above Camp 6 (27,300ft) which made it difficult to handle cameras.

Speaking now for myself, there comes also the saddening realisation that the view from the top of Everest which I now have in my mind's eye is very possibly no longer the magnificent pure naked wholly coloured vision of the moment, but consequently wholly coloured by the slides I then took and have seen so many times since.

The photographs we took are owned by the expedition, and copyright does not revert to the photographers for two years. Apart from that, the demand for the photographic material is such from sponsors, for lectures, for publication in books, etc. that it is a long time before the actual photographer receives a full set of his own original photographs back again – by which time he may well be embroiled in another expedition.

We were particularly fortunate that Wendy Bonington was able to devote a great deal of time to sorting through the slides and returning all those not required. Those she kept for lecture sets were duplicated and copies sent back to each photographer for his records.

We were also grateful for the care with which Wendy Bonington treated our colour slides and Down Town Darkroom our black and white negatives. Would that all others who handled our material so roughly had paused to consider it took a lot of getting.

Cinematography by Ian Stuart

The BBC film unit consisted of the two producers, Ned Kelly and Chris Ralling; Mick Burke and myself as cameramen; and Arthur Chesterman as sound recordist.

Our brief was to film and record a 75-minute documentary programme and to send back TV news reports and sequences for the 'Blue Peter' programme. A total of 39,000ft of film was used.

EQUIPMENT

1. Sound equipment (by Arthur Chesterman)
Lightweight, reliability, and convenience of use were the prime factors that influenced my decision to use the Nagra SN as the main recorder on the expedition, although I did have a Nagra 4.2 and Nagra IS as alternatives. By running the machine at 3¾" per second and using double play tape I achieved a recording time of 54 minutes per reel without sacrificing quality. I had a lightweight mixer built which provided two microphone inputs and full monitoring facilities which gave the same versatility and capability to the SN as a full-size Nagra. The total weight of the equipment was four pounds and it was small enough to leave in my sleeping bag overnight, to keep it warm. Mallory alkaline cells were used throughout and, although they gave reduced performance under very cold conditions, their performance was superior to ordinary batteries under the same conditions.

The SN gave no trouble at all, in spite of rough treatment and, although it would sometimes take up to three seconds to reach speed, this was almost certainly a battery problem and only happened when it was extremely cold. I used Sennheiser 415 microphones – the 415 is a short gun mike – for most work and Audio Engineering Radio Microphones. These gave no problems and are probably the best microphones for this kind of work.

2. Camera Equipment included the following:

    Cameras
        2 Eclair NPR, 10-1 Angenieux zoom and 10-1 Zeiss zoom
        1 Eclair ACL with spare body and 10-1 Angenieux zoom
        2 Arriflex ST with 10-1 Angenieux zooms
        1 Bell Howell 70 DR
        5 Bell Howell 200T autoloads with either single-lens or two-lens turrets
        1 Bell Howell 200T with electric drive and crystal sync. facility (adapted by the BBC)
    Tripods
        2 Ronford fluid 2
        2 Miller
        1 Satchler and Wolfe heavy duty

Additional lenses included
> 20-1 Angenieux zoom
> Novaflex outfit 140mm–600mm
> Telestigma telephoto

also 2 Ferranti solar battery chargers (developed specially by Ferranti Ltd and the BBC Research and Development department)

Film Stock
> Kodak Eastmancolor 7247

Filters
> A range of 85 and 85B with neutral density was taken

PROBLEMS

1. Logistics

Having our own team of BBC porters meant that we had no serious logistical problems below Camp 2. Above this camp manpower is at a premium and climbing the mountain obviously takes precedence. The BBC front line was kept supplied, but, due to the speed at which this expedition moved, by a very narrow margin. Some means of making camera loads immediately recognisable (brightly coloured bags?) would have been a help at high camps.

2. Temperature

The effect of cold on film equipment is cumulative. At night all gear with moving parts and batteries was kept inside tents and as warm as possible. At altitude the sun's radiant heat is tremendous and equipment was exposed to this for as long as possible each day. The great range of temperatures experienced can give rise to condensation if care is not taken. Cameras, magazines and lenses were always brushed clean of snow and stored at night in closed plastic bags.

3. Batteries

Maintaining a stock of fully charged batteries is a big worry when working in remote areas. We left a petrol driven battery charger at Khumde Hospital (a six-day round trip by runner) and had sufficient batteries to depend on that source if necessary. Blessed as we were with good weather, however, our two Ferranti solar chargers made good use of the intense sunlight at Camp 2 and kept us fully charged. This was probably the first time that solar chargers had been used to support a film unit.

4. Rushes

Approximately every six days exposed film was taken by runner to Kathmandu (12 days) and airfreighted to London by Liz Hawley, our press agent, where they were processed by Denham Laboratories. Naturally this results in a long delay before reports are received.

5. Photographic Exposure

Throughout the expedition I relied heavily on a Pentax spot meter, generally relating exposure to flesh tones, especially above the snow line. A Weston Master and a Spectra were also taken. None of these meters were winterised and all jammed if allowed to get cold.

6. Oxygen

The lack of oxygen at altitude makes camera operating difficult, and a tripod essential for prolonged shooting. Hand-holding above 17,000ft might well be made easier if the operator used an oxygen system. One's ability to sustain creative effort is also drastically reduced. For me six hours' filming at 17,000ft was more than enough for one day.

7. Personalities

Personal relationships can make an expedition an enjoyable or a harrowing experience. Compatibility is extremely important within an expedition film unit. On this expedition relations between the unit members and between them and the climbers were excellent. In particular the friendly, co-operative and frank attitude of the climbers played no small part in making the film a success.

The 3 Eclair Cameras were provided by Soromec of Paris and not winterised; they were guaranteed to function at –30°C. The 10-1 Zeiss zoom was not winterised either but also worked sharply and smoothly throughout the expedition. The bulk of the rest of the equipment was provided by the BBC who winterised it (degreased and regreased with low freezing point grease) and carried out modifications where necessary. The Bell Howell 200T with crystal sync. made sync. shooting with the Nagra SN, at high camps or even the summit, a possibility. All the 200T cameras had film identification codes consisting of holes drilled through their gates on the sound track side.

The 600mm Novaflex took effective shots of climbers above Camp 6 from a position near Camp 2. For camera movement to be successful with this lens a geared head or equivalent is necessary.

Eastmancolor 7247, with its good latitude characteristics, coped well with the extreme contrasts above the snowline. On exteriors it was usually used in conjunction with a wratten 85N6 filter at f11 or f16.

FILMING

The camera equipment used on the expedition can be divided into four main categories.
1. Equipment used on the walk in.
2. Equipment used at Base and Advanced Base Camps.
3. Equipment used for professional coverage of climbing.
4. Summit and amateur use.

1. Two camera teams filmed the approach march, generally working independently of one another, one team using an Eclair ACL, the other using an Eclair NPR and Arriflex ST. Filming a walk in is difficult. Mountaineers tend to walk rapidly and are usually impatient of delay, some can be downright camera shy. Film units therefore need to start ahead of the main body and have the energy to overtake them once they have passed. The problems are obviously compounded by ill health, as few people complete the walk in without experiencing one or two days below par. The ACL proved to be an ideal sync. camera for this work, being much lighter, more compact and faster to bring into operation than the NPR.

On the approach our cameras were carried by porters. This was not as satisfactory as using Sherpas for this job. Although Sherpas consider it below their dignity to work as porters on the walk in, they can be persuaded by argument and bonuses if these are organised at the time of their engagement. The BBC employed 48 porters and 6 Sherpas on the march in and 6 camera Sherpas at Base Camp and above. In addition to his many better known abilities, the Sherpa can quickly grasp some of the technicalities of filming and can become an indispensable camera assistant. Pasang Temba of Khumjung is such a man.

Our in-service equipment was carried in rucksacks, padded with foam plastic. A more convenient arrangement would have been zip-around canvas cases, fitted with cut out Ethafoam and mounted on pack frames.

2. The NPR and ST Arriflex were chosen for use at Base and Advanced Base Camps, as they had proved their reliability on Everest in 1971. The NPR generally worked well, but at very low temperatures (−15°C) the mechanism itself functioned normally, but the centre drive sprocket in the magazines seized. It is absolutely essential that cold room tests should simulate actual working conditions as nearly as possible. Magazines need to be loaded with film and all equipment left to freeze for twelve hours before testing for such tests to be meaningful. That old war horse the ST behaved impeccably. The shock wave from an avalanche that hit Camp 2 destroyed the camera tent and spread gear far and wide, where it lay unprotected from the cold for some time. At dawn it was the ST Arriflex that recorded the scene.

3. Mick Burke used an ACL for sync. filming on the mountain. This camera with its push-on 200ft magazines, although untried, was considered to be the best available for the job. The ACL appears to have functioned well, but detailed information is unavailable due to Mick's tragic death.

4. Amateur coverage on the mountain was photographed with Bell Howell 200T 50ft autoload cameras. These are clockwork, cassette loading, pocket sized, robust and easy to operate. Their reliability was proved on Everest in 1971. Martin Boysen used an autoload to shoot effective material at Camp 6, the highest cine film used in the documentary. The same type of camera was used by Mick Burke to film Pete Boardman and Pertemba on the summit ridge.

Medicine *by Dr Charles Clarke*

The benefit which every Everest doctor derives from his predecessors is considerable and both Dr Barney Rosedale and Dr Peter Steele gave much useful advice, thus saving a considerable amount of time. At early expedition meetings it became clear that a team of our size, which could be spread over a vast distance and altitude, would need two medical officers. We felt this particularly because of the logistic problem of having the expedition divided between the face and Base Camp by bad weather. Dr Jim Duff from Kendal, a graduate of Liverpool University, was soon recruited and it was most helpful to have as a partner someone who had worked in Nepal – he had spent the previous year working on the British section of the East–West highway through the Terai and foothills of Nepal.

No two doctors would plan for Everest in the same way; for example, in the United States, I feel sure, the preparations would have been more elaborate. The team members had no formal medical examination but a careful medical history was taken with particular reference to illnesses on previous expeditions. A dental check was strongly advised and all had a chest X-ray, a full blood picture and urinalysis. Blood grouping with antibody screening was also carried out so that we could, in an emergency, consider transfusion. The usual inoculations for smallpox, cholera, typhoid, tetanus and polio were carried out, largely by local general practitioners. BCG (against tuberculosis, which is common in Nepal) would have been given had not all the members reacted to the appropriate skin test. Gamma globulin – excellent short-term protection against infectious hepatitis – was also given and although there is relatively little malaria in Nepal, pyrimethamine (Daraprim) tablets were issued weekly before and during the monsoon approach march.

From this somewhat sketchy prelude there emerged no current illness, although some chest pain and an unusual electrocardiogram, in the case of one member, did in the end lead him to investigation with a coronary arteriogram which was normal. Later he went well to Camp 5. Previous severe occult gastro-intestinal blood loss had occurred in one member.

The accumulation of the ten porter-loads of medical supplies took place almost entirely through the generosity of the pharmaceutical industry. The only point which revolutionised the packing was the large variety of polythene boxes we were given; this made it easy to pack delicate equipment for the varied terrain of the journey overland and the approach march.

Insurance is becoming costly as the numbers of Himalayan casualties rise. We had a Life and Medical Insurance for £6000 per head at a premium of under £50 each.

Although rescue attempts by air are possible in the Western Cwm, the case would have to be exceptional to justify an attempt. It would, anyway, require elaborate liaison in Kathmandu before the expedition. We chose to rely on evacuating patients on foot (their own, if possible) or by stretcher to Base Camp, thence to Khumde (by yak if necessary) where there is the small, but very well-organised, hospital founded by Sir Edmund Hillary. There Dr Paul Sylvester and his wife, Glen, kindly agreed to help us if the need arose. Only exceptionally would we use the home-made ice and rubble helipad at Base Camp to fly a patient direct to Kathmandu – although at the end of the expedition we did use this route to fly out Chris Ralling with some of the film. It is worth remembering that the payload of most of the helicopters operating in Nepal is small, and it may be that no more than two passengers could be airlifted at this altitude. For expeditions elsewhere in Nepal, it would be well worth while contacting the helicopter pilots before leaving Kathmandu and specifying a potential rescue site near one's Base Camp.

ILLNESS ON THE APPROACH MARCH

The usual discomforts of the monsoon came our way: diarrhoea, a few blisters, infected wounds. Apart from being aggressive about sterilising drinking water, we took no special precautions and ate anything and drank tea and chang locally. Oddly, the most severe case of sunburn on the whole trip occurred early in the approach march – the 'cloudy-bright' conditions being deceptive.

ILLNESS ON THE MOUNTAIN

1. Acclimatisation
The leisure of our stay in Khumde (about 13,000ft) and the march to Base Camp – about eight days for most of us – undoubtedly contributed to the scarcity of serious symptoms of altitude sickness up to 18,000ft. On our return it was alarming to see trekkers planning to do the journey in less than half the time, and easy to understand why pulmonary and cerebral oedema are so common in the Khumbu Valley.

2. Pulmonary Oedema
We had one case of serious altitude sickness at Base Camp. Keith Richardson, in spite of leisurely acclimatisation, developed pulmonary oedema five days after arrival. I chose to evacuate him on foot to Khumde and with oxygen as far as Pheriche, where he made a rapid recovery. Thus, sadly for Keith, there was no possibility of his returning to join the expedition and take part in reporting for the *Sunday Times* from the Western Cwm, as he had planned.

3. Cerebral Oedema
Two Sherpas became drowsy and listless after several carries from Camp 2 to Camp

4. Both had early papilloedema (swelling of the head of the optic nerve) and retinal haemorrhages. One was disproportionately breathless. Recovery was rapid with oxygen and descent to Base Camp; both were treated with the potent steroid, Dexamethasone.

4. Frostbite and Hypothermia

The combination of the team's experience of cold and high altitudes, together with superb equipment, contributed to making frostbite a relatively trivial problem. Dougal Haston, Doug Scott and Martin Boysen had minor frostbite of fingertips at the end of the trip but they recovered rapidly as we came home with no specific treatment. Doug and Dougal's bivouac on the South Summit deserves special mention here as the model of 'how to avoid cold injury'.

We also had an ingenious device for warming oxygen, designed by Dr E. Llewellyn Lloyd from Edinburgh. This would have been invaluable in the treatment of hypothermia.

5. Sunburn and snowblindness

We carried a variety of anti-sunburn creams (Piz Buin and Roche Eversun 7 were the most popular) and several members also wore silk masks. No one was incapacitated by severe sunburn but several noses became very painful. A simple nose-guard – easily made from tape – gives an adequate shadow.

Many of the Sherpas complained of minor snowblindness, largely because they disliked wearing goggles in the morning heat in the Icefall. With steroid eye drops they recovered rapidly.

6. Other illnesses

Two members developed severe chest pain at Camp 2, which was later shown to be due to rib fracture; one man passed a renal stone at Camp 2. One Sherpa had a severe attack of migraine, also at Camp 2: he had had similar attacks at altitude in previous years.

Mike Cheney, our Base Camp Manager, suffered much severe pain caused by a form of arthritis in the thoracic spine. It later turned out that he had an infection in a vertebra at the site of a previous operation. He bore his symptoms with great courage and only at the end of the expedition did he accept being carried by yak to Khumde.

Hamish MacInnes inhaled part of a soft snow avalanche above Camp 4 and took several weeks to recover. He returned home before the summit bid.

High-altitude cough was almost universal, a difficult symptom to alleviate – particularly at night. A variety of cough lozenges, of which Mac and Fisherman's Friend were the most popular, were used freely by everyone. The old-fashioned Dr Nelson's Inhaler (now banned from hospitals because it is unhygienic!) filled with a mixture of Macs, rum and hot water was particularly helpful.

It is interesting to note how long after the expedition the coughs and sore throats persisted in the European members – some of us were still troubled several weeks after returning to Britain.

Morale was high throughout the trip and this certainly contributed to the lack of serious illness. The doctors hoped to keep a low profile on the expedition and our task was made relatively easy by the excellent relations we maintained amongst ourselves and with our Sherpas.

RESEARCH

It is often said that a medical officer contemplating serious altitude research on a pure mountaineering expedition should direct his interests elsewhere. It is frequently unpopular, equipment is hard to maintain and there may be much routine or emergency work to do. Our work was correspondingly modest and determined by personal interests. We carried out the following studies which will be briefly mentioned here:

1. A survey, with photographs, of the symptomless haemorrhages in the retina which occur at high altitude.

2. Measurement of the intra-ocular pressure during the early part of the expedition – up to 20,000ft.

3. Some observations on the use of soft contact lenses (Permalenses) at high altitude.

The results of these studies will be published in the medical press. We found a tendency for relative newcomers to high altitude to develop multiple retinal haemorrhages (which were symptomless) whereas in those members who had been over 24,000ft in previous years they were a rarity, as indeed were symptoms of altitude sickness.

There was no change in the intra-ocular pressure during acclimatisation – and in particular during the development of the retinal haemorrhages.

Two members of the team were able to use soft contact lenses up to 24,000ft.

MEDICAL EQUIPMENT

The choice of supplies was determined largely by our predecessors on Everest and in particular, the 1972 British and 1971 International expeditions. Where possible, drugs were chosen which would serve two or even more purposes. The surgical and anaesthetic equipment must depend on the experience of the medical officers rather than on their enthusiasm; our equipment was certainly less than others have carried.

We took particular care to distribute supplies widely in small quantities, clearly labelled – almost all the packing was done before leaving Britain – and the details which follow, though long, do give information which may be useful in the future.

DIAGNOSTIC KITS *Packing: polythene boxes. Numbers: two.*

1 Littman stethoscope; 1 aneroid sphygmomanometer; 1 auroscope/opthalmascope (Keeler pocket set); 2 low temperature thermometers; 6 pen torches; 1 bottle Multistix diagnostic strips; 20 spatulas.

RESUSCITATION KITS *Packing: Vickers Laerdal boxes. Numbers: two.*

1 Vickers Laerdal resuscitation kit; 2 mucous extractors; 6 needles and syringes; 4 Medicuts; 2 scalpels + blades; 1 crêpe bandage; 10 skin swabs; 1 wound dressing; 1 Steristrip.

Drugs: packed in empty Fortral boxes.

8 Diazepam 10 mgm inj; 6 Omnopon 20 mgm inj; 4 Pentazocine 60 mgm inj; 4 Scoline 50 mgm inj; 4 Atropine 1 mgm inj; 8 Frusemide 20 mgm inj; 2 Digoxin 0.25 mgm inj; 4 Nalorphine 10 mgm inj; 2 Chlorpheniramine 10 mgm inj; 4 Dexamethasone 4 mgm inj; 4 Haloperidol 5 mgm inj.

INTRAVENOUS AND ANAESTHETIC EQUIPMENT *Packing: polythene boxes. Number: one.*

4 I.V. giving sets without needles; 2 6-pack Fenwal bags (blood taking), 6 Rheomacrodex 500ml in saline; 2 1 litre Intravenous Dextrose 5%; 2 500ml intravenous normal saline; 8 Butterfly needles; 8 Medicuts; 2 crêpe bandages; 2 Micropore tape 2.5cm; 2 LP needles; 20 Marcaine 0.5% 10ml inj; 10 Ketamine 100 mgm inj; 100 small gauze squares; 20 antiseptic wipes.

DOCTORS' READY KITS *Packing: polythene boxes. Numbers: two.*

50 Codeine Phosphate 15 mgm tablets (sachet); 100 Lomotil tablets (bottle); 24 Panadol tablets (box); 30 Superplenamins (multivitamins) (tin); 500 water sterilising tablets (bottle); 30 Fortral 50 mgm capsules (sachet); 10 Frusemide 40 mgm tablets (sachet); 20 cough lozenges (foil strip); 2 Omnopon 20 mgm inj + syringes + needles; 30 Ampicillin 250 mgm tablets (sachet); 1 pair of scissors; 1 Elastoplast doctors set; 6 safety pins; 1 lint dressing no. 6; 1 eye dressing; 2 Elastocrêpe 7.5cm bandages; 1 elastic adhesive bandage; 1 theatre and ward dressing; 1 Steristrip sutures ¼"; 10 assorted Melonin dressings; 1 pack of moleskin; 1 suncream; 1 lipsalve; 1 antiseptic cream (M&B); 1 Otrivine 0.1% nasal spray; 10 Welldorm capsules (foil strip); 10 insect repellent wipes; 1 insect repellent gel; 1 Tineafax powder 25G; 1 Iodex with Wintergreen; 4 Benoxylate minims; 4 Sulphacetamide minims; 4 Anusol suppositories.

CLIMBERS' PERSONAL KITS *Packing: polythene boxes. Numbers: twenty-eight.*

30 Codeine Phosphate 15 mgm tablets (sachet); 20 Lomotil tablets (foil strip); 12 Panadol tablets (box); 100 water-sterilising tablets (Puritabs bottle); 20 cough lozenges (foil strip); 1 tin assorted Elastoplast, code 7291; 3 safety pins; 1 crêpe bandage 7.5cm; 4 Melonin dressings; 3 Elastoplast wound dressings; 1 suncream; 1 lipsalve; 1 antiseptic cream (M&B); 1 Otrovine 0.1% nasal spray; 10 Welldorm

capsules (foil strip); 10 insect repellent wipes; 1 insect repellent gel; 1 Iodex with Wintergreen; 1 Tineafax powder 25g; 2 Benoxylate minims; 2 Sulphacetamide minims; 4 Anusol suppositories.

CAMP FIRST-AID KITS *Packing: polythene boxes. Numbers: ten.*

50 Codeine phosphate 15 mgm tablets (sachets); 100 Lomotil tablets (bottles); 48 Panadol tablets (boxes); 30 Superplenamins (multivitamins – tin); 30 Fortral 50 mgm capsules (sachet); 10 Frusemide 40 mgm tablets (sachet): 40 cough lozenges (foil strip, polythene bags); 2 Omnopon 20 mgm inj + syringes + needles; 30 Ampicillin 250 mgm capsules; 1 pair of scissors; 20 Mogadon 5 mgm tablets; 20 Dalmane 30 mgm capsules; tin, assorted Elastoplast, code 7291; 1 triangular bandage; 3 safety pins; 1 lint dressing no. 9; 1 eye dressing; 2 crêpe bandages; 1 Sleek 2.5cm; 1 Elastoplast strip 7.5cm; 8 assorted Melonin; 10 antiseptic wipes; 2 suncream; 2 Lipsalve; 1 Otrovine 0.1% nasal spray; 1 antiseptic cream (M&B); 1 Anusol cream; 1 Otosporin drops; 4 Benoxylate minims; 4 Sulphacetamide minims; 1 Chloram-phenicol eye ointment; 1 zinc and castor oil cream 112g.

DRESSING PACKS *Packing: fibre medical boxes. Numbers: two.*

6 Elastoplast theatre and ward dressings; 10 assorted crêpe bandages; 7 Elastoweb bandages; 80 Melonin dressings 4" × 4" and 2" × 2"; 18 Elastoplast dressing strip 3" × 1 yard; 10 Elastoplast adhesive bandage 3"; 120 Carbonet dressing 4" × 4" (in foil packs) pieces; 200 Airstrip dressings, 3" × ⅞" and 3" × 2"; 5 Airstrip assorted dressings (tins code 7291); 3 Sleek 7.5cm strapping; 6 Duropore 2.5cm strapping; 12 Micropore 1.25cm strapping; 6 Micropore 2.5cm strapping; 5 packs digit sized Tubinette bandages + applicator; 12 plaster of paris emergency packs 3" × 3 yards; 24 safety pins; 500G sterile gauze; 1kg cottonwool; 100 4" × 4" gauze swabs; 10 assorted sterilised lint dressings; 12 eye pads; 240 antiseptic wipes; 4 dressing packs.

SURGICAL KITS *Packing: large polythene boxes. Numbers: two.*

1 scissors 7" sharp; 1 scissors 7" blunt; 2 artery forceps 6"; 1 forceps 5" toothed; 1 forceps 5" non-toothed; 1 needle holder; 1 scalpel handle no. 3; 12 assorted catgut and silk sutures with needles; 12 no. 11 blades; 3 catheter bags; 2 urinary catheters (Foley 16 and 20 FG); 2 spigots; 1 tourniquet; 1 disposable proctoscope; 1 dental upper forceps; 1 dental lower forceps; 1 excavator, large; 1 dental spatula; 1 dental mirror; 1 dental forceps; 1 PhisoMed 150 ml; 3 surgical gloves size 7½; 20 Disposagloves; 1 Rikospray antibiotic; 1 nasogastric tube; zinc oxide, clove oil, Cavit quickset; 1 neurosurgical Burr Hole kit; 2 collars (padded polythene, adjustable); 8 scrubbing brushes; 3 dressing packs; 11 pairs scissors.

Packing: Zimmer splint box. Numbers: two.

8 assorted ¾" and 1" Zimmer splints; 2 Argyll trochar cannula sets (thoracic).

Packing: small polythene boxes. Numbers: two.

1 Heimlich chest valve; assorted rubber tubing and connectors.

STOCK DRUG PACKS *Packing: polythene boxes. Numbers: two.*

400 Ampicillin capsules 250 mgm; 400 Oxytetracycline tablets 250 mgm; 200 Septrin (dispersible) tablets; 400 Phthalylsulphathiazole tablets 500 mgm; 30 Triplopen vials; 10 Ampicillin inj 500 mgm; 100 Flagyl tablets 200 mgm; 300 Daraprim tablets 25 mgm; 50 Chloroquine tablets; 100 Griseofulvin tablets 500 mgm; 25 Alcopar sachets 5 G; 4 Mycota cream; 50 Digoxin tablets 0.25 mgm; 10 Digoxin 2 ml inj; 100 Frusemide tablets 40 mgm; 20 Frusemide inj 20 mgm; 100 Opilon tablets; 12 Opilon ampoules; 100 Ronicol tablets; 100 Ventolin tablets 4 mgm: 1 Ventolin inhaler; 100 Praxilene tablets; 20 Praxilene ampoules; 300 Veganin tablets; 300 Panadol tablets; 1000 Codeine Phosphate tablets 15 mgm; 100 Fortral capsules 50 mgm; 20 Fortral inj 60 mgm; 100 Pethidine tablets 50 mgm; 10 Omnopon inj 20 mgm: 500 Lomotil tablets; 100 Senna tablets; 100 Dulcolax tablets: 36 Anusol suppositories; 4 Anusol cream; 500 Mag Trisil tablets; 50 Stemetil tablets 5 mgm; 10 Stemetil inj 12.5 mgm; 1500 G Kaolin powder; 200 Diazepam tablets 5 mgm; 10 Diazepam inj 10 mgm; 250 Mogadon tablets; 250 Dalmane capsules 30 mgm; 200 Soneryl tablets: 50 Largactil tablets 50 mgm; 25 Haloperidol tablets 5 mgm; 5 Haloperidol inj 5 mgm; 25 Kemadrin tablets 5 mgm; 100 Phenobarbitone tablets 30 mgm; 5 Phenobarbitone inj 200 mgm; 8 Chloromycetin eye ointment 1%, 4 g tubes; 20 Pilocarpine minims 2%; 20 Mydrilate minims 1%; 20 Phenylephrine minims; 40 Chloramphenicol minims 0.5%; 20 Sulphacetamide minims; 40 Benoxylate minims (local anaesthetic); 4 Betamethasone eye/ear/nose drops 5 ml; 2 standard eye dressings; 2 eye patches; 20 fluorets; 180 Fersaday tablets; 360 Superplenamins tablets; 200 Redoxon tablets 500 mgm; 1 Clinitest set; 15 Dexamethasone/Betamethasone inj 4 mgm; 200 Dexamethasone/Betamethasone tablets 0.5 mgm; 5 Piriton inj 10 mgm; 50 Piriton tablets 4 mgm; 40 water for inj 2 ml; 15 Lignocaine plain 1% 5 ml; 30 Assorted syringes and needles; 1 Set Vickers inflatable splints; 2400 water-sterilising tablets (Puritabs); 100 dispensing labels; 100 polythene dispensing bags; 1 Mercurochrome crystals 25 g; 1 Crystal Violet crystals 25 g; 1 Brilliant Green crystals 25 g; 12 Swarm insect repellent tubes; 60 Mijex insect repellent sticks; 48 insect repellent gel (tubes); 600 insect repellent wipes (sachets); 6 Caladryl cream; 36 Tineafax powder 25 g; 6 olive oil cream shampoo; 12 Lenium shampoo; 13 bars of soap; 5 E45 cream (tubes); 3 Ascabiol 200 ml; 4 M&B antiseptic cream; 8 zinc and castor oil cream (112 G pots); 6 Lorexane powder; 12 Vapona insect repellers; 30 Iodex with Wintergreen (tubes).

SUNCREAM, LIPSALVE, COUGH SWEETS *Packing: fibre boxes. Number: one.*

200 tubes suncream (Vanda, Uvistav, Piz Buin, Eversun 7); 250 lipsalves (Little Princess, Piz Buin, Uvistav, Pickles); 3000 cough lozenges (Mac, Dequadin, Bradasol, Fisherman's Friend); 2 Dr Nelson's Inhaler.

HYPOTHERMIA KITS *Packing: loose. Numbers: two.*

1 hypothermia treatment kit (Dr Lloyd); 1 mummy survival bag.

EVEREST:
THE UNCLIMBED RIDGE

with Charles Clarke

Authors' note

A library on Everest already exists, recording many attempts, successes, failures and tragedies. In adding to this we record the story of a small expedition, pieced together from our own thoughts and memories and the diaries of those who kept them. We are indebted to Hilary Boardman for allowing us to use Peter's diary freely, and to Maria Coffey for Joe's letters.

CHRIS BONINGTON
CHARLES CLARKE
May 1983

Contents

1

'A worthwhile objective'

April 1981 – 1 March 1982

Charles Clarke

'You *are* coming to Everest next year, aren't you?' was how Chris put it. It was the first I knew of it. It was April 1981 and we were spending the weekend at the Glenridge Hotel on the shores of Ullswater in preparation for the 1981 British Mount Kongur expedition to China. While we talked logistics and tested tents, filmed and held a press conference, I sensed that our meeting had two roles. Its overt purpose was to plan our visit to Mount Kongur on the southern border of Xinjiang, China's western province: more surreptitiously, the seeds were sown for the first British expedition to the Tibetan side of Everest for over forty years. Peter Boardman, Al Rouse, Joe Tasker and I slipped off downstairs on the Sunday morning to hear Chris unfurl the plans to attempt the little-known North East Ridge of Everest from Tibet the following year.

The highest mountain in the world lies between two Himalayan nations, a giant pyramid astride the frontier of Nepal and Tibet. It's southern flank, bounded by the West Ridge and the South East Ridge, lies in Nepal and has been visited extensively since the second world war. The Tibetan side is at present less well known but was explored thoroughly by British expeditions in the 1920s and 1930s. Between the 3000m (10,000ft) East, or Kangshung Face, and the north wall of the mountain lies the North East Ridge, three miles long. Unclimbed, obvious, long and elegant as a route, it was a magnificent virgin line, the only ridge left for a new route on Everest. Thus it remains.

It is often difficult to explain the choice of a route on a mountain. If the peak is unknown or unclimbed there seems little need to justify the intention to attempt a first ascent. For second and subsequent ascents of peaks above 8000m (26,000ft), such is the scale of the undertaking that the choice becomes of crucial importance. Why, for example, was it more attractive to us to attempt the North East Ridge of Everest from Tibet rather than an unclimbed route on Lhotse, Everest's 8500m (27,900ft) neighbour, from Nepal? First, geographical innovation makes a route attractive. Nepal, whilst being a fascinating, hospitable and delightful country, is now very much on the tourist routes to the Far East, with Kathmandu connected by frequent flights to several Indian cities and to Bangkok. Kathmandu with its quaint Hindu charm is no longer a place few Europeans have visited. All of us had been to the Himalaya during the previous fifteen years on several occasions – we once calculated we had been on over forty expeditions between us – and had cast longing glances to the northern border of Nepal, to Tibet, the forbidden land under Chinese rule. In the late 1970s, in keeping with the change of policy in the People's Republic of China, Tibet was, for the first time in forty years, becoming a country a foreigner could visit. First a few privileged invited guests were taken to Lhasa, the capital, and Xigaze and Gyantse, central Tibet's major towns. The writer Han Suyin described her visit in 1975, and, in her view, the great improvements in the country since the Chinese had taken over in 1950. A few tourists were allowed to visit in 1978 and 1979 and in that year an event took place which was to revolutionise mountaineering in Central Asia.

With little warning to outsiders, though with great internal preparation, in October 1979 the Chinese government opened selected high mountains to foreign expeditions. Great peaks which had almost disappeared into climbing mythology could once again be reached; within months of the announcement teams from Europe, the United States and Japan were deep in conference with the officials of the Chinese Mountaineering Association in Beijing. In addition to Chomolungma or Everest (8848m/29,028ft), there were Shisha Pangma (8012m/26,250ft) in Tibet, Anyemaqen (6282m/20,610ft) in Qinghai Province, Minya Konka (7566m/24,800ft) and Siguniang (6250m/20,500ft) in Sichuan Province, Bogda (5445m/17,864ft), Mustagh Ata (7549m/24,767ft), Kongur Tiube (7595m/24,918ft) and Mount Kongur (7719m/25,325ft) in Xinjiang Province. Each of these mountains was geographically very attractive to a small group of climbers and high-altitude scientists who had come together under the leadership of Michael Ward, a London surgeon and veteran Himalayan climber from the 1950s and early 1960s. At the time, in the early months of 1980, we chose Mount Kongur, an almost unknown peak in the far west of Xinjiang. In 1980 Kongur was one of the highest unclimbed peaks in the world, in a forgotten corner of Central Asia. It satisfied the instinct in all of us for exploration, to attempt to climb a very high, almost unknown peak and to mount a high-altitude scientific expedition. The story of *Kongur, China's Elusive Summit* has already been told and on this happy and successful expedition we explored the Kongur massif, the only mountain group on the 'Chinese List' which still seemed surrounded with an air of mystery. How we longed for more peaks to be available.

For a second expedition to China within the confines of the bureaucratic rules, the North East Ridge of Everest was an obvious choice. An approach through Tibet would be intriguing and whilst in the Everest region we would be following routes explored by the British expeditions which visited the Tibetan side of the mountain between the two world wars. The ridge itself was elegant, unknown and looked, from the few photographs we had, difficult but possible. The route of our choice had to satisfy one other, purely self-imposed, criterion. It had to be climbable by a small expedition without high-altitude porters and without oxygen. There were alternatives on Everest, for example an attempt on the Kangshung Face on its eastern side. We rejected this – the route seemed too dangerous because of avalanches. There are other firsts to be done on Everest (though it has been climbed alone, alone without oxygen, at night and by at least six different routes). One colossal undertaking would be a traverse of the mountain from Nepal to Tibet and doubtless one day this will be done.

If Everest were to be the successor to Kongur there was one catalyst essential to both ventures – money. Through a stroke of genius, luck and excellent advice, Michael Ward and Chris Bonington had met David Newbigging, Chairman of one of Hong Kong's greatest companies, Jardine, Matheson & Co., Ltd. Jardines, originally a Scots trading company, was established in the Far East just over 150 years ago and had not only a large financial stake in the prosperity of Hong Kong but links with China which, though established in Chinese Imperial days, lasted (with some hiccups) through the changes of the Kuomintang, Civil War, Liberation and Cultural Revolution. Jardines agreed first to underwrite the Kongur expedition and showed interest in Chris Bonington's proposals for Everest. Without them it is doubtful whether either expedition could have taken place but with them there was finance on generous terms, a deep knowledge and understanding of China and their own managers, agents and friends in many of the principal Chinese cities.

While we travelled across China to Kongur in May 1981, accompanied by David Newbigging and a small group of Jardines' personnel, we discussed the plans for Everest. Thus before Kongur was even attempted, we had a loose agreement that Everest might be a going concern. Martin Henderson, Financial Director of Mathesons, their London-based company, had taken to climbing and expedition organisation with enthusiasm. 'It's certainly a worthwhile objective,' he said, slipping into climbing jargon. For many multi-national companies could there be anything *less* 'worthwhile' than sending six men to Tibet to climb a mountain?

It seemed odd to be travelling across China in 1981 to a remote part of Xinjiang and to be already discussing the next expedition, but such is the pace of modern Himalayan climbing and the insistence by the Chinese for clearly defined plans that we needed to have made firm arrangements for the following year before returning to Britain.

Kongur taught us many things. Visits to mountains within the People's Republic are experiences very different from trips to the southern Himalaya. The Chinese love order and insist upon precise logistic details, such as bookings for trucks, jeeps, porters and yaks well in advance. The weight of expedition administration, the time-consuming arguments with Customs officials, airlines, Sherpas and porters, do not, or should not exist in China. Superficially this is very attractive for an expedition is almost guaranteed to reach its mountain on time and in good order. Experience on Kongur had taught us how efficient this system could be – but how well organised we needed to be to take advantage of it. My only reservation was that such relentless efficiency lacked a little of the familiar charm and chaos of many a southern Himalayan scene and also that China is grotesquely expensive for foreigners.

On Kongur, we had made very real friends in China. Mr Shi Zhanchun, Vice-Chairman of the Chinese Mountaineering Association, who had himself led two successful Everest expeditions, went out of his way to help us, advising us in detail about logistics in southern Tibet. Our relationship with Jardines, too, had matured. We had grown to understand each other and real friendships had formed. David Newbigging, a man of immense personal charisma and power had, it seemed, taken to the climbing scene, to our unruly dress in the immaculate air conditioned offices of Hong Kong and the curious aspirations of mountaineers, so different from the material dedication of the Jardines' empire. Relationships between a team and its sponsors are beset with potential difficulties; whilst recognising with immense gratitude the financial backing from any organisation, an expedition needs to feel that it is itself the master of its destiny. Though as dependent as an infant, a team does not want to be dominated by the Great Provider. Jardines sensed this almost instinctively and gave us freedom. In turn we felt we behaved towards the company with a filial loyalty without feeling that we were under coercion to act unnaturally in the many public and private engagements we shared. A good example of this were the trekking parties of non-climbers organised by Jardines which accompanied us happily on both expeditions as far as Base Camp and explored with us until we acclimatised. In the sense that after a liaison of three years we are still firm friends, the relationship has been very successful and certainly without Jardines' backing, successive instalments of the 1980 Kongur Reconnaissance, the 1981 Kongur expedition and this Everest expedition would have been a very different, disjointed and, I suspect, far less fulfilling experience for all of us.

Peter Boardman, Chris Bonington, Al Rouse and Joe Tasker reached the summit of Kongur on 12 July 1981. Scarcely had they returned to Base Camp than my own thoughts turned to the following year. The Kongur equipment, all well travelled and battered, needed reorganising. I had the unusual task of packing the main supplies for Everest in Western Xinjiang in the few days' rest we had at Kongur Base Camp before returning home. A complex baggage manifesto, varying from scientific equipment bound for Britain, tents for Hong Kong, oxygen cylinders to await our return in Beijing, was typed in quadruplicate at Base Camp, boxes checked, sealed and finally abandoned in Kashgar. 'Don't worry,' our liaison officer, Mr Liu Dayi, announced, 'if it is labelled correctly there is no problem.' It was true. It is a tribute, indeed, to the Chinese that our only permanent losses in three years of expeditions through the People's Republic and Hong Kong occurred in London at Heathrow Airport, a sad reflection on the capitalist world.

The Kongur expedition returned to Britain on a sunny morning early in August 1981. I realised with a surging sense of panic that there were to be but six months in Britain before we were off again. There was much to do. Chris immersed himself in the Kongur book with his usual dedication, dividing time sparingly between his life as author, lecturer and Everest leader.

Whilst many of the details of our plans for Everest were similar to Kongur, the form of the expedition was to be very different. Our team was to be six instead of ten and the whole emphasis was to be on as small, self-sufficient and light a scale as the objective would allow us. The climbing team was to be four in number, supported by two 'low-altitude staff' of which I was to be one.

Chris was now forty-eight, one of the most experienced high-altitude mountaineers. Expeditions have been his life since 1960, following at almost annual intervals, notably the first great face climb of an 8000m peak, Annapurna South Face in 1970, his attempt on Everest's South West Face in the autumn of 1972, its successful ascent in 1975, Brammah in 1973, Changabang in 1974, the Ogre in 1977. I had known Chris well since Everest in 1975. I had been impressed both with his power as a leader, which he liked to exercise from as near the vanguard of an expedition as possible, and by the meticulous attention he paid to detail. In contrast Chris's ability to change his mind about major decisions is perhaps a source of amusement to those who know him well. At its best it reflects the unusual quality of being able to listen to advice and it ensures that those who know him don't miss expedition meetings by sleeping late.

Coupled with his undoubted abilities there are sides to Chris's intimate life that few of us envy and even fewer wish to share. He is a deep sleeper whose snores can be heard from a great distance and have once been mistaken for the approach of wolves, and an execrable chef whose nadir of culinary achievement was to ruin an entire and most precious meal high on Kongur by mistaking lemonade powder for potato powder.

Peter Boardman was a relative newcomer to the Himalayan scene when I met him on Everest in 1975. He had then been twenty-four. His outstanding performance there was to make the second ascent of the South West Face with Sherpa Peremba. It was Peter who had waited in vain on the South Summit of Everest in appalling weather for Mick Burke to return, struggling back to Camp 6 in a storm which marked the closing stages of the South West Face expedition. He had been pushed to fame and followed Everest with a succession of extraordinary high-altitude climbs, typified by bold routes on great mountains with minute expeditions, several shared with Joe Tasker.

I had known Peter for seven years and had seen him emerge into maturity. I learnt that beneath what was at first sight a veneer of relaxation was an almost superhuman driving force, spurring on each expedition. On a trip Peter was a tidy, clean, organised man who valued his solitude and during long hours alone would write profusely and study his subject in depth. On Kongur and on Everest he was the natural mountain historian, collecting information in an ordered and interesting way. His concentration on writing had already borne fruit. His first book, *The Shining Mountain*, an account of climbing the West Wall of Changabang with Joe Tasker, had won the John Llewelyn Rhys Memorial Prize. While he attempted the North East Ridge of Everest the proofs of his next book, *Sacred Summits*, the story of his remarkable climbs in 1979, were already with his publishers.

If Chris Bonington was to be the example of the public persona on this expedition, Dick Renshaw would be the gentle recluse, ultimately disciplined, dedicated wholly to mountaineering. He had established a particularly strong climbing partnership with Joe Tasker, who wrote of him: 'In smoking, as in all things, Dick was completely controlled. He would take along one cigarette for each bivouac, so friends could estimate how long he thought a climb might take by the number of cigarettes. Three meant a serious route.' Dick had proved himself as a mountaineer with major contributions to make, first by his winter ascent of the Eiger with Joe in 1975 and later that year in their extraordinary two-man ascent of Dunagiri (7066m/23,182ft) in the Garhwal Himalaya. This was one of the first difficult routes attempted by a two-man team and with similar ventures of others pioneered a new era of high-altitude mountaineering – small expeditions climbing alpine-style.

While Dick survived Dunagiri he was not unscathed: exhausted near the summit, he had lost his gloves in the descent and his hands were severely frostbitten. My introduction was a telephone call to the Middlesex Hospital in 1975. 'Hello, I'm Dick Renshaw. A surgeon at home wants to amputate my fingers and says I'll never climb again. Do you agree?' We saw a lot of each other during the treatment for his frostbite and he managed to avoid all but trivial amputation. He has certainly climbed again.

The fourth of the climbing team was to be Joe Tasker. His climbing life was inextricably linked, first with Dick, on the Eiger and on Dunagiri, and later with Pete on Changabang and Kangchenjunga. He had also been to K2 with Chris and Pete in 1978, an expedition which was abandoned after the death of Nick Estcourt. He returned, undeterred, to K2 with Peter, Dick and Doug Scott in 1980, when they were all but swept from the mountain by avalanches. An attempt on the West Ridge of Everest in the bitter cold of the winter of 1980–1 also failed, but success on Kongur followed in 1981. Spare, with a halo of thinning, dishevelled hair, Joe had a reputation for argument, a brittle veneer that vanished quickly as I grew to know him – usually on excited evenings in our house as he left for the Himalaya.

With the wealth of expedition experience, Joe, too, turned to writing. I wondered sometimes if he felt upstaged by the success of Peter's *The Shining Mountain*. If so, there was no need. In 1981 he was correcting the proofs of *Everest the Cruel Way* as we flew to China and he followed this with a moving climbing autobiography, *Savage Arena*. Joe's second creative talent was in photography and filming. With characteristic enthusiasm and order he had, in 1981, learnt the skills necessary for high-altitude filming and throughout this trip to Everest thought, shot and lived the film he was never to see.

Adrian Gordon, thirty-five, was to be my companion on the lower slopes of Everest. Being an executive of the Royal Hong Kong Jockey Club is an unlikely background for a member of a major Himalayan expedition, suggesting either a bookmaker or an expert trainer. Adrian loves neither gambling nor horses but has a passion for the Far East. From a military family, he served in the Seventh Gurkha Rifles both in Nepal and Hong Kong before leaving in 1972 to work for peaceful ends with the Gurkha Reintegration Scheme in Nepal. We had met in 1975 in Nepal when with his fluent Nepali he had organised Sherpas, camps and equipment on the South West Face. Like myself he had few aspirations to go high but knew that expeditions require organisers as well as a summit team. It was Adrian's thankless task to sort out our grubby gear from Kongur, mend tents, check equipment as it arrived either by sea from China or by air from Britain, and organise much of the food and camping equipment in Hong Kong.

I regarded my own selection as something I did not wholly deserve. Though I had already made several modest Himalayan climbing trips, the 1975 Everest South West Face expedition taught me for the first time the flavour of a large expedition, its tensions, the meaning of total commitment, the joy of success and the pain of death. I learnt by attrition of the fears and failings of some great climbers and gained useful knowledge of illness at high altitude. For six years I longed to return, particularly to Central Asia. My medical career did not seem to suffer from my previous absences, indeed they may have helped it, and having to my surprise been appointed as a neurologist at St Bartholomew's Hospital in London in 1979, I found support from my colleagues when I planned to visit Kongur in 1981. Once again I failed to distinguish myself as a climber, being unwell above 5500m (18,000ft) and having a close brush with a windslab avalanche on an easy peak near Base Camp. I thought frequently that three months in Tibet would be too much for me and waited to be told by the others that a stronger replacement would be necessary. As it turned out, nobody seemed worried about my failures and when we returned to London in August 1981 I found myself once again immersed in food lists, medical supplies and organisation for Everest.

This then was our team; a party of six very different people all related by a common cause and unanimous in the goal we had set ourselves. We seemed, for Everest, to have one great asset. Almost all of us knew each other well, trusted each other implicitly and were intent upon success. Neither bravado, internal jealousy nor over-confidence were components in the family atmosphere of this expedition. We were not without argument but we were free of the seeds of bitterness. It seemed to me that at least we would enjoy ourselves in Tibet.

I often feel that the preparations for an expedition are like the description of a first pregnancy – of intense interest and importance to the participants but certainly not unique. While Adrian packed in Hong Kong, Chris, Pete and Joe organised the high-altitude equipment in Britain; Dick and I looked after the food. There were no committee meetings. We packed early in January during a weekend when Britain was paralysed under a layer of ice and snow. Somehow we all reached Manchester and I slept on crates outside the Jardines' warehouse, snug in several sleeping bags with the temperature at –12°C.

There was a sombre undercurrent, an element of finality as we packed our belongings – most of which we would next see in the Rongbuk Valley of Tibet. For Joe, Pete, Chris and Dick there would be high risks near the summit of Everest. I wondered how they felt, that icy weekend. For myself awareness of the dangers of high-altitude mountaineering are never far from the surface. I had seen death on one expedition and had lost friends on others. So had we all. It is well known that a fatal accident occurs more often than not on expeditions over 8000m. Together we felt we shared the responsibility for the task we had chosen to undertake. Fear colours my own climbing and has made me gradually less ambitious, content with modest climbs and to expand my interest in high-altitude medicine rather than pursue ever-increasingly challenging objectives.

In Manchester we read the Bonington masterplan, fresh from his Wang word processor.

1 March	*Depart London Heathrow, Flight No. BA003*
2 March	*Arrive Hong Kong*
7 March	*Fly Chengdu – Lhasa, Flight No. CA4403*
16 March	*Arrive Everest Base Camp with Jardines' trekking team*
Mid-May	*Attempt summit*

It all had a familiar ring – we would be leaving in six weeks.

Goddess Mother of the World

1 March – 8 March

Charles Clarke

Parting becomes harder each time we go. A strange distance begins to build up the week before with each decision about my patients, house, friends and family having an uncanny finality. I shop at Sainsbury's for the last time, bringing home food that I won't be eating. I clean the drains and pay the telephone bill. Ruth, my wife, finds it hard and does not hide her feelings. 'I wish you were gone and have done so for months; for when you've gone I can at least look forward to the time of your return getting shorter.' My two daughters have their own defences. Total immersion or separation. Ruth keeps apart, as if expedition affairs are part of a religion she wishes to forget. Wendy Bonington keeps apart, too, looks forward to making pots and painting, isolated in her Cumbrian cottage.

Hilary Boardman is different; a climber herself and no stranger to the Himalaya. When we were on Kongur last year she was in India some 300 miles away, climbing new peaks and before, on a pre-marital honeymoon of magic, she had with Peter tramped with the pygmies, clad only in their spectacular penis gourds, through the rain and steam of New Guinea to climb the Carstenz Pyramid. Hilary is involved, part of the fabric of knowledge of our routes, maps, equipment, almost to the extent of being a member of the team. I sometimes feel she is cross she isn't coming with us.

Joe's Maria, slim, fine and rather fierce, has become a part of the outfit too. She knows more of Joe's inner thoughts than anyone else, but not everything for there's always a private side to Joe.

Dick's family I know less well. Jan seems maternal, friendly and quietly resigned to our departure while Daniel, the twenty-month blond image of Dick, potters about in his nappies, chuckling like his dad.

Frenda Gordon is in Hong Kong, their second baby due during the expedition. I dare not think what she will have to go through, all alone while we're away. But she seems to have accepted it readily and doesn't, I believe, realise that expeditions are dangerous. Of course, they shouldn't be for Adrian and me, I repeat to myself constantly, but know that there will be times when I shall be very, very frightened.

The days drag on. A week to go till Monday, 1 March. There are important things to do. The oxygen sets from the States are delayed. Are we really going on an Everest expedition *again* without checking the system, even if we hope not to use it? We had so many oxygen failures on the South West Face in 1975 that more might have cost us the summit. It is extraordinary that there is still no good light high-altitude oxygen set. We can send man to the moon... but there's no demand for ten sets a year for the Himalaya. Everything comes separately from different firms. From the USA masks from Scott Sierra, regulators from Robertshaw, helmets from Protection Incorporated, adaptors from Rowe Engineering in Islington, bottles from Life Support Engineering in Sussex. Will they all fit together? With the inevitability of Sod's Law, they do not. Friday evening and we leave on Monday. They're not too good at this sort of thing in Tibet, either. Eventually a raid on the anaesthetics laboratory at Barts sorted out the couplings and we had, it seemed, 'a system', yet untested as the oxygen bottles were already in Lhasa. I felt guilty and hoped the boys wouldn't find out.

The weekend was like the closing scenes of a play you hope will end. It was cold and clear in London. I ran on Hampstead Heath on Saturday, a crisp, glittering morning with London stretching out below, its skyline cut out of cardboard, stark in a morning free of haze. An attractive Hampstead-looking couple with Old English sheepdog stroll by, fashionably clad in sheepskin and high boots. I looked at them with a mixture of envy, lust and faint disdain, thinking that they'll be walking their dog next Saturday while I shall be far away, probably in Lhasa.

By Sunday the clan is gathering. Joe telephones to complain bitterly that I have given over our spare double bed to Dick and Jan. Half mocking, 'You know who your real friends are,' he says. 'I expect I'll see you on the 'plane, if you've kept me a seat.' But within a couple of hours Maria and he are around with beer and wine and laughter. Pete flies in from Geneva, alone. Dick, Jan and little Dan. The booze flows as we have a faintly strained evening, torn between two closely cherished loves. One is a wayward mistress, seductive beyond belief. We all want to get moving, to cut the bonds that tie us to work, telephones and responsibility and come to Tibet, to Lhasa, to the mysteries of the northern side of Everest and the North East Ridge. The other mistress is more constant, homely, warmer and reliant. Home, Ruth and two young girls who I put to bed. Rebecca, nine, blonde and thoughtful, insists I promise I shall not venture above Base Camp and volunteers in turn to work hard at school. Naomi, tousled, dark, rowdy and five, simply demands a present from Hong Kong. They scream for Joe to come and kiss them.

We all drank too much to allay our anxieties, turned in too late and woke too early in the tense over-organised fervour of last-minute packing, trying to fight clear of a hangover. The black Jardines' limousines arrived on time and we climbed aboard, watching a silent group on my doorstep. The strain of parting would soon be over and we'd all feel better for it.

Chris keeps somewhat apart on these occasions. He'd stayed the night before 'at his military club in town', which though it sounds like an abode of Biggles in the thirties is no more than a sensibly priced and friendly hotel.

It is Chris who has masterminded the publicity of the expedition, helped design a brochure and inform the press. Some climbing purists shun this sort of thing, but we all felt a certain need to explain our aims to the press. Climbing by foreign expeditions is still a very new phenomenon in China and it allows small groups of individuals to penetrate hitherto forbidden areas of the People's Republic – southern Tibet, Xinjiang and remote areas of Sichuan. We were thus in a position of privilege within China, freer than any usual tourist in Tibet. In a genuine, though minor, way our relations with our Han Chinese staff and the local people were also important and could further future co-operation between two countries with histories and aspirations so disparate.

Jardines, our sponsors, were a further reason for the expedition being known. With 150 years of trading and negotiating in China, and a large stake in the economic stability and prosperity of Hong Kong, we wanted to establish in Britain, Jardines' role as sponsors of two major expeditions to China – to Kongur in 1980–81 and to Everest in 1982. Lastly we felt a small part of climbing history, the first expedition from China to Tibet, following the steps of the 1921 Everest Reconnaissance and seven subsequent expeditions. But more than to fulfil a role in an Everest chapter of some encyclopaedia, we wished to see for ourselves a country and a mountain range which had held itself apart, almost untouched for forty years.

For Peter, Chris, Joe and me aboard the British Airways 747 for Hong Kong it was just seven months since we had returned from Kongur – it seemed a little unreal to be going back so soon. I felt poorly informed about the details of the northern approaches to Everest, having had little time to do more than collect the books.

Today there is a vast Everest literature and we had with us many of the major volumes. I settled down like a schoolboy revising for exams to glean the essential information about the northern side. I was soon reading *Mount Everest, the Reconnaissance, 1921*, Sir Francis Younghusband's *The Epic of Mount Everest* and a delightful light-hearted book of Bill Tilman's 1938 Everest expedition – small like our own.

Everest is, to our generation of climbers, a mountain viewed largely from the south, seen through the haze of the plains of India or from Tiger Hill above Darjeeling. The imperial Survey of India who, under Sir Andrew Waugh, computed in 1852 that Peak XV was, at a little over 8848m (29,028ft), the highest mountain in the world, viewed the mountain from the Nepalese foothills in India. Waugh named the peak after his mentor and previous Surveyor-General, Sir George Everest – a fine example of the authority of the Raj which renamed a peak on the border of two foreign countries, Tibet and Nepal, with a name from village England, quite disregarding its various native names, the most familiar of which was Chomolungma.

To the Tibetan villager, travelling with his yak to new pastures below the Rongbuk foothills, to the Khamba brigand, hiding from pursuing bands of a local warrior lord, or the illegal surveyor from India disguised as a monk, the North Face of Everest would, however, be but one of a group of great peaks in the dry high-altitude rolling plateau of southern Tibet. Even today the traveller might fail to identify the world's highest mountain from the north until he is well into the Rongbuk Valley.

Perhaps the earliest photographs of Everest from the north were taken from Khamba Dzong, some ninety miles away, by J. C. White, a member of the British Mission to Lhasa led by Colonel Younghusband in 1904. Later in this expedition Major Ryder and Captain Rawling saw the mountain from some sixty miles due north and thought it might be approached from that direction.

Although the Mission to Lhasa established a British presence in Tibet, the xenophobic monastic oligarchy which ruled the country did not warm to the idea of an expedition to Chomolungma, the Goddess Mother of the World. It was not until 1921, after a successful application by the Viceroy, Lord Chelmsford, had been presented in Lhasa by the British Resident of Sikkim, Sir Charles Bell, that the first Everest Reconnaissance was permitted, led by Lieutenant Colonel Charles Howard-Bury, an Indian Army officer with a passion for Tibetan exploration, and in particular Mount Everest. He was a tenacious, if opinionated, organiser. Harold Raeburn was climbing leader with George Leigh Mallory, G. H. Bullock and Dr A. M. Kellas, a veteran Himalayan explorer. Majors H. T. Morshead and E. O. Wheeler of the Survey of India, Dr A. M. Heron of the Geological Survey and Dr A. F. R. Wollaston, explorer, naturalist and physician, completed the party.

The achievements of the Reconnaissance were considerable for they explored, mapped and climbed around several thousand square miles of unknown ranges and glaciers on the northern and eastern sides of Everest. Travelling largely on horseback, they first crossed the Himalaya from Darjeeling and travelled west along the southern fringe of the Tibetan plateau. Illness struck early on the trip and Dr Kellas died, it was thought of pneumonia, shortly before reaching Khamba Dzong – thus depriving the team of the most experienced Himalayan mountaineer of the day. Raeburn also fell ill and played little part in the expedition thereafter.

The northern approaches to the mountain were first explored, the West and Central Rongbuk Glaciers. They confirmed the impression from distant views that Everest was a huge pyramidal peak of three great ridges and three faces. The West Ridge and North Face were felt to be out of the question for a first ascent. The upper reaches of the long North East Ridge above 8400m (27,560ft) did, however, look feasible and from the northern side of the mountain it was clear that a straightforward secondary ridge joined this arête, leading from a col at 6990m (22,933ft) to the crest at about 8230m (27,000ft). The western approaches to this col (the North Col or Chang La) looked hazardous and the climbing party, comprising by this time only of Mallory and Bullock, believed that the only way to explore the eastern side of the North Col was to travel north around Everest to the Kharta and Karma Valleys, which they assumed would in some way lead to the North Col. Having travelled to Kharta by the Doya La, they crossed a 5300m (17,389ft) pass, the Langma La, to Karma, a broad fertile valley with a spectacular southern wall formed by the precipices of Chomo Lonzo, Pethangtse and Makalu. Filling the head of the Karma Valley was the huge Kangshung Face of Everest, framed to the south by the South Col (7986m/ 26,200ft) and South East Ridge, and to the north by the long North East Ridge and the Raphu La (6510m/21,358ft). Neither looked a feasible proposition. The eastern side of the North Col was still elusive, although the expedition survey party had outlined a route there from the Rongbuk Valley via the East Rongbuk Glacier. The team ended their stay in the autumn of 1921 by travelling up the Kharta Valley over the Lhakpa La, a pass at 6705m (21,998ft). From there Mallory, Bullock and Wheeler, accompanied by their porters, descended to the head of the East Rongbuk Glacier and made a spirited climb to the North Col of Everest. Above lay the buttresses of the North Ridge which looked reasonable ground for a future attempt on the mountain.

In three months of intense activity the Tibetan side of Everest had been explored. Only the Western Cwm and the South West Face remained as unknown pieces of the jigsaw but these lay in the forbidden land of Nepal – and would be, in any case, extremely difficult of access from Tibet by either the South Col or the Lho La. Mountaineers were to wait some thirty years before approaching the massif from the south. The mountaineering achievements of reaching the North Col and climbing several 6000–7000m peaks were considerable and the detailed surveys of Morshead and Wheeler were to form the basis of all maps of the Everest region. Heron had carried out a geological survey (much to the distaste of the Tibetans who thought he would disturb the deities of the rocks with his hammer) and Wollaston had made a valuable record of the flora and fauna of the region.

The composition and prejudices of the 1921 Reconnaissance were those which would mark many succeeding expeditions to Everest. The team was chosen not by the leader but by the Everest Committee, joint child of the Royal Geographical Society and the Alpine Club, who naturally chose gentlemen who were Army officers or graduates of the older universities. The press at first were rigorously excluded by A. R. Hinks, Secretary of the Royal Geographical Society, although under pressure he relented. His attitude is summed up in a letter to Howard-Bury during the expedition. 'We don't know the way about among all these sharks and pirates...we are having a devil of a time over these sharks who want photographs. No one regrets more sincerely than I do that any dealings with the press were ever instituted at all.'

An aloofness seems to have pervaded the Reconnaissance, exemplified in the closing chapter of the 1921 book. Here Norman Collie, the President of the Alpine Club, wrote his appreciation in which he omitted to mention at all four members of the team – Raeburn, the climbing leader, Wollaston, a notable explorer and naturalist, Heron the geologist, and poor Dr Kellas who lost his life.

Most of the expedition members had at least one personal target of detestation. For Mallory, it was Howard-Bury and Raeburn, both of whom he found irritating. The team's actions seem to exemplify this lack of harmony with Mallory and Bullock's failure to find the East Rongbuk Valley which can only be regarded as an error of major proportions – forcing the expedition to march nearly a hundred miles to its new Base Camp at Kharta. Surely a team with a specialist, highly experienced survey party (Wheeler was later to become Surveyor-General of India) should use it to liaise with the climbing team in finding a route to the mountain, rather than leave it to work as a separate unit?

For life at high altitude there seems to have been little overt preparation. Although Trisul (7120m/23,359ft) had been climbed in 1907 and many of the effects of lack of oxygen and cold documented on previous expeditions to the Himalaya and Andes, there seems to have been little rigorous emphasis on acclimatisation. The choice of equipment was even left to individuals, an allowance of £50 being made for each man to buy his own boots and clothing.

The 1922 expedition led by Brigadier-General Bruce was a team of thirteen Britons who followed the East Rongbuk Glacier route and camped on the North Col on 18 May – the first time man had camped above 6900m. On 27 May George Finch (the father of the actor, Peter) and Captain Geoffrey Bruce (the General's nephew) reached 8320m (27,296ft), using oxygen – the first time that it had ever been used on a climb. On a subsequent assault on 7 June seven porters were killed in an avalanche en route to the North Col, an indication of how dangerous these slopes could be after fresh snowfalls. General Bruce recorded his interpretation of the Tibetan reaction tersely in his account of the expedition. 'If it was written that they should die on Everest, they should die on Everest; if it was written that they would not die on Everest, they would not, and that was all there was to be said in the matter.' Despite this accident, plans were soon afoot for the 1924 expedition.

It was on this famous assault, again led by General Bruce (though he had to retreat with malaria on the march in), that Norton reached 8550m (28,052ft) without oxygen. This was followed by Everest's most famous tragedy, the loss of George Leigh Mallory and Andrew Irvine. They were last seen near the crest of the North East Ridge, above the North East Shoulder, at a height greater than 8500m (27,888ft). Their bodies were never recovered, though an ice axe belonging to the pair was discovered later. Two other deaths took place on this expedition, almost forgotten in the drama of the loss of the favourite sons of England – Lance-Naik Shamsherpun died following a stroke and assistant boot-maker Bahadur died of pneumonia following frostbite. Their names were recorded on a memorial cairn with those of the dead of 1921 and 1922.

Political troubles, caused in part it is thought by the behaviour of the 1920s parties (shooting wildlife, collecting geological specimens and travelling to unspecified areas) and in part by the loss of life (Everest expeditions had already claimed twelve lives), prevented further visits to Tibet for nine years. British expeditions again tried Everest by the North Col route in 1933, 1935, 1936 and 1938 but each, usually because of bad weather, turned back below the 8550m record set by Norton in 1924. Such failures served only to increase the mystique of this, the highest mountain.

Two other events in Everest's history before the second world war should not be forgotten. In 1933, still in the period when the history of aviation was fired by personal ingenuity and courage, sometimes to the point of lunacy, two aircraft flew over the summit of Everest. It was not the first time the idea of flying to Everest had been mooted, for Howard-Bury had visited the Air Force in India in 1920. Initially he was given a cold shoulder, although later enthusiasm seems to have been rejected by the Everest Committee on the grounds of finance. The Houston Everest flight on 3 April 1933 was carried out in two Westland aircraft powered by the new supercharged Pegasus S3 engines. The Everest flight deserves to be remembered, not for its achievement as a high-altitude stunt, but as an expedition which was organised with exemplary efficiency. Oxygen equipment, cameras and clothing were all heated by ingenious low-voltage systems (modified for the specific purpose) and great attention given to the preparation of weather reports from Calcutta and from the expedition's own high-altitude balloon.

Another pre-war visit to Everest had a less happy ending. Maurice Wilson, an eccentric Yorkshireman with almost no climbing or flying experience, decided to pilot himself to Everest and climb the mountain solo, relying on a diet of rice and spiritual determination achieved by meditation. Despite every step of his journey being forbidden or frustrated by the British government or the government of India, he eventually flew to India, smuggled himself to Tibet in 1934, and died, presumably of hypothermia, below the North Col. His body was discovered by Charles Warren, doctor and climber on the 1935 expedition, led by Eric Shipton.

In the decade following the second world war Everest's Tibetan side received little attention, when Nepal, previously a country even more secretive than Tibet, began to open its borders. A little was known of the southern side, for Mallory had seen it from the West Rongbuk Glacier in 1921 and before, in 1907, Nata Singh of the Survey of India had visited the Dudh Kosi Valley and mapped the snout of Khumbu Glacier. In the summer of 1950 an Anglo-American reconnaissance expedition reached the Khumbu Glacier from Nepal, and was followed next year by a British and New Zealand team led by Eric Shipton. The first and second attempts on the mountain by the South East Ridge by the Swiss expeditions of 1952 were unsuccessful. The following year the summit was reached via the South East Ridge by the Sherpa, Tenzing Norgay and the New Zealander, Edmund Hillary, members of the British expedition led by John Hunt. The southern side of Everest has had, since then, almost annual visits and the original route has been climbed by nineteen expeditions, with ascents by ninety-one individuals to date.[1] The other frontier ridge – the West – was climbed by the Americans in 1963 by a route that included several hundred metres on the North Face – and later by the Yugoslavs in 1979. The South West Face of Everest, rising out of the Western Cwm, was climbed in 1975 after five previous attempts. On this expedition, led by Chris Bonington, Dougal Haston, Doug Scott, Peter Boardman and our sirdar Pertemba, reached the summit. Adrian Gordon and I had been part of the support team. Our success had been marred by the tragedy of losing Mick Burke, climber and cine photographer, who was last seen heading upwards, a few hundred metres below the summit. The South Buttress of the South West Face was later climbed by a Polish expedition in 1980.

In contrast the Tibetan faces and ridges of Everest seem almost to have been forgotten in the fervour of the fifties, sixties and seventies, the 'Golden

1 Since 1982 ascents of Everest have totalled around 1500, predominantly by the South East Ridge.

Age' of mountaineering in Nepal. Several parties made illegal visits to the Tibetan side; in 1947 Earl Denman, Canadian by birth and by account a loner with little mountaineering experience, travelled through India to Tibet, reaching a point below the North Col with his Sherpas, Tenzing Norgay and Ang Dawa, both so famous in later years. Again in 1951 another clandestine trip to Everest and Tibet was made by a Dane, Klaus Becker-Larsen, who travelled illegally through Nepal to Khumbu. He first attempted the dangerous Nepalese face of the Lho La (6006m/19,604ft) and narrowly escaped being hit by rockfall. Later, with four Sherpas, he crossed the Nangpa La (5716m/18,753ft) into Tibet and, like Denman, made his way by the Rongbuk Valley to the East Rongbuk Glacier. Again this ill-conceived attempt failed below the North Col and Larsen returned, alive but undetected by the Chinese, to Namche Bazar.

A further sortie into Tibet from Nepal took place in 1962. An American expedition of four, led by Woodrow Wilson Sayre, grandson of the former President, set out with Sherpas and a liaison officer, ostensibly for Gyachung Kang (7922m/25,900ft), a neighbour of Everest. Their aim was to climb a huge icefall below the Nup La, cross this 5985m pass and descend to the Rongbuk Glaciers. In a sense this small team was brilliantly successful, proving that a team unsupported by Sherpas can travel and be self-sufficient over long distances at high altitude. After a series of attempts they reached the North Col and finally abandoned the expedition at about 7600m (24,935ft). They were lucky to return to Nepal alive and undiscovered by the Chinese. The sequel to this illegal journey, and several other flagrant violations of 'the rules', led to the Nepal Himalaya being closed to expeditions from 1964 to 1969 – a reminder of how mountaineering can depend upon the fickle whim of governments.

I had hoped to read of the Chinese' own expeditions to Everest before we touched down at Hong Kong on the morning of 2 March. We were, as ever, made to feel VIPs by Jardines as we were ushered through the airport into several waiting Mercedes. Little was new here for most of us, from the chauffeurs who knew us by name and the immaculate Jardines offices in the Connaught Centre, to the measured luxury of the Excelsior Hotel. Friends from the previous year greeted us and with bearded smile Adrian Gordon told us soon after our arrival that Frenda had had their baby, another son, and all was well.

A typed programme was in our room; there would be little time to think about jet lag after a twenty-hour flight. Within two hours we were reporting for duty at the helicopter pad of HMS *Tamar* for a flight around Hong Kong. Skyscrapers flashed by, ships in the harbour grew small like toys in a game – 'You know what separates the men from the boys? The size of their toys.' We had left the commercial centre and were skimming green hills, thinly wooded slopes running to remote beaches, out towards the New Territories, and the Chinese mainland. Here, at the eastern end of the frontier, is the town of Lo Wu, pierced by the railway and road to the People's Republic. From the air Lo Wu exposes an uneasy contrast between the People's Republic and the colony of Hong Kong not, on the face of it, flattering to Hong Kong. To the northern side are the grey and white blocks of an ordered town with empty streets, bicycles and few vehicles; this is the People's Republic. Yards away in Hong Kong there is a bustling mixture of apartment blocks, offices, bazaars and a sprawling shanty town seething with people, cars, bicycles and carts.

We flew along the deserted land border where a high fence now marks a No Man's Land. Illegal immigration to Hong Kong has, to a large extent, been curbed by increased Chinese vigilance and constant patrols by land, sea and air from Hong Kong. We saw no fugitives but the previous year Peter told me that he had seen two corpses huddled half-sunk in the mud flats near the border.

The pace of these two days was hectic. A serious beer session with our pilots was followed by a ceiling writing competition. Joe won with an unlikely poise from his belt slung over the girder above the bar. Dinner in the mess with Gurkha stewards, chicken and chips and too much wine. I fell asleep in the car on the way home to the hotel and awoke, over-excited but ready for more, the night ending in an excess of alcohol for us all in the hotel. Perhaps wiser than the rest of us, Chris slipped off to bed, he usually does.

Chris and I had one more day in Hong Kong before leaving for Beijing. Adrian, Dick, Joe and Peter and the Jardines' trekking party who were coming to Base Camp were to fly to Chengdu, capital of Sichuan Province, where we were all to reunite before flying to Lhasa. March 4 was a hurried day of meeting the Hong Kong press, last-minute shopping in the land of plenty, refills for ball pens, diaries, the final additions to the Canon and Olympus camera paraphernalia – and more over-excited entertainment far into the small hours.

By noon next day we were in Beijing, re-united with more friends from Kongur: David Mathew, a languid Old Etonian, who was the Jardines Beijing Manager, his assistants, Alison Hardy and Peter Po – an émigré from mainland China whose home was now Hong Kong.

Despite being amongst friends, I felt uneasy to be back in China and anxious to leave for Lhasa. What a contrast to the year before when every aspect of Chinese life fascinated me in this Third World nation which is so different from the rest of Asia. Previously I had been impressed with the order, health, civility and efficiency. Here was Beijing, a city with streets cleaner than London, free of beggars and where appointments were on time. It was, however, now the drabness which overwhelmed me. Beijing seemed a grey city, all the greyer in March before the green of spring, sprawling without form around the vastness of its central Tian-an-men Square.

We were not in Beijing to see the sights, but to put together the pieces of the bureaucratic jigsaw which are an integral part of any expedition to China. The Chinese Mountaineering Association with headquarters in Beijing, is an organisation which includes amongst its functions the supervision of the day-to-day management of all foreign expeditions.

The meeting with the CMA was, as usual, formal and to the point. We met Mr Shi Zhanchun, the Vice-Chairman, a warm and enthusiastic man who welcomed us back as old friends. Mr Chen Rongchang, who was to be our liaison officer, had had his nose, hands and ear frostbitten on a previous visit to Everest. He was impressively efficient and through our interpreter, Mr Yu Bin, asked us questions about our own plans which we could not answer in the detail required. 'On what date exactly will you require the nine yaks at Base Camp?' Three thousand miles away in a land where neither the British nor most Chinese could speak the language.

Mr Shi has been associated with mountaineering in China since the 1950s and particularly with Everest. He led the first Chinese Everest Expedition in 1960 – a massive affair with over 200 members. Mr Shi himself climbed above 8000m and his mountaineering experience is abundantly obvious in conversation. In our meeting with the CMA and at a banquet which followed in the evening, we wanted to piece together a few missing links in the story of Chinese activity on Everest on the Tibetan side.

We still knew very little about the early visits of the 1950s. It was widely rumoured that a Russian expedition went to Everest in 1952. A forty-man team, led by Dr Pavel Datschnolian, was believed to have reached 8200m (26,900ft) before six members were lost, including the leader. Whether or not this report has any foundation will probably never be known: the very existence of the expedition was formally denied in 1974 by the President of the USSR Mountaineering Foundation. Tactful questions to the Chinese – for Sino-Soviet relations are still a subject which may provoke embarrassment and hostility – brought the response that Mr Shi was unaware of any Russian expedition to Everest, although it was agreed that Russia 'helped' in a reconnaissance expedition of 1959.

We shall probably never know all the details of Chinese visits to the mountain, but we seem to have some fairly definite events on which to build a Chinese Chomolungma calendar.

In 1958 the First Chinese Reconnaissance took place, a multi-disciplinary scientific and mountaineering expedition. The Second Reconnaissance followed the next year and the road to and beyond Rongbuk was built. In 1960 the First Chinese Chomolungma expedition, led by Mr Shi Zhanchun, climbed the mountain by the North Col route. For the first time yaks were used instead of porters to carry loads to Advanced Base Camp at 6500m (21,326ft).

On this expedition, after a determined first assault by Mr Shi and Wang Feng-Tung, who almost reached the top of the Second Step on the summit ridge at 8600m (28,216ft), the mountain was climbed by Wang Fu-Chou, Chu Yin-Hua and Konbu during the night of 24–25 May. The account of this expedition, whose success was doubted for many years in the Western climbing press, is still hard to follow. This is explained, I believe, by poor translation and a total lack of experience of the expedition's press agents, accompanied by incomplete photographic corroboration. Looking back nearly twenty-five years later and having now met the leader, Mr Shi, and others who were on the trip, I find every reason to applaud the very considerable achievements of the party.

During our visit to Beijing we learnt for the first time of a Second Chinese Chomolungma expedition in 1964 and later checked our interpretation of the facts with Mr Chen, our liaison officer, who had been a team member. This pre-monsoon expedition was the first to set foot on the North East Ridge from the Raphu La and reached about 7000m (22,966ft) before turning back. There was also an unsuccessful attempt by the North Col route. We were told that this expedition was in preparation for one on a larger scale in 1965 – a trip that never took place, probably because of the Cultural Revolution.

Mystery surrounds the events of the next decade. A report in *Alpinismus* in 1967 rumoured that a Chinese expedition had suffered a massive accident the previous year in which twenty-six people had died and there was a suggestion in *Mountain* (No. 8, 1970) that a team of three surveyors had reached the summit, apparently separately, in 1969. My hunch is that these tales are both untrue, but that several small expeditions of scientists and surveyors visited Chomolungma in the late sixties and no ascent was made or even intended. For these were troubled times in recent Chinese history with the Cultural Revolution at its height and internal difficulties within Tibet.

The most recent Chinese ascent was in 1975. This expedition was again led by Mr Shi and was a large team accompanied by scientists and a film crew. Nine climbers – seven Tibetan men, one Tibetan woman and one Han Chinese – reached the summit on 27 May 1975, using intermittent oxygen. The ascent was filmed, including the final steps to the summit, by telephoto. Important and unusual scientific work was carried out – for example an electro-cardiogram was recorded on the summit. An aluminium survey pole was left on the top (if doubt remained for outsiders!) and was discovered by Doug Scott and Douglas Haston after the first ascent of the South West Face from Nepal that autumn.

In 1982 ours was the fourth expedition since 1975 on the Chinese side. A joint Sino-Japanese team climbed a new route in the North Face in 1979 and was followed by Reinhold Messner's remarkable solo ascent without oxygen by the North Col route in 1980. A large French military expedition attempted the North Col route in the spring of 1981 but failed because of bad weather, reaching a height of 8200m. In the autumn of the same year an American team were the first to attempt the huge Kangshung Face. They succeeded in climbing a steep and very difficult rock buttress at the foot of the face, reaching a height of about 7000m before turning back.

This in outline was the sum of our knowledge about the Chinese side of the mountain – and I was relieved to discover that there had been no further activity on the long North East Ridge. I had half expected that we would be told gently and in passing that the Chinese climbers went barefoot from the Raphu La to the North East Shoulder on several occasions!

And so on the morning of 6 March, Chris and I left Beijing along the long avenue to the airport with Mr Chen, our liaison officer, and Mr Yu, our interpreter. David Mathew, hating air travel as much as I do, would accompany us as far as Xegur, our last town in Tibet. We were off at last for Chengdu, en route for Lhasa.

3

Lhasa, once forbidden city

8 March – 16 March

Charles Clarke

A turbo-prop Ilyushin roared into the darkness of a warm, soggy Chengdu dawn; within an hour we were in daylight, not too far above the ground which was a spectacular range of peaks in eastern Tibet, many over 6000m high. I was unprepared for both the fierceness and scale of the terrain below us. How different from the Tian-shan range (in Xinjiang) which the previous year had seemed fairly gentle hills, sometimes covered with snow. But these Tibetan peaks stretched as far as the eye could see on either side of the aircraft, for forty-five minutes' flying at 350–400 knots, and were the sharpest range of mountains I had ever seen – viciously sharp, towering ridges with knife edges, fluted ice gutters and spiky summits so thin that it looked as if you could scarcely straddle them. They are, I suppose, 6000–7000m high; not one of the major peaks has ever been visited.

We dropped then through lower hills, sandy, barren wastes, and flew along the Tsang Po which, renamed the Brahmaputra, takes an unscheduled turn south into Assam. The airfield is two hours' drive from the rest house (why, I wondered – because it's easier to defend?), which is just over a mile out of central Lhasa, tucked into a military complex. There were ten field guns next door to us. There, across the valley floor, the Potala Palace loomed in the distance like some vast fortress, its features blunted by haze, rising incongruously out of the modern Lhasa of corrugated roofs and concrete blocks. We came to see the Potala in its true beauty as we drove to town that afternoon. It was saved from appearing dull and monolithic by a subtle tapering in all its dimensions, in every fold of the walls. The result is a vast structure poised lightly on a hill. It is one of the most beautiful buildings I have ever seen.

Our large party was feeling the strain of the altitude at 3600m. The climbing team seemed well enough but some of the trekkers looked tired and ill. I felt lethargic, too, barely able to drag myself the 200m to the compound's dining room. From now on I had to be vigilant about our health and hoped that in the week to come we could avoid the more unpleasant forms of altitude sickness. We began to get to know the trekking group better and enjoy the company of ten people who were largely from a world of high finance and commerce. David Newbigging, Chairman of Jardines, with his wife Carolyn had been with us in Xinjiang: we were now used to the idea of living with the 'Taipan' whose word almost alone had, it seemed, financed both the Kongur and Everest expeditions. Martin Henderson, who had personally organised much of this Everest trip, and been with us to Kongur Base Camp, was with us again; previously a stranger to climbing, he had absorbed much of its history and jargon, even taking a course at Peter's International School of Mountaineering in Leysin. There was Piers Brooke, an English banker living in New York, and his wife Suzy who writes children's books; Robert Friend from Jardines in Hong Kong, Andrew Russell from Jardines in Manila and Michael Jardine (no relation), a fluent Mandarin speaker who ran the Jardines office in Shanghai. 'The Pygmies', Steven McCormick and David Livermore, two six foot three American conservationists who were having their first glimpse of Asia, completed the party.

Tibet is, and always has been, a land of mystery and despite having been opened by the Chinese government to selected tours, it is still one of the countries least visited by travellers. For each of us this was to be a treasured experience, probably never to be repeated, and each of us would feel the power of this country, smell it, touch it and perhaps just begin to understand it. In European literature Tibet has been a country which has excited two emotions – inquisitive fascination or disgust. Travellers for centuries, and there have only been a handful until recent times, remarked upon the filth, squalor and disease of Lhasa. Certainly many of the early Everesters did not share our fascination with Tibet. Mallory, who loathed the country and the people, wrote: 'A usual and by now welcome sound in each new village is Strutt's [Deputy Leader of the 1922 expedition] voice, cursing Tibet – this march being far more dreary and repulsive even than the one before, and this village being more filthy than any other.'

Even as recently as 1955 the journalist Alan Winnington, on a remarkable journey through eastern Tibet to Lhasa, wrote of the capital: 'Open heaps of rubbish – which are traditionally cleared once a year – lie along some streets, a mixture of rotting substances from which the purple green carcass of a decomposing dog juts out. Dogs are everywhere...'

The two aspects of Tibet which provide much interest to the traveller of the late twentieth century are the incomparable relics of its monastic past and relations between Tibetans and the Han Chinese. Whereas a fable, extolling national virtues and vices, relates that the Tibetan people are descended from the union of a mountain she-devil (deceit, theft and cruelty) and a monkey (wisdom, humanity and piety), the truth of their origins, although more mundane, is far from clear. Nomadic tribes are thought to have settled in Tibet, particularly in the fertile eastern regions, in the first five centuries AD, or possibly earlier. In the seventh century the country was united under a dynasty of warrior kings, Namri and his son, Songsten Gampo (c.627–650AD) who began an era of martial expansion and initiated the relationship with the Chinese throne by marrying Wen Cheng, a princess of the Tang Dynasty. He also married a Nepalese princess and took a Tibetan wife. The Tibetan empire of the seventh and eighth centuries extended far beyond its present frontiers, into Kashmir, Xinjiang, China proper, Bhutan, Sikkim and Nepal; Tibet was a major Central Asian power during this period and dominated the Silk Road through Xinjiang.

The Tibetan empire collapsed in the ninth century and the last Tibetan king was assassinated in about 842. During the internal strife in the three centuries that followed there emerged the religious leaders and the monastic overlords who were to lay the foundations of the country's future theocracy. From the thirteenth to the seventeenth century Tibetan history was influenced by the rise of the Mongols in Central Asia and the country became a vassal state after the Mongol conquest of China at the beginning of this period.

Buddhism, evolving its unique Tibetan form, can be seen as the motive force behind the nation's more recent history. Buddhism became the royal religion with the Chinese princess, Wen Cheng; it replaced but also incorporated much of Bon-Po, a primitive animistic religion which existed in many of the Himalayan countries.

In 1260 Kublai Khan, the Mongol Emperor, invited to Beijing, Basba, a prelate of Tibetan Lamaism, leader of the Sakya (Red Hat sect). He is said to have performed many miracles and converted many princes to Buddhism, the Mongolian form of the religion developing thereafter with its headquarters in the holy city of Ulan Bator, the present capital of Outer Mongolia. Basba also created an alphabet for the Mongolian language. In return he was invested with power, both secular and religious, in Tibet which became a part of the Chinese Empire. A century later another powerful prelate, Tsong-kha-pa, initiated a reform movement in an attempt to purge Lamaism of devil worship, corruption and sexual vices. Celibacy was enforced. This reformed sect, the Gelugspa, or Yellow Hats, spread throughout Tibet, monasteries were built, often becoming fortresses, each with a standing army of warrior monks. Rivalry was the rule and in one such period, about 1642, the Gelugspa Head Lama, Ngawang Lobsang, having solicited help from his Mongol overlord, was installed as Dalai Lama – 'The Ocean of Wisdom' – in the Potala Palace in Lhasa. Ngawang Lobsang, the Great Fifth Dalai Lama (the title being conferred retrospectively on his four predecessors), became the religious and secular head of state and succession by reincarnation became a definite doctrine. The office of Panchen Lama, the head of the area around Xigaze, Tibet's second city, was also created about this time.

The inauguration of the Dalai Lamas conferred upon Tibet a monastic dynasty which was to both mould and restrain future development. The monasteries increased in size and wealth, exacting taxes and labour from the peasantry in return for spiritual protection. It was in the interests of the spiritual leaders to eschew all change within Tibet and to resist the influence of foreigners. Lhasa became a Forbidden City, visited by only a handful of travellers until the twentieth century. This policy of isolation, though it created both the unique architectural and artistic splendour of Tibet, paved the way to the country's decline. Because of celibacy the population dwindled. Recorded as 10,000,000–12,000,000 in the twelfth century, it was around 2,000,000 at the Imperial Census of 1795. By the 1953 Chinese census it was 1,000,000 with a further 2,000,000 Tibetans living within Chinese provinces outside Tibet. Meanwhile a poverty-stricken peasant class was maintained on the borderland of slavery by the monks and lay nobles. They were landless, without suffrage, diseased and, it must be surmised, discontented with their lot. Tibet had few relations with foreign countries except China which regarded the Himalayan state as part of its empire. China, under the Manchu Dynasty, occupied Lhasa and in 1788 the Manchu armies were again in Tibet, this time to defend the country against an invasion from Nepal. In the century that followed China maintained its suzerainty over Tibet with varying degrees of strictness, but it was only in 1912 that the Chinese Amban, or Resident, was expelled from Lhasa at the time of the decline and demise of Imperial Peking.

British interest in Tibet increased towards the end of the nineteenth century. There were rumours of Russian influence north of the Himalaya and clandestine visits between St Petersburg and Lhasa, in particular by a mysterious Russian monk named Dorjieff. Prevalsky, the Russian explorer of the nineteenth century, visited the more remote areas of the country, and Britain grew nervous. The British Raj became obsessed with the vision of neutral buffer states to protect the Himalayan frontier of its Indian Empire and determined to establish relations with the Tibetan capital. Having been rebuffed on many occasions, a British force actually invaded Tibet in 1903. Thinly disguised as a political legation, this Mission to Lhasa led by Colonel (later Sir) Francis Younghusband fought several pitched battles, inflicting losses of several thousand on the Tibetan army before it reached Lhasa in 1904, and the Thirteenth Dalai Lama fled to Ulan Bator. This expedition was a large affair, as Peter Fleming records in *Bayonets to Lhasa*:

ANIMALS	NUMBER	CASUALTIES
Mules	7096	910
Bullocks	5234	954
Camels	6	6
Buffaloes	138	137
Riding Ponies	185	24
Pack Ponies	1372	899
Nepalese Yaks	2953	2922
Tibetan Yaks	1513	1192
Ekka Ponies	1111	277

The final entry on the list dealt with two-legged animals:

Coolies	10,091	88

Francis Younghusband, who was later to become a driving force behind the pre-war Everest expeditions, had an affection for Tibet but was under no illusion about the inflexible attitudes of the lamas.

The British, having established a presence in Lhasa, retired to India. Thereafter they had a degree of influence and even started an English school in Gyantse and a permanent British Residence in Lhasa. Relations became more cordial and in the great war Tibet offered support to Britain, an offer politely declined. Until the end of British rule in India in 1947 Tibet remained a remote if civil neighbour north of the Himalaya.

The twenty-five years that followed Indian Independence have been momentous in the history of Tibet. In 1950 the emergent People's Liberation Army, intent on uniting all the former states of Imperial China, invaded eastern Tibet and defeated a Tibetan army at Chamdo. The Fourteenth Dalai Lama fled to India, returning to Lhasa a year later and in September of 1951 the PLA, we are told, 'now entered Lhasa without a shot being fired, with a music band and a concourse of Lamas from the monasteries blowing great silver conches in welcome'.[1] Under the terms of the agreement with China, Tibet was to become a region with local autonomy, freedom of religion and the status and office of the Dalai Lama guaranteed. Changes were, however, to take place which would alter the face and structure of the nation. Roads were built, and a modern communications system set up. Collective farming was introduced and land taken from the monasteries and given to the farming communes. Religion, although not actively suppressed, was not encouraged by the Chinese. Immigration by Han Chinese workers, officials and soldiers took place on a large scale. These changes and the stress imposed upon the old unflinching monastic order, led to conflict between the Tibetans and Chinese. A revolt in eastern Tibet

1 *Lhasa, the Open City*, Han Suyin. Jonathan Cape, 1977.

took place in 1956 and a more widespread but equally unsuccessful uprising in 1959. The Dalai Lama fled to India and, though still the spiritual head of Tibetan Buddhism, lives in exile and has never returned to Lhasa.

But Tibet's troubles were not over, for in 1966 the Cultural Revolution was to cause havoc, bloodshed and destruction throughout the land. Bands of Red Guards, most of whom were young Tibetans, destroyed much of the nation's artistic and architectural heritage which had been preserved by the unchanging order of its clergy and the dry cold climate. Of over 2000 monasteries and shrines, we were told that under a dozen remain – and we were to see most of them on the journey to Everest.

Passions run high over the rights and wrongs of these unhappy years. Tibet was never, as some suggest, a serene land-locked Himalayan Switzerland and with its heritage and people cared for lovingly by its lamas. It was a fierce country, cruel and impoverished, held together by the bonds of a religion which, though once a comforter, had become an oppressive force which had sown the seeds of its own demise.

China is today impressively honest about admitting the difficulties it has had with Tibet, although there are dark areas where detail is sketchy. What was apparent during our three months' stay was that Tibet is still nationally remarkably intact, despite the destruction of many of its monuments, and there is no attempt on the part of the Chinese to regard the country or the people simply as an extension of the central provinces of the People's Republic. Tibet was, and is, an enigma.

Close to the Potala Palace in central Lhasa is the Jokhang Temple. It is the shrine built to commemorate the coming of Princess Wen Cheng from China in the seventh century and houses the golden Buddha she brought with her. On her arrival at the site of the temple, so the story goes, a spring welled up in response to her presence, beauty and piety. Indeed, in the courtyard there is a well. The Jokhang is encircled by the Parkhor, a bustling array of market stalls, selling shawls, boots, carpets, jewellery and rancid yak butter. Pilgrims mingle in the crowd, walking slowly clockwise round the temple, chanting, 'Om mani padme hum' (Hail to the jewel in the lotus), spinning prayer wheels and plucking rosaries. To gain advancement along the Path of Enlightenment, a few progress by prostrating themselves along the flagstones.

The temple was packed; there must have been about 3000 people inside. The entrance courtyard is black with the grease of prostrating bodies, while a queue, six deep, orderly and mostly silent, wound round the court and disappeared into its inner sanctum. The Jokhang is a place of superlatives and extravagance. In the courtyard were two copper vats some metre and a half across to provide molten rancid yak butter for some 10,000 lights set in rows upon the floor, tended by a few monks. It was once thought that between a quarter and a third of Tibet's butter production went to fuel the lights of its monasteries.

The central hall is about 30m square, covered and gloomy, its cloisters supported by pillars fully fifty centimetres square, carved and painted in vivid red and gold. Between the pillars hang thankas, the silk paintings, soiled by grease and smoke but of incredible richness. Thirty-five of these priceless paintings, some said to come from the Tang Dynasty, hang along each of the four walls. From the central roof in swirling smoke, pierced by shafts of sunlight, hang five giant thankas 9m long and ending high above our heads. Surrounding this hall above the pillars are carved lions, twenty-five to a wall, and signifying either the wrath waiting for the unfaithful or perhaps the might of Imperial China.

Within the hall stands a small shrine filled by the 2m-high Buddha Princess Wen Cheng brought from China. It is gold, 1200 years old, encrusted with turquoise, coral and other jewels, filling a shrine supported by stone pillars, carved with Tang reliefs. There were other shrines, prayer halls, Buddhas and effigies to monarchs, all rich, dimly lit and filled with the smell of rancid butter smoke, incense, sheepskin and sweat. There was the sound of clashing cymbals, tinkling bells and the low humming prayers of monks and pilgrims.

The Jokhang, packed with people on each day we were in Lhasa, is now clearly a place of fervent prayer, and not at all as described in 1975 by Han Suyin: 'It is obvious that the Jokhang is no longer a place of worship; no crowd is there and except for some incense burning in front of some of the statues, I only noticed one old woman who seemed to be doing some praying.'

From the roof of the Jokhang we peered between the golden domes and spires, looking out on multi-coloured Lhasa. I had never realised that the shutters would be reds and blues, the dresses carmine, purple, green and brown, the high felt boots richly embroidered. The old town surrounds the temple, whitewashed, two-storey houses with painted sills and lintels, each with a frill of cotton fluttering in the breeze. This has changed little, though we saw some fine modern buildings, replicas of old houses recently completed and destined to be dwellings. Above, half a mile away, towers the Potala. The rest of Lhasa is less enticing. Tin roofs and concrete blocks of apartments line the main streets, looking incongruous, ugly and, beside such history, temporary structures.

There is another facet of Tibet's religious past – tolerance. Tucked behind the Parkhor market rises the tiny crescent moon which marks the Lhasa mosque. A bearded old man greeted us with 'Salaam aleikem' and we conducted a halting conversation in smiles and patchy Urdu. The mosque is painted inside in Tibetan style, with Tibetan pictures of Mecca, and adorned by many clocks each telling a different time. Islam has flourished in Tibet for several centuries, apparently untouched by recent troubles. They came, the old man told us, from Kabul. Today a small Moslem community of under a hundred still live, trade and pray in the Lhasa markets.

'Gob smacking, eh?' was Pete's conclusion, covering his literary prowess with language from a childhood in the Scouts. Dick, usually silent, murmured, 'Best sightseeing I've ever had.' We were all impressed but there was more to come.

Next morning we climbed the steps of the Potala, with Joe filming us. The steps end in a simple entrance some 120m above the city. Above it towers the Potala for another 180m – it was said to be the tallest building on earth for many centuries. From a distance it may appear to rest lightly upon its hill, but close to it is like standing beneath a mountain rather than a building. For some reason we were not to use the Tibetan entrance at the front but were taken round the back, climbing a steep drive to the back door. Under the old regime nobles on horseback would ride up this hill for a limited distance only, in direct proportion to their rank – while for the common people of Lhasa the palace itself was a Forbidden City. Neither were they permitted even to catch a glimpse of their reincarnate deity, the Dalai Lama. Within the Potala lie the tombs of six Dalai Lamas, and, scattered in a thousand rooms, thousands of little shrines. A morning's visit does little more than convey a general impression of the place; of the thirteen storeys connected by rickety stair ladders; of rows of golden statuettes and of a central shrine, somewhere in the depths of the palace, built as a memorial to King Songsten Gampo and his three wives – Chinese, Nepali and Tibetan. This is the oldest remaining part of the Potala begun in the seventh century. The main structure dates from the seventeenth, when it was rebuilt.

Our visit was conducted through the gloom of dusty passages, half lit by dim electric bulbs. I felt that though the Potala had indeed been lucky to survive the troubles in Tibet, it was no less lucky to have survived its wiring. The electricity system is a maze of exposed cables and frayed insulation all coated with a layer of dust and grease. Some rather hesitant fire extinguishers lurk in the corners, but if the Potala goes up in flames it will be like a torch. I was thinking about the fire risk in a dark corridor when we were suddenly ejected into dazzling sunlight. We were on the roof, perched some 300m high above the city, in the courtyard surrounding the Dalai Lama's chambers. 'His palace or his prison?' I wondered, for he had been rarely permitted to leave it.

The last afternoon in Lhasa we spent at the Norbulingka, the Summer Palace, where in shaded, ordered gardens are the summer residences of the previous Dalai Lamas. We saw the Fourteenth's, empty since his departure in 1959. This was a modern Tibet I did not care for. Amid the painted pillars and wall hangings, a broad mirrored staircase swept up to the bedrooms along carpeted corridors. Within the suite there were two Art Deco armchairs, a vast 1940s radiogram with its Garrard turntable upon which rested one HMV 78rpm record of, of all things, Tibetan Folk Songs. A portable, leather-bound wind-up gramophone lay beside it. Next door a rudimentary bathroom with some fine Shanks 'sanitary ware' – which we were told could not be connected to the plumbing when it arrived – an international, not Tibetan, problem. For me a sense of garish vulgarity pervaded this house and the Summer Palace and I was glad to leave for more earthly pleasures.

Joe, Dick, David Mathew and I, helped by a Tibetan film crew of children, went off to film the Parkhor market. Tourists, though now common enough in Lhasa, are a summer attraction and in March we were the first of the year. Friendly crowds quickly surrounded us, some chanting, others laughing, others trying to sell jewellery, daggers or hats. We were alone for our Chinese staff had, quite wisely, left us to get on with it. We arrived home dusty and exhausted but happy to have had a glimpse of Tibet to ourselves.

We left for Xigaze next morning in the icy dawn of the end of winter. The weather was fine but bitterly cold with night temperatures of −12°C. First we crossed the Tsang Po River and drove up to the Khamba La, a 4800m pass above the magnificent frozen turquoise lake, Yamdok Tsamdo. We dropped quickly to its shores past a tiny fishing village. Dry hills capped with ice surrounded us. The lake was a haven for migrating wild fowl and quickly the party's ornithologists vied with each other to name nearly twenty species. I tried to join in but, knowing only a few Himalayan birds from previous trips, fell quickly behind Martin Henderson and Andrew Russell – red crested pochard, mallard, hen harrier, Tibetan snow finch, Eurasian kestrel, common pochard, Eurasian widgeon, rock bunting, little bunting and Guldenstadt's redstart, great crested grebe, ruddy shellduck, merganser, bar-headed geese, coots, hill pigeon, dark kite, magpie. We drove on, round the lake for some thirty miles, heading for high mountains and climbed a pass of over 5200m (17,000ft), the Kharo La. We were following, albeit backwards, the road of the invading British seventy-eight years earlier. The Kharo La has the dubious distinction of marking the site of the highest battle ever fought by British troops: a lonely defile flanked by glaciers where hundreds of Tibetans died for four deaths on the invading side.

We drove on, past Gyantse, scene of another British engagement. This is Tibet's third largest city and perhaps 10,000 people live within it and the surrounding country. We passed by the fine monastery which I visited on a later journey, to be fascinated to see the remodelling of damaged Buddhas being carried out by craftsmen using mud and straw.

We stopped at Xigaze and drove into a compound on the outskirts of the town, the rest house for Chinese officials, drivers, tourists; a friendly place, but faceless. Xigaze is Tibet's second city, the see of the re-incarnate Panchen Lama. It has one of Tibet's most famous monasteries, the Tashilumpo, founded in 1445. This survives, partially rebuilt. Chris and I slipped out of the rest house next morning and walked over to the monastery. We clambered on to the wall of the Tashilumpo like naughty schoolboys, helped up there by a passing Tibetan, to photograph the golden roofs and the fine long shadows of the early morning. We later paid a more formal visit to the monastery with a Chinese guide who told us that there were now six hundred monks in residence and that children were, once again, being recruited: we saw several boys, their heads shaven, in monks' robes. There were many pilgrims in the courtyard and once again the fervent activity of worship.

Above Xigaze stretches the line of tottering walls of the fort, now in ruins. Martin, the two American 'Pygmies' and I climbed the hill above the town in the afternoon, pleased to be getting some exercise again and relieved that it seemed possible without becoming rapidly exhausted, for we were now at about 4500m (14,760ft). The golden roofs of the monastery were far below us, surrounded, as in Lhasa, by an ugly town of modern zinc-roofed buildings.

The road to Xegur, the last town on our journey was memorable only for its monotony, relieved and enlightened by the Sajia monastery. Sajia, off the main Xegur–Xigaze highway some 250 miles from Lhasa, was once one of the largest monasteries in Tibet, on the main yak route south. Once there were two monasteries, north and south. Huge and monolithic, it is the southern shrine which survives today. Sajia is an example of ecclesiastical architecture with a military purpose. A castellated square, 200m across, flanked by four corner turrets, defends the inner monastery, itself a square of 80m. We were conducted inside to an upper dining room with low tables and fine blue and white canvas shutters. After a picnic lunch we entered the inner courtyard through a two-storey portico. Two 6m-high grotesque figures faced each other across the entrance – a black demon on the left, a red dragon opposite – beckoning us into the main shrine. Inside twenty huge tree trunks (in this treeless land), the largest four fully a metre in diameter, supported the roof and beneath on low carpeted benches was seating for 400 monks. Frescoes stretched from floor to ceiling, nearly 12m high, some from the Yuang Dynasty (fourteenth century), but others more obviously Indian and Nepalese. Seven golden Buddhas formed the centrepiece of the shrine, surrounded by hundreds, if not thousands of vases, presents from China long ago. Strangely there were no tankas in this fine hall.

A side hall housed a collection of hundreds of miniatures – Buddhas, statues in gold and a curious plan of the southern monastery housed in a glass case some two metres square. In this the outline of the walls, its entrance and rooms, was etched in powder, made from different coloured salts. There is also a fine library housing several thousand books, mostly printed in blocks on hand-pressed paper, but some were handwritten, illuminated with gold on thin slivers of wood. Much of the southern monastery has been finely restored (or possibly never damaged). Not so the northern shrine. David Mathew and I slipped away from our guide, crossed a rickety bridge and climbed quickly into the ruins. Now totally destroyed, a photograph fifty years ago showed that the structure rose in tiers up the hillside, housing 6000 monks. Nothing remains except here and there a patch of wall with the outline of a battered fresco. We were perhaps moved more by this destruction and pillage than by the splendour of the southern buildings.

Xegur Dzong (fort) was still four hours' drive over the dusty rolling highlands. Xegur, which had once been one of the most spectacular dzongs of Central Asia, a military city clinging to a steep hillside, is now a small administrative centre with only the walls of the dzong remaining, etching the skyline in ruined fingers. Tibetans still climb the steps behind it to small shrines, encircling the fort clockwise in a pleasant three-mile hike. We were still acclimatising around 4000m before the final lift to Rongbuk at 5200m (17,000ft). We stayed two days, resting, reading, walking or, in the case of Chris, Adrian and myself, lying in bed with the 'flu.

On 16 March we were up before dawn, blow torches trained on the trucks' engines, lighting the barracks with spurts of flame in the bitter cold. The engines, as if to surprise us all, did not explode but burst into life and purred, howled or spluttered through the day. We were off, huddled in duvets, masks and boots, most of us in an open truck, but Joe filming out in front in the jeep. The road to Rongbuk soon left the Friendship Highway from Lhasa/Xigaze/Xegur to Nepal, turned left and headed over a 5000m pass. Here we had our first view of the main Himalayan chain, Makalu, Lhotse, Everest, Nuptse, Gyachung Kang and Cho Oyu. We stopped to photograph them all. David Newbigging asked Peter and Chris to identify the peaks and looked a little uncertain as there was disagreement about which was Everest. 'Well, you should know if anyone does.'

We dropped steeply to the valley floor along which the Dzakar Chhu, the river from the Rongbuk Glaciers of Everest, flows eastwards. Soon the river turns south to Kharta on the eastern side of Everest and then cuts through the Himalaya in the gorge of the Arun River, thus delivering all the melt water from the snow and ice of Everest to Nepal. The Dzakar Chhu was beginning to thaw but the ford was iced over, hazardous for trucks. Mr Chen, our liaison officer, had already preceded us and secured, in this unlikely place, a caterpillar tractor which dragged one of our trucks across when it broke through the crust of ice.

We were but a few hours from Everest and the holiday was nearly over, the splendour of a surfeit of monasteries behind us. I felt that these treasures, the glittering jewels luring the sentimental European magpie, had blinded us to another Tibet, a Tibet much harder to reach but more positive. It is difficult to get excited about a tractor, but here was one, not thirty miles from Everest. In two months we would see it ploughing the ground now frozen around us. At Xigaze in the alluvial plain, which is the most fertile land in central Tibet, there are many tractors, ploughs and combine harvesters for the barley – material gains in a country which may have lost its spiritual leadership but also perhaps its former terrible poverty.

The track climbs gently into the Rongbuk Valley, easier and safer than many Himalayan hill roads. It was late afternoon and the weather cloudy as we entered the wide stony floor below the ruined Rongbuk monastery. Suddenly, it was there, the massive, sombre pyramid of the North Face of Everest, being the only great peak in view, filling the head of the valley ten miles away and 4000m above us. True, we had seen photographs, paintings, sketches and even models of the North Face and perhaps we did not have the thrill of Bullock and Mallory's first glimpse in 1921 but here, on a windy afternoon in southern Tibet we were all fulfilling a dream, to visit the northern side of this, the highest mountain. It looked very, very cold.

An hour later, having cut a track through two iced rivers with the help of some local Tibetans (they did it, we watched), and having passed the ruins of Rongbuk, we arrived at a stony plain which was to be our Base Camp at 5200m (17,000ft). It was nearly dark, snowing and the wind howled. We had arrived.

4

An icy start

17 March – 4 April

Charles Clarke

The first night at Base Camp was a miserable affair. We struggled with the huge mess tent in the wind and snow – we had forgotten how its complex frame of poles clipped together until Martin Henderson, who had solved the problem on Kongur, was summoned to instruct the climbing team. Food was long in coming and meagre when it arrived. There were two events; one which filled us with distaste for fellow mountaineers, the other with anger at our Tibetans. First we realised that we were camping on ground which, though fairly flat, resembled the outskirts of a municipal rubbish dump. Yak dung was acceptable, indeed expected, but not the debris of tins, glass, beer cans, batteries, shreds of clothing, polythene binding, boxes and gas cylinders – their origins all too obvious. 'Principal nocturnal hazard of Base Camp, broken glass.'

Secondly, in unloading the three trucks, we had enlisted the aid of some Tibetan boys who had helped us with the road: within half an hour or so our 220 boxes were in orderly lines but also within that time a remarkable quantity of food and equipment had been slipped deftly into the folds of their clothing. Adrian spotted some losses but first disregarded them – there seemed nowhere the Tibetans could hide much of value. In the end we searched them, each proclaiming his innocence. From a pile of grubby bags and blankets we dug out sweaters, socks, chocolate, film, towels and tins of fruit. The temptation of our array of wealth had been too great and, as if to remind us of their creator, the she-devil of the mountains, they had succumbed. Mr Chen firmly and sensibly told them off but didn't overdo it.

We planned to spend the last two weeks of March acclimatising, staying below 6000m, for with a high Base Camp at 5200m and easy terrain above, it would have been tempting to rush high too quickly. Even so, following a week at around 4000m, acclimatisation was being hurried, for after three days at 5200m, headaches, lack of appetite and that torpid feeling of exhaustion affected us all. The trekking team were to take part in our high-altitude forays. On 19 March Joe and Pete, with Piers and Suzy Brooke,

Robert Friend and Andrew Russell, set off slowly up the Central Rongbuk Glacier to look at the glacial pinnacles below the North Face of Everest. They saw from unusual angles peaks which Joe and Pete knew so well from Nepal – Lingtren, Pumo Ri, Nuptse, Everest's neighbours.

The East Rongbuk team of Chris and Dick, with David Newbigging, Martin Henderson, Michael Jardine, David Livermore and Steve McCormick, moved up the valley which had seemed so small as to be disregarded by the 1921 Reconnaissance. They placed a camp some three miles away at a point a third of the way between the pre-war expeditions' Camps 1 and 2. So we called it Camp 1½ (5650m/18,537ft). The next day some of them climbed on to about 5850m (19,190ft).

Adrian and I, exhausted after the 'flu, and Carolyn, with laryngitis, stayed at Base but it was so cold, even there. Joe had told us all chilling tales of Everest in winter but we never really listened, thinking that by late March and April winter would be behind us and spring – whatever that meant here for there were no flowers or grasses – would be on its way. The first night was below –20°C and by day, though the weather was fine, the temperature was barely above zero with a blustery wind cutting deep into layers of warm clothing.

On 21 and 22 March the trekkers returned, mostly bearded, grubby and smiling after their trips to high altitude. Joe and Pete carried a load of old tins down from the Central Rongbuk and looked tired. It does one good to remember the stress of early days at altitude where already there is half as much oxygen as at sea level. Everyone looked rotten. Mr Chen was unwell and the cook demoralised by altitude sickness from which I think he never really recovered – the menu for the farewell banquet for the trekkers was not a great success. Next morning we waved goodbye to them and stood, our small team of six, alone with the mountain for the first time.

The plan was simple but we could not carry it out alone: to establish an Advanced Base at about 6500m (21,326ft) on the upper moraines of the East Rongbuk Glacier we needed yaks. We planned to make three ferries which, with the three-day journey up, descent, rest days and bad weather, would take all of a month. Adrian and I were to organise this while the climbers were to push along the North East Ridge. We sat in the mess tent with Mr Chen and our interpreter, Mr Yu, to have the first of many meetings, each of which had an unhurried formality commencing with tea, biscuits and cigarettes. I liked Mr Chen from the start. In his late forties, with a frostbitten face, efficient, quiet, sensible and determined, he was a man whose attitude to our problems, which were legion, was to solve them rather than to ask us to change our minds. Unexpected changes of plan, although part of any expedition, are anathema to the Chinese and it amused me on many occasions to see his look of resigned anguish as he wrote out methodically in a small notebook the third and fourth alteration to a particular phase of the expedition. Mr Chen also knew his ground in the hills: he had been on the mountain twice and had travelled widely in the Everest region. He had earned his position as a committee member of the CMA by long years of hard work.

Mr Yu, a sports interpreter from Beijing, was in his early thirties. This was his first visit both to Tibet and to high mountains and his first expedition of any kind, though he had travelled widely with sporting teams to Hong Kong, Pakistan, France and Cuba. His command of colloquial English was excellent and he was prepared to lend a hand with anything – from chipping ice in the frozen river beside camp, loading trucks, cooking, washing-up or helping in major administrative decisions.

The Chinese expedition staff was completed by Dawa, a Tibetan truck driver from Lhasa who acted as a Tibetan interpreter, and Cheng Wenxin, the jeep driver for whose skill and restraint we were to feel grateful on some of the hill roads. Wang Chouhai, the cook, who seemed unwell and sulky for much of our stay, perked up a little towards the end and produced some reasonable meals.

It is no secret that some foreign climbing teams have had difficulty with their staff and it is important to record that we did not. They worked hard in the monotonous routine of Base Camp life and never hurried us to finish, though it was obvious that they would be glad to get home.

We were not alone for long. Big Lou Whittaker, a giant guide from Seattle, and Jim Wickwire were leading an American team to the North Face. We met them all that evening; fresh faced and friendly, they seemed to have relatively little experience of extreme altitudes. Almost all were guides from Mount Rainier and Marty Hoey, a tall attractive girl, was among them. 'She's just there because she can climb,' drawled one expedition sponsor, Texan Dick Bass. His co-sponsor Frank Wells agreed. Dick and Frank had personally sponsored this American expedition largely to take part in it themselves as a training exercise for a larger project – to climb the highest peak in each continent. With them was a figure from Everest's history, Sherpa Nawang Gombu. He had studied for a year or so in childhood at the Rongbuk monastery and at the age of seventeen he was on the 1953 expedition, with the nickname of 'Roly Poly', when he worked for Michael Ward, the expedition doctor. He later climbed Everest twice, once with Lou's twin brother, Jim, the first American to climb the mountain, in 1963 and again with the third Indian expedition in 1965. Rotund and jovial, he made no secret that he did not plan to do it all again. We grew to like and respect the American team and our fears for their inexperience were groundless, for they stayed as a cohesive unit to the end, pushing high up on to the North Face, though they failed to climb to the summit.

The yaks were due on 29 March. In the intervening days we needed to reconnoitre the route to Advanced Base and to become more acclimatised. We left on the 25th as Peter recorded:

THURSDAY, 25 MARCH 1982: BASE CAMP TO CAMP 1½

We're not ones to rush off in the mornings, despite a faintly big plan. Charlie kindly has sorted out the food. Choosing tent partners – a vegetarian, a snorer or someone who won't make breakfast? Eventually chose Joe – Dick and Chris need to get to know each other. Mr Chen, our LO, goes down to Xegur this morning with the jeep – he's not been feeling too good for a number of days – stomach upset. The weather's rather poor today which puts us all off hurrying anyway. Fully clad in one-piece Biffo suit plus Gore-tex/Thinsulate salopettes and jacket. I suppose it's easier to walk when it's cool. The trekking team left the tents and some gear up there – Chris and Dick don't even have to carry pits, because they're up there. We become fairly widely spread out. Turn left, see walls of pre-war Camp 1. I'm carrying Koflachs, wearing KSB 3s. 32 lbs. What's that about a pound of weight on your feet? Starts to snow. After a few hours, find Dick where the trekking team left their tents. 'Camp 1½.' Dick has a brew ready, Joe misses the way, then Charlie. Chris goes back to help Adrian. Eventually all ensconced. The altitude gets me. I can't remember much 'at height', anyway my writing's wobbly. I'm sharing with Joe – it seems better to read *Manchu*. Dick and Chris eating gluey tsampa.

FRIDAY, 26 MARCH: TO PRE-WAR CAMP 2, 6000 METRES

This is only our fourth or fifth day's exercise and here we are carrying over forty-pound loads from between 5500 and 6000m. This morning's weather still snow. These nights are long, sound sleep for a while then fitful with long periods of wakefulness – just roll over and try lying the other way. So we appreciate the lie-in and I read more *Manchu*. Eventually we do pack up and leave, early afternoon. With Charlie and Adrian out for the walk (they both turn back fairly soon). Our camp is the other side of the Changtse Glacier, wherever that is. Guess how we're finding the way up here? We're following telephone lines! – Chinese, perhaps French, perhaps Japanese, lying on the ground, occasionally twisted by the wind around ice cliffs and moraines. When Dick took his trekking group through this way they made a mistake which we don't have to make again – and they wasted four hours. But they saw Big E – no chance of that this time. Like yesterday, a few worrying spots for yaks with loose stones on top of ice. Now we follow those amazing giant blue-green fins of ice in the glacier (differential melting, of course). This moraine now a broad highway. Find a lot of stuff – the French must have stopped here and we want to also, since we are tired. Still snowing lightly. Camp beside a tower of ice like Froggatt Pinnacle – but at least ice is easier to melt than snow – but everything has a bit of grit in it because of the winds up here ... and in the evening the weather clears. Feeling the altitude and not feeling very hungry and tonight it's intensely cold despite wearing all my clothes. Cold, starry and still.

SATURDAY, 27 MARCH: PRE-WAR CAMP 2 TO PRE-WAR CAMP 3
(OUR ADVANCED BASE) AND BACK

Whilst we're walking up have to remind ourselves how high up we are, higher than Kohi Mundi[1] ... the sun comes up earlier here than at Base – nine fifteen – and it is a perfect day. The Yanks seem impressed that we set off in that bad weather to come up here the other day but – 'do the unexpected' and now we're vindicated. We shall walk up unladen today – a clear way but high up. Chat. Chris has very good feelings about this trip, as good as he's ever had about the team. I say, 'And we all know what we're taking on.' It's been funny listening to them next door. Chris talking a lot but Dick holding his own with his usual devastating one-liners ... The mountains and glacier are swept clear and hard by winter winds – the glacier is glassy, translucent, hard. We stop often and look up as the ridge appears in pieces before us (through cloud and gaps in the ice pinnacles). Oh, yes, I managed to finish *Manchu* before we left this morning. Looks a very long way – and still winter so clear of snow. Find a good spot from where we can contour to the Raphu La. Here we hope will be our Advanced Base. It seems at the moment the highest, bleakest, most windswept place on earth. At first through the Raphu La we can see Pethangtse and then from higher up, Chomo Lonzo with its unclimbed North West Summit that looks like the Dru ... I don't think this is going to be the most comfortable Advanced Base but at least it's high up. We'll have to wear crampons just to walk across to the Raphu La, the ground's so icy! A few pre-war tins here (the French camped higher up). But the ridge continues to make a great line ... Decided not to have a brew up here – we scuttle off back down to Camp 2, it only takes one and a half hours. Chris has his little tape recorder for the BBC programme and asks for a few comments! He lingers behind to record his own thoughts in whispered ecclesiastical tones. Back at the camp ahead of Chris we chat briefly. 'There's no one else like him,' says Dick, 'he's unique – always doing something even if its projecting plans on the route or writing his diary.' Chris has named one nasty-looking tooth on the ridge 'the Fang' – still a question if we'll find a straightforward way round it. But we'll certainly get some good photos, it being a ridge ... Difficult to eat properly up here with the unappetising food and altitude – and the time to melt ice also. We'll have to get organised for our Advanced Base. Perhaps it'll just have to be a hunter's return at Base. Tonight I start and finish the thriller, *Gorky Park* – it grips me so much I read until half past midnight. I sleep well.

SUNDAY, 28 MARCH: PRE-WAR CAMP 2 TO BASE CAMP

A month today I left Leysin – looking forward to the post but I can wait. I suppose time away depends upon how long you *expect* to be away and, expecting this to be a long campaign, this last month has gone very quickly – and the next month should

---

1 A 6248m peak in Afghanistan Peter climbed in 1972.

see us working our way up the route – and, hopefully, poised ... it's another lovely still morning, prelude to a windy afternoon blowing up the valley ... We leave everything except that which we walk about in at camp and set off down. 'The Fang' appears again. It's important to give things names ... Rapid progress downhill, about four hours, 11.30 to 15.30 with rests and looks. High mountains, looks low here and dry ... At the East Rongbuk junction we meet two Yanks, the camera man and Mr Warner Bros., they give us a cool sip. Carrying enormous loads. Thank goodness we don't have to do that or prove that. The authors discuss – only Dick not publishing a book this year! Hope they're not reviewed together. Ask Dick if he's thought about alpine guiding; he thinks he might not be immediately sociable enough ... Back at Base – the flocks of alpine choughs which now live here race off. Some yaks and yak men – the Yanks are shifting their stuff now. Watch for wandering Tibetans; they'll pick up anything you leave around. Tang orange juice (so much better than Rise 'n Shine) – three loaves of Charlie's bread and his cheesecake. A lovely afternoon – I have my first proper wash (except hair) since Xegur. Charlie flies his kite from the frozen lake; from my tent door it looks higher than Everest! Eat a lot.

MONDAY, 29 MARCH

1900 hours. A pleasant day. Handwriting improving as I acclimatise. Dick spends his hours carving a swan from a block of mahogany and sketching. I write up my diary, wash pants and socks, do a cross section of Big E on the graph using Schneider's map and compose a little poem about Everest's Flag Clouds. Now the sun comes up on the tent at 9.58! After supper the Americans come round and I shall give them this to post ... a great evening, successful entertainment. Had a long, far ranging chat with Jim Wickwire for about two hours. About K2, Peter Goodwin, Dalai Lama, Charlie Houston, Jim Morrisey's expedition to the East Face of Everest last year which made such a profit, K2 summit view, Namche Barwa and so on. He has a library of 3000 climbing books ... It was great to talk to someone so interested in the same things – though he is rather intense. They liked the 'I'm a wanker' song. We're a very happy expedition and they absorbed that from us I think. An hilarious time but too stimulating and not a good night's sleep.

The yaks had not yet arrived: it was nobody's fault for things move slowly in Tibet. Our jeep was away in Xegur so we waited, reading and resting. The weather at Base Camp was mixed, usually fine and blustery but very cold. I recorded the temperatures carefully, always having omitted to do so regularly before. Before the sun hit us at about 9.45 a.m. at Base it was −12°C both within my tent and in the shade outside. An hour later, within, it would rise to 20°C, although in shade outside it would be only 2°C. Sunset beyond the hills west of Rongbuk was shortly before 7 p.m.

On 31 March I strolled down the valley with Chris for half an hour to the first evidence of the highest previous inhabitants, the Rongbuk nunnery. Perched on the tongue of a huge landslide, its fifty or so dwellings were in ruins, destroyed by man, not rockfalls. A few walls remained with flecks of fresco but hidden away there was a tiny shrine.

A wooden trap in a sandy floor led in the darkness down a flimsy ladder. With a headlamp a simple clay Buddha peered at us through the gloom. Around were some cast figures, old prayerflags, coins and carved slates. A butter lamp was still warm, the low vault smoky. This shrine, easily concealed in a cellar, had escaped destruction and was still in use. Chris and I looked down towards the Rongbuk monastery a mile or so away and decided to go a little further. Within a few minutes we met thirteen yaks and five yak herders camped by the stream. They greeted us with smiles, some with the old Tibetan custom of pushing forward their tongues, gently, through an open mouth rather than sticking them out like rude children. These were our men and they would meet us next day at Base.

Dusk was approaching so we turned and walked home, more tired than we expected. Chris was relaxed, happy with the team but keen to get moving. We both felt that this expedition, although it might have hidden dangers, contained no personalities in which there lay the seeds of discontent. We knew each other well, knew of our weaknesses, could sniff the signs of irritation or the wish to be alone. There was a fraternal atmosphere, by no means always one of agreement, but one of intuitive understanding. There was much laughter too.

We left in the early afternoon of 2 April for the pre-war Camp 1, tucked round the corner at the end of the East Rongbuk Valley. Travelling together seemed a new experience. Joe filmed the yaks on a steep corner which turns into the East Rongbuk, causing a minor stampede. Peter carried the huge cine tripod and Chris helped with a load of films. An easy walk to the mess of the old French camp site. Peter sat in silent fury with an ice hammer flattening over two hundred empty Camping Gaz canisters, the manufacturer's label advertising in vain 'Leave No Litter' in three languages. We sat, cooked and read a while in the heavy military mess tent that was to be home at Advanced Base. We were impressed by our yak herders, a gentle lot who looked after their animals well. They had already shown us a new route to the camp, crossing the ice lake of the glacial stream instead of fighting up the moraines along its left bank.

The next day saw us to the old Camp 2 along the screes of the left bank with a rough track marked with red paint splashes on the rocks by the Japanese. This was a hillside on the move with many red boulders swept away below the route. It looked safe enough, though, until a steep scree slope to a shelf. Here the path had been lost and needed rebuilding for the yaks who, though agile, cut their feet on sharp stones. The Tibetans leapt into action hurling boulders from the slope and creating in minutes a zig-zag path for 45m. Joe and Peter filmed while Adrian and I pushed on.

We would have done better to have waited, for a rattle from above warned of a stonefall. We ran for cover and the air was filled with rocks, several scoring direct hits on my personal bodyguard, a large though unstable boulder. 'They're not aiming at us anyway,' I thought. We hurried along the remaining section, pausing to avoid further stonefalls and arrived in a rather breathless, shaky sweat on a moraine above the previous Camp 1½, mid-way between the pre-war Camps 1 and 2. The others came through with no problems but I avoided this section in future by a safe but exhausting scramble in the ice and boulders of the glacial stream.

'Quite acceptable alpine risks', was the consensus of opinion and I felt a bit wet. It is so often, I thought, on easy ground that accidents happen, on paths, on easy abseils and apparently straightforward glaciers – and I seem to have been involved in more than my fair share, explaining, perhaps, my lack of progress as a hard climber.

This was my first journey along the Rongbuk moraines to Advanced Base at 6400m (21,000ft). There can be no easier route to this altitude on a great mountain, a gentle walk along moraine, rather monotonous and, apart from the short Rockfall Alley, entirely safe. Above, to the right, towers the wall of Changtse (7553m/24,780ft), a peak opposite the North Face of Everest, rising from the North Col. The northern skyline is of lower peaks, many of them easy and climbed on pre-war trips – Kellas's Peak (Ri-ring), Khartaphu and several unnamed 7000m peaks. The moraine route winds first between the East Rongbuk and Changtse Glaciers and then, finding the left bank of the East Rongbuk, runs between sérac walls, the edges of two dry glaciers, before turning south and up to Advanced Base to look out over the vast expanse of ice which forms the head of the East Rongbuk Glacier, draining the slopes of the Lhakpa La, several smaller northern glaciers, the Raphu La and the séracs of the North Col. Smooth in places, almost like polished glass, there was a fine dust of spindrift blowing across it. In sunlight and calm, a friendly place but in cloud and blizzards, fierce, hostile and forbidding. 'The highest golf course in the world,' Dick said later, when the route was picked out by marker flags across to the Raphu La.

Above, the North East Face of Everest with its crest, the ridge, towered like a huge sail, furrowed by couloirs of green ice. The scale had been hard to comprehend from photographs for this was a country of giant features with ourselves like Lilliputians beneath it. It was two miles from the Raphu La to the North East Shoulder (8393m/27,536ft) and just under a mile further to the summit – great distances at these extreme altitudes. We could see the crest almost in its entirety, beginning as snow and looking easy to 7300m. There were then two steep sections, rock buttresses which looked harder – we thought the Chinese had stopped at the first of these in 1964. Thereafter, 2000m above us was a series of jagged pinnacles, rock on the north eastern side capped by a crest of snow, the corniced head wall of the Kangshung Face of the eastern side of Everest. The Pinnacles looked hard and dangerous.

Adrian and I helped unload the yaks and left for Base Camp. The work had now begun. It was 4 April.

First steps

5 April – 14 April

Chris Bonington

The site of Advanced Base was indeed a bleak spot, a tumbled stony moraine at the edge of the glacier. On one side were crumbling cliffs that guarded the lower slopes of Changtse and on the other our immediate view was barred by a swell of ice. Below, the rocky tongue of the moraine that had provided our highway curled round the corner, leading the eye down the wide open sweep of the glacier. It wasn't a dramatic view. Everest, fore-shortened as it was, seemed shapeless and sprawling, hardly the highest mountain in the world, while the peaks on the other side of the glacier, most of them over 7000m, were more like snow-clad hills. It had a polar feel to it and reminded me of pictures I have seen of Antarctic ranges. The weather certainly felt Arctic. There was a bitter wind tearing down the glacier and although it was a bright, sunny day, there was no warmth in the sunlight.

Our pile of boxes and kit bags and, for that matter our numbers, seemed puny compared to the vast scale of what was before us. We were already at 6400m, yet it did not feel particularly high, perhaps because we were still in the bed of the valley and there was so little snow around us due to the low precipitation on the north side of Everest. As a result we had the luxury of a camp on bare rocks. But once we started shifting rocks for a tent site we were quickly reminded of the altitude, for any sudden exertion caused immediate breathlessness.

Adrian Gordon had borrowed our mess tent from the Army in Hong Kong. It was made from heavy canvas and was intended to fit on to the back of a Land-Rover but it was ideal for our purposes, being extremely strong and roomy. Pete dubbed it 'the big Greenie'. It took us most of the afternoon to erect the tent, mooring it to the ground with climbing ropes criss-crossed over the canvas and tied to large rocks. We also built a wind-break in an ineffective effort to shelter the entrance. Inside it was dark and gloomy, with draughts seeking out every chink, but at least it gave us some protection from the elements.

That night there were just three of us at Advanced Base, for Joe had returned to our previous camp with Charlie and Adrian to annotate and pack the film he was sending back to Independent Television News in London. We did not bother to put up any other tents but slept in the base tent amongst a mess of food packages, dirty pans and cookers. Dick had walked that day all the way from Base Camp, the ten and a half miles and 1200m in height gain, to catch us up. He had stayed behind hoping that our mail would arrive with our jeep but two days had elapsed with no sign of it and he had been forced to walk up empty-handed. Even so we were very impressed by the speed of his journey which he had completed in under six hours.

He did not even appear tired, doing as much as any of us to erect the base tent and, that evening, cooking supper. This was all the more commendable since Dick is a vegetarian and he plopped some foil-wrapped meat dishes into the water he was using to cook lentils for himself.

Next morning Pete was feeling ill and unable to eat anything. He complained of pains in his chest and nausea: whether it was altitude or some bug we could not tell, but he managed lethargically to clear a site for his own personal tent, pitch it and then crawled into it to sleep out his malaise.

Dick and I were keen to reach the Raphu La and investigate the approaches to the North East Ridge. We set out just after mid-day, roping up and putting on crampons for the first time on the expedition. I had a feeling of fresh excitement that submerged all the doubts I had held both in the preparatory period and during the approach. At forty-seven, was I too old for this? Could I keep up with the other three? Could I reach the summit without using oxygen? But all this rolled away in anticipation of actually setting foot on the North East Ridge. We took with us a few alloy wands to mark the route and started out. The snow was hard and crisp underfoot, compressed and beaten by the wind. The Raphu La (6510m/ 21,358ft) seemed little higher than our own Advanced Base but first we had to lose height crossing a gentle depression in the glacier. It was a great open sweep of white, unsullied by open crevasses, though the occasional crack in the snow showed that there might be some hidden chasms lurking.

We strode across steadily. I was delighted that I seemed to be fully acclimatised and that I did not need to pause for rests, though we stopped frequently to gaze up at the ridge to pick out the best route on to it. There was a subsidiary buttress stretching up to a shoulder which was marked on the map as 7090m. Pete had suggested that this might be an ideal route, bypassing the lower part of the ridge and taking us straight up to our first camp on the crest. I had my doubts. It now seemed a long way and, looking at it from close by, we could see dirty streaks of black ice and broken rocky steps barring the way. It did not look easy.

We plodded on, breasting a gentle slope that led towards the col. The rocky head of Chomo Lonzo peered over the crest and then, as we reached the col, everything opened out. The slope before us dropped dizzily out of sight. This was no mountain pass and it was hardly surprising that it had never been crossed for the Kangshung side was steeply glaciated in a series of sérac walls. The Kangshung Glacier itself, 1200m below, was dirty rubble-covered ice seamed with open crevasses. Looking down the glacier an array of peaks, most of them unclimbed, even unnamed, stretched into the distance but on the far horizon, some eighty miles away, squatted the great bulk of Kangchenjunga (8598m/28,208ft), third highest mountain of the world. The fact that Pete and Joe had climbed it with Doug Scott in 1979 gave us a point of reference. To its right, dwarfed but nonetheless shapely and steep, was Jannu (7710m/25,294ft), also climbed by friends, Roger Baxter-Jones, Rab Carrington, Brian Hall and Al Rouse, in the autumn of 1978.

The peaks on the southern side of the Kangshung Glacier were fiercely dramatic. Chomo Lonzo (7790m/25,558ft) dominated the horizon for it was closer and more rugged than Makalu (8475m/27,806ft), its taller neighbour. Even closer was the shapely summit of Pethangtse (6710m/22,014ft) which led the eye along and up the great eastern ridge of Lhotse (8501m/27,890ft) whose huge and threatening South East Face jutted into wind-driven clouds. But most impressive of all was the back, or south eastern aspect, of our ridge which we would just see from the col. The Kangshung Face thrust its way into the cloud base some 1500m above us, in a slope that was crazed with erratic fluting and runnels, sérac walls and naked black rock.

The sight was both daunting and immensely exciting. It showed just how serious the North East Ridge was to be, but we hoped to avoid the south eastern side and follow easier slopes on the north west.

We set foot for the first time on the North East Ridge that afternoon. From the Raphu La the slope swelled up like the face of a gigantic wave with the occasional cornice breaking at its crest. At first the angle was easy, around thirty-five degrees, and the snow crisp and hard, giving us a feeling of security as we zig-zagged our way across it. I quickly forgot the intimidating aspect of the other side of the ridge in the joy of movement, in such superb surroundings. That afternoon we climbed about 200m, traversing well below the crest to find a spot where we could gain safe access to the slopes leading to it and thus find a short cut to the ridge, avoiding the Raphu La.

We did not go far that day; just enough to reassure ourselves of the quality of the snow and the line of the route before dropping down the slope to a point where we could safely cross the bergschrund at its foot. At the bottom we found a good viewpoint from which to pick out the best route to the crest. We favoured a compromise between the subsidiary arête that had attracted Pete and the crest of the ridge from the Raphu La. Inevitably we worried about the cornices but finally resolved that they were reasonably safe.

Dick and I returned well satisfied with what we had done and seen, though on the way back we discovered that the glacier was not as innocent as it had seemed. What appeared on the surface as little more than a crack opened out into a vast, bell-shaped crevasse whose depth and sides were lost in a black void. We traced our journey back in a wide arc to avoid any risk of avalanche from the flanks of the North East Ridge. This detour had a sting in the tail, however, for there was a gentle though exhausting climb near the end, followed by a long plod to the very edge of the glacier before suddenly our Advanced Camp came into sight, tucked away in a hollow of the moraine. Pete and Joe had used the day to erect tents for all of us so that the base tent could be used for living and cooking together.

Next morning the wind howled down the valley ceaselessly so we used it as an excuse to spend the day making our camp slightly more comfortable, draping a tarpaulin over the base tent, making a table of stones inside it for cooking and eating and building windbreaks in front of our personal tents. By evening the camp had at last begun to feel habitable though it was still desperately cold and we never took off our down suits. Feet were chilled and frozen even inside our sheepskin camp boots. We felt very much alone.

We had spent a lot of time both back in England and in the early stages of the expedition poring over photographs, discussing strategy and tactics. Being a team of four ruled out the use of oxygen as a major part of the plan, for we could never have carried the cylinders, each weighing about 7 kilos, up to 7900m or so. Pete, Joe and Dick wanted to climb the mountain without oxygen, though my own attitude was more ambivalent. I wanted to get to the top of Everest and had fairly serious doubts about my ability to do it without the help of oxygen, which was why I insisted on bringing a stock of cylinders and masks as far as Advanced Base. There was the chance of changing our policy if circumstances suggested it later.

There were two ways we could have tackled the ridge. One was by conventional siege methods with a series of camps linked by fixed ropes until we had a camp close enough to the summit for one or two to make a summit bid. The other way was to climb the mountain alpine-style which meant packing our rucksacks at the foot of the mountain with about ten days' food, a tent and all the climbing gear and keeping going, camping and bivouacking on the way. On Everest, Reinhold Messner had used alpine-style tactics in his incredible solo ascent from Tibet in 1980. He had made a reconnaissance to the North Col but then climbed the mountain in a single push, camping twice on the way up, reaching the summit, getting back to his top camp on the third day and returning to Advanced Base on the fourth. Messner was climbing a known route that was comparatively straightforward. We, however, would be on new ground with the additional problem which we knew from photographs that the principal difficulties started at around 7900m and went on up to 8380m, over a series of pinnacles that barred the way to the upper part of the ridge.

It seemed to make sense, therefore, to adopt a compromise between the two approaches, establishing a series of camps – we hoped just two – to the foot of the Pinnacles and then to make an alpine-style push from this high base with one or more bivouacs up to the summit. We hoped this would enable us to acclimatise on the route itself, coming down for rests at Base or Advanced Base, until we were ready to make that summit push. We would only be able to use a little fixed rope because of the problems of carrying it but we were hoping that the lower part of the ridge would be sufficiently straightforward for us to do without this safeguard. In view of the high winds we had already experienced we were hoping to dig snow caves, certainly as far as the Pinnacles, since they would be more stable, less noisy and certainly very much more restful than tents.

The dawn was clear on 7 April and even the wind had dropped a little. Loading ourselves with a few ropes, deadmen snow anchors and pitons, we set out over the glacier following the line of marker flags that Dick and I had left on our reconnaissance. We kept up a good steady pace, plodding over the ice without a rest until we were just short of the ridge. I could not help being relieved that Pete and Joe agreed with our assessment of the best route on to the ridge. We each dumped one of our ski sticks at the foot but carried the second to use in one hand, an ice axe in the other. On this occasion we remained roped, Dick and I on one rope, Pete and Joe on the other.

This, our first sortie, took place three weeks after reaching Base Camp. We were fresh, rested and acclimatised and plodded steadily, moving together in a series of zig-zags up the crisp snow towards the crest of the ridge. The snow was so crisp and firm it felt very secure as we followed it up to the spine of a subsidiary spur which gave way to broken rock on the other side. A basin of steep snow below the crest of the corniced ridge led to another spur. It was steep enough to justify moving one at a time and Dick set out to lead the first pitch, taking a line about 30m below the crest, where the angle was easiest.

Pete and Joe watched but Pete was unhappy about the line, pointing out that if there was a heavy snowfall the weight of an avalanche could be considerable. Pete favoured a higher line, just below the cornices, and set out to prove his point. He climbed steeply to a small notch in the ridge. Peering over the brink on the other side he was confronted by a terrifying drop. Sheer flutings of rotten snow clung to steep black rock, dropping away for over 1000m into the heavily crevassed and dirty snows of the Kangshung

Glacier. It was four rope-lengths to the top of the next spur – another rocky spine projecting out of the snow. The next basin looked even steeper than the one we had just climbed, and beyond it was yet another, to bar our way before we reached the top of the shoulder on which we had hoped to set our first camp. I was beginning to tire and announced, 'I don't know what you lot think but I've gone far enough for one day. This is a good spot for a snow cave and I think we should stop here.'

Even as I said it I realised that I was being defensive about my own fatigue, anticipating Pete's drive to achieve planned objectives, particularly when they were well within his own reach. On this occasion, however, I think I was being unnecessarily sensitive for the others readily agreed with me and I suspect that everyone had had enough for that day. I dug into the snow and though it was very compact, it did not seem excessively icy; more important, it seemed deep enough for us to be able to dig out a snow cave. We draped our load of ropes around a rock and started back down, climbing unroped now that we knew the route.

We took one rope down with us and all four of us roped up on the glacier in case there were any hidden crevasses. That evening, still quite fresh, we strode back to Advanced Base in just over half an hour. The camp itself was still exceedingly uncomfortable with the gear and food once again a chaotic shambles. The following day dawned blustery and grey so we had another session of clearing up the camp site and preparing climbing equipment, food and cooking gear that we were going to need for our first serious sortie. Once assembled, we assessed it would come to about ten loads, for we now had to start ferrying the rope we would probably need higher up the mountain.

On 9 April, therefore, we set off with our first carry and started to dig out the snow cave. Although I had estimated that this would be straightforward, it proved much harder than we had anticipated since almost immediately we hit ice. Chipping it away was a long laborious process. Only one person at a time could get into the hole we had dug. He worked flat out for about five minutes and then crawled out to allow the next one in line a turn; and it went on throughout the day.

By late afternoon the cave was barely large enough for two people to squeeze inside. Joe was determined to get everything on film, both inside and out. He crouched down outside the hole, asking Pete to shovel the snow straight at him to get a dramatic effect. Pete did so with such energy that the blade of the shovel shot off the end of the handle, hit Joe in the face, nearly knocking him off his precarious footholds and then bounced down the steep slope, coming to rest about 100m below. It was characteristic of Pete that with simply a mutter of apology to Joe for nearly decapitating him, he immediately set off to retrieve the shovel, cramponing down steep snow, teetering across some exposed rock and then climbing back up without even pausing to rest. We continued digging for an hour or so before descending to Advanced Base. We returned the following day with the plan that Joe and Dick, who had drawn the short straws, should stay at our First Snow Cave while Pete and I would carry up loads of food and climbing gear, then return to Advanced Base to move up with our personal gear the following day.

On the way back down on 10 April, Pete and I paused on top of the slight spur where we left the single ski stick we used on the lower slopes. It was a magnificent late afternoon with the cloud building up in a huge wall behind us, somehow contained by the barrier of the North East Ridge. The sky to the north was clear, a cold pale blue over the russet folds of the Tibetan plateau.

'You know,' Pete said, 'I really enjoy this business of going up and down the route, slowly getting to know it better. It was like that on Kangch, where we ended up doing the same thing. I find I don't get bored with it. It's getting to know the mountain itself better and better.' I shared his feelings.

The following day, while Pete and I plodded for the third time up to the snow cave, Dick and Joe set off on the next section of the ridge. There was a fierce wind with the cloud closing in at an early stage. The incline was now steeper, dropping dizzily for 700m to the glacier below. Being on new ground they climbed roped, moving one at a time, front pointing, with ice axe and hammer in either hand. It was a slow, cautious process, and it took them some hours to cross the security of the broken rocky spur that dropped down to the glacier from the shoulder. They were then able to move together, scrambling over broken rocks, picking their way from one strip of hard snow to the next, to the crest of the ridge. Visibility was down to a few metres. It was a strange, frightening world of screaming wind and scudding snow, of a slope that dropped precipitously into a boiling cauldron of cloud. And then they reached a point where the snow had peeled away from the rocky ridge, forming a series of crevassed holes. Joe wondered whether this could be made into the site of a camp but quickly dismissed the idea, for it all seemed too precarious. It was too close, anyway, to our First Snow Cave. Giving the holes a wide berth they picked their way up the ridge. This now broadened into a whaleback which, but for the thinness of the air and the bitter cold, could have been somewhere in the Cairngorms, contained as they were in blanketing cloud. They followed the ridge for nearly a quarter of a mile until, unsure of where they were, they returned.

Pete and I had waited at Advanced Base for as long as possible, hoping vainly that Charlie and Adrian would arrive with the yaks and, most important of all, with some mail, for we had now been away from home for over a month without any letters. In Pete's words: 'Our heads turn constantly down the valley, looking for the signs of a few yaks, a few welcome black heads with wide spaced eyes that glow from a great distance in the torch light. So we dawdle and reluctantly pack up and leave at 3 p.m. after watching the lads on the ridge; wondering if they're doing the right thing – usually it's best to go as near the crest as possible.'

But there was no sign of the yaks, so we set off back up to join the others. When our small cave was filled with bodies there hardly seemed room for four. I crawled in last and settled into the routine of snow cave living, unrolling my foam sleeping mat, taking off my overboots and boots, brushing each free of loose snow, then crawling into the welcoming sleeping bag to start cooking. One of the advantages of a snow hole is that there is always plenty of snow available in the walls to melt for drinks, though here it was so hard that we needed the ice axe to chip it away.

We had only been separated for a day and yet it was good to be a foursome again, immensely exciting to hear what Dick and Joe had seen and what they thought of our prospects. One of the great advantages of digging snow holes rather than pitching tents, quite apart from the greater security and comfort, was that we were always together and could therefore discuss everything. It meant that there was little danger of any kind of schism within the team and that the pairing always remained flexible. We could thoroughly talk over our plans for the climb. It was important that we all agreed to the general principles of our approach. Inevitably there were frequent differences about immediate tactics but these we were able to mull over until we came to a conclusion with which we could all agree.

There was also an affectionate badinage that helped hold us together and defused any tension or argument. It was born from previous trips and a mutual liking and respect for each other. I had knowm Pete since our expedition to the South West Face of Everest in 1975 but it was on Kongur the previous year that we had come to know each other really well. This was even more the case with Joe for I had shared a tent and climbed with him throughout that expedition. I had first been on an expedition with Joe to K2 in 1978 but the expedition had ended so prematurely when Nick Estcourt had been killed in an avalanche that I had hardly got to know him, and had even disliked him for his constant questioning of every decision. It was a mistrust that was probably mutual, but on Kongur we came to know and like each other, establishing a steady easy relationship. Although Dick was a friend of Joe and Pete, I had not met him before this expedition. But I got on so well with Pete and Joe I felt I could trust their judgment. With Dick this certainly proved the case. Quiet and thoughtful, and lacking worldly ambition, he unobtrusively got on with any work that needed doing. All too often it was he who cooked the evening meal, went out to get ice to melt for water or did the washing-up. Pete commented in his diary: 'Chris thinks Dick is saint-like – makes him feel quite humble.'

By the time all four of us were in our sleeping bags it was a tight squeeze inside the cave. The entrance was blocked by rucksacks but even so the insidious spindrift found its way in. With both stoves going and the entrance blocked, the temperature quickly rose above freezing and, as a result, a steady trickle came down from the roof. Even so it was much more comfortable than a tent. Although the wind was raging outside it was silent within. There was a feeling of cocoon-like security in this tight little cave.

Next morning we were slow in getting ready for the day. There was an element of Lifemanship in trying to avoid being the first pair out of the cave. Pete commented:

Had hoped they'd show the 'newcomers' the way but they don't seem too keen, so I lead off and belay on an ice axe. Chris follows very slowly and so I offer to do the leading so that he can recover in between rope-lengths. Eventually we reach the little rocky ridge running up to Point 7090m but Chris is depressed at how slow he is going. 'I'll do all I can to support you on this climb but ...' and I tell him to shut up – we've a long campaign ahead with plenty of time for all of us to fade and recover. He gets a burst of energy and it is all I can do to keep up with him to Point 7090.

I was able to keep in front, roped up but moving together, once we had reached the crest of the ridge. It was strange how strength ebbed and flowed. Once on the crest the gaping holes on the south east side of the ridge no longer seemed so threatening. Nevertheless, none of us fancied the thought of trying to use them for shelter. It was easy walking, crampons crunching into firm snow, but the very ease of it made the altitude all the more noticeable; we were now over 7100m (23,284ft). I set myself a steady rhythm of fifty steps and then a rest, found I was able to keep ahead of the others and was childishly pleased about it. I reached Joe and Dick's previous high point where there was a little pile of rope tucked into a hollow in the snow, added some of my load and continued up the slope. By this time the cloud had closed in and the wind was gusting fiercely. Just before setting out that morning Dick, whose eyesight was so much better than any of ours, had picked out the tiny black dots of the yaks arriving at Advanced Base. Pete and I had left a note asking Charlie and Adrian to open up on the radio as soon as they arrived. While Pete and I were starting the route, Joe was trying to contact them and eventually got through to hear the welcome news that the mail had arrived and that each one of us had several letters.

We were now heading for what looked like the first real difficulties on the climb, a steep step in the ridge, and we wanted to get our next snow hole as close as possible to it. We also had to find a bank of snow sufficiently deep in which to dig a cave. We found what we hoped would be a suitable spot in a slight dip in the ridge, dumped the ropes we had carried up and started back down. It had taken us five and a half hours to reach this point. That night I could manage to eat hardly anything. It was Pete's turn to cook and he had made chilli con carne from a freeze-dried packet, spiced up with extra chilli powder and garlic. Normally it was the tastiest of all the freeze-dried food but that night neither of us could force down more than a few mouthfuls. Were we building up a resistance to the uniform bland flavour of freeze-dried food or was it simply the altitude? Whichever it was, we were only absorbing a few hundred calories each day yet were expending several thousand. Fatigue was beginning to set in and it was Joe who suggested that we should carry only light loads up to our high point until we had finished the snow cave.

We had returned unroped the previous day, so now set out independently, each at his own pace, without the worry of delaying one's partner. Dick was away first and I quickly dropped behind, needing many more rests than the previous day, plodding up in misery of effort. Were the others feeling the same strain? Joe had a racking cough and was sometimes coughing up blood. But he also had that hard, self-contained sense of discipline and never complained. Perhaps he was feeling just as bad as I but had a greater tolerance to suffering and pushed himself on where I sank into the snow for a rest. Pete, who appeared to have an inexhaustible strength, plodded up the ridge with what to me seemed an effortless ease, and yet he also had his doubts:

A dullness seems to come over me at altitude. It is so difficult to think about the past or about any aspects of life – beyond the summit, staying alive, little hypochondrias. I try to remember what it's like to feel normal, to be able to concentrate on words, thoughts and ideas (though conversation is stimulating and wide-ranging on this climb). How long we've been at it already – so long – and so long, so long to go. Do I really enjoy it? However much I look around and try to absorb and wonder, try to keep my eyes open, the thought 'How much of this climb we have yet to do; will I be able to match up to it?' threatens to overwhelm me all the time.

Pete and Dick arrived first at the site of the Second Snow Cave and probed the hard snow with a ski stick to find a suitable spot. By the time I got there half an hour later there was a hole deep enough to crawl into and a cascade of dirty snow, with lumps of ice and grit, being thrown out between Dick's legs. He was like a terrier down a rabbit hole.

We tunnelled away through the afternoon, each taking turns in the hole. After we had been at it for a couple of hours and had a chamber that was barely large enough for one, we hit a wall of shattered rocks. There were three choices, find another spot and start again, bring up tents and use these or just carry on and mine away the rocks. After some discussion we decided on the latter since there seemed no better site for a cave and we had already committed so much time and effort to this one. By mid-afternoon there was just room for two people to work inside. Fortunately the rock was already shattered by frost and could be prised and levered from a bed of close-packed fragments. Even so there was obviously a lot more work to be done before all four of us could move in.

Pete commented:

It's cold and bleak and windy outside; Dick's first to voice the obvious fact that there's not enough work for four at a time up here. I suggest that Dick and I stay, but Joe says: 'Why you?' Chris sets off down alone; I do a bit of digging but then Joe and Dick say I should follow him – 'You know what his route finding is like.' I did promise Wendy I would look after him, and so I rush off down and catch him up as he's leaving the rock rib below Point 7090 – and take over the track finding in the cloud and fresh snowfall.

Certainly all the alpine guiding I've done has helped me walk on snow, without facing inwards with two ice tools all the time, but familiarity with this ground must not breed over relaxation – it's a long bouncy drop down to the glacier.

That night back in our First Cave, we discussed strategy. I was all for going back down for a rest the next day. The thought of mail from home as much as my growing fatigue was a strong influence. Dick, quietly determined, was adamant that we must finish the cave before going down. It made sense and I resigned myself to another day of effort, though that night I could only force down a few mouthfuls of the vegetarian meal of cheesy mashed potato with sweetcorn that Pete had prepared.

At least I was bright in the mornings, and uncurled myself at about seven when it was still dark, to turn round to get my head at the same end as the entrance. I pushed Pete's slumbering feet up out of the way and shook the pan and stove free from the chill dusting of spindrift that covered everything at the bottom of the snow hole. A struggle with the lighter and soon the stove was melting the snow for the first brew of the morning. It was a slow, painful sequence. It never took less than three hours to make three brews, to force down some cereal and perhaps some biscuit and cheese, then to crawl out of the warmth of the sleeping bag and grapple with boots and overboots ready for another day's toil.

It was a fine, windless morning, the best so far, and we got going at half past ten, our earliest so far. I was full of good intentions and away first. I cramponed up the snow just beyond the cave but I had no strength in me and had to use every ounce of will power to make each step. It was not so much a case of breathlessness but rather a heavy lethargy that had taken over my limbs. I knew I could not make another journey without having a real rest, so I turned round and dropped back to the cave where Pete was just putting on his crampons. I told him I would have to leave them to it for the day and go down by myself. There seemed no point in waiting for them in the cave and I was prepared to risk crossing the glacier without a rope, as much as anything to get the letter I longed for.

I set off down. It was so easy once I started descending. I could not help feeling guilty. My logic told me that if I was to last the course I would have to nurse myself, yet I hated doing it, hated admitting that I no longer had the stamina the others had.

As I dropped down the other three climbed towards the Second Cave. It had been our plan to return to Advanced Base after putting in a day of work. They took only two hours to reach the previous high point and spent the rest of the day mining the rock and snow. Pete commented:

I slowly put on my oversuit and start digging. It's a bit limited because Dick has the only good axe for chopping and the snow and rocks are getting a bit hard for the shovel ... We had a full afternoon's work at nearly 7300m, with those familiar little hallucinations as we chop. Nicer to be working inside than emptying the long approach trough because of the afternoon wind. We're all feeling the strain now of many days on the trot of hard work without much food ... and, most worrying, we've all got cold feet.

Around 5 p.m. we come to a stop – had enough digging really for today; there is still quite a bit of work to do but that can wait till next time. Once more snow has fallen; what tracks are visible are tricky to follow – place axe at every step.

We pile into the snow cave and leave most of the gear, including down suits, here. Dick, last to arrive, smells as much as I do in the enclosed space as he changes. Joes sets off down first. I wait for Dick and follow him along the 'Ramp' cornice.

Meanwhile I had reached Advanced Base. It was a delight seeing Adrian and Charlie, to be pampered and spoilt with a soup made from fresh vegetables and bread cooked that day in a makeshift oven, but most exciting of all was the prospect of letters from home. Charlie handed over a little pile to me. There was one I wanted and needed above all, the one from Wendy. At a glance at the envelopes no sign of her handwriting but maybe it was in the typewritten one. I tore them open, a sense of growing desolation overwhelming me. There were letters from my secretary, from friends at home but there wasn't one from Wendy. I had noticed the effects on others when they failed to get letters from home. I was now experiencing it at first hand. It was particularly hard that evening when the others, desperately tired but fulfilled and satisfied with what had been a long weary day, opened their letters and exchanged news from home. Pete noticed: 'Chris has no letter from Wendy. He's quiet all evening and reads while we chat.'

I went to bed early, to my cold little tent and although I tried to rationalise that a letter could have been delayed or could have just missed the post, although I was secure in Wendy's love, I nonetheless wrote a bitter, hurtful torrent of words that, of course, would reach home weeks later, out of all sequence with what had happened, and after Wendy had written me several letters whose love and reassurance were to do more than anything else to keep me going.

Next morning the sun warmed the tent and we each lay cocooned in our sleeping bags and thoughts until Charlie and Adrian came round with mugs of steaming tea. It was good to be cosseted, good to be back in the comparative luxury of Advanced Base and we had the satisfaction of knowing the Second Snow Cave at 7256m (23,805ft) was nearly ready for the next foray.

6

The Second Snow Cave

16 April – 23 April

Chris Bonington

We were sorry to see Adrian and Charlie leave for Base Camp two days later. It was not just cupboard love. True they looked after us, preparing delicious meals, chiding us for not eating more, collecting ice from the glacier, washing up, but it was their company that was most precious. Charlie, relaxed and amusing, helped us escape from the tense seriousness of our task, while Adrian, much quieter, lent reassuring support. I could not help thinking what it must have been like for Pete and Joe on Changabang in 1976, for they had been on their own for three months while climbing its West Wall. There had been no respite from each other's company and the fact they had come through this had given their relationship a particular strength, though they often bickered at each other like an old married couple. There was a strong element of competition in their relationship, and this was perhaps getting stronger as they expanded their ambitions and talents in writing. Each wanted to write the book describing this expedition. So many mountaineering partnerships and friendships have been destroyed by the pressures of fame and ego, and yet I had a feeling that this particular one had a durability that could withstand these stresses.

Dick's relationship with both Pete and Joe was slightly different. There was no question of competition, for Dick's ambitions seemed entirely within himself, as a test or perhaps a quest to discover what he could achieve for his own fulfilment. He did not, as they did, need to communicate his experience to a wider audience.

The three days went all too quickly. We frequently gazed up at the ramparts of the North East Ridge, focusing on the two buttresses immediately above the Second Snow Cave. These looked as if they would present the first serious difficulties of the climb. Through the telescope we could see what appeared to be a steep snow gully going through the First Buttress, but the Second Buttress seemed to present a rocky barrier stretching across the full extent of the ridge.

Our last day, 17 April, was spent in sorting out food and climbing gear for our second foray. We hoped not only to climb the two steps but also to establish a third snow cave on the conspicuous shoulder just below the Pinnacles, which we thought would be the crux of the climb. Next day we spent a dilatory morning finishing off our packing, unconsciously delaying the end of our relaxation and the moment of toil.

The wind was as cruel as ever, picking up clouds of fine snow, as we trailed across the glacier. I had taken the precaution of being in front so that I could set a steady pace. The slopes leading up to the crest of the ridge, blown clear of snow, were once again firm and secure as we zig-zagged up them, a ski stick in one hand, an ice axe in the other.

We had left a foam mat pinned in place across the entrance of the First Snow Cave, so only a little spindrift had leaked in. We were able to install ourselves quickly and settle back into the routine of high mountain living. There was still a lot of food, fuel and climbing gear to be ferried up to the Second Snow Cave and more work to be done to make it habitable. Pete and I attended to that the next day, descending to our First Cave at night.

Pete describes the evening ritual:

Life inside the cave: Chris and I swop positions and cooking duties. It's warm in here, five degrees above freezing, with condensation dripping from the ceiling. Warmest between Dick and Chris – Chris has now taken the hints about animal farm noises, and he coughs and clears his nose inside his sleeping bag... sleep is getting a bit better (avoiding pills, unlike Chris and Joe) but appetite not much. Funny how an 'us and them' mentality, based on cooking pairs, comes out even when four of us are all crammed together in the cave.

Managing to keep regular (though put it off an hour or so yesterday 'cos of the wind). This entrance is a bit short, so some spindrift problems, but it's a good cave and a haven, though there is not much of a ledge outside. We can only get down bland foods, usually powdered potato and cheese, spiced up with onions, garlic and chilli.

The following morning we loaded up our sacks and set out for the Second Snow Cave. This time we were going to stay. The previous day, I had travelled light, something noticed by the others, which meant that I now had an extra quantity of food as well as my sleeping bag and spare clothes. We all tended to watch each other to ensure that work was fairly divided.

Pete observed:

Chris leaves behind some of his Gaz canisters but is spotted: 'You can't get away with anything on this trip,' he says cheerfully and loads them into his sack. Dick's away first again. He's always willing to have a go first, but looks tense and uncertain and ponderous on steepish ground... I usually try thirty paces at a time up here, but it's hard work with a load. Dick reaches the snow cave first and plunges in and starts hacking. He gets crabby around 7300m sometimes and makes a comment that I should start clearing the debris he's made, but I'm hacking a big platform outside on which to stack the polythene bags of food we carried up yesterday.

Eventually all four of us are hacking and clearing. The slopes and fall line outside are stained with the mud, rock chips and dust from our excavations. We can cut very near the surface because the sugary snow-ice is so hard. Joe is a good shovel hacker...one rock is particularly big and stubborn and I declare war on it. Joe eventually shifts it using an ice hammer as a lever. Dick gets stroppy about this misuse of an ice tool until he realises that it is not his own. Joe is really funny on this trip and rarely misses an opportunity to tease.

One of us had to stay outside in the cold to clear the rubble from the entrance and kick it down the slope. It was Dick's turn when, once again, he picked out the tiny black specks of the yaks returning to Advanced Base. Even though Charlie and Adrian were so far away and could not possibly do anything to help us in an emergency it was reassuring to know that they were back. That night they brought us up-to-date on the Falkland Islands crisis and told us the news we were really waiting for, that there was some more mail for all of us.

There is always a tendency to declare a snow cave large enough when it barely is and this occasion was no exception. We were tired and cold and longed to creep into our warm sleeping bags. The prized position in any snow cave is obviously as far as possible from the entrance. Not only is this the warmest spot but it also means that no one crawls over you. I suggested that we drew lots, but Dick, with typical selflessness, volunteered to take the uncomfortable door position. I'm afraid the rest of us took no persuading. Joe, still cooking with Dick, was next in line, then me, and Pete was on the inside since it was his turn to cook for us.

While Pete and I had a comfortable night, next morning Dick was almost completely covered in snow from spindrift blown in from the partly blocked entrance. He was cold and shivery and just lay still in a stupor. I could not help wondering why Dick had not done more to protect himself from the snow, even if it had meant waking the rest of us. Pete felt the same way: 'To me this is stupid silent suffering, since he had access to two closed cell foam mats and all those polythene bags full of food with which he could easily have blocked off the entrance and kept warm. There seemed to be a touch of "This high altitude is suffering, therefore I must suffer" about it all. I say this to Chris later, but he is much more tolerant than I am.'

We were all sluggish that morning and talked around the problem. The snow cave was so uncomfortable, that I suggested two should remain behind to do something about it while the others went out and attempted our First Buttress.

'But what are two people going to do all day here?' asked Pete.

'There's a lot of work in just making that ruddy passageway fairly snow proof. And just getting all the food sorted out, and when they've done all that they can have a brew, they can lie down, they can dream,' I replied.

'And read *Daniel Martin*,' said Pete.

'They can read *Daniel Martin* as long as they let me have it back.'

'Well, I don't mind what I do but I do think it is very important that this place is sorted out. It's just ridiculous lying here covered in snow all night,' said Joe.

'I wouldn't know about that,' said Pete from the security of his space at the end of the cave.

'I know. You've got no spindrift on you. This is from the last half hour, not from all night,' said Joe.

'I'm having a marvellous time over here; I've no idea how much you lads are suffering over there,' said Pete.

'I'm glad you appreciate it, I'm glad you are seeing the luxury of your situation,' replied Joe.

'Well,' I suggested, 'I think it just makes life simpler if two people know that their function in life is to get this place sorted out ...'

'And get smacked on the bottom if it's not done,' riposted Joe.

'By Daddy Boardman,' I said, to keep it light.

'Well,' said Pete, 'I'm going to check what page Bonington's on in *Daniel Martin.*'

'Let's draw straws for who does what,' I suggested. 'I think two people should have the function to make this place liveable in.'

'Do you agree with that, Joe?' asked Pete.

'Yeah, but I'm not sure about drawing straws. I think people who are better at doing snow caves should do the snow caves.'

'I'm inclined to agree to that,' I interjected.

'I'm not saying this because I think I'm better at snow caves, I'd just as soon go on the hill.'

'I know I'm not very practical,' I observed. 'I'm not very good at that sort of thing. Dick's very good at sorting out snow caves because he's practical. I would say, as a suggestion, Dick and Joe are both rather good at it. Pete's very good at charging over the hills and I'm a kind of a dead weight to hold him back.'

'Don't you agree, Pete?' checked Joe.

'Yes.'

'I mean, would you prefer to stay here or ...'

'No, I'll go with the flow. I'm just feeling guilty that I had such a comfortable night over here.'

And so it was decided. Pete and I were to push the route out, while Joe and Dick improved the snow cave. This was how most of our decision-making took place and it worked well.

It was exciting to venture on to new ground next morning and I found the fatigue that had almost overwhelmed me the previous day vanish with the prospects of some real climbing. As always the distance to the foot of the First Buttress was much further than we had anticipated. It was up a gentle wave of snow and we did not bother putting on the rope. I was even able to keep ahead of Pete as we plodded over the crisp surface towards a rocky prow that barred our way on the crest of the ridge. A traverse over easy-angled, slabby rock led towards a snowfield which, in turn, led up to the gully which we hoped would take us through the Buttress at about 7300m. Looked at head-on it seemed very steep.

We continued to climb solo up increasingly steep snow-ice to a small, rocky island. It was time to rope up but the rock was very compact and there were no cracks for pitons. I ended up putting a deadman snow anchor into the snow just above the island, and Pete started to front point up towards the rocks above. It was a lovely cold clear day, and I had time to gaze around me. The North Col was far below, the summit of Changtse seemed almost level with us, and we could see over the peaks guarding Everest to the north and east, to the rolling purple hills of the Tibetan plateau, broken by the occasional white cap of some distant snow peak.

Pete's progress was slow. All movement is at that altitude. On reaching the rocks he probed around trying to find a suitable crack for a piton and eventually found one. He then led on up the side of the rocks until the rope had nearly run out. I followed, using my Petzel ascendeur for security. My turn to lead. Once in it, the gully did not seem quite as steep as it had done from below; the average angle was probably around sixty degrees, but there were bulges that were considerably steeper.

My progress also was slow, but the climbing was enthralling. Fatigue was banished not just by the risk of falling but by the fascination of breaking new ground, of working out a route, assessing the security of the deep packed snow. It took me over an hour to run out fifty metres of rope. To Pete the time crawled, but for me it raced by. I had nearly reached the end, was halfway up the gully and could see a sloping rock ledge to one side of it with some hairline cracks running into it. Just enough for a knife-blade piton. I tapped one in and wondered whether it would hold Pete when he came up. He reached me and led on up the gully. The angle began to relent and he climbed out of sight. Another long pause, a distant hammering and it was my turn to move once more. Pete had gained the top of the First Buttress and had hammered an angle piton as an anchor into a crack beneath a huge boulder just below the crest of the ridge. We crouched in the shelter of the rock and nibbled some chocolate before pulling out on to the ridge itself.

'You know,' I said, 'that's the first time we've actually been on the same rope together.'

'Not quite,' Pete replied. 'Don't you remember when I came up to your place before the '75 trip to be vetted. We did a climb then.'

'What was it?' I asked.

'Haste Not, on White Ghyll in Langdale.'

Broken rock and ribbons of snow led across towards the Second Buttress. It would have been good to look over the other side of the ridge to the east, but it was now getting late and we were tired. We cached the remaining rope under a rock and started back down. It had been an immensely satisfying day with some real progress to show for it.

Back at the Second Snow Cave, the other two had also achieved a lot. The entrance was now guarded by blocks cut out of the hard snow, with a door made from a sleeping mat to stop the spindrift blowing in. They had seen us coming down and had a brew ready. That night it was my turn to cook and next morning Pete and I could laze away the early hours, for it was to be Joe and Dick's turn to go out in front to force the Second Buttress. We were to follow carrying more ropes and climbing gear.

It was 11.30 before Dick and Joe were ready to start. We followed an hour later but caught them up on the first fixed rope. It was a much warmer, hazy morning, with almost no wind. The mist drifted over the ridge, softening its outline. It was possible to rest without becoming chilled to the bone. Pete even dropped off to sleep at the top of the First Buttress whilst waiting for me. We picked up the gear we had left behind the previous day and added it to the ropes we had carried up from the Second Snow Cave. I seemed to have used up my quota of energy the previous day and dragged behind the others whilst Pete stormed on, quickly catching them up. They were now on the Second Buttress, and had found a gangway that cut through it. It was little more than scrambling over loose rock, but they left a rope in place to ensure a safe descent.

On reaching the top of the Buttress at 7620m (25,000ft), they anchored the rope and carried on for a short distance, but soon it began to snow heavily. The top of the shoulder could only be glimpsed through the flurries and it was impossible to pick out the best route to it. As usual it was Pete who was keen to push on even so.

'Come on, lads, where's the determination? Really we are going to have to get a grip of this route soon. D-Day's not just a build-up on the South Coast, we've got to go on the offensive.'

'That's all very well,' replied Joe, 'but there's a bloody great smoke screen and we can't see where the hell we're going. There's no point pushing on blind.'

Pete comments in his diary: 'The Falkland Islands crisis and all the war books on this expedition, combined with living at close quarters with ex-Sandhurst Chris and ex-Ghurka Adrian, have given a lot of war and battle discussions to this trip – all, it must be said, part of the wide ranging political conversation.'

But the flurries of snow quickly brought us back to the qualities of the North East Ridge of Everest. As I reached the top of the second fixed rope they were already returning and by the time I had dumped my load they had vanished in the enveloping snow. There were no tracks, just the glimpse of a flag which marked the high point of the previous day. The sensation was strange; I could have been coming down Striding Edge in a Lakeland blizzard. There was no point of reference except my own exhaustion, a leaden lethargy which made each physical effort supremely difficult.

To my surprise, I caught up with the others at the top of the first fixed rope. I came upon them suddenly, as I rounded the huge boulder to which the rope was anchored. There was a sense of alarm amongst them for Pete had just had a very narrow escape. He had arrived first and had clipped a karabiner and piton brake on to the fixed rope. He was about to lean back to start the abseil, and had just grasped the rope, when the piton anchoring it pulled out in his hands. Had this happened when he had his full weight on it he would almost certainly have fallen backwards and off the end of the rope to his death. This time we had been very lucky. By the time I joined the others they had put in two deadmen snow anchors and Pete was again ready to descend. At the end of the fixed rope we had to traverse the slabby rocks, now covered in a layer of treacherous snow. Pete, perhaps shaken by his narrow escape, suggested we needed a fixed rope here but there was none available so Joe simply walked across. Pete followed with uncharacteristic caution, slipping and fumbling. He shouted at Joe heatedly and they had a short slanging match which seemed to release some of the tension.

That night in the Second Cave we were all tired and subdued. The following morning we had a discussion of what we should do next which verged on the acrimonious. Even Pete wanted a day off since he and I had now been on the go for five days without a rest.

A morning with some suppressed anger from me. Not much sign of determination or movement from Joe and Dick. Chris finds a diplomatic way of saying these things. Perhaps we are running out of guts and drive and we need to go down for a rest – down to Base Camp this time. Joe sees the strategic sense of this. But we haven't even seen the Pinnacles from close up. The weather's not helping of course, clouding up in the afternoons and obscuring the view.

Dick proposes staying up, which irritates me a bit because I've been rather disappointed with his dwindling dynamism up here ... I slowly see the sense of Chris's arguments; he comes up with a clever solution to Joe's now out-dated let's-go-light-with-just-a-shovel strategy – to put two people up there with a tent and try to dig the snow cave from that, so alleviating the need to travel backwards and forwards from the Second Cave with all the accompanying waste of energy.

The discussion lasted the better part of the morning. I was very aware that it was I who tended to call a halt first but I suspect that this acted as a useful counterbalance to Pete's forceful drive which was due in part to the fact that he was probably by far the strongest of us. The close nature of Joe and Pete's relationship meant it was also a competitive one in which neither of them admitted weakness to the other. On Kongur the previous year, I had on occasion felt that Joe had welcomed some of the arguments for delay I had put up, even though he would not have been prepared to initiate such an argument himself.

We eventually decided to go down for a good rest at Base Camp and then follow my plan on our return, to carry a tent up to the shoulder at 7850m and for two of us to sleep up there and dig the snow cave. It was mid-day before we were ready to move. We had to take stock of our supplies of food, fuel and climbing equipment, barricade the cave so that it would be habitable and mark it so that we could find it on our return.

It started to snow as we set off. At first it was easy enough, just walking down the crest of the ridge to Point 7090, but below that the angle steepened and the piled fresh snow was close to the critical point of avalanching. Joe and Dick roped together and, climbing one at a time, set out across the slope. Pete and I were still climbing unroped. We had no choice for we had brought only one rope down with us. It was slow, nerve-racking climbing with the constant threat of a slab of snow breaking away around or above us. It took three hours to get back to the First Snow Cave and another two to reverse the steep slopes below, but the angle then eased and we were able to take the rope off and climb independently down the lower slopes. Even here, though, there was a threat of avalanche and there was no real relaxation until we were back on the glacier.

Although there was now little danger, it was snowing hard and we could only just see the ghostly shape of the next marker wand in this featureless, grey-white world. Dick took the lead of our camel train and we plunged through the white, pausing at each marker to search for the next. Once we set out hesitantly from a wand into the void and suddenly realised, from the way the wind had changed, that we had probably gone in a circle. We retraced our steps, found the last wand and tried again, this time glimpsing a flag over the brow of a slight rise. We were back on track. Advanced Base seemed lonely and derelict. We missed Charlie and Adrian's warm greetings, cups of tea and soup and the friendly cosseting we needed after those days on the hill.

They had obviously left for Base Camp in a hurry. But where was the mail? We lit a stove for a brew and started searching. Surely Charlie and Adrian had not taken it back down with them. The thought of setting off tomorrow for Base Camp leaving our precious letters undiscovered up here was almost unbearable. We angrily searched both the communal 'greenie' tent and all our personal tents several times over but there was still no sign of any letters. It was now dark. Dick had quietly got down to organising our meal and, in looking for ingredients, found the precious bag of mail in one of the food boxes outside the tent. There were letters for all of us. I had three, warm fresh loving ones from Wendy, telling of the day-to-day events at home. I felt remorse for my previous angry and reproachful words to her. We spent the evening happily reading our mail, eating and drinking endless cups of tea and coffee. Tomorrow we were going down to Base Camp; it felt as if we were going back to civilisation.

7

Of yaks and men

5 April – 25 April

Charles Clarke

For nearly two months after establishing Advanced Base Adrian and I lived at a pace very different to that of the four climbers. We had, of course, a task to fulfil, to support the team by keeping the stream of supplies moving to Advanced Base, by coping with illness and looking after four tired men when they returned. We also had plans of our own which we rarely discussed, lest they appeared to dilute the climb.

Base Camp was a lonely windswept place as we trudged in on 5 April, the Americans had all set out for the North Face, our trekkers had been gone two weeks. The Chinese staff seemed miserable and many hadn't been well. Mr Chen, the liaison officer and the senior Chinese official with us, had already been taken to hospital in Xegur. Our jeep driver, Mr Cheng, was in Lhasa and so was Dawa, the Tibetan truck driver. Mr Wang, the cook, was demoralised. Mr Yu, the interpreter and thus our only linguistic link with anyone, was, however, pleased to see us. There was no outside news of interest (apart from what sounded like a minor problem in the Falkland Islands) and I felt sorry for the Chinese during their lonely vigil at Base Camp. Apart from Mr Chen none had any personal interest in mountaineering and their work, solely at Base Camp, was monotonous. Western travellers such as ourselves have an inquisitive mentality, an interest, however fitful, in anything unusual, so that each day seems to have only half the waking hours we need for fulfilment. Such was my attitude to Tibet and the Everest region but this was not shared by the Chinese. They were far from home in a country they did not find fascinating. They had to endure cold, hardship and boredom. Yet our Chinese staff worked very hard and consistently. If their ambivalence towards Tibet sometimes angered us, their true worth and feelings were exemplified by patience and, when tragedy occurred, both by humanity and enthusiasm to help in any way. I often wondered how I would feel being an English liaison officer on a Chinese expedition to Northern Ireland.

While the yaks rested for three days among the barren moraines around Base Camp, Adrian and I set about exploring our surroundings. With a file of pre-war photographs from the Royal Geographical Society and a set of hand-coloured slides lent by Jack Noel of the 1924 expedition there was a possibility of finding relics from the past. Where was the old British Base Camp? Where was the memorial left to Mallory and Irvine? Where were the former treasures of Rongbuk? Was there any wildlife in these treeless hills?

We first looked for the pre-war Base Camp. One moraine mound looked like another but by aligning the photographs with views of Everest and Changtse we found a flattish area tucked away in the rocks with some old tent sites, a few tins and broken wooden poles. This was clearly the old camp site, and a better and more sheltered spot than our own. The account of the 1924 expedition relates how, following the loss of Mallory and Irvine, Howard Somervell and Bentley Beetham supervised the construction of a memorial cairn, originally over 2m high. This fine monument with the twelve names of those who had lost their lives before the 1924 accident, was badly damaged by the time the British revisited Everest in 1933. Little at all remained of it by the last expedition in 1938. There seemed almost no chance of finding it. Adrian and I wandered around turning over rocks and then set off for the crest of a prominent moraine. There indeed was a minute shrine, a disused pot of ashes within a tiny cairn. Our initial hopes went unrewarded – there were no slates, no carvings and no names. Perhaps it was the tomb of a hermit who once lived high in the Rongbuk Valley, the ruins of whose house we had seen. Disappointed we sauntered down the moraine. I kicked over a slate fragment and the light fell on it obliquely, throwing a shadow around the numerals '192'. I felt it must refer to a 1920s expedition. Thus encouraged, we turned up further shards. 'MA ..., SHER ... EMBA ...' A few yards away were larger slates, at the side of an old fire and here was a 20-kilo slab, the broken headstone of the monument which had once read, '... IN MEMORY OF THREE EVEREST EXPEDI-TIONS'. We pieced together as much as we could and built a fresh cairn. I wrote rather laconically to David Newbigging that I thought it best to leave it there ... 'Assuming one of us doesn't join the In Memoriam, God forbid.'

Wildlife and flowers were our other interest in this remote region on the northern side of the Himalaya. How very different was the terrain to the lush lands of Nepal and India, where pine forests climb into the foothills and give way first to birch, rhododendron and juniper, and then to alpine meadows where grow primulas, saxifrage, potentilla, iris and blue poppies – and many more alpines. In those southern jungles there are bear, tiger and civet cats, while higher snow leopard hunt ibex, blue sheep and musk deer, hares, marmots and pika.

No spring flowers grew at the head of this barren valley. There were no trees for miles around. A few grasses were sprouting when we left in June. We saw blue sheep twice, and there were many hares around Rongbuk.

Apart from a vole we were to meet and befriend later, birds were our only animal companions. A lonely Himalayan griffon flew up and down the valley many times and yellow-billed choughs were common scavengers both at Base and up to 8000m. We saw around Base Tibetan snow finch, hill pigeon, raven and a striking pale pink bird, the great rose finch. Among the moraines Tibetan snow cock chuckled, while at Rongbuk we saw Tibetan partridge, Guldenstadt's redstart and horned lark.

We left Base again with the yaks and the five Tibetans on 10 April and wandered slowly up the East Rongbuk Valley. Adrian was clearly better acclimatised than on the previous trip: I felt terrible. Perhaps it was because of the Diamox I was using – usually a useful drug in the prevention of altitude sickness but which, in my case, had some unpleasant side effects. Ang Nuru, the leader of the yak herders, took my sack for the last hour. We camped at about 5 p.m. at the site of the pre-war Camp 1 and the five Tibetans, being now the majority, looked after us. It is easy to be impatient with porters and yak herders on a march: living with them makes it easier to understand their ways. That afternoon they chipped the ice and boiled water on a yak dung fire, breaking bricks of tea and adding coarse salt. Dirty Tibetan bowls came out of grubby bags and were ladled gently full. A knob of yak butter is dropped into each bowl, smelling fatty and rancid. It floats on the surface and makes the Tibetan tea taste a little like a rotten, salty chicken soup: I almost grew to like it at the end. Ang Nuru motioned us into the makeshift shelter and fed us tea. There were ten or twelve pints between seven of us. He said the butter helps chapped lips. Then out came the meat. Raw leg of sheep, dried in the cold winds of the Tibetan plateau. They ripped slivers off the bones and chewed them, hard; we followed and once the art of eating raw lamb from a dirty sack had been accomplished the meat tasted quite good.

Two hours passed. The younger men gave buckwheat to the yaks, pounding up the grain with water into little cakes and mixing in a little coarse brown sugar. Ang Nuru brought out his prayer book and chanted for an hour, licking tsampa (roasted barley flour) from his bowl between verses. By nine, 'the meal' was being prepared. Wet tsampa was being rolled into little balls (incidentally cleaning the cook's hands in the process); the tsampa dumplings were thrown into the cauldron of water with fragments of sheep, salt and chilli – and boiled for an hour or so. We slipped off to bed by ten, before this feast was ready but, generous as ever, Ang Nuru woke us at 11.30 with mugs of stew. We could not stomach the flavour but, trying hard not to upset our employee, we forced a little down before managing to pour the rest away. I feel I can eat almost anything but had to confess the tsampa stew had beaten me. The candles were out at twelve, the great yaks' eyes glinting in the moonlight, fearsome but harmless – perhaps the source of many a yeti scare. It was a cold night, –13°C in the tent.

Dawn came with a grey glimmer around seven. The yak men struggled out of sheepskins, drew on their coarse wool trousers and jackets, socks and felt boots and were up, fetching ice and water, feeding their animals and checking their hoofs. The tea brewing ritual began again and, as before, we were looked after as part of the family. Tsampa, tasting faintly like dry Weetabix, is made into a paste with salt tea. This is the Tibetan breakfast cereal – how similar the carbohydrate breakfast is the world over.

We were off about nine. I was frightened of the falling stones above Camp 1½ and wanted to explore a safer route among the boulders of the frozen East Rongbuk stream. I spent an hour on thin ice slithering around – an unpleasant, longer, though safer alternative. We reached the walls of Changtse and the old Camp 2 by mid-afternoon, feeling energetic in a brilliant morning free of wind. The ritual of the previous night followed. It was bitterly cold, down to –26°C in the tent and, typically, the Tibetans had brought no extra clothing or sleeping bags, preferring to hoard the down gear we gave them rather than soil it. They snuggled together under sheepskins and emerged stiffly in the morning, grinning. They hurried and left early. Two yaks had already dropped off at Camp 1, four more were lame and I waited anxiously to see what would happen but I need not have worried. Three Tibetans picked up the yak loads, fully 40 kilos apiece, and carried them themselves, arriving at Advanced Base without complaint. They were good men.

We learnt much on that second yak carry. Our Tibetans were among the most friendly companions we'd ever had in the mountains: they cared about their animals and about us as if both were extensions of their families. Conversation was, however, a bit thin. Adrian speaks Nepali and they knew a few words learnt from traders. For the rest we had to learn Tibetan, soon mastering the words for spoon, mug, stew, yak, load and road. Merriment and obscenity were not far below the surface and this international language soon became part of the vocabulary, an unusual event in China where there is a strange prudishness about it all. We soon knew the Tibetan for farts and that Ang Nima had a very pretty sister.

Advanced Base was empty when we arrived but the barren windswept rocks beside the glacier now seemed more friendly. The others had worked hard, building tent platforms and walls – the main mess tent was firmly anchored with rocks and ropes. The western sides of all the stones were blasted with frozen powder snow which had penetrated any opening in the tents and left a fine film of powder. It had clearly been windy. We looked across the glacier to the ridge, rising like a huge dorsal fin from the bare ice. Two little figures were working hard on the Second Cave at about 7256m (23,805ft), and two more were higher on the ridge. I felt impatient that things were not going faster and thought worriedly about when I said I would be home – we had already been away six weeks.

At six in the evening I talked to Joe on the radio. I am a pessimist about radio communication and seem to have had endless problems with radios on other expeditions. The tiny Sony sets which Joe had brought were already battered – they had been on two previous trips. It was a surprise to get through immediately and to hear that all was well. They would be down in two days.

Adrian and I settled down for our first night at 6400m (21,000ft). It was snowing slightly and the wind rising, roaring across the East Face of Changtse above us, crashing with explosive fury at the protruding rock buttresses. We heard the noise first like a distant peal of thunder, then the blast would sweep unchecked across the glacier, blowing a fine ice dust like powdered glass. A second explosion as it hit the tents, rattling the fabric with harsh, aggressive noise. The wind is never a friend here, it cannot serve us to fill our sails. My only use for it was to fly my kite at Base Camp.

The Advanced Base mess tent was a gloomy dark green military box tent, battened down and reinforced with a rough stone table in the centre and food boxes, ropes, harnesses, cameras, books and radios scattered around. A smoked ham and salami hung from the roof, delicacies which we thought we might enjoy but which proved too rich for the inevitable loss of appetite which occurs above 5500m. Outside were more food boxes, fixed ropes and pitons, crates of film and boxes of personal gear beside each single tent. Each of our tents was so different, instantly recognisable, reflecting the personality of the owner. Joe's, Peter's and Adrian's were organised and tidy, Dick's spartan and half the size of the others. Chris's and mine were rather a mess.

The choughs, yellow-billed black birds like crows, were our only companions, scavengers ready to eat anything. They seemed to nest – or at least to roost – in the rock turrets of the East Face of Changtse at 7000m, a windy spot for a home.

On our second evening, after a day spent organising loads, cooking and baking bread in a makeshift oven, it was less windy, even silent at times except for the pistol shots of the glacier as the ice groaned round the corner from the North Col. Suddenly there was a rustle within the tent, as if small stones were moving in the moraines beneath us. It continued and became more persistent and was obviously a creature. We waited excitedly to meet our unexpected companion and laid a trail of food away from the box beneath which the noise originated. We were soon rewarded when a pointed nosed brown rodent with a whiskered face popped up, saw us and vanished. 'Nibbles' was soon to become a firm friend. Probably a vole (a Sikkim vole seems most likely) and clearly living permanently at 6500m – the site of these old camps, quite what he ate in the lean years I do not know. As the weeks passed we saw 'him' grow fat and become quite tame;

he would come out when called to be fed and by the end of the expedition he had even found a mate. I suppose he originally came up in a load but, living there now permanently, we'd seen what was almost certainly the highest mammal on earth.

Chris returned on 14 April, alone and tired; the others were down by the evening. It was good to be together again and hear the news that work on the Second Snow Cave was advancing. They all looked exhausted but happy with the progress and I expected that we would all descend as planned to Base Camp the following day. There was, however, need to push out the route fast and they'd decided, perhaps unwisely, to rest at Advanced Base for several days, rather than at Base, in order to save time. I thought they all picked at the food I prepared, even the fresh warm bread from the 6400m oven, rather than devouring everything edible like wolves.

'Deterioration' at high altitude due to persistent lack of oxygen occurs whenever man tries to live for long periods much above 5500m. Appetite falls off, sometimes dramatically. Sleep is fitful and one's energy gradually flags. Despite the relative comforts of Advanced Base, plentiful food and enough warm clothing, it was perhaps an error to think that we could ever live there without our physical resources running slowly downhill. In retrospect, I feel sure that the long periods spent above 6000m in the 1920s and 1930s, particularly with the terrain so disarmingly easy, contributed to the failure of the expeditions. Certainly later on this trip there was unanimous enthusiasm for resting at Base Camp, despite a twelve-mile walk.

Adrian and I left on 16 April to pick up the third and last yak carry. Pleased with ourselves we took six hours to get down and fell upon a large Chinese meal. Morale had improved. Mr Chen, the liaison officer, was back from Xegur, fit and well, and there was more mail from Lhasa.

We planned to rest and then return to Advanced Base with the yaks and later attempt a peak of almost 7000m to the north. If we needed to justify what appeared to be a jaunt, our peak seemed to afford a remarkable view of the North East Ridge. We could also keep in radio contact.

It was not to be. We sensed something was wrong with the third yak carry early in the three-day journey. There was unnecessary argument about loads and we found that our five Tibetans had again brought no expedition clothing. As we left the pre-war Camp 1, two of the yak herders stayed behind while the three who came said that they wanted to reach Advanced Base that day instead of the next. We agreed. We had finished our journey by early afternoon, leaving ample time for the yak herders to drop back to reach pre-war Camp 2 or, even at a stretch, Camp 1. No, they wanted to stay; yes, they'd like some whisky. We agreed.

Lom Sangu, the eldest Tibetan – and we were never good friends – eagerly grasped a bottle of White Horse and promptly drank it in one. His two companions huddled around the stove eating aspirins for their headaches, now quite unable to leave because Lom Sangu could not walk. Six hungry yaks shivered in the wind outside. They would leave at day-break, about seven. We agreed. They could make us tea. We lent them a tent and sleeping bags which belonged to the absent climbers.

I had a fitful, headachy night, and pottered around after sunrise, brewing endless cups of tea. The Tibetans snored, two surfacing about nine, while one remained firmly inside the tent, coughing and groaning. We were irritated with them for they had outstayed their welcome. We were keen to get moving ourselves but could not leave them alone in the camp. In an effort to hurry them I poked by head inside their tent to glimpse an extraordinary scene. There was the entire expedition's rations of chocolate, several climbing ropes, tins, sweets, biscuits, adhesive tape, all being packed feverishly into Tibetan woollen bags by the man who was apparently sick.

My fury was uncontrolled. We hustled them out of the camp, having searched grubby folds of clothing and all their belongings. I felt cheated, hurt and intensely angry that our excellent relationship had been soured by this deception. We cancelled our plans for a peak, radio-ed the ridge and set off after them to Base Camp. By nightfall on 21 April we were back at Base Camp. Mr Chen listened patiently to our problem with resignation born of many expeditions. Next day he harangued the Tibetans who seemed to apologise for their behaviour. We wished not to exact retribution but rather to make certain that they returned at the end of our stay to help us down with the loads. As usual on an expedition we were entirely dependent in some way upon the local people.

Three days later the others came down to rest.

8

Idle days

24 April – 28 April

Chris Bonington

It was a brilliant sunny morning at Advanced Base on 24 April but the entire mountain was plastered with freshly fallen snow and we all felt we had made the right decision in coming down. There was a holiday atmosphere as we sorted out our gear and packed light sacks with exposed film to take back down to Base. I was the first away and I strode alone down the scoop of snow between the ice of the glacier and the rocky moraine. You can never relax completely above the snow line and suddenly I plunged downwards into a hidden crevasse. A momentary terror engulfed me but I came to a halt with my head just above the surface, my shoulders jammed between the narrow walls of ice. I, too, had been lucky; it had been just narrow enough for me to stop. Another 15cm wide and I could have gone all the way down.

Shaken and chastened, I struggled out and scuttled across to the rocks. It was harder walking, but at least they were safe. The others noticed the hole as they came down and were relieved to see my tracks emerging on the other side. Pete, plugged into the stereo sound of his little cassette player, felt good:

Walking down into oxygen always makes me feel strong. Locked into music the walk speeds past. It seems obvious now that we should have done this last time. I have eaten so little in the past three weeks. Full of thoughts and excitement as I go down, really a feeling of return. We haven't done badly up there, but we have been away such a long time; it is such a long time since I flew a kite at Xegur, even since we were last at Base Camp.

I purposely blind myself to much of the beauty – our ridge must be all that matters for a while.

Each landmark brought us closer to safety and comfort. The glimpse of the ice lake by the first camp that we had used on the way up and then, much closer, the tent we had left in place there, the cairn with the prayer-flag that marked the junction with the Central Rongbuk Glacier, the sight of the spur at whose foot lay Base Camp and, at last, the stretch of flat shingle that led to the little tent village. There were so many tents for so few of us. Just the long walk across the flat and then Mr Chen and Mr Yu came out to get me, warmly shaking my hand. Charlie and Adrian were down at the Rongbuk monastery for the night. Then there was a big base tent with stacks of papers and magazines sent by David Mathew from Beijing and cans of Budweiser beer brought in from Lhasa. There were tiny new potatoes boiled in their jackets.

Halfway through the afternoon there was a roar of a truck; we momentarily though that this was Charlie coming back, but then there was the sound of Americans voices. We knew that the American Everest team were all up the Rongbuk Glacier. Could these be trekkers? We groaned at the thought, having no desire to make polite conversation, or to talk to lay people asking endless obvious questions. But we'd have to greet them. I ventured out of the tent, to be met by a vaguely familiar figure, big and slightly shambling with a long, rather battered face framed by a traditional Tibetan hat. It took a second or so for it to dawn on me. It was Jim Bridwell, the American climber who had stayed at our house a couple of years before. He was a legendary figure, with many new routes in Yosemite to his credit and, more recently, routes in Alaska and Patagonia. He had also climbed Cerro Torre, one of the steepest and most difficult rock peaks in the world, with a complete stranger, after his own companions had returned home.

After the first greetings, we found that Jim was part of a small expedition whose object was to ski around Everest. Leader and creator of the project was Ned Gillette, a well-known cross-country skier who had been in the American Olympic team and had written one of the best handbooks on the sport before branching into expeditions, skiing across the Karakorum in 1980 and then skiing up and down Mustagh Ata in China the same year. He had with him his girlfriend, Jan Reynolds, also a strong competitive cross-country skier, and another skier, Rick Barker. Jim Bridwell was both climbing expert and film-maker, and had led them up a new route on Pumo Ri the previous winter.

All this came out as we sat and talked and drank wine and beer around the table in the base tent. It was wonderful having fresh people to share our experience and friends to talk to. We reminisced, exchanged tales of mutual friends, swapped music cassettes and relaxed in a way that we had been unable to do for some weeks. The Americans were sponsored by Camel cigarettes, though Jim Bridwell was the only member of the team who smoked. They had made the Nepalese part of the trip the previous winter but had not been allowed to cross the frontier and were therefore now completing the Tibetan side, having flown in through Beijing to Lhasa.

Ned was very much the organiser, in constant consultation with their liaison officer, juggling plans and possibilities in an effort to fix their trip from the Lho La, back down the West Rongbuk Glacier, up the East Rongbuk, over the Lhakpa La, which Mallory had crossed sixty years before and then into the Kangshung Valley by the Karpo La. It sounded an enjoyable, interesting trip, during which they would cover much exciting ground. In some ways I envied them, for they were doing something that was well within their powers, yet both Ned and Jim envied us and were already talking of plans to go to Everest, such is the lure of the highest point on earth. We spent the days relaxing at camp, sleeping much and eating well but also wondering about the immediate future.

Pete wrote in his diary:

As far as equipment, food and support (Charlie and Adrian) we couldn't have better. No expense or thought spared. Funny, despite all my hypochondria, I am going by far the best, am certainly the strongest of all those up there on the hill. For the first time, this was actually frustrating during this last go. But it is encouraging that the two steps were so very easy, and so, possibly, the big towers and gendarmes are also going to be easier than we think.

But this mountain is so big, our project so vast, so long, that all our energies are consumed by it and have to be directed towards it. Even Chris has little left over for other things. I find books difficult to read, when on other trips I have always found reading to be a useful distraction. It is even difficult to concentrate on photography, as if it is an energy drain. And now other Everest books, other people's experiences on Everest – their dates, their efforts, their carries have a dwindling relevance as we build up our own experience of the mountain and the pattern of our own attempt becomes increasingly defined.

I learnt a lot on K2 in 1980. Before that I believed nothing could resist if I tried hard enough; but I do want so much to succeed this time. Kongur, in contrast, was playing. As Kissinger said to Nixon, 'A victor has a thousand relatives, but a loser is an orphan.'

And later that same day:

An idle morning drifting by; now listening to Fleetwood Mac, Bare Trees. Sort of weary, but not the same aches and pains, the same racking cough that I have up there on the ridge; it is so difficult to be fully aware at altitude. Life inexorably becomes blinkered – 'Yes, I know I must eat, must force it down, must make a big effort each day' ...

And yet we are a great compact little team, hardly a cross word ever between us. In a way, we all respect, sort of love each other, for we know that when the crunch comes each of us will do the right thing.

While Pete wrote, Dick worked on the swan he was carving. He had brought the mahogany with him and was slowly, patiently, chiselling out its gently curved neck. Joe either slept through the day or worked on the notes of his film, and I just slept and slept. That first night had developed into a spontaneous, happy party of talk and drinking, and stories that became increasingly maudlin, but I had not been able to stand the pace and had staggered early to bed, to lie listening to the steady beat of the stereo, awake yet too tired to join in.

The following day, 26 April, Charlie and Adrian returned from Rongbuk, relaxed and satisfied with their ascent of a minor peak. True, as we all gazed down the valley from Base Camp their 6200m summit did not look impressive. 'You mean that dramatic peak that dominates the western side of the valley, to which the eye is drawn like a magnet?' was the way Pete put it teasingly.

Charlie's diary:

Adrian and I set off from Rongbuk, climbed a steep scree gully to the west and soon look down on the monastery. After four hours we reach a crest, a fine line of shattered rocks like a Lakeland ridge bare of snow. The weather looks appalling with tongues of dense black cloud shooting down like sabres, pouring snow on to nearby hills. There seems little point in staying on this bleak and windswept ridge at 6000m but, having carried a tent here, we felt compelled to. We cook and settle down. The idiot in me has brought a lightweight sleeping bag and I sleep little, shiver and feel restless. Adrian snores peacefully as I wait for dawn.

It is clear. We look across to Nepal and from this unusual angle can see the three ridges of Everest, the South East as a jagged silhouette and the West in profile as well. Our peak is several hundred metres above us. By ten we are on the top bathed in warm still sunlight. A delicate heave on to the tabletop of a rock pinnacle for a few seconds' photography. 6200m on the altimeter and just over that on the map. Away to the west the ranges of Gyanchung Kang and Cho Oyu, new and exciting views. But Rongbuk was beckoning and we sped off down, down a steep scree ridge, down through the rocks and across a stream in three hours.

Oh Rongbuk, the stream and the grass to lie on. How can anyone have thought this is a barren, inhospitable place? It felt like Paradise that quiet afternoon as we lay in the sun outside our tent. The monastery seems to have been destroyed with unparalleled savagery. Not a room remains undamaged. We know little about its remote past but Tilman, talking to the High Lama in 1938, concluded that it was built in the early part of this century. There seems no way of telling but the surrounding walls look reasonably new. The Chinese told us that its destruction took place in 1969 and at that time the valley was uninhabited, except by the monks and nuns – separated from each other only by forty minutes of trail.

The central hall is about 18 x 24m and the surrounding walls about 180m square.

Many Mani stones and just a few terracotta clay miniatures. And no efforts at restoration. The stupa outside the monastery is split in two to ransack the relics within.

Recent visitors (which include many Europeans) appear to have decided that the destruction of the building is inadequate – so they have used it as a rubbish dump and lavatory, filling the place with tins, excrement and lavatory paper ... we have a long way to go to educate ourselves.

We stayed lazily on the river bank and talked to Chris at 6 p.m. on the radio. They had come down to Base Camp from the ridge for another rest. A truck drove past. Some figures in red waved. We waved back. They looked rather smart, macho, aggressive and flashy and I suppose they thought we were trekkers. We, of course, felt rather superior!

The next three days slipped away agreeably. We even had a picnic at the site of the old British Base Camp. A picnic was something our Chinese staff found difficult to understand, it being altogether too frivolous. Lying in the sun, the ubiquitous tape deck rolling, nibbling salami and Stilton, swilling red wine, it was easy to forget, at least for a short time, the presence of Everest towering there at the head of the valley. It was concealed by the low moraine ridge on which had once stood the memorial to Mallory and Irvine.

'Pass those nuts over, please.'

'More pâté?'

'Want some more wine?'

'I'll borrow *Flesh Wounds* when you've finished it, if I may.'

Charlie flew his kite with the exuberance of a small boy. A lammergeyer circled overhead. Conversation became blurred as I dropped off into a doze. I could be lying on the grass in the Lakes during a family picnic. Dimly I longed for the end of the expedition, longed to be home, to see my Lakeland hills and walk up High Pike, to get out rock-climbing with the lads on the long summer evenings.

The three days' rest were nearly over. It was 28 April. Charlie and Adrian walked up to pre-war Camp 1 that afternoon. We were to follow the next morning, walking straight through to Advanced Base in the day. Time was galloping past all too quickly. April had all but gone and we still had not reached the Pinnacles – but at least the weather was getting kinder. The ice lake beside Base Camp was beginning to break up; each day the stream ran higher. It was even possible to wander around the camp in shorts and a T-shirt during the middle of the day. Surely the ridge would be kinder to us than last time?

9

The third foray

29 April – 7 May

Chris Bonington

The holidays were over. On 29 April Pete, plugged into his cassette, was away first: 'I'm listening to classical for the walk up. It's less imposing than pop music and I can choose my own rhythm... I've at least had some reasonable food; fried eggs inside my tum, Mars bars in my little sack to keep me going on this long walk; I feel fit, though light.'

Dick was close behind, but Pete was determined to keep his own pace, and quietly strode on to the music of Mahler's Resurrection Symphony. On the way up, each of us tended to walk in his own little world. Joe had set out last of all, but overtook me before the junction of the East Rongbuk Glacier. I plodded up slowly, following the trail of scattered yak dung, the abandoned telephone wires of previous expeditions and the occasional daubs of Japanese red paint.

It was noticeable how a tenuous path had formed in the few weeks of use. The journey to Advanced Base which originally had taken three days was now just a matter of hours. Dick took a mere six hours, I a more modest nine. Next morning we packed polythene bags full of food and Gaz cylinders and set off for the ridge. Charlie and Adrian were going to accompany us as far as the foot of it, carrying the big 16mm cine camera so that Joe could get some good close-up action shots. It was typical of the thought and work he put into the filming. He had already spent some time with Charlie and Adrian, briefing them both on the working of the camera and also basic film techniques.

It was a savage return to the mountain. The wind blasted across the Raphu La, sweeping the fresh snow from the ridge and giving us perfect cramponing conditions, but it was so strong that in the worst gusts we had to stop, crouched, clinging to our ice axes. I could not help feeling discouraged, for I seemed to have gained no benefit at all from our rest. Pete commented:

Chris walks very slowly, resting it seems at every step, and eventually not far from the 'schrund, the others overtake us. 'Does Chris always go slow?' whispers Adrian...

I'm worried about being 'type cast' as always climbing and cooking with Chris and have made little hints to Dick and Joe. But it's not up to me to suggest, 'cos I don't want to hurt CB. Chris arrives late and says he feels he's hardly had a rest at all – he does get depressed easily. But he does bounce back and says, 'It's my turn to cook, you did it last time.' I'd forgotten.

This was a feeling I was never made aware of. Although I had doubts about my own ability to get to the top, I never had any about the others. I was convinced we had a good chance of success. On my good days I dreamed of getting there myself and on the bad ones wondered at what stage I might have to drop back to a purely supporting role.

The following day, 1 May, was an easy one. It took barely two and a half hours to reach the Second Snow Cave. This time it was to be the turn of Pete and me to sleep near the entrance and, since I had cooked the previous night, Pete had the unenviable spot on the outside, though with the snow-proof door it was less of a hardship. We had the entire afternoon to cook, read and discuss our plans for the next few days. We had settled on my proposal to move one pair straight up to the top of the shoulder at 7850m (25,755ft), and for them to camp if necessary while they dug the cave. The other pair would drop back to the Second Snow Cave and rejoin them the following day.

Pete commented: 'I'm agitated about how the teams will be split up; very agitated but not so much that I dare risk saying anything and being misunderstood. So I trust that Providence will guide us – and we draw bits of paper for the next couple of days' sportsplan.'

Pete's prayers were answered. He and Dick were to stay on the shoulder, while Joe and I did the second carry.

'Well, I'm glad, anyway,' said Joe, 'at least it'll give me another night sleeping at a lower altitude.'

We let the afternoon slip away, even though there was a lot to do, for we had all the food to sort out and pack. It was Dick who had the innate self-discipline to urge us into action. We sorted out five days' food and fuel, leaving behind much of the freeze-dried meat, which we all found unpalatable. Our standard diet had become a handful of muesli in the morning and cheesy mashed potato at night. We divided the food into two poly bags for Joe and me to carry the next day.

In the morning, as usual I got away first. We had brought with us a length of rope to leave across the easy-angled slabs leading to the snow slope of the First Buttress, but now clear of snow, it was once again straightforward and anyway there was nowhere to anchor the rope, so it was left at the far end in case we should ever need it.

Pete caught up with me at the top of the First Buttress and he and Dick moved steadily together towards the second length of fixed rope. Joe had been filming, but he also passed me. I was determined not to let them get too far ahead, and stayed doggedly behind them.

Pete had now pulled away from the rest of us:

Wonder how long it will be to the top of this long-sought landmark? Can we really just traverse around it to the col on the other side? It looks no worse than the sort of ground we have been traversing for miles down below … but soon I'm out of sight of the others, solo-ing with a lot of pauses for gasps, across an intricate bit of ground, across steep slopes only tenuously attached, it seems, to the rock of the mountainside, over little steps, round bulges, picking out a line traversing about 30–60m below the crest of the ridge.

By this time the afternoon cloud had rolled in, filling the great bowl of the Kangshung Face and overflowing on to our side of the ridge in breakers that enveloped us and then dissipated in the tearing wind. It was like the incoming tide, getting imperceptibly deeper until each one of us was enclosed in a world of driving snow. Pete had disappeared from sight around a corner. Joe and Dick were just ahead, Dick having difficulty on a steep little overlapping wall that barred the way. To avoid it, I took a slightly higher line and as a result overtook him. This is how Dick felt: 'As the others pulled away I gave up the struggle to keep up. Bugger it, I'll go at my own pace and forget the unspoken recriminations. I put it down to an off day. Funny how you feel bad about it, as though you're not pulling your weight.'

The steps made by Pete and Joe were vanishing under the fresh snow as Dick and I stumbled up over snow-covered rocks probing our way through the mist. Out in front, Pete was thrusting forward on to new ground:

At last I can see round the corner, into the col, the rest of the ridge looming through the clouds towards the Pinnacles and what now appears as a prominent inset gully, plunging down towards the glacier … No, it's steep round the corner, and I climb straight up. There is no way we can avoid going round the top of this summit. Also there is the spur running up from the Kangshung side. It gives us our only hope for a snow cave. We can't afford to pour all that effort we did last time into hacking a cave out of ice and rock.

Some rocks, a snowy plateau; I dump my sack and feel a different person – what a difference without that unwelcome weight, to be able to move about. No one has been up here before and I can breathe and look around. There must be a cornice somewhere. I walk near the rocks, down a few feet to the col on the other side. Good, quite safe, we can walk to the foot of the steep part where we'll have to fix ropes at the start of the Pinnacles.

I come back and Joe arrives. I uncoil a rope and he belays me as I peer over the east side. By a stroke of luck I find the top of the spur coming up the other side, although there is no indication along the edge to tell where it could be. Enthused, I kick down it. Below the slope goes down quite steeply and then broadens into a shoulder. I get the shovel and dig a bit, yell back up that it should be fantastic for snow caving.

Joe has a long way to go back down and leaves. As I start shovelling he points out that I'm a bit near the cornice that runs into the main ridge from this subsidiary spur but says, 'It should be OK.'

I reached the top of the shoulder at 7850m just as Joe was about to start down, dumped by bag full of food and Gaz cylinders, and peered over the edge to see Pete's boots sticking out of the slope. He had burrowed the entrance passage to the cave. I wished him the best of luck and started back down, to pass Dick a short way below the crest. The tracks were now completely covered and the visibility so bad, that I gave him explicit instructions on the route so that he would be sure of finding the cave. He was going very slowly and was obviously tired. When Dick reached the top of the shoulder, he also noticed how close to the cornice was the hole that Pete had started. He suggested putting up the tent, but Pete hated the idea of leaving the relative shelter of the lee side of the ridge. 'It's so windy on the ridge, and here, just a few feet down, it's so warm and quiet and the snow is so good.'

Dick reluctantly agreed they should dig on but complained, 'I don't know what happened on the way up; I just ran out of steam above the top of the Buttresses.'

He started to dig, but became increasingly worried by the proximity of the cornice and persuaded Pete to have a careful look. They decided to abandon excavation for the night and pitch a tent on top of the shoulder. Pete dug out a rectangular depression in the snow in which to sink the tent, as some protection from the driving wind.

Damn, it's so cold and I forgot to tie on the guy lines to the outer skin of the tent. I have to shelter inside and tie loops and then go outside and tie them on to the tent loops with freezing fingers, anchoring the tent walls with everything I can stick into the snow – poles, hammers, axes, anything that will stay. I'm determined that we shouldn't take off. Dick goes straight inside and doesn't budge again.

It's not very pleasant inside, with the snow and ropes weighing down the valance and the tent flapping madly in the wind ... Prop the stove precariously in the middle – a couple of spills, but we manage to eat a couple of packets of noodles each.

While Pete and Dick were getting installed for the night, Joe and I dropped back to the Second Snow Cave. Joe quickly vanished from my sight and I went down on my own, the footprints already covered in fresh snow. The occasional marker wand and our two lengths of fixed rope were the only reminders that anyone had ever been here before. I had reached that level of weariness, when even in descent, I needed to stop for a rest every few yards. How long could I go on pushing myself to this degree? Could I make it back up to the top of the shoulder tomorrow, and after that, the Pinnacles? Could I keep going at over 8000m? I was now at the top of the First Buttress. Come on, concentrate on the ropes, clip in correctly. I slid and stumbled down, left my harness and ascendeurs clipped to the rope at the bottom, and carefully front pointed down the final stretch. I go so much more nervously when exhausted. I teetered across the snow-covered slabs, crampon points scraping ineffectively on the smooth rock and was grateful for the final easy slopes leading to the snow hole.

Joe was already in his sleeping bag, the stove in the corner purring quietly, heating water for a brew. I slumped on to my mat and just could not stop myself crying. They were tears of exhaustion, of frustration, of despair at my own weakness. Joe didn't say anything, just quietly let me get over it, and then offered me a brew. I muttered apologies but he sympathetically dismissed them, saying I'd feel better in the morning. That night he did the cooking, but I raised the energy to crawl out of the cave to make the evening radio call. We could hardly hear Pete up on the shoulder, for there was too much mountain between us, but Charlie was very clear. He and Adrian were off on another climb. They had crossed the East Rongbuk Glacier and were camped near Khartaphu, beneath a peak of almost 7000m, which they hoped to climb the next day. They could see us clearly and had a fine view of the entire North East Ridge. After the usual queries about the progress of the Falkland Islands war, Charlie was able to relay messages from Pete, asking us to pick up all the gear dumped at various spots on the way up.

After a good night's sleep in our now roomy cave, my resolve returned, and I was the first away, carrying my personal gear and a few items of climbing equipment that were still to go up. Joe soon caught up with me and, on the slopes above the Second Butress, he chose a slightly different route from mine and began to pull away. Soon my progress had slowed to a crawl but at last I reached the crest and flopped down for a rest. Gradually it pervaded my consciousness that someone was below me and I glanced back to see Joe coming up behind. He had reached the top about an hour before and, realising that I was having a struggle, had decided to come back to help me with my rucksack on the final stretch. Unfortunately, because of the slight difference in our routes, he'd missed me. It was too late to let him carry my sack but I felt immensely touched by his kindness. Going back to help someone at that altitude shows a very real concern. We plodded slowly those last few metres up over the rounded snow dome and there below us on the other side of the ridge, was a ledge carved out of the snow and the gaping hole dug by Dick and Pete during the day. It was a superb snow cave. The snow was just the right consistency, firm, but not too hard. The chamber had an alcove at either end for the cooking stove, it was easy to scoop out snow for making our brews and, being on the lee side of the ridge, was sheltered from spindrift.

Joe and I were cooking at one end, Pete and Dick at the other. As so often happened, once all four of us were squeezed in, the cave was barely big enough. We discussed what to do the next day and decided that Dick should drop back down to the top of the Second Buttress where we had left some ropes, bring them back up and then enlarge the hole, while the three of us should go to the foot of the Pinnacles and start climbing them.

Next morning dawned fine. The Kangshung Face dropped beneath us in a huge concave bowl. We could see the South Col on the other side of the summit at about the same height as ourselves. From there it was a mere five or six hours to the summit. We, on the other hand, were nearly two miles from the summit, with the jagged Pinnacles between us and the comparatively easy ground of the upper part of the ridge. We could now see the top clearly but this seemed remote, dwarfed by the immediate threat of the Pinnacles. The ridge curved gently and easily to the foot of the first one, a triangle of snow-veined rock, leading to a shapely point.

Pete was first away from the cave, striding steadily over the crisp snow, keeping a few feet below the corniced crest. Joe and I followed, carrying some ropes and pitons. Pete reached the foot of the First Pinnacle in about two hours. Joe and I were three-quarters of an hour behind him. I scrambled out in front, clambered up a small rock wall and looked round for a belay. The rock was hard, black and slaty, with very few cracks. There was nowhere for a piton belay, but there was a huge block iced into the slope, and I draped the rope round the top of this. Pete was obviously raring to get at the Pinnacle, so Joe and I tossed for who should hold his rope. I won so Joe set off back to the cave to get a brew on.

Pete started up the bottom snow slope of the Pinnacle. This led up to a rocky buttress, split by a shallow ice groove at about 30m. He hunted around for a crack in which to hammer in a piton anchor, but they were all blind, so he had no choice but to continue up the groove, bridging out on sloping rock holds on either side, looking constantly for a suitable crack. The time crept by and I stamped and shivered, watching Joe wander back along the ridge. The rope crept out through my fingers. It was nearly at an end. No alternative but to tie on another rope. Had Pete slipped, nothing could have saved him and he'd probably pull me off as well.

A deeper ringing tone echoed down. He had at last got in a decent peg, but he didn't stop there. Obviously it was not a good stance. Another couple of pitons and he reached some broken ledges and hammered in a final anchor. It had taken nearly three hours. Cold and shivery, I followed, trying to put as little weight as possible on the rope. It had been a fine lead and one that Pete had enjoyed. As I followed, jumaring up the rope, he carried on, unbelayed but towing a rope behind him. I joined him when he paused. He now moved diagonally over quite easy ground and ran out another 30m. I set off, hammering in an intermediate anchor to make the rope easier to follow. This at last was real climbing. By the time I reached Pete the cloud had closed in and it was beginning to snow but he was determined to reach a little notch in the ridge about 30m above.

And the straight-up pitch is great fun – solid rock; don't put in a runner for a while, in case Chris has to attach another rope; eventually I reach the ridge. Great, it's firm. I can sit astride it, uncomfortable but safe. Snow softish on the other side. Rocks near, but crackless. Can I climb higher? Seems OK. The next bit doesn't look too steep. That was my objective for today, but time is running out. It's around 6.30.

Chris yells up asking me to decide what I'm doing. He's getting cold. My hands were intensely cold down there, but now with the grip and the climbing, everything's warmed up … I put two deadmen in, one on the ridge, the other through the cornice of the ridge and start off down; scrape around and get a kingpin in; good, need the deadman higher up. I then abseil, using full body harness.

Put out a lot of effort today and feel very, very weary. It is misty and snowy and even Joe's tracks have disappeared and I can only follow Chris for a short distance. I'm staggering with fatigue, particularly when I have to go uphill for that little bit to the top of the shoulder and can see Chris through the cloud arriving spectacularly at the Snow Cave. Big relief to arrive there myself.

Joe records our encouraging comments and coughs. So much coughing; I've never coughed or retched so much before in my life. Where does the mucus come from? It's because we're in the Death Zone or the 'regrettable' zone, as Joe calls it. When cells are dying the phlegm comes, to move it on and out.

Dick, bless him, has a brew ready. I'm even going off tea at altitude, but liquid always revives and slowly we settle to almost normal and can face the thought of a little food … Chris can't stand the smell of milk powder and retched twice at the entrance. Dick has had peas and rice prepared for a long time and I spoon it painfully down until it becomes cold and impossible.

We're going back up tomorrow. I'm sure this sort of thing hasn't been done before at such an altitude, but I think this is the only way at the moment to progress, for two people to think, 'This is my day, my responsibility.' We must get going early and go all out and do our maximum in this time.

It was to be the turn of Dick and Joe next morning, while Pete and I took it easy, having a leisured breakfast and then following them with a load of ropes and tents. By the time we had emerged from the snow hole, they were only halfway across the easy stretch leading to the Pinnacles. Fresh snow had fallen during the night but they were also tired and moving slowly. Dick had now been up here at 7850m for three nights, Joe two. As soon as we set off Pete pulled ahead, reaching the foot of the Pinnacles by the time I was halfway across, while Dick, followed by Joe, was moving very slowly up the fixed rope. They were going no faster than we had the previous day when we had pushed the route out for the first time. It was the insidious effect of altitude, the gradual slowing up caused by sleeping at nearly 8000m without any oxygen. Plodding in their wake, I certainly felt it. At last I reached the foot of the Pinnacles but could not face the prospect of that long slow toil up the fixed ropes. Hardly thinking, I dumped the tent and ropes on the boulder at its foot, and, racked with guilt, fled back down the ridge. At least I could have a meal ready for them when they returned. Dick had now reached the high point and sorted out the ropes and climbing gear, while Joe came up the final rope-length. The ridge jutted steeply above them, looking threatening, even dangerous. The day had started fine but a scum of high grey cloud now blanked out the sun and the very flatness of the light increased the feeling of threat.

Since Dick was first at the high point, and had therefore had the longest rest, it was his pitch:

I hope that Joe will offer to take this pitch as I've been in front up to now. I can't ask him but I console myself with the fact that the pitch after will be his lead. Personal survival; it's hard to think beyond oneself. This self-absorbed suffering must be a cardinal sin.

I select my gear – we are short of deadmen. Hopefully, I take some ice screws. Joe is encouraging and we decide on a system of communication. I set off, wary. The steepness becomes alarming. I thrust in both tools. There's a crusty layer which gives a false sense of security, but soon that disappears and I'm left floundering. The trick is to kick a step that will not collapse into the lower one. I sink both arms deep into the snow; gaining little height but quite a lot of horizontal ground and I'm feeling the lack of protection. It's going to be a monster swing if the snow collapses. I become increasingly aware that I might be on a corniced ridge that could collapse. It's a frightening pitch and I have to fight hard.

But the angle began to relent and the snow became firmer. Dick had run out the full length of rope. By this time Pete had caught up with Joe and from the shoulder I could watch their slow progress, three tiny dots clinging to the corniced ridge.

Pete wondered:

The surface crust sounds, and is, hollow and underneath it is deep, collapsing and insubstantial. Why didn't Dick even squeal, 'Hey, watch me, Joe, this is really unstable and dangerous'? A very cool lead and I (as Joe did) find even following it up a rope very frightening.

When Dick reached the end of the rope, he managed to find a placement for a deadman, and called down to Joe; 'It's safe, you can come up now.'

He was able to sit down and rest while Joe jumared up the fixed rope. On arrival Joe immediately started to set up the cine camera while Dick sorted out the belay so that he could safeguard Joe for the next rope-length. The angle looked easier and the ridge had broadened, giving the promise of firmer snow. It was while doing this that Dick became aware of a strange sensation of numbness spreading down his left arm and leg. At first he thought it was just the cold, but then his left cheek and even the left side of his tongue became numb. He bit it, and there was no feeling and yet when he bit the right side it felt normal.

'There's something funny going on with me, Joe,' he said.

'What is it?'

And Dick described the symptoms.

'You'd better go down. Pete can belay me on this pitch. There's no point three of us being up here.'

As Dick waited for Pete to come up the rope, he couldn't help remembering the story of Art Gilkey, the American climber who had had a thrombosis in his leg high on K2 in 1953. They had been trapped by a storm at their top camp and when it ended his five team mates had tried to evacuate him, lowering and hauling him down the steep slopes. They had had one narrow escape when one of them slipped, pulling off the others, to be saved by the belay of their anchor man. It was shortly after this that Gilkey somehow slipped out of his harness and fell to his death. It seems quite possible that he did this on purpose, realising that the others would almost certainly lose their lives if they continued their attempt to save him. These were Dick's thoughts as he huddled on the crest. Once Pete arrived he could start down. By the time he got back to the snow cave he felt perfectly normal, even a little shamefaced at having made a fuss and having come back early.

At the high point Joe, belayed by Pete, had started up the next stretch of the ridge. The snow had now improved and he was able to make good steady progress, kicking methodically into the snow just below the crest. Another 50m of rope and he slotted in a deadman to bring up Pete. Just two pitches that day. They were still 60m short of the top of the First

Pinnacle; they dumped the ropes and the tent Pete had carried up and started down.

Back at the Third Snow Cave, I had started melting snow for brews, when Dick crawled in. Diffidently he described what had happened to him, saying that he felt perfectly all right again. He was also worried about frostbite.

'Does my nose look funny?' he asked.

'It's a bit purple. Let me feel it.'

It was warm to the touch, not cold and frozen.

'It'll be all right. I think you've just had a nip.'

I was puzzled, a little worried about the other symptoms, but had no idea what they could be and anyway was preoccupied by my own fatigue. Joe and Pete got back about an hour later, tired, but elated with the progress they had made.

I had started a large panful of cheesy potato, by now our staple food. By the time they had brushed the snow from their down suits and boots and had crawled into their sleeping bags it was ready. I lifted if off the stove by its handle to pass it over Joe, who was next to me, for Pete to have the first spoonful. As I lifted it above Joe, the handle gave way, and the pan toppled into his sleeping bag, covering it in a gelatinous yellow goo – Oh shades of Kongur! I'd spilled boeuf Stroganoff all over him on that expedition; but this was worse for it was like glue, clinging greasily to both our sleeping bags and setting in the cold.

Joe, ever self-controlled, said nothing at all, just lay back and left me to spoon up the fast-freezing mess. I scraped it back into the pan and eventually recovered about a quarter of it, which I reheated, but somehow we had lost our appetites. Pete, however, cooked a rival meal for himself and Dick. That night we did not talk much about plans for the next morning. I think we were all too tired. I had been in favour of going back down for a rest, feeling that we were now exhausting ourselves just getting up to the high point and then, as had happened that day, only pushing out two rope-lengths. Pete and Dick, however, felt that we must, at all costs, get the route run out further along the Pinnacles to be sure of crossing them and making an effective bid for the summit on our return.

It was only next morning, 6 May, after a couple of brews and a half cup full of muesli, that we discussed seriously what to do next. It was ten o'clock before we finally came to the decision to descend. I left my sleeping bag, all my spare clothes and some camera equipment in the cave. It was a form of demonstration to myself that I was going to return, that I would not give up, though in the back of my mind there were now some very serious doubts.

The slopes below were covered with nearly half a metre of fresh snow, making the descent slow and insecure. Even so we climbed unroped, picking a way down slowly. Back at the Second Snow Cave we paused for a few minutes. We were late for the mid-day call that we had arranged, but after several attempts managed to raise Charlie. It was good to make contact and we told him that we'd be back down at about six o'clock that evening.

Then we set off once more, Dick first, me just behind. He stopped half-way down the long easy slope towards the top of the spur at Point 7090 and I quickly caught him up. His crampon had fallen off and he was struggling to push it back on. I crouched in the snow beside him, tried to give him a hand and, holding the crampon, thrust it up against the sole of his over-boot. Dick toppled off balance, grabbed me, and pulled me over as well. We rolled over, did a somersault in the soft snow, both clawing at its surface to stop ourselves. What a stupid lunatic way to go, but we came to a stop, laughing nervously. I apologised for my over-eagerness and Dick, strug-gling with his crampon without further help from me, eventually jammed it back on his boot. We continued down, roping up over the steep slopes immediately above the First Snow Cave, moving now even more cautiously, until at last we could relax at the crest of the arête leading down to the glacier. Even this though, required care. There was a very real danger of avalanche as we picked our way down it. Once back on the glacier we roped up and plodded back towards Advanced Base.

Pete wrote:

And what a weary little gang we must look as we topple across – call them moun-taineers? They can't even walk across the horizontal! Such a close relationship between us all on this trip; a closely knit group of mates.

Joe, dedicated as ever to the film, had instructed Charlie and Adrian to come out and film our return. Charlie commented in his diary:

And so they're back, shortly after 6 p.m., captured on celluloid by Adrian and me as budding cameramen. Oh, they came up that slope so slowly. At first we thought something had happened to them because we could see their tracks coming down from the Raphu La into a piece of dead ground and then we waited and waited and waited. The answer was quite clear; they were exhausted and crept in like old men, but rallied a bit like soldiers, for the last few yards to Advanced Base – which is exactly what we didn't want on the film!

We sat outside the big greenie tent and told Charlie what had happened, particularly what had happened to Dick. He asked briefly about symptoms but was non-committal, murmuring that he'd have a look at Dick back at Base Camp. And there were all the good things of Advanced Base, fresh bread and a fresh vegetable broth that slid down deliciously after our almost inedible dehydrated foods of the mountain.

We all had sore throats and that night Charlie made for us his own brand of inhaler, bashing a hole in the lid of a mess tin and pushing through it a length of rubber tubing so that we could breathe in the steam from a brew of honey, lemon and whisky. We looked like a group of opium smokers crouched round the stone table in the middle of the mess tent, as we coughed and hawked and spoke of our adventures of the previous days. Adrian and Charlie told us of the latest exploits of our mascot 'Nibbles' and of how he was growing even fatter on his rich diet. Whatever would he do when we left?

Observing us, Charlie commented in his diary:

All are fucked, sore-throated and so on, but well. Dick had a strange turn yesterday. Numb left face, left tongue, left arm for five or ten minutes while on the climb. No headache or visual disturbance. I haven't examined him, other than his eyes, where he has florid papilloedema[1] with haemorrhages and ghastly dilated veins. The diagnosis is easy – a small stroke. What's to be done now?

Chris seems quiet, much quieter than usual and I put this down to tiredness. Peter is, I think, very pent up without much to show for it and his 'act' of being helpless palls a bit. He seems to have less fun in him than before but I think this is merely the state of the climb.

Joe, however, seems an easier person this time, possibly because he and filming fit in well together – I think this will be a superb film. Perhaps because we have to help him very specifically, like walking over to the bergschrund and doing some cramponing in that foul gale – he turns round and is helpful back in turn. I find, in fact, that having been more cross with Joe in the distant past, I do feel very much more warm to him than I used to be.

After a lazy morning we set off at around two o'clock, just after Jan Reynolds and Rick Barker of the American ski team arrived with their yak herders. They were planning to use our camp for a few days before completing their circumnavigation of Everest. We chatted for a short time and then went our different ways.

On the way down Charlie told me that he was sure that Dick had had a stroke and that it was most unlikely he would be able to go back on to the ridge. And what about me, I wondered? Had I the strength to make it to the summit or, for that matter, could I keep up with Pete and Joe?

The sun had a real warmth and everywhere we could hear the sound of running water. The summer had arrived and conditions seemed perfect but had we the strength to return, to climb the Pinnacles and then go for the summit?

---

1 Swelling of the optic nerve in the retina – a problem which occurs occasionally at extreme altitude.

10

Everything is changed

7 May – 12 May

Chris Bonington

As I walked slowly into Base Camp, our Chinese staff came out to greet me, shaking me warmly by the hand. Joe and Pete were in the base tent, reading their mail. For a few moments Everest was forgotten as I skimmed through my letters, digging out first the ones from Wendy, so that I could transport myself back to our Lakeland home and fells, then letters from the children and from friends. There were cans of beer, a Thermos full of hot water for tea and a bowl full of delicious new potatoes.

Charlie was with Dick, examining him. We were subdued in spite of our pleasure at being back in the comparative warmth and luxury of Base. We were all waiting for Charlie's verdict but instinctively avoided talking about it, turning, once we had read our letters, to the old newspapers and magazines that David Mathew had sent us. For once the cassette recorder had been left off. All you could hear was the gurgle of running water, the rustling of the wind and the chatter of our Chinese staff. The atmosphere was charged with foreboding, but I did not want to rush into any rash decisions which we might regret later, and therefore suggested that we waited till the morning before we discussed anything.

Charlie completed the examination of Dick in his tent, told him that he had had a mild stroke and that he would have to consider seriously whether or not he should return to altitude. Dick did not sleep much that night as he tried to determine what he should do. He had felt wonderfully fit on the way down from Advanced Base. As usual he had arrived back about half an hour in front of anyone else. He desperately wanted to go on with the expedition, both to share in the work of the team and to fulfil his personal ambitions. He seemed to have absolute confidence in his own and the team's ability to complete the climb and passionately wanted to be part of this. Charlie had left him with the onus of making the decision and at first Dick resolved to carry on with the climb, convincing himself that the stroke had only been a very minor one and that he was now fully recovered.

Charlie had very little sleep that night either, for he was worried that he had not spelt out sufficiently clearly the seriousness of what had happened to Dick. He was up early the following morning and went over to Dick's tent.

'I've been thinking it over, Dick. I'm afraid I've got to tell you not to go back up again. You've got to think of what would happen if you did have another stroke. If you were paralysed, it wouldn't just be your life at risk, it'd be the others as well, because they'd have to get you down. I'm sorry.'

'How likely is it to happen again?'

'It's difficult to say. But it is a distinct possibility. I don't think it's a risk you're justified in taking, if only for the sake of the others.'

Dick was silent for a long time. There were so many implications. Would he ever be able to return to the high peaks of the Himalaya? How could he adjust to a life without mountaineering? He then agreed with Charlie that this was the only possible course.

Later on that day, Charlie recorded:

It's strange how at altitude, or in the heat of the moment, it's difficult to make obvious decisions. At Base Camp I had a good look at Dick and superficially he was perfectly well, admitting to, rather than complaining of, his left hand feeling somewhat 'thick' – no more.

There were, however, definite signs of his stroke when I examined him. The implications are heavy:

Descent to sea level is the only way to sort this out properly, and messing around here at Base is unacceptable.

He really should have a medical escort, but I don't see how I can leave the rest of the team without medical cover.

The question of his return in future years is knotty. In his place, I wouldn't go above 6000m, particularly as he has had what sounds like papilloedema several years ago at very high altitude.

It was with a heavy heart that I decided all this and told him, but he does understand. Thank God we didn't have a paralysed man on our hands. This is all that can be said.

Charlie suggested to Dick that it might be easier for him if he went for a walk after breakfast while the rest of us were told and decided what to do. Charlie's voice slipped into that unemotional, slightly clinical tone of all doctors as he explained the position. It was something that we had expected but nonetheless the formal acknowledgement of the inevitable was still grim. This also seemed the right time to tell them of a decision I'd just made myself. We could at least then discuss how we were going to cope with this new set of circumstances.

'I'm afraid I've got yet another bombshell,' I told them. 'I've been thinking about it ever since we got back down to Base Camp and, the more I go into it, the more I realise I just can't keep up with Joe and Pete. Quite honestly I'm not at all sure I could even get back up to our high point.'

'Don't you think you'll be all right after a few days' rest?' said Pete. 'You know, we're all shattered at the moment. I don't think any of us should make any decisions for the time being.'

'But I really have thought this out, and I think we do need to start think-ing of what we are going to do. I'm not going to change my mind on this one. You know we've always thought it'd be useful to have a line of retreat down to the North Col, but we've just never had the time or energy to go there. If Charlie, Adrian and I establish a camp on the North Col, you and Joe could drop down the North Ridge once you've climbed the Pinnacles – either after getting to the top or, if you take too long getting over the Pinnacles, you could come straight down to the Col, have a rest and then go back again. You never know, I might even have rested enough to go with you.'

'That's a lot to take in at the moment,' said Joe. 'I agree with Pete. We shouldn't make any decisions in a hurry.'

'You know, Chris, all our recent trips have been hard work like this,' said Pete. 'We're not supermen. We're probably just as tired as you are.'

'You've no bloody idea how much I've been pushing myself!' I exploded, almost tearful in the violence of my own sense of doubt and emotion. 'I've never pushed myself so hard, never felt so out of control. I'm sorry. I know my own limits and I've reached them.'

The conversation waxed and waned. Pete apologised for being flippant and I said I realised he didn't really mean it. It was halfway through the morning when Dick came into the tent. He had shaved off his beard, it was as if he was already in a different world. We all stopped talking. What could one possibly say. I just muttered: 'We're terribly sorry, Dick.'

He could not hold back his tears. It was not only Everest, or a matter of leaving the close companionship of our little group, it was his entire life that was altered. Dick was not interested in fame or money but he loved the mountains, needed to stretch himself to his own limits – and now, all that seemed closed to him. But he quickly got hold of himself.

'I'll be all right. It's just getting used to it that's difficult.'

We talked around it and then I asked him whether he wanted to stay on at Base Camp, but he replied that there seemed no point.

'If I can't take part in the climb, I think I'd rather get home to Jan and Daniel. There's just no point in hanging around here. It's not as if I could do anything to help you all.'

And so it was decided that Dick should set out for Lhasa in a few days' time, just before we returned to the climb. This would enable Charlie to keep him under observation a little longer and Dick to rest before his journey. We talked around the problem a while and then trailed back to our tents to read, write diaries or worry.

Pete observed:

Lying in my tent you can tell exactly who it is; Chris, from the snuffle breathing; Joe from his groans. He's on his way over the gravel towards our windy bog. But Joe returns and arouses Charlie and they go and inspect his stool. I think; 'Oh no; blood in his stool; ulcer. Chris is out too, and Dick. I'll have to solo the North Col route, damn it!' Feel worried the whole trip is falling apart.

Charlie wrote in his diary:

And Joe, poor Joe. What on earth is going on? Dull, central and abdominal pain, tarry black stool which can only mean blood. The easiest conclusion is an ulcer, but he has a very bloody throat with a hard black crust right across the pharynx. I suppose this could have seeped down and caused the problem. We'll have to wait to see the outcome but clearly he cannot go anywhere with a bleeding bowel. I've told him he mustn't go up unless he's really better.

And so we bathe our wounds and hope for a reasonable enough recovery to get three up high and I suppose two on the summit. One would do. Trying to look at it all objectively, I do not think we have a hope in hell. The days required to kill the Pinnacles, added to the summit ridge, cannot be less than six and this is simply too long without oxygen. I think:

Pete could do it.

Joe probably could, but is ropey.

Chris has said he doesn't think he can and I'm sure he's right.

Dick can't because of illness.

Adrian has had severe chest pains.

Me? Well, as usual, I'm apprehensive about being drawn into something much too big for me and really a bit apprehensive about the North Col, particularly as the weather is getting warmer. Still, I'll be pleased to have to go up there and back.

This leaves two alternatives, either go for it, as Pete would like – or abandon it and go for the Col route as a threesome. The first seems the purer – for two to climb as far as they can on the ridge – and I expect that is what will happen on the day.

I was more optimistic than Charlie, feeling that Joe and Pete had a very good chance of completing the Pinnacles. They had only to make a height gain of about 300m over a distance of around a quarter of a mile. With the knowledge that they could drop down to the North Col on the other side and would not have to return over the Pinnacles, they could surely make the traverse in a couple of days. We could even see what looked like an easy line of traversing ledges that bypassed the Final Pinnacle.

I was less sanguine about their chances of reaching the summit, since it did seem that they would need at least one night, maybe two, on the Pinnacles before they reached the final section of the ridge. It was reasonably easy but there was a lot of it – a mile in horizontal distance and 450m of vertical height to gain. But even if they only managed to climb the Pinnacles, this would have been a comparative success, for they would have crossed the unclimbed part of the ridge.

And what of my feelings? I was not depressed by my own failure and was even relieved that I had made the decision to withdraw from the summit bid. I had been so extended, so out of control. Now that I had finally decided to drop back into a support role I felt a vast release of tension and actually looked forward with an excited anticipation to our trip to the North Col. This was something which seemed a useful contribution to the expedition, was within my capabilities, and a goal in itself. In a letter to Wendy I wrote: 'I have no regrets. I desperately want them to succeed and, much more important, come back safely. I realise it's above my ceiling without oxygen and I want to get on with OUR LIVES!!! I only hope I haven't addled my brain already; I don't think so.'

We were all worried about possible brain damage through extended periods of effort at high altitude. We tried to make a joke of it, laughing about the grey cells we might have lost. Charlie had actually noticed some symptoms: 'Chris's short-term memory is appalling. He is capable of forgetting whole conversations we've had only a few hours previously. It's taken as a giggle, but I cannot really put this down to tiredness.'

The atmosphere that day had been oppressive. We were overwhelmed by the sudden change from slow, steady progress up the ridge to the collapse of fifty per cent of the climbing team. But the following day, our second back at Base Camp, we had begun to pick ourselves up. Joe was feeling remarkably better, reassured that his black stools were probably caused by all the blood he had swallowed from his throat.

He quietly reassured Pete: 'Don't worry, I'll be OK. I'll be with you.'

I was beginning to make my own plans for our trip to the North Col. Dick borrowed a telephoto lens so that he could go for one last walk and get some fresh pictures of Everest from around the ruined nunnery. It was a lovely clear morning, the sky, a far-flung vault of blue with Everest towering at the head of the valley with its characteristic cloud-banner blowing out from its summit. Dick felt as well and fit as he had ever done on the expedition and strode down the jeep track, resolving almost to walk out to Xegur, and pick up the jeep there. In that way he could remain close to the mountains for that brief period longer. The track wound round and down the glacial debris to the flat of the valley some three miles away and 150m below Base Camp. The ruined nunnery was just a short way up a slope and for the first time that morning he had to climb uphill.

His strength suddenly drained from him and he slowed down to little more than a crawl. He sat down on a rock; his vision became distorted, his heart pounded; he could hardly breathe. On the previous occasion he had not been frightened because he had not really known what was happening. Now he did. These were the symptoms of another stroke. He was alone; it would be hours before anyone found him. By that time it could be too late. 'Sit still, relax. You'll be all right.' He remembered that he had told Joe that he was going to the nunnery. Someone would come and look for him.

He sat there for about quarter of an hour. His heart had returned to a more steady beat and he could now see clearly. He could get back to Base if he took it steadily. But he was so very, very weak. He dropped back to the track but it was now all uphill and seemed to go on for ever. He needed all his determination to just put one foot in front of the other.

Back in the base tent we were getting worried. It was past lunch time and Dick had been gone for several hours. We were just beginning to discuss sending out a search party, when he quietly slipped into the tent.

'Could I have a word with you?' he asked Charlie.

Once again everything was changed, turned up on end. There was now no question of Dick lingering at Base Camp for a few days, or of his being able to travel back on his own. Charlie was very worried about him having another more serious stroke and told us that he would have to accompany Dick at least as far as Chengdu. I could only agree, even though I was worried at losing our medical cover over the period of the summit bid. Joe and Pete would be pushing themselves so hard. After all only a few people had reached the summit of Everest without oxygen and they would be attempting something even more exacting. They would be several days above 8000m, pushing themselves to extremes.

'You will come straight back, of course,' I exhorted Charlie.

We broke up and wandered to our tents. Pete nudged Charlie. 'Thought you were going home, didn't you, you bugger!'

Mr Chen was, as always, calm and helpful, making sensible suggestions to help Dick and Charlie on their way. On the morning of 10 May, Dick, Charlie and Mr Yu piled into the jeep on the first stage of their journey. We all shook hands with Dick, slightly embarrassed, emotion pent up and inhibited, and then silently watched as the jeep bumped over the shingle road in the washed out grey of the early dawn.

Charlie recorded their journey:

On the evening of 11 May, Dick and I drove into Lhasa in a sandstorm. Dick had improved steadily and his health gave me no more cause for concern. He contin-ued to make a complete recovery. We stopped for the night at the Lhasa rest house: the storm had settled and the air was warm. We had entered a different world; the cherries were in blossom and willows in leaf; yaks ploughed, their decorative plumes waving in the wind. Tired and a little dejected, we flew to Chengdu next morning and were soon on the telephone to London, Hong Kong, to Beijing and Cardiff. The Chinese could not have been more helpful – Everest Base Camp to Hong Kong in four days must be nearly a record. On the 13th Dick and I parted rather solemnly at Chengdu Airport and I turned once again towards Everest. I suddenly wanted to go home.

Back in the big base tent the tiny size of our team really hit us. We missed Dick's strength and Charlie's caring cheerfulness. On a more material level, it was Charlie who baked the bread, who cooked the delicious fresh veg-etable broths which we had so enjoyed at Advanced Base. We were a sombre bunch but, at the same time, felt we could now start planning posi-tively for the future. Joe and Pete were poring over photographs of the upper part of the ridge, calculating heights and distances. There was a hidden level of communication between them from which, inevitably, I now felt excluded. And yet they never made me feel unwelcome. There was no resentment in their manner, nor was it recorded in their diaries. Joe in a letter to Maria, merely stated:

Chris is feeling a bit slow on the mountain … There is a big job for Pete and me to do but hopefully it could go well next time we go back up and if fortune, weather and spirit favour us we could be up the mountain in a few days from when we start … I'll write again soon, hopefully with more cheerful news, but as you can imagine – having come down for a rest – it has been quite a re-adjustment twice over in the last thirty-six hours to the new state of affairs and the situation does rather seem to dominate all.

And Pete to Hilary:

Chris more relaxed now he's changed his role, which is a great help to Joe and me. From the 7.30 meal onwards we keep each other amused with chat and alcohol for three hours. One more day of forgetfulness, and the problem returns and all is on our shoulders … Wish more letters from you would arrive; I need a bit more assurance before I launch on this great, committing adventure.

We celebrated Joe's thirty-fourth birthday on the evening of 12 May, our last night at Base Camp. Our cook had risen to the occasion, baking a birth-day cake and preparing a lavish feast. We decided to open one of our bottles of champagne but in the rarefied atmosphere the pressure difference was so great that most of the contents jetted out in a great streamer of foam, leaving little more that a few teaspoonfuls of wine. We opened another bottle, this time holding a plastic bucket ready to catch the exploding bubbles. It was a happy, boozy night with Joe in fine form, wryly funny, Pete gentle and very boyish, Adrian quiet and serious but with a twinkle of humour. 'Adrian's climbing career is rising like a phoenix,' said Pete. 'At this rate he'll be the first Englishman since the war to reach the North Col.' I had a feeling of immense affection for all three of my companions.

That night, in his tent, Pete wrote: 'A great birthday for Joe ... whatever may happen on this trip, we'll be able to say we've had some good times.'

11

They walked out of our lives

13 May – 21 May

Chris Bonington

Back at Advanced Base the big green tent was as bleak and gloomy as ever, with the wind screaming down the Rongbuk Glacier, clutching and buffeting the fabric of the walls. We had walked up that day. Pete, Joe and Adrian covering the distance in a good fast time, with me bringing up the rear, trailing in a couple of hours later.

Our original plan had been for Pete and Joe to set out the following morning, but now they were having second thoughts. They talked around it and eventually decided to have a rest day. It proved a wise choice, for the 14th was cold and blustery. There was not much organising to do, for much of the food and all the climbing gear was already in place at the Third Snow Cave or at the high point. We spent a quiet day, most of it in our own tents, reading, writing our diaries or just sleeping.

Pete wrote:

Not missed anything today – a blustery night and though it became still first thing this morning, it started snowing soon after and has been blowing about wildly all morning... I slept deeply and got up about 10.30. Had a big breakfast, cereal and fried ham. But you do feel different up here, a slight heaviness in the head. You do deteriorate.

Perhaps this general bad weather will subside, and a great spell of sunshine lasting five days will arrive. Chris is much more relaxed on this trip since he changed his role – cheerful and jokey and supportive.

The 15th dawned clear though windy. Pete and Joe fussed around with final preparations, packing their rucksacks and putting in a few last-minute goodies. Then suddenly they were ready, crampons on, rope tied, set to go. I think we were all trying to underplay the moment.

'See you in a few days.'

'We'll call you tonight at six o'clock.'

'Good luck.'

And then they were off, plodding up the little ice slope immediately beyond the camp, through flurries of wind-driven snow. They were planning to move straight through to the Second Snow Cave, to avoid spending longer than absolutely necessary at altitude. This would mean they would reach the Third Cave on their second day, and then on the third they hoped to traverse the Pinnacles and reach the North Ridge. If they could do this they would be in a very good position to make their bid for the summit on the fourth or fifth day. To have any chance of success they had to keep to this schedule, for they could not afford to spend more than two nights above 8250m before going for the summit.

Adrian and I were hoping to find a way up to the North Col that same day. We left shortly after the others and our route took us up the piled rocks of the moraine past the site of the French Camp, the skeleton of an old frame tent a reminder of the former expedition. They had been defeated by the North Ridge and it was as if the mess they had left was a futile revenge on the mountain, or was it that they had no feeling for the empty beauty of the glacier and peaks around them, for their rubbish was spread all the way up the East Rongbuk Glacier?

We followed the thinning moraine to a rocky corner which forced us on to the glacier itself. It was time to rope up. The glacier was easy, sloping gradually in a series of gentle waves to the great wall of the North Col. To our surprise, the way was marked with bamboo poles, to which still clung the shreds of yellow flags. Had these, too, been left by the French, or perhaps by the Japanese the previous year? It meant that we could plod, unthinking, towards our goal. But as we approached it, the wall at the end of the valley loomed ever steeper. I had thought of 'just nipping up to the North Col', but now I began to realise that I had underestimated it. Adrian's climbing experience was strictly limited. He had come with us to the South West Face of Everest in 1975 to help run our Advanced Base since, as an officer in the Gurkhas, he spoke fluent Nepali, but he had done practically no ice climbing. At the end of the expedition he had spent a night at our fourth camp at 7300m, then, in a hasty evacuation in the dark, had very nearly lost his life, when he descended much more slowly than the Sherpas who had accompanied him and had lost the route. When we had reached him at around midnight, he was beginning to show signs of hypothermia and certainly would not have lasted much longer. He had done very little snow and ice climbing since then and had only envisaged being in a support role on our expedition this time. Nevertheless, he was glad of his new task, commenting:

At last I'm doing something positive and feel better and stronger that I have done for over three weeks; even the pain in my chest seems to have subsided to a dull ache. And yet despite my renewed vigour and enthusiasm I'm not without fear, for the North Col has claimed a fair number of casualties in the last sixty years. The first time I set eyes on it, I thought, 'I'm bloody glad I'm not going up there.' But here I am.

Adrian quickly showed that he was fresher than I. He had a spring in his step that I lacked. After an hour's walk we reached the crest of a slight wave in the glacier and stopped to examine the route. I could see that the line of the flags led up to a smooth convex slope of ice that continued up towards a wide snow ramp which, in turn, led up to a barrier of sérac walls. There seemed a way through these, but it was undoubtedly complex. To the left of the Col, the slope was uninterrupted by séracs or crevasses, but it was very much steeper. This was the route that Mr Chen had recommended and the one that Reinhold Messner had used when he climbed the mountain solo, but it looked rather steep for someone as inexperienced as Adrian. The easiest angle route was on the right but this was obviously threatened by avalanche.

I was finally influenced by the presence of the marker flags and followed these to the foot of the ice slope. Once there we quickly realised that this was a route only for a party with plenty of rope to fix in position. The ice, though not steep, was smooth and polished. We retreated and took stock once again. I decided to go for the left-hand route, took a wide circuit round the foot of the face, and started up the slope. By this time the day had galloped away and it was now nearly four in the afternoon. We had arranged to call Pete and Joe on the radio at 6.30, but had left it back at Advanced Base – a good excuse for retreat.

That day Pete and Joe had made a good fast time to the Second Cave and told us they felt they were going well. I told them we would try to reach the North Col the next day and arranged to open up once again at 6.30 in the evening. The following morning we took with us the radio, a tent and some food, hoping to dump the gear on the Col, so that when we moved up the following day we should only have to carry our sleeping bags and personal gear.

We quickly reached the previous day's high point, but almost immediately found ourselves on steep ground, crossing ice covered by powdery, insubstantial snow. This led up to a bergschrund, with a long stride on to a steep wall of crusty snow; certainly not the easy slog that I had promised Adrian. How about getting back down? Above, the slope smoothed out, but it was consistently steep. In addition, some 450m above us, a series of huge cornices loomed threateningly. If they collapsed we were in their direct line of fall.

I glanced across to the right and saw a route we could have taken to turn the convex ice slope that had deterred us the previous day. The angle was altogether easier over there and much more within the range of Adrian's experience. But to reach it we should have to go beneath a shattered sérac wall, over a slope littered with huge ice blocks. It seemed worth it and I headed across, with Adrian in tow. He was none too happy:

My confidence in Chris's ability to select the safest route received a setback today. We had begun our ascent slightly to the left when Chris decided to cut back under a horrendous-looking sérac. 'Quite stable,' says he, while I peered into the bowels of this monster, muttering the Buddhist mantra 'Om mani padme hum' faster than a Tibetan can twirl his prayer wheel!

But this took us on to an easier line that led up through the centre of the slope. The snow now became quite soft and deep, for we were on the lee side, but the angle was sufficiently easy for Adrian to take over the lead. He was undoubtedly going more strongly that I and I was very glad to let him do the trail-breaking for a while until once again the slope steepened. I went out in front, cramponing up steep hard snow.

We had now reached the area of sérac walls in the upper part of the face. I had observed what seemed to be a gangway between two of the séracs which eventually led to the final slopes just below the North Col. I struck up this, stepping very gingerly over some windslab to the top of the slope, and was appalled to find a huge, moat-like crevasse between me and the sérac wall, stretching as far as I could see in either direction. I first had a look to the left, but the crest narrowed to a fin-like arête, falling away into another giddy drop. Glancing back to the right, I noticed a ladder hanging precariously from the sheer ice wall on the other side of the crevasse. If we could only reach it. This surely must have been the route used by the French. I followed the lip of the crevasse until I was opposite the ladder. The crevasse was about two and a half metres wide at this point and another ladder, like a drawbridge, was dangling provocatively from the other side, just out of reach. But it was getting late. The sun had already dropped behind the North Col, leaving us in cold shadow. The depths of the crevasse were blue-black, its lip crumbling. I move tentatively on to a fragile snow bridge that spanned the chasm.

'Watch the rope, Adrian, the whole bloody lot could go.'

But what if I did get to the other side? I should have about 4 or 5m of sheer ice to traverse to reach the foot of the ladder, and how secure was that? I was tired and frightened.

'It's nearly 6.30, Chris. Hadn't you better call the lads?'

Respite! I fled from the brink of the crevasse, and traversed back along its edge so that we could see round the corner and have a direct line of sight with the crest of the North East Ridge.

'Hello Snow Cave Three, this is Chris just below the North Col, can you hear me? Over.'

There was no reply. We tried again a few minutes later and Pete's voice came through, telling us that they had reached the Third Snow Cave in good time and would be going for the Pinnacles the next morning. I replied that we had not managed to reach the North Col that day, that we would be having a rest day tomorrow, and would move up to the North Col on the 18th, ready to receive them if they came down that way. We arranged to have a radio call at three o'clock the following afternoon and then again at 6 p.m. A hurried 'good luck' for the morrow and the radio was dead.

We dumped all the gear we had carried up on the lip of the crevasse, marked it with an alloy wand and started down. We were both very tired and Adrian, who had never been on snow as steep as this without the reassurance of a fixed rope, was understandably nervous. On the way we were able to avoid the dangerous sérac wall by making a long traverse towards Changtse. Even here we had some moments of excitement, when the snow ran out and Adrian had to pick his way down the smooth icy crest. He slipped, but fortunately I was ready, and was able to hold him. Eventually we reached the comparative safety of the glacier and were able to plod through the gathering gloom back to the rocky moraine. We trailed slowly back to the camp, reaching it in the dark. It had been a fourteen-hour day and we were both exhausted. That night we were too tired to cook any food. We just melted some snow for tea, and collapsed into our sleeping bags.

It was always difficult getting up before the sun warmed the tent, which happened at about nine. Even then, I lay for a long time in a stupor before thirst and hunger drove me out of the warmth of my sleeping bag. It was another perfect day, cloudless, almost windless, a pleasure to be out. I staggered over to the mess tent and for the first time that morning, peered through the telescope. I started at the snow shoulder, behind which hid the Third Snow Cave. No sign of them there, so I swung the telescope along the crest of the Ridge leading to the First Pinnacle. Still no sign. Could they have overslept? And then I saw them, two small, distinct figures, at the high point they had previously reached on the First Pinnacle. To get there they must either have travelled very fast, or perhaps had even set out before dawn. They certainly knew that they had to cover a lot of ground that day, for to have a good chance of reaching the summit they had to reach Point 8393 that evening.

The image through the telescope was so sharp I could actually see their limbs. For the rest of the day, either Adrian or I watched through the telescope as Pete and Joe slowly made their way along the ridge. But now their progress had slowed down. They were on new, and presumably, difficult ground. We assumed they were leaving a fixed rope behind them for they had with them about 300m of rope. Their slowness was not surprising. They were now at around 8250m above sea level. They must have had around 15 kilos each on their backs, with their sleeping bags, tent, stove, food, fuel and climbing gear. It was difficult to tell how hard the climbing was but I suspect it was harder than they had anticipated. I wondered if anyone had ever climbed to that standard at that height before. They were now higher than all but five peaks in the world.

We spent the day cooking, drinking and eating, but constantly going back to the telescope to gaze up at those tiny figures. I longed for three o'clock, so that we could turn on the sound, have some kind of contact with them, hear how they were, what the climbing was like – but most of all just to hear them. It was five to three. I opened up the radio and started calling.

'Hello climbing team, hello climbing team, this is Advanced Base, do you read me? Over?'

The set crackled in my hand, but it was just some distant voices speaking Chinese. The Pinnacles, etched black against the sky, were stark and jagged. I tried again. It was now past three but there was still no reply. I was not unduly worried. Perhaps their set had failed, but more likely they were so engrossed in the climbing they either forgot to open up, or just did not have time. I could clearly see one figure on the ridge, outlined against the sky, halfway between the crest of the First Pinnacle, and the black tooth of the Second. The other figure was just below the skyline, moving very slowly.

We now called on the half hour through the rest of the afternoon but there was no reply. At nine that evening, the sun already hidden behind Everest, we looked up at them for the last time and called them yet again on the radio. One figure was silhouetted in the fading light on the small col immediately below the Second Pinnacle, whilst the other figure was still moving to join him.

They had been on the go for fourteen hours. It was only twenty minutes or so before dark, so they had to find somewhere to spend the night at the foot of the Second Pinnacle, either a snow cave, or more likely a small ledge cut out of the snow on which they could pitch the tent. But what was it like up there? The ridge was obviously narrow and the slopes on either side seemed steep, but there was plenty of snow on the eastern side. The only problem, perhaps, could be that it was too soft and insubstantial.

We had our evening meal, looked up at the ridge, whose black serrated edge could be seen clearly against the inky blue of the clear, star-studded sky. There was no twinkling of a light and presumably they were camped or holed up on the other side. I slept deeply that night but next morning immediately went over to the telescope.

There was no sign of them. Perhaps they were already on their way. It was another brilliant, clear day and the absence of a snow plume from the summit indicated that there was little wind to trouble them. We knew that they would be out of sight on the other side of the ridge for 100m or so, since on the north side the way was barred by the sheer rocky buttresses of the Second Pinnacle. I had a feeling that they would try to get back on the north as quickly as possible, both because the snow on the east would probably be insecure and also to have some kind of contact with us, even if their radio was no longer working. There also seemed to be interconnecting ledges across rocky slopes on this side.

At this stage we were not unduly worried. We leisurely packed our rucksacks, had one last brew, and then, leaving a note for Charlie to let him know what was happening, set off for the North Col. This time we retraced our descent route and made steady, uneventful progress. I had brought with me a pair of binoculars and every ten minutes or so I gazed up at the ridge, hoping to see Joe and Pete. From the slopes leading up to the Col we had an excellent view. Beyond the Second Pinnacle there was a very small col. The crest of the ridge then levelled out for what, I estimated, were about three rope-lengths, before dropping away to the col beneath the Final Pinnacle. We knew from photographs that they then had to come on to this side of the ridge, for there was a sheer rock buttress on the eastern side. To the north there was a line of ledges which we thought would give easy access on to the North Face.

I explored each point where I thought they might come into sight and then swung the lenses back down the ridge. Our field of view was so good that they would have been clearly visible had they returned to the crest or northern side of the ridge. But there was nothing. Just rock and snow and ice. I could not stop myself praying that they were all right. I found myself crying in the intensity of an anxiety that had crept up on me almost unawares. I chided myself. Nothing to worry about yet. They're just on the other side of the ridge.

We were now on the ramp leading up the centre of the North Col. Our steps from two days ago were covered with wind-blown snow and again I was very happy to let Adrian do the trail-breaking. It was six in the evening before we reached our previous high point. I took a tentative look at a narrow arête of snow. It looked feasible, but steep and frightening, something to be attempted in the morning when we'd be feeling fresh.

'Come on, Adrian, we'll stop here for the night. It's safe enough with this crevasse between us and the slope.'

I started digging a platform beside the crevasse. Adrian was appalled at the exposure of our perch but I tried to reassure him that it was perfectly safe. 'Once in the tent you can forget the drop.'

It was a wonderful dusk, the sky cloudless, with hardly a breath of wind.

To one side the North East Ridge was black and massive, while below us the East Rongbuk Glacier swept away in a vast white highway. On the other side of the glacier stretched the gentle snow peaks flanking the Lhakpa La and behind them towered the solid rocky triangle of Khartaphu. The very peace of the scene was soothing. I was glad to be high once again, glad to be climbing with Adrian and sharing with him our modest adventure of reaching the North Col.

The following morning we struck the tent and I set out along the fragile crest of the arête which we hoped would bypass the crevasse. As so often happens, it was easier than it looked, and although it steepened into a nearly vertical drop into the huge crevasse below us, I had the security of the rope paid out by Adrian. Cutting big bucket steps, I worked my way down, then shouted to Adrian to anchor the rope so that he could follow. We now had the rope in position for our return. Soon we had both cautiously abseiled down it and were able to break out on to the easy ramp we had seen from below. Once more I was pleased for Adrian to take the lead on straightforward ground. As we went up, we were still searching the ridge every few minutes but still there was no sign. Although we were getting anxious, we could not help enjoying the sensation of being on new ground, of finding our way up to the North Col. There were intriguing reminders of our predecessors. An old cable-laid nylon rope hung from a huge overhanging boss of snow. Could it have been left by the Chinese in 1975? Further up, by a formidable narrow ice chimney, projected a butane gas cylinder, French 1981 vintage, no doubt. This route seemed too hard for us and we continued up the ramp to the foot of an acutely angled snow slope that seemed to lead to the crest of the ridge. Once again I went into the lead, kicking my way up the steep, but secure snow, until suddenly my head poked over the crest. I had reached the North Col.

It was a sharp knife-edge, dropping away steeply on the other side with the fresh vista of Pumo Ri, shapely and elegant, in the near distance and behind it the great bulk of Cho Oyu. I moved cautiously along the knife-edge to where it broadened into an easy slope, and buried a deadman snow anchor. While Adrian jumared up the rope I was able to look around. The ridge opened out into a wide dome just above the lowest point of the Col. It would provide both a good camp site and an excellent viewpoint of the North East Ridge. In the concentration and very real joy of climbing that final pitch to the Col, there had been no room for my growing worry about Pete and Joe, but now it came creeping back. I got out the binoculars and searched the line of ridge again but to no avail.

But what of the Americans in the Great Gully of the North Face? I started searching for them and picked out a collection of tents, tiny coloured boxes, clinging beneath a sheer sérac wall. There was no sign of movement, but a line of tracks wound sinuously across the slope, taking a route round the huge icefall that barred the Great Gully at about half height. There was another camp, tucked below a rocky overhang just near the side of the couloir, and I could just discern some more tracks. Surely they also would be going for the summit in such perfect weather?

By this time Adrian had joined me. He shared with me a sense of elation very similar to that which I experience on reaching a summit. I suppose it was because this was our chosen objective. Just after he arrived we saw two tiny figures descending the fixed ropes on the American route. Could they be Pete and Joe, who had somehow got across on to the North Face without us seeing them? But this was clutching at straws. Our logic quickly told us that these were Americans, perhaps on their way down from a successful summit bid.

We dug out a platform for the tent and spent the rest of the day taking it in turns to examine the North East Ridge. It was now 19 May and I was very worried. Pete and Joe had been out of sight for two nights and almost two days. From this viewpoint we could see just how short a distance they would have had to cover before we could expect them to come into sight on our side of the ridge after turning the Second Pinnacle.

That afternoon, Adrian picked out some movement at Advanced Base. Could it be *them*? Could they somehow have retreated all the way down without us seeing them? But no. There were three figures. It could be the American skiers, or perhaps it was Charlie who had come up with some Tibetans. We opened up on the radio at six o'clock. There was no reply from Pete or Joe, but Charlie, reassuring and cheerful, came on the air. I immediately told him of my fears. Charlie recalls:

At 6 p.m. on 19th I had a crackly radio link with the col. I was about to berate Chris about the mess but his message was anxious, high pitched, almost unintelligible. They had not seen them … 'I am concerned …'

'I share your concern,' I replied.

I share your concern … my world of elation was quick-frozen, replaced, not yet by sorrow or pain, but by a curious reality. I was in a high camp, with two Tibetans for the night. Three miles away on the North East Ridge something had happened or was happening. Two miles away on the North Col Chris and Adrian were safe. We were 6000 miles from home. I talked bleakly to my diary:

The ridge is very much a spectator sport from down here up to the Second Pinnacle. Then there is obviously some dead ground. I'm not sure how the view compares from the North Col. I think we must prepare for a disaster. But there is still hope. If the situation is the same tomorrow I shall have almost given up.

However, we had all this on Kongur last year and everyone was OK.[1] On the

---

1 The summit party were out of contact for ten days in 1981.

positive side they could have shot off early on the 18th, gone out of sight, conquered the 'great problem'. On the 19th they could be out of sight still, in all probability camped between the two steps, summit tomorrow and back to the North Col.

The outcome will be quite simple. They'll either come bouncing in or drag themselves in in various degrees of injury or illness: or, we'll never see them again. I cannot really accept them as lost, but then it took a while for Mick's loss to sink in.[1] Oh God.

I did not sleep well that night and as soon as it was light enough I was gazing up anxiously through the binoculars. Another perfect day but still no sign. We opened up on the radio on the hour throughout the day, but with little hope of a reply since it was unlikely that we should hear them unless they were in direct line of sight. I now searched not only the crest but the glacier at its foot, just in case they had fallen.

That night Adrian went outside for one last look up at the ridge.

'Chris, come and have a look at this, I think I can see something. It could be a tent.'

He handed me the binoculars.

'It's about a third of the way along the ridge, above and beyond the Pinnacles, just below the crest. Look, there are three slight bumps. Go down from the left-hand one. There's a bit of a gully, and there it is, on a kind of ledge. It's just a little orange blob. It could be a tent, couldn't it?'

It was certainly on the line from the Final Pinnacle on to the North Face. Then why hadn't we seen them? They would have been in view, moving slowly, for a long time. But that little orange blob was a slender strand of hope. I pushed logical doubts aside. That could be Pete and Joe. Perhaps they had reached the top and were on their way down. They could be with us tomorrow. Neither Adrian nor I slept that night. I imagined what they would have to say, what they had done, how they would look, convincing myself that it was undoubtedly their tent and that they were on their way down. The night crept away so very slowly. We had arranged a call to Charlie at eight and I expressed my hope.

'There's a faint ray of hope. Last night Adrian saw a small red patch that could be a Sumitomo tent. It's on about the right line. But we haven't seen any figures and, of course, it's possible that it's a ruined tent from a previous expedition. It's on rock rather than snow, which means it doesn't stand out quite so well. It's not a hundred per cent but at least it's hopeful. Over.'

But as the light on the North Face improved and we gazed at the distant little blob, our hopes dwindled. There was no sign of movement. It was the

1 Mick Burke's death on Everest in 1975.

wrong colour, being orange when the outer of the Sumitomo was a deep red and its inner a bright yellow. It was also the wrong shape, looking more square than domed. It was perhaps a box tent abandoned by the French the previous year. The weather had been so clear and our viewpoint so good, surely we should have seen them if they had reached the end of the Pinnacles? Our hopes vanished and despair set in. They had now been out of sight for four days – four days to cover a distance of about three rope-lengths at the least, eight or so at the very most. Four nights above 8250m. If their progress had been so slow, surely they would have decided to retreat. We had already seen the effects of spending four nights at 7850m.

The only explanation must be that a catastrophe had occurred. What if one of them had fallen and was injured? Surely the other would have retraced his steps to signal us for help, particularly since we assumed they had left a line of fixed rope behind them? It would have meant retreating only two or three rope-lengths. Or could both of them have fallen sick or be so incapacitated by exhaustion that neither could move? This seemed unlikely. They were well acclimatised, and though perhaps tired from our long siege, they knew how to pace themselves and had been at these altitudes without oxygen before, on Kangchenjunga and K2. One of them could perhaps have collapsed, but not two. That left a grim interpretation. That they were both dead. Either one had fallen, pulling off the other, or perhaps one of those fragile ice flutings had collapsed, sweeping both of them down the huge Kangshung Face. I could remember its immense scale, just how steep the upper part of the ridge had seemed, and how insubstantial and dangerous Dick had found that pitch on the First Pinnacle.

Below us Charlie had also spent a sleepless night.

I was washed over by different waves of emotion. I fought with pain because I loved them. They were the personification of what I had once wanted to be, but I had not that combination of physique, skill and drive to push high on great peaks. They courted danger, yes, in the huge scale of the undertaking but not because they were reckless. Not Pete and Joe. There are, I think, some climbers who can – in the fervour of their ambition, intoxicated by danger and excited by the prospect of success – push aside all fear and feelings, take great risks and, moving fast, often alone, survive enough times to gain a reputation. To me these climbers are as one of the faces of Buddha, who lived as a hermit practising extreme asceticism, emaciated beyond measure before gaining enlightenment by this supreme sacrifice. I wondered if Pete and Joe, like Buddha returning after his enlightenment, would come back to the world of man and accept the dish of fresh curds from the village girl on the Full Moon Day of May. For Peter and Joe there was, I feel, that Middle Way: they believed that hard high-altitude climbing was a reasonable sport within mountaineering. Statistically dangerous, yes, but with care, stealth and speed, within reason. They had affirmed their faith in high altitude by repeated visits, they knew and respected the arena of avalanche, storm and stonefall. They had pushed hard and fast at the summit of Kangchenjunga, retreated in the face of avalanches from K2. They were wily and sometimes very frightened. They never showed self-indulgent elation when successful.

I talked it over with Adrian and then at mid-day with Charlie. There seemed nothing to gain by staying on the North Col. We left the tent in place, anchored to a snow shovel and its valence securely wedged down with snow. We also left the radio, the cooking gear, all the remaining food and a note welcoming them back and telling them what we had done.

We held ourselves tightly in control. Although I had very little hope of their survival I could not bring myself to admit it. Besides, we were still on the mountain and needed all our concentration to return safely to Advanced Base. By the time we reached the sérac wall where I had left a fixed rope, the clouds had engulfed us and the wind was beginning to whip stinging snowflakes into our faces. Adrian, who wears glasses, was almost blinded as they misted up. He was also feeling the debilitating effects of spending three nights at around 7000m. We were both very, very tired as we stumbled down the slope, thankful for the marker wands we had placed to guide us down.

Back on the glacier we could begin to relax, and then, having reached the rocky moraine, we were able to take off the rope and walk down in our own time. I pulled ahead, forcing myself over the broken rocks covered in fresh snow, to get back to the camp. At last it was in sight and Charlie was coming towards me.

'They've had it, I'm sure they've had it,' I muttered.

'I know.'

We held each other and wept.

12

A fruitless search

21 May – 1 June

Chris Bonington

It was all so familiar. Adrian sat quietly in his usual corner. Charlie cut some bread. The big kettle bubbled on top of three Gaz stoves, the pressure cooker hissed quietly, the canvas of the big green tent rattled in the wind. Books, gloves, karabiners, cine equipment, packages of food were piled on the boxes round the cluttered stone table. Some of the gear belonged to Pete and Joe. We had to decide what to do and the very urgency of this demand was a therapy in itself, helping us to control our grief.

In front of us was the picture file, so meticulously collected by Pete before the expedition, some of them from the pre-war expeditions, others taken by the Americans who had attempted the Kangshung Face the previous year. The stark black and white pictures emphasised the ferocious steepness of those snow flutings on the East Face. We thrashed over the possibilities and arguments that we had all been grappling with in the last few days.

'You know, when you look at the face,' I said, 'it's just great clusters of snow plastered on to very steep rock so that the whole lot could come away. If they did fall, it wouldn't have been 100m, it'd be nearer 1000m. It's horrendously steep.'

'But it's just possible, isn't it, Chris, that they could have survived in some huge slide of snow, and could somehow have got all the way down on to the Kangshung Glacier?' said Charlie.

'It'd be a one in a million chance,' I replied. 'I just can't believe they could have survived a fall on that, and even if they did, just look how steep the bottom is. They'd never get down it.'

'But it's still just possible,' persisted Charlie. 'Look at Messner on Nanga Parbat. There've been other instances as well when people have fallen and got down into another valley. However unlikely it is I think we must go up the Kangshung Valley.'

'I agree,' I said, 'but we've also got to keep this side under observation, just in case they do get back this way. Someone's going to have to sit out here as well.'

'I don't mind doing that,' volunteered Adrian.

'You know, I suppose we should really go back up the ridge itself and try to reach their high point.'

'Come on, Chris, be realistic,' said Charlie. 'I don't think Adrian or I could make it, and for that matter, could you? And anyway, would we see anything?'

'I know. I know all that. But you can't help feeling that you should. And I suppose that's the question everyone will ask. We've got to tell Hilary and Maria what we've done. We've got to try to eliminate every possibility, however strongly we feel they're dead, however certain we are that they've fallen down the Kangshung Face.'

'Yeah, but even if you managed to get all the way to the Second Pinnacle, how much would you see? Would it confirm anything?' asked Adrian.

'I suppose if we found a broken rope at their high point, that'd be some kind of confirmation. But at least we'd know they weren't there, that they hadn't collapsed from exhaustion or were sick. But quite honestly, I don't see how they could be. I could believe that one of them might be sick, but not both of them. They'd have such a short distance to get back into sight, and they should have had a fixed rope as well. I'm afraid the only real explanation is that they've both fallen.

'The trouble is as well that, unless we actually reached their high point, we'd learn no more than we know now. And you're right; quite honestly I don't think I could make it again up to the Pinnacles. I was shattered just getting up to the North Col. There's no way you or Charlie could be expected to go on to the ridge without any fixed ropes.'

'Well then, it's the Kangshung Valley,' said Charlie.

'I agree. I think we'll see more from there with the telescope than we ever would on the ridge itself.'

We discussed the plan in detail. To reach the Kangshung Valley we could have followed the American skiers over the Lhakpa La and Karpo La, but this would have meant carrying mountaineering gear and coming back the same way. If Pete and Joe had somehow managed to get down into the Kangshung Valley, it was most unlikely that they would be in a fit state to climb back over a high pass. On the other hand, if we returned to Base Camp we could drive to the Kharta Valley and trek over the Langma La, into the Kangshung Valley. At the same time we could warn Mr Chen of our fears.

This raised another problem. We needed to keep news of our fears to ourselves until we had exhausted every possibility. We talked late into the night, trying to think of every eventuality, before collapsing into drugged sleep.

Next morning Charlie and I set off, leaving Adrian to his solitary vigil. It was typical of his selflessness that he had volunteered to stay. He was going to remain there, keeping the ridge under observation until 28 May, when we promised to send up the yaks to carry down our equipment. He was to have a week of complete isolation clearing up the camp, burying our rubbish and packing loads.

On the way back to Base Camp I wanted to make a diversion to the American Camp, to tell them of our fears and to ask them to keep an eye out for our two friends. There was just a chance that they might see something from high on the North Ridge during a summit bid.

Charlie and I walked together to the junction with the Central Rongbuk Glacier. He pushed on towards Base Camp while I turned south up the side of the glacier. I felt very much alone. 'It's not far at all,' Charlie had said, but the glacier seemed to stretch away endlessly. There was just an occasional paint-daubed rock to indicate the route. And what if no one was there? If they were all away climbing? At last I noticed a little cluster of tents on the glacier below. I had over-shot. There was no sign of any activity and the site had a desolate, empty feel to it. I approached, full of dread that there would be nobody around. A head appeared from a tent doorway, and soon I was sitting among friends in their mess tent. I had indeed been lucky for they had come down from their Advanced Base that day, and were going back up the next.

I told them of our fears for Pete and Joe; they heard me out and then told me that they also had had a tragedy. Just a few days before on 15 May, Marty Hoey had fallen to her death. Four of them had been climbing the fixed ropes to establish their top camp for a summit bid, when somehow she had fallen out of her harness, all the way down the Central Gully. I could see they were still stunned by what happened, though they had decided to make one more bid for the summit. I expressed my sympathy and asked them to keep an eye out for Joe and Pete if they did manage to reach the crest of the ridge. They promised to do so, and invited me to stay the night at their camp, for it was now past six in the evening.

But I did not want to stay. I felt the need to be in our little world at Base Camp and, by walking there that night, driving myself to the point of exhaustion so that I might get some sleep.

It was dark by the time I got back and Charlie had already told Mr Chen. There was no criticism, no questioning, only sympathy and offers of help. Next morning we made our plans in detail. Mr Yu was going to accompany us when we took the truck round to the Kharta Valley. In the meantime Mr Chen was going to organise our flights back to Hong Kong, reassuring us that in no circumstances would our fears about Pete and Joe be revealed prematurely.

On 24 May we drove the hundred miles on bumpy dirt roads to the Kharta Valley. It was now summer, and the fields were lush with newly sprouting barley. We were following the broad valley that drains the Rongbuk Glacier, the Dzakar Chhu which curls round to the east into the great Arun River and flows through the Himalaya into Nepal. The village of Kharta is described as a leafy paradise in the early Everest books, such a contrast from Rongbuk that several expeditions seem to have been lured this way because of its beauty. Now the terrain has changed with the woods thin and many fields barren, the result of ruthless deforestation for fuel. We paused at the Kharta Commune Headquarters – a soulless, corrugated courtyard in a windswept dusty valley. Where were the hedges of rhododendrons, where were the flowers? Trees had been demolished here on a huge scale. We bought potatoes, arranged porters for the next day and drove on six miles up the Kharta Valley.

Suddenly, around a corner we saw some familiar tents. The American ski team were pitched on a grassy bank by the Kharta stream. Ned, Jan, Jim and Rick greeted us wildly at first – they had become great friends – then we told them tersely of our fears. They asked questions, voiced their sympathy.

Whilst we had been on the ridge they had not been idle; they crossed the Lhakpa La and Karma La, dropping into the Kangshung Valley, aiming to descend it and then turn north along the Arun Gorge at a village marked on the map as Sakyetang. A track was also shown, running down the Kharta Valley floor, through Sakyetang and on over lower hills to Kharta. They had searched for a week for this route, battled through forests of rhododendrons and finally, short of food, they had turned back in an attempt to find another route out. Luckily they had met several porters whom their Chinese staff had sent from Kharta. These guided them back over a 4870m pass, the Langma La. As far as we could establish there had never been a route down the Karma to Sakyetang and the entrance to this valley from the east can only be reached over the Langma La, crossed by Mallory and Bullock in 1921. This was the route we were to follow – entailing a three-day journey to the Kangshung Glacier.

Charlie and I pitched our tent and started cooking some supper. The four Americans were obviously in conference, and Ned eventually walked over and told us that they would be very happy to keep us company in our search, even though it would mean retracing their steps. We were delighted. Not only would it mean that we should have someone with us who knew the way but, perhaps even more important, they would be able to help in the remote event of a rescue.

We set out the following day, accompanied by three cheerful Tibetans who were going to act as guides and porters. The terrain was so different from the Rongbuk side. On the valley floor azaleas were in bud, rhododendrons already in flower, while alpine flowers were beginning to bloom in the grassy meadows beneath the Langma La.

On the second day we crossed the pass, getting a glimpse of the huge snow-clad Kangshung Face of Everest for a few minutes through the clouds. We descended to the glacier past frozen lakes and then over hillsides covered in coarse, tussocky grass and azaleas. To the south the walls of Chomo Lonzo and Pethangtse fell precipitately to the valley floor, huge spires looming out of the mists. Sometimes we caught glimpses of Everest some ten miles up the valley but with a high rainfall the Karma Valley is often filled with cloud, sucked in by the huge face which blocks its western end.

On the third night we arrived at the head of the valley, Base Camp site for the 1981 American expedition that had attempted the Kangshung Face. It had clouded over that morning and the mist was clinging to the tops of the moraine ridges all around us, hiding the mountain peaks and revealing only a desolate expanse of jumbled rock, dirty grey ice and dark crevasses. We looked with distaste at the Western litter of empty boxes, torn paperbacks and tins scattered over a meadow of sparse grass on the side of the glacier. The boxes provided fuel for a huge bonfire. The Great Carton Festival, Ned called it. He had an infectious enthusiasm that had lifted Charlie and me from our preoccupied introspection but that night, gazing into the patterns of the flames, I felt the tension mounting within me.

Would the fog clear during the night? Would we see anything? I didn't know whether to dread seeing no trace at all, or to be confronted with irrefutable evidence of what had happened. And what of Adrian? He was on his own in that tomb-like tent, so full of memories. He couldn't escape into the brief, if brittle, laughter that we were able to share with our companions. The fire was dying, the rubbish that had fuelled it exhausted. We trailed back to the tents, and I quickly dropped off to sleep, to be woken by Ned in the pallid pre-drawn. It was 28 May. The fog had cleared and the huge Kangshung Face was now clearly visible at the head of the valley.

We mounted the telescope on a tripod and took turns to stare through it. I could pick out the shoulder where we had dug the Third Snow Cave, the First Pinnacle and the col below the Second Pinnacle where, eleven days before, I had seen that small figure outlined against the darkening sky. Near-vertical ice flutings dropped away below the Pinnacles, sheer runnels swept clear of snow. Below were the tiers of séracs, icefalls and finally rock buttresses which form the 3000m-high face. Nothing moved other than the occasional avalanche. There was no sign of Pete and Joe. We walked back quietly, often apart, wrapped in thought. There was little to say. The faint hope we had lived with for over two weeks was now gone.

Three days later Charlie and I were back at Base Camp. Adrian had arrived from Advanced Base: he had no news. There remained a final act. Charlie had chosen a large slate from near the 1924 memorial and during the evenings had picked and chiselled away at a simple epitaph. As in 1924 the Tibetans built a cairn upon a hill near Base Camp. We placed the tablet and stood silently, tearful in the wind. Next day we left to bring our bad news home.

Epilogue

To Wendy Bonington in Cumbria and Martin Henderson in Jardines' London office fell the task of breaking the news. There was already a sense of foreboding in the air. We had sent no news for three weeks at a critical stage of the expedition, perhaps explicable enough in itself. Whilst our unhappy tale remained a private one, the details of our probable travel arrangements did not. Hilary, Ruth, Maria, Wendy and Frenda were anxious when they heard that Chris was due 'to fly to Beijing on 5 June'. There was no news of success or failure. Experienced expedition watchers, they felt strongly that something was gravely amiss.

Dick travelled to Manchester to tell Maria. Hilary's telephone in Switzerland was answered by Dougal Haston's widow, Annie. Betty Prentice, an old friend of us all, told Peter's mother in Bramhall and the local priest broke the news to the Taskers in Billingham.

Now, almost a year later, I can, I think, look back upon death in three ways. I mourn the loss of two close friends. I mourn, too, their great lost talents, singly and combined, their skills of climbing, writing, filming, humour, warmth and drive. Lastly, I question the nature of our journey – to venture with a small team on unknown ground on the highest mountain in the world. The outcome answers the question, 'Was it worth it?' It would not have been had we been able to peer even dimly into what was to happen. Since we are not granted this faculty I can only look back on the spirit of the venture.

I believe that with the mysteries of our personalities, our curious drives and our self-appointed goals, we could not have turned down this opportunity for fulfilment without denying ourselves a glimpse of the very meaning of existence. In time I expect we shall do the same again and be lured back perhaps by another Goddess Mother of the World.

CHARLES CLARKE
May 1983

PETER BOARDMAN AND JOE TASKER
WERE LOST TOGETHER ON CHOMOLUNGMA (MOUNT EVEREST).
THEY WERE LAST SEEN ON 17 MAY 1982
AT 8250M ON THE NORTH EAST RIDGE

Peter Boardman

1950–82

Peter David Boardman was born on Christmas Day 1950, the younger son of Alan and Dorothy Boardman of Bramhall, Stockport. He first went to Nevill Road County Primary School and then on to Stockport Grammar School in 1956. While there he began climbing, visiting the mountains of Corsica in 1964 and 1965. Here he first enjoyed the flavour of the wilderness, 'the freedom of moving, lightweight, through mountain country, carrying shelter, warmth, food and fuel on my back'. In 1966 he joined the Mynydd Climbing Club which then met in the Manchester Arms, Stockport. He began climbing seriously with Barry Monkman, a friend from school, and later with Dave Pownall. Once enrolled in the Mynydd he quickly became a highly competent rock-climber, leading VS routes within a year on grit-stone and Welsh and Lakeland crags. He visited the Swabian Alps in 1966, youth hostelling, and two years later went to the Pennine Alps to climb. He graduated quickly through alpine classics to become a leading British alpine mountaineer. He made the first British ascents of the North Face Direct of the Olan, the North Face of the Nesthorn and the North Face Direct of the Lauterbrunnen Breithorn.

From Stockport Grammar School he went to the University of Nottingham where he became President of the University Mountaineering Club. He took a degree in English, followed by a teaching diploma at University College of North Wales, Bangor, in 1973, where for a time he learnt Welsh. He was never to teach in any formal sense of the word but he joined Glenmore Lodge, Aviemore, in 1973 as an Instructor and gained the Mountain Guide Carnet in September 1977. He joined the British Mountaineering Council as National Officer in 1975 and, despite little experience in the world of committees, he quickly mastered this demanding post, adding greatly to the BMC's contact with young climbers and climbing clubs, ex-perience which would stand him in good stead when he was elected President of the Association of British Mountain Guides in 1979. His skill in negotiation and his knowledge of international mountaineering bureaucracy facilitated the entry of British Guides into the Union Internationale des Associations de Guides de Montagne. In January 1978, following the death of Dougal Haston in an avalanche, he was invited to take over the International School of Mountaineering in Leysin. As Director he helped continue the tradition of the school and found his metier as a guide and teacher of the sport he loved so much. Instructing climbing for Peter was never a necessary chore but a positive pleasure; he allowed his knowledge and affection to diffuse freely to those around him.

His first expedition was to Afghanistan in 1972, the University of Nottingham

Hindu Kush expedition, with Martin Wragg, Chris FitzHugh, Bill Church, Margaret and the late Oliver Stansfield, their baby Esther and Bob Watson. On this trip he demonstrated something of his own power – he was immensely strong and skilful, a man who valued speed as a means of safety. As a training climb his small party chose the North Face of Koh-i-Khaaik and followed this with the first ascent of Kohi-Mundi, a great achievement for a first expedition.

In 1974 he visited Alaska and with Roger O'Donovan made the first ascent of the South Face of Mount Dan Beard. Early in 1975 he went to the Caucasus and in July he left to go to the South West Face of Everest, the youngest member of the team and in many ways the least known. It was here that I first met him. Large expeditions were also a novel experience for him as an extract from his diary on the approach march shows: 'We round a corner and there is the British Raj in all its glory, neatly lined up erected tents, crowds kept at a distance, and we sit down at tables in the mess tent and are brought steaming kettles full of tea. For a mountaineer surely a Bonington Everest expedition is one of the last great Imperial experiences that life can offer.' Peter was a diligent, disciplined member of the team, a little retiring on a sociable expedition. He was certainly one of the strongest members and this led to his selection for the second ascent of the South West Face, following Dougal Haston and Doug Scott. Peter was paired with the expedition sirdar, Sherpa Pertemba and set off from Camp 6 in front of a second pair, Mick Burke and Martin Boysen. Martin turned back after a short distance with faulty oxygen equipment while Mick continued alone. Peter and Pertemba reached the summit of Everest in deteriorating weather at 1.40 p.m. on 26 September 1975. Peter was wearing, loyally, a Mynydd T-shirt for the summit photograph. With the conditions worsening rapidly they returned along the South East Ridge and to their amazement met Mick Burke ascending the ridge alone, about 30m below the summit. They exchanged a few words and agreed to meet up at the South Summit. Peter, despite deteriorating weather and poor visibility, insisted on waiting for over an hour and a half below the South Summit: in the storm that was to follow they were struck twice by avalanches while crossing the exposed slopes of the South West Face and struggled into Camp 6 in the dusk. Mick was never to be seen again.

In the months that followed it fell to Peter to record those moments many times, at lectures and at interviews. He did so with frankness and great sympathy, although it was obviously painful to him to recall what had been the momentous hours of his life.

After Everest '75, expeditions followed with frightening speed. In 1976 he visited the Polish High Tatra and later that year joined Joe Tasker for the West Wall of Changabang, the legendary climb which followed the lead of Joe and Dick Renshaw on Dunagiri a year later. Changabang was an example of meticulous forethought – for example the sleeve hammocks which were to dangle precariously on the face were first tested in a deep freeze – and much of the special equipment was designed and made by Mynydd members. This expedition, too, gave Peter a further share of tragedy, as

Joe and he buried the bodies of four members of the American Dunagiri expedition.

Peter had a companion as constant as his travels would permit for the last six years of his life. Acquaintance, girlfriend and finally wife, Hilary Collins had first met him as she took part in a course in Aviemore in 1974. In 1976, after Changabang she organised his first lecture, at Belper High School where she ran the School's Outdoor Activities Department. They climbed together shortly afterwards at the Torrs in New Mills (where Peter fell but was held by her) and later in the winter of 1976–7 in Torridon. There they planned a visit to New Guinea, Hilary then leaving for a post in Switzerland to teach in a private school. In 1977, unable to visit New Guinea, they climbed together on Mount Kenya (the second winter ascent of the Diamond Couloir) and Kilimanjaro. Peter was soon to follow Hilary to Switzerland, to Leysin, in 1978 when he took over the International School of Mountaineering. They were married in August 1980.

In 1978, by now firmly one of the most respected high-altitude mountaineers, he took part in the K2 expedition led by Chris Bonington. Little was achieved; Nick Estcourt died in an avalanche early on the trip and the expedition was abandoned.

The following year was as full a climbing year as is possible. He spent Christmas 1978 in the Snow Mountains of New Guinea with Hilary, climbing the Carstenz Pyramid and Dugundugu. Peter spoke little about this small expedition, preferring perhaps to keep this tender memory to himself. 'Back from the Stone Age' in the New Year, he was ready to leave for Kangchenjunga in March with Joe, Doug Scott and Georges Bettembourg. They climbed the North Ridge of Kangchenjunga, reaching the summit without oxygen on 15 May. Returning for the alpine summer season and guiding from Leysin, a further expedition was in preparation. Again a trip that was wholly in Peter's style – small, forceful and elegant to a mountain of mystery. This time it was Gaurishankar in Nepal. Peter was openly disappointed that an American/Nepalese expedition, led by Al Read, had made the first ascent of the North Summit. The West Ridge to the virgin South Summit, looked hard and committing and with John Barry, Tim Leach and Guy Neidhardt (from Leysin), Peter left in September on the third extraordinary expedition of the year. This was as long, fine and intricate a ridge climb as has ever been done in the Himalaya, exposed for long sections and demanding sustained care. Despite John Barry falling from the crest and injuring his arm, the others reached the summit with Pemba Lama on 8 November.

For 1980 the unsettled score, K2, remained. It was not in Peter's nature to try to recreate a large expedition in the style of 1978. This trip was to be a foursome with Joe, Dick Renshaw and Doug Scott. Having attempted the West Ridge, they moved to the Abruzzi but once again the Savage Mountain struck, all but sweeping the expedition from the Abruzzi Spur in a succession of avalanches. They survived, reaching 7975m, but poor weather and exhaustion prevented a further attempt on the summit.

Mount Kongur followed in 1981, a large expedition by Peter's standards, but one which satisfied his keen interest in mountain exploration. He researched in great detail the history of climbing in Xinjiang and contributed important material to the expedition book. He reached the summit on 12 July with Chris Bonington, Al Rouse and Joe Tasker and narrowly escaped serious injury during an abseil near the top. A stone dislodged by his own abseil rope knocked him unconscious and he slid almost to the free end until, by chance, his thumb jammed in the descendeur.

Everest followed in March '82 and on this, our third expedition together, I sensed more of his feelings. Outwardly he was placid, apparently relaxed among high mountains with high risks. Growing to know him better I realised how aware he was of the dangers of his existence. He wore no blinkers about immortality and had no sense of fatalism – he wished to make sure he stayed alive. I thought he felt fear deeply but was somehow able to overcome it to achieve his extravagant climbing ambitions.

A further talent emerged through his climbing career – writing. He spoke and wrote well about Everest in 1975 but could not avoid the label of successful new boy. Changabang, his first shared experience with Joe, seemed to me to be an event of such magnitude that *The Shining Mountain* leapt from him as part of all his inner experience, an outstanding document of endurance, pain, pleasure and a closeness to another human being. The success of the book was immediate in the climbing world and won him wider acclaim with the John Llewelyn Rhys Memorial Prize for literature in 1979.

Sacred Summits, published shortly after his death, described his climbing year of 1979, the trips to New Guinea, Kangchenjunga and Gaurishankar. A book which captured both the variety and intensity of three very different expeditions, it will, I believe, be held in years to come among the greatest of climbing literature, for its merit rather than for its author's untimely end.

Although Peter's achievements with his partners will be recorded in the archives of mountaineering, it is his warmth, humanity and wisdom which will be so sorely missed by those of us who loved him. He did not agree with Howard Somervell's epitaph, 'There are few better deaths than to die in high endeavour'. Nor did Joe. And as I carved a headstone for their memorial in the Rongbuk Valley my only wish was for the last few moments of their lives to be unravelled.

CHARLES CLARKE

Joe Tasker

1948–82

Joe was born in Hull in 1948 and five years later moved to Teesside where his father worked as a school caretaker until his retirement. Joe was one of ten children in a very close-knit family from which a strong sense of consideration and thoughtfulness for others seemed to develop. Several members of his family were usually at the airport when Joe left on an expedition or returned. Just before leaving on this last expedition to Everest Pete wondered whether Joe, noted for turning up at the last minute, would be on time to meet the press. 'He will be,' said someone else. 'Joe might keep the press of the world waiting but never his family.'

As the oldest son of a strongly Catholic family, Joe was sent to Ushaw College, a Jesuit seminary, at the age of thirteen. His seven years there were to have a lasting effect on him in many ways. It was there that he started climbing when he was fifteen, in a quarry behind the college, with the encouragement of Father Barker, one of the priests, and in the well-stocked library his imagination was fired by tales of epic adventures in the mountains. He was always grateful for the excellent education he had received and his amazing will power and stoicism may perhaps have been partly due to the somewhat spartan way of life and to the Jesuit ideals of spiritual development through self-denial. He started his training as a priest but at twenty realised that he did not have the vocation and decided to leave – the hardest decision of his life.

In complete contrast to his life at Ushaw was his first job – as a dustman. He enjoyed the hard physical labour and the friendly banter with his workmates and his forthright nature and ability to communicate with people from all walks of life broke down any barriers. He then went on to work in a quarry in the Lake District, where he was near the crags, for by now climbing had become a major part of his life. Feeling the lack of intellectual stimulation to which he had become accustomed at Ushaw, he decided to go to Manchester University to take a degree in sociology. The thin, fresh-faced youth looked the most unlikely of climbers but he soon made a big impression in the University Climbing Club with his keenness and drive, doing hard routes and often climbing solo. His climbing career almost came to an early end whilst he was soloing Three Pebble Slabs at Froggatt. His ancient pair of worn Kletterschuhe were not up to the thin friction and he fell, breaking his wrist so seriously that the specialist said the flexibility would be permanently impaired, curtailing his climbing. Never one to accept the hallowed words of experts without testing their veracity, Joe regarded this as a challenge and within a year was back climbing again with renewed enthusiasm and a brand new pair of EBs.

Whilst at university he was still finding his feet after so many years at the seminary and, although he was conscientious and absorbed by his studies, it was a time of experimentation and exploration. He was fascinated by the people living in their various ways, on the fringes of society, such as down-and-outs, alcoholics and gypsies. He had a deep concern for others and his understanding and genuine warm nature made him a very good friend. However, this side of him was not easily discernible as it was often hidden by an abrasive, hard shell. Despite his gregariousness and his ability as a raconteur he was also, in many ways, a very private person, sometimes appearing quite secretive and even enjoying creating a sense of mystery by making partial disclosures. During decision-making, whether personal or at a group level, he would not air his thoughts until he had fully mulled over the problem, often preferring to do so in solitude.

Although we were at the same university, we never climbed together during that period. Our first real encounter was in Chamonix in 1970 when, on a wet, dreary day, Joe's curly red head appeared through the door of my tent and he asked me if I fancied doing the North Face of the Dru. Having overcome his initial awe of the Alps, it being his second season, he seemed ready to tackle anything. It being my first, however, I was not and I demurred. The ice had been broken and we spent our first alpine season together the following summer, climbing classic routes. The following year we again teamed up and developed a taste for North Faces. Joe really took to the mixed alpine routes, relishing the insecure, delicate climbing. We were very different in personality and two seasons seemed enough but, nonetheless, we ended up climbing together again in 1973 after a chance meeting in Chamonix. We were both very ambitious and that season we climbed the Walker Spur, the Bonatti-Gobi Route on the Eckpfeiler Buttress, the North Face of the Nesthorn, the North Face of the Dent Blanche and the North Face of the Eiger.

Joe had got a good degree earlier that year but had decided not to settle into a career in order to be free to climb. At the end of the season all his money had gone and he decided to stay on in the Alps and find work in the Swiss vineyards in the autumn. He said that the penniless period between the end of the climbing season and starting work was one of the happiest times of his life. He survived on the refunds from empty wine bottles and on tins and packets of food left by departing climbers. He was able to relax and enjoy the mountains totally free from any cares about work, study or even climbing. After working in the vineyards he joined a group of young people at an archaeological site at Beaume in Switzerland and later on we had an abortive attempt at winter climbing in the Alps.

In the summer of 1974 we met in Chamonix or, as Joe put it, 'There was the unplanned but inevitable encounter with Dick, alone and looking for a partner. It doesn't do to fight one's fate and we arranged a climb together.' We did what Joe thought was one of the most memorable alpine climbs – the East Face of the Grandes Jorasses, an intricate and demanding route. Joe had been stretched intellectually by academic life but the mountains provided the challenge to stretch mind and body to the full although I was continually amazed that someone who was so attached to his creature comforts should become involved in a sport which entailed so much physical hardship. At home he loved warmth and comfort: it was as though in times of plenty he was storing up an excess to help him through leaner times on the mountains. Frequently it seemed as though only his will power and determination drove his body on and it was not unusual to see him, at altitude, bent double over his ice axe racked by fits of coughing and spitting blood. The vast physical effort needed for mountaineering did not come easily but here, as in all his other activities, he had a powerful drive and restless energy.

Our ascent of the North Face of the Eiger in the winter of 1974–5 was a landmark in Joe's mountaineering career. It was an exhilarating climb and provided a stepping stone to the Himalaya, giving us the necessary confidence to tackle a Himalayan peak as a two-man team. In 1975 we left Manchester in an overloaded Ford Escort van, our destination Dunagiri, a 7000m peak in Northern India. It was an adventure from the start, fraught with problems and difficulties, but Joe seemed very much in control and methodically overcame one obstacle after another. He had the uncommon knack of going straight to the heart of a problem and solving it in the most expedient way. By September we were at 6400m on the South Ridge but were insufficiently acclimatised, tired and, with few supplies and little fuel left, should have retreated. We both suppressed our doubts and fears, however, and this almost cost us our lives. We struggled on to the summit, leaving no resources for the descent which evolved into a four-day epic and left me with badly frostbitten fingers. Joe was becoming more at ease and more appreciative of the mountain environment and, having a natural eye for photography, was rapidly developing this talent and was able to record the mountains' changing moods. He was later to give a vivid description of the whole trip in his book, *Savage Arena*. In it he also describes the impression made on him by Changabang.

> The days on Dunagiri were days of continual exposure to the subliminal presence of that stupendous mountain. It had been a thing of beauty beyond our reach, a wall of difficulty beyond our capabilities, it had been the obstacle which blocked the sun's warming rays in the early morning and the silent witness to my delirious wanderings.

He conceived the audacious idea of climbing the awesome West Wall as a two-man team. In Pete Boardman, Joe sensed a kindred spirit and the two of them combined to make a formidable driving force. Their success was a source of great delight to Joe, particularly as a number of established climbers had deemed the climb impossible, and it was the start of a brilliant partnership and a firm friendship. The rivalry between them was often evident, both of them setting very high standards in their goals which the other felt he had to attain or better. There was continual banter between them in which each tried to open up the chinks in the other's armour. Pete's presence seemed to induce in Joe a show of hardness and outrageous behaviour. They sometimes seemed like an old married couple but their banter would not have existed without a deep mutual respect and a strong affection.

In 1977 he attempted, without success, the North Ridge of Nuptse with Mike Covington and Doug Scott. That summer he went to the Alps but found that their allure was no more and thereafter he applied himself wholeheartedly to Himalayan expeditions. In 1978 he went with Chris Bonington's team to attempt the West Ridge of K2 and he witnessed the huge avalanche which swept his friend, Nick Estcourt, to his death, after which the expedition was abandoned. The following year, 1979, he went to Nepal with Doug Scott, Pete Boardman and Georges Bettembourg to attempt the North Ridge of Kangchenjunga (8598m) without oxygen. Until then Joe's highest climb had been to 7000m and to try to climb the third highest mountain in the world aroused in him many doubts about his ability to perform at altitude. Beneath Joe's appearance of confidence was a vulnerability which was very rarely expressed and which was counteracted by his ability to detach himself from his emotions. He proved himself capable of coping with the altitude and this exciting and successful ascent was, for Joe, an important personal achievement.

Frequent expeditions were taking their toll on his private life and his long absences and total involvement with mountaineering were too much for his personal relationships to withstand. In 1979 he began to organise an expedition to attempt, once again, the West Ridge of K2. At about this time he met Maria Coffey, who was to become a constant companion and a great source of strength to him. I had not climbed with Joe since 1975 but we had kept in touch and he had always been ready with his kind support. Valuing his friendships highly, he made great efforts to keep in touch with his many friends. Joe, Pete and I reached a height of 7975m on the Abruzzi Spur of K2 in very unsettled weather. It was one day's climbing to the summit from our tent, perched in a precarious position on a small ledge hacked out from a steep snow slope. During the night, after many hours of snowfall, an avalanche thundered down the slope, engulfing the tent, but miraculously not knocking it off the ledge. Joe was completely buried, Pete managed to extricate himself, dragged me out and we both dug out Joe. We had escaped death from the avalanche but there were a further three days of harrowing descent down slopes which after continual snowfall had become extremely avalanche-prone, with annihilation seeming imminent at each step. Back at Base Camp each of us individually decided to go back up for another try, and it was this decision which made Joe realise the depth of his commitment to mountaineering. It was an experience which had a profound effect on him.

Shortly after coming back from K2, Joe went off on an expedition to attempt a winter ascent of the West Ridge of Everest. Despite being still very weak and not having fully regained his weight, it was an example of his incredible will power that he was able to find the strength to apply himself fully to the task in hand. Conditions on the mountain were brutal and the cold more intense than he had ever experienced. They did not get to the top but it was an innovative step and showed the feasibility of winter climbing on the world's highest peaks. This expedition was the theme for Joe's first book, *Everest the Cruel Way*. It was an exciting account and revealed Joe's talent for writing. He wrote it in a very short time and under great pressure as he was also running a climbing shop and preparing for yet another expedition. He was also becoming more involved with filming and this was probably more suited to his gregarious nature.

In 1981, Pete and Joe were again together, with Chris Bonington and Alan Rouse, on the expedition to Mount Kongur.

The North East Ridge of Everest offered a double challenge for Joe – not only to climb it, but to film the entire expedition. He seemed to be living life at a cracking pace and sometimes felt frustration that there was not enough time to do all the things he wanted. He had just finished *Savage Arena* before leaving for Everest, and he completed his equipment appendix for the Kongur book just before we flew to Lhasa. There didn't seem to be enough hours in the day to pack everything in but it was evident that he was totally happy in what he was doing. At Base Camp there was the time and space to relax more fully and Joe amused us with funny stories and by appearing in the most bizarre clothes we had ever seen on an expedition. Life was never dull with him around and the constant jibes between him and Pete kept them on their toes and us entertained. I was very happy climbing with Joe: he had a fine judgment and I felt totally safe with him. He impressed us all with his professional attitude to filming and with his dedication, persevering in the foulest conditions. It was a bitter blow to me to have to leave the expedition after suffering a mild stroke and the night before I left everyone went off to their own tents after an early supper to write letters for me to take with me the following day. Joe had a heavy work-load to get through, completing his film reports as well as writing letters, but he must have sensed my desolation and, although it meant him working through most of the night, he stayed chatting with me and keeping me company for a couple of hours.

This thoughtfulness was typical of Joe and through his sometimes frenetic lifestyle there shone a very special warmth and vitality. He was an outstanding mountaineer and a very good friend.

DICK RENSHAW

Both these obituaries also appear in the *Alpine Journal* 1983.

British Everest Expedition 1982

CLIMBING TEAM

Peter Boardman
Chris Bonington
Dick Renshaw
Joe Tasker

SUPPORT TEAM

Charles Clarke
Adrian Gordon

TREKKING PARTY

David Newbigging
Carolyn Newbigging
Piers Brooke
Suzy Brooke
Robert Friend
Martin Henderson
Michael Jardine
David Livermore
Steven McCormick
Andrew Russell

CO-ORDINATING OFFICE/SPONSORS

London
Martin Henderson
Philippa Stead
Elaine Edwards

Cumbria
Louise Wilson
Alison Lancaster
Norma Atherton

Hong Kong
T. T. Harley
P. A. Farnell-Watson

Peking
David Mathew
Alison Hardie
Peter Po

Canton
Rita Chan

CHINESE PERSONNEL

Chen Rongchang *Liaison Officer*
Yu Bin *Interpreter*
Tang Huanzing *Trekker's interpreter*
Wang Chouhai *Cook*
La Ba *Cook*
Cheng Wenxin *Jeep Driver*
Dawa *Truck Driver*

Diary of Events

1 March	Boardman, Bonington, Clarke, Renshaw, Tasker fly from Heathrow to Hong Kong.
4 March	Bonington and Clarke fly to Beijing.
5 March	Boardman, Gordon, Renshaw, Tasker and trekkers fly to Chengdu.
6 March	Bonington, Clarke, Mathew fly from Beijing to Chengdu.
8 March	All team fly from Chengdu to Lhasa.
9–16 March	Team drive to Base Camp.
17 March	Organising Base Camp.
18 March	At Base Camp.
19 March	Bonington, Renshaw, David Newbigging, Henderson, Jardine, Livermore and McCormick set out for East Rongbuk Glacier, camping at 5500m at junction of Central and East Rongbuk Glaciers.
	Boardman, Tasker, Friend, Russell, Piers and Suzy Brooke set out for Central Rongbuk Glacier and camp just below, by river.
	Clarke, Gordon and Carolyn Newbigging remain at Base.
20 March	East Rongbuk party reach Camp 1½ (5650m), a third of the way between Camp 1 and Camp 2.
	Central Rongbuk party walk up Central Glacier to approx. 5600m and return to their camp.
21 March	Bonington and Livermore return to Base Camp.
	Henderson, Jardine, McCormick, David Newbigging and Renshaw walk up East Rongbuk Glacier to 5850m and return to Camp 1½.
	Central Rongbuk party return to Base.
22 March	East Rongbuk party return to Base.
	American Everest team reach Base Camp.
23 March	Trekkers leave.
24 March	Team at Base.
25 March	Team go to Camp 1½.
26 March	Climbing team move to pre-war Camp 2 (6000m) in 4 hours.
	Support team go short way and back to Camp 1½.
27 March	Climbing team go up to Advanced Base (6400m) and return to pre-war Camp 2.
	Support team go to level of Changtse Glacier and return to Base.
28 March	Climbing team return to Base (4 hours).

29 March	At Base.
30 March	At Base. American jeep goes out with mail.
	Yaks due but do not arrive.
	Americans move up to their Operational Base.
31 March	At Base. Bonington and Clarke visit nunnery.
	13 yaks plus 5 herders reach camp just below nunnery.
1 April	Yaks arrive at Base.
2 April	Team (less Renshaw waiting for mail) go to pre-war Camp 1 with yaks.
3 April	Team go to pre-war Camp 2. Renshaw at Base.
4 April	Team reach Advanced Base. Bonington and Boardman stay.
	Clarke, Gordon and Tasker return to pre-war Camp 2.
	Yaks return to pre-war Camp 1. Renshaw walks from Base to Advanced Base in 6 hours!
5 April	Bonington and Renshaw recce Raphu La and bottom of N.E. Ridge.
	Tasker moves to Advanced Base.
	Support team return to Base.
6 April	Climbing team at Advanced Base.
	Support team at Base.
7 April	Climbing team climb ridge to site of First Snow Cave (6850m).
	Support team at Base. Discovery of pre-war Everest memorial.
8 April	Climbing team at Advanced Base making it windproof.
	Support team at Base.
9 April	Climbing team carries to First Snow Cave, starts digging and returns to Advanced Base.
	Support team at Base.
10 April	Renshaw and Tasker move to First Snow Cave.
	Bonington and Boardman do a carry, returning to Advanced Base.
	Support team to pre-war Camp 1 with yaks.
11 April	Renshaw and Tasker push route short way beyond Point 7090m.
	Bonington and Boardman move up to First Snow Cave.
	Support team to pre-war Camp 2.
12 April	Climbing team carry rope and push route to site of Second Snow Cave, 7256m.
	Support team to Advanced Base.
13 April	Climbing team carry rope and food to Second Snow Cave.
	Support team at Advanced Base. Yaks return.
14 April	Boardman, Renshaw and Tasker carry to Second Snow Cave and dig it out, then return to Advanced Base.
	Bonington goes straight down to Advanced Base.
	Support team at Advanced Base.
15 April	Climbing team and support team at Advanced Base.

16 April   Climbing team at Advanced Base.
                Support team to Base.

17 April   Climbing team at Advanced Base.
                Support team at Base.

18 April   Climbing team return to First Snow Cave.
                Support team at Base.

19 April   Climbing team to Second Snow Cave.
                Support team with yaks to pre-war Camp 1.

20 April   Climbing team move to Second Snow Cave.
                Support team with yaks to Advanced Base. Yaks stay up.

21 April   Bonington and Boardman climb First Buttress, reaching 7560m.
                Renshaw and Tasker snowproof Second Snow Cave.
                Support team returns to Base (because of theft).

22 April   Renshaw and Tasker climb Second Buttress, reaching 7640m.
                Bonington and Boardman follow, carrying rope.
                Support team at Base.

23 April   Climbing team return to Advanced Base.
                Support team at Base.

24 April   Climbing team return to Base.
                Support team to camp at 6000m west of Rongbuk.
                American ski team arrive.

25 April   Climbing team at Base.
                Support team climb Point 6200, camp at Rongbuk.

26 April   Climbing team at Base.
                Support team return to Base.

27 April   All team at Base.
                Picnic at pre-war Base Camp.

28 April   Climbing team at Base.
                Support team move to pre-war Camp 1.

29 April   All team reach Advanced Base.

30 April   Climbing team move to First Snow Cave.
                Support team at Advanced Base.

1 May   Climbing team move to Second Snow Cave.
                Support team at Advanced Base.

2 May   Boardman and Renshaw move up to Third Snow Cave at 7850m.
                Bonington and Tasker carry to Third Snow Cave.
                Support team camp on Kartaphu Glacier.

3 May   Boardman and Renshaw dig Third Snow Cave.
                Bonington and Tasker move up from Second to Third Snow Cave.
                Support team attempt Point 6919 and return to Advanced Base.

4 May   Bonington and Boardman climb 4 rope-lengths on First Pinnacle to
                8100m, leaving fixed rope in place.

	Tasker carries rope to foot of First Pinnacle.
	Renshaw goes back to gear dump above Second Step.
	Climbing team return to Third Snow Cave.
	Support team at Advanced Base.
5 May	Renshaw and Tasker force route on First Pinnacle to 8170m.
	Renshaw has minor stroke after leading very hard pitch.
	Boardman carries to high point and belays Tasker.
	Bonington carries to foot of First Pinnacle.
	Support team at Advanced Base.
6 May	Climbing team return to Advanced Base.
	Support team at Advanced Base.
7 May	Team return to Base.
8 May	Team at Base.
9 May	Team at Base. Renshaw has second stroke.
10 May	Bonington, Boardman, Gordon and Tasker at Base.
	Clarke and Renshaw drive to Xigaze with Yu.
11 May	Bonington, Boardman, Gordon and Tasker at Base.
	Clarke and Renshaw reach Lhasa.
12 May	Bonington, Boardman, Gordon and Tasker at Base.
	Clarke and Renshaw fly to Chengdu.
13 May	Bonington, Boardman, Gordon and Tasker walk to Advanced Base.
	Renshaw flies to Hong Kong.
	Clarke in Chengdu.
14 May	Bonington, Boardman, Gordon and Tasker at Advanced Base.
	Clarke flies back to Lhasa.
15 May	Boardman and Tasker reach Second Snow Cave.
	Bonington and Gordon reach foot of North Col slopes.
	Clarke reaches Xigaze.
16 May	Boardman and Tasker reach Third Snow Cave.
	Bonington and Gordon at 6900m, just short of North Col.
	Last radio contact with Boardman and Tasker at 1800 hrs.
	Clarke reaches Base.
17 May	Boardman and Tasker last seen at 2100 hrs, at foot of Second Pinnacle at 8250m.
	Bonington and Gordon at Advanced Base.
	Clarke at Base.
18 May	Bonington and Gordon reach and camp at previous high point at 6900m.
	Clarke walks to pre-war Camp 1 with two Tibetans.
19 May	Bonington and Gordon reach North Col.
	Clarke reaches Advanced Base with 2 Tibetans.
20 May	Bonington and Gordon on North Col.

Clarke at Advanced Base.

2 Tibetans return to Base.

21 May   Bonington and Gordon join Clarke at Advanced Base.

22 May   Bonington and Clarke return to Base, Bonington calling in at American Base.

Gordon at Advanced Base.

23 May   Bonington and Clarke at Base.

Gordon at Advanced Base.

24 May   Bonington and Clarke with Yu drive to Kharta. Meet American ski team.

Gordon at Advanced Base.

25 May   Bonington, Clarke, Ned Gillette, Jim Bridwell and Rick Barker reach yak pasture below Langma La (c.4850m) with 3 porters.

Gordon at Advanced Base.

26 May   Search team cross Langma La and camp beyond Karma Bridge at 4390m.

Gordon at Advanced Base.

Yaks leave Base for pre-war Camp 1.

27 May   Search team reach head of Karma Valley (American 1981 Base).

Gordon at Advanced Base.

Yaks reach pre-war Camp 2.

28 May   Search team examine Kangshung Face through telescope, then return to Karma Bridge.

Yaks reach Advanced Base, clear it, returning to Camp 1.

Gordon walks to Base.

29–30 May   Search team return to Base.

31 May–

1 June   Team at Base.

2–4 June   Bonington to Chengdu, breaks news by phone.

5–6 June   Clarke and Gordon to Lhasa.

Bonington in Beijing.

7 June   Bonington reaches Hong Kong.

8 June   Clarke and Gordon to Chengdu.

9 June   Clarke and Gordon reach Hong Kong.

10 June   Press conference in Hong Kong.

Bonington and Clarke fly to London.

11 June   Bonington, Clarke and Renshaw attend London press conference.

A Select Bibliography

HISTORY AND TRAVEL

Perceval Landon, *Lhasa* (2 vols), Hurst & Blackett, 1905.

L. Austine Waddell, *Lhasa and its Mysteries*, John Murray, 1905.

Fosco Maraini, *Secret Tibet*, Hutchinson, 1952.

Sir Charles Bull, *Tibet Past and Present*, Clarendon, 1924.

—*People of Tibet*, Clarendon, 1928.

—*Religion of Tibet*, Clarendon, 1931.

Sir Francis Younghusband, *The Epic of Mount Everest*, Edward Arnold, 1926.

Alan Winnington, *Tibet*, Lawrence & Wishart, 1957.

Peter Fleming, *Bayonets to Lhasa*, Hart-Davis, 1961.

Han Suyin, *Lhasa, the Open City*, Cape, 1977.

David Snellgrove and Hugh Richardson, *A Cultural History of Tibet*, reprinted by the Prajna Press, Boulder, Colorado, 1980.

Frank Steele, 'A journey to Tibet and the Northern Side of Everest', School of Oriental and African Studies, University of London, 1982.

Glossary

A

abseil method of descending a rock face by sliding down a rope, usually doubled so that the rope can be pulled down afterwards.

acclimatisation process of physiological adaptation to living and climbing at high altitude.

aid climbing using equipment such as pitons, ice screws, bolts directly to assist progress; also called artificial climbing.

alpine-style climbing at high altitude in one continuous push from the foot to top of the mountain, carrying minimum gear, bivouacking en route as necessary, but not returning to base to restock, nor using fixed camps or fixed ropes.

anchor the point to which a fixed abseil or belay rope is anchored; either a natural feature or a piton, bolt or nut.

arête a sharp ridge of rock or snow.

B

belay a method of safeguarding a climbing partner from falling by tying oneself to a firm anchor from which one can pay out or take in the rope. A lead climber may safeguard himself with a running belay (runner) by putting in a piton, nut or, in earlier days, placing a rope loop over a natural rock spike or round a chockstone, then letting his rope run through a karabiner (or sling and karabiner) attached to it.

bergschrund the gap or crevasse between the glacier proper and the upper snows of a face.

bivouac to spend a night in the open or in a snow hole on a mountain, or in a minimal bivvy sack or tent, as opposed to a proper tent or fixed camp.

bolt an anchor point hammered into a hole drilled in the rock, which expands to create a friction grip.

bouldering exercising or training by climbing boulders that require a high level of technical expertise.

C

chang Sherpa beer brewed from rice or sometimes millet.

Cheyne-Stokes respiration disordered and irregular breathing pattern experienced by the unacclimatised at altitude.

chimney a fissure in the rock or ice wide enough to climb up on the inside.

chockstones stones found wedged in a crack or placed there specially to hold a running belay, or belay, the natural precursors of manufactured wedges and nuts.

climbing roped climbers rope together on difficult or dangerous ground for safety, and can either all move together or move one at a time, leaving other member(s) of the team constantly belayed.

col a pass or dip in a ridge, usually between two peaks.

cornice an overhanging mass of snow projecting over the edge of a ridge, formed by prevailing winds.

couloir an open gully.

crampons steel spiked frames which can be fitted to boots to give a grip on ice and firm snow slopes.

crevasse a crack in a glacier surface which can be both wide and very deep, made by the movement of the glacier over the irregular shapes in its bed, or by bends in its course.

cwn a deep, rounded hollow at the head or side of a valley, formed by glacial action.

D

deadman small alloy plate which is dug into the snow to act like a fluke anchor, digging deeper the harder it is pulled.

descendeur alloy device used for belaying and abseiling.

E

étrier portable rope and metal or webbing loop ladders of a few rungs used in aid climbing.

F

face a steep aspect of a mountain between two ridges.

fixed ropes on prolonged climbs up steep ground the lead climber, having run out the full length of rope, ties it to an appropriate anchor, and subsequently all climbers move independently up and down the fixed rope, clipped on to it, using it either as a safety line or, on very steep ground, for direct progress. The rope is left in place for the duration of the climb.

front pointing climbing straight up steep snow or ice by means of kicking in the front points of crampons and supporting balance with an ice axe, or, on steep ground, using the picks of an ice axe and ice hammer in either hand.

G

gendarme a rock pinnacle obtruding from a ridge, often surrounded by snow.

H

headwall steep rock barrier at the head of a valley.

I

icefall where a glacier falls steeply and creates a series of crevasses and pinnacles of ice.

J

jumar clamps devices that lock on to fixed rope to support a climber's weight when subject to downward force, but which can be slid up the rope as a method of climbing, or jumaring, it.

K

karabiners oval metal snap-links used for, among other things, attaching rope to an anchor.

L

la pass (Tibetan).

M

monsoon the monsoon reaches the Himalaya and climbing is impossible by the middle of June, so expeditions are made in the pre-monsoon season (mid-May to mid-June) or the post-monsoon season (mid-September to mid-October). The Karakoram is not affected by the monsoon in this way.

moraine accumulation of stones and debris carried down by a glacier.

N

névé permanent snow at the head of a glacier.

nuts originally were nuts (of nuts and bolts) with the thread drilled out, but progressed to alloy wedges. Used in cracks to support belays.

O

oedema a high-altitude illness in which water accumulates in the brain (cerebral oedema) or the lungs (pulmonary oedema). Immediate and swift descent is imperative for survival.

off-width cracks too wide to fist jam, too narrow to take more than an arm and leg. Difficult to protect.

P

pitch section of climbing between two stances or belay points.

piton a metal peg hammered into a rock crack to support a belay.

powder-snow avalanche caused by freshly fallen snow on steep surfaces before it has had time either to thaw or freeze; one of the most spectacular and dangerous avalanche conditions.

protection the number and quality of running belays used to make a pitch safer and psychologically easier to lead.

prusiking a method of directly ascending a rope with the aid of prusik knots, or friction hitches, with foot loops.

R

rakshi Sherpa spirit usually distilled from rice.

ridge the line along which two faces of a mountain meet.

running (running belay) an intermediate anchor point between the lead climber and the main belay, when the rope runs through a karabiner attached to this anchor, thus reducing the distance a leader would fall.

S

sérac wall, pinnacle or tower of ice, often unstable and dangerous.

seige-style the method by which the 8000m (36,250ft) summits were first climbed. It involves establishing fixed camps up a mountain, connected by fixed ropes. These camps are stocked by porters and/or climbers who move up in relays, taking turns out in front making the route and establishing the next camp, then returning to Base camp to rest while another team moves up to continue from the new high point. The use of supplementary oxygen on the higher 8000m peaks and using large porter teams are other regular features of siege-style climbing.

Sherpas an ethnic group of Tibetan stock, living in the Everest region, who have obtained an effective monopoly of high-altitude portering in Nepal.

sirdar head Sherpa on an expedition.

sling a loop of rope or nylon tape used for belays or in abseiling.

spindrift loose powder snow carried by wind or small avalanche.

spur rock or snow rib on the side of a mountain.

stance place where a climber makes his belay, ideally somewhere comfortable to stand or sit.

step vertical or short steep rise in a gully or ridge.

T

top rope a rope secured from above.

traverse to move horizontally or diagonally across a rock or snow slope. Also the ascent and descent of a mountain by different routes.

tsampa barley flour, a staple or Sherpa diet.

U

undercut low horizontal crack or pocket with a lip on its upper surface around which a hold or pinch grip can be attained.

W

wedge made from wood and used for hammering into wide cracks for belays or runners.

white-out condition of driving snow and mist with a snow background, which makes it impossible to judge distance or distinguish between solid ground and space.

windslab avalanche occurs when a snow layer formed by wind-compacted snow settles insecurely on top of old snow and descends in enormous blocks, or slabs.

Index